Three themes embedded in *Exceptional Children and Y*  an interactive and effective approach to teaching based on cooperation, support, and problem-solving.

 THEME 1 **Commonalities** unite all students more than differences separate them. Seeing the similarities among all individuals breaks down the barriers that set people apart.

 THEME 2 **Collaborative relationships** enhance student learning and make the job of teaching richer and more enjoyable. This book says "You are not alone." It emphasizes the importance of the links among professionals and the links between professionals and families.

 THEME 3 **You "Can Do" the work that will make a difference.** There may be a sense of uneasiness or nervousness about working with students who are exceptional. This book demonstrates how to make a significant difference in helping all students reach their potential.

Families of Exceptional Children

SPECIAL education professionals have increasingly based their decisions about services and programs on the knowledge that the family's involvement can make their work much more effective. In this chapter, you will learn how exceptionalities affect families, how teachers and other professionals can involve parents and family members in making educational and life choices, and how to provide support to the entire family.

As you read, look for answers to these questions:

Collaboration: How can family members and professionals learn to work together as partners?

Commonalities: How does the family participate in the exceptional child's development at every stage of life?

Can Do: What are some of the ways in which exceptional children contribute to the strength and richness of a family?

USING YOUR KNOWLEDGE

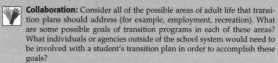

Commonalities: What are your rights to education and housing? What legislation exists to protect the rights of adults with disabilities? Consider why legislation is necessary in this country to identify and protect the rights of individuals with disabilities and others. Find out what legislation currently is under consideration at the state or national level.

Collaboration: Consider all of the possible areas of adult life that transition plans should address (for example, employment, recreation). What are some possible goals of transition programs in each of these areas? What individuals or agencies outside of the school system would need to be involved with a student's transition plan in order to accomplish these goals?

Can Do: Does your school or university employ individuals with disabilities? What types of support services are available at the school site or in your community to support individuals with disabilities in the workplace?

Feb/1999

Exceptional Children and Youth

Exceptional Children and Youth

An Introduction to Special Education

SECOND EDITION

NANCY HUNT

California State University
Los Angeles

KATHLEEN MARSHALL

University of South Carolina

HOUGHTON MIFFLIN COMPANY   BOSTON   NEW YORK

For Maggie
N. H.

To my parents
Vivian and Harold Marshall
K. M.

Senior sponsoring editor: Loretta Wolozin
Associate editor: Lisa Mafrici
Senior project editor: Rosemary Winfield
Senior production/design coordinator: Jill Haber
Senior designer: Henry Rachlin
Senior manufacturing coordinator: Marie Barnes
Senior marketing manager: Pamela Laskey

Cover design: Rebecca Fagan; cover image: copyright Keith Haring.

Chapter opener photos: Chapter 1, Jeff Greenberg/The Image Works, Inc.; Chapter 2, John Schoenwalter/Jeroboam; Chapter 3, Lydia Gans/Impact Visuals; Chapter 4, Mary Harrison/Jeroboam; Chapter 5, Mary Kate Denny/PhotoEdit; Chapter 6, Robert Finken/The Picture Cube; Chapter 7, Ellen Senisi/The Image Works, Inc.; Chapter 8, Bob Daemmrich Photo, Inc.; Chapter 9, Will & Deni McIntyre/Photo Researchers, Inc.; Chapter 10, Lydia Gans/Impact Visuals; Chapter 11, Ellen Senisi/The Image Works, Inc.; Chapter 12, Lawrence Migdale; Chapter 13, Ellen Senisi/The Image Works, Inc.; Chapter 14, Michael Kagan/Monkmeyer Press Photo Service.

Figure on page 406: From *In Search of the Human Mind* by Robert J. Sternberg. Copyright © 1995 by Harcourt Brace & Company, reproduced by permission of the publisher.

Printed in the U.S.A.

Library of Congress Catalog Card Number 98-72046

ISBN 0-395-90408-0

123456789-QH-02-01 00 99 98

Brief Contents

Contents

FRAMEWORK 1: Common Issues for All Exceptional Children and Youth in Special Education **95**

part two *Learning About the Potential of Exceptional Children* *105*

4 *Children with Mental Retardation* 107

5   *Children with Learning Disabilities* 139

6   *Children with Behavioral and Emotional Disorders* 193

7 Children with Communication Disorders   227

8 Children Who Are Deaf and Hard of Hearing   259

12 *Children Who Are Gifted and Talented*

FRAMEWORK 2 **Common Issues for All Developing Professionals in Special Education and Related Fields** **437**

Preface

In a time when most advocates believe in the importance of seeing children with disabilities first as children, and as children who will benefit from schooling and experiences that are as normal as possible, this book attempts to accomplish a difficult goal. We expect that our readers—teachers, future teachers, and professionals in related fields—will come to appreciate both the commonalities between children with disability labels and their age peers *and* the unique learning characteristics they may have as a result of their disability.

The emphasis on *commonalities* is important for several reasons. For too long, an "us" and "them" attitude relative to children receiving special education services has prevailed in schools, and it has resulted in children and their teachers, parents, and programs being segregated from the normal experiences of a school community. In addition, focusing on differences may lead teachers to believe that they do not have the skills to teach children with disability labels, or that such children are not their responsibility, rather than emphasizing that *all* children are *our* children. Both assumptions are, at best, counterproductive and, at worst, destructive.

Yet learning about uniqueness is important, too. Children who are deaf or blind *will* learn more efficiently with specific teaching strategies adapted to their disabilities that have been developed over years of teachers' experience. Children identified as having learning disabilities *do* need a focused, deliberate, and individualized emphasis on learning to read and write. And the field of special education has developed such a focus, such strategies, over the last decades. Furthermore, these strategies may improve learning for many children who are *not* eligible for special education services.

The goal for this book has evolved from a commitment to both commonalities and uniqueness. We hope that our readers will recognize the need to work with other professionals in the schools to improve educational achievement for *all* students—those who learn without struggle and those who need a specialized and individualized focus. And in the second edition of this textbook, our goal is that our readers will have the attitudes, the knowledge, and the skills needed to do just that.

Approach of the Text

As a teacher (and we believe all professionals who work in schools are teachers, at one level or another), your classes will reflect all of the injustices, strengths, and questions faced by individuals with disabilities in our society: they are mirrors of our communities. Your voice, behavior, and example will set the stage for how individual students are treated, whether differences are appreciated and respected, and whether students learn to work together.

Because of this, we believe that the most important characteristic you can acquire as a teacher is the ability to be a good problem-solver within cooperative and supportive contexts. The desire and ability to identify learning problems, find the best teaching strategy for a situation, or discover the best way to break down a social barrier is the strength of the most effective teachers. As we present the many puzzles, challenges, and opportunities in the field of special education, we hope you will experience the desire to investigate and grow as individuals and educators.

We want to share our commitment to individuals with disabilities and do our part to help you become effective and confident teachers. Our goal is to communicate our feelings of optimism and determination to our readers.

To help you develop an interactive and effective approach to teaching based on cooperation, support, and problem solving, the text often presents information that draws on our personal experiences. And to help you understand the bases of our philosophy, we have identified three themes that underlie all the book's content and are addressed throughout the text:

- **Theme 1** *Commonalities* unite all students more than differences separate them. We hope that our book helps teachers recognize the commonalities among all students. Seeing the similarities among all individuals breaks down the barriers that set people apart.

- **Theme 2** *Collaborative relationships* enhance student learning and make the job of teaching richer and more enjoyable. This book says, "You are not alone." It emphasizes the importance of the links among professionals and the links between professionals and families.

- **Theme 3** You *"can do"* the work that will make a difference. You may feel uncertain or nervous about working with students who are exceptional. This book demonstrates how you and other professionals can make a significant difference in helping *all* students reach their potential.

These themes play an important role in bringing together all the parts of the book and providing an integrated approach for the introductory course in special education. We expect that through this book you will see and feel differently about yourself and your future students and act on these new understandings as a teacher.

Organization of the Text

Exceptional Children and Youth is presented in three major parts:

- *Part One*, "Building Blocks for Working with Exceptional Children," introduces major topics in special education. Chapters 1–3 address the history and development of special education, factors that put children at risk for a disability and early intervention, and the importance of including the family in the educational process. These three chapters are grouped together because these factors are critical elements for all areas of special education—and for all individuals with disabilities.

- *Part Two*, "Learning About the Potential of Exceptional Children," discusses students with specific types of disabilities within the context of early life experiences and schooling. We continually point out the similarities in learning characteristics among students with different categorical labels and the similarities in most effective instructional procedures. When you work with individuals with disabilities, we encourage you to focus on the level of support a student needs to learn critical skills, to identify the most effective way to present those skills, and to recognize that categories and labels have limited value. Chapters 4–12 provide basic background on the definition and prevalence of the exceptionality. Most of each chapter is devoted to understanding the effects of the exceptionality on the child and family and to educational issues such as placement, assessment, and appropriate teaching strategies.

- *Part Three*, "Considering Cultural Diversity and Lifespan Factors," expands the context of special education by spanning a range of ages and cultures. Chapters 13 and 14 discuss how issues of exceptionality are addressed in diverse cultures and as children with disabilities become adults. The chapters address major issues related to educational, vocational, and civil rights.

Revisions in This Edition

The second edition of *Exceptional Children and Youth* has been updated and made more concise for our readers. We have added two new **Framework** sections:

- "Framework 1: Common Issues for All Exceptional Children and Youth in Special Education" and
- "Framework 2: Common Issues for All Developing Professionals in Special Education and Related Fields."

These discussions appear before and after the categorical chapters (before Chapter 4 and after Chapter 12) to help students identify the common issues across the categories in special education. The Frameworks also provide students with strategies and resources to become reflective practitioners.

Each categorical chapter (Chapters 4–12) has a clear emphasis on strategies for inclusive classrooms. In addition, each chapter has been revised as follows:

- Chapter 1, *A Context for the Individual in Special Education*, has been updated to include a description of the major components of the 1997 IDEA.

- Chapter 2, *Risk Factors and Early Intervention*, features a streamlined conceptualization of biological and environmental risk and contemporary references to the most common risk factors. The topic of early intervention is now covered in this chapter, where it seemed to flow from the discussion of risk factors naturally.

- Chapter 3, *Families of Exceptional Children*, has been updated to provide new coverage of families under stress. A focus on perceptions of culturally diverse family members strengthens the chapter.

- Chapter 4, *Children with Mental Retardation*, has been updated and presents a new emphasis on classroom teaching strategies.

- Chapter 5, *Children with Learning Disabilities*, has been trimmed and focused so that important instructional recommendations are highlighted and made more accessible to the reader.

- Chapter 6, *Children with Behavioral and Emotional Disorders*, includes updated material related to the 1997 amendments of IDEA, added methodological coverage, and featured coverage of ADHD.

- Chapter 7, *Children with Communication Disorders*, has been pared down to focus more clearly on types of communication disorders. There is new coverage of language delay in young children and updated research on the major chapter topics.

- Chapter 8, *Children Who Are Deaf and Hard of Hearing*, presents an updated, comprehensive view of educational issues for children with hearing loss.
- Chapter 9, *Children Who Are Blind or Have Low Vision*, has updated research, methods, and strategies for use with students with vision loss.
- Chapter 10, *Children with Physical Disabilities and Health Impairments*, reflects new medical and technological information and contains new coverage of child abuse.
- Chapter 11, *Children with Severe Disabilities*, has expanded methodological coverage and features a separate section on autism.
- Chapter 12, *Children Who Are Gifted and Talented*, has new topic coverage on gifted girls and gifted students with disabilities. Since most teachers have some students considered gifted, there is an emphasis on strategies that can be used in all classrooms—often to benefit all children.
- Chapter 13, *Exceptional Children from Diverse Cultural Backgrounds*, has been redesigned to include expanded coverage on assessment and instructional procedures.
- Chapter 14, *Exceptional Individuals Through the Lifespan*, has been updated to reflect recent outcome data and transition programming.

Special Learning Features of the Text

In the second edition we have emphasized teaching *strategies* that our readers can use in their work with children. They are based on both research and practice, and they are infused into the narrative of the textbook and also presented in boxes set apart from the narrative. While an introductory course in special education is not generally considered a methods course, we think we can lay the groundwork here for successful teaching strategies:

- *The First Person* section in each chapter lets the reader experience the topic of the chapter through the story of someone who has "been there."
- *A Closer Look* sections examine subjects of special interest to the topic at hand—sometimes model programs, treatments, or professionals who work with specific groups of children.
- *What You Can Do Now* sections at the end of each chapter provide the reader with specific suggestions exemplifying our *can-do* theme: ideas for learning more about a topic, volunteering with a group, or putting new learning into action through an activity.

Other Learning and Study Features

In addition to the special features, *Exceptional Children and Youth* contains useful learning tools such as

- *Orientations* Chapter-opening overviews that provide both a coherent narrative and focusing questions to point readers to key material.
- *Chapter summaries* Comprehensive summaries of major points for review.
- *Margin notes* Main ideas and definitions for easy reference.
- *Key terms* For review at the end of the chapter.
- *"Using Your Knowledge" discussion questions* More "hands-on" activities related to chapter topics and discussion.
- *"Multimedia Resources"* Lists and descriptions of organizations, books, journal articles, and web sites on the Internet related to each chapter topic that are relevant for personal interests and professional development.

Ancillaries to Accompany the Text

Instructor's Resources Guide

The second edition of *Exceptional Children and Youth* is accompanied by the *Instructor's Resources Guide*. Part 1 of the *Resources Guide* provides model syllabi for organizing course materials and activities for either a 10-week or a 15-week term. It is particularly useful for new instructors or those who are using an experiential approach for the first time.

Part 2 includes chapter-by-chapter materials for the instructor and the student. For the instructor, complete coverage of the best available materials for teaching is provided—including learning objectives, chapter and lecture outlines, class activities, references, and resources that provide useful information (such as major publishers' names and addresses and the names and addresses of organizations that work with individuals who are exceptional).

Part 3 is a complete set of assessment materials. The test bank contains multiple-choice and essay questions for each chapter.

Part 4 includes guidelines for using *Frameworks 1 and 2*, which support the categorical chapters (Chapters 4–12) and the accompanying case study, *The Story of Lucy and Nell*.

Computerized Test Bank

Computerized versions (IBM and Mac) of the *Test Bank* items are available on adoption of the text.

Overhead Transparencies

A set of colorful overhead transparencies has been prepared to help present key concepts and graphics to your class. These transparencies include text art and additional representations to support the text and your teaching and are available on adoption of the text.

The Story of Lucy and Nell

The Story of Lucy and Nell, the case study booklet, is included free with every student text.

Teacher Education Station Web Site

The Teacher Education Station web site (go to http://www.hmco.com/college, and then click on "Education") provides additional pedagogic support and resources for beginning and experienced professionals in education, including the unique "Project-Based Learning Space." For more details on all that this web site offers, see the site map on the back inside cover of this book.

Acknowledgments

We would like to acknowledge the contributions of the authors who contributed either complete or partial chapters in the first edition: Dr. Elaine Silliman and Janet Stack, University of South Florida, Chapter 7, "Children with Communication Disorders"; Dr. Cay Holbrook and Dr. Mary Scott Healy, University of Arkansas, Little Rock, Chapter 9, "Children Who Are Blind or Have Low Vision"; Dr. Emma Guilarte, University of South Carolina, Chapter 10, "Children with Physical Disabilities and Health Impairments"; Dr. James Delisle, Kent State University, Chapter 12, "Children Who Are Gifted and Talented"; Dr. Philip Chinn, California State University, Los Angeles, Chapter 13, "Exceptional Children from Diverse Cultural Backgrounds."

We also appreciate the many constructive suggestions and feedback provided by the reviewers of the text, including the following:

Sherwood J. Best, *California State University, Los Angeles*
Maria E. Bove, *Castleton State College*
Ruth M. C. Buehler, *Millersville University*
John S. Childers, *East Carolina University*
Gloria Contreras, *University of North Texas*
Suzanne D. Cormier, *Winthrop University*
Rosemary R. Davis, *Palomar College*
Daniel Fasko, Jr., *Morehead State University*
Diane L. Fazzi, *California State University, Los Angeles*
Shernaz B. García, *University of Texas, Austin*
Beth Harry, *University of Miami*
Martha Miller Henemier, *Cumberland College*
Aileen Lau-Dickinson, *University of South Carolina*
Shane Martin, *Loyola Marymount University*
Gayle Mindes, *DePaul University*
Suzanne M. Morin, *Shippensburg University*
J. David Smith, *University of South Carolina*
Deborah M. Switzer, *Clemson University*
Stephen Trotter, *University of the Pacific*
Julianne C. Turner, *Pennsylvania State University*

Most authors do not have the luxury of collaboration that we do with our colleagues at Houghton Mifflin. Lisa Mafrici has helped us at every stage of our work with warmth, humor, and grace. Elaine Silverstein, our developmental editor, has been a top-notch professional and contributor. Rosemary Winfield and her colleagues in the production department shepherded us through that process artfully. Finally, we recognize our great good fortune in having worked with Loretta Wolozin from the inception of this project, now more years ago than any of us want to remember. No author in any domain could have a better collaborator or a better mentor and friend.

Both of us have people we would like to thank individually. Nancy Hunt particularly appreciates the knowledge and support of her colleagues and friends at California State University, Los Angeles, particularly M. Diane Klein, Diane Fazzi, Diane Haager, Christine Givner, Jamie Dote-Kwan, Mary Falvey, Sherwood Best, Barbara Clark, Simeon Slovacek, and Allen Mori. The staff and students at The Accelerated School in Los Angeles kept me grounded in the real world as I did this work. I'm also grateful to Leslie Geffen of the Mirman School, Mary Ann Lane of the Lighthouse, and Jeff Girion of Marlborough School for their help with the "First Person" sections. Maggie Gram provided concrete help along with her love and support, and Lucy, Nell, and Dewey Gram entertained me and thrived despite my preoccupation.

Kathleen Marshall expresses appreciation to her colleagues at the University of South Carolina, particularly William Brown, Erik Drasgow, and Mitchell Yell, and to Dr. Edward A. Polloway of Lynchburg College. I would also like to thank Richard Sribnick and the rest of my family for their continuous support and encouragement.

Nancy Hunt
Kathleen J. Marshall

Building Blocks for Working with Exceptional Children

PART ONE introduces you to the major topics in the field of special education. You'll learn how special education has evolved during the past three decades and its implications for your future classroom. You'll learn about the factors that may affect individual students' educational experiences: their individual strengths, their families, and their exposure to risk. In your role as a teacher, you will need to take all of these factors into account. As you will see, the building blocks we discuss here are a vital foundation for your work with exceptional individuals.

$\mathcal{A}$ Context for the Individual in Special Education

THE goal of this chapter is to introduce you to the context of special education—the rewards and challenges, the diversity of students' needs and abilities, the historical and legal roots from which contemporary special education has developed, and the ongoing questions of how and where we can best help exceptional students reach their potential. As you read, look for answers to these questions:

■ **What is special education?**

■ **How have legislation and litigation opened doors for exceptional individuals?**

✔ **Can Do:** What can be learned from teachers of the past that will improve present practices?

Collaboration: How can general and special educators collaborate to improve educational outcomes for all children?

Commonalities: What needs do *all* students share, whether or not they are classified as having a disability?

Schools are filled with children—dark and light, quiet and loud, happy and sad—with special needs. For some it's the need for warmth, patience, and support to weather a tough emotional time; for others the need for someone to take time to find out what really interests and motivates them. We are about to embark on the study of some of those children, those who present special challenges to their teachers by virtue of their disabilities and their special gifts and talents. But each child in school will challenge you, and we hope to show you that the differences among children are simply variations on a theme of *commonalities*. You can reach and teach every one of them.

More and more, American schools are becoming places of great student diversity. The changes that result from this diversity are sometimes unsettling to us. If you cannot speak Korean, can you teach a child who does? If the new child in your class is in a wheelchair and cannot speak, will you be able to communicate? How can you best *collaborate* with other professionals in your school in order to meet the needs of these children? With so much expected of teachers, so much responsibility resting on your shoulders, will you be able to respond, to teach, to see progress in each of your students?

We think you will. We hope to help you to get to know some of the characteristics of your students who are considered exceptional. We believe that our teachers are up to the challenge of teaching all students—you *can do* it, and do it well.

Definitions and Terms

Like other fields of study, special education has its own terminology. We use several terms to describe the group of students we work with. Among them is **exceptional,** used in the title of this book. We use this word to describe the range of students—those who are called blind, gifted, deaf—who receive special education services in the school. It does not simply refer to students who are gifted but to any student who may be an "exception" to the rule.

Some of these students have a **disability** (students who are gifted do not fall into this category). A disability is a limitation, such as difficulty in learning to read or the inability to hear, walk, or see. A **handicap** is not the same as a disability; a handicap results from the limitations imposed by the environment and by attitudes toward a person with disabilities.

Some examples will help here. Some adults who are deaf, for example, admit that they are disabled—they hear very little. But they do not consider themselves handicapped. Their disability does not limit them in ways that they consider significant. They associate with a community of other deaf people with whom they can communicate freely; they do not often encounter people who manifest prejudice against them. They are satisfied with their lives, their abilities and limitations. The deaf schoolchild, however, may be considered handicapped; she may not yet have learned an efficient communication system or to read English well, which considerably limits her ability to communicate with others and to achieve in school.

A young person who has experienced a spinal cord injury may emerge from the hospital unable to walk—a serious disability and perhaps a handicap. Through physical therapy and rehabilitation, however, that person can often learn strategies to cope with the handicap associated with the disability. Use of a wheelchair and adaptive devices in the car will enable him to become mobile again; modifications of work space and the home may make those places acces-

Exceptional students are all those who receive special education services in the school.

A disability is a limitation; a handicap is the limitations imposed by the environment and by people's attitudes.

Major league pitcher Jim Abbott, born with one hand, has not allowed his disability to become a handicap. (AP/Wide World Photos)

sible to him using a wheelchair. Nowadays, a physical limitation does not prevent a person from participating in sports, from wheelchair racing to mountain climbing.

Overcoming the attitudes of others toward that disability may be a more difficult fight. Will the behavior of friends and family change? Will job opportunities be there? Will new acquaintances think of him or her as a disabled person, or as a person who happens to have a disability?

You will notice that we try to use **people-first language** in this book; first we describe the person, then the disability (see the examples in the box "People-First Language"). This is so that we can think about individuals who have disabilities, such as the young person just described, as *people* who happen to have the characteristic of having disabilities.

People-first language focuses on the person, not the disability.

Naturally, within special education there is an emphasis on prevention of disabilities and on starting services as early as possible. **Early intervention** is the provision of services for children from birth to age 3 and their families. It has the goal of optimizing each child's learning potential and daily well-being and increasing the child's opportunities for functioning effectively in the community (Cook, Tessier & Klein, 1996). We use the term **at risk** to describe those infants and young children who have a greater likelihood of developing a disability because of factors such as extreme prematurity, chronic poverty, or early medical problems. Some educators also use the term to describe older students who may be more likely to drop out of school; however, in this book we use it to describe infants and young children only.

Early intervention helps reduce the impact of disabilities on young children.

What *is* special education, you may wonder, and what is so special about it? **Special education** is simply the educational program designed to meet the

Special education is the education program designed to meet the unique needs of exceptional children.

Although I am, by birth and cultural experiences, a midwestern Lutheran German/Norwegian American, I have oftentimes felt I also came from a foreign planet, by virtue of also having been born with a rare disability. The intertwining of these two exceptionally diverse vantage points has made me the person I am today.

Being born with a disability brings with it its own unique culture. Thus, any baby born with spina bifida, cerebral palsy, Down syndrome, or any other congenital condition is, by virtue of his or her birth condition, "cross-cultural." Although the baby's heritage is Anglo, Hispanic, Native American, etc., his or her birth condition is NOT. The "NOT" part is the accumulation of knowledge and attitudes that family members have about individuals with this particular condition. Since no one "plans" to have a baby born with this disability, this "NOT" part is filled with unsaid thoughts and feelings . . . remnants that seem to arise out of nowhere as everyone (affected child and his or her family) copes with such an unplanned "complication."

I have come to believe that, of all the difficulties inherent in growing up with a disability, a family or community's combined ignorance of what it means to have a disability is, by far, the most painful aspect of the entire condition. This familial ignorance produces an intense loneliness that transcends all cultural aspects. It is this very ignorance that often enables someone with a disability to find more commonalities with someone from another culture who also shares the same disability.

unique learning and developmental needs of a student who is exceptional. What is special about special education is the recognition of the unique nature of each individual and the accompanying design of an educational program specifically planned to meet that person's needs. Special education is not limited to a particular "special" place; most special educators believe that it should take place in the most normal, natural environment possible. That may be in a baby's home, in a general education classroom, or in the Pizza Hut in the student's community; sometimes it may occur in a hospital or a special school designed for a particular group of students, such as a school for deaf students. This book is designed to help you learn more about special education; we hope that it will assist you in finding your own role in serving students who are exceptional.

Although at a distance I can be seen as "white," up close and personal it is quite obvious that I have a facial difference. . . . When I taught general education (for twenty-five years), I was oblivious to my disability difference, unless it was helpful in understanding a difference from a child's point of view. I can't recall any situation where the reality of my facial paralysis seemed insurmountable to parent, child, or professional peer. And now, working specifically with families that have children with disabilities, I can use what I have learned living in the "disability culture" to advocate for the well-being of the young child.

People need to realize that young children with disabilities will ultimately grow up to become *adults with disabilities*. And, as an adult with a disability, one needs to feel comfortable with one's whole self, even the part that "doesn't work right." This insight is best taught by another adult with the same (or similar) disability—someone who has "walked the walk" and truly knows the questions that a child or teen may ask when coping with a particular disability. In the final analysis, for the *child with the disability*, one must become aware of the TWO cultures from which he or she comes.

Sandy Goodwick

Sandy Goodwick was born with Moebius syndrome, a rare genetic disorder that causes facial paralysis.

Prevalence of Exceptional Children

Prevalence figures reflect how many students within a given category need special services.

Every year the Office of Special Education and Rehabilitative Services (OSERS) in the U.S. Department of Education prepares a report for Congress that describes the prevalence, or number, of students with disabilities receiving special education services. Chapters 4 through 12 will give you more information on some of the issues surrounding how we identify and count individuals within categories. What's important to note here is that prevalence figures reflect how many students need special services and so are used to allocate funds, to determine whether there are enough teachers, and for many other purposes.

The *Eighteenth Annual Report to Congress on the Implementation of the Individuals with Disabilities Education Act* (1996) reported that there were 5,439,626

8

A closer look

People-First Language

In speaking or writing, remember that children and adults with disabilities are like everyone else—except that they happen to have a disability. Here are a few tips for improving your language related to disabilities and handicaps.

1. Speak of the person first, then the disability.
2. Emphasize abilities, not limitations.
3. Do not label people as part of a disability group.

4. Don't give excessive praise or attention to a person with a disability; don't patronize.
5. Choice and independence are important; let the person do or speak for him/herself as much as possible.
6. A disability is a functional limitation that interferes with a person's ability to walk, hear, talk, learn, etc.; use the word *handicap* to describe a situation or barrier imposed by society, the environment, or oneself.

Say	**Instead of**
child with a disability	disabled or handicapped child
person with cerebral palsy	palsied, CP, or spastic person
person who has . . .	afflicted, suffers from, victim
developmental delay	slow
emotional disorder, mental illness	crazy, insane
uses a wheelchair	confined to a wheelchair
person with Down syndrome	mongoloid
has a physical disability	crippled
condition	disease (unless it *is* a disease)
seizures	fits
paralyzed	invalid
chronic illness	sickly
has paraplegia, hemiplegia, quadriplegia	paraplegic, hemiplegic, quadriplegic

Source: "It's the 'Person First'—Then the Disability," *Pacesetter* (September 1989), p. 13. Reprinted by permission from *Pacesetter. Pacesetter* is published by PACER Center, Minneapolis, Minnesota.

children from ages 3 to 21 receiving special education services during the 1994–1995 school year. Table 1.1 shows the breakdown of students between ages 6 and 21 by disability group. Notice that 51 percent of the total number of school-age students being served is classified as learning disabled, and 92 percent of the total number fall into the four largest categories: learning disabilities, speech or language impairments, mental retardation, and serious emotional disturbance. Overall, about 12 percent of elementary and secondary students in the United States receive special education services (Eighteenth Annual Report to Congress, 1996).

Foundations of Special Education

Although there have always been exceptional children, attempts to teach them are relatively recent. As Hewett and Forness (1984) put it, "Throughout

Table 1.1 **Students Age 6 to 21 Served Under Part B of IDEA by Disability: School Year 1994–1995**

Disability	Number	Percentage
Specific learning disabilities	2,513,977	51.2%
Speech or language impairments	1,023,665	20.8%
Mental retardation	570,855	11.6%
Serious emotional disturbance	428,168	8.7%
Multiple disabilities	89,646	1.8%
Hearing impairments	65,568	1.3%
Orthopedic impairments	60,604	1.2%
Other health impairments	106,509	2.2%
Visual impairments	24,877	0.50%
Autism	22,780	0.46%
Deaf-blindness	1,331	0.03%
Traumatic brain injury	7,188	0.15%
All disabilities	4,915,168	

Source: *Eighteenth Annual Report to Congress on the Implementation of the Individuals with Disabilities Act* (Washington, DC: Department of Education, 1996). Adapted from Table 1.5, p. 9.

recorded history, perhaps the only categories that mattered were the *weak*, the *odd*, and the *poor*" (p. 3). The first known attempts to teach children with disabilities came in the sixteenth and seventeenth centuries, when priests and other religious men and women taught small groups of deaf and blind children, usually the offspring of the aristocracy.

Early History: Great Teachers and Their Legacy

A series of curious, innovative, dedicated men and women in Europe and the United States pioneered the teaching techniques that are the foundation of special education. First among them was **Jean-Marc-Gaspard Itard.** In 1799, Itard was a 25-year-old physician in Paris when an 11- or 12-year-old boy emerged from the woods near the French town of Aveyron. The boy was unclothed, scarred, and covered with dirt; he did not walk, but ran; he knew none of the conventions of human civilization and did not speak. This boy became the focus of a great controversy in France between the "nativists," who believed that a person's potential was determined by genetic heritage and was therefore unalterable, and the "sensationalists," who believed that environmental input in the form of sensory experience could change a person's intellectual development. Who would venture to teach this "wild boy"—to civilize him?

Itard, who bore within him the optimistic legacy of the French Revolution, volunteered for the task. For five years, he and the boy, whom he named Victor, lived at the school for the deaf in Paris while he attempted to teach him. His greatest hope was that the boy would learn language, which Itard considered the hallmark of civilized society. Through daily, painstaking lessons, Itard rewarded Victor with small amounts of food when he accomplished a task. After nine months, Victor had accomplished Itard's first goals for him: He developed normal eating, sleeping, and personal hygiene routines (Lane, 1976).

Jean-Marc-Gaspard Itard tried to teach the "wild boy of Aveyron" to speak.

After five years, however, Itard considered his work a failure; although Victor could recognize some words in print and had acquired many of the behaviors of "civilization," his only words were *lait* and *oh Dieu* (French for "milk" and "oh God"). With great disappointment, Itard abandoned his work with Victor, who was cared for by the wife of a groundskeeper at the school for the deaf until his death at around the age of 40.

Although Itard felt he had failed because he had not made Victor "normal," others found both teaching techniques and encouragement in the changes that had occurred in Victor. Among those were Edouard Seguin, who became a student of Itard; he built on Itard's methods to form his own approach to teaching children we would now say have mental retardation. Maria Montessori translated a book that Seguin wrote about his own methods and materials and made them the foundation of the Montessori method, first used with children with mental retardation. Montessori's teaching methods involve the development of the child's natural curiosity and the training of the senses through materials that are manipulable, three-dimensional, and concrete (Cook, Tessier & Klein, 1996).

> Edouard Seguin and Maria Montessori applied Itard's methods to the teaching of children with mental retardation.

The ideas and methods of these great European teachers reached several Americans who were influential in setting up special education services in the United States. Samuel Gridley Howe (1801–1876) was a graduate of Harvard Medical School and a political reformer. He taught Laura Bridgeman, a young deaf and blind woman, and his teaching techniques became the foundation for the methods used at the Perkins School for the Blind in Watertown, Massachusetts, the first school for students with disabilities in this country, which Howe helped to found.

> Samuel Gridley Howe developed methods of teaching students who were both deaf and blind.

Thomas Hopkins Gallaudet (1787–1851) was a graduate of Yale and Andover Theological Seminary when he attempted to teach 9-year-old Alice Cogswell, the deaf daughter of a neighbor, some simple words and sentences (Moores, 1997). Gallaudet traveled to Europe to learn from teachers there and returned home with a deaf teacher, Laurent Clerc. Gallaudet then became the principal at the first school for the deaf in the United States, founded by Alice Cogswell's father and others. The first teacher at the school was Laurent Clerc. Clerc trained many of the teachers at the early schools for deaf children in this country. Gallaudet University in Washington, D.C., was named for T.H. Gallaudet. Some groups would like the name changed to Gallaudet and Clerc University, to acknowledge the early role of a deaf teacher in the education of deaf children.

> Gallaudet, Clerc, and Bell pioneered methods of teaching children who were deaf.

Alexander Graham Bell (1847–1922) did not think of himself as the inventor of the telephone but as a teacher of children who were deaf. Bell came from a family of speech teachers, and his mother was deaf, so it was natural for him to use his skills to teach deaf children to speak. Bell's views on enhancing speech and residual hearing in deaf children are still alive today, exemplified by members of the Alexander Graham Bell Association for the Deaf, headquartered in Washington, D.C.

> The dedication and ingenuity of Annie Sullivan, Helen Keller's teacher, have inspired many to become teachers.

Anne Sullivan Macy (1866–1936), Helen Keller's beloved "Teacher," has been an inspiration to many entering the teaching profession. Sullivan, who had a serious vision impairment until her teenage years, attended the Perkins School for the Blind and was recommended to Helen Keller's mother through Alexander Graham Bell. Annie Sullivan carefully studied Dr. Howe's records from teaching Laura Bridgeman before she went to work for the Keller family. Those methods, and Annie Sullivan's intelligence, dedication, and ingenuity, helped Helen Keller to become the person that she was. The intricate and remarkable

Alexander Graham Bell was a mentor and friend to Helen Keller and her teacher, Anne Sullivan Macy. (Corbis-Bettman)

relationship between this teacher and her student is detailed in Joseph Lash's fascinating book, *Helen and Teacher* (1980).

Later History: Advocates for Social Change

After the initial surge of interest in education of children who were deaf and blind and had mental retardation in the United States, school services for children with disabilities plateaued for many years. It was not until the 1960s that two events converged to reignite national interest in the needs of children with disabilities. The first of these was the election of John F. Kennedy as president in 1960. Kennedy had a sister, Rosemary, with mental retardation, and he was openly committed to improving the quality of life for people with mental retardation. He did two concrete things to accomplish this goal: He set up the President's Commission on Mental Retardation, a group of expert researchers and practitioners who identified the issues and priorities in the field, and he supported the use of federal funds to educate teachers of children with disabilities. Kennedy's greatest contribution was less concrete. His acknowledgment of mental retardation in his family and his dedication to improving services for people with disabilities played a large part in lessening the stigma of mental retardation and added prestige to the career of teaching children with disabilities.

Kennedy's commitment to improving services for people with disabilities helped lessen the stigma of mental retardation.

The other event of the 1960s that influenced families and other advocates of children with disabilities was the civil rights movement. The political and social demands of African Americans for equal rights and access to opportunities at all levels of society provided an example to families and groups working with

A Context for the Individual
in Special Education

The joy of victory is infectious for the second-place winner in the 200-yard dash at the Special Olympics. (H.L. Delgado/Impact Visuals)

With normalization, people with disabilities have the opportunity to lead typical lives.

Deinstitutionalization has helped end the segregation of people with mental retardation from the community.

Inclusion refers to placement of the child with disabilities in the general education classroom, with the supports the child needs also provided in the classroom.

children with disabilities of what could be accomplished on behalf of disenfranchised groups.

In 1972, Wolf Wolfensberger articulated the principle of **normalization**—that people with disabilities should have the opportunity to lead as close to a normal life as possible. This philosophy implies that no matter how severe an individual's disability, he or she should be integrated into society. The normalization principle implied that special institutions for people with mental retardation, which tended to be segregated from the community, should be deemphasized. This movement, known as **deinstitutionalization,** has led to the establishment of many small group homes and other community residential facilities in towns and cities.

In schools, the application of the concept of normalization has also led away from segregation—the education of exceptional children in special schools or separate buildings—and toward the goal of education in the least restrictive environment (see the next section). After the landmark special education legislation P.L. 94-142 was passed in 1975, educators used the term **mainstreaming** to describe the participation of children with disabilities in the general education classroom. Today, the word **inclusion** is used. Although it would be satisfying to be able to provide the "correct" definition of inclusion, in fact the word means different things to different people. It is usually used to refer to placement of the child with disabilities in the general education classroom, with the supports the child needs also provided there. In practice, there appears to be a continuum of inclusion, ranging from full-time, complete membership of the student with disabilities in the general education classroom to part-time participation for nonacademic subjects and activities.

The practice of inclusion makes considerable demands on both the general educator and the special educator. The collaboration that must occur is often

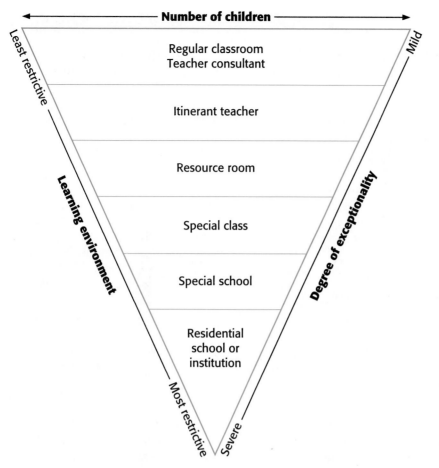

Figure 1.1
Learning Environments for
Exceptional Children

Source: E. Deno, "Special Education as Developmental Capital," *Exceptional Children* 37 (1970), 229–237. Copyright 1970 by the Council for Exceptional Children. Reprinted with permission.

new to both, and it is a skill that requires time, patience, and willingness. Certainly, not every teacher is in support of inclusion—in fact, the practice can be quite controversial. Many special educators strongly believe that inclusion should simply be one option in the continuum of program options and that the individual needs of the child, rather than a "one-size-fits-all" philosophy, should determine the child's placement (see Figure 1.1). Court decisions over the past several years have affirmed the need for the continuum of program options (U.S. courts affirm, 1996).

General educators have sometimes objected to inclusive practices, maintaining that they are not prepared to meet the individual needs of children with disabilities, that the practice is too time-consuming, and that it takes time from other children. But there are many special educators who believe that placement in segregated settings like a special school or even a special day class has interfered with the social and academic growth of children with disabilities and also limited the opportunities of children who are not disabled to learn from those who are. Recent research has indicated that the majority of general educators and administrators support the idea of inclusion, given the appropriate supports and collaborative practices (Scruggs & Mastropieri, 1996; Villa, Thousand, Meyers & Nevin, 1996) (see the accompanying box).

The practice of inclusion requires collaboration between the general educator and the special educator, as well as time, patience, and willingness.

～ Supports for General Education Teachers

A synthesis of research studies on inclusion has identified these supports needed by general education teachers who are including students with disabilities in their classrooms:

- *Time*: Teachers report a need for one hour or more per day to plan for students with disabilities.
- *Training*: Teachers need systematic, intensive training, either as part of their certification programs, as intensive and well-planned inservices, or as an ongoing process with consultants.
- *Personnel resources*: Teachers report a need for additional personnel assistance to carry out objectives. This could include a one-half time aide and daily contact with special education teachers.
- *Materials resources*: Teachers need adequate curriculum materials and other classroom equipment appropriate to the needs of students with disabilities.
- *Class size*: Teachers agree that their class size should be reduced, to fewer than twenty students, if students with disabilities are included.

- *Consideration of severity of disability*: Teachers are more willing to include students with mild disabilities than students with more severe disabilities, apparently because of teachers' perceived ability to carry on their teaching mission for the entire classroom. By implication, the more severe the disabilities in the inclusive setting, the more the previously mentioned sources of support would be needed.

These needs may be greater for secondary teachers than for elementary teachers. Overall, it seems clear that many teachers have reservations or concerns about mainstreaming and inclusion and believe that substantial supports are necessary to enable these efforts to succeed. The ultimate success of mainstreaming/inclusion efforts, then, may well depend on the extent to which such supports are made available.

Source: T.E. Scruggs & M.A. Mastropieri, "Teacher Perceptions of Mainstreaming/Inclusion, 1958–1995: A Research Synthesis," *Exceptional Children*, *63*(1) (1996), 72. Copyright © 1996 by The Council for Exceptional Children. Reprinted by permission.

Regardless of your personal experiences or beliefs about inclusion, it is important to understand what the "best practices" for including children with disabilities in general education classrooms are. They rest on three assumptions: First, that all teachers receive appropriate preparation and education about meeting the needs of children with disabilities; second, that children with disabilities are productive learners in the general education classroom; and third, that the appropriate supports are provided to both the student with disabilities and the teacher.

Legislation

Federal law now mandates that children with disabilities be educated in the **"least restrictive environment"**—that which provides the child the greatest number of options for interactions with nondisabled peers and the same opportunities as those peers.

P.L. 94-142, now known as IDEA, requires that children 3 to 21 with a disability be provided a free, appropriate, public education in the least restrictive environment.

■ **Public Law 94-142**   The law that has had the most profound impact on children with disabilities is Public Law 94-142, formerly known as the Education for All Handicapped Children Act (1975) and now known as the **Individuals with Disabilities Education Act (IDEA).** It requires that every child between the ages of 3 and 21 with a disability be provided a free, appropriate public education in the least restrictive environment.

Before P.L. 94-142 was passed, only one-fifth of the children with disabilities in the United States were enrolled in school programs at all (U.S. Department of Education, 1995); the remainder were either excluded from school, received inappropriate education, or were housed in institutions that did not provide edu-

Table 1.2 **Foundations of Special Education Law**

1973	P.L. 93-112	Section 504 of the Rehabilitation Act
1975	P.L. 94-142	Education for All Handicapped Children Act (now known as IDEA)
1986	P.L. 99-457	IDEA amendments
1990	P.L. 101-336	Americans with Disabilities Act
1990	P.L. 101-476	IDEA amendments
1997	P.L. 105-17	IDEA amendments

cational programs at all. Now we are much closer to enrolling all children with disabilities, although that is still an elusive goal. Congress has amended the law several times (see Table 1.2); as a result of the 1975 law and its amendments, children with disabilities and their families have well-defined rights. Among these are:

1. *Zero reject.* No child, no matter how severely disabled, shall be refused an appropriate education by the schools.

2. *Nondiscriminatory evaluation.* Evaluation procedures must be conducted with fairness in the child's native language.

3. *Due process.* Families and school districts can exercise their Fourteenth Amendment rights to due process under the law; that is, they may resort to mediation and appeal procedures when they do not agree with one another over issues such as the child's placement.

4. *Least restrictive environment.* Each child must be educated with nondisabled peers to the maximum extent appropriate. We discuss the differing perspectives on this concept later in the chapter (see page 25).

5. *Individualized education program (IEP).* The plan for each student's education is at the heart of special education law. We describe its key components on page 20 of this chapter and refer to its use in the classroom throughout this book.

The individualized education program is at the center of P.L. 94-142.

■ Major Amendments to P.L. 94-142

Public Law 99-457 *The Extension of Special Education Services to Infants and Young Children* In 1986, Congress amended P.L. 94-142 with P.L. 99-457. This amendment extended the provisions of P.L. 94-142 to all children between the ages of 3 and 5 through the Preschool Grants Program. Now states receiving federal funds under these laws *must* provide a free and appropriate public education to preschoolers as well. In addition, under the Handicapped Infants and Toddlers Program, states are provided incentives to develop early intervention programs for infants with disabilities and those who are at risk for developing disabilities from birth through age 3. We will learn more about these provisions in Chapter 2.

P.L. 99-457 extends the provisions of P.L. 94-142 to children between the ages of 3 and 5.

Public Law 101-476 These 1990 amendments used "people-first" language to rename the Education of the Handicapped Act the Individuals with Disabilities Education Act (IDEA). This law also recognized the importance of preparing

IDEA now mandates an individualized transition plan (ITP) for each student receiving special education.

∿ Key Components of Public Law 105-17: The 1997 Amendments to IDEA

- Teachers must have access to research findings on effective educational practices.
- States will establish performance goals for students with disabilities and include these students in state- and districtwide assessments.
- General education teachers who are responsible for implementing the IEP must be included on the IEP team.
- IDEA '97 underscores the fundamental idea that students with disabilities should be learning what other children are learning in school. Schools will be required to assume greater responsibility for assuring that students with disabilities have access to the general education curriculum.
- Individualized transition plans are now mandated at age 14.
- The educational rights of students with disabilities who are violent or dangerous are protected, although schools are

able to more quickly remove those students from the classroom.
- There is an emphasis on the need for qualified personnel in special education.
- The eligibility category of *developmental delay* has been added for children ages 3 to 9.
- The general education teacher must be part of the IEP team whenever appropriate.

Source: Adapted from N.D. Safer, "IDEA Opens the Door to a Better Future for Students with Disabilities and Special Educators," *Teaching Exceptional Children, 29*(6) (1997), 1; and J.E. Heumann and T. Hehir, "Believing in Children: A Great IDEA for the Future," *Exceptional Parent* 27(9) (1997), 38–42.

students for life and work after school. It mandated the creation of an individualized transition plan (ITP) for each student receiving special education services.

Public Law 105-17   The 1997 amendments to IDEA provided the most substantial revision of the law relating to the education of children with disabilities since P.L. 94-142 was passed in 1975. The following box, "Key Components of Public Law 105-17," lists some of the changes in these amendments.

■ **Section 504**   Are you taking class in a building that has ramps leading up to it? Are there elevators as well as stairs and escalators? In the elevators are there Braille cells next to the numerals indicating each floor? Is there a wide stall, a low sink, and a low mirror in the restroom? Is one of the public telephones set low on the wall? Are there plenty of special parking places for people with disabilities outside?

Let us hope that all these adaptations make your school building accessible to students, faculty, and staff with disabilities. Most public facilities have not become accessible out of the goodness of anyone's heart. They are accessible because of Section 504 of the Rehabilitation Act of 1973, a civil rights law that requires that institutions not discriminate against people with disabilities in any way if they wish to receive any federal funds.

Section 504 of the Rehabilitation Act of 1973 requires that public facilities be accessible to people with disabilities.

Section 504 has had considerable impact on architecture and construction in the United States, since it requires changes in building design for physical access. It has also been used to prohibit discrimination against a person simply because he or she is disabled. For example, if you had a newborn baby who needed corrective surgery to open a blocked trachea, would you hesitate about having it performed? Well, that surgery cannot be denied to a baby with Down syndrome, either, simply because she will have mental retardation. Section 504 prohibits discrimination on the basis of disability.

■ **The Americans with Disabilities Act** On July 26, 1990, President George Bush signed into law Public Law 101-336, the Americans with Disabilities Act (ADA), with these words: "Today, America welcomes into the mainstream of life all people with disabilities. Let the shameful wall of exclusion finally come tumbling down." The ADA is civil rights legislation for people with disabilities, and it is patterned on Section 504 of the Rehabilitation Act of 1973. The provisions of the ADA cover four major areas: private-sector employment; public services, including public facilities, buses, and trains; public accommodations, including restaurants, hotels, theaters, doctors' offices, retail stores, museums, libraries, parks, private schools, and day-care centers; and telecommunications, making telephone relay services available twenty-four hours a day to people with speech and hearing impairments. Table 1.2 presents a summary of key legislation in special education.

> The ADA protects the civil rights of people with disabilities in four major areas: private-sector employment, public services, public accommodations, and telecommunications.

Litigation

The landmark *Brown v. Board of Education of Topeka, Kansas* (1954) decision set the stage for several important court cases concerning children with disabilities. In the *Brown* decision, the U.S. Supreme Court ruled that separate schools for African American and white students cannot be considered equal and are therefore unconstitutional. This ruling provided the precedent for parents and advocates who maintained that children with disabilities were being unfairly denied equal educational opportunities.

> In *Brown v. Board of Education*, the Supreme Court ruled that "separate but equal" schools were unconstitutional.

The first two court cases we will discuss addressed the overrepresentation of children from minority backgrounds in special education classes. First, let us examine the assumptions behind these cases. If your school district has a population of children that is 33 percent African American, 33 percent white, and 33 percent Latino, you might logically expect that the population of children in special classes would be approximately the same. If you examined those numbers and found that, in fact, the children in special classes were 50 percent white, 25 percent African American, and 25 percent Latino, you might say that white students were overrepresented in those classes; that is, their number is out of proportion to what we see in the population of students in the district.

Diana v. Board of Education (1970) was a state class-action suit that addressed the overrepresentation of children from non-English-speaking backgrounds in special classes in California. It was filed on behalf of nine Mexican-American children who had been placed in classes for students with mental retardation based on results of IQ tests given in English. Advocates for the children argued that their assessment had been unfair, since it was not conducted in Spanish, their native language. The case was settled with the agreement that children must be tested in both their primary language and in English when special education placement is being considered. When the children involved in the case were retested more appropriately, seven of the nine were no longer eligible for special education.

> *Diana v. Board of Education* mandated that children be tested in their primary language for special education services.

In *Larry P. v. Riles* (1979) the issue was the disproportionate number of African American students in classes for students with educable mental retardation in California. The plaintiffs maintained that standardized IQ tests, used as the basis for placement of these students, were culturally biased against African American children. The *Larry P.* ruling eliminated the use of IQ tests to place African American students in classes for students with mental retardation in California. The overrepresentation of African American children in special

> *Larry P. v. Riles* dealt with the fairness of IQ testing for African American children.

A good day at school means
having fun with friends.
(Evan Johnson/Jeroboam)

education remains a cause of great concern, despite changes in assessment practices spurred by the *Larry P.* decision (see Chapter 13 for more discussion).

Two other important state court cases addressed the need for schooling for children with disabilities who at the time were not provided with any education at all. In *Pennsylvania Association for Retarded Citizens (PARC) v. Commonwealth of Pennsylvania* (1972), parents of children with mental retardation sued to procure an education for their children. The courts decided in their favor and required Pennsylvania to provide a free, appropriate public education for students with mental retardation. In *Mills v. the Washington, D.C. Board of Education* (1972), a similar decision was reached in regard to all children with disabilities in the District of Columbia.

PARC required Pennsylvania schools to provide a free and appropriate education to students with mental retardation.

Since the passage of P.L. 94-142, there have been several cases in which the courts have interpreted various aspects of the law. The first case to reach the U.S. Supreme Court, *Board of Education of Hendrick Hudson School District v. Rowley* (1982), concerned the question of what constitutes an "appropriate" education. The parents of Amy Rowley, a deaf child, requested that she have a sign language interpreter in order to benefit fully from her placement in a regular class. The court wrote that an "appropriate" education did not mean that the student must reach her maximum potential, but that she have a reasonable opportunity to learn. Since there was evidence presented that Amy Rowley could derive some benefit from regular class placement without a sign language interpreter, she was denied that additional service.

The *Rowley* and *Tatro* cases concerned the schools' responsibilities to provide "related services."

In *Irving Independent School District v. Tatro* (1984), the Supreme Court explored the school's responsibility to provide catheterization, a medical service,

Table 1.3 **Important Litigation Involving Special Education**

1954 *Brown v. Board of Education* In this case, the U.S. Supreme Court decided that the concept of "separate but equal" schools was unconstitutional and declared that all children must have equal opportunity for education.

1970 *Diana v. Board of Education* (California) This state case established that California schools could not place students in special education on the basis of culturally biased tests or tests given in the student's nonprimary language.

1972 *Pennsylvania Association for Retarded Citizens v. Pennsylvania* This state case established the right of children with mental retardation to a public education in Pennsylvania.

1972 *Mills v. Washington, D.C. Board of Education* This state case established that all students with disabilities were entitled to a public education in the District of Columbia.

1979 *Larry P. v. Riles* (California) In this state case, it was decided that IQ tests could not be used to identify African American students with mental retardation.

1982 *Board of Education of the Hendrick Hudson Central School District v. Rowley* The U.S. Supreme Court, in its first decision interpreting P.L. 94-142, defined an "appropriate" education as one that provides a child with a reasonable opportunity to learn.

1984 *Irving Independent School District v. Tatro* The U.S. Supreme Court decided that procedures that could be performed by a nonphysician (such as catheterization) qualified as related services, not medical services, and must be provided by the school district, so that a child can attend school and benefit from special education.

1988 *Honig v. Doe* The U.S. Supreme Court ruled that a student receiving special education services cannot be excluded from school indefinitely (expelled), particularly if the behavior is related to the student's disability.

to a child with spina bifida who needed this service in order to remain in school. The Court decided that since this procedure could be performed by a school nurse, and the child needed it to remain in school, it should be considered a related service rather than a medical service, and the schools must provide it.

In 1988, the Supreme Court, in *Honig v. Doe*, ruled that a student receiving special education services cannot be excluded indefinitely from school and from receiving the services specified in the IEP. In addition, the student cannot be expelled from school if the behavior in question is related to his or her disability. Table 1.3 summarizes these and other court cases that have significantly affected special education.

In *Honig v. Doe* the Supreme Court ruled that a student receiving special education services cannot be expelled if the behavior in question is related to his or her disability.

Individualized Education

At the core of the laws pertaining to the education of exceptional children is the concept of individualized education: Each student should have a program tailored to his or her unique needs. P.L. 94-142 and its amendments have instituted a system of planning that can now extend from birth to the postschool years. Table 1.4 describes the components of individualized education. In the following sections we'll look at each of these individualized programs.

With individualized education, each student has a program tailored to his or her unique needs.

Table 1.4   Documentation for Individualized Education

The individualized family service plan must include the following components:

- A statement of the infant's or toddler's present levels of development (physical, cognitive, speech/language, psychosocial, motor, and self-help)
- A statement of the family's strengths and needs related to enhancing the child's development
- A statement of major outcomes expected to be achieved for the child and the family
- The criteria, procedures, and time lines for determining progress
- The specific early intervention services necessary to meet the unique needs of the child and family, including the frequency, intensity, and method of delivering services
- The projected dates for the initiation of services and expected duration of those services
- The name of the case manager (service coordinator)
- The procedures for transition from early intervention into the preschool program provided under Part B of IDEA

The individualized education program must include the following components:

- A statement of the child's current educational performance levels
- Annual goals and benchmarks or short-term objectives
- A description of the special education and related services provided
- A statement describing the program modifications and supports the child needs to benefit from the general education curriculum
- A statement of the extent to which the child will be able to participate in regular education programs
- The date on which services began and their anticipated duration
- Appropriate objective evaluation criteria and evaluation procedures and schedules for determining, at least annually, whether the short-term objectives are being achieved
- A statement of transition services needed by students who are 14 and over

The individualized transition plan might include the following components:

- A statement of transition services needed (career planning, self-advocacy, social life, community participation, postsecondary education, leisure services, advocacy/legal services, daily living, physical care)
- Annual goals in each service area, accompanied by objectives designed to meet those goals
- Statements of educational and related services needed to enable the student to meet the goals and objectives
- Statement of interagency responsibilities and linkages, including the agency, purpose, contact persons, and the time by which the responsibility or linkage must be established

Source: "Legal Foundations: The Individuals with Disabilities Education Act (IDEA)," *Teaching Exceptional Children* (Winter 1993), pp. 85–87. Copyright © 1993 by The Council for Exceptional Children. Reprinted with permission. Updated by authors, 1998.

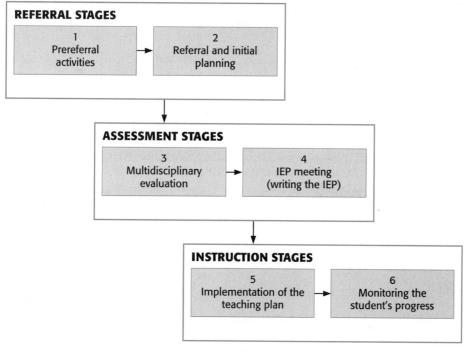

Figure 1.2
Stages of the IEP Process

Source: Adapted from J. Lerner, D. Dawson, and L. Horvath, *Cases in Learning and Behavior Problems: A Guide to Individualized Education Programs* (Salem, WI: Sheffield Publishing Co., 1980), p. 3. Used by permission.

The Individualized Family Service Plan (IFSP)

Exceptional children and their families can first receive individualized services through the IFSP. The writers of P.L. 99-457, recognizing the importance of early intervention for young children in the context of the family, mandated that an **individualized family service plan (IFSP)** be drawn up by an interdisciplinary team that includes family members. The major components of the IFSP are listed in Table 1.4. The IFSP is meant to ensure that young children from birth to age 3 who are identified as having disabilities or who are at risk receive the services they need to develop skills and prevent additional disabilities. Chapter 2 will provide more detail on the IFSP.

> The IFSP ensures that the youngest children and their families receive the services they need.

The Individualized Education Program (IEP)

The **individualized education program (IEP)** is the basis for special education programming in preschool, elementary, middle, and high school. IDEA calls for a team of people to draw up a written IEP at a meeting called for that purpose. The team is typically made up of the parent(s), the special education teacher, the regular education teacher, and the school principal. When it is appropriate, the student is also present at the IEP meeting. Other school professionals become involved, too, when the student needs supportive services: The school nurse, speech-language specialist, adaptive physical education teacher, and others may participate in the IEP process. According to the law, the IEP must have the components listed in Table 1.4. Figure 1.2 illustrates the stages of the IEP process, and Figure 1.3 shows a sample IEP.

> The IEP outlines the educational plan for each student.

INDIVIDUALIZED EDUCATION PROGRAM

Student's name _Sara Austin_

Student ID# _72348_   DOB _10/8/88_

Current assignment _Queensbury School, 4th grade_

DATES

Initial IEP _9/94_

Current IEP _9/97_

IEP review _6/98_

Exceptional Education Assignments (Location/Program/Organization/Time)	Initiation Date	Anticipated Duration	Person Responsible
Learning disability resource room	9/97	6/98	Roberta Chase
15% of time/week at Queensbury			
school			

Related Services			
Speech and Language therapy			
1/2 hr. 3x/week	9/97	6/98	Phyllis Find
Occupational therapy			
1/2 hr. 3x/week	9/97	6/98	Paul Cecil

Extent to Which Student Will Participate in General or Vocational Education

85% in general education program

Required Special Aids, Services, or Equipment

_N.A._

Subject (hours/% of time)

English, Social Studies, and Science

20 hrs./week

Art/Music 1 hr./week

Vocational edcuation _____

Physical education: _X_ Regular ___ Adaptive

In Attendance at IEP Meeting	Signature	Date	Signature	Date
LEA representative (title: _Principal_)	Louise Fischer	9/97		
Parent(s), Guardian(s) or Surrogate Parent(s)	Gina Austin	9/97	Robert Austin	9/97
Student				
Teacher(s)	Anna Chase	9/97		
Evaluator(s)				
Other(s)				

Figure 1.3

A Sample Individualized Education Program

Source: Adapted from Winifred Anderson, Stephen Chitwood, and Deirdre Hayden, *Negotiating the Special Education Maze: A Guide for Parents and Teachers*, 2d ed. (Rockville, MD: Woodbine House, 1990), pp. 122–123. Reprinted with permission.

Student's name Sara Austin

Student ID# 72348

Exceptional education assignment _____

LD Resource Room

Performance or Subject Area: Math

Present Level: Adds and subtracts 2 digit numbers

Counts to 50 by 5's

Identifies penny, but confuses nickels, dimes, quarters

Annual Goal: Sara will be able to make change for a dollar using pennies, nickels, dimes, and quarters by June.

Short-Term Instructional Objectives	Evaluation of Short-Term Instructional Objectives		
	Criterion for Mastery	Evaluation Procedures and Schedule to be Used	Results/Date
1. Sara will discriminate between the four different coins.	Accurately name the coins – 100%	Teacher observation using real coins by October 29.	
2. Sara will identify the coin and its value.	Write number value under picture of coin.	Worksheets on coins completed accurately in independent work by Jan. 1.	
3. Sara will make change for a dime in three ways.	Demonstrate with real coins.	Teacher observation by March 1.	
4. Sara will make change for a quarter in three ways.	Use pennies, nickels, and dimes to make a quarter accurately – 100%.	Teacher observation by April 6.	
5. Sara will purchase a box of crayons at school store and count change.	Purchase completed with 100% accuracy.	Crayons and correct change given to teacher by May 27.	

Figure 1.3

(Continued)

The ITP helps prepare students for life and work after school.

The Individualized Transition Plan (ITP)

As noted earlier, the Individuals with Disabilities Education Act mandated transition services for all students receiving special education services. Transition plans are now required from the age of 14. The **individualized transition plan (ITP)** includes the components listed in Table 1.4.

The Pros and Cons of Labeling

We use terms that we call "labels" to describe groups of exceptional children. In this book, you will read about students with mental retardation, learning disabilities, physical and health impairments, speech and language impairments, and emotional disturbance, as well as students who are deaf and hard of hearing, visually handicapped, or gifted and talented.

Think of the labels that could be applied to you. Are you a Caucasian female? A Latino male? A Catholic, Protestant, Jew, Muslim? Would you want those labels to be the first piece of information other people learn about you? People with disabilities and their families and advocates have worked very hard to erase the "disability-first" perception that has often pursued them.

Why use labels at all? Many people feel that we should not. But labels do serve some useful purposes. First, they help us count individuals with exceptionalities. Just as the United States government wants to know your sex, race, and age in order to provide representation and services to your community, the federal government and the states count the numbers of students with disabilities in order to plan for and provide educational and supportive services.

Labels also help professionals differentiate methods of instruction and support services to different groups. Children who have visual disabilities learn to read with materials that are quite different from those used by children who have learning disabilities. Children who are deaf or hard of hearing need the support services of an audiologist and possibly a speech-language specialist. Gifted and talented students may learn more from a differentiated curriculum tailored to their learning strengths and needs (Clark, 1997). Many special educators would argue, however, that instructional methods do not vary significantly for students who are identified as having learning disabilities, mild mental retardation, or severe emotional disturbance, although the emphasis of instruction might vary from student to student, depending on individual student learning needs. We will pursue this topic further in the Framework section that follows Chapter 3.

Labels can lead to prejudging and stereotyping.

Labels enable professionals to communicate efficiently about children and their needs. But they are frequently misused and can carry an enormous stigma. Words like *hyperactive*, *autistic*, and *dyslexic* are often used freely to describe children who are having academic or behavioral difficulties in school. Using such terms may make a professional sound knowledgeable, but labels like these may alter the perceptions of others about the learning potential of such a child. Labels often obscure individual differences among children, as well (Hobbs, 1975); we assume that all children identified as "learning disabled" are somehow the same. (Table 1.5 shows how labels have changed over time.)

Special education professionals would like to replace current labels with terminology directly related to instruction.

Many professionals within special education see categorical labels as a necessary evil and would like to replace current labels with terminology that is directly related to instruction and that minimizes negative connotations (Adelman, 1996).

Table 1.5 Terms Reflecting Social Changes

Areas of Disability	Past	Present
Mental Retardation	idiots, feebleminded, cretin, mentally deficient, educably retarded or trainably retarded, morons, high level or low level	mild, moderate, severe retardation and intermittent, pervasive, extensive, and limited retardation
Learning Disabilities	dyslexia, minimal cerebral dysfunction, specific learning disabilities, learning disabilities	learning disabilities
Emotional Disturbance	unsocialized, dementia, emotionally disturbed, acting out, withdrawn	emotional/behavioral disorders (E/BD)
Attention Deficit Disorder (with or without hyperactivity)	hyperactivity, specific learning disabilities	ADD (Attention Deficit Disorder without hyperactivity) or ADHD (with hyperactivity) and combined
Head Injuries	strephosymbolia, brain crippled children, brain injured, closed head injury	traumatic brain injury
Deafness	deaf and dumb, deaf mute	severely/profoundly hearing impaired
Persons with Orthopedic Disabilities	crippled children, physically handicapped	physical disabilities
Learning Disability in Reading	dyslexia, minimal cerebral dysfunction, specific learning disabilities	dyslexia
Autism	childhood schizophrenia, children with refrigerator parents, Kanner's Syndrome, autoid	autism (high functioning or low functioning)
Placements for Individuals with More Severe Disabilities	Asylums, institutions, residential schools, group homes	community living, assistive living, and supportive employment
Placements for Individuals with Mild Disabilities	normalization, mainstreaming, Regular Education Initiative, integration	inclusion
Assessment	testing, measurement	assessment, normal referenced or authentic/performance based assessment
Preassessment	diagnosis, child study teacher assistance teams	preferral teams, student support teams

Source: G. Vergason and M.L. Anderegg, "The Ins and Outs of Special Education Terminology," *Teaching Exceptional Children*, 29(5) May/June (1997), p. 36. Copyright © 1996 by The Council for Exceptional Children. Reprinted with permission.

Educational Setting

P.L. 94-142, which is also known as IDEA (Individuals with Disabilities Education Act), requires that each school district provide a range of program options for students with disabilities. As you saw in Figure 1.1, these programs range from what is considered the least restrictive to the most restrictive environment. Remember that the concept of "least restrictive environment" is based on the opportunities available for interaction between the student with a disability and nondisabled peers. In practical terms, this means that a family attending an IEP meeting must have the option of choosing from this range of programs in order to obtain the most appropriate education for the child. The family and the

The least restrictive environment, which may be different for each child, allows the most interaction with nondisabled peers.

Friendships like the one between these two students are an important outcome of the inclusion of children with disabilities in the regular classroom. (Therese Frare/NYT Pictures)

Inclusion of students with disabilities in the general education classroom requires collaboration between general and special educators.

school district must come to an agreement about the setting in which the child's educational needs can most appropriately be met.

The concept of the least restrictive environment was originally envisioned as a relative one—that is, one that must be interpreted anew for each student based on his or her unique learning characteristics. Some professionals today, however, interpret the least restrictive environment in a more general fashion and argue for the inclusion of students with disabilities in the general education classroom, along with curricular adaptations and the collaboration and teaming of professionals from special and general education (Stainback, Stainback & Ayres, 1996). Others call for maintaining the continuum of educational services (Council for Exceptional Children, 1997; Leiberman, 1996).

Let's consider an example. Ana is a student who has engaged in violent and self-destructive behavior. These behaviors have been decreased in the special school for students labeled seriously emotionally disturbed that she has been attending, but this is considered a relatively restrictive setting for Ana, since she has no opportunity there to interact with her nondisabled peers. At her IEP meeting, her family and teachers decide that Ana's educational goals could best be reached in a less restrictive setting: a special class for students labeled severely emotionally disturbed on an elementary school campus. There she will

∼ Defining Characteristics of Collaboration

- *Collaboration is voluntary.* People cannot be forced to use a particular style in their interactions with others.

- *Collaboration requires parity among participants.* Each person's contribution is equally valued, and each person has equal power in decision-making.

- *Collaboration is based on mutual goals.* Professionals do not have to share all goals in order to collaborate, just one that is specific and important enough to maintain their shared attention.

- *Collaboration depends on shared responsibility for participation and decision-making.* Collaborators must assume the responsibility of actively engaging in the activity and in the decision-making it entails.

- *Individuals who collaborate share their resources.* Sharing resources of time, knowledge, and materials can enhance the sense of ownership among professionals.

- *Individuals who collaborate share responsibility for outcomes.* Whether the results of collaboration are positive or negative, all participating individuals are responsible for the outcomes.

Source: Adapted from M. Friend & L. Cook, *Interactions: Collaboration Skills for School Professionals* (White Plains, NY: Longman, 1996), pp. 6–9.

have opportunities to participate in social and academic activities with her peers, with her special-class teacher planning and overseeing those experiences. With success she will have the opportunity for more and more of those experiences.

Advocates of inclusion might suggest that Kimberly be placed at her grade level in her neighborhood school, with a special education teacher or instructional aide available to monitor her behavior and make curricular adaptations as they are needed. They would argue that only with the models of appropriate behavior available in the regular class and the opportunities for meaningful social interaction provided there can Kimberly be motivated to change her behavior. This picture of inclusion can succeed only if professionals from special and regular education team up to provide individualized educational services for Kimberly and each included student.

Inclusion is not yet a reality for most students with disabilities. Nonetheless, the majority of students identified as exceptional *are receiving their instruction primarily in the regular classroom.* A number of different kinds of programs have been developed to ensure that these students and their teachers receive the support they need. Many involve the special educator and the regular educator collaborating. **Collaboration** between the general and special educator—"working together in a supportive, mutually beneficial relationship" (Friend & Cook, 1996, p. 5)—is the foundation for successful inclusive practices. The accompanying box describes key characteristics of collaboration.

Special and regular educators also work together in **team-teaching** situations. Team teaching, also called co-teaching, can involve shared instruction of a lesson, a subject area, or an entire instructional program. At the TRIPOD-Burbank program in southern California, for example, teachers of deaf students pair with elementary teachers in classrooms with three to six deaf students and twenty-two hearing peers. Both teachers sign and speak at all times, and many of the hearing students learn to understand and use sign language quite well. According to Vaughn, Schumm, and Arguelles (1997), co-teaching is "a bit like a marriage" (p. 5); it can be very rewarding once some of the common issues are worked out.

Most exceptional students receive the majority of their instruction in the general education classroom.

Collaboration is the foundation of successful inclusion.

Team teaching can involve shared instruction of a lesson, a subject area, or an entire instructional program.

The prereferral intervention team
works to keep students in the general education classroom.

Another arrangement is the **teacher assistance team** (also known by many other names, such as the *intervention assistance team*). This is a group of teachers and other school professionals who work together to assist the regular classroom teacher. Under some circumstances, a team concentrates on keeping children in the regular classroom instead of referring them to special education; a team like this is sometimes known as a **prereferral intervention team** (Graden, 1989; Safran & Safran, 1996). In other situations, team members provide consultation to teachers or direct services to students who are identified with special needs but are in the regular classroom.

These arrangements are designed to maintain the student's instruction within the regular classroom. Other kinds of services for students with special needs are called **pullout programs,** since they involve the student leaving the classroom to receive specialized instruction. The traditional organization of the resource room, for example, involves students leaving the regular classroom for specialized instruction in academic areas of need. In many parts of the country, however, this is changing, and the resource teacher is operating on the **consultation model**—meeting with teachers to plan instructional adaptations for students as well as providing direct instructional services within the regular classroom. Some other examples of pullout programs are speech and language services, orientation and mobility for students with visual handicaps, and physical therapy for students with physical disabilities.

Sometimes students are educated within **special classes** in regular schools. These classes group children by exceptionality—gifted, deaf, learning disabled—and a specialist teacher instructs them together. Individual students may leave the special class for part of the day to receive instruction in the regular classroom, but the majority of their time is usually spent in the special class.

Special schools are designed exclusively for students with exceptionality, and the related services that the students need are usually housed under the same roof. Since the emphasis of P.L. 94-142 is on education within the least restrictive environment, special schools, which usually provide no opportunity for their students to interact with nondisabled peers, have been considered viable alternatives only for students with the most severe disabilities. Many professionals believe that even for those students, complete segregation from the mainstream cannot be justified; others believe strongly in the importance of maintaining the special school option (Cohen, 1995).

Residential schools are special schools where the students live during the school year. This is considered the most restrictive educational environment for exceptional students, since they have no opportunity to interact with their nondisabled peers.

Some students, because of chronic illness or other medical needs, are taught at home or while they are hospitalized. **Home- or hospital-based instruction** is provided by a special education teacher and is usually temporary, until a student is ready to attend school again.

In today's schools, the great majority of students with disabilities are receiving their education in a regular school building: The *Eighteenth Annual Report* (1996) put that number at 95 percent of students aged 6 to 21. At the classroom level, 43.4 percent were served in regular classrooms, 29.5 percent were served in resource rooms, and 22.7 percent were served in separate classes. The remaining students received their educational services in public and private separate school facilities (3.1 percent), public and private residential facilities (0.7 percent), and homebound/hospital settings (0.6 percent) (see Figure 1.4).

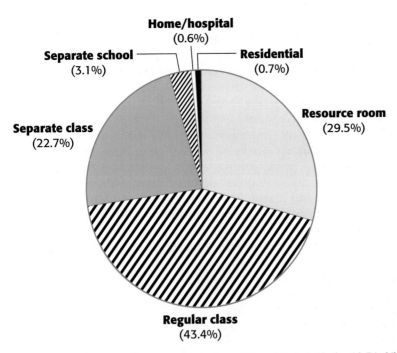

Figure 1.4
Percentage of All Students
with Disabilities Age 6–21
Served in Six Educational
Placements, School Year
1993–1994

Source: Eighteenth Annual Report to Congress on the Implementation of the Individuals with Disabilities Education Act, U.S. Department of Education, Office of Special Education Programs, Data Analysis System (DANS).
Notes: Includes data from 50 states, the District of Columbia, and outlying areas. Separate school includes both public and private separate school facilities. Residential includes both public and private residential facilities.

Measuring Progress and Identifying Ongoing Challenges

You can see from what you have read so far in this chapter that the last twenty-five years have been a very rich period in the United States for people with disabilities and their families and advocates. New laws and new attitudes have opened up many opportunities for learning, growth, health, and friendships.

We are beginning to see documentation of the improvements in outcomes for students with disabilities as a result of IDEA and its amendments. Those who have been educated under IDEA are more likely to complete high school than those who came before them and more likely to be competitively employed; employment rates of high school graduates who have been educated under IDEA are twice that of the overall population of people with disabilities. Today, 44 percent of all adults with a disability have completed some college or received a degree, compared to 29 percent in 1986 (U.S. Department of Education, 1995).

Students educated since IDEA was passed are more likely to have completed school and found employment than their predecessors.

Progress in Community Settings

The philosophy of normalization has had a significant effect on the residential options available to people with disabilities. Through the deinstitutionalization movement, over the last twenty-five years a large number of individuals with disabilities have successfully moved from institutions to community settings

Many believe that adults with disabilities should be permitted to live in the least restrictive, most "normal" environment.

Schools must work to improve the educational achievement of students with disabilities.

such as group homes and apartments. Presently, only about 1 percent of children with disabilities live in expensive and isolated institutions (U.S. Department of Education, 1995). The concept of the least restrictive environment can also be applied to housing; many feel that the least restrictive community settings—that is, those that allow greatest access to normal daily life experiences and interaction with one's neighbors—are the most desirable for adults with disabilities (Walsh, Rice & Rosen, 1996).

Although impressive improvements have been made, challenges still remain. Too many children are being served without the supports they need in order to succeed; too many young people, particularly those identified with learning disabilities and emotional disturbance, are dropping out of school. Children of color, and those from non-English-speaking backgrounds, are still being overidentified, stigmatized, and misserved. Too many teachers are inadequately prepared to serve children with complex teaching and learning needs. Our problems in special education remain daunting, despite our progress.

But we cannot become discouraged. The hoped-for result of the changes and trends within special education and its related fields is not simply to extend opportunities and access to people with disabilities. It is to provide an improved overall quality of life. We have come a long way toward providing the rights guaranteed by our Constitution and Bill of Rights to people with disabilities, but there are still many goals we have yet to attain. Through reading this book and working with students with disabilities we hope you will join us in our quest to reach those goals.

SUMMARY

- Special education can be understood as providing an educational program to meet a student's unique learning needs.

- When describing exceptional students, we distinguish between a disability (which refers to a student's condition) and a handicap (which refers to a limitation imposed by his or her environment). We also use people-first language, which decreases the negative impact of the labels that are used to categorize exceptional children in school.

- Exceptional children make up about 12 percent of the school-age population, but advances in their education have been made only recently. Despite pioneering work by early advocates and educators, it was not until the civil rights movement of the 1960s that significant movement toward full acceptance and participation in society by people with disabilities began.

- Progress has been made through both litigation and legislation. Cases such as *Diana v. Board of Education* and *Larry P. v. Riles* challenged the disproportionate representation of students from minority groups in special education. Major legislation includes Public Law 94-142, the Individuals with Disabilities Education Act, and the Americans with Disabilities Act.

- These laws guarantee people with disabilities specific educational and civil rights. Among the most important are the individualized education program and the continuum of educational settings ranging from the least to the most restrictive environment.

■ The options for educational settings for students with disabilities include regular classrooms, resource rooms, special classes, special schools, residential schools, or other placements such as home or hospital.

Key Terms

exceptional
disability
handicap
people-first language
early intervention
at risk
special education
Jean-Marc-Gaspard
  Itard
normalization
deinstitutionalization
mainstreaming

inclusion
least restrictive environment
Individuals with Disabilities Education Act (IDEA)
individualized family service plan (IFSP)
individualized education program
individualized transition plan (ITP)
collaboration

team teaching
teacher assistance team
prereferral intervention team
pullout programs
consultation model
special classes
special schools
residential schools
home- or hospital-based instruction

Multimedia Resources

Anderson, W., S. Chitwood, D. Hayden. *Negotiating the Special Education Maze* (3rd ed.) (Bethesda, MD: Woodbine House, 1997). A guide to help parents and teachers understand the special education system.

Brightman, Alan J. *Ordinary Moments: The Disabled Experience* (Syracuse, NY: Human Policy Press, 1985). A series of essays that describe in rich, vivid language the daily physical and spiritual lives of people with disabilities.

Carballo, Julie B., et al. *Survival Guide for the First-Year Special Education Teacher, Revised* (Reston, VA: Council for Exceptional Children, 1994). Developed by special education teachers who survived their first five years, this guide offers tips on many aspects of teaching, from organizing your classroom to managing stress.

Council for Exceptional Children (CEC) website: http://www.cec.org. CEC is the major professional organization in special education, serving children with disabilities through their families, teachers, and other advocates.

Getskow, Veronica, and Dee Konczal. *Kids with Special Needs: Information and Activities to Promote Awareness and Understanding* (Santa Barbara, CA: The Learning Works, 1996). This is a guide to promoting awareness and knowledge of childhood disability among children, teachers, and parents. It contains valuable suggestions for classroom activities aimed at nondisabled children.

National Information Center for Handicapped Children and Youth (NICHCY) website: http://www.nichcy.org. NICHCY is a treasure trove of information about children with disabilities and their educational needs, for teachers and families.

Teaching Exceptional Children, 29(5) (May/June 1997) (Seventy-fifth Anniversary Issue). This journal, published by the Council for Exceptional Children, has useful and timely articles for all teachers six times a year. This particular issue focuses on the history of special education in the United States.

USING YOUR KNOWLEDGE

 Can Do: What is special education? Conduct a survey of regular and special education teachers to collect their responses to this question. What are some elements mentioned by all (or most) of them? Get together with others in your class to compare survey results and create a "real-life" definition for yourselves.

 Commonalities: How do people in your community refer to exceptional individuals? During the first few weeks of this semester, keep a file of newspaper clippings of articles that relate to exceptional individuals, special education, or related services. You might also keep a journal. What types of issues are discussed? What types of language are used? What conclusions can you draw about the role of exceptional individuals in the community, their acceptance, and their visibility?

 Collaboration: Are there any legal cases in progress that have to do with the rights of exceptional individuals? If so, try to attend a court hearing. Or find out if your local government is working on legislation related to people with disabilities or exceptional students. Try to schedule an informal interview with a city council member or legislator to talk about the goals of the legislation and any obstacles it must overcome. If you feel it is appropriate, write a letter to your representative supporting or opposing the legislation, detailing the reasons for your position.

How do teachers adjust to mainstreamed exceptional students? Visit a local school that has adopted an inclusion policy and see if you can talk to a regular education teacher. Some questions you might ask include: How do you prepare for an IEP meeting? What are some ways you collaborate with other professionals? Do you find it difficult to manage your time? What are the rewards of having exceptional students in your class? After meeting with a teacher, get together with others in your class to share results.

WHAT YOU CAN DO NOW

1. **Begin a journal in which you reflect on your own attitudes and feelings toward people with disabilities. Which of your feelings are based on experiences, and which on media reports or stereotypes? What do you hope to learn from this course that might change your attitudes?**

2. **Visit a classroom setting where students with disabilities are served. How is it different from what you are used to? How is it similar? Perhaps you could spend time as a volunteer in such a setting.**

3. **Volunteer at a service agency that serves children with disabilities in the age range that interests you. Call your local United Way, March of Dimes, or children's hospital, and ask about volunteering opportunities.**

4. **Observe media coverage of people with disabilities or issues important to them. Do newspapers and television newscasts cover these topics in a fair and unbiased manner? Write a letter to the editor suggesting more coverage or more positive coverage, perhaps concerning access, bias, aging, employment, or medical advances.**

5. **Invite a person with a disability to speak to your class (with your instructor's permission!) and tell his or her story.**

Risk Factors and Early Intervention

IN this chapter, we introduce you to the factors and conditions that put children at risk for developmental disabilities. These factors can result in any of the specific disabilities that are discussed in later chapters, but it is also possible that a child will have the experiences and resilience to overcome the risk without developmental delay. You will also learn what *early intervention* can do for young children and families. As you read, look for the answers to these questions:

■ Why is it important to identify children at risk?

■ How does early intervention work to prevent disability or lessen its impact?

 Can Do: What can be done to prevent disabilities?

 Commonalities: Why are prevention and prenatal care important for *all* children?

 Collaboration: How can teachers and early intervention specialists work with other professionals to minimize the effects of a child's risk status?

Many factors can place a child at risk for the development of a disability.

Happily, the great majority of pregnancies result in healthy babies who will not require any special educational services when they reach school age. Yet each woman, each couple conceiving a child, also takes a chance that the child will develop differently from "the norm" and as a result have special needs that will require extra help and support at home and at school.

Why do some pregnancies produce children with special needs? Why do some children who have difficult starts in life do just fine, while others who begin life under ideal circumstances develop problems? The answers are complicated—many times no medical or psychological expert can answer them for bewildered parents. But in this chapter we will describe some of the circumstances that place a child at risk for the development of a disability.

The information in this chapter should have meaning for you as a teacher or other professional working with exceptional children. First, it should help you decide whether the cause of a student's disability has any bearing on the kind of instruction or support you will provide. Second, it should help you give more complete information to family members who come to you for advice and counsel. This information will be relevant to each of the specific disabilities discussed later in the book. We encourage you to review this chapter as you learn about children with specific disabilities.

We also expect that this information will have personal meaning for each reader. Some of you may be making decisions about whether or when to begin a family. Others may be watching your own children have children. We hope that the information presented here will help you to plan for a healthy family and to make intelligent, well-informed decisions that can enhance the possibilities for a healthy baby. Ultimately, the message of this chapter is that we can all have an impact on the prevention of disabilities in children. Each one of us has a responsibility to do whatever is within our power to *prevent* disabilities in the children of our country—and that is part of what this chapter is all about.

We must all help prevent disabilities in children.

Definitions and Terms

Public Law 99-457, which amended P.L. 94-142 in 1986, identifies three groups of children from birth to age 3 who may be eligible for early intervention services. They are:

- Children with developmental delay
- Children with a physical or mental condition that carries a high probability of developmental delay
- Children who are medically or environmentally *at risk* for developmental delay if early intervention is not provided

Let us look at how the term *risk* is used.

Psychologist and researcher Claire Kopp (1983) defined **risk factors** as "a wide range of *biological and environmental conditions* [emphasis added] that are associated with increased probability for cognitive, social, affective, and physical problems" (p. 1). Biological conditions generally arise from factors related to pregnancy or maternal and child health, such as low birthweight, exposure to drugs or toxic substances, or a chromosomal abnormality. Environmental conditions include negative influences in the child's physical or social surroundings after birth such as extreme poverty, child abuse, or neglect.

Risk factors are biological or environmental conditions associated with cognitive, social, affective, and physical problems.

The second part of Kopp's definition contains a crucial concept. These conditions are *associated with increased probability* for a variety of later problems. It is more probable that these adverse outcomes will occur if there are risk factors present—but the presence of one or more risk factors *does not guarantee* developmental problems in children. Children may be at risk for developmental problems, but they will not necessarily have them. The severity of the risk factor as well as the nature of the environment in which each child grows will determine whether developmental problems will occur.

The presence of risk factors increases the probability of adverse outcomes but does not guarantee them.

Some children overcome both biological and environmental hurdles and, because of their own characteristics and the outside support that they receive, emerge as strong and productive adults. We refer to these children as especially *resilient*. You will see, however, that the existence of clusters or combinations of risk factors makes it more likely that developmental problems will occur and that *early intervention*—comprehensive, individualized services provided to children from birth to age 3 and their families—can have a significant impact on a child's development.

Types of Risk

Since the concept of risk is wide-ranging, it is helpful to have a framework within which categories of vulnerable infants can be described. We will use the categories of **biological risk** and **environmental risk** to describe the potential impact of specific factors on young children (see Figure 2.1).

Biological Risk

Biological risk exists when events occur before, during, or after birth that may be associated with damage to the child's developing systems, increasing the likelihood that he or she will experience developmental problems. Biological risk factors can be divided into three categories that correspond with the earliest periods of development (Kopp, 1983): the **prenatal** period, from conception to birth; the **perinatal** period (which overlaps the prenatal period somewhat), from

Biological risk exists when prenatal, perinatal, or postnatal events occur that may increase the likelihood that the child will experience developmental problems.

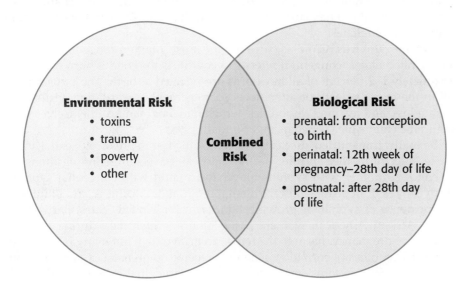

Figure 2.1
Types of Risk

the twelfth week of pregnancy through the twenty-eighth day of life (Gorski & VandenBerg, 1996); and the **postnatal** period, covering events of early childhood that occur after the twenty-eighth day of life.

■ **Prenatal Factors**   Prenatal factors are those that affect embryologic and fetal development before birth. Adverse prenatal events often account for the most severe developmental outcomes among the infants who survive them. If they have their impact during the **first trimester** (first three months) of pregnancy, they may compromise the organs and body parts developing at that time; if they occur later in pregnancy, they may affect the growth and differentiation of those organs that are still developing, such as the brain and central nervous system. Prenatal factors include maternal illnesses and maternal use and abuse of substances, including drugs and alcohol. These factors—alcohol, drugs, illnesses, infections, and so on—are often called **teratogens,** substances that can cause birth defects. We will discuss some of the most common factors that research tells us can affect embryologic and fetal development during pregnancy (see Figure 2.2).

Teratogens are substances that can cause birth defects.

Maternal Illness and Infection   Not every illness of the pregnant mother will affect her unborn child, but some illnesses and infections are known to have a devastating impact on embryologic and fetal development. **Rubella,** for example, sometimes called "German measles," is a highly contagious virus. Rubella is particularly damaging if contracted by a woman during the first sixteen weeks of pregnancy. It can result in blindness, deafness, heart malformation, and/or mental retardation in surviving infants, depending on the fetal organ developing at the time the rubella virus strikes. Moores (1996, p. 101) describes the impact of the virus:

Illness of the mother during pregnancy can cause damage to the developing fetus.

> If a pregnant woman contracts rubella, particularly during the first trimester . . . of pregnancy, the virus may cross the placental barrier and attack the developing cells and structures of the fetus, killing or crippling the unborn child. The virus can kill growing cells, and it attacks tissues of the eye, ear, and other organs.

Fortunately, immunization against rubella (see the section of this chapter that discusses prevention) has virtually eliminated this disease as a cause of disability in the United States.

Cytomegalovirus (CMV) is currently the most common congenital infection in the United States (**congenital** refers to a condition the child is born with). Approximately 1–2 percent of all newborns are infected at birth. The virus can result in the infant's death or aftereffects such as mental retardation, vision and hearing loss, and learning disabilities, which may not manifest themselves until later in the child's life (Hutchinson & Sandall, 1995).

Sexually transmitted diseases (STDs), which are spread by sexual intercourse, affect a mother and her partner and can have serious implications for the child. A mother with syphilis may have a child with congenital syphilis, which can result in death or severe mental retardation, deafness, and blindness. The incidence of syphilis is growing rapidly in the United States, particularly among African American women. If the illness is identified during the first trimester of pregnancy, harm to the fetus can be avoided, but many infants with congenital syphilis are born to women who receive no prenatal care. Herpes, another STD, has symptoms such as cold sores and vaginal infections. Although

When STDs are identified and treated during the first trimester of pregnancy, harm to the fetus can be avoided.

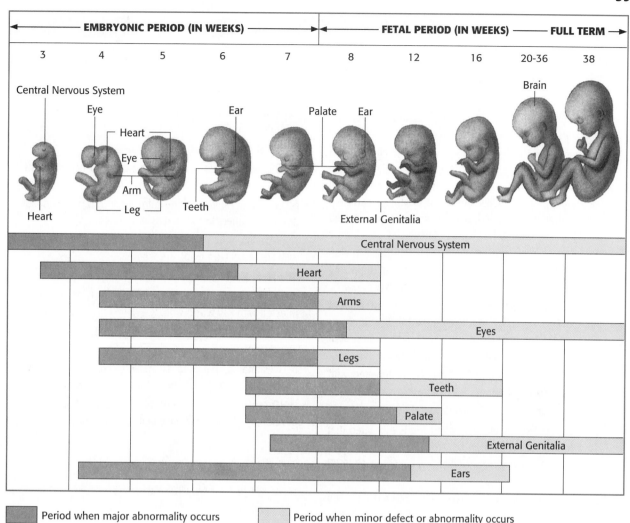

Period when major abnormality occurs   **Period when minor defect or abnormality occurs**

Figure 2.2
Sensitive Periods in Prenatal Development
Source: Adapted from *Before We Are Born,* Fifth Edition by K. L. Moore. Copyright © 1998. Used by permission of W. B. Saunders.

the risk of transmitting herpes to an unborn child is relatively low, if transmission does occur during a vaginal delivery it can have severe consequences for the infant, such as neurological, vision, and hearing impairment (Hutchinson & Sandall, 1995). Other STDs, including chlamydia, can also affect fetal development and the health of the newborn. STDS are a particular risk for pregnant adolescents (Rosenthal, Cohen & Biro, 1994).

From 15 to 30 percent of U.S. women with **acquired immune deficiency syndrome,** or **AIDS,** or those who test positive for the human immunodeficiency virus (HIV), transmit HIV infection to their offspring during pregnancy, birth, or breastfeeding (Working Group on Mother-to-Child Transmission of HIV, 1995). AIDS is a disease that weakens the immune system and ultimately results in death. HIV infection causes central nervous system damage in children, so children who are HIV positive may experience significant developmental difficulties. Improvements in treatments for infants and children with HIV

AIDS and HIV can be transmitted during pregnancy, birth, and breast-feeding.

～ Pediatric HIV/AIDS Fact Sheet

Children

- It is estimated that the number of children with HIV in the United States is between 10,000 and 20,000.

- AIDS is the seventh leading cause of death for children 1 to 4 years of age in the United States.

- Between 15 and 30 percent of infants born to HIV-infected women become infected with the virus, resulting in an estimated 1,300 to 2,000 children born with HIV annually in the United States. Studies show that treatment can help reduce the rate of HIV transmission from an infected woman to her baby to less than 10 percent.

- Today, nearly 100 percent of new HIV infections in children result from an HIV-infected pregnant woman passing the virus to her baby either before or during birth.

- Approximately 30,000 American children have already lost their parents to AIDS, and it is estimated that by the year 2000 the overall number of orphaned children and adolescents will exceed 80,000 in the United States.

- UNAIDS estimates that 1,600 children are infected with HIV each day worldwide.

- 1,200 children die of AIDS each day worldwide.

- Since the start of the global epidemic, it is estimated that close to 2.6 million children have been infected with HIV worldwide. Of these, an estimated 1.4 million children have died.

- Of the adults estimated to have been infected with HIV worldwide, 17 percent have died. Of the children estimated to have been infected with HIV worldwide, 54 percent have died.

Adolescents

- Twenty-five percent of new HIV infections in America occur in people under 20 years of age. This represents two new adolescent HIV infections every hour.

- Fifty percent of newly infected adults worldwide are between 15 and 24 years of age.

- Every year, 3 million American teenagers acquire a sexually transmitted disease, leaving them more susceptible to HIV infection.

Women of Childbearing Age

- AIDS is now ranked as the leading cause of death among African American women ages 25 to 44.

- AIDS is now ranked as the third leading cause of death among all American women ages 25 to 44.

- Approximately 42 percent of the 21.8 million adults living with HIV/AIDS worldwide are women.

In the Next Three Years . . .

- It is estimated that as many as 10 million children may be infected with HIV worldwide.

- It is estimated that 3 million children will die from AIDS worldwide.

- It is estimated that 5 to 10 million children will be orphaned by the death of one of their parents due to AIDS.

- WHO projects that 30 to 40 million people, 90 percent in developing nations, will have been infected with HIV.

Source: Pediatric Aids Foundation website: http://www.pedaids.org/PAF: 1311 Colorado Ave., Santa Monica, CA 90404 (310) 395-9051. Data are from the Centers for Disease Control and Prevention and the World Health Organization, April 8, 1998.

appear to be lessening the severity of early appearing symptoms (Cohen, Grosz, Ayoob & Schoen, 1997), but many children with HIV or AIDS will qualify for special education services; those services should focus on enhancing the quality of life for eligible children and their caregiving families (Bruder, 1995).

AIDS is rapidly increasing among women and children all over the world. In the United States, women infected with HIV are more likely to be young, poor, urban, non-Caucasian, and intravenous drug users (Widerstrom & Nickel, 1997), and therefore their children may be subject to multiple biological and environmental risk factors. The accompanying box, "Pediatric HIV/AIDS Fact Sheet," provides some data on pediatric AIDS.

Maternal Substance Abuse   Maternal drug use during pregnancy continues to generate great concern among professionals, politicians, and the general public. Doctors recommend that even the most common legal drugs, whether they are over-the-counter or prescription, should not be taken by pregnant women or be taken only with a doctor's recommendation. Many over-the-counter or prescription drugs have been associated with birth defects, particularly congenital malformations such as heart defects, ear damage, and cleft lip and palate (Dixson, 1989); the effects of others on the developing fetus have not been adequately investigated by researchers.

The caution of medical professionals about over-the-counter and prescription drugs comes in part from the experience of many Europeans with **thalidomide** in the late 1950s. Thalidomide was prescribed to pregnant women for nausea; over time it was learned that taking it during the first trimester of pregnancy caused shortened or missing arms and legs in the child (Graham & Morgan, 1997). The thalidomide experience taught medical researchers and practitioners that great care is needed with drug ingestion during pregnancy (Dixson, 1989).

The thalidomide tragedy of the 1950s demonstrated that great care must be taken with all drugs during pregnancy.

The long-term effects of illegal drug use during pregnancy are only beginning to be known. Babies of mothers who used cocaine, heroin or methadone, marijuana, PCP, or amphetamines (substance-abusing mothers who use combinations of drugs, as well as alcohol, are referred to as **polydrug users**) appear to be at significant short-term risk and may be particularly vulnerable to the effects of an unstable environment.

Polydrug users are those who use a combination of drugs as well as alcohol.

Cocaine and marijuana are currently the drugs most commonly used by women of childbearing age (Widerstrom & Nickel, 1997). Babies prenatally exposed to cocaine are more likely to be born early and to have a low birthweight and a smaller head circumference. Some research indicates that they are also more likely to have congenital malformations, to die during the perinatal period, and to die of sudden infant death syndrome (SIDS) during the first year of life, but studies are contradictory in these areas (Myers, Olson & Kaltenbach, 1992).

The long-term effects of cocaine exposure on preschool and school-aged children remain unclear. One study found that the majority of a group of cocaine/polydrug-exposed children whose mothers received prenatal care, nutritional counseling, and therapy for chemical dependence had normal intellectual, social, emotional, and behavioral development through age 3 (Griffith, 1992). Studies now indicate that the majority of children prenatally exposed to cocaine will not experience cognitive or physical problems by the time they enter school, but they may be at greater risk for emotional and behavioral problems (Batshaw & Conlon, 1997). In addition, cocaine use significantly affects the family environment; more than half the women who are dependent on cocaine will experience physical abuse, STDs, or separation from their children by imprisonment (Richardson & Day, 1994). It appears that substance-exposed children who are most likely to develop problems in life are those who also experience additional risk factors, such as family instability and absence of medical care. Since these outcomes are so variable, we can do these children and their families a service by avoiding the use of sensationalized labels that may become self-fulfilling prophecies.

The long-term effects of prenatal cocaine exposure on the child are difficult to predict.

Maternal alcohol intake during pregnancy can have grave effects on the developing fetus. Most seriously for surviving children, it can result in **fetal alcohol syndrome (FAS).** The child with FAS has altered facial features such as a small head, widely spaced eyes, upturned nose, large ears, and a small chin; he or she

Maternal alcohol use during pregnancy can result in fetal alcohol syndrome or fetal alcohol effects.

Fetal alcohol syndrome results in specific physical characteristics along with behavioral and cognitive deficits. (George Steinmetz)

will also have developmental delays in language and cognition and may have behavior problems such as oppositional and defiant behavior, poor judgment, and social withdrawal (Batshaw & Conlon, 1997). Some children have the cognitive and behavioral characteristics associated with FAS but not the physical abnormalities; they are said to have **fetal alcohol effects (FAE).** Alcohol-related birth defects (FAS and FAE) occur in about 1 in 200 births worldwide, making them one of the leading causes of mental retardation today (Batshaw & Conlon, 1997). Although not all offspring of women who drink alcohol experience these significant aftereffects, researchers have not identified a "safe" level of alcohol intake during pregnancy. As a result, doctors now recommend that pregnant women drink no alcohol at all.

Smoking can result in pregnancy complications as well as low birthweight and physical abnormalities in the infant.

Prenatal exposure to tobacco also has a serious impact on the developing fetus. Maternal cigarette smoking during pregnancy is the single most important cause of low birthweight (Shiono & Behrman, 1995); pregnant women who smoke have a relatively high number of pregnancy complications that can result in perinatal loss, premature delivery, and physical abnormalities. Studies of the long-term effects of smoking during pregnancy on child development are inconclusive, but it is clear that maternal smoking results in more colds, asthma, other respiratory problems, and middle-ear infections for children (Cook, Petersen & Moore, 1990).

Young mothers and older mothers are at risk for different pregnancy complications.

Extremes of Maternal Age Mothers at the beginning and at the end of their reproductive span are at the greatest risk for potential pregnancy problems. Young mothers, particularly those in the earliest teenage years, are more likely to have pregnancy complications resulting in prematurity or low birthweight, as well as other medical complications that could endanger the life and health of their babies (Smith, 1994). Among the biological factors that place the infants of adolescent mothers at risk are poor maternal nutrition, small maternal size, and,

Table 2.1	Maternal Age and the Risk of Having a Baby with Down Syndrome

Age of Mother	At Any Pregnancy	After a Previous Baby with Down Syndrome
29 or below	1 in 1,000	1 in 100
30–34	1 in 600	1 in 100
35–39	1 in 200	1 in 100
40–44	1 in 65	1 in 25
45–49	1 in 25	1 in 15

Source: From Matson, J. L. and Mulick, J. A., *Handbook of Mental Retardation*, Second Edition. Copyright © 1991 by Allyn & Bacon. Reprinted/adapted by permission.

most important, limited access to prenatal care (Meisels & Wasik, 1990). The children of very young mothers are also considered at risk because of characteristics of their caregiving environment.

Older mothers may present a different set of problems. They are more likely to have a child with **Down syndrome,** a condition caused by an extra twenty-first chromosome that results in mental retardation and physical anomalies in the child (see Table 2.1). Since the older a mother is, the more likely the possibility of her having a baby with Down syndrome, the American Medical Association recommends that pregnant women aged 35 and older undergo amniocentesis or other prenatal testing. We will discuss prenatal testing procedures later in the chapter in the section on prevention of disabilities.

Women over 35 are also more likely to have health problems such as diabetes and high blood pressure, which can complicate a pregnancy. Older mothers, however, are also more likely to have access to early and consistent prenatal medical care, and, given such care, many potential pregnancy complications can be managed, and a healthy baby is born. Access to good prenatal care can minimize the effects of maternal age.

■ **Perinatal Factors** Perinatal factors are those that occur from the twelfth week of pregnancy to the twenty-eighth day of infant life. It is here that medical research and technology have had a profound impact on both the survival and the quality of life of small and sick babies. Nevertheless, perinatal stresses still increase the risk status and, at times, call for special treatment and follow-up (Keogh, Wilcoxen & Bernheimer, 1986).

The perinatal period ranges from the twelfth week of pregnancy to the twenty-eighth day of life.

Oxygen Deprivation For a variety of reasons during pregnancy, labor, delivery, and newborn life, the infant can experience **hypoxia,** or a decreased availability of oxygen in the body tissues. Hypoxia can cause cells in the brain to die, resulting in brain damage and, sometimes, death. The long-term effects of oxygen deprivation can be severe or minimal, but among the handicapping conditions associated with prolonged hypoxia are cerebral palsy, mental retardation, seizures, visual and auditory deficits, and behavior problems. Most affected infants, however, experience mild episodes of hypoxia and, therefore, do not develop disabilities (Robertson & Finer, 1993).

Prematurity and Low Birthweight The average length of pregnancy, or gestation, is forty weeks. Babies born before thirty-seven weeks' gestation are called

Premature babies are born before thirty-seven weeks' gestation; low birthweight babies weigh less than five and a half pounds.

Nancy Hunt's twin daughters, Lucy and Nell, were born fourteen weeks early in 1989, each weighing under two pounds. After a series of medical complications common to infants born so prematurely, and after three months in the hospital neonatal intensive care unit, they came home to their parents and older sister, Maggie. What follows is an excerpt from the case study that accompanies this textbook, "The Story of Lucy and Nell," and then an update.

With both babies home, our family could get back to normal. Of course, *normal* would have to be redefined, but we could do that together. We knew that we were lucky that neither Lucy nor Nell had been born with or developed an identifiable disability. But I also knew we were a long way from being out of the woods. Nell, particularly, with all her medical complications, worried me. I knew our pediatrician felt the same worry. But only time would tell whether our girls would be "normal." I would have to wait and see.

Update, 1998:

When I discuss Lucy and Nell with my students, I often relate the following incident, which occurred shortly after I wrote the case study. I was invited, along with several other parents of children at risk or with disabilities, to speak to a class at a neighboring university.

premature, or **preterm.** Although the timing of a birth is important, the baby's weight may be even more crucial. Babies born weighing less than about five and a half pounds (2500 grams) are said to be **low birthweight.** Even full-term babies can be low birthweight; thus, prematurity and low birthweight can be independent of one another. Think of it this way: A premature baby, born at thirty-four weeks' gestation, might already weigh six pounds; a baby born on her "due date" might weigh only four pounds.

Some of the conditions that have been associated with prematurity in the research literature are lack of prenatal care, the mother's prepregnancy health and illness during pregnancy, her nutritional status before pregnancy and weight gain during pregnancy, her age, height, and weight, smoking, use of drugs, uterine and cervical problems, social class, ethnic group membership, multiple births, and geography (Bernbaum & Batshaw, 1997; Kopp, 1983). Women who are poor and young are in particular danger of delivering prematurely; they are also more likely to receive little or no prenatal care and be undernourished (Paneth, 1995; Scholl, Hediger & Belsky, 1994).

Each of us would tell our "stories" to the class, then participate in a group discussion. Before class started, I chatted with the young mother sitting next to me, and we discovered many commonalities between us. Her son had been born at the same time as my girls, and he and Nell were born at the same weight, one pound eleven ounces. Both he and Nell had had serious respiratory problems, the same heart problem, and a grade 3 intraventricular hemorrhage, or "brain bleed." But while Nell was by then walking and talking, this mother's son had severe cerebral palsy.

And that is what risk is all about. Some children develop disabilities, and some do not—and it's often not clear why. This wasn't about environment: this mother, 19 years old and single, was clearly bright, competent, and in love with her child. As I talked with her, I felt very lucky and very guilty, and recommitted myself to my work with young children with disabilities.

Lucy and Nell are now 8 years old and in the second grade. They learned to read last year, and that brought me such joy—of course I worried that it would never happen. But now Lucy calls herself a "bookworm," and Nell writes long, detailed letters to friends and family—no punctuation and creatively spelled—but full of her ideas. We are lucky people.

Nancy Hunt

What are the dangers of premature birth? Premature babies are more likely to be low birthweight, and the lower the birthweight, the more likely a baby will have serious complications or die. Premature babies' systems are sometimes not ready to function independently; the babies need to gain weight but often have not developed the ability to coordinate sucking and swallowing, and their intestines are not yet ready to digest food normally, so feeding and weight gain are complicated; and their immature immune systems make them very vulnerable to infection. In addition, the lower the birthweight, the more likely it is that the baby will develop complications of prematurity, such as respiratory distress syndrome (extreme difficulty in breathing), brain hemorrhage (bleeding), and retinopathy of prematurity (an eye condition that can lead to blindness), which place their long-term development at risk.

Advances in **neonatology,** the study of newborns, have dramatically changed the prognosis for even the tiniest surviving premature babies. The specialized care given to these fragile infants in the **neonatal intensive care unit,** the area of the hospital that provides care for sick and premature newborns, has

Advances in neonatology and high-risk infant care have ensured the survival of many low birthweight babies.

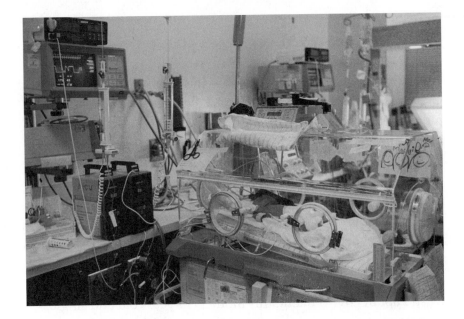

The neonatal intensive care unit provides the constant monitoring and life support systems needed by infants who are premature, fragile, or ill. (Dorothy Williams)

ensured the survival of many babies who, even a few years ago, would have died. Until recently, babies weighing three and a half pounds and under (now called very low birthweight) routinely died; now most are routinely saved. The limits of survival have changed dramatically over the last few years; currently, the majority of infants born at twenty-four or more weeks gestational age survive. Most of those babies weigh less than two pounds; the smallest survivors weigh around one pound. New drugs that successfully treat respiratory distress syndrome are helping to increase those numbers (Shiono & Behrman, 1995). Premature babies are much more likely than full-term babies, however, to have conditions such as cerebral palsy, mental retardation, seizures, and vision and hearing impairments.

The number of premature survivors with disabling conditions increases as the birthweight drops. Current research suggests that from 10 to 30 percent of very low birthweight babies who survive are chronically ill or disabled. Their disabilities range from school learning problems, particularly those related to hyperactivity and attention, to severe disabilities (Hack, Klein & Taylor, 1995; Teplin, Burchinal, Johnson-Martin, et al., 1991).

■ **Postnatal Factors** Among the postnatal biological factors of early childhood that place a child at risk for school learning problems are *chronic diseases and infections* and *severe nutritional deficiencies.* Chronic diseases like asthma or juvenile arthritis may cause the child to miss too many school days or may have more serious consequences, as we will discuss in Chapter 10. Infections of childhood like **meningitis** that are accompanied by a high fever can also cause damage to the brain, resulting in a range of disabling conditions such as hearing and vision loss and mental retardation. Conditions like **chronic otitis media,** the most serious form of the middle-ear infections so common in early childhood, can have subtle but important effects on language learning and later school performance (Medley, Roberts & Zeisel, 1995).

Diseases like meningitis and conditions like chronic otitis media can result in disabilities that affect school performance.

In the United States, nutritional deprivation is usually associated with extreme poverty, and it is difficult to separate the effects of poor nutrition from the

The halls outside the neonatal intensive care unit (NICU) are not places of frivolity. Nurses, doctors, and respiratory therapists step quickly through. Family members wait with anguished faces. The walls are lined with pictures of the "success stories"–babies who started out very small and are now pudgy infants and toddlers. These pictures are a source of hope for the parents whose babies lie inside the nearby doorways, sometimes wavering between life and death.

The NICU itself is a smallish room dominated by ten large rectangular Lucite boxes–the incubators. Next to each one is machinery, some of which extends by wires into the incubator itself. For each incubator there is a small screen, like that of a computer terminal, with two or more sets of moving lines on it, measuring heart rate, respiratory rate, and oxygen saturation–how pink or blue the baby is. There are numbers flashing quickly by on those monitor screens, their meanings indecipherable to the layperson.

Although voices are quiet, strange sounds are everywhere . . . beeps of varying pitch and loudness. Some seem to be ignored, and you wonder what they are for. Others cause the nurses to call to each other–"Don't worry, it's just me." Still others summon the nurses quickly to an incubator–"Come on, Melissa, breathe!"

Melissa is so small that your heart jumps to your mouth in fear . . . thirteen inches long. Her eyes are covered by a white mask, protecting them from the harsh blue lights. A tiny yellow hat is on her head, and attached to it by strings is a plastic band that covers her cheeks and is inserted in her nose. The other end is connected to a long tube leading to one of the machines. A long, thin tube extends from her tiny mouth. She is naked, but her arm is held down by a bandaged splint to keep the intravenous tube in place. Her foot is covered by white bandages, which stem the bleeding from the many needle pricks required to take blood. Patches cover the right and left sides of her chest, with wires protruding and leading out of the incubator. Her skin hangs from her bones, with not a gram of fat underneath.

Melissa's mother carried her for just short of twenty-six weeks, and she weighs less than two pounds. Her chances for survival are 50-50. Right now, though, at age two days, her vital signs are stable, and she is breathing on her own, with some extra oxygen being provided. The doctors are voicing cautious hope to her parents.

In the next incubator is a baby who looks huge by comparison–he is a full-term seven-pound newborn. He was born with a serious heart defect and will be wheeled to surgery this afternoon.

On the other side of the room a young couple stand next to their first-born's incubator. The mother's hand reaches through the porthole and strokes her baby's back. Their daughter, born at twenty-five weeks gestation, is now six weeks old and doing well. They know, however, that her status could change at any minute, through an infection or another calamitous medical event. Right now they are both singing softly to their daughter.

The NICU nurses and doctors must be aware of the latest in medical research and technology as it pertains to the neonate, or newborn. Today they are sending premature babies home, often slightly before their expected due date, who five years ago would have had a far poorer chance of survival. But they are not simply committed to these babies' survival. They know about the increased risk in their patients for cerebral palsy, blindness, mental retardation, seizure disorders, and other problems, and they make every effort they can to prevent those conditions from occurring.

The nurses and doctors are not miracle workers. Babies do die. Sometimes it seems clear that others will have serious medical and developmental problems. Still more will develop school difficulties later in life. The nurses and doctors, then, do much more than provide intensive medical care. They must support and counsel each baby's terrified parents through the roller coaster of their child's life in the intensive care unit.

Note: Support for families with babies in a neonatal intensive care unit is often provided by parent-to-parent groups and support networks within the hospitals. For information on these groups and other support services for families, contact the Association for the Care of Children's Health, 19 Mantua Road, Mount Royal, NJ. Phone: (609) 224-1742; email: amkent@smarthub.com.

other deprivations of poverty (Kopp, 1983). In many Third World countries, however, there is dramatic evidence that malnutrition alters brain development in children. There is little doubt that chronic poor nutrition can cause learning problems in school.

Environmental Risk

Environmental risk includes all the risk factors related to the environment in which the child develops.

The second risk category that we will examine, environmental risk, includes risk factors related to the environment in which the child develops (Garbarino, 1990; Sameroff & Chandler, 1975). Environmental factors can influence development at any stage; our discussion will first refer to prenatal events that may affect the environment of the mother before birth.

■ **Environmental Factors That Influence Prenatal Development** Studies from Hiroshima and Nagasaki, as well as ongoing observation of the aftereffects of the fire at the nuclear reactor at Chernobyl, suggest a strong relationship between exposure to radiation in pregnant women and such birth defects in their offspring as mental and growth retardation and congenital malformations (Dixson, 1989). The effects of radiation depend on the distance from the source, the intensity of the source, and the time during pregnancy of the exposure (Graham & Morgan, 1997). Although the diagnostic x-rays that would most commonly be experienced by pregnant women are rarely strong enough to harm the fetus, exposure to any form of radiation during pregnancy should be avoided because of the increased risk of childhood cancer for the fetus (Dixson, 1989).

Since many women today continue to work during pregnancy, they must consider the **occupational hazards** associated with some workplaces. Some occupations expose workers to low levels of radiation, while others expose them to low levels of lead and mercury. Exposure to these and other substances has been linked to reproductive loss and birth defects (Sparks, 1984).

Traditionally, physicians and researchers have looked to mothers as the source of risk in their children, but some recent research has attempted to identify the role of the father in contributing to biological risk (American College of Medical Genetics, 1996). The research has found that older fathers account for a small percentage of all cases of Down syndrome (Skinner, 1990). Also, investigations of exposure to toxic substances in the environment have intensified because of the conviction of many veterans of the Vietnam War that their exposure to the defoliant Agent Orange increased the number of birth defects such as spina bifida and the incidence of childhood cancer in their offspring.

■ **Postnatal Environmental Factors** The characteristics of the child's immediate caregiving environment are vital to optimal development. That environment must provide protection from exposure to dangerous toxins and disease as well as opportunities for learning and social growth and a stable home and family. We'll look at each of these areas.

Most researchers agree that the results of adverse biological risk events can be exaggerated or improved upon by the characteristics of the environment. For example, although AIDS is classified as a biological risk factor, and it occurs in all sectors of our population, it is clear that AIDS is more likely to occur among those living in poverty. Children who are "at risk" develop as they do because of a complex interaction between their risk history and their caregiving environments.

Other agents within our environment can cause problems for children that may affect their school learning. Some of these, such as exposure to radiation and toxic chemicals, we are aware of, although hard data verifying the effects of these substances on the developing nervous system in children are difficult to come by.

Lead One substance scientists are learning more about is lead. There are at least 2 million homes in the United States where lead-paint-covered surfaces are chalking and flaking, and almost every child in such a home has elevated levels of lead in the blood (Needleman, 1992). Although poverty significantly increases the risk of lead exposure, excessively high levels of lead are found in children of all social classes and racial backgrounds. African American children living in poverty are at greatest risk: 55 percent have elevated lead levels (Agency for Toxic Substances and Disease Registry, 1988).

Early exposure to lead is associated with a greater likelihood of school problems.

Children with high lead levels have decreased IQ scores and poorer language and attention skills; their teachers find them more distractible and less well-organized and persistent (Needleman et al., 1979). Long-term follow-up of these children indicates that early lead exposure is associated with a substantially elevated likelihood of having a reading disability and dropping out of school (Needleman et al., 1991).

There are, no doubt, other substances within our environment that cause damage to the developing nervous system in children that have not yet been identified. Many of the causes of childhood learning problems, as we shall see in future chapters, are unknown.

Accidents Accidents of all kinds are examples of environmental risks. Car accidents are the most common, but accidents may also happen on bikes, in swimming pools, and anywhere else that active, curious young children play and explore. Accidents that involve head trauma, oxygen deprivation, or spinal cord injury can cause severe physical disability as well as learning and behavior problems. Caregivers must be extremely watchful and observant of their children's play areas and their risks.

Accidents are the most common postnatal risk factor.

The characteristics of the social environment are also crucial for optimal development: the nature of the medical technology available to support a sick newborn or child, the availability of public health services in the community, and the emphasis on educational achievement within the society as a whole. The next part of our discussion of environmental risk concentrates on the social aspects of poverty and family issues. You will see, however, that there is a great deal of overlap among these areas, and they are often interrelated.

Poverty Biologically normal infants who live in poverty may be at risk for problems of development because of characteristics of their caregiving environment. This environmental risk can occur as a result of inadequacies in their interactions with their caregivers, their access to health care, and their opportunities for stimulation and life experiences. These inadequacies are more likely to exist in impoverished families—money *does* buy health care, food, and quality day care for working or absent parents—but they are by no means exclusive to poor families.

Poverty—which can include both economic and social factors—is a major cause of environmental risk.

In the United States today one out of five children lives in poverty; a baby is born into poverty every 35 seconds, and child poverty rates are two to nine times as high as those in other industrialized nations (Children's Defense Fund, 1997). The children of poverty are more likely to die in childhood, to be in

Adult supervision might prevent skateboarders from taking risks that can lead to disabling accidents. (Mimi Forsyth/Monkmeyer Press Photo Service)

special education programs, and to drop out of school; the girls are more likely to become pregnant during adolescence and the boys to engage in criminal behavior.

What is it about living in poverty that leads to poor outcomes for children? The obvious answer, lack of access to good medical care and nutrition, as well as to experiences and opportunities, is only partly right. Most of us can cite several examples of people who grew up in such circumstances who have reached significant levels of achievement in our society. Garbarino (1990) made the point that some families are economically impoverished but have a "socially rich family environment": family members, neighbors, and friends who provide support for both children and parents—the "informal helping relationships" that are the foundation of some communities. Other families are both economically and socially impoverished. According to Garbarino (1990, p. 90),

> These are the environments in which prenatal care is inadequate, intervals between births are often too short, beliefs about child care too often dysfunctional, access to and utilization of well-baby care inadequate, early intervention for child disabilities inadequate, and thus in which child mortality and morbidity are rampant.

These conditions are more likely to occur in our inner cities, where families must also live with the reality of frequent violence that respects no target—not even a small child. The stresses in such communities can become unbearable; neighbors may be afraid and distrustful of one another, and little sense of community may exist.

Social impoverishment can occur at every economic level, but more affluent families can pay for supportive services when they are not available through friends and family. Many poor families, frequently headed by single mothers, are left with few resources to help with the considerable stresses of child-rearing.

Families come in all shapes, sizes, and configurations. We can no longer assume that a child will grow up in a traditional nuclear family, nor do we insist that there is one "right" way to raise children. We do know, however, that there are characteristics of the caregiving environment that appear to help children develop optimally. Emotional and physical safety, responsive and sensitive caregivers, and stability of family members are all tied to the healthy development of children.

We will discuss issues related to families in the next chapter. But here it is important to describe two characteristics of families that place the child at risk: maltreatment and family instability.

Child Maltreatment   Child abuse and child neglect are grouped together under the term *maltreatment*, and reports of both are abundant in the United States today. Although hard economic times and high rates of unemployment no doubt increase the likelihood of child maltreatment (Garbarino, 1990), reports of the murder, abuse, and neglect of children are as old as recorded history and appear in all cultures.

Children with disabilities are overrepresented in samples of abused children, but it is difficult to determine how many children with disabilities are abused (Turnbull, Buchele-Ash & Mitchell, 1994). Professionals suspect, however, that child abuse is responsible for a proportion of the cases of mental retardation, physical disability, and emotional disturbance in the United States today: One group estimates that over 18,000 children are seriously disabled every year as a result of abuse or neglect by parents or caregivers (U.S. Advisory Board on Child Abuse and Neglect, 1995).

Child abuse may be responsible for a proportion of the cases of mental retardation, physical disability, and emotional disturbance in the United States today.

Family Instability   Although we now know that the two-parent family is not a necessary condition for optimal child growth and development, it does seem clear that children need at least one stable caregiver throughout their childhood in order to develop well (Werner & Smith, 1982). That caregiver may not be a parent—often, a grandmother or other relative can provide the ongoing stability a child needs. As developmental psychologist Urie Bronfenbrenner reminds us in his often-quoted statement, "The critical factor in a child's development is the active involvement of at least one adult who is simply crazy about the child" (1993, p. 47). Children who experience many changes in the adult makeup of the household appear to do less well in school (Hunt, 1982) and may be at greater risk for dropping out of school and engaging in criminal behavior.

It is important to emphasize that the existence of one risk factor alone does not ensure developmental problems. Rather, those problems occur because of the existence of multiple risk factors, most often a combination of biological and environmental events.

Developmental problems most often stem from a combination of biological and environmental risk factors.

Research on risk factors has shown us that children with some of the previously described biological risks, such as prematurity, are more vulnerable to environmental stresses than other children are. It is the combination of biological and environmental risk factors that places that developing child in jeopardy for future school problems.

Prevention

Fortunately, many steps can be taken to prevent or minimize the occurrence of risk factors and developmental problems in infants and children. Some of these steps can be taken for our children; some we can take ourselves; some are questions of public policy, and we can work within our political system to advocate for important changes (Simeonsson, 1994).

Major Strategies for Prevention

Inoculation, or vaccination against infectious diseases, is a prevention strategy that should be available to every child.

■ **Inoculation** Inoculation—vaccination against infectious diseases—starts in the first year of life and should continue through early childhood. Children are inoculated against diphtheria, tetanus, pertussis (whooping cough), measles, mumps, rubella, and polio, among other diseases. An effective, wide-reaching immunization program can virtually eliminate these diseases, many of which can also harm pregnant women. In addition, many adults have not been immunized against rubella. Administration of a rubella titer test can determine whether you have had the disease, which can be easily confused with other common illnesses. If you have not had rubella, you will be doing a service to your community by becoming immunized against it, so you will not contribute to the spread of this destructive virus. It is not only women thinking of having children who should be immunized—men can spread this virus too!

Genetic counseling can also be a step in preventing disability.

■ **Genetic Counseling** Couples who have reason to be concerned that they might have a child with a disabling condition will find that **genetic counseling** can provide them with helpful information. With information from a couple's

Not everyone enjoys inoculations, but they do prevent illnesses that historically led to disability and death. (Andy Levin/Photo Researchers, Inc.)

family and personal health history, a genetic counselor can often discuss the likelihood that their child will inherit a genetic condition (see the Closer Look box).

The role of the genetic counselor is a neutral one; the counselor provides prospective parents with information and possible options, but the parents are then left to make their own decision about whether or not to have a child (Chedd, 1995). The prospective parents must often make some difficult choices, since rarely can a genetic counselor guarantee what the outcome of a pregnancy will be.

■ **Early Prenatal Care**   The easiest, most routine step a pregnant woman can take to reduce the risk for her baby may also be the most effective. Early **prenatal care,** the care an expectant mother receives from her physician during pregnancy, can provide a prospective mother with crucial but routine tests and observations that can drastically affect her baby's health. Blood tests that rule out the presence of sexually transmitted and other diseases, information about proper nutrition and activity level during pregnancy, and counseling and treatment based on the prospective mother's needs significantly lower the level of risk in each pregnancy.

Early and consistent prenatal care is the most effective way to prevent many disabilities.

Despite the effectiveness of early prenatal care as a preventive measure, thousands of women give birth each year without ever seeing a doctor or visiting a clinic. Many of them are young, and most of them are poor. Babies born to women who do not receive prenatal medical care are more likely to be premature or sick at birth. There is also a higher likelihood of miscarriage, stillbirth, and early infant death in these pregnancies (Mechaty & Thompson, 1990).

The availability of free or low-cost prenatal care varies from state to state. Federal and state governments have, for the most part, failed to implement policy that would make these services available to all women, despite persuasive data that document the cost-effectiveness of such action. In countries where free prenatal care is routinely available, infant mortality and morbidity are considerably lower (Garbarino, 1990).

■ **Prenatal Testing**   For those who have received genetic counseling or are concerned about the health of their growing fetus, two procedures can provide more information: **amniocentesis** and **chorionic villous sampling (CVS).**

Amniocentesis was the first technique developed for prenatal diagnosis (Batshaw & Rose, 1997). It is performed between the fourteenth and eighteenth weeks of pregnancy by inserting a needle through the mother's abdomen into the amniotic sac and withdrawing less than one ounce of amniotic fluid. The amniotic fluid contains cells shed by the fetus, and these are cultured. A karyotype (a study of the number and description of the fetal chromosomes) is generally available in two weeks or less. Examination of the fetal chromosomes can lead to identification of chromosomal abnormalities like Down syndrome. Evidence of neural tube defects like spina bifida can be seen in the analysis of the amniotic fluid cells. The risk to the fetus and the mother from amniocentesis is quite low.

Amniocentesis and chorionic villous sampling can provide information on the health of the fetus.

In chorionic villous sampling (CVS), which is performed between the eighth and tenth weeks of pregnancy, a thin catheter is inserted through the vagina into the uterus and used to remove a small portion of the cells from the chorion, part of the developing placenta (Batshaw & Rose, 1997). Those cells, which contain genetic material from the fetus, are cultured. In two to three days a karyotype is obtained. Evidence of Down syndrome and other relatively common genetic abnormalities can then be determined. CVS is slightly less safe than amniocentesis; there is an approximately 1 percent greater risk of miscarriage following CVS

A closer look

Genetic Counseling: "The Science Is the Easy Part"

What is genetic counseling? The mother of a 6-year-old with Down syndrome put it well when she said, "In two one-hour sessions, our counselor taught me everything I wished I had remembered from Biology 101, Psychology 101, and Philosophy 101." Genetic counseling draws on knowledge from these fields and others in an effort to provide the most accurate, up-to-date information on the causes and treatment of genetic disorders, the tests available for identifying them, a possible prognosis for a child with a genetic condition, and the prospects for future pregnancies.

A good genetic counselor should have first-rate knowledge of genetics. But he or she should also be able to communicate that knowledge in easy-to-understand language. And, according to Barbara Bowles Biesecker, genetic counselor and section head at the National Center for Human Genome Research, National Institutes of Health, genetic counselors must be able to listen as well as talk. "People are terrified when they get a diagnosis," she explains. "They often ask, 'Why did this happen?' They already know the scientific explanation; what they are really asking are the more soul-searching questions How will I cope? Will I be able to love and accept this child?' Genetic

counseling is much more complicated than explaining percentages. Actually, the science is the easy part."

Possibly the most important thing families can get from a genetic counselor is time—time to process a lot of information, time to grieve the considerable losses they may experience.

A genetic counselor can provide a tremendous amount of information about local and national resources. He or she may also be able to explain the practical implications of recent research results.

Genetic counselors are also familiar and comfortable with conditions other medical professionals rarely see. While your pediatrician might see two children a year with your child's disability, a genetic counselor may see two a week. "One of the best things our counselor did was hook us up with other parents. Nobody can understand what we're going through except other CF parents," says the mother of a child with cystic fibrosis.

Different families seek genetic counseling for different reasons. A couple with a newly diagnosed infant or young child, for example, will probably want a comprehensive explanation of the child's condition and likely prognosis. They

than following amniocentesis (Burton, Schulz & Burd, 1992), but with further research and refinement it may be used more frequently than amniocentesis.

One mother who had prenatal testing before the birth of her daughter, who has spina bifida, reminds us that prenatal testing is often helpful no matter what a couple's views are on the termination of pregnancy:

> I will always be grateful that when I finally gave birth to my daughter, it was in a setting where she could get the best of care from the moment of her first breath, and that my husband and I were fully prepared to welcome her into our lives with open arms. At the time of a prenatal diagnosis, it may be hard for families to see the value of the opportunity they have been given, but ultimately I believe families and their children benefit most by knowing about problems as early as possible. (Reichard, 1995, p. 131)

Early Intervention as Prevention

As we have emphasized, the presence of risk factors does not guarantee a developmental delay or disability. **Early intervention** plays an important role in preventing additional deficits in children who are at risk. Early intervention pro-

may also want to know the chances of this or another birth defect occurring in future pregnancies.

According to Phillip R. Reilly, M.D., clinical geneticist, lawyer, and president of the Shriver Center for Mental Retardation, the following people may benefit from consulting a genetic counselor:

- Families in which there is a known genetic disorder, such as cystic fibrosis, Huntington's disease, or hemophilia

- Couples that come from the same ethnic group, when that group is known to have a high incidence of certain disorders. Tay-Sachs disease is common among some ethnic groups, such as Ashkenazi Jews, for example, and one in twelve African Americans carries the gene of sickle cell anemia.

- Families in which there have been multiple miscarriages, stillbirths, or a childhood death from unknown causes

- Women older than 34 who are pregnant or planning a pregnancy

- Relatives—especially siblings—of a child with a genetically transmitted disorder

How do you find a genetic counselor?

A pediatrician or the geneticist at your HMO or local hospital may be able to refer you to a qualified genetic counselor. Or contact one of the following organizations:

National Society of Genetic Counselors
233 Canterbury Drive
Wallingford, PA 19086-6617
http://members.aol.com/nsgcweb/nsgchome. htm#marker

Alliance of Genetic Support Groups
35 Wisconsin Circle, Suite 440
Chevy Chase, MD 20815-7015
(800) 336-4363
http://medhlp.netusa.net/agsg/agsup.htm

Source: Adapted from "Genetic Counseling—The science is the easy part" by Naomi Angoff Chedd, *Exceptional Parent*, August 1995, pp. 26–27. Copyright © 1995. Reprinted with the expressed consent and approval of *Exceptional Parent*, a monthly magazine for parents and families of children with disabilities and special health care needs. Subscription cost is $32 per year for 12 issues; call 1-800-562-1973. Offices at 555 Kinderkarnack Rd., Oradell, NJ 07649.

grams may lessen the effects of risk factors on a child by enlisting the support of a team of professionals and family members in the child's care and development.

■ **Early Intervention Programs** What is early intervention? What are its goals? These are vital concerns for the parents or caregivers of a child with a disability or a child at risk for developing a disability. Hanson, Ellis, and Deppe (1989) define early intervention as "a comprehensive set of services that are provided to children from birth to age three and their families" (p. 211).

The basic component of early intervention is a teacher (often called an early intervention specialist) working collaboratively with other professionals, the family, and the child, to provide information, support, activities, and strategies designed to minimize the effects of the child's risk status or disability on his or her development.

As you learned in Chapter 1, early intervention services for infants and toddlers and their families are authorized by P.L. 99-457. Early intervention includes efforts to improve the child's performance in all major functional areas—language, cognition, fine and gross motor skills, and social-emotional development. And because research shows that early intervention yields significant results (Guralnick, 1997), availability and comprehensiveness of early

Early intervention is the set of services provided to children from birth to age 3 and their families, designed for their unique characteristics and needs.

Research documents the effectiveness of early intervention services.

intervention programs can have a great impact on the lives of children who are at risk and those with disabilities.

Gallagher (1992) describes the assumptions underlying Part H of P.L. 99-457 (now Part C of the reauthorized IDEA of 1997), the section of the law that outlines services for infants and toddlers from birth to age 3. These assumptions provide a useful summary of the goals of early intervention:

1. The earlier the treatment, the better.
2. The more professional disciplines that participate, the better.
3. Families are important.
4. Qualified personnel are needed.
5. Children who are at risk should be helped.

Hanson (1996) describes the defining characteristics of early intervention:

- Services are individualized, based on the varying needs of children and their families, and the individualized family service plan (IFSP) is the document that outlines these services.

- Services are provided in varying locations, either the child's home, a center, or a combination of home- and center-based settings.

- Services should be cross-disciplinary and coordinated with one another.

- Depending on child and family needs, disciplines represented may be education, medicine, nursing, nutrition and dietetics, social work, speech-language pathology and audiology, occupational therapy, physical therapy, and psychology.

- Since no one agency can provide all those services, an interagency, collaborative approach is necessary.

- A continuum of services must be available, from comprehensive and intensive services to those that may be short-term and limited, and those services must be enmeshed in the broad range of community services available to young children.

Early intervention can be provided in the family home or at an early intervention center.

■ **Models for Early Intervention Programs** Early intervention services are generally delivered through either a home-based program, where the early intervention specialist provides services to the family in its own home, or a center-based program, where the family brings the child to an early intervention center. Often, services to infants and medically fragile toddlers are provided in the home; as children grow older and stronger, they are more likely to attend a center-based program. There are no definite rules, though, about how a program is designed. Some influential factors include geography (for example, whether caregivers need to travel long distances to reach the center) and the nature of the population being served (for example, an urban center serving many teenaged parents and their children might include classes in basic child care).

Cook, Tessier, and Klein (1996) identified eleven elements in the early intervention literature that are associated with effective early intervention programs. Among them are:

- A well-defined program model and philosophy with staff commitment to the approach being implemented

- A consistent system that promotes a high level of family involvement and support with an emphasis on caregiver-child interaction

- Extensive and cooperative team planning and program implementation
- Facilitation of functional skills to enable children to cope with environmental expectations as determined through individualized program and service planning
- Flexible adaptation of intervention techniques to determine those most effective in meeting child- and family-focused outcomes and objectives
- Strong emphasis on language and social skill development
- Incorporation of "best practices" as they are continually determined through practice and research in the field
- A well-designed system for staff and parent training and development

The best early intervention programs will reflect these elements, as well as the practices identified in "A Closer Look: Commonalities: Best Practices in Early Childhood Education."

■ **The Role of the Family in Early Intervention** With the growing appreciation of the importance of viewing the child within the context of the family, the focus of early intervention has shifted from the child to the entire family system. This broadened focus is reflected in the law, which mandates that each family receive an **individualized family service plan (IFSP)**, a written account of the personal and social services needed to promote and support each family member for the first three years of the child's life.

Each IFSP must include a statement of the family's strengths, as well as needs related to the child; a description of the major outcomes to be achieved by the child and the family; a description of the family's current resources, priorities, and concerns; and a list of the specific services needed to meet the unique requirements of each child and family. These services may include family training, counseling, respite care, and home visits, as well as physical, occupational, and speech therapy, audiological services, and so on (Sandall, 1997a, 1997b).

Most families need information related to their child's condition, assistance in learning to identify their child's unique cues, guidance in handling the child in a more therapeutic and easy manner, and referrals for other services. The focus of early intervention is typically on facilitating and coordinating this range of activities so that the family may experience more satisfying and rewarding relationships with the child and the child may develop more fully (Hanson, 1996).

Remember that three groups of young children (from birth to age 3) are eligible for early intervention services:

- Those with an identified condition related to developmental disability, such as hearing or vision loss or Down syndrome
- Those who are experiencing developmental delay in motor, cognitive, communication, psychosocial, or self-help skills
- Those who are at risk for significant developmental delay because of biological and/or environmental events in their lives

Let's look at a hypothetical baby, Sarah, who has Down syndrome. Down syndrome is a condition that carries with it an extremely high probability of mental retardation, and often involves physical abnormalities (such as organ defects) as well. Sarah is 8 months old and is recovering from heart surgery that successfully repaired a congenital heart defect. In the next year, Sarah's physical

Family involvement and family support are the foundation of effective early intervention.

The IFSP must describe the family's strengths as well as its needs.

Three groups of infants and toddlers are eligible for early intervention services under the law.

 closer look

Best Practices in Early Childhood Education

The best practices for the field of early childhood special education must be built on those well-established principles of practice that are best for *all* young children. These are perhaps best stated in the 1986 position statement offered by the National Association for the Education of Young Children (NAEYC, 1986). Two major themes have guided the development of these best practices: (1) that early education must meet the individual developmental needs of each child, and (2) that the best medium through which to do this is children's play.

Several key recommendations emerge within this NAEYC framework related to curriculum, adult-child interactions, family involvement, and evaluation that are essential to high-quality early intervention programs. These are summarized below. However, . . . early interventionists must move beyond the criteria of NAEYC's best practices to ensure specific instructional techniques necessary to meet the unique needs of young children with disabilities and their families. The field of early childhood special education is built on best practices from the fields of both early childhood and special education. . . .

Curriculum

- Educational goals are incorporated into all daily activities. Objectives are not taught in isolation but are integrated into meaningful activities and events.

- Curriculum planning and intervention are based on the teacher's specific observations of each child in natural contexts.

- Learning is an *interactive* process. Children's interactions with adults, peers, and the physical environment are all important.

- Learning activities and materials must be concrete and *relevant* to children's lives. Teachers should make use of real-life objects and activities (e.g., make a trip to the fire station, not just read a story about fire engines).

- Programs must be able to meet a wide range of interests and abilities. Teachers are expected to *individualize* instructional programs.

- Teachers must increase the difficulty and challenge of activities gradually and skillfully.

- Teachers must be able to facilitate *engagement* of each child by offering choices, making suggestions, asking questions, and describing events in ways that are meaningful and interesting to the child.

- Children should be given opportunities for *self-initiation, self-direction,* and *repeated practice.*

- Teachers must accept and appreciate cultural differences in children and families and avoid ethnic and gender stereotypes.

- Programs must provide a balance between rest and activity, and they should include outdoor activities each day.

- Outdoor activities should be *planned,* not simply opportunities to release pent-up energy.

- Programs must create careful *transitions* from one activity to the next. Children should not be rushed, and schedules should be flexible enough to take advantage of impromptu experiences.

Adult-Child Interaction

- Adults should respond quickly and directly to children's needs and attempts to communicate. Whenever possible, adults should be at eye level with children.

Source: *Adapting Early Childhood Curricula for Children,* Fourth Edition by Cook et al, © 1996. Reprinted by permission of Prentice-Hall, Inc., Upper Saddle River, NJ.

- Children must be provided with a variety of opportunities to communicate. Interaction is best facilitated on a one-to-one basis, or in groups of two to three children. Large-group instruction is less effective in facilitating communication.

- Professionals must be alert to signs of stress and provide sensitive, appropriate assistance to children.

- Adults must facilitate the development of self-esteem by "expressing respect, acceptance, and comfort for children, regardless of the child's behavior" (NAEYC, 1986, p. 14).

- Adults must use disciplinary techniques that enhance the development of self-control. These include setting clear, consistent limits; redirecting inappropriate behavior; valuing mistakes; listening to children's concerns and frustrations; helping children solve conflicts; and patiently reminding children of rules as needed.

- Adults must be responsible for all children at all times. Health and safety issues must be addressed constantly.

- Adults must plan for gradually increasing children's independence.

Family Involvement

- Parents have the right and responsibility to share in decision making regarding their children's care and education. Professionals must maintain frequent contact, and parents should be encouraged to participate.

- Professionals must regularly share information and resources with parents, including information regarding stages of child development. They must also obtain and respect parents' views of individual children's behavior and development.

Evaluation

- Child evaluations should not rely on a single instrument.

- Evaluations should identify children with special needs and provide information that will lead to meaningful educational modifications.

- Evaluations must be culturally appropriate.

Additional Best Practices for Children with Special Needs

In addition to the NAEYC recommendations just summarized, certain other recommendations are particularly important for young children with special needs. McDonnell and Hardman (1988) have suggested the following:

- Services for young children with disabilities should be provided in integrated settings within the local community.

- A transdisciplinary model of service delivery should be utilized; isolated therapies should be minimized.

- Artificial reinforcement and aversive control techniques should be avoided.

- Training should emphasize function rather than form of response.

- Program planning should include planned enhancement of the child's skill development within daily family routines.

- Curriculum should be developed with reference to the individual child, as well as to family, peers, and the community.

- Program evaluation and child assessment should be accomplished using a variety of outcome measures.

- Transitions from one educational setting to the next should be planned carefully.

health must be monitored closely to ensure her complete and successful recovery. Her family will need help facilitating Sarah's speech and language development, usually delayed in children with mental retardation. Sarah is not sitting or crawling, which suggests a delay in her motor development, and we know that her cognitive development is likely to be delayed. Because of Sarah's varied needs, the design of her intervention program, or the outcomes on her IFSP, will benefit from the input of a team consisting of health-care professionals, a speech-language specialist, a physical therapist, and a teacher skilled in activities that will facilitate cognitive development. And we haven't even mentioned her parents' needs!

The IFSP outcomes for Sarah and her family might look like this:

1. Sarah's parents will learn more about Down syndrome and meet other parents of children with Down syndrome through participation in a parent-to-parent support group.

2. Sarah's parents will feel confident in their ability to facilitate their daughter's healthy growth and development, particularly in the area of communication skills.

3. Sarah will begin to use pointing and vocalizations to indicate her needs.

4. Sarah's parents will learn more about the impact of her surgery and recovery on Sarah's overall development, particularly her motor development.

5. Sarah will sit and crawl independently. (Cook, Tessier & Klein, 1996)

According to the IFSP, Sarah will receive weekly home visits from an early intervention specialist and a speech-language pathologist, and her parents will take her to physical therapy twice weekly. Sarah's parents will be given the name of their local Down syndrome parent group, and respite care will be provided so that they can attend the meetings. The team expects that Sarah will be attending a center-based early intervention program by the time she is 18 months old, with one or both of her parents attending with her.

With the help of an **interdisciplinary team** of professionals, Sarah's parents will make sure that she is off to a healthy start in life.

Identification and Assessment of Infants at Risk

Since most states have developed early intervention programs for infants and young children under P.L. 99-457, criteria must be designed to identify children who are eligible for these services. Clearly, young children with identified disabilities are eligible. Also eligible are those children described as developmentally delayed. It is the group of children we discuss in this chapter, those who are categorized as biologically and environmentally "at risk," who have presented the most significant problems to the state teams working on eligibility criteria, and, based on our previous discussions in this chapter, we can begin to see why. We have developed a considerable list of biological and environmental risk factors, and there are many others we have not had the space to present. Deciding which risk factors or how many factors will qualify a child for services has presented a considerable challenge to the states. Many states require that multiple risk factors be used to qualify children for programs, since we know that as risk factors multiply, their combined effect is likely to be greater than that of any single factor.

Techniques for Identification and Assessment

We obtain information about a child's risk status from a number of sources: hospital and health records, family interviews, observation of the child, developmental and health screenings, and diagnostic assessment. **Screening** refers to quick and efficient procedures whereby large numbers of children can be evaluated to determine whether more in-depth assessment is required; screenings of young children's development, hearing, vision, and overall health can identify children with a high probability of delayed development. **Diagnostic assessment,** a more in-depth look at the child's development, provides a more definitive picture of whether the child has special needs; in diagnostic assessment, formal assessment tools are used by a multidisciplinary team, with considerable input from the child's family (Meisels & Provence, 1989).

No one source of information should be used to make any decisions concerning a child's eligibility for services; "best practices" in assessment demand that multiple types of data from multiple sources be used for good decision-making. Foremost among these sources is the family. Meisels and Provence (1989) put it this way:

> One should not try to screen or assess young children without the active participation of those most expert about them—their parents. All parents know a great deal about their children, and the task of those conducting the screening and assessment is to enable parents to transmit that information productively. (p. 15)

"Best practices" in assessment demand that multiple types of data from multiple sources, especially the family, be used for good decision-making.

The Problems of Predicting Disabilities from Risk Factors

Despite the large number of studies that identify biologically at-risk infants and follow their development over time, researchers have found that their ability to predict which children will develop disabilities is relatively poor. Children with severe disabilities, often caused by massive central nervous system insult, are an exception to this rule, but they are the very small minority. Fortunately, many of the early complications of biological risk status are transient—that is, they disappear over time. Many infants can and do recover from the trauma of premature birth and early medical complications.

But, once again, the child's ability to recover from these early experiences appears to be mediated by the caregiving characteristics in his or her environment. Cohen and Parmalee (1983), for example, found that for most of their premature subjects, neonatal complications did not necessarily predict scores on the Stanford-Binet IQ test at age 5. But children whose developmental performance improved the most had caregiving that was more responsive, more reciprocal, and encouraged more autonomy than those children whose performance did not improve. We can begin to see why early intervention for infants at risk must focus on the infant within the context of the family.

Children with responsive and consistent caregiving have the best chance of recovering from the effects of risk factors.

The Resilient Child

The impact of risk factors varies a great deal in different children, families, and environments. For example, there are many healthy young children doing well in school today who were born at very low weight; other low-birthweight children are striving to overcome disabilities ranging from mild learning disabilities to severe mental retardation. Many children grow up in poverty and go on to lead productive adult lives; others develop school problems that lead to dropping out of school or to special educational programming. On the other hand, few children born with serious chromosomal abnormalities grow up without developmental delays (although many of them can, as we shall see, become productive citizens).

So far in this chapter, we have identified a large number of biological and environmental risk factors that increase the likelihood of poor developmental outcomes in children. No single risk factor satisfactorily predicts or explains what will happen to a child, but the accuracy of our predictions increases with the number of risk factors that the child experiences, and the most vulnerable children of all are those who experience both biological and environmental risk factors. In fact, most children who experience a series of biological risk factors (with the exception of those that clearly damage the central nervous system) but grow up in a stable, supportive environment develop very well.

There are also the remarkable children who, despite a multitude of adverse biological and environmental events, overcome the odds and become healthy, productive adults. Werner and Smith (1982) called them "vulnerable but invincible." What is it about these children that protects them from the school failure, emotional distress, early parenthood, and criminal behavior demonstrated by other children from similar backgrounds?

To find these protective factors, we look first within the child. Werner (1986, p. 16) defined the characteristics shared by the **resilient,** or "stress resistant," children of several studies:

> (1) An active, evocative approach toward solving their developmental tasks, enabling them to negotiate successfully an abundance of emotionally hazardous experiences; (2) the ability, from infancy on, to gain other people's positive attention, and to recruit "surrogate parents" when necessary; (3) a tendency to perceive and interpret their experiences constructively, even if they caused pain and suffering; and (4) a strong "sense of coherence," a belief that their lives had meaning.

Werner described the most resilient subjects of her longitudinal study of the children of Kauai: One out of three grew up in chronic poverty, had experienced perinatal stresses or had congenital defects, were raised by mothers with little formal education, and lived in families with serious instability, discord, or parental mental illness. But one out of four of these children "escaped the ill effects of such multiple risks and developed into stable, mature, and competent young adults who 'worked well, played well, loved well, and expected well'" (Werner, 1986, p. 13). There were ameliorative personal factors within these children and protective factors within their caregiving environments, among them positive parent-child relationships during the first two years and emotional support provided by other family members (such as siblings and grandparents) during early and middle childhood.

As Werner's research indicates, risk factors are not the only significant variables capable of influencing the course of children's development. Dunst (1993) suggests that it is not simply the absence of risk factors that help us predict which children develop well; there are also "opportunity factors" that can occur within a family and community and that may enhance and strengthen a child's development. According to Dunst, research demonstrates that positive development outcomes are influenced by the power of factors such as high education level of parents, stimulating and warm caregiver-child interaction, and a sup-

Some resilient children overcome the odds and become healthy, productive adults.

Personal factors within resilient children and protective factors within their caregiving environments may help them overcome early risk factors.

portive extended family. The influence of these opportunity factors increases when multiple factors are present.

The fact that there are children who can experience many stressful biological and environmental events and emerge as healthy, competent adults provides us with hope and encouragement. We must use the results of this research to support other at-risk children and families so that they, too, can develop protective personal characteristics despite stressful caregiving environments.

SUMMARY

■ Risk factors include a wide range of biological and environmental conditions associated with increased probability of developmental problems in young children.

■ Risk factors can be categorized as biological risks and environmental risks. Biological risks are a threat to a child's developing systems and can include diseases, maternal substance abuse, and oxygen deprivation. Environmental risk stems from damaging physical and social surroundings of the child and his or her caretakers, such as exposure to lead, accidents, or limited access to health care.

■ Some steps that help prevent risk status and disability include inoculation, genetic counseling, prenatal care, and prenatal testing. Early intervention is another means of preventing the negative impact of risk factors.

■ Early intervention consists of a comprehensive set of services for infants and toddlers aged birth to 3 and their families, designed for the unique needs and built on the unique strengths of each child and family. Early intervention has a strong family focus and can consist of services offered by a range of professionals across disciplines.

■ At-risk children can pose a challenge for early intervention personnel because the range of possible risk factors is so great and because the presence of one or more risk factors does not guarantee a developmental delay. Techniques used to identify children for early intervention include screening and diagnostic assessment.

■ It must be remembered that no absolute predictions can be made regarding at-risk children. Some children are exceptionally resilient and succeed despite seemingly large odds. Positive parent-child relationships and emotional support from other family members can help a child overcome biological and environmental stresses.

KEY TERMS

risk factors
biological risk
environmental risk
prenatal
perinatal
postnatal

first trimester
teratogens
rubella
cytomegalovirus
  (CMV)
congenital

sexually transmitted
  diseases (STDs)
acquired immune
  deficiency syndrome
  (AIDS)
thalidomide

polydrug users

fetal alcohol syndrome (FAS)

fetal alcohol effects (FAE)

Down syndrome

hypoxia

premature (preterm)

low birthweight

neonatology

neonatal intensive care unit

meningitis

chronic otitis media

occupational hazards

inoculation

genetic counseling

prenatal care

amniocentesis

chorionic villous sampling (CVS)

early intervention

individualized family service plan (IFSP)

interdisciplinary team

screening

diagnostic assessment

resilient

MULTIMEDIA RESOURCES

Centers for Disease Control (CDC) National AIDS Clearinghouse website: http://www.cdcnac.org. For general information about HIV/AIDS-related resources and services, prevention materials, referrals and publications, funding information, and clinical trials, call (800) 458-5231. For general questions about HIV and for educational materials, call the CDC National AIDS Hotline at (800) 342-AIDS.

Dorris, Michael. *The Broken Cord* (New York: Harper & Row, 1989). This book relates the emotionally wrenching story of the author's adoption of a young Sioux Indian child who is later diagnosed with fetal alcohol syndrome.

Healthtouch website: http://www.healtouch.com. This website offers information on a wide variety of health-related topics. Look under Health Information for sexually transmitted diseases and AIDS; see Drug and Alcohol Abuse for information about drug and alcohol use during pregnancy.

National Maternal and Child Health Clearinghouse website: http://www.circsol.com/mch/. This clearinghouse gathers and disseminates material on topics related to the health of mothers and children, such as prenatal care and nutrition, in the form of pamphlets, bibliographies, and other resources. The clearinghouse can be reached by phone at (703) 356-1964.

Streissguth, Ann. *Fetal Alcohol Syndrome: A Guide for Families and Communities* (Baltimore: Brookes, 1997). This book by one of the foremost researchers on FAS reviews the research and interventions for a popular and professional audience.

USING YOUR KNOWLEDGE

 Can Do: Can you identify risk factors? Contact the local branch of a human services agency like the Department of Social Services or the Department of Youth Services. Find out if any case histories of previous clients are available. If so, read through several of them and make note of risk factors that were addressed. Get together with others in your class and compile a list of the most common risk factors.

 Commonalities: Visit a neonatal intensive care unit. Write a narrative report of what you observed and present it to your classmates.

 Collaboration: How much can be done to prevent disabilities? Divide the class into several groups. Have each group role-play talking to a professional from a multidisciplinary team, including a genetic counselor, a social worker who assists families under stress, a doctor or nurse who provides inoculations at community health centers, an early intervention specialist, and so forth. Ask the professionals how they view their role in preventing disabilities. Are there any limitations that they would like to overcome? Get together as a class and write a list of recommendations for the prevention of disability.

WHAT YOU CAN DO NOW

Each of us has a personal and a social responsibility to help prevent disability in our communities. Here are some ways for you to help.

1. Participate in fundraising and awareness campaigns.

- Pledge or organize a team of volunteers for a fundraising event. Major fundraising organizations like the March of Dimes, the United Way, or the United Cerebral Palsy Association would love to have your help.
- Working as a class, design posters illustrating risk factors and related prevention strategies for display in a community education program.
- Hold a "risk awareness" education day at your local high school or community center.

2. Promote early prenatal care and early recognition of risk and disability.

- Invite a genetic counselor from a local hospital to come and speak to your class or your parent group.
- Find out about the low-cost prenatal care services in your community and, in a small group, devise a plan to publicize them in your community.
- Find out where you can refer parents who are concerned about their child's early development in your town or city. Make a list for your school and local pediatricians.

3. Take care of yourself and the people you care about.

- Avoid alcohol use when considering pregnancy.
- Remember that modeling of responsible behavior for others can be a powerful influence.

Families of Exceptional Children

3

SPECIAL education professionals have increasingly based their decisions about services and programs on the knowledge that the family's involvement can make their work much more effective. In this chapter, you will learn how exceptionalities affect families, how teachers and other professionals can involve parents and family members in making educational and life choices, and how to provide support to the entire family.

As you read, look for answers to these questions:

■ **What is the legal basis for family involvement in special education?**

■ **How does the birth of an exceptional child affect the family?**

Collaboration: How can family members and professionals learn to work together as partners?

Commonalities: How does the family participate in the exceptional child's development at every stage of life?

Can Do: What are some of the ways in which exceptional children contribute to the strength and richness of a family?

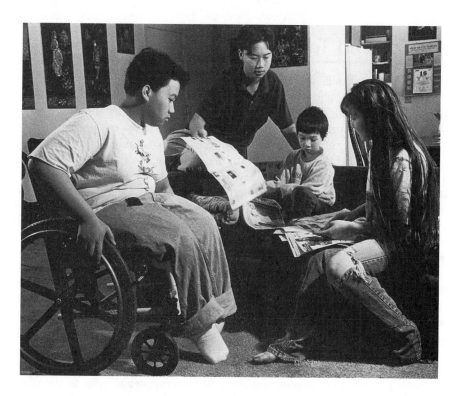

The emotional pull of the family is like nothing else we ever experience in this world. Thoughts of your family may fill your heart with love and longing or with regret and bitterness—most people, realistically, feel a combination of all those emotions. No one can inspire love like a mother, father, husband, wife, son, daughter, brother, sister. And no one can inspire anger in the same way, either.

Families with exceptional children are like other families. Parents love their children fiercely and become fiercely impatient with them. Sisters and brothers play together, fight, are jealous of one another, grow up to be friends or distant relations. Families weather the storms of life together or fall apart under the stresses.

This is not to say that living with an exceptional child does not set a family apart. It often does. Parents of children with disabilities often spend a great deal of time in a public relations effort—"explaining" their children to doctors, teachers, psychologists, neighbors, and other shoppers in the supermarket. Yes, she is different . . . special . . . exceptional . . . gifted . . . disabled . . . whatever. This can become difficult for all the family members. And sometimes families must watch their children suffer without being able to help—whether it be from lack of acceptance by others, hospitalizations and surgeries, or missing out on one of life's experiences.

Those of you without an exceptional family member may tend to focus on those unhappy experiences when you think of children with disabilities. But a family has difficult times with every child. This chapter will help you understand more about the inevitable stresses involved with being the parent of an exceptional child. It should also help you to appreciate the options and supports that are available to families, and the joy that exceptional children, like other children, bring into their families' lives.

Definitions and Terms

The team of professionals working with exceptional children in the schools today—the general education teacher, the special education teacher or consultant, the school nurse, the speech specialist, and all the others—generally works more closely with the families of its students than is the norm in "regular" education. At their best, our efforts as educators occur in partnership with the families of our students, and the goals that families have for their children are foremost in our planning. Our involvement with families, as we saw in Chapter 1, is mandated by law. The law and amendments that make up the Individuals with Disabilities Education Act (IDEA) require that families be given every opportunity to participate in each step of their child's school program. In addition, it is just good common sense that families be involved: They are the best source of information about the abilities and needs of their child, and they often know what goals are most important for their child's successful functioning (Allen & Petr, 1996). Our collaboration with families requires that all professionals working with exceptional children understand the stresses and strengths of families and know how best to communicate with family members.

Educators' involvement with families of children with disabilities is mandated by law.

A note about terms: Clearly it is not always the biological parent who raises the exceptional child—it may be one biological parent, a grandparent, a foster parent, another relative, or a family friend. Acknowledging these diverse possibilities, many professionals prefer to use the term **caregiver** to refer to the person who assumes that role. That term seems relatively impersonal to us, so in

The caregiver is the person who raises the child.

this chapter we use the word *parent* generically, to include all those caregivers who take the responsibilities traditionally associated with being a parent.

Much has been written about the fact that there is no "average" American family any more. Perhaps it used to be Mom, Dad, and the two kids, but nowadays the family can take myriad forms, from a single mother raising her children independently to a foster family with four or five at-risk children to an extended family with three generations living under the same roof. A home can provide love, care, and stability to a child without a biological mother and father being present. In addition, we know that the majority of women with children work outside the home, often because of economic necessity. Although this reality may change the nature of the parent-school relationship, it does not mean that no relationship exists. Our criteria for what constitutes a "good" family have evolved and broadened, and our expectations for families must become more flexible in response to the increased demands on them.

Family Reactions to Exceptionality

We all have fantasies about our unborn children—which the experience of having a real child soon erases. We may think of a curly-haired toddler holding our hand and walking contentedly by our side. We may look at other people's children behaving irritably or having a temper tantrum and think, "*My* child will never behave like that." We may picture our future offspring winning the science fair, writing the Great American Novel, or competing in the Olympics.

Most of the time, our children don't fit those fantasies. They may excel in ways that surprise us and show no interest in areas in which we imagined they would achieve. We seldom live up to our own dreams of being perfect parents, either. Our children love us anyway, and we usually come to accept each other, imperfect as we all are.

The discovery that a child is exceptional may come at birth or soon after, or it may come later in a child's life—perhaps, as with giftedness or learning disabilities, at school age. Although parents may experience similar feelings at either point, the age of the child does appear to make a difference in the family's initial response. First we will discuss early diagnosis. Keep in mind that the more severe the disability, the earlier it is likely to be identified.

When a child with a disability is born into a family, the family's expectations are violated in at least two ways. First, the child may not look like or behave like the child they imagined. The doctor's predictions about the future may be dour and depressing or frightening in their vagueness. Grandparents and friends may not know how to react and may offer no congratulations, send no flowers, make no phone calls. Instead of imagining a bright future for the child, the parents imagine the worst—or don't know what to imagine.

Second, the parents' expectations for caring for the child may not match with reality. Nearly all families underestimate how much work is involved in having a new baby and how much of their own lives they are required to give up. Although all newborns are demanding, a baby with a disability may have special equipment, require special feeding techniques, be particularly irritable or fussy, and not respond predictably to being cared for. As a result, first-time parents may not be able to benefit from advice from friends and relatives, and experienced parents may not be able to rely on their experiences with their other children for some aspects of caregiving.

More severe disabilities tend to be identified earlier.

Families who have access to parent support groups when their children are identified with a disability are fortunate: Other parents of children with disabilities can often provide both emotional support and specific ideas for easing the burdens of child care. Organizations founded by parents of children with a specific disability, like the Association for Retarded Citizens-United States (ARC-US), the Cystic Fibrosis Foundation, or the Down Syndrome Congress, are often a great help to families with newly identified young children. (See the Multimedia Resources section at the end of this chapter for a list of useful organizations.)

The birth of a child with a disability may violate a family's expectations.

When parents of exceptional children look to the future, their dreams and expectations may also be violated. During childhood, the parents may be required to advocate for their child in order to ensure that he or she receives an appropriate educational program. As an adult, their child may still need their care. Parents must prepare for what will happen to that child—no matter what age—when they die.

This is not what we bargain for when we begin to dream about having a child. But it is not the catastrophe that it might seem to be at first glance, either. Many families become stronger and wiser for the experience of having an exceptional member. As usual, those virtues do not arrive without pain and struggle.

As an illustration, let us observe a hypothetical family:

Marcus and Maria's baby is whisked away from them the minute she is born and soon surrounded by green-coated medical personnel who work over her quietly but urgently for many minutes. Returning from the huddle, their ashen-faced obstetrician tells them that their baby appears to have Down syndrome and is having difficulty breathing. The doctors suspect that she has a heart problem, and she is being taken to the neonatal intensive care unit, where she will undergo tests and be evaluated.

Before they can think about what questions to ask, Marcus and Maria are in the recovery room, looking at each other. Down syndrome? Doesn't that mean mental retardation? And a heart problem? Will she survive? Do we want her to survive? Will she need surgery? Why is this happening to us?

In describing the experience of learning that their child had a disability, many parents remember the initial feeling as one of *shock*. Parents sometimes describe themselves as standing over the situation, looking down on it and watching themselves. These feelings can be short-lived or persist for some time. Because of this, professionals are encouraged to repeat the information they have about the baby or child at another time, or in a different way, as often as possible over the first few days. It is crucial for professionals to be available to parents as they ask questions and the import of the news slowly dawns on them.

Some authors describe a stage of *denial* that parents reportedly experience when grappling with the initial news that their child has a disability. According to this theory, denial may result in a refusal to acknowledge the implications of the child's disability and therefore an unwillingness to begin intervention or treatment for the child (Luterman, 1979). What is seen by some as denial, however, may simply be a lack of understanding of the implications of the disability.

When the shock diminishes, parents may begin to feel a deep *grief*. Their "dream child" is gone, and they don't know what they are left with. This is a feeling that many parents continue to feel for a long time, although it is not a constant feeling. For many, this grief is alleviated by the beginnings of attachment to their child. Let's go back to our hypothetical situation . . .

> Late that night, Marcus and Maria are able to visit their new daughter in the neonatal intensive care unit. The doctors have told them that their baby has a congenital heart defect that will require open-heart surgery. Although the baby is wearing a heart monitor and receiving some oxygen through a nasal tube, the nurse takes her out of her incubator and places her in Maria's arms. She's adorable! Marcus and Maria exclaim with surprise as they notice her fuzzy hair, her smooth skin, her tiny hands. Marcus notices that her nose is tiny and her eyes appear to have an upward slant. She opens those eyes, and suddenly the baby and her parents are looking at each other for the first time. Despite the sadness and anxiety in their hearts, Marcus and Maria fall in love with their new daughter. They decide to name her Angelica.

Another feeling that parents must often struggle with is *anger*. They look at friends and family members with normal, healthy babies and wonder why their baby couldn't have been that way. They look for someone to blame for their dilemma, and if they find no one, they may turn the anger inward and blame themselves, often without reason.

Anger is another common emotion parents grapple with.

Despite the pain, most parents eventually reach a point at which they accept the fact that their child has a disability, which Jan Blacher (1984a) described as *adjustment and acceptance*: "a constructive adaptation to the child's handicap and realistic expectations of his or her progress" (p. 28). Although feelings of anger, guilt, and sadness do not disappear, the parents are able to recognize and rejoice in their child's progress and to act as advocates for their child.

Most parents reach a point of adjustment and acceptance.

Our story of Marcus and Maria depicts a hypothetical example of a family learning shortly after birth that their child will have a disability. In some instances, early diagnoses like these do occur. Some disabilities are present at birth and are identified immediately or in the first few days of life. For many other families, however, the knowledge that their child has a disability comes later. Parents may suspect that something is wrong, but they sometimes have difficulty getting professionals to confirm their suspicions. Parents typically suspect hearing loss in their child, for example, before the age of 12 months, yet the average age at which the diagnosis is confirmed is $2\frac{1}{2}$ years (Northern & Downs, 1991). Learning disabilities typically do not appear until the child is in school and must begin to learn to read; children with autism may develop normally for the first months of life. The worry that something is wrong with their child is very stressful for parents; they often veer back and forth between reassurance and deep anxiety.

Not all disabilities are diagnosed at birth; many are diagnosed later.

Many parents and professionals have concluded that although feelings of shock, denial, grief, anger, and acceptance may be part of the experience of adjusting to the diagnosis of a child with a disability, it is inaccurate to assume that they appear in sequence, one following the other (Blacher, 1984b). Instead, these feelings may appear and reappear throughout child-rearing. A stage theory does not adequately explain the complexity and individuality of a family's response to the identification of disability in their child.

Shock, denial, grief, anger, and acceptance may recur throughout child-rearing.

The Family Systems Approach

The family systems approach provides a useful framework for understanding the diverse situations of U.S. families.

Recently, professionals writing about families with exceptional members have borrowed and expanded on a framework used by sociologists to understand family life; that framework is known as the **family systems approach** (see Figure 3.1). Family systems theory is a framework for understanding the family as an interrelated social system with unique characteristics and needs. It is based on the assumption that an experience that affects one family member will affect all family members (Turnbull & Turnbull, 1997).

Factors Affecting the Family's Reaction

We know a great deal about families and how they work from our own experiences, and the components of the family systems approach provide us with a conceptual framework for discussion. Foremost among these is the first component, **family characteristics,** which includes the characteristics of the exceptional child as well as the family itself. Let us examine how this information has specific implications for families with a child with a disability.

■ **Characteristics of the Child's Exceptionality**   Clearly, various abilities and disabilities will have differing effects on family life. For one thing, the *nature* of the exceptionality will determine the family reaction. The child who is deaf challenges the family to alter its communication system; will family members use sign language or speech for communication? If the choice is sign language, is each family member willing to take on the commitment of attending sign language classes? The child who is chronically ill places financial as well as emotional stress on the family; the child with a learning disability requires extra academic support and may cause a family to examine the emphasis they place on school achievement.

The *degree* of exceptionality may also have an impact on the family reaction. Children with more severe disabilities may look and behave quite differently than other children. Although on one hand these factors might stigmatize a family, on the other they clearly communicate that the child has a disability, relieving the family of the need to explain. Some disabilities, like deafness and learning disabilities, are "invisible"; they are less likely to be apparent from looking at the child. Families of children with disabilities often describe the stress and frustration that accompany the constant explanations of their child's disability that are expected by family, friends, and strangers. Berry and Hardman (1998) provide a poignant example of this in their excerpt from Kathryn Morton's description of going grocery shopping with her daughter, Beckie: "I took her shopping with me only if I felt up to looking groomed, cheerful, competent, and in command of any situation. . . . to look tired and preoccupied with surviving . . . would have turned both of us into objects of pity" (Morton, 1985, p. 144).

Responses differ with the nature, degree, and demands of each child's exceptionality.

The *demands* of the exceptionality will also affect the family's ability to respond. Children who are medically fragile, needing special equipment such as ventilators, oxygen, or gastrointestinal tubes, present great caregiving demands on a family. Children in wheelchairs or who use other equipment require special accommodations in their homes. Children with behavioral and emotional disorders may be destructive of themselves, of others, or of objects within the home. Each exceptionality places its own unique constraints on family life. Even giftedness is no exception; the needs of the talented child, for example, for

Each exceptionality places its own constraints on family life.

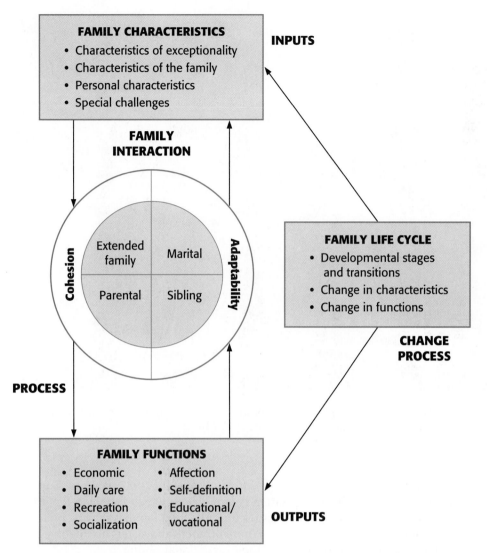

Figure 3.1
Family Systems Conceptual
Framework

Source: A. P. Turnbull, J. A. Summers, and M. J. Brotherson. *Working with Families with Disabled Members: A Family Systems Approach* (Lawrence: University of Kansas, Beach Center on Families and Disabilities, 1984), p. 60. Adapted by permission.

lessons, tutoring, or special attention may create difficulties for other children in the family.

■ **Characteristics of the Family**   In addition to the nature and demands of the child's exceptionality, each family has qualities and characteristics that make it unique. Among these characteristics are family configuration and family size. Family configuration refers to the adults present in the family. These can include one or both parents, stepparents, or foster parents, and **extended family** members such as grandparents, aunts, uncles, cousins, or family friends. There may be one adult living with the child or many. For children of working parents, the caregiver during the parents' work hours may also be essential to the family configuration. Children who experience many changes in family configuration (such as several foster placements) appear to be particularly vulnerable to

Configuration refers to number of adults present in the family.

The word *family* has a unique meaning for the Giraldis, who have adopted 17 children with disabilities. (Andy Levin/Photo Researchers, Inc.)

school problems later in life (Baker, Mednick & Hunt, 1987; Werner & Smith, 1982). Related to family configuration is family size, which usually refers to the number of children in the family. Issues for only-child families may be quite different from those of larger families. Where brothers and sisters are involved, we must consider their needs in light of their exceptional sibling.

Another important family characteristic, one determined by income, education, and employment, is its **socioeconomic status** (SES), which may affect its ability to participate in the child's educational program. Although most families have periods of financial strain, for some it is a more chronic problem than others. As this is being written, more than one in five of all urban children in the United States live in families below the poverty line (Children's Defense Fund, 1997). As we noted in Chapter 2, poverty can affect a child's health and nutrition as well as access to experiences.

The cultural backgrounds of our families and the families we work with will influence beliefs about child-rearing, education, and family life, as well as attitudes toward an exceptional family member. You will see in Chapter 13 that culture means different things to different people. One useful definition calls **culture** a framework that guides life practices (Hanson, 1998a). The term does not refer to a rigid or prescribed set of characteristics but "a set of tendencies or possibilities from which to choose" (Anderson & Fenichel, 1989, p. 8). The practices and traditions that arise from family culture may provide a source of pride and comfort to family members . . . and sometimes a source of misunderstanding or confusion for the professionals who work with them.

Socioeconomic status is determined by family income, education, and employment.

A family's cultural background influences its attitudes toward exceptionality.

Culture is a multifaceted and complex family characteristic. One of its components, **ethnicity,** refers to membership in a particular racial or national group. Descriptive terms such as Latino, American Indian, or Japanese refer to ethnic background, but within these groups even finer distinctions can be made, such as those referring to tribe or country of origin. Another component of culture that is very much related to school learning is the *language* of the family. Whether it be Spanish (the most common language spoken in American homes after English), Cantonese, Vietnamese, American Sign Language, or another language, the child's home language will affect your ability to communicate with family members and the child's ability to profit from instruction in English. In 1996, the Los Angeles Unified School District's Home Language Survey identified seventy-nine different home languages or dialects used by pupils in the district, which is the second largest in the United States with approximately 681,505 pupils. Although your area may not be quite as diverse, you must always consider this important variable when planning educational programs for students and asking for the involvement of their parents.

Religious background is another family characteristic that will affect the perception of disability. Churches, temples, and other religious communities often provide a significant source of support for families, and religious beliefs can shape a family's strategies for coping with a disability.

A child with a disability may be perceived quite differently from culture to culture. Many American Indian groups, for example, believe in accepting all events as they are; this value is based on the Indian belief that these events occur as part of the nature of life, and one must learn to live with the good and the bad in life (Coles, 1977; Joe & Malach, 1998). As the result of these values, attitudes toward children with disabilities are often open and accepting; difference and disability may be viewed as a natural part of life (Dorris, 1989). Other groups define a broader spectrum for "normal" behavior, and therefore have difficulty with a school label such as "mental retardation" for their child (Harry, 1992a). In some Latino cultures, however, strong beliefs in the powers of good and evil, reinforced by religious beliefs, may lead a family to believe that the birth of a child with a disability has resulted from a curse put on the child or the effects of an evil spirit (Zuniga, 1998). Families with Anglo-European roots are more likely to use the tradition of scientific explanation to understand the cause of a child's disability. But each of us must take care not to make blanket assumptions about families' beliefs and practices based on their cultural background. According to Zuniga:

> The central principle is to view each family as an individual unit to ascertain what meaning they ascribe to the illness or disability. Assumptions should not be made without first getting to know the family since so many variables contribute to views on causation and disability, particularly related to children. (p. 235)

Impact of Exceptionality on Family Function

Think about the list you may currently have—either in your head or written down—of "things to do." Going to the bank, shopping for groceries, registering for a class, buying a book, calling a friend to arrange an outing, having your eyes examined—all of these tasks are related to personal needs. If you are a parent, your own list is probably at the bottom of an infinite list of things to do for other family members.

Ethnicity refers to membership in a racial or national group.

Family functions include all the life tasks the family performs to meet its needs.

Families with exceptional children are often responsible for complex **family functions.** Family finances can be strained by the need for ongoing professional evaluation and services. Taking care of the everyday needs of an exceptional child can be a full-time job in itself: Feeding, dressing, toileting, and transporting a child with a severe disability is labor-intensive. The socialization and self-definition needs of parents are often sacrificed to the needs of children, and families are expected to devote a great deal of time and energy to the educational and vocational needs of their exceptional child. When needs of family members are not met, stress may result.

When you work with the family of an exceptional child, you must take into account the needs of the entire family and the responsibilities for fulfilling family functions that parents already carry. These responsibilities are challenging for any parent, and sometimes feel overwhelming in economically secure two-parent families; they are compounded in single-parent families and in those families where economic strains are real. Your expectations for families of children who are exceptional must be tempered by your appreciation for the responsibilities involved in meeting their overall needs. Your most useful suggestions to parents will help them incorporate effective strategies for facilitating their child's development into their daily routines; there will also be times when you can offer families additional means to cope with the demands of their family life and the stress that results from unmet needs.

Exceptionality and Family Interactions

Family interaction addresses the relationships among family members.

All the relationships within families can be touched by the presence of a child with exceptionality; traditionally, conventional wisdom assumed that relationships would be affected negatively. More recently, researchers have begun to examine the possibility that the presence of such a child can affect **family interactions** in positive as well as negative ways, and we have begun to alter many of our long-held assumptions and views.

■ **Between Marriage Partners** Research on the lifespan of a typical marriage suggests that most marital partners report a decrease in satisfaction with marriage in the years following the birth of children (Belsky, Lang & Rovine, 1985). With the presence of any child adding to strain in a marriage, some researchers have assumed that the presence in a family of a child with a disability would lead to increased stress and family breakdown. A large-scale study done in England by Pahl and Quine (1987) described a more complex situation, in which a number of specific factors led to unusually high levels of stress in parents of children with severe handicaps. Some factors were related to the child's disability, such as the child's behavior problems, and some to general family problems, such as parents' money worries. The highest levels of stress were reported by the families of children with the most severe disabilities. Breslau, Staruch, and Mortimer (1982) found that the best predictor of mothers' distress was the intensity of the child's daily needs—the amount of help, for example, that the child needed with eating, dressing, grooming, and so on. You can see that the weight of these factors within each family would vary depending on the nature of the child's disability and other family characteristics, and on the coping strategies and sources of support available to each family.

Families of children with the most intensive caregiving needs appear to experience the most stress.

The research on divorce in families of children with disabilities is somewhat equivocal; some studies have found higher levels of divorce (Gath, 1977); others have found no difference in divorce rates between families with and without

Family support for people with disabilities can take many forms. Here a father and daughter read together from a book that has typed words for her and a braille overlay for him. (Linda Eber/Impact Visuals)

children with disabilities (Williams & McHenry, 1981). We know from research, then, that having a child with a disability does increase parental stress, particularly when the child has severe disabilities and intensive daily care needs. Whether the increased stress is related to higher levels of divorce in these families is still unclear.

Having a child with a disability increases parental stress, but whether it increases the probability of divorce is unclear.

■ **Between Parents and Children**   Researchers have identified some differences in parent-child interaction when the child has a disability or is at risk for the development of disability. (The interaction between mothers and their children is studied much more frequently than that of fathers and their children.) These differences vary according to the characteristics of each mother and each child and appear to change somewhat over time, particularly during the first year of life. In general, it appears that mothers of young children with disabilities dominate the communication interactions with their children more than mothers of children without disabilities, perhaps because it is more difficult to interpret infant cues and responses (Barnard & Kelly, 1990). Klein and Briggs (1987) demonstrated through their Mother-Infant Communication Project that effective communication techniques could be facilitated through indirect modeling in a group of mothers and high-risk infants.

■ **Among Siblings**   What happens to the brothers and sisters of children with exceptionalities? Do they suffer from lack of parental attention? Are they given too much responsibility for caregiving? The impact of a sibling with a disability on brothers and sisters seems to depend on a number of factors, such as the attitudes and expectations of parents, family size, family resources, religion, the severity of the disability, and the pattern of interactions between siblings

(Powell & Gallagher, 1993). Some studies have cited the negative aspects of the experience. Increased need for child care, for example, may make particular demands on older sisters (Stoneman, Brody, Davis & Crapps, 1988). Brothers and sisters of children with disabilities may react to related stress with changes in their behavior or feelings of loneliness, insecurity, or incompetence (Milstead, 1988).

Most professionals today believe that it is important to invite siblings to participate in decisions concerning their brother or sister with a disability, and sometimes to help with the exceptional child's educational programs. Swenson-Pierce, Kohl, and Egle (1987) taught siblings to instruct their brothers and sisters with severe handicaps and found that they were successful teachers: Their siblings with severe handicaps increased independent performance of the skills taught. Teaching is not appropriate for every sibling; some will enjoy the process and some will not. But many brothers and sisters are natural teachers of their exceptional siblings, and the family benefits from these positive interactions.

Siblings can play a key role in the rearing of their exceptional sibling.

■ **The Extended Family**   Families with effective support systems seem to cope better with the stresses of daily life (Garbarino, 1990). For many, this group includes extended family members who provide help and support. The extended family includes grandparents, aunts, uncles, nieces, nephews, and other relatives. Extended family members may live with parents and child or apart from them. They can be respite caregivers as well as sources of emotional (and sometimes economic) support to overstressed parents. Family support programs should consider the impact of a child with a disability on grandparents as well as more immediate family members; many parents of children with disabilities worry about how their own parents will accept their grandchild (Seligman & Darling, 1989).

Extended family members can provide support for overstressed parents.

■ **Families Under Stress**   Raising children today presents special challenges to families in environments that Garbarino (1997) calls "socially toxic." Garbarino believes that elements of children's social world—violence, poverty, disruption of family relationships, substance use, the proliferation of guns, the threat of AIDS—have become poisonous to their development and undermine their sense of security. In addition, researchers tell us that adults are spending less time with children, and "the lack of adult supervision and time spent doing constructive, cooperative activities compounds the effects of other negative influences in the social environment for kids" (Garbarino, 1997, p. 14). The children who may be most vulnerable to the "social toxins" are those who already have the most developmental risk factors (see Chapter 2), especially those who live in poverty.

Some families have difficulty withstanding these social stresses—Hanson and Carta (1996) call them **"families with multiple risks"** and suggest strategies for educators working with them (see the box "Principles of Support and Intervention for Multiple Risk Families").

Families with children with HIV infection, for example, must deal with many stressful issues (Lesar, Gerber & Semmel, 1996). The negative social climate and stigma still associated with HIV and AIDS caused 70 percent of the families in the Lesar study not to disclose the cause of their child's illness to anyone outside their immediate families. The amount and nature of the social support they received was therefore diminished, leaving them isolated, and the intense caregiving demands of the child's illness isolated them further.

Families with multiple risks experience social and economic risk factors that can be overwhelming.

Family dinners provide structure and support for all family members. (Jeff Dunn/The Picture Cube, Inc.)

Coping Strategies and Sources of Support

Despite the responsibilities and strains we have described, many families of children with disabilities survive and thrive:

> These are the families who roll up their sleeves and get on with the task of finding the best available services for their child; who both accept the reality of the disability and are able to love the child for who he or she is; who

---

➤ Principles of Support and Intervention for Multiple Risk Families

1. *Provide opportunities for positive caregiving transactions.* Providing support at the earliest point for children and parents or caregivers in establishing positive and mutually satisfying relationships with one another holds promise for preventing or relieving sources of stress.

2. *Shift focus from deficits to emphasis on individual and family strengths.* Services to children and families will be best served by identifying and supporting strengths, rather than by fault-finding and blaming.

3. *Recognize and encourage informal sources of support.* Friends, community members, teachers, and others may be natural supports for families.

4. *Become cross-culturally competent.* Professionals must be sensitive, respectful, and knowledgeable about the family cultures.

5. *Provide comprehensive, coordinated services.* Services to families must be community-based, appropriate, and valued by families; agencies must work together to provide coordinated services to families.

6. *Recognize the need to offer families a broad spectrum of services.* Schools and other agencies must recognize that families with multiple challenges may require assistance in numerous areas before they can make use of other interventions that address specific child needs.

7. *Deliver flexible, usable services.* Service providers must individualize services based on family needs.

8. *Cross professional boundaries and overcome bureaucratic limitations.* Agencies and professionals must break through bureaucratic boundaries to work together on behalf of families.

Source: Adapted from M.J. Hanson and J.J. Carta, "Addressing the Challenges of Families with Multiple Risks," *Exceptional Children,* 62(3) (1996), 201–212. Copyright © 1996 by The Council for Exceptional Children. Reprinted with permission.

manage to have successful marriages and emotionally well-adjusted children, both with and without disabilities. Many of them have enough energy left over from coping with the demands of their own lives to provide support to other families, and even to give encouragement now and again to weary educators and service providers. These families are said to have made a positive adaptation to their child with a disability. We meet these parents every day in the course of our educational or health practices. (Summers, Behr & Turnbull, 1989, p. 27)

Recently researchers have begun to study how people cope with stress and adversity. **Coping strategies** are the things people do to enhance a sense of well-being in their lives and to avoid being harmed by stressful demands (Turnbull & Turnbull, 1993).

Coping strategies help people avoid the harmful effects of high levels of stress.

Some of the resources that have been found to assist families in successful coping include problem-solving and behavior-management skills; negotiation and communication skills in working with professionals; informal social support, including other family members; and community support. In addition, Summers, Behr, and Turnbull (1989) note that a family's coping strategies have a great impact on how well they adapt to their child's disability. Families that cope successfully tend to use three key coping strategies:

- They attribute a cause to the event in order to establish a sense of personal control.
- They acquire mastery, or a feeling of control, in order to keep the adverse events from occurring again.
- They enhance self-esteem by finding the benefits or positive experiences that can result from adverse events. (Taylor, 1983)

Turnbull and Turnbull (1993) describe these strategies as "cognitive coping"—"thinking about a particular situation in ways that enhance well-being" (p. 1). Thus, successful support of families incorporates strategies that increase not only the families' understanding of the causes of disability but also their sense of control over the events of their lives and their self-esteem related to the presence of their children with disabilities (Summers, Behr & Turnbull, 1989).

■ **Parent Support Groups**   At times, organizations, school programs, or agencies offer support groups for parents of children with similar disabilities or ages. These groups may have a specific goal, such as teaching advocacy skills, or they may be formed to provide parents with an opportunity to get to know other parents who have similar concerns. Parents often feel most comfortable among a group of peers and can discuss their very private fears and worries about their children among other parents who may have shared their experiences and feelings. Participation in support groups appears to help many parents feel less isolated; often parents report that until they participated in a group they felt they were the only people in the world with their problems. Participation in groups can also help parents form a network of new and understanding friends, and this helps families fulfill the often-neglected socialization function previously mentioned.

Support groups can provide comfort and information for parents.

The parent-to-parent support model links experienced parents with parents who are new to programs and procedures.

One effective model for parent support is the **parent-to-parent model,** which links experienced parents of young children with disabilities to parents who are new to the programs and processes (Slentz, Walker & Bricker, 1989).

Through phone conversations and group meetings, experienced parents listen, comfort, and share their experiences with others just beginning to learn about their children. Parents who have had similar experiences are often the most empathic and knowledgeable source of support for new parents.

Turnbull and Turnbull (1997) point out that support groups are common in early intervention programs, somewhat less so in school-age programs, and almost nonexistent for parents of older children and adults. Parents of older children and adults with disabilities often need information, communication, and sharing as well, and programs designed to meet their needs could fill a void that leaves many parents isolated.

Parents of older children and adults with disabilities can also benefit from support groups.

■ **Respite Care** For many families, the constant vigilance and caregiving required by a son or daughter with a disability can become overwhelming. A young child with intensive medical requirements, for example, may need to have equipment cleaned, adjusted, and monitored throughout the day; parents may even sleep lightly, perhaps with an intercom to the child's room next to them, in order to be able to hear if equipment "beeps," indicating that the child (or the equipment) is having a problem. The child may be on several different medications or require special treatments that must be administered day and night. The child's care can be so complex that parents cannot simply leave the child with a babysitter. Children with unusual or demanding behavioral characteristics, such as those typical of some children with autism, for example, can also be particularly difficult to care for.

Most parents benefit from spending some time without their children in order to build up their spirits for the relentless requirements of being a parent. This is the case for parents of *all* children. For some families of children with very intensive caregiving needs, this time is much more difficult to obtain, and single-parent families are especially hard-hit. It is for families like this that the concept of **respite care** was developed. In respite care, trained substitute caregivers take over the care of the family member with a disability for a period of time that can range from an hour to a weekend. Respite care is usually provided in the family home, but it can also occur in the caregiver's home or in another facility such as a day-care center or a group home. Respite care is not yet widely available all over the country for families of children with disabilities; when it is provided, however, families report that it positively benefits their families and helps reduce stress levels (Benson, 1989).

Respite care provides substitute caregivers to families with children with disabilities.

The Role of the Family in Special Education Services

As we saw in Chapter 1, the laws pertaining to the education of children with disabilities (IDEA and its amendments) allow for parent partnership in every stage of the educational process. Parents choose to collaborate with professionals to varying degrees—some participate a great deal, some not at all.

The concerns of families with exceptional children change as their children grow and develop, moving from infancy through the school years. Sometimes their children receive special education services from the first year of life through age 21. Let us take a look at the programs available for children with disabilities throughout the school years, and the provisions and expectations for parent involvement within those programs.

Teachers and parents play and sing with young children in an early intervention program. (Laura Dwight)

Early intervention services are delivered by a team of professionals to children up to age 3 and their families.

Under IDEA, parents are encouraged to be active members of their child's decision-making team.

The Early Years

In Chapter 2 we described the **early intervention** services that can be provided when a child under the age of 3 is identified with a specific disability or developmental delay or is considered at risk for the development of a disability. Parents of young children in early intervention services are typically concerned with meeting the day-to-day needs of their child and learning more about the implications of their child's developmental status or disability. As we discussed in Chapter 1, the strengths and needs of the family are identified in the **individualized family service plan (IFSP)**, which is developed cooperatively by the family and the family service team (Sandall, 1997a, 1997b).

During the School Years

Starting school is an important event in every child's life, and it means adjustments for every family. For parents of typically developing children, school entry usually means that they will play less of a role in their child's education. Although they will help with homework, confer with teachers, and possibly attend school meetings, the decisions about what their child will learn, how he or she will learn it, and where learning will take place are all made by the school.

This process is quite different for parents of a child with a disability. Under the provisions of IDEA, educational decisions, including those relative to program planning and placement, are made by a team that includes one or both parents. This process may begin as early as age 3, when a child who has been in an early intervention program or who has been recently identified with a disability transitions into a preschool program.

■ **The Parents' Rights** Built into P.L. 94-142 is an acknowledgment of the parents' *right to be informed and to consent*. Before a child can be evaluated to determine whether he or she is eligible for special education services at all, parents must receive a written assessment plan that thoroughly describes, in clear, everyday language, what kind of evaluation will be conducted and for what purpose. They must sign and return the assessment plan before an evaluation can take place. In fact, parents' right to an informed consent must be considered at every educational decision point for their child. Ask yourself these questions when considering how this operates in the school in which you teach:

- Are the written materials that explain procedures and alternatives available in the parents' native language? Verbally translating or paraphrasing this information may not constitute informed consent.

- Are the explanations on those written documents suitably simple and straightforward enough for a layperson to comprehend? Educators, like many other professionals, are notorious for their use of jargon; sometimes we are so immersed in it that we assume that everyone else understands it, too.

- Do parents understand that they have the option *not* to consent? Sometimes this information is not emphasized by professionals who talk with parents, or it is "buried" on consent forms.

As we said earlier, parents also have *the right to participate in placement and program decisions* through the individualized education program (IEP) process. Parents are equal members of the IEP team, as discussed in Chapter 1. They can express preferences for where their child will attend school and what the primary goals and objectives of their child's educational program will be. If parents do not agree with the IEP team's recommendations, no change in placement or program can be made until the disagreement has been settled.

When parents and school personnel disagree about a child's evaluation, placement, or program, parents must be informed of their **right to due process.** Either the parents or the school may call for a hearing (usually called a **due process hearing**) in order to resolve the conflict. Under the 1997 amendments to IDEA, **mediation** must be available to families and the school district before they go to a due process hearing, although participation in mediation in order to resolve disputes is voluntary (The new IDEA, 1997). At the due process hearing, both parties may be represented by lawyers and have the opportunity to call witnesses who will testify for their point of view. The decision is made by an impartial hearing officer. Usually both parties accept the decision of the hearing officer, but if either side still strongly disagrees, the decision can be appealed to the state educational agency and to state and federal courts.

Because of the many opportunities for parent participation that P.L. 94-142 provides, some professionals come to believe that parents are under an obligation to play a part in this process. This assumption is not correct. Parents also have the *right not to participate* in this educational decision-making. Some parents are not comfortable in such a situation; others are not able to take part, and so they waive their rights. Cultural considerations come into play here, too. Parents from some cultural groups may prefer to leave educational decision-making to the schools. When parents choose not to become involved in the IEP process, you must be sure that they understand all their options. Perhaps transportation is difficult for them, and telephone participation would be easier. Has it been made clear to them that an interpreter will be available?

MacMillan and Turnbull (1983) point out that teachers sometimes equate parents' noninvolvement in schooling with noninvolvement with the child who has a disability. This is usually an inaccurate perception. Parents of children with disabilities, especially those with more severe conditions, have strenuous demands on their time and energy; they may see the time the child is in school as their only respite. In addition, family factors such as lack of child care, lack of

Parents have the right to be informed and to consent, to participate in placement and program decisions, to due process, and not to participate.

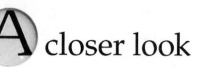

A closer look

Commonalities: Collaborating with Families

Successful family-teacher collaboration requires trust, commitment, work, appreciation, and communication. Family members and teachers should be equal partners who work together to set goals, find solutions, and carry out and evaluate those solutions. Here are some strategies for achieving a successful partnership.

1. *Evaluate your communication skills.* Good communication is based on effective listening. Teachers should maintain an open and nonjudgmental attitude and avoid giving advice, sermonizing, analyzing, or persuading. A noncritical stance will allow families to provide the teacher with all the information necessary for effective collaborative problem solving.

   Use effective questioning. Avoid close-ended questions, which can be answered with "yes" or "no" or a single-word response; ask open-ended questions that allow family members to focus on what is important to them. For example, asking, "Can you tell me about Stephanie's mealtimes?" will provide more information than asking "Does Stephanie eat dinner at the same time every night?" Make sure you ask only questions necessary for providing services to the student and family; avoid intruding into private areas for the sake of curiosity.

   Empathize with family members and assist them in recognizing their feelings and attempting to solve their problems. Be able to restate the main ideas in a family member's conversation and summarize what has been said in a conversation or meeting. This shows family members that you have recognized and understood their input. Effective communicators express empathy and acceptance while collecting information necessary for achieving intervention goals.

2. *Be flexible in your expectations and requirements for families.* Family members have varying responsibilities and tasks, which may prevent them from attending school events. Some parents may find that a lack of transportation, a support system, or an inflexible work schedule may make participation in the child's educational programming nearly impossible for some familes (Shea & Bauer, 1991).

   The work of Beth Harry and her colleagues (1992b, 1995) has identified some of the factors that may contribute to the relatively low level of participation in special education procedures on the part of African American families. Harry's longitudinal study identified several factors that discouraged the parents' participation and advocacy for their children:

   - *Late notices and inflexible scheduling of conferences.* Despite mandated timelines, parents did not always receive notices of meetings in a timely manner.

   - *Limited time for conferences.* Meetings averaged twenty to thirty minutes in length unless parents expressed many concerns.

   - *Emphasis on documents rather than participation.* According to Harry and her colleagues:

   When parents were asked how they perceived their role in the conferences, the majority consistently replied that their main role was to receive information about their child's progress and to sign the documents. . . . Observations revealed that parents' participation in conferences usually consisted of listening, perhaps asking a question (usually regarding logis-

ents are intimidated and uncomfortable in school. If a parent cannot participate in school events, consider the following:

- Increase and improve written communication with the family. Frequent notes, journals, or notebooks that the child can carry home, written commendations for the child, and reports of the child's work can help parents be involved in meeting the educational goals for their child.

- Increase telephone contact. An occasional call at a mutually convenient hour to convey important information about the child's progress connects parents to the educational program. Make sure the family does not hear from you only when there is a problem!

- Consider a home visit with the family's permission. Sometimes transportation problems or demands of young children keep a parent housebound.

3. *Build on strengths rather than focusing on negatives.* Families are imperfect, but most parents work hard for their children in the best way they can. Find the strengths within each family and build on those to develop other areas that need strengthening. Teachers, too, are imperfect and have practices and attitudes that we would like to improve. Give yourself the opportunity to learn from family members how to be a more effective professional.

Sources: J. M. McGonigel; R. K. Kaufman; and B. H. Johnson, eds., *Guidelines and Recommended Practices for the Individualized Family Service Plan,* 2d ed. (Bethesda, MD: Association for the Care of Children's Health, 1991), pp. 34–37; T. M. Shea, and A. M. Bauer, *Parents and Teachers of Children with Exceptionalities: A Handbook for Collaboration* (Boston: Allyn & Bacon, 1991), pp. 110–131; P. J. Winton, "Effective Communication between Parents and Professionals," in D. B. Bailey and R. J. Simeonsson, eds., *Family Assessment and Early Intervention* (Columbus, OH: Merrill, 1988), pp. 218–222.

tical issues such as transportation), and signing papers. A typical view, expressed by one mother, was: "They lay it out [the IEP]. If you have questions, you can ask them. Then you sign it." (p. 371)

- *The use of jargon.* The use of unexplained technical terms by professionals can have a silencing effect on parents and can cloud their understanding of information and decision-making.
- *The structure of power.* When conferences are structured so that professionals report and parents listen, there is an implication that power is in the hands of the professionals.

Research tells us that teachers can unwittingly make family members feel powerless.

Practices like these violate the spirit of the law when they diminish parents' incentive to participate as partners in assessment, planning, and placement issues regarding their children.

■ **The Parent-Teacher Relationship** The laws mandating educational programs for exceptional children require that parents and professionals work together, or collaborate, in order to meet the best interests of the child. Although most teachers see the importance of this collaboration, some may not have the skills or the persistence needed to help parents become involved. Turnbull and Turnbull (1997), Brinckerhoff and Vincent (1986), and Walker (1989) have re-

Children seem to learn best when their families and teachers work together to meet their goals. (Bob Daemmrich Photography, Inc.)

ported success in increasing parent-professional collaboration through some of the strategies described in the box "Collaborating with Families."

Beth Harry (1992b) suggests that new roles for parents need to be developed in order to restructure parent-teacher communication:

Deliberate steps must be taken to help family members feel like part of the team.

- *Parents as assessors.* Parents' participation in the assessment processes that occur before the IEP meeting legitimizes their roles as providers of meaningful information about their children.

- *Parents as presenters of reports.* A parent report could be a formal part of the process, signaling to parents that their input is valued and necessary.

- *Parents as policymakers.* Harry recommends school-based, advisory parent bodies for special education programs, and active recruitment of parents as teacher's aides.

- *Parents as advocates and peer supports.* Parents serving in policymaking and support roles within schools may be more inclined to share their learning with other parents.

Despite gains, most schools and school districts have a great deal of readjustment to do before parents feel like true partners in their children's education.

Leaving School

Parents of children with disabilities may be worried about their child's future.

When the young person with a disability has completed school or reached age 22 (remember that P.L. 94-142 allows for schooling through age 21), the family must face a new bureaucracy and new issues. How will the child, now a young adult, spend his or her time? Is he or she prepared for employment? Can he or she find a job? How will he or she spend leisure time? What kinds of friendships and relationships will he or she have? Will there be a place for him or her in the community? Where will he or she live? Most of these issues confront any young adult seeking to separate from the family and achieve a sense of personal identity and independence, but they often assume a special degree of intensity and poignancy when faced by young adults with disabilities. Whitney-Thomas and Hanley-Maxwell (1996) found that parents of students with disabilities have less optimistic visions about their son or daughter's future than do parents of students without disabilities. They suggest that parents' feelings may realistically reflect the more narrow range of choices in adult life for students with disabilities.

■ **Transitions to Work and Higher Education**   Although many in special education equate **transition** with employment opportunities, Halvorsen, Doering, Farron-Davis, Usilton, and Sailor (1989) broaden the concept of transition to include the needs of the whole person across all life areas.

In the past, many families had to make the difficult decisions about the needs of their young adult child with little help. To compound the problem, few alternatives were available for quality residential and employment opportunities for young adults with disabilities. Over the past fifteen years, however, the federal government has turned its attention to postschool choices for individuals with disabilities (Will, 1984), and since 1990, special education professionals have been required to focus on the provision of transition services to families at times of change. Preparation for the transition from school to work must begin long before school ends. In fact, many experienced parents and professionals believe that for some students, particularly those with severe disabilities, preparation should begin very early in the child's schooling (Falvey, 1995) (see the accompanying box).

> More services are available now to help young adults with disabilities make the transition to life after school.

The services for students with disabilities that have been provided since the passage of P.L. 94-142 in 1975 have led to an increased number of those students attending higher education programs (U.S. Office of Special Education: http://www.ed.gov/offices/OSERS/IDEA/overview.html/). Section 504 of the Rehabilitation Act of 1973 and the Americans with Disabilities Act (1990) require that higher education opportunities be extended to all qualified individuals with disabilities.

> Because of IDEA, more students with disabilities are going to college.

■ **Family Concerns for the Future**   The future of their children with disabilities is often a source of great concern for parents. Many parents, recognizing that they are not immortal, worry about what will happen to their child when they are no longer able to take responsibility for his or her care.

> Transition planning helps parents understand how their exceptional child will live as an adult.

Participation in the process of transition planning can allay some of the natural anxiety about future options (Clark & Patton, 1997). Along the way, the parents become aware of the resources available to help plan for the long-term future of their son or daughter. Families need information and support in order to confront the intricacies of financial planning and government benefits, guardianship, making a will, and finding and evaluating residential options for their son or daughter. Decisions relating to these crucial areas should be made, whenever possible, with the input of the son or daughter with a disability and should be based on his or her personal preferences (Turnbull, Turnbull, Bronicki, Summers & Roeder-Gordon, 1989). Even individuals with the most severe disabilities have ways of communicating personal preferences, and family members are most likely to be able to interpret their signals.

The ties that bind family members usually persist throughout a lifetime. When a son or daughter has a disability, those ties may involve more responsibility for decision-making and caregiving than a family anticipates. But despite

first person

I believe that as professionals you can make a difference in our lives as parents of children with special needs.

You have the opportunity not to be intimidated when we blow off steam. You should not personalize these angry negative feelings. The great challenge for you is to give us the opportunity to fall apart once in a while.

You have the opportunity to decrease our profound sense of loneliness. . . . So often we want to talk about "it," but few people appear to want us to talk. You will often be the ONE person who will say: Tell me more. And then what happened? And how did that feel?

You have the opportunity to help us know our child. In the beginning, most of us know very little about their special needs. . . . You can model for us how to say the words, how to tell others. You can take us into our children's lives.

You have the opportunity to share books, pamphlets, and resources. Take the articles out of your file cabinets and off the shelves and spread them to the parents who have no idea where to find the stories and facts about our children.

You have the opportunity to help us recognize and celebrate our victories. They are often small for the "normal" population to appreciate. You know that awful-sounding "grunt" made by our child is truly a miracle. Often it is only you who knows that a new movement is significant and indicates a renewed sense of hope.

∼ Critical Aspects of the Transition Process

Halvorsen and her colleagues (1989) define transition planning as a process that includes longitudinal, comprehensive planning that results in effective and satisfying outcomes when certain quality standards are met. Critical aspects of this process include:

• Parent collaboration in all decisions regarding school and postschool preparation and placement

• A quality, integrated, community-intensive educational program

• Systematic planning that begins early in the school years and becomes more comprehensive as graduation nears

• Involvement and collaboration with all appropriate school and adult service agencies

• Placement into meaningful, integrated employment and living opportunities with participation in natural community and leisure activities (p. 256)

You have the opportunity to remind us how far we have come and how much we have accomplished. You, often more than our closest friends, know the details of our successes. Over and over, you can highlight those changes and celebrate the growth.

You have the opportunity to allow us those moments when our souls fall into deep despair. We will, at times, feel that we cannot and don't want to continue for another moment.

You can give us the space to be in that dark place. It is one of the greatest "interventions" you can give us.

If at times you can do some of these suggested activities, then you will have the opportunity to help us feel hope. We must feel hope if we are to get to our next appointment or face the next birthday party or use the words *special needs*.

Partnership is a collaboration. Plopped right in the middle of that word you will find the word *labor*. Partnership is labor. It is hard work. You are the midwives helping us to give birth to a new relationship. Let us begin.

Janice Fialka

Source: Excerpted and adapted from "You Can Make a Difference in our Lives," *DEC Communicator*, November 1996 23 (1), p. 8. Reprinted by permission of the author. Janice Fialka is the mother of two children, Micah (who has developmental disabilities) and Emma. This excerpt is published in a collection of her writings called "It Matters: Lessons from my son." To obtain a copy or to receive information about her speaking engagements, contact her at 10474 LaSalle Boulevard, Huntington Woods, MI 48070 or by email: ruaw@aol.com.

these responsibilities, and despite the stresses and strains that can accompany them, many family members describe the benefits gained by living with a son or daughter or brother or sister with a disability. Ann and Rud Turnbull (1990) and their colleagues have identified six categories of positive contributions made by young people with disabilities cited by families. They are

- being a source of joy
- providing a means of learning life's lessons
- giving and receiving love
- supplying a sense of blessing or fulfillment
- contributing a sense of pride
- strengthening the family (p. 115)

Although it is important to stress that the journey isn't easy and families must be supported through their very real times of crisis, professionals in special education are finding that, given support, information, and strategies from professionals and other parents, most families can come to recognize and experience the positive contributions made by their family member with a disability.

Having a child with a disability can bring joy, love, and pride to a family.

Our role is to support and inform families in that process. Most of us find that families are our best teachers.

SUMMARY

■ Family involvement in special education is mandated by IDEA because families are the best source of information about the abilities and needs of a child who is exceptional.

■ The family systems approach uses the characteristics, interaction, function, and life cycle of each family to describe its unique dynamics, including initial reaction to the child who is exceptional, the child's impact on the family, and the family's ability to cope and find support.

■ The initial reaction to a child with a disability may be influenced by the nature and degree of the disability, family size and socioeconomic status, and cultural and religious background.

■ Some of the most important sources of support for parents are parent-to-parent support groups, respite care, and early intervention and special education services.

■ Parents continue to play a key role through the school years. They have the right to be informed and to consent to evaluation of their child and to participate in placement and program decisions through the IEP process. Families are the focus of transition services and resources for planning for their child's future needs.

KEY TERMS

caregiver

family systems approach

family characteristics

extended family

socioeconomic status

culture

ethnicity

family functions

family interactions

families with multiple risks

coping strategies

parent-to-parent model

respite care

early intervention

individualized family service plan (IFSP)

right to due process

due process hearing

mediation

transition

MULTIMEDIA RESOURCES

Beach Center on Families and Disability, 3111 Haworth Street, University of Kansas, Lawrence, KS 66045, (785) 864-7600, website: http://www.lsi.ukans.edu/beach/beachhp.htm. The Beach Center provides resources, information, and family support on a variety of issues of interest to families.

Fadiman, Anne. *The Spirit Catches You and You Fall Down: A Hmong Child, Her American Doctors, and the Collision of Two Cultures*. (New York: Farrar, Straus, & Giroux, 1997). This book tells of the impact of cultural misunderstanding on the health of Lia Lee, the child of Hmong Laotian refugees who has epilepsy.

Exceptional Parent magazine publishes articles especially for families of children with disabilities and provides a forum for the exchange of information by families with children with rare or unusual conditions. The address is 555 Kinderkamack Road, Oradell, NJ 07649, Phone: (201) 634-6550, Fax: (201) 634-6599, website: http://www.eparent.com/news/resource/eparent/eparent.htm/.

Featherstone, Helen. *A Difference in the Family: Life with a Disabled Child* (New York: Basic Books, 1980). The author, a parent and educator, discusses openly and honestly how it feels to raise a child with a disability. This remains one of the most powerful books on the topic.

Harry, Beth. *Cultural Diversity, Families, and the Special Education System* (New York: Teachers College Press, 1992). Harry's work has provided a voice for families who have not traditionally been heard in the special education system.

Simpson, Richard L. *Working with Parents and Families of Exceptional Children and Youth: Techniques for Successful Conferencing and Collaboration* (Austin, TX: Pro-Ed, 1996). Lots of ideas for improving conferencing and collaboration with families.

Organizations Providing Useful Resources for Families

Autism
Autism Society of America (ASA)
7910 Woodmont Avenue, Suite 650
Bethesda, MD 20814-3015
Phone: (301) 657-0881; (800) 328-8476
Fax: (301) 657-0869
Website: http://www.autism-society.org

Behavioral and Emotional Disorders
Research and Training Center on Family Support and Children's Mental Health
Portland State University
P.O. Box 751
Portland, OR 97207-0751
Phone: (800) 628-1696; (503) 725-4040
Fax: (503) 725-4180
E-mail: bas@rri.pdx.edu
Website: http://www.rtc.pdx.edu/

Federation of Families for Children's Mental Health
1021 Prince Street
Alexandria, VA 22314-2971
Phone: (703) 684-7710
Fax: (703) 836-1040
E-mail: ffcmh@crosslink.net
Website: http://www.ffcmh.org

Cerebral Palsy
United Cerebral Palsy Associations (UCPA)
1660 L St., NW
Washington, DC 20036-5602
Phone: (202) 776-0406; (800) 872-5827
Fax: (202) 776-0414
E-mail: ucpanatl@ucpa.org
Website: http://www.ucpa.org

Cystic Fibrosis
Cystic Fibrosis Foundation (CFF)
6931 Arlington Road
Bethesda, MD 20814
Phone: (301) 951-4422; (800) 344-4823
Fax: (301) 951-6378
E-mail: info@cff.org
Website: http://www.cff.org

Deafness
Alexander Graham Bell Association for the Deaf
3417 Volta Place, NW
Washington, DC 20007-2778
Phone: (202) 337-5220 (V/TT)
E-mail: agbell2@aol.com
Website: http://www.agbell.org

DB-LINK, the National Information Clearinghouse
on Children Who Are Deaf-Blind
DB-LINK Western Oregon State College
345 N. Monmouth
Monmouth, OR 97361
Phone: (800) 438-9376
Fax: (503) 838-8150
E-mail: dblink@tr.wou.edu
Website: http://www.tr.wou.edu/dblink

Health Impairments
Association for the Care of Children's Health (ACCH)
7910 Woodmont Avenue, Suite 300
Bethesda, MD 20814-3015
Phone: (301) 654-6549; (800) 808-ACCH
Fax: (301) 986-4553
E-mail: acch@clark.net
Website: http://www.ACCH.org/ACCH/

Learning Disabilities
National Center for Learning Disabilities (NCLD)
381 Park Avenue South, Suite 1420
New York, NY 10016
Phone: (212) 545-7510

International Dyslexia Association (IDA)
8600 LaSalle Road, Suite 382
Baltimore, MD 21286-2044
Phone: (410) 296-0232; (800) 222-3123
Fax: (410) 321-5069
E-mail: info@interdys.org
Website: http://www.interdys.org

Mental Retardation
The Arc of the United States
500 E. Border Street, Suite 300
Arlington, TX 76010
Phone: (817) 261-6003; (800) 433-5255
Fax: (817) 277-3491

E-mail: thearc@metronet.com
Website: http://thearc.org/

National Fragile X Foundation
1441 York Street, Suite 303
Denver, CO 80206
Phone: (800) 688-8765 (V; toll-free)
Fax: (303) 333-4369
E-mail: natlfx@aol.com

National Down Syndrome Congress (NDSC)
1605 Chantilly Drive, Suite 250
Atlanta, GA 30324
Phone: (404) 633-1555; (800) 232-6372
E-mail: ndsc@charitiesusa.com
Website: http://www.carol.net/~ndsc/

Severe Disabilities
TASH
29 West Susquehanna Avenue, Suite 210
Baltimore, MD 21204
Phone: (410) 828-8274
Fax: (410) 828-6706
E-mail: info@tash.org
Website: http://www.tash.org

Visual Impairment
Blind Children's Center
4120 Marathon Street
Los Angeles, CA 90029
Phone: (213) 664-2153; (800) 222-3566
Fax: (213) 665-3828
E-mail: info@blindcntr.org
Website: http://www.blindcntr.org/bcc/

This list was compiled from

**National Information Center for Children & Youth
  with Disabilities (NICHCY)**
P.O. Box 1492
Washington, DC 20013-1492
(800) 695-0285 (Voice/TT)
(202) 884-8200 (Voice/TT)
Website: http://www.nichcy.org/

You can search their database yourself for other organizations, using the name
of the specific disability and "families" as the key terms.

USING YOUR KNOWLEDGE

Can Do: Are you acquainted with the family of an exceptional child? If
so, how do the components of the family systems approach apply to this
family? Are they useful in identifying areas where services might be provided? Do they help you recognize the family's specific strengths and

needs? Use the family systems framework to write a brief description of this family.

 Commonalities: Read about families of exceptional children. Many accounts have been written by parents, family members, and exceptional individuals themselves. What does the family provide to the child? What does the child contribute to the family? Create a list of positive contributions of the child to the family and the family to the child.

 Collaboration: Interview the parent or parents of a child with a disability. How much of the caretaking role does the parent currently undertake? Have the demands of caretaking increased or decreased during the past ten years? Have the parents sought support services, or do they rely on informal support from other family members, volunteers, and so forth? After completing the interview, summarize your results and present them to your classmates. Brainstorm some possible resources for the family.

WHAT YOU CAN DO NOW

1. **Visit an early intervention center and observe the programs provided there. How are they designed to promote the children's development? How are family members involved? Ask if you can examine several IFSP forms. Look for examples of how outcomes are tailored to individual family needs. When you return to class, discuss your impressions with your classmates. Try to devise an IFSP for one of the families you've read about.**

2. **Think about the way you communicate with parents. Do you**

• use the primary language of the family or have an experienced interpreter present?
• avoid jargon?
• allow time for questions and unexpected concerns to be addressed?
• provide complete, unbiased information about the child's strengths and needs?
• know how to relax and listen attentively? Many family members need and enjoy an opportunity to talk about their child.

3. **Do you think you could be trained to provide high-quality respite care to families with an exceptional child? Find out where respite care services are provided in your community, then call and see if your services are needed.**

Common Issues for All Exceptional Children and Youth in Special Education

Introduction

In five of the chapters of this book (Chapters 1, 2, 3, 13, and 14) we present topics that are relevant to the lives of all students with disabilities. In Chapters 4 through 12, we present information relevant to students with a particular category of disability. These categories, such as mental retardation and learning disabilities, reflect the definitions, terms, and descriptions that have evolved since the inception of the field of special education. Categories were created primarily because of suspected or documented differences in the causes, manifestation, or treatment of observed disabilities. Before we describe the categories of special education, which are the topics of Chapters 4 through 12, we want to point out some important similarities among students with various disabilities. We will also discuss cross-categorical educational structures such as service delivery models, assessment, and curriculum. After you have read this introductory framework, and all of the categorical chapters, we will present another framework section in which we pull together the information you have learned and show you how it all relates to the three themes of our book: commonalities, communication, and can do.

Categorical/Noncategorical Special Education

When the term *category* is used in the context of special education today, it refers to one of the thirteen types of disabilities described and defined in the Individuals with Disabilities Education Act (IDEA) of 1991. These categories are mild mental retardation, moderate mental retardation, severe mental retardation, profound mental retardation, learning disabilities, emotional/behavioral disorders, deafness/hearing impairments, blindness/visual impairments, physical/orthopedic disabilities, autism, traumatic brain injury, speech and language disabilities, and other health impairments. According to federal regulations, students must fit into one of these categories before they are considered eligible for special education services and before states can receive federal funding for the students' needs. Other groups of students (for example, students who are gifted and students with attention deficit disorder) may receive services through other federal or state funds but they do not belong to the categorical groups described in IDEA. Although, as you will see, there are many proposed reasons for categorical identification, whatever name or label we give to a specific disability a student might have, we must always address first and foremost the individual and specific needs of each student.

The number of categories in special education, and the definitions of the disability areas, have changed considerably over the years. Categories were developed because of the assumed differences in the causes of learning difficulties and the perceived differences in the types of educational programs needed by students in each group. The number and nature of categories changes as professionals in medical, psychological, and educational fields learn more about disabilities, develop opinions about educational strategies, and identify desired educational outcomes for students.

Some of the information gathered over the past few years, however, has caused a number of professionals in the field of special education to question the need for categories. Some of their concerns relate to philosophical issues. For example, must we label children in order to serve their educational needs? Another area of concern relates to practical issues, such as educational programming. If the same instructional strategies are used to teach most children with disabilities, why should we categorize them? Another practical concern focuses on the selection of only certain children to receive special education services. Other children, who do not meet the federal definition, may "slip through the cracks" and fail to receive special services even though they are not succeeding in the school environment. These, and related concerns, have resulted in changes in the way special education services are delivered in approximately half of the states in this country.

In some states, students with disabilities are served according to categorical label, while in other states, they are not. If students are served based on their category, it means that they are grouped together and served by a teacher who is certified in that particular area. For example, students with learning disabilities would receive specialized services by a teacher who is certified in learning disabilities. If those students receive services outside of the general education classroom, only students with learning disabilities will be in that educational setting. States that provide categorical programming adhere to the philosophy that students with different types of disabilities require different specialized services and/or learning environments.

Some individuals agree with the categorical model for service delivery, because they believe it increases the probability that the students in a class will have similar needs. They feel that teaching procedures, or at least the primary emphasis of instruction, is different for students with, for example, mental retardation, learning disabilities, and behavior disorders. Some people, however, disagree with the emphasis categorical special education places on labels, as opposed to services. They argue that often the differences among students within a category are as great or greater than the differences among students with different categorical labels. This philosophical disagreement has led to other types of identification practices for service delivery.

Although students must be identified according to category to meet federal regulations, a school does not have to use that category as a guideline for providing services. In many states, for example, special education services are provided using a noncategorical approach. Students are grouped according to the level or amount of services needed rather than a specific category. For example, if a number of students who have been identified as needing special education all are experiencing reading difficulties and require specialized reading instruction, a teacher may provide instruction for all of those children together, even though one may have a behavior disorder, one may have a learning disability, and two students may have mild mental retardation. In some instances, students may be grouped according to level of service required, for example, in-class support, pull-out support, or separate curriculum. In other settings, students may simply be identified as having mild or significant disabilities. Teachers in states that use a noncategorical approach to special education may be certified according to general level of disability rather than category. For example, certification may be in the area of mild disabilities rather than learning disabilities.

Individuals who support noncategorical special education believe that this approach is based more on instructional needs and prevents having an arbitrary label dictate instructional setting or services. Others, however, feel that noncategorical special education makes incorrect assumptions about the similarities of educational programming required by teachers and for students. They are also concerned about the range of skills and disabilities teachers may be required to address in a specific setting.

Is it better to use a categorical or noncategorical service delivery approach? This is one question we hope you will keep in mind as you read the following chapters. Consider the points we've discussed and how they relate to your own ideas about categories of special education and teaching. You can also expect your ideas and opinions to adjust at least a little once you enter the school setting.

Evaluation and Assessment

As we've discussed in earlier chapters, all individuals must go through an evaluation process before they can receive special education services. This process may take a variety of forms. Most students who receive services are not identified as having a disability until they reach school age. For these children, it is their interaction with the academic and social requirements of the school setting that brings their learning difference or disability to light.

School evaluations across the country follow a similar format. The first step in the evaluation process is the recognition—usually made by classroom teachers or parents—that the student is not doing well or not adjusting to school. The child may not be able to perform at the same rate or level as other students in the class; or he may have difficulty socializing with his classmates or teachers. At this point the classroom teacher, perhaps with the help of the parents, may try some new teaching techniques or may try adapting some classroom tasks or activities. If the teacher's attempts are not successful in addressing the student's difficulties, he or she may seek additional assistance. Schools typically have a team, often called the Child Study Team, consisting of teachers and support personnel that serves as a resource for teachers who are attempting to address a child's specific needs in the classroom. After the classroom teacher refers a student to the Child Study Team, the team evaluates the student's performance and the learning environment and comes up with some suggestions for the teacher, the child, and perhaps the parents. These suggestions are called prereferral interventions, because they are designed to eliminate, if possible, the need for the referral of a child for special education. If the prereferral interventions are not successful in remediating the problem, the teacher or parent may refer the child for a special education evaluation.

Once a referral has been made, and the parents have approved the referral process, a school psychologist is brought in to test the student. The purpose of the initial evaluation is to see if the student qualifies for special education services in any category under the federal guidelines. As you read through each categorical chapter, you will see what the guidelines are for each type of disability. Typically, a number of tests are given—each state has a list of approved tests for a special education evaluation. The battery of tests usually will include an IQ test, academic achievement tests, a test or tests of adaptive behavior (age-level breakdowns of expected skills in areas such as self-help and socialization) and social behavior, and checklists for teachers and parents to rate the student's performance and behavior. Other, specialized tests may be given if the child is having difficulty in a particular area, such as language development or speech. Most of the tests are designed to compare the student's performance with the performance of other students of the same age. From the testing data, information from teachers, parents, and the student, and clinical judgment, the psychologist makes a recommendation regarding the student's eligibility for special service.

For example, in most cases, before a child can be identified as having mental retardation, the student must have an IQ in a certain range, must show a pattern of significant difficulty in academic work, and must have a certain number and range of difficulties in adaptive behavior. The psychologist's recommendation is brought to a group or team, which should include the child's parents and teachers, and a final decision is reached. It is important to realize that a parent can cancel the process or refuse the services at any time. A school would then have to find alternative methods for assisting the student. Sometimes parents will go outside of the school setting to get another evaluation, particularly if they are unhappy with the procedures or results of the school evaluation.

Once the student has been identified and determined eligible for special education services, the teachers and parents work to develop an Individualized Education Plan (IEP). This plan describes the educational placement, services, and skills necessary to address the student's learning needs. This occurs regardless of whether the child will receive categorical or noncategorical services. All students receiving special education services will have an IEP. Further informal assessment often is necessary to derive the specific educational goals for the student.

Evaluation and assessment procedures vary somewhat for students with certain types of disabilities. For example, individuals with severe disabilities will be evaluated very early in life, and the evaluation may initially focus less on IQ and academic areas and more on movement, health management, communication, and socialization. Evaluations of students who have visual impairment would include an ophthalmologist's examination as well as an evaluation of the student's mobility. We discuss specialized assessment in each relevant categorical chapter.

The assessment procedure seems fairly straightforward, but professionals have raised a number of questions. Should only one set of test data be used to identify and label a child? How appropriate are the tests used? How valid are the specific eligibility criteria found in the federal regulations? As you read the following chapters, you will see that the eligibility criteria for some special education categories appear vague and subjective. Although some people like this ambiguity, because it allows personal and clinical judgment to play a role in identification, others find it is problematic, because it allows for variability within categories. This is another good topic upon which to reflect as you read the categorical chapters. Consider the impact of eligibility criteria on the identification process and, finally, on who can or cannot receive special education services.

Service Delivery Models

As we explained in Chapter 1, federal legislation requires that a continuum of services be available for all students receiving special education services. Traditionally, a continuum of services has been defined as not only the amount of services a student receives but also the setting in which those services are delivered. Typically, therefore, the two components are looked at together, with professionals and parents operating under the assumption that certain types or amounts of services require a setting other than the general education classroom. As we look at the different models available to students under the continuum of services, it may help to recall one more requirement from federal legislation—placement in the least restrictive environment. This guideline reminds us that we always place students in the setting that is both the least removed from the general education setting and the most appropriate for educational opportunity.

The Classroom

Many students with disabilities receive special education services in the general education classroom. This setting has increasingly become the model of choice in many schools, particularly for students with mild disabilities, because of increased opportunities for collaboration between the general education and special education teachers. Within the general education classroom, the classroom teacher may adapt or modify teaching methods or testing methods, adjust classroom organization, or develop behavior management strategies so that an individual student's need may be met. Special education teachers, itinerant specialists (for example, Braille teachers), or therapists may consult with the general education teacher or enter the classroom to provide in-class specialized services. Special education teachers may co-teach with general education teachers, coming to a classroom for a period or two a day and delivering instruction with the classroom teacher. Co-teaching allows information to be provided to students in a variety of ways and encourages alternative classroom structures to enhance a child's success in the classroom setting.

Resource Class

The resource model, also called the pull-out model, has traditionally been used for students who require specialized support in a specific area or different and intense instruction in a particular academic skill. In the resource model, a student or group of students is pulled out of the general education classroom to meet with a special education teacher or therapist in a separate setting. Typical examples of resource programs could include a class in reading instruction for elementary students with learning disabilities who are reading a year or two below grade level, a social skills class for adolescents with behavior disorders, or a class for children with articulation difficulties. Many students in resource programs receive one to three periods per day of services. The majority of their classroom time is spent in the general education classroom.

Self-Contained Class

The self-contained class model provides the majority of a student's instruction in a classroom separate from the general education classroom. As you might expect, this model is recommended when the student experiences great academic and/or behavioral difficulties and appears to receive no benefit from the general classroom. The student in a self-contained class receives all primary instruction from the special education teacher. Often, a self-contained placement is used when an alternative curriculum is thought to be beneficial to the student. For example, it may be determined in the IEP that a student's educational program should focus on life skills. Sometimes, a self-contained class may be selected because of the anticipated need for a consistently small teacher-student ratio, as when specific skill instruction in multiple areas requires intensive teacher involvement and attention.

Separate School

Although separate schools are infrequently used as a placement option in the continuum of services, they remain an option. Some school systems continue to have separate schools, but many do not. Those that remain typically are designed to address the needs of students with severe and profound disabilities, sensory disabilities, or severe behavior disorders. Most separate schools today are private schools, which may be used as placement options by the public school systems. Some of these placements may be temporary—for example, a school in a psychiatric hospital—others are long term and may be residential. Private schools are used as a placement option if the school district cannot provide an appropriate education for the student. Separate school placements often are initiated by the parents.

Life Setting

When we examine appropriate educational options and placements for students with disabilities, we must go beyond the classroom and even the school setting. For some students, particularly those with severe disabilities, skill instruction should take place in the same environment in which the students need to display those skills. If students need to learn domestic skills, such as cooking, or transportation skills (riding a bus), or vocational skills, instruction can be much more effective if it actually takes place in the kitchen, the neighborhood bus, or the workplace. Often adolescents with mild disabilities (or no disabilities!) will receive job training at the actual job site.

As we described the placement options, you might have recalled our discussion of inclusion in Chapter 1 and wondered how it fits in to the continuum of services. The term *inclusion* today most often refers to the placement of a student in general class setting. For example, if a student with learning disabilities is in a resource class for one period per day, you might hear that she is included for five periods a day. Inclusion as a philosophy, however, is a more comprehensive concept. Individuals who believe in inclusion as a philosophy have challenged the traditional way of looking at the continuum of services. From their perspective, level of services, not setting, is the only critical factor. In other words, regardless of how much support a student needs, those services must be delivered in the general education classroom setting. Supporters assert that it is each student's right to receive an education in the same environment as his or her peers. What do you think? Consider your opinions on inclusion and appropriate service delivery models for individuals with disabilities as you read the following chapters.

Instruction

There is no single set of instructional strategies that is common to the education of all students with disabilities. In the categorical chapters, we have attempted to consider a range of educational philosophies, as well as our own. There are, however, some commonalities in the way that instruction for individuals with disabilities is approached. These are broad groupings that may help you understand the rationale or purpose of the specific instructional strategies you will come across later. We will look briefly at academic skills instruction, specialized skills instruction, adaptive skills instruction, and life-skills instruction. Some students will receive only one type of instructional focus, while others will receive several. Factors such as the type of disability a student is experiencing, the student's age, long-range goals, and previous instructional success will all figure into the equation as instructional decisions are made.

Academic Skills Instruction

Many students who receive special education services experience disabilities that affect their ability to acquire basic academic skills. Therefore, many students with disabilities have some degree of difficulty in learning reading, arithmetic, and writing skills. Students who have difficulty in these areas are likely to experience problems in other academic subjects as well, because subjects such as history rely heavily on the basic skills, particularly reading. Many special education programs, therefore, have a heavy concentration on basic skill instruction. This is particularly true for students with mild learning disabilities, mental retardation, and behavior disorders. The purpose of this type of instruction, of course, is to teach students the basic academic skills so that they may have the benefit of these skills as learning and life tools.

Specialized Skills Instruction

Some students with disabilities require direct instruction in specific skills that are not academic in nature. Specialized skills instruction encompasses a wide variety of student needs; it could, for example, be instruction related to appropriate behavior or anger control, instruction related to developing or maintaining muscular movement, or instruction that teaches a child how to pronounce words beginning with the letter *r*. As in academic skills instruction, the purpose of specialized skills instruction is to remediate the difficulty caused by the student's specific disability.

Adaptive Skills Instruction

Sometimes the skills students need or would benefit from most are those that allow them to work around their disability to access information or social interaction. A focus on adaptive skills instruction is designed to teach individuals how to get what they need to know or do in a different way. Adaptive skills instruction encompasses a variety of things. One example of adaptive instruction would be teaching a student with severe cerebral palsy who is unable to speak how to use a voice synthesizer. Another example is teaching a high school student with a severe reading disability to use a strategy for acquiring as much content as possible from a biology text that is too difficult for him to read.

Life-Skills Instruction

Life-skills instruction refers to direct instruction in the skills necessary to increase the probability of independent living. Life-skills instruction is provided when students require extensive educational support and when the general education curriculum does not include the skills an individual needs to acquire. Typically, life skills include domestic skills, self-care skills, work skills, recreational skills, and transportation. Life-skills instruction is often paired with a community-based instructional setting. When planning life-skills instruction, we attempt to look to the future of the individual student and instruct the student in skills he or she needs now, as well as those he or she will need in the future.

A Look Ahead

In this Framework, we have explored topics and ideas that are important in your reading of and reflection on the following eight chapters, which cover specific special education categories. At the end of those chapters (following Chapter 12), we will revisit all these topics in the second part of the Framework. The focus of that section will be on your own reflections about working with exceptional students. Whether you go on to become a practitioner of general or of special education, your knowledge and reflections about the ideas presented here will be vital to your professional development and professional practice.

Learning About the Potential of Exceptional Children

THE CHAPTERS in Part 2 emphasize ways of teaching students with specific disabilities. In addition to information on each category of exceptionality, Chapters 4 through 12 focus on helping you understand the educational issues for each group of exceptional students. These include placement, assessment, and the selection and use of appropriate teaching strategies.

Children with Mental Retardation

STUDENTS with mental retardation demonstrate a range of abilities and increasingly are included in the general education classroom. In this chapter we will look at how curriculum and teaching strategies are modified to help these students reach their potential in academic and life skills. We will also focus on the community as a source of instructional materials, employment, and independent living arrangements both during and after the school years. As you read, think about the following questions:

■ What are the criteria for classifying a student as having mental retardation?

■ What is adaptive behavior, and why is it significant?

■ How does mental retardation affect a student's learning patterns?

Collaboration: How can educators work with businesses within the community to plan effective instruction?

Can Do: What teaching methods can you use in your class to help students with mental retardation achieve their learning potential?

Commonalities: How are the educational goals of individuals with mental retardation similar to the educational goals of all students?

Mike Silvert loves to use the camera that he received as a present for his thirteenth birthday. As a photographer for his school newspaper, he conveys his unique view of the world through his photos. This successful, ambitious, and creative student has moderate mental retardation.

When you think of people you consider intelligent or smart, you probably focus on their competence—their ability to handle situations. You probably do not base your judgment on their IQ test scores or the grades they received in school. Yet people with mental retardation are often categorized by just these types of criteria rather than—like Mike Silvert and his classmates—their success in real-life situations.

You will discover in this chapter that the great majority of people with mental retardation are not so different from the rest of us, and they are frequently well assimilated into everyday life. Their primary source of frustration is the classroom, a place where, as you know, the definition of "smart" can be very narrow. So, in this chapter, we hope to help you broaden your concept of successful learning as you learn what you can do to help these students reach their full potential.

Definitions and Terms

The definition of **mental retardation** has been revised numerous times to reflect our evolving understanding and philosophy. Currently, the most widely accepted definition comes from the American Association on Mental Retardation (AAMR). It was accepted as the new federal definition in 1993:

> Mental retardation refers to substantial limitations in present functioning. It is characterized by significantly subaverage intellectual functioning, existing concurrently with related limitations in two or more of the following applicable adaptive skill areas: communication, self-care, home living, social skills, community use, self-direction, health and safety, functional academics, leisure, and work. Mental retardation manifests before age 18.

The four following assumptions are essential to the application of the definition:

1. Valid assessment considers cultural and linguistic diversity as well as differences in communication and behavioral factors.
2. The identification of limitations in adaptive skills occurs within the context of community environments typical of the individual's age peers and is indexed to the person's individualized needs for supports.
3. Specific adaptive limitations often coexist with strengths in other adaptive skills or other personal capabilities.
4. With appropriate supports over a sustained period, the life functioning of the person with mental retardation will generally improve.

Mental retardation is characterized by subaverage intellectual functioning and deficits in adaptive behavior.

Intelligence and General Cognitive Functioning

The concept of intelligence is critical to the definition of mental retardation and to our characterization of all individuals. Each reader of this book will have different ideas about what constitutes intelligence. Researchers, too, have difficulty

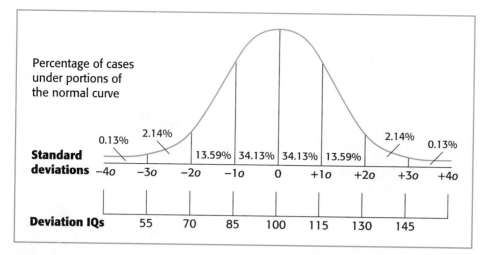

Figure 4.1
The Theoretical Distribution
of IQ Scores

Source: S. A. Kirk and J. J. Gallagher, *Educating Exceptional Children*, 6th ed. (Boston: Houghton Mifflin, 1988), p. 11. Copyright © 1988. Used with permission.

agreeing on a definition of intelligence. Salvia and Ysseldyke (1991) wrote that "No one . . . has seen a thing called intelligence" (p. 145). It is what psychologists call a *construct*, defined by theorists and test makers and determined by their ideas, beliefs, and cultural values.

Even though no universal agreement exists on what constitutes intelligence, a number of tests have been developed to measure it. The model for the intelligence tests used today was designed by two French scientists, Alfred Binet and Theodore Simon, in 1905. Binet and Simon were asked by the French government to find a way to distinguish between children who could achieve in school and those who would fail. The children identified as likely to fail were to be placed in special schools for slow learners. The test that these two men created was not based on a theory of intelligence, but it did accurately predict school achievement. Louis Terman of Stanford University adapted the Binet-Simon test for American use in 1916, and it became known as the **Stanford-Binet**. The test, which has been revised three times since then, is still widely used by American psychologists (Patton, Beirne-Smith & Payne, 1990). It places great importance on verbal judgments and reasoning.

Another test frequently used to predict academic achievement in school-age children is the **Wechsler Intelligence Scale for Children, Third Edition (WISC-III)**. This test is divided into two scales: One measures verbal skills and the other performance skills, which are theoretically not influenced by verbal abilities. David Wechsler, who wrote this test, also developed preschool and adult intelligence scales.

The intelligence test scores for the population at large can be represented in what is often described as a bell-shaped curve (see Figure 4.1). This distribution, also known as the normal curve, illustrates the range of scores that can be expected in any representative population. An average intelligence test score of 100 represents equivalence between mental age and chronological age.

The phrase *subaverage intellectual functioning* in the AAMR definition refers to performance on one or more intelligence tests resulting in an IQ score of about 70 or below. It is possible, however, for a student with an IQ score higher than 70 to qualify as having mental retardation, given clear deficits in adaptive behavior. Conversely, it is possible for a student with an IQ score of 65 not to be

Speaking isn't the only way to communicate personal needs. Students can make important contributions to their IEP meetings when given the opportunity. (Laura Dwight)

identified as having mental retardation if he or she has good adaptive behavior. A critical point to remember is that the word *significant*, which is used in the 1993 definition ("significantly subaverage intellectual functioning"), is subjective.

Adaptive Behavior

Adaptive behavior, the other key element of the AAMR definition, includes those social, maturational, self-help, and communicative acts that assist each individual in adapting to the demands of his or her environment (Patton, Beirne-Smith & Payne, 1990). They are *age-appropriate* and *situation-appropriate*; that is, they are different at each age and in each situation. Adaptive behaviors present a more comprehensive picture of a child's abilities than do IQ scores alone. Let us examine some examples of adaptive behaviors found in different developmental periods to see how they vary.

During the infancy and preschool period, the most rapid and dramatic changes in adaptive behavior occur. The infant learns to reach, roll over, sit, stand, walk, and run; to finger-feed and then to use a spoon and drink from a cup; to draw others into close social relationships; and to communicate—first through vocalizing, then, gradually, through understanding and repeating single words, two words together, short phrases, and finally sentences that increase in length and complexity. By preschool, many of these milestones have been mastered. The child becomes toilet-trained, and then many of the adaptive behaviors focus on social goals: learning to play and interact successfully with other children and with new adults, sharing, and making friends.

In the elementary school years the child must become socialized to the expectations of school and learn to adapt to those demands: to sit quietly until spoken to, to raise a hand to be recognized, to follow the teacher's directions. Other adaptive behaviors are refinements of earlier milestones in motor, social, and language development; also included are academic skills that apply to everyday functioning in the environment, such as reading danger and warning signs.

Adaptive behavior is not easy to measure. Expectations for age-appropriate and situation-appropriate behavior may differ from city to city, state to state, and from culture to culture. Geography, local behavior norms, and cultural differences all interact to determine if a child's behavior is appropriate in a particular locale. These factors contribute to the variability of classification status from one school district to the next.

Expectations for appropriate behavior may differ from place to place and culture to culture.

To avoid misplacing children in special classes for students with mental retardation, the concept of adaptive behavior was developed. Now, in order for a child to be classified as having mental retardation, he or she must demonstrate deficits in adaptive behavior that are comparable to the child's measured IQ. By incorporating the measure of adaptive behavior, the definition acknowledges that the child functions in various environments and potentially possesses many types of skills.

Adaptive behavior is usually measured through observation and interviews with the child's parents, guardians, or teachers. Two of the most widely used instruments are the **AAMR Adaptive Behavior Scale** (Nihara, Foster, Shellhaas & Leland, 1981) and the **Vineland Adaptive Behavior Scales** (Sparrow, Balla & Cicchetti, 1984). Adaptive behavior scales enable the teacher, parent, or observer to determine the child's competence in a wide range of functional behaviors. The AAMR Adaptive Behavior Scale measures two major areas—independent performance of daily living skills and inappropriate or maladaptive behaviors, such as self-abuse or destructive behavior. The Vineland Adaptive Behavior Scales, Interview Editions, measure the domains of communication, daily living skills, socialization, motor skills, and maladaptive behavior. Figure 4.2 shows a section from one of these scales.

Manifestation During the Developmental Period

Mental retardation must be present before the age of 18. This element is included in the AAMR definition in order to distinguish mental retardation from conditions in which adults suffer from impairment of brain functioning, such as from a head injury or a stroke. A child with an IQ test score of 70 or lower might not be identified until he or she reaches school age and deficits in adaptive behavior become apparent. It can also be decided that a child no longer has mental retardation if gains are made in adaptive behavior or in measured intelligence level. The term *mental retardation* can thus refer to a current state of functioning or performance rather than a permanent condition.

Mental retardation must be identified before age 18, but a child can show gains in adaptive behavior or measured intelligence.

Classification Issues

Scientists and teachers have to differentiate among individuals with varying degrees of mental retardation. Scientists study the effects of degrees of severity on the characteristics and behavior of people with mental retardation; administrators must determine which students need special programs; teachers plan educational programs for students based on the levels of functioning. As with most categories, or groups of exceptional individuals who share a common label, there is tremendous variety within the group of people identified as having mental retardation.

DOMAIN 1: Independent Functioning

A. Eating Subdomain

Item 1: Use of Table Utensils (circle highest level)

Uses table knife for cutting or spreading	6
Feeds self neatly with spoon and fork (or appropriate alternate utensils, e.g., chopsticks)	5
Feeds self causing considerable spilling with spoon and fork (or appropriate alternate utensil, e.g. chopsticks)	4
Feeds self with spoon—neatly	3
Feeds self with spoon—considerable spilling	2
Feeds self with fingers	1
Does not feed self or must be fed	0

Item 2: Eating in Public (circle highest level)

Orders complete meals in restaurants	3
Orders simple meals like hamburgers and hot dogs	2
Orders single items, e.g. soft drinks, ice cream, donuts, etc. at soda fountains or canteens	1
Does not order in public eating places	0

Item 3: Drinking (circle highest level)

Drinks without spilling, holding glass in one hand	3
Drinks from a cup or glass unassisted—neatly	2
Drinks from a cup or glass unassisted—considerable spilling	1
Does not drink from a cup or glass unassisted	0

Item 4: Table Manners (circle all answers)

If these items do not apply to the individual, e.g., because he or she is bedfast and/or has liquid food only, place a check in the blank and mark "Yes" for all statements.

	Yes	No
Throws food	0	1
Swallows food without chewing	0	1
Chews food with mouth open	0	1
Drops food on table or floor	0	1
Does not use napkin	0	1
Talks with mouth full	0	1
Takes food off others' plates	0	1
Eats too fast or too slow	0	1
Plays in food with fingers	0	1

Subdomain total (add items 1–4)

Figure 4.2
AAMR Adaptive Behavior Scale

There are varying degrees of mental retardation.

Since 1961, the American Association on Mental Retardation has used the terms *mild, moderate, severe,* and *profound* to denote degrees of mental retardation. People with mild mental retardation may require support services to enable them to graduate from high school, get appropriate job training, and get married and raise a family. Most individuals with mild mental retardation easily blend in to school and work environments. People with moderate mental retardation typically require support services and often supervision to enable them to live and work in independent or semi-independent community settings.

People with moderate mental retardation have characteristics that are probably the ones you think of when you hear the phrase *mental retardation.*

Individuals identified as having severe or profound mental retardation require more extensive educational services. In this chapter, we will discuss the needs of students with mild and moderate levels of mental retardation. You will learn about individuals with severe and profound mental retardation in Chapter 11.

Some educators in this country continue to use the terms *educable mental retardation* (EMR), *trainable mental retardation* (TMR), and *severely and profoundly handicapped* (SPH) to describe learners with mental retardation. Table 4.1 shows the relationships between the two sets of terms.

Classification and Placement

Traditionally, the terms *educable mental retardation* and *trainable mental retardation* were used to place children into two different curricula. Students in the classes for educable mental retardation were exposed to a more academic curriculum, with an emphasis on reading and arithmetic. Those in classes for students with trainable mental retardation concentrated more on a functional curriculum, which stressed the learning of self-help and independent-living skills. Today, the terms *educable* and *trainable* have fallen out of favor, although you will still see them used in some public school settings.

In recent years, we have seen some changes in the way students with mild and moderate levels of mental retardation are classified and grouped for instruction and in the content of their curriculum. Many children who used to be served under the classification of mild mental retardation are no longer being identified as having mental retardation (MacMillan, 1989). Increasingly stringent application of the adaptive behavior criterion has resulted in fewer children receiving the label of mild mental retardation. Those children who are identified are increasingly exposed to a curriculum that stresses preparation for life skills rather than the traditional remedial academic program. The expanded curriculum of life skills, vocational instruction, and basic academics now offered to many students with moderate mental retardation is often suitable to students in both groups and may make the distinction between moderate and mild mental retardation less important from an educational perspective.

Now that we've made these comments, we would like to caution you about making assumptions about the ability levels of students identified as having mild mental retardation. As a teacher, you will always need to make your own careful assessments about what and how to teach an individual child. In addition, keep in mind that the purpose behind labels and categorical grouping is to provide better educational services to children.

With fewer children classified as having mild mental retardation, the mild and moderate categories are merging.

Table 4.1 Degrees of Mental Retardation

Mild mental retardation	Educable mental retardation (EMR)
Moderate mental retardation	Trainable mental retardation (TMR)
Severe mental retardation ⎫	Severely and profoundly handicapped (SPH)
Profound mental retardation ⎭	

Classification and Intelligence Tests

From the beginning of intelligence testing, it was clear that children's experiences influenced test performance. In fact, debate over the role of experience in intelligence test performance has been at the core of the allegations made about bias in IQ testing.

In addition to experience, other factors may influence how a student with disabilities performs on standardized tests (Patton, Beirne-Smith & Payne, 1990). First, IQ tests are often focused on language skills. This emphasis has serious implications for many exceptional learners, since language difficulties go hand in hand with many disabling conditions and also may exist in children from economically or culturally different backgrounds.

Second, differences in students' physical capacities may interfere with test performance. Sometimes responses to test items are timed, and the child with a physical disability may be penalized in such a situation. His mind may be able to solve a problem as fast as anyone else, but his body will not cooperate. A blind child may not be able to tell what's "missing" in a picture; a deaf child may not have a wide vocabulary, but these limitations do not mean that these children are not "intelligent." This kind of testing will not give an accurate picture of the abili-

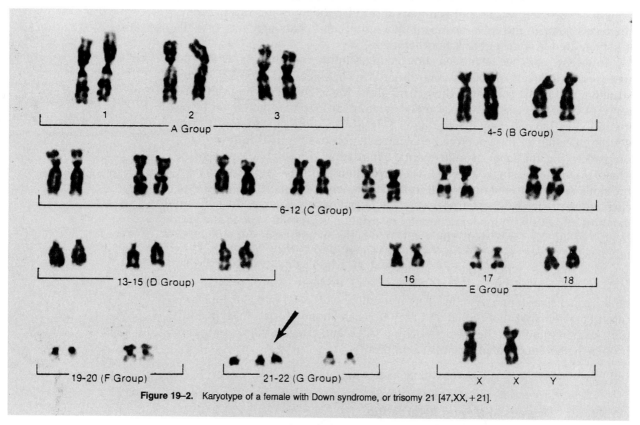

Figure 19–2. Karyotype of a female with Down syndrome, or trisomy 21 [47,XX,+21].

An extra chromosome can result from an incomplete division of the 23 pairs of chromosomes during the formation of an egg cell. The extra chromosome at the 21st position results in trisomy 21—the most common form of Down syndrome. (From "The Child with Down Syndrome," by S. Pueschel. In *Developmental Behavior Pediatrics* by Mel Levine, W. Carey, A. Crocker, and R. Gross, eds. [Philadelphia: Saunders, 1983]. Copyright 1983 by W. B. Saunders & Co. Reprinted by permission.)

ties of many exceptional learners. Some alternative intelligence tests, such as Raven's Progressive Matrices and the Hiskey-Nebraska Test of Learning Aptitude, are designed for nonverbal students, and some adaptations, such as computerized response systems, are used for students with some disabilities.

As you learned in Chapter 1, representatives from minority groups have objected to the use of IQ tests with children from both racial and language minority backgrounds (*Larry P. v. Riles; Diana v. State Board of Education*) because they believe that these children do not have equal access to the middle-class American cultural experiences that may be measured by these tests. Both the law and good practice dictate that no one test shall ever be the sole grounds for diagnosis of a disability or for special class placement.

Other objections to the use of IQ tests have been raised by concerned professionals. These tests sample a relatively restricted range of behaviors: They do not measure motivation, creativity, or special talents. Also, there is no correlation or relationship between IQ and a person's success after school (Henley, Ramsey & Algozzine, 1993). There is currently a lively debate within the field of educational psychology about the nature of intelligence that we will explore in Chapter 12. Despite a tremendous amount of scholarship and research, we still do not have a widely agreed-upon definition of intelligence.

Prevalence

A strict interpretation of the normal curve (see Figure 4.1) would suggest a prevalence rate for mental retardation of about 3 percent; that is, 3 percent of the total population would be identified as having mental retardation. According to the *Eighteenth Annual Report to Congress on the Implementation of the Individuals with Disabilities Act* (1996), however, the U.S. Department of Education reported that approximately 1 percent of the school-aged population, or 11.6% of all students with disabilities, was identified as having mental retardation. Factors affecting the prevalence rate include the procedures and recommendations used in school referral processes, changes over time in federal and state regulations, and the identification and elimination of potential risk factors through early intervention.

> Approximately 1 percent of school-age children have mental retardation; most are classified with mild mental retardation.

The great majority of people with mental retardation—about 80 to 85 percent—are "invisible": They do not look "different." These individuals have mild mental retardation, and the majority of them are integrated naturally into the community. This fact adds to the difficulty in determining accurate prevalence rates and reveals one of the reasons many children aren't identified until they reach school. Children with moderate mental retardation, however, are more likely to exhibit distinguishing physical or developmental characteristics and, therefore, be identified at an early age or at birth. Often the delay of certain developmental milestones, such as walking, the onset of speech, and the acquisition of self-help skills, alerts the parents and physician. Only about 7 to 10 percent of the people with mental retardation fall into this category.

Causes

There are a number of possible causes of mental retardation, many of which can be linked to the risk factors described in Chapter 2. In Table 4.2, we list ten potential causes. The list includes causes for all levels of mental retardation. With

Table 4.2 Causes of Mental Retardation

1. *Infections and intoxications* Examples include rubella, syphilis, meningitis, and exposure to drugs, alcohol, or lead. The child may be exposed through the mother during pregnancy or may contract infections after birth. Unfortunately, fetal alcohol syndrome and drug addiction are major causes of mental retardation.

2. *Trauma or physical agents* Injuries to the child that occur before, during, or after birth fall into this category. Hypoxia (deprivation of oxygen) and injuries received through child abuse are examples.

3. *Metabolic or nutritional disorders* Examples of these disorders include phenylketonuria (PKU), Tay-Sachs disease, and galactosemia. In disorders of this type, the child's inability to metabolize or tolerate certain elements in food results in brain injury.

4. *Postnatal gross brain disease* This refers to tumors that occur after birth.

5. *Prenatal diseases or conditions of unknown origin* Examples of conditions found in this category include hydrocephalus and microcephaly. Hydrocephalus refers to the presence of cerebrospinal fluid in the skull, which increases the size of the skull while causing pressure on the brain; microcephaly describes a condition in which the skull is significantly smaller than normal.

6. *Chromosomal abnormality* Chromosomal abnormalities refer to an unusual pattern of genetic material on one or more of the child's chromosomes. Two of the more well-known syndromes associated with chromosomal abnormalities are Down syndrome and fragile-X syndrome. Both of these syndromes usually result in distinct physical characteristics and mental retardation. Fragile-X syndrome is found mostly in males (because of the defective X chromosome). Females carry the chromosome and some may experience mild mental retardation. In some instances, these syndromes appear as recessive genetic traits; in others (such as the most frequently occurring type of Down syndrome), the abnormality is associated with other factors, such as the age of the mother.

7. *Other perinatal/gestational conditions* Two prominent examples in this category are prematurity and low birthweight. Although many infants do not suffer negative effects from these conditions, both prematurity and low birthweight are risk factors for mental retardation. As you might expect, the more extreme these conditions are, the higher the level of risk.

8. *Presence of psychiatric disorders* A few psychiatric disorders may be associated with mental retardation. The most prominent example of this category used to be autism; however, autism is no longer considered to be a psychiatric disorder.

9. *Environmental influences* This category includes causes that are described as cultural-familial. We will describe this category in greater detail later in this section.

10. *Other unknown causes* Because it is difficult to identify the causes of mental retardation in many children, we suspect that there are causes that have yet to be discovered.

Source: H. J. Grossman, *Classification in Mental Retardation* (Washington, DC: American Association on Mental Deficiency, 1983).

the exception of category 9 (associated almost exclusively with mild mental retardation), the conditions listed can result in any level of mental retardation.

Biological Factors

Table 4.2 shows that many causes of mental retardation appear to be tied to biological factors. The more severe the level of mental retardation, the more likely it is that a cause can be pinpointed. For persons with moderate or severe mental retardation, biological causes can be pinpointed in 60 to 75 percent of the cases (McLaren & Bryson, 1987).

As we mentioned in Chapter 2, prenatal care, genetic counseling, and appropriate immunizations can help prevent many disabilities, including mental retardation. The medical community continues to identify ways to prevent or ameliorate mental retardation through genetic research or very early (often prenatal) treatment. For example, the effects of hydrocephalus can be greatly minimized by surgery in which a shunt is implanted in the head of the infant prior to birth, allowing the fluid to drain away before brain damage occurs. Another example involves the identification of phenylketonuria (PKU), a metabolic disorder. All hospitals now require a test for PKU at birth. If the condition is present, the child is put on a specific diet and mental retardation can be avoided.

Despite these advances, however, Patton, Beirne-Smith, and Payne (1990) point out that there is no certain cause in at least 50 percent of cases of mental retardation. This is particularly true for individuals with mild mental retardation.

Many causes of mental retardation appear to be related to biological factors, but cause is uncertain in over 50 percent of cases.

Environmental Factors

We may not be able to ascertain the causes of mental retardation precisely, but we know that a great many children with mild mental retardation come from low socioeconomic backgrounds, which might lead us to believe that environmental influences are contributing or causal factors. Other possible factors could relate to family expectations, preparation for school, or the cultural values experienced by and passed down to the child through the family. These influences are sometimes described as cultural-familial causes of mental retardation.

It is difficult to pinpoint specific causal relationships between cultural differences, socioeconomic conditions, and mental retardation. Most children from such backgrounds develop normally. Cultural differences may, however, result in a child's inability to respond to questions normed on a white, middle-class population or to work effectively in traditional school environments. Although poverty alone does not imply poor nutrition, poor health care, or a poor social environment (just as wealth does not necessarily imply good nutrition, good health care, or a good social environment), many of these risk factors do tend to occur together.

You may have heard about the ongoing debate over the role of environment versus the role of heredity in determining intelligence. Do smart parents have smart children because the children inherit intellectual ability, or do their surroundings encourage the fullest possible development of their intelligence? Could students with mild mental retardation inherit low intellectual ability from their parents, or could even a bright child be affected by adverse environmental conditions? The relative roles of heredity and the environment in intellectual development have been discussed, debated, and researched for many years.

The relative importance of heredity and environment in intellectual development has been debated for years.

The current thinking in this area represents a compromise of sorts. Each child probably comes into the world with a range of intellectual ability, and the environment in which the child is reared helps to determine the extent to which that ability is expressed (MacMillan, Semmel & Gerber, 1994). In other words, it is likely that heredity and environment *interact* to form the demonstrated intellectual ability of most children. Certainly the environment (including teaching) can affect how any child's cognitive, behavioral, and physical skills develop throughout his or her lifetime.

Effects of Mental Retardation

When we look at the effects of mental retardation on any individual, we must keep in mind not only the obvious things, such as severity and complicating factors, but also the child's own personality and determination. The effects of mental retardation may be perceived as limiting by some and as challenging by others. The impact on the family may be seen as devastating, enlightening, exhausting, or unifying—sometimes a combination of all these and more.

Effects on the Child

Mental retardation is a developmental disability; that is, it affects a child's overall development in a relatively uniform manner. Remember that all of the strands of development (cognitive, language, social, and so on) that are described separately in books like this one are, in life, very much intertwined. For purposes of study, however, it is easier to separate them; so let us examine development in individuals with mild and moderate levels of mental retardation.

■ **Cognitive Development** By definition, mental retardation can be interpreted to mean a low level of cognitive ability. Intelligence tests are used to pro-

Participation in exercise and competitive sports can result in high spirits and self-confidence as well as better physical conditioning. (T. L. Litt/Impact Visuals)

vide an overall measure of cognitive ability, and persons with mental retardation are identified as having deficits in the ability to learn.

The ability to learn can be described in many ways. One aspect of learning
is capacity—how much information can be processed at one time. Typically,
children with mental retardation process smaller amounts of information than
their average classmates. Another aspect of learning is the ability to engage in
problem solving. Individuals with mental retardation may rely on a limited set
of problem-solving strategies, which can cause difficulty when new, different,
or complex problems arise (Wehmeyer & Kelchner, 1994). Students with mental
retardation may also have difficulty using such cognitive skills as metacognition, memory, and attention.

Metacognition and Memory   Most students with learning problems, including
mental retardation, have difficulty in the areas of metacognition and memory,
particularly short-term memory. **Metacognition** refers to the ability to identify
how one learns and to evaluate, monitor, and adapt the learning process. These
difficulties in metacognition and memory, therefore, translate into problems in
planning, evaluating, and organizing information.

Let's look at a student studying a list of spelling words. The student will
look through the words to find similarities or patterns (knowing to look for a
mnemonic aid is an example of metacognition), practice spelling and writing
the words several times (rehearsal—a memory strategy), determine if she needs
more time to study the words (performance evaluation—metacognition), and
decide that reviewing the words right before the spelling test will improve her
probability of remembering them (awareness of how to improve performance—
metacognition).

A student with mental retardation is more likely to have difficulty realizing
the conditions or actions that will help her learn or retain the material. Given a
list of spelling words, the student might not think to rehearse the words, not notice similarities or letter patterns, have difficulty evaluating his or her performance, and not realize that a review might be helpful. Because of these cognitive effects, we must focus instruction on *how* to learn as well as on *what* to learn
so that the student can achieve the greatest possible level of independence.

Memory and metacognitive skills are closely related in some instances. Before students can use strategies for aiding memory, they must be aware that
such strategies are needed. Consequently, a very important aspect of improving
the learning abilities of students with mental retardation is teaching when specific strategies for remembering need to be used.

Attention   Mental retardation is often characterized by **attentional deficits**—
the child has difficulty coming to attention, maintaining attention, and paying
selective attention (Brooks & McCauley, 1984; Zeaman & House, 1963, 1979). In
many instances, the problem is not that the child *won't* pay attention, but that he
or she *can't* pay attention or doesn't know how to attend. It is possible, however,
to minimize the effects of attentional deficits on learning.

A student with a deficit in the area of coming to attention will experience
difficulty focusing on the task at hand and, in the case of independent work,
will have problems getting started. For some students this may be a result of
having difficulty breaking their attention away from distractions or previous activities. Other students may have difficulty recognizing the signs, directions, or
task requirements for a new activity. It is often helpful for teachers to use clear
and unambiguous signals that indicate the beginning or ending of activities and

Teachers must focus instruction on
how as well as what students learn.

that specify task requirements. These signals may be phrases, like "Eyes on me," or actions, like clapping the hands.

Many students with mental retardation have a shorter attention span than other children their age. A child experiencing difficulty maintaining attention will do much better on long tasks (such as practicing problems in arithmetic) if the task is broken into shorter segments that can be done throughout the day rather than all at once. Sometimes, gradually increasing the amount of time a child is required to pay attention will help to lengthen a child's attention span. Children with mental retardation, like all children, will be able to attend longer to material that is interesting and attractive.

A student with problems maintaining attention may need frequent direction to reorient him or her back to the task at hand. One way teachers try to deal with this problem is to establish a signal that can be used instead of constant verbal direction. A clap, or a tap on the board or desk, can be used to remind the child to refocus. Teachers also try different types of written cues, including colored marks, underlining, arrows, and so on, to help children focus on starting points in written material.

In the area of selective attention—attending to the key issues—students with mental retardation often have difficulty identifying the critical aspects or content of information. A young child might not be able to identify the distinguishing characteristics or dimensions of a letter or word. An older student might miss the key words in the directions for a test.

Some ways you can accentuate important information for students include:

- Underlining key words, using color or exaggeration to help draw attention to the words
- Using key words to cue the student that what you are about to say is important
- Present less extraneous information during initial teaching
- Teach the student to recognize and use the cues you have provided

Generalization, or transferring skills from one setting to another, is often difficult for students with mental retardation.

Generalization Many students with mild mental retardation and most students with moderate mental retardation experience difficulty transferring skills from one context to another. In other words, once a student has learned a specific skill in the classroom using certain materials, he or she may have difficulty performing that skill another way, in another setting, or with other materials (Agran, Saltzberg & Stowitchek, 1987). Sometimes the problem of **skill transfer**, or **generalization**, can be relatively minor and easy to remedy. Some children simply become confused by a change in format or materials and just need to be told that they can use the same skill or strategy in the new situation.

Teachers thus need to anticipate the possibility that students will need an explanation before performing the skill in the new format. For example, a student who can work single-digit addition problems successfully but has only been presented with problems in a vertical format may not realize that the same process applies to problems in a horizontal format (2 + 3 = __). This child will need additional instruction and demonstration.

You can maximize the potential for generalization by incorporating real-world materials into your instruction. For example, a student who has learned all of the basic addition and subtraction skills may not realize that those same skills can be used to balance a checkbook, so you can have students practice using real checkbooks. Use real materials whenever they are readily available—

～ Strategies for Enhancing Cognitive Skills

Metacognition and Memory

- Teach memory strategies, such as rehearsing and chunking information, if students are not using them.
- Teach students when to use memory strategies or provide cues for using them.

Attention

- Establish clear signals to orient students to the task or lesson.
- Break up long instructional segments or tasks into several short sessions.

- Gradually increase the amount of time you expect children to attend to a task.
- Accentuate key content and directions for the students through the use of response prompts or cues.

Generalization

- Teach students to use the skills they have learned in one class in other classes or settings.
- Use real-world materials to help students generalize basic skills to realistic situations.

---

it makes learning more meaningful for all students and addresses the problem of poor skill transfer.

The child with moderate mental retardation may experience a great deal of difficulty understanding that the pencil-and-paper addition he or she does in the classroom is the same basic skill used in counting money or adding up points in a board game. For students with moderate mental retardation the use of actual materials to teach needed or desired skills has even more importance. Teachers should never assume that a generalization of responses will occur without specific instruction. See the box "Strategies for Enhancing Cognitive Skills" for a summary of instructional strategies.

■ **Language Development** One early sign of mild or moderate mental retardation is a delay in the acquisition of communication skills. Children with mental retardation acquire language at a slower rate than other children, usually have limited vocabularies, and tend to use a restricted number of sentence constructions. Their language is structurally similar, however, to the language of other children and develops in the same way (Polloway, Patton, Payne & Payne, 1989).

Speech problems are also found more frequently in children with mental retardation. In a survey of services provided to elementary-age students with mild mental retardation, Epstein, Polloway, Patton, and Foley (1989) found that 90 percent of the population they surveyed had been identified as needing speech or language services, especially in the area of articulation. Structural differences, such as tongue size or facial musculature, can affect the way some individuals pronounce certain sounds.

Children with mental retardation may experience a delay in language development.

Individuals with mental retardation also may experience difficulty in nonverbal communication skills. Many children with mental retardation demonstrate appropriate nonverbal skills (proximity, gestures, eye contact), yet may display inappropriate skills or engage in appropriate skills at an unusual level (Bufkin & Altman, 1995). For example, a pat on the shoulder is appropriate during most interpersonal conversations. If someone were giving you a pat on the shoulder every few seconds, however, you would probably view the behavior as inappropriate. Nonverbal communication skills can be as important as verbal language in providing opportunities for and success in communication with peers.

People with mental retardation may have physical health problems and impaired motor skills.

■ **Physical Development** People with mild retardation may, as a group, be less physically fit than others—they may weigh somewhat less and be of smaller stature, have poorer motor skills, and have more health-related problems than their peers (Drew, Logan & Hardman, 1992).

The physical health and motor skills of individuals with mental retardation are more likely to be impaired as the degree of mental retardation increases. Thus, people with moderate mental retardation are more likely to have noticeable differences. The same rule holds true when we consider the existence of additional disabling conditions, many of which, like cerebral palsy and epilepsy, involve physical ability and overall health. The greater the degree of mental retardation, the more likely it is that another disabling condition will accompany it.

Some of the specific syndromes that cause mental retardation result in accompanying physical impairments. The most common of these, Down syndrome, frequently results in structural heart defects, which in most cases can be corrected surgically. Individuals with Down syndrome are also prone to lung abnormalities, which makes them susceptible to upper respiratory infections (Patterson, 1987). The incidence of hearing and visual impairments in children with Down syndrome is also considerably higher than in the general population. Although there was a time when these physical disabilities greatly shortened the prospective life span of people with Down syndrome, medical technology has enabled most individuals to live well into adulthood.

Many students with mild retardation require no extra programs or assistance to participate in sports or physical education activities. Other students, however, require more specialized physical activities—such as adaptive physical education—which include specific activities designed to improve strength and coordination. There are also organized activities designed specifically for persons with mental retardation or other disabilities, such as the Special Olympics. These programs provide opportunities for persons with mental and physical disabilities to compete in adapted track and field events.

■ **Social and Emotional Development** Research has indicated some variability in the extent to which students with mild mental retardation are accepted and liked by their peers (Sabornie, Kauffman & Cullinan, 1990; Siperstein, Leffert & Widaman, 1996). It is important to remember that every child or adolescent, with or without mental retardation, has personal and physical characteristics that can assist or detract from that individual's popularity and acceptance.

Students with mental retardation may have difficulty with self-esteem, peer relationships, and maladaptive social behaviors.

Students with mental retardation may have difficulties with peer relations, have low self-esteem, and lack motivation (Cegelka & Prehm, 1982). They may also display delays in the development of communication, self-help, and problem-solving skills, all of which contribute to effective interaction with others (Wehmeyer & Kelchner, 1994). In some cases, students with moderate mental retardation exhibit **maladaptive behaviors**, which may range from body rocking or hand flapping to aggression toward themselves or others. These behaviors do not occur in the majority of students with moderate mental retardation; often they are associated with specific syndromes, such as autism (see Chapter 11).

Always evaluate a child's behavior in the context of his or her environment. Difficulties in social and emotional development often occur as the result of ongoing frustration about relationships with others and failures in school. Behavior must also be considered in relation to the attitudes teachers and other students display toward the child.

Commonalities: Working Toward Tolerance

Diana Zernone's new doll is the first she's ever had that looks like her: The 14-year-old New York City girl has Down syndrome, and so does Dolly Downs, a pigtailed blonde who went on the market in 1992, assembled by workers with mental retardation and developmental disabilities at Camp Venture Inc.

The idea for a doll resembling a child with Down syndrome came from a Rockland County couple who have a 31-year-old son with autism and have run programs for people with mental retardation for twenty-three years. Dr. John Lukens, a child psychologist, and Kathleen Lukens, the executive director of Camp Venture, said their inspiration was a former client who once asked her parents why she did not look like them.

Seeing people with Down syndrome on television's "Life Goes On" and in advertisements convinced the Lukenses that the public might be ready for the doll, which is also intended to teach children who do not have a handicap to be more tolerant of those who do.

The building where the doll is assembled is off a country lane. The workshop itself is a huge open room. A number of those seated around long tables wave and shout greetings to visitors before returning to their work, but the hall was surprisingly quiet on a recent afternoon, with most people concentrating on putting together pens, packaging cameras, and in one corner assembling the dolls.

The job has been divided into fifteen steps, not including the stitching, which is done by several seamstresses who work at machines along the workshop's back wall. And after the last worker on the assembly line ties the red ribbons into Dolly's hair, all of those who have participated in making the doll take turns signing the cards attached to the finished product, which say, "I made this doll."

So far they have made about 100 of the dolls, which are sold for $24.95 and shipped directly from the workshop. The information numbers are 914-624-5330 and 800-682-3714. Eventually, Camp Venture directors hope that their new product will help secure steady employment for the 150 adults with disabilities in the sheltered workshop.

Source: Melinda Henneberger, "Doll Gives Identity to Down Syndrome Children," *New York Times*, December 12, 1992. Copyright © 1992 by The New York Times Company. Reprinted by permission.

Learning to use money has important implications for independence in many community settings. (Bob Daemmrich Photography, Inc.)

Simple frustration in academic and learning situations can account for many instances of poor self-concept and lack of effort in school. If your instructional strategies are designed to prevent numerous failure experiences, you will help strengthen the child's perceptions of himself and his abilities.

Most social behaviors are learned, just as other skills are learned. Sometimes, students with mild and moderate mental retardation display **immature behaviors**, which generally reflect an inability to control emotions and delay gratification. Students with immature behaviors may have a low tolerance for frustration, cry easily, and do socially inappropriate things (Epstein, Polloway, Patton & Foley, 1989; Pollaway, Epstein & Cullinan, 1985). These behaviors may indicate a lack of appropriate social learning. A student with a problem in the area of selective attention, for example, may not have learned or may have difficulty identifying the relevant cues in a social situation, such as the nonverbal signals many of us use to judge how other people are reacting to us. When you enter a library, for example, you notice the low volume of speech and adjust your level of speech accordingly. If you don't, you probably notice the looks other people give you and then make the adjustment; if you do not, your behavior is interpreted as disruptive or inappropriate.

Studies have demonstrated that the behavior of students with mild and moderate mental retardation can be changed through behavior modification techniques and social skill instruction. With instruction, students can learn appropriate behaviors by modeling the behavior of peers in the classroom. This can pay off in improvement of social relations with others and an improved perception of self.

Effects on the Family

The realization that a child has mental retardation may be either sudden or gradual, as you learned in Chapter 3. Sometimes, when the child is very ill at birth or when recognizable physical signs are present, the parents know about their child's disability before they leave the hospital. These children most likely will have a severe disability (although predictions made at birth about the child's later functioning are notoriously unreliable).

More often, however, the clues come slowly. The child may not sit, stand, and walk at the expected ages and may not understand language or use words at the expected times. But there are many differences in the way children develop, and parents often postpone acknowledging that their child is different from others.

Most children with mild mental retardation are first diagnosed at school.

It is in the school environment that most children with mild mental retardation are identified and the effects on the family are fully realized. Parents may confer with their child's teacher or receive a letter from the school administrator requesting permission to assess their child for possible provision of special education services. A discussion with the school psychologist after testing, or the IEP meeting, may be the first place that the parents hear the words *mental retardation* applied to their child.

For some parents, diagnosis, labeling, and the provision of special services will come as a relief; they usually are the ones who have suspected that their child has learning difficulties. Others will react negatively to the term *mental retardation*. These words evoke a special set of reactions from parents, perhaps because most people have little knowledge of mental retardation or of persons with mental retardation. It is a well-known adage that we often fear what we do not understand.

Another possible cause of negative reactions by parents is that their concept of mental retardation includes an inability to learn and limited potential for a fulfilling life. It can be particularly difficult for parents who have perceptions of this type to attach the label of mental retardation to their child—a child who seemed just like all of the other children until he or she reached school. Accepting mental retardation, for many parents, involves a significant adjustment in their expectations and hopes for the child. Of course, these adjustments are often based on the parents' perceptions of mental retardation rather than their knowledge. Once parents acquire a more realistic concept of mental retardation, they are often able to raise their expectations and focus on the strengths and abilities of their child.

Parents of children with mental retardation, like most parents of children with disabilities, often seek support from parent groups, gain knowledge from classes, books, and journals, and become aware of available services through contact with schools, associations, and service agencies (see the Multimedia Resources section at the end of this chapter). In general, higher-income families experience less stress than other families with children with mental retardation (Stoneman, Brody, Davis & Crapps, 1988). Many factors, such as the ability of the family to provide extra programs or training for the child and to hire helpers for child care or housekeeping, may account for this difference.

The presence of a child with mental retardation can affect family interactions and the relationships among parents and other family members. Although a common concern has been that children with mental retardation monopolize their parents' attention and disrupt sibling relationships, research indicates that the effects are minimal when children have mild or moderate mental retardation. Stoneman, Brody, Davis, and Crapps (1987) compared pairs of same-sex siblings and found no evidence that mothers attended to children with mental retardation at the expense of their siblings. Nonetheless, individuals with moderate mental retardation may demand more time of their parents than do other children.

Overall, the research in this area seems to suggest that siblings of children with mental retardation find ways to get the attention and social interaction they need (Stoneman, Brody, Davis & Crapps, 1988). The interactions of siblings within families reflect the added child-care responsibilities of older siblings, and the sibling relationships are often characterized by a strong caregiving or dominant role on the part of the sibling without mental retardation. As individuals with mental retardation continue to receive educations that increasingly stress independent activities and functional skills, it will be interesting to see how sibling relationships change.

Educational Issues and Instructional Strategies

Because of our improved knowledge of effective educational technology, our changing philosophy toward inclusion, and a greater awareness of the rights of all individuals, educators are now rethinking the way we should educate individuals with mental retardation. As teachers, we now expect to provide meaningful educational experiences—experiences that will help prepare the students for life on their own—and to do it in the most inclusive setting possible. In many educational settings, the classroom teacher is responsible for the majority of service delivery to students with mental retardation. Interaction, communication, and professional cooperation between the special education teacher and

Educational programs for many students with mental retardation emphasize preparing students for life after school.

classroom teacher are becoming the most important factors in the successful educational experience of students with mental retardation. Many current and upcoming educational issues, therefore, focus on the cooperative nature of educational programming and the development of challenging educational environments for full inclusion.

Early Intervention

Although diagnosis of severe mental retardation is typically made at birth or within the first year of life, children with moderate or mild mental retardation are more likely to be identified at a somewhat later age. With the advent of Public Law 99-457, however, which stresses early identification of children with disabilities and provision of appropriate services, identification may take place much earlier.

P.L. 99-457 (see Chapter 1) states that children identified as developmentally delayed, at risk, or having an identified disability between birth and the age of 3 are eligible to receive services. Most students in this age range receive services from the agency designated by the state to handle infant programs. Identified 3- and 4-year-olds are eligible for preschool programs through the local educational agency. As you might expect, one of the goals of early intervention is to reduce the effects of mental retardation on learning and basic skill acquisition.

Curriculum

Curriculum includes the basic skills (reading and math) and content-area skills (science and social studies) taught in the regular classroom as well as functional life-skills content designed to help students learn the work, domestic, or leisure skills needed for independent living.

Curriculum decisions should be based on the anticipated outcomes, or expected goals, of education. For example, the anticipated outcome for a student who is capable of doing classwork in the regular class and has a high level of basic skills is to receive a high school diploma. This student may be best served by taking basic academic courses in the regular curriculum, which might also include some vocational classes and training. The anticipated outcome for another student might be to live and work in a supervised community setting. The student would follow a full-time curriculum devoted to life skills, which might include training in social skills; interpersonal communication skills; domestic skills such as cooking, managing finances, and cleaning; using community transportation; and prevocational and vocational preparation, including on-the-job training.

A functional or life-skills curriculum provides the skills necessary for students to live and work independently.

A functional or **life-skills curriculum** is intended to provide the skills necessary to maximize a student's ability to live and work independently. Curricula for students with mild mental retardation generally include instruction in basic academic areas with a focus on functional academics. **Functional academics** are basic academic skills, such as reading, writing, and arithmetic, taught in the context of real-life or community activities. For example, reading skills might be presented in the context of reading menus, clothing labels, signs and directions; and arithmetic skills in the context of paying for food in restaurants or grocery stores, planning a weekly budget, or balancing a checkbook.

Other functional curriculum components considered important for students with mild disabilities include health, sexuality, and family care; job preparation;

science and social studies—again with a functional emphasis; social skills; using community resources; and independent living skills (Drew, Logan & Hardman, 1992; Morgan, Moore, McSweyn & Salzberg, 1992; Patton, Beirne-Smith & Payne, 1990).

Students with moderate mental retardation may require more support and have more difficulty in transfer or skill generalization. These students can benefit from a more comprehensive curriculum that includes self-care skills, community access skills, social interaction and communication skills, physical and motor development—including recreation and leisure skills, and specific job training (Drew, Logan & Hardman, 1992; Patton, Beirne-Smith & Payne, 1990). In the next section, we will discuss how the student's future goals affect his or her class placement.

The curriculum for students with moderate mental retardation encompasses the essential areas of everyday life. These areas are referred to as *domains*. Although you may see different terms used to describe these areas, they can be identified as domestic, recreation and leisure, vocational, and community living. The development of the curriculum involves:

- Looking at the specific skills that the student needs in these areas
- Identifying the specific skills in which the student needs instruction
- Providing that instruction in the context of the particular domain

In other words, the curriculum is generated by the student's environment rather than by a list of skills found in basal texts or regular curriculum guides. Instruction involves presenting the skill in a naturally occurring context and integrating it with other skills found in that setting (Browder & Snell, 1987; Snell, 1988). Instead of teaching students a list of sight words or a few arithmetic operations or a series of social skills, a targeted activity would be identified, such as grocery shopping, going to a movie, applying for a job, or going to a fast-food restaurant. Then, the needed skills in reading, math, social behavior, transportation, communication, and organization related to the specific activity would all be taught in conjunction with practicing and performing that activity. All instruction is therefore useful, meaningful, and motivating to the student; teaching is focused on usable skills that can be practiced often. (See the accompanying box, "Environmental Assessment of Skills for Instruction," for an example of curriculum planning.)

The community itself is playing an ever-increasing role in curriculum content for students with mental retardation. One goal of **community-based instruction** is the placement of students in job settings found in their local community. In addition, the community provides opportunities for the functional application of basic skills. For example, teachers can use menus, job applications, store names, movie theater marquees, bank books, bowling scorecards, and city maps (to name a few items) from the local community to assist in developing skills that can be used immediately and practiced repeatedly in the student's home environment. The regular classroom teacher should find that using these resources facilitates learning and provides motivation for all the students in the class! A third role for the community is to serve as a source of activities. A series of local activities—using the post office, visiting the doctor and dentist, applying for a job, using the public recreation center, and eating at a favorite restaurant—could be the basic curriculum components for the school year, and all of the academic, social, communication, and self-care skills needed for each activity could be taught as the class participated in that activity.

The curriculum for students with moderate mental retardation emphasizes self-care skills, social interaction, recreation and leisure skills, and job training.

Community-based instruction allows students to receive instruction in meaningful and motivating settings.

∼ Environmental Assessment of Skills for Instruction

Student: Patricia Kelly, age 16
Environment: Home
Domains: Domestic/Vocational
Rationale: Patricia is responsible for watching her two younger siblings (ages 8 and 10) every day from 3:30 to 5:30. Many of the skills required can also be used as a basis for employment in child-care fields. All of the skills can be used to address future parenting needs.

Area 1: **Recreation**–Skills for instruction

Suggest activities appropriate for indoor play.

Check toys and play materials to make sure they are safe and age-appropriate.

Check on children playing indoors every 15–20 minutes if they are not in sight.

Keep children in sight or hearing distance at all times when they are playing outside.

Recognize and prohibit rough or dangerous outside play.

Guide children in their selection of afterschool snacks or prepare suitable snacks for them.

Play with children.

Area 2: **Child Management**–Skills for instruction

Know household rules for indoor/outdoor play.

Remind children of rules when they return from school.

Enforce rules.

Know and use only management strategies suggested by parents.

Know and use a few plans or "tricks" for diverting children's attention.

Give accurate report of children's behavior to parents.

Area 3: **Safety**–Skills for instruction

Identify and clear away unsafe debris, broken toys, etc., both inside and outside.

Check premises to ensure that potentially harmful materials are out of children's reach (matches, firearms, cleaning materials).

Be familiar with and experienced in administering emergency first aid procedures.

Know how to administer emergency procedures when a child is choking.

Distinguish between a mild incident and emergency, and act according to plan.

Read labels to determine if substance is poisonous.

Locate and use fire extinguisher and know fire evacuation plan.

Locate and call appropriate persons in case of concern or emergency (includes neighbor, parents, local emergency number).

Educational Setting

Students with mild and moderate levels of mental retardation attend school in a variety of settings, ranging from the regular classroom to the special school (see Framework, Part 1). Remember that a child may be classified as having mild mental retardation during one evaluation, and three years later be identified as having a learning disability. Students, therefore, can move from one educational setting to another, usually to one that is less restrictive.

As we've mentioned, however, these options should be considered in relation to the future goals or desired outcomes of education. The setting for instruction is closely related to the curriculum. For example, the regular classroom may be the best setting for a student in a diploma-track program, while a special classroom or community setting might be the most appropriate instructional site for a student receiving instruction in social or vocational skills.

Professional disagreement exists over the most appropriate instructional setting for students with mild mental retardation. This conflict involves questions about the efficacy of programs offered in special education classes, the current emphasis on maximizing integration of students into regular education classes, and the need to provide a specialized curriculum (MacMillan & Hen-

The focus of a student's instruction will often determine his or her educational setting.

drick, 1993). Many schools emphasize including students with mental retardation as much as possible. Thus, students with mild mental retardation may spend most of the day in regular classes and receive special education services during one or two class periods in a resource class.

Sometimes, students with mild mental retardation remain in the resource class for several class periods, and some may be served in self-contained classes. In these instances, inclusion is often limited to nonacademic periods such as gym, music, lunch, and study hall. A curriculum that focuses more on functional or life skills can then be delivered in the special education class. Students also may receive related services, such as adaptive physical education, speech and language therapy, or counseling. If your school has a program for students with mild mental retardation, you should expect anything, from a child who is in your class for the entire school day, with consultation provided by the resource teacher, to a child you see only during nonacademic periods.

Students with moderate mental retardation are more likely to be placed in full-time or self-contained special education classes than are students with mild disabilities. Keep in mind, however, that many schools do have programs that include systematic inclusion of students with moderate disabilities, particularly, but not exclusively, in nonacademic subjects. The rationale often used for placing students with moderate mental retardation in self-contained classes is that the teacher is able to develop and deliver an alternative curriculum. For example, the students can receive more intensive programming in life-skill activities or in community-based training when they are in a self-contained program. Nonetheless, interaction with peers is a major focus of education—an important consideration for successful community integration in later years as well as during school.

Students in self-contained programs may be mainstreamed into lunch or arts classes in order to provide at least minimal interactions with peers. Many educators, however, feel that more complete assimilation in regular classes is necessary. Sometimes the need for special instruction and training must be weighed against the philosophy of integration and the need for social interaction as educators and parents try to decide on the most appropriate program for an individual child.

The need for specialized instruction must be weighed against the need for inclusion.

Because of the current emphasis on community-based instruction, many secondary students with moderate mental retardation are receiving instruction outside of the school setting for part of the school day (Nietupski, Hamre-Nietupski, Donder, Houselog & Anderson, 1988). As we discussed earlier, community-based instruction not only can provide students with appropriate educational experiences, it can also maximize opportunities for social and physical integration.

Teaching Strategies

■ **Methods**   We see many commonalities in the instructional procedures used for students with mild and moderate mental retardation. A basic instructional technique focuses on the clear and straightforward presentation of tasks that have been carefully analyzed and sequenced. The process of breaking down a task or skill into its component parts is called **task analysis** (Alberto & Troutman, 1990). The ability to identify the set of skills required to complete a certain task (from preparing a sandwich to reading a newspaper article) and to develop an appropriate instructional sequence to teach them is an important skill for teachers of students with mental retardation.

Teaching students with mental retardation includes a focus on clearly presenting carefully sequenced tasks.

Cooperative learning is a strategy that involves providing children of various skill levels with a task to complete together. The teacher structures the activity to allow each child to make a significant contribution to the task. Cooperative learning is a good strategy to keep in mind when teaching students with mental retardation in an integrated classroom.

Prompts are clues or guides that maximize the probability that the student will answer correctly or attend to the appropriate material. Prompts are an important aspect of instruction in special education and are used extensively during initial instruction. If you underline the key word in a series of directions, you are prompting the student to attend to that key word. If you model the correct way to sound out a word, you are providing a prompt for the correct response. Prompts are then faded, or eliminated, over time. You may remember tracing dotted lines (which gradually disappeared) when you were learning cursive handwriting. The dots were prompts that were faded as you became more competent in the task.

Many teachers focus on prompting students' awareness of their learning. Students with moderate mental retardation may need content-specific prompts, such as a series of pictures or photographs to remind them of what needs to be done. Le Grice and Blampied (1994) taught students with moderate mental retardation to operate a video recorder and personal computer using color videotapes of a familiar staff member doing the steps of the skill. The videotape served as a sequenced series of prompts corresponding to the task analysis. We are only touching on the types of prompts that can be used in the classroom. The important thing for you to remember is that prompts can be easily integrated into regular classroom instruction.

Prompts can help overcome selective attention deficits. Providing fewer items at a time and teaching mnemonic strategies can facilitate memorization, and providing steps or strategies to follow can help organization and evaluation—key aspects of metacognition. These same procedures also apply to nonacademic tasks. Students receiving instruction in a functional curriculum also have many learning experiences that require attention, remembering, and organizing. These activities can range from something as simple as learning a telephone number and address to remembering the steps involved in following a recipe, writing a check, or going shopping for groceries. Instruction also needs to be sequenced and structured carefully, with reliance on prompts to illustrate how to do the task as well as when to do it (see the box on "Simple Strategies for Teaching Students with Mental Retardation").

■ **Materials**   Because of the issue of skill transfer and generalization, the types of materials used in instruction can be very important—particularly when life skills or vocational skills are being taught. Both simulated materials and real-life materials have their uses. If you were teaching sight words found in the envi-

---

～ Simple Strategies for Teaching Students with Mental Retardation

- Teach students in small groups (three or four students).
- Teach one concept or skill at a time.
- Teach steps or strategies for learning (a plan for remembering or sequencing information).
- Provide ample opportunity for practice (practice often, but don't overload).
- Use prompts to promote correct responding (examples, modeling, physical guidance).

ronment, an example of a simulated material would be the word *exit* printed in red capital letters on a rectangular card placed over the doorway of the classroom. An alternative would be to use the real thing and conduct your lesson using the actual exit sign over the door at the end of the hallway.

The use of real materials can motivate as well as facilitate generalization. As we've mentioned, using an actual checkbook folder and checks can provide a good way to practice subtraction and addition skills that can easily be integrated into the regular curriculum. Many schools have had success at integrating the more functional objectives of a student's curriculum into their regular classroom curriculum.

Students who are in the regular classroom for the academic curriculum will probably use the same materials as everyone else. The resource or consulting teacher may work with the classroom teacher to develop strategies for helping the student interact with the text and other materials. There are materials designed specifically for curriculum packages for students with learning difficulties. At the elementary level, these materials often are found in programs for basic skills instruction (reading or math) such as the SRA Corrective Reading Series. At the secondary level, these materials might include low-vocabulary, high-interest reading material such as teen magazines or plays. The regular education teacher can ask the resource teacher or consultant about available materials or catalogs.

> Instruction using simulated or real materials can help students generalize skills.

Computer-Based Instruction

Computer-based instruction has provided teachers of students with mild and moderate mental retardation with a number of instructional options. The availability of computers can augment a curriculum, expand opportunities for practice, and facilitate new instruction. Hasselbring and Goin (1989) have identified the following most common and important uses for computer-based instruction:

> Computer-based instruction provides teachers with additional resources for teaching students with mental retardation.

1. *Drill and practice* The computer is used to provide a range of practice activities, such as math problems to perform or words to read. Although this is the most common educational use of the computer, you should remember that drill and practice activities reinforce previous learning rather than teach new skills.

2. *Tutorial plus drill* In this type of lesson, some initial instruction takes place and then drill and practice activities follow. It is important for the teacher to evaluate the type of instructional strategies used in the lessons.

3. *Word processing* Using word-processing programs to produce written work may help develop students' skills in written language. The computer eliminates many of the problems students have with the actual production of letters, and the ease with which words can be moved or erased can also help to encourage more fluent writing.

4. *Thinking and problem solving* Some computer programs (such as Logo) can provide the student with exercise in developing higher-level thinking and problem-solving skills.

5. *Simulations* Computer simulations of real-life situations can provide students with practice making decisions without the risk of real consequences, dangers, or tight time constraints.

Technology also can be used as a means of delivering instruction and instructional prompts to students in areas other than academic skills. For example, Mechling and Gast (1997) used a Digivox, an augmentative communication device, to teach skills such as using a dishwasher to students with moderate mental retardation. The Digivox contains pictures or symbols that the student presses to release a corresponding digitized speech recording. A series of photographs of the student or teacher performing each step of the task was placed over the computer symbols, and the verbal directions for each step were recorded, enabling the students to use the Digivox to learn the series of tasks.

It is important for you to evaluate software carefully and determine its appropriate instructional use. The types of available software are growing rapidly, and many companies are now producing exciting learning programs as well as the frequently used drill and practice activities. The computer can be a powerful teacher's aid in the classroom, as well as a motivating activity for many students. Computer programs can provide introductions and basic skill reviews of many areas that may not be a part of the regular classroom curriculum.

Transition to Adult Life

Many people with mild mental retardation integrate themselves successfully into the life of their community with little or no outside assistance. They find jobs and do them well; they marry and begin their own families. Others, though, continue to need the help and support of social agencies. In Robert Edgerton's study of the lives of adults with mental retardation, *The Cloak of Competence* (1967), adults had difficulties in three major areas: making a living, managing sexuality and marriage, and using leisure time. Although over thirty years have passed, these areas of concern remain (Edgerton, Bollinger & Herr, 1984).

More and more, emphasis is being placed on the skills that young people need to make the transition from school to the working world. Also, there is a focus on the factors that are related to quality of life: social adjustment and integration into all aspects of the community. Research suggests the importance of community employment and living to the self-esteem of individuals with men-

Everyone has a job helping prepare lunch to take to school or work. (M. Greenlar/The Image Works, Inc.)

A closer look

Can Do: Preparing Special Needs Students for Employment

The Institutional and Home Management class at Spring Valley High School is designed to prepare high school students with mild and moderate mental retardation for transition to jobs after graduation. The classroom business concept was begun fifteen years ago. The class is used to teach the students specific job skills, but an equally important goal is to provide meaningful, creative work that contributes to a positive self-image.

The students are divided into three classes of eleven to thirteen students. Two of the classes are one hour long; students preparing to exit school take class for two hours. The classroom is conducted by a teacher and one teaching assistant.

The class is designed and run as a bakery and catering business. Students fill orders on a daily basis for customers in the school and the community. Cake orders vary from birthday cakes to elaborate wedding cakes. The variety of foods prepared for customers ranges from simple individual orders to catered receptions. The students also prepare and serve luncheons to faculty and community members.

A high volume of business requires the students to perform meaningful work the entire time they are in the classroom. They gain valuable job-related skills such as following directions, gaining and maintaining a high level of production, working well with co-workers, accepting constructive criticism, and arriving on time. They also learn the consequences of improper work-related behavior—students who behave inappropriately are fired from their classroom jobs. The student then spends the class period in a designated area of the classroom called "unemployment." Before returning to "work," the student must complete a simple job application and be interviewed by the teacher.

As the students gain job skills and positive attitudes, they move through a leveling system that culminates with a transition class. They are given interest and aptitude tests and are exposed to a variety of jobs in the community. When ready, individual students are then placed in supported, competitive employment. When the students have gained the skills necessary to perform the job without the aid of a coach, they exit school. After the students graduate, adult service providers follow up and carry on the transitioning of the special needs students into the adult world.

Source: Sue Dillon, transition coordinator, Spring Valley High School, Columbia, SC. Reprinted by permission of the author.

tal retardation (Griffin, Rosenberg, Cheyney & Greenburg, 1996). The educational experiences that address the movement from school to work and from home or residential school to independent community living are referred to as **transitional programming**. Transitional programming has become an integral part of the educational plans of most students with mental retardation, as the box "Preparing Special Needs Students for Employment" illustrates.

Transitional programming addresses the experiences students need to move on to life after school.

Employment Opportunities

People with mild mental retardation continue to face serious problems finding meaningful work that uses their skills and pays above the subsistence level (Edgar, 1987; Hasazi, Gordon & Roe, 1985). Because the needs of some students with mild mental retardation are not always obvious, many have not received the necessary preparation for transition.

Recent research on the adjustment of students with mental retardation to the world of work suggests that more comprehensive and long-range transition support is necessary (Hasazi et al., 1985; Neubert, Tilson & Ianacone, 1989). All secondary students with mental retardation now have a separate component of their IEP that identifies and describes the transition training they will receive. The importance of transition in the curriculum of students with mental retardation is likely to continue to increase as specific needs of adults with mild mental retardation are identified. Greater cooperation among the educational system, the business world, and adult social agencies will help to improve transition services.

People with moderate mental retardation are more likely to receive comprehensive preparation in the transition process related to employment. In the past, many students with moderate levels of mental retardation worked in **sheltered workshops**—large facilities that provide simple contract work. Sheltered workshops provide work experience, but they continue to segregate people with mental retardation from the community throughout their adult lives. Although sheltered workshops are still regarded as an option for adult employment, particularly for persons with severe disabilities, many students with moderate mental retardation are now being prepared for work in the community.

As we have seen, community-based instruction is becoming an important component of the curriculum for students with moderate mental retardation. **Community-based employment** is one aspect of this educational preparation and the transition to work process. Students are placed in actual job sites, and on-the-job training takes place while the student is still in school. Some examples of typical jobs include working in fast-food restaurants, gardening or nursery work, and maintenance or cleaning work. The goal is for the students eventually to be able to perform the job with minimal (if any) extra supervision.

The transition process has generated a new professional role—that of a **job coach.** A job coach is a person trained in special education and sometimes vocational education who trains people on the job and works with on-site supervisors to help them integrate the person with mental retardation smoothly into the employment setting. Many school systems now hire job coaches as a part of their special education personnel.

Given appropriate support, individuals with mild and moderate mental retardation can work successfully in the community.

Residential Options

When today's adults with mental retardation were born, many of their parents were encouraged to place them in institutions as soon as their disabilities were diagnosed. These institutions seldom had educational programs and often simply provided custodial care for their residents. Over the last twenty years, however, three factors have contributed to the trend we now call **deinstitutionalization**—the movement from residential or institutional settings to community environments. First, the publication of books such as Blatt's *Christmas in Purgatory* (1966), which documented the abuses suffered by some residents of institutions, spotlighted those conditions for the general public. Second, a series of studies demonstrated the superior functional levels of persons with mental retardation who lived outside institutions (MacMillan, 1982). Third, the courts became involved in mandating alternatives to residential institutions. For example, in *Pennsylvania Association for Retarded Citizens v. Commonwealth of Pennsylvania* (1971), all children with mental retardation were determined to have the right to a free and appropriate public education.

As a result of these and other factors, a variety of community-based residential alternatives for people with mental retardation have been developed.

Among them are **group homes**, in which several people with mental retardation live together, learning to care for themselves under the guidance of a trained supervisor. Another option is some form of apartment living, where smaller groups of people might live, again with support from trained supervisors. Sometimes people choosing to live in apartments may live alone or with a roommate with mental retardation. Supervisors might check to see that bills are being paid on time, that there is food in the refrigerator, or that the laundry is being done. Other times, the support person might just provide occasional transportation or help organize community-based activities.

Many adults with mild mental retardation support themselves and live in their own apartment or home. Preparation for community living, however, can be an important facet of the transition process. We have discussed the importance of teaching students the ways in which learned skills can be applied to real-life settings. Keeping a home, raising a family, and budgeting money are areas that can and should be addressed in school. An important part of the transition process is helping students with mild mental retardation achieve and maintain contacts with adult social service agencies that can provide assistance and information through adulthood. This can be particularly valuable in the areas of financial management, health care, employment counseling, and insurance.

Individuals with moderate mental retardation should receive systematic preparation for the transition to independent community living. A curriculum that addresses domains similar to those we discussed earlier will provide direct, on-site instruction in domestic and community living skills. Research supports the positive effects of community living on the social and cognitive development of persons with moderate retardation (Inge et al., 1988). By providing early and effective transition programs during the school years, we can maximize the probability that adults with mental retardation will adjust successfully in community residences.

> Research reports the positive effects of community living on the social and cognitive development of people with moderate mental retardation.

Personal and Civil Rights

The history of educating individuals with mental retardation includes acts and philosophies that ignore personal and civil rights. Today, many legal and ethical dilemmas remain unresolved. The right to life and the right to education are issues still being addressed by advocates and the court system. (See Chapter 11 for further discussion.) Many adults with mental retardation also have to fight for access to fair housing, for the right to marry and have children, and for the opportunity to work in community settings.

> The battle for personal and civil rights for people with mental retardation is not yet over.

It is difficult for most persons with mental retardation to wage an effective campaign for personal rights—often the mental competence of the individual is determined to be unknown or insufficient and the parents or other legal surrogate must legally represent the individual. Often, the wishes of the parent and the individual may be different, resulting in decisions that are at odds with the individual's preferred outcomes. Another issue receiving a lot of attention today is the fact that the judicial system does not consider persons with mental retardation a protected class. This means that persons with mental retardation are eligible for, among other things, the death penalty. The apparent inequities in the legal system and the potential for abuse through representation suggest that advocacy is an important function for everyone interested in the fair treatment of *all* people.

SUMMARY

■ The AAMR definition of mental retardation includes three criteria: subaverage intellectual functioning, impairments in adaptive behavior, and manifestation during the developmental period.

■ Mental retardation is usually classified as mild, moderate, severe, or profound. Approximately 1 percent of school-age students are identified as having mental retardation. Of these, 80–85 percent have mild mental retardation. The causes of retardation include both biological and environmental factors.

■ Students with mental retardation may have trouble learning how to learn (metacognition), remembering, coming to and maintaining attention, and generalizing. Language development may be delayed, although most differences are quantitative rather than qualitative. Students may be smaller and more prone to health problems, although physical differences generally are not visible. Students may also exhibit inappropriate social behavior.

■ Parents and siblings adjust their familial roles to accommodate a child with mental retardation. Siblings often spend more time on child care, though not at the expense of peer relationships.

■ A functional curriculum emphasizes independent functioning, incorporating academic skills such as reading in a real-life context. Teaching strategies that can be used by regular or special educators include task analysis, cooperative learning, metacognitive strategies, and using prompts and concrete materials. Computers provide drill and practice, word processing, tutorials, and other instructional assistance.

■ Transition programs are designed to help students achieve as much independence as possible through employment, living arrangements, and social relationships.

KEY TERMS

mental retardation
Stanford-Binet
Wechsler Intelligence Scale for Children, Third Edition (WISC-III)
adaptive behavior
AAMR Adaptive Behavior Scale
Vineland Adaptive Behavior Scales

metacognition
attentional deficits
skill transfer (generalization)
maladaptive behavior
immature behavior
life-skills curriculum
functional academics
community-based instruction
task analysis

cooperative learning
prompts
transitional programming
sheltered workshop
community-based employment
job coach
deinstitutionalization
group home

MULTIMEDIA RESOURCES

ARC National Headquarters, 500 East Border, Suite 300, Arlington, TX 76010; (817) 261-6003. Information about programs and national policies affecting individuals with mental retardation and the ARC newsletter can be obtained from ARC Headquarters.

Down Syndrome News. Newsletter of the National Down Syndrome Congress; (800) 232-6372. This newsletter can serve as a source of information and support for professionals, parents, siblings, and individuals with Down Syndrome.

Edwards, Jean; and David Dawson. *My Friend David: A Source Book About Down Syndrome and a Personal Story About Friendship* (Austin: Pro-Ed, 1983). David Dawson, a man with Down syndrome, tells his story through taped interviews. In addition, the book offers a section on strategies, education, residential, and vocational options, and resources for people with Down syndrome.

Kaufman, Sandra Z. *Retarded Isn't Stupid, Mom!* (Baltimore: Brookes, 1988). The mother of a girl with mild mental retardation describes her growth to adulthood and her struggle to achieve independence and normalization.

Scheerenberger, R. C. *A History of Mental Retardation* (Baltimore: Brookes, 1983), and *A History of Mental Retardation: A Quarter Century of Progress* (Baltimore: Brookes, 1987). These two books provide a comprehensive background of events and people in the field of mental retardation from earliest times through the 1980s.

Seltzer, Marsh Mailiick; and Marty Wyngaarden Krauss. *Aging and Mental Retardation: Extending the Continuum* (Washington, DC: American Association on Mental Retardation, 1987). A monograph covering issues relating to programs and services for people with mental retardation over the age of 55.

Siblings for Significant Change (support group), 105 East 22nd Street, Room 710, New York, NY 10010; (212) 420-0776. This organization presents strategies and support contacts for brothers and sisters of individuals with disabilities.

Sibling Information Network Newsletter. A. J. Pappenikou Center on Special Education and Rehabilitation, University of Connecticut, 249 Glenbrook Road, Box U-64, Storrs, CT 06269.

USING YOUR KNOWLEDGE

Collaboration: How do regular and special educators collaborate in schools that require full inclusion of students with mild mental retardation? In what ways do the educational strategies used by special educators complement the regular teacher's class activity? Visit a school that uses a full inclusion model and observe a student with mental retardation in several classes. Talk to the special education teacher and classroom teachers to learn what they do to support the student's academic and social needs.

Can Do: How is a functional curriculum designed to meet the needs of an individual with moderate mental retardation? What areas are covered? After talking to several educators, try to design the framework for a functional curriculum that has a goal of developing residential and employment independence for the student.

Can Do: What is a day on the job like for a person with mental retardation? What types of jobs are held? Interview an employee who has mental retardation. Does he or she have a job coach? What are the job's responsibilities? What does he or she like or dislike about it? Get together with others in your class to design a job profiles guide.

Commonalities: What teaching strategies are appropriate for both students with and without mental retardation? Consider both individual, group, and small-group instructional methods. Would some types of material adaptations for students with mental retardation be beneficial for all students? Why?

WHAT YOU CAN DO NOW

1. Plan an "education awareness day" to highlight achievements in inclusion and normalization in the school, setting a positive example for the community.

2. Send out a survey to local business people to find out their needs and attitudes regarding disabilities. Would they want to hire a person with a disability? For what type of job? Expectations? Support? Pay? Security?

3. Visit a group home and talk with its residents and staff. Find out what type of contact residents have with the community (for example, shopping in local stores, riding public transportation). Discuss their views on the value of community living.

Children with Learning Disabilities

5

IN this chapter we discuss students with learning disabilities, the largest group of children served in special education and the group most likely to be included in general education classes. Although these students require special education services, their learning needs are often balanced by excellence in other areas of life, and their ability to reach their potential can be dramatically enhanced by appropriate teaching and learning strategies. As you read about students with learning disabilities, think about the following questions:

- What are learning disabilities? What distinguishes a learning disability from underachievement?

- What do we know about the causes of learning disabilities?

- What specific strategies are most helpful for teaching students with learning disabilities?

Collaboration: What kinds of professional support are available to help classroom teachers work with students with learning disabilities?

Can Do: What specific adaptations will enable students with learning disabilities to achieve in the classroom setting?

Commonalities: What interventions or adaptations presented in this chapter might be used to help *all* students learn?

Do you remember having to read aloud in school as a kid? Or sitting in a difficult foreign language class, sweating in fear of being called on to translate a passage? Many of us remember vividly the feelings of panic, fear, and anxiety that those situations evoked—particularly if we were not good readers, or if we hadn't done our language homework the night before. Even now we can remember what it is like to feel inadequate in school.

Some students feel this way in school every day. The most ordinary classroom tasks are problematic for them. The students may be popular with others or rejected by their peers; they may be athletic or have two left feet; they may have wealthy parents or poor, but they share one characteristic. Although they have average intelligence, they do not do well in school. The majority of them read very poorly, and reading competently is the keystone of school success. You know some of these students; you may have worked with them. Let us find out more about them.

Definitions and Terms

Children with learning disabilities have probably always existed, but for many years their unique problems and characteristics went unrecognized by educators. Their concerned parents would have no problem finding a label to describe their child, but the label varied depending on the training of the professional whose help they sought. To physicians, these children were *neurologically impaired* or had *minimal brain dysfunction*. To speech and language pathologists, the same children might be called *aphasic* or *dyslexic;* psychologists might call them *perceptually handicapped* or *hyperactive*. This proliferation of terms and specialists did not help parents find appropriate educational programs for their children. But in 1963, a group of parents met in Chicago and invited the noted special educator Dr. Samuel Kirk to address them. When Kirk described the "specific learning disabilities" that their children shared, the parents seized on that term to describe and unite their children (Lerner, 1993).

The Federal Definition

A number of definitions of learning disabilities have been put forth over the years; most of them are quite general in order to accommodate the wide range of beliefs related to learning disabilities. The most widely used definition of **learning disabilities** was originally written in 1968 by the National Advisory Committee on Handicapped Children. It was slightly adapted for inclusion in Public Law 94-142 (1975), now Public Law 101-476, the Individuals with Disabilities Education Act (1990). This definition attempts to unify this group of students by including some of the earlier labels used to describe students with learning disabilities, such as perceptual handicaps, brain damage, and so on. It reads:

> "Specific learning disabilities" means a disorder in one or more of the basic psychological processes involved in understanding or using language spoken or written, which may manifest itself in an imperfect ability to listen, think, read, write, spell, or to do mathematical calculations. The term includes such conditions as perceptual handicaps, brain injury, minimal brain dysfunction, and developmental aphasia. The term does not include learn-

The current federal definition of learning disabilities refers to a disorder in one or more of the basic psychological processes of understanding and using language.

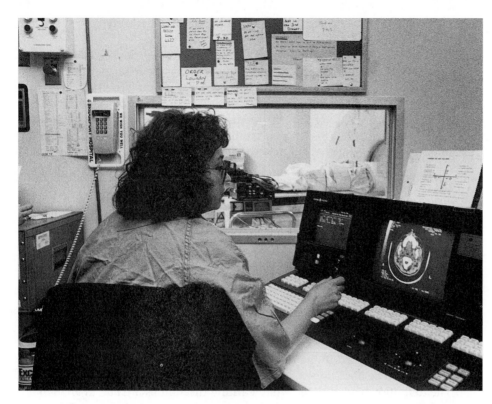

Advances in technology may one day give us more specific information about the causes of learning disabilities. (Gale Zucker / Stock, Boston, Inc.)

ing problems which are primarily the result of visual, hearing, or motor handicaps, of mental retardation, of emotional disturbance, or of environmental, cultural, or economic disadvantage. (p. 22)

The federal law goes on to state that a student has a learning disability if he or she (1) does not achieve at the proper age and ability levels in one or more of several specific areas when provided with appropriate learning experiences, and (2) has a severe discrepancy between achievement and intellectual ability in one or more of the following areas: (a) oral expression, (b) listening comprehension, (c) written expression, (d) basic reading skill, (e) reading comprehension, (f) mathematics calculation, and (g) mathematics reasoning.

Students with learning disabilities do not achieve at their age and ability levels in one or more specific areas.

Key Elements in the Federal Definition

The federal definition emphasizes that the performance of students with learning disabilities is often tied to their ability to receive or express information—reading, writing, listening, and speaking are some of the ways we take in information or communicate what we know. The academic areas listed in the definition illustrate how this disability can be manifested. It is important to note that a child may have a learning disability in all of the skill areas mentioned or just in one area. For example, a student may find it difficult to learn to read and spell, yet do quite well in math. Some individuals can speak and write in an organized and effective manner, yet become quite confused when dealing with number concepts and algorithms. Knowing that a child has a learning disability tells you only that the child is experiencing some difficulty processing information. You must learn much more about the child before you can tell how much difficulty he or she is experiencing or what impact the disability has on specific academic subjects or tasks.

Another key element of the federal definition is that the students demonstrate a severe **discrepancy** between achievement, or their performance in school, and their intellectual ability or potential. For example, a 9-year-old child with an average IQ who reads on the first-grade level would be exhibiting a discrepancy between what we expect (reading on the third-grade level) and the way he or she performs (reading on the first-grade level). A discrepancy is determined by examining the differences between intelligence and achievement tests.

All that really is needed in most states to obtain a diagnosis of learning disabilities is a discrepancy between achievement and ability. The extent of the discrepancy necessary for identification varies from state to state because the size of the discrepancy is not spelled out in the federal definition. A significant discrepancy is usually about equal to one or two years below expected performance level or two standard deviations below average performance. Although most states identify this discrepancy by comparing scores on standardized achievement tests with scores on intelligence tests, some states use a formula that takes into account factors such as IQ, achievement level, and age, while others use simple differences in grade-level performance (Frankenberger & Fronzaglio, 1991). It is important to remember that this discrepancy has only to occur in *one* of the areas listed in the definition (mathematics, reading, or writing) for identification to be made.

A diagnosis of learning disabilities calls for a discrepancy between achievement and ability.

The definition also outlines what learning disabilities are *not*, in an element of the definition that has come to be known as the **exclusion clause:** "The term does not include learning problems which are primarily the result of visual, hearing, or motor handicaps, of mental retardation, of emotional disturbance, or of environmental, cultural, or economic disadvantage." This sentence, which has caused a great deal of disagreement among professionals in the field, has important implications for identifying students with learning disabilities.

Because a number of other disabilities or life situations may also result in problems in learning, some professionals feel that it is important to ensure that the difficulties a child is experiencing cannot be attributed to the fact that she comes from a deprived family or suffers from a physical or other disability. As you might imagine, it is difficult to tease out the effects of a socially or economically deprived environment on a student's performance. Consequently, you may find few psychologists or child study teams who will deprive a child of the opportunity to receive special education services because they suspect the environment contributed to her learning problems. On the other hand, this clause can be used to help prevent the improper labeling of children from distinct cultures who have acquired learning styles, language, or behaviors that are not compatible with the academic requirements of schools in the dominant culture.

The exclusion clause also reflects the opinion of some professionals that learning disabilities cannot exist in children with other disabilities. Other experts, however, do feel that there are children with sensory disabilities or cognitive disabilities who do not achieve up to the level of their ability and that they, too, can be considered to have learning disabilities.

Because many children achieve below grade level, and it is often difficult to determine *why* a child is underachieving, the criteria for learning disabilities allow large numbers of children to be classified. As you might expect, this results in great diversity among the children identified as having a learning disability. Some children are one year behind in one subject while others are four years behind in three subjects. Although all of these children are identified as having a learning disability, their educational needs and programs may be very different.

Prevalence

In 1963 the term *learning disabilities* was newly coined; twenty years later it described the largest group of children served in special education. Learning disabilities was first included in public law as a disability area in 1975. Since that time the number of students identified as having a learning disability has grown by 160 percent, from approximately 800,000 students to over 2 million students (U.S. Department of Education, 1991; 1996).

A number of reasons have been suggested for the enormous growth in the identification of students with learning disabilities. The following are some of the most frequently suggested:

1. Children who are underachieving are incorrectly identified as learning disabled. The evaluation and identification criteria are too subjective and unreliable, and there are few, if any, alternative programs for many of these students (Frankenberger & Fronzaglio, 1991; Henley, Ramsey & Algozzine, 1993).

2. The classification of learning disabilities is more socially acceptable than many other special education classifications, particularly mild mental retardation and behavior disorders. Consequently, parents and teachers advocate for this classification (Frankenberger & Fronzaglio, 1991; Lerner, 1993).

3. Greater general awareness of learning disabilities has resulted in more appropriate referrals and diagnoses. Teachers and parents are more aware of the types of services that are available (Lerner, 1993).

4. The number of students identified as learning disabled parallels the increased social and cultural risks that have arisen during the past two decades. Biological and psychosocial stressors may place more children at risk for acquiring learning disabilities, and, therefore, more children are identified (Hallahan, 1992).

> The criteria for learning disabilities allow large numbers of children to be classified.

Although we have no way of knowing the extent to which any of these reasons are accurate, it is likely that they all have contributed to the expansion of the population of students with learning disabilities.

Theories on Causes of Learning Disabilities

In a great majority of cases, the cause of an individual's learning disability is unknown. This is true despite a vast amount of research investigating the possible causes of learning disabilities. Many educators and researchers disagree with the research emphasis on finding the cause or causes of learning disabilities (Wallace & McLoughlin, 1988). What help does it provide a teacher or another professional, they ask, to know what caused the problem? Knowing the cause of the disability does not necessarily tell us how to teach a student; in fact some people believe that it may hinder the teaching process, particularly in the case of vague and poorly defined terms like *brain damage*. Nevertheless, the search for the causes of learning disabilities continues to occupy many researchers in

> In most cases, the cause of a child's learning disability cannot be determined.

Class participation by students with learning disabilities depends on interest, confidence, and the ability to attend to the information being presented. (Elizabeth Crews/The Image Works, Inc.)

language, psychology, and medicine, and there is at least one good reason why this should be so. If we can identify the factors that cause learning disabilities, we may learn to prevent them.

The speculation and research about the causes of learning disabilities can be grouped into two categories: internal factors, such as organic, biological, or genetic factors, and external factors, sometimes referred to as environmental factors. Keep in mind, however, that when we are talking about possible causes of learning disabilities, we are referring mainly to hypotheses rather than facts.

Internal Factors

■ **Brain Damage Theories** Since the brain is the center of learning, many professionals have assumed that students with serious learning problems have some type of brain damage. Although this explanation makes sense intuitively, there has been very little supporting research evidence. If brain damage exists, it has been too negligible to be identified through available technology, such as an electroencephalograph (EEG), a test used to measure brain activity. Therefore, the theory of minimal brain damage has not received any physiological support.

Recently, however, there has been a renewed interest in neurological evaluations and brain research in the area of learning disabilities. Certainly one reason for this interest is advanced technology, which has improved our ability to get more detailed information. Although there have been no definitive breakthroughs in identifying causes for learning disabilities, some researchers have reported interesting findings. For example, Bigler (1992) used a procedure called magnetic resonance imaging (MRI) to get a picture (similar to an x-ray) of the brains of individuals who had severe reading disabilities and also of some people who did not have learning disabilities. He found that some of the individuals with learning disabilities had similar structural irregularities of the left hemisphere of their brains. This structural difference was not present in all of the individuals with disabilities, so Bigler could not draw any specific conclusions. Many people feel, however, that as technology advances, neurobiology will provide some answers about the causes of learning disabilities.

■ **Other Physiological Factors**   Medical researchers have suggested that other physiological factors have a role in causing learning disabilities. Many possible causes have been proposed over the years, including malnutrition and biochemical imbalances, such as allergies or the inability of the blood to synthesize a normal supply of vitamins (Cott, 1972; 1977). Cott's suggestion that some children were unable to synthesize vitamins triggered attempts to treat learning-disabled children with massive doses of vitamins, called megavitamin therapy. The **Feingold diet** (Feingold, 1975) is the best-known example of the belief that allergies to certain substances found in foods (particularly artificial colorings and flavorings) cause hyperactivity and learning disabilities. None of these theories, however, has stood up to scientific experimentation (Arnold, Christopher & Huestis, 1978; Kavale & Forness, 1983). A review of studies on malnutrition did suggest, however, that severe malnutrition can affect the development of the central nervous system and, therefore, can affect learning (Hallahan & Cruickshank, 1973).

When we look back on the birth histories of students with learning disabilities, we do see that many of them experienced more **perinatal stress** than other babies. That is, during the perinatal period (from labor and delivery through the age of twenty-eight days) there were more traumatic events in their lives, such as difficult or prolonged labor and delivery, hypoxia during the birth process, low birthweight, or illness. Many babies with those same problems, however, do not have learning difficulties later in life, so perinatal stresses cannot be the sole cause of learning disabilities.

Several researchers have postulated that learning disabilities are inherited. As a teacher, you will often hear the parent of a child with learning disabilities say, "I had that same problem when I was in school—we just didn't have a name for it then." Although you may discover a lot of anecdotal evidence for inheritance, the empirical evidence is in dispute (Gelfand, Jenson & Drew, 1988). The strongest evidence for a genetic basis for learning disabilities comes from studies of identical twins reared apart, which showed that both twins were likely to have a learning disability (Bonnet, 1989), and studies of the rate of disability occurrence within families (Lewis, 1992). Much more conclusive research needs to be done, however, before a link between heredity and learning disabilities can be established.

No link between heredity and learning disabilities has yet been proved.

External Factors

If we look at learning disabilities as differences in **learning style**, or the way a student approaches learning, we may see the interaction between the student and the environment as the critical causal factor of learning disabilities.

The learning styles of children with learning disabilities may be incompatible with school requirements.

Learning style can have a definite effect on the ways we fit into certain learning environments and the types of things we are most likely to learn. Some students approach learning in an organized and sequential way. They are prepared, want direction, and are expert at categorizing and relating information they receive. Other students approach learning in a haphazard or disorganized way; these students pick up information from what they see or hear, not necessarily what they are supposed to be learning and not necessarily in the order or way their teachers or parents designed. Still other students can be found between these two extremes. It is probably easy for you to look at these descriptions and figure out which students would be most likely to succeed in school and which would be likely to fail.

Some people believe we need to consider the possibility that children identified as having a learning disability are really those children whose learning style is not compatible with the learning requirements of most school settings (Hall, 1980). In other words, rather than experiencing a deficit or disability, the students simply don't fit the mold. If teaching procedures and task requirements were different, the students wouldn't have a disability at all. Students with learning disabilities do often demonstrate a disorganized approach to learning; however, this may be a characteristic of the disability rather than a cause.

Today, some educators believe that external factors are the major cause of learning disabilities (Morsink, 1985). The factors that are most frequently implicated are lack of motivation; inappropriate methods, materials, and curricula (Wallace & McLoughlin, 1988); and, simply, poor teaching. This theory is attractive to many people because many students with learning disabilities *can* learn when they receive direct, systematic instruction. Through careful assessment of the student's academic strengths and weaknesses, the skills that are missing or weak can be identified and taught.

We can also look beyond the school to the family environment in our search for causal factors. Of course, the federal definition excludes the identification of students whose learning problems are primarily a result of cultural differences or impoverished conditions. We also mentioned, however, that it is difficult to measure the extent to which a factor such as poverty influences a child's learning problem. In a recent study, Lorsbach and Frymier (1992) compared students with and without disabilities on five risk factors for school failure: personal pain, including experiences such as suspension and drug use; academic failure; family socioeconomic status; family instability, including divorce and number of residence changes; and family tragedy. This study indicated that students with learning disabilities were at greater risk on all factors. This study is one in a body of research that identifies children with learning disabilities as being more at risk than students without learning disabilities. Although some of these factors, such as academic failure, could be anticipated given the nature of the disability, many of the other factors suggest that effects of a child's home situation or environment cannot be automatically disregarded as potential contributors to some learning disabilities. In spite of the requirements of the definition, it is clear that some children have disabilities that may be tied to their environment.

Perhaps someday we will learn that some children, because of internal factors, are more vulnerable to external events and as a result develop what we now call learning disabilities. But since these learning disabilities range along a continuum, from mild to severe, and consist of many different types, it is probably foolhardy to search for *one* cause of a complicated group of learning problems (see the accompanying box, "Possible Causes of Learning Disabilities").

∾ Possible Causes of Learning Disabilities

Internal Factors
The following causes have been suggested, but little hard data are available:

- Brain damage
- Malnutrition and biochemical imbalances
- Perinatal stress
- Genetics

External Factors
Many educators believe that external factors are major causes; others believe that they predispose children to learning disabilities. Major external factors include:

- Learning style
- Classroom factors (lack of motivation; inappropriate materials, methods, and curriculum)
- Environmental stressors (personal pain, family instability, poverty)

Characteristics and Effects of Learning Disabilities

It is difficult to identify a few characteristics that describe all people with learning disabilities. In the following section we will examine what is known about how individuals with learning disabilities learn—how they receive, process, and produce information. We will also look at the potential impact of learning disabilities on academic performance, social behavior, and the family.

Learning Disabilities and Cognition: Approaches to Learning

As you remember, the federal definition of learning disabilities specifies that it is "a disorder in one or more of the basic psychological processes involved in understanding or using language." In this definition, *language* refers to the symbols of communication—spoken, written, or even behavioral. Although *psychological processes* is a vague term, think of it as referring to all the things we do when we take in information (listen, read, observe), try to learn information (classify, remember, evaluate, imitate), and produce information (speak, write, calculate, behave). These psychological processes are aspects of *cognition*, the wide range of thinking skills we use to process and learn information (Henley, Ramsey & Algozzine, 1993).

In this section, we will look at five cognitive processes: perception, attention, memory, metacognition, and organization. These processes are vital to our ability to understand and use language. All students who have difficulty learning are probably experiencing a problem in one or more of them. You will notice that most of the processes we mention, as well as the related learning characteristics of students with learning disabilities, are similar to those we discussed in Chapter 4. This overlap exists because learning is learning, no matter who does it. Everyone uses the same basic processes to learn information. We don't always use them the same way, however, or with the same degree of efficiency.

Learning disabilities can affect cognitive processes—thinking skills used to process information.

■ **Perception** Perception, as defined here, is the ability to organize and interpret the information we experience through our senses, such as visual or auditory abilities. Perception is important to learning because it provides us with our first sensory impressions about something we see or hear. When we hear a note or a sound, we are able to identify and appreciate its uniqueness. When we see the letter *B* we identify its structure (overall shape), orientation (direction of the letter), and component parts (one straight line and two curved lines). Later, if we see the letter *D*, we are able to see that *D* has its own set of properties, and some are similar to *B* and some are different.

A student who is listening, reading, or observing relies on his perceptual abilities to help him recognize, compare, and discriminate information (Wallace & McLoughlin, 1988). The ability to hold the image of a letter, word, or sound is necessary before information can be recognized, recalled, or applied. Let's look at an example of a young child who is just learning to read. If this child has difficulty discriminating sounds, she may confuse similar sounds, such as those made by the letters *m* and *n*; *b, p,* and *d*; and *f* and *v*. This confusion may make it difficult for the child to decode words by "sounding them out" and make the connection between written letters and spoken sounds (Nix & Shapiro, 1986). This connection, so important for reading, will be more difficult for her because, in her mind, the relationship seems to change. Sometimes she sees *m* and hears *mmm*; other times she sees *n* and hears *mmm*. This means she may begin guessing when asked to read a word such as *man*. (Is it *man, nam, nan,* or *mam*?)

Right away you can see the importance of two essential teaching approaches for a child with difficulty in perception; first, do not present pieces of information that are perceptually confusing (for example, that sound alike or look alike) together or right after each other. Second, point out the important characteristics of information. The student must be encouraged to attend to and recognize the identifying aspects, since she may have difficulty picking them out herself (see the accompanying box, "Teaching Strategies for Students with Perceptual Difficulties").

Some children with learning disabilities reverse letters, words, or whole passages during reading or writing. Occasional letter or word reversal is typical of all young children because prior learning of shapes and colors doesn't involve the added dimensions of directionality and orientation. A square is a square no matter which way you point it or draw it. When learning to write, however, it becomes important to notice the direction of symbols; this takes a little while to get right.

Children who reverse words while reading typically reverse words that can be read in either direction (*saw* and *was*). You will seldom see a child try to read *firetruck* as *kcurterif*. The most common letter reversals are also those that are letters in either direction (*b* and *d*). If we think about how close these two letters are in the alphabet and recognize that often they are taught close together, we can understand why they are often reversed. The child hasn't had time to learn one completely before being introduced to the other.

■ **Attention** The importance of attention to learning seems fairly obvious to most of us. It is the underlying factor in our ability to receive and process information. How can you take notes on a lecture if you can't tell what's important? How can you work a long division problem if you can't stay on task? As we discussed in Chapter 4, *attention* is a broad term that refers to the ability to focus on information. Students who experience attention difficulties to a considerable degree may be identified as having **attention deficit disorder** (ADD) or **attention**

Attention deficits are frequently associated with individuals with learning disabilities.

~ Teaching Strategies for Students with Perceptual Difficulties

- If two pieces of information are perceptually confusing, do not present them together. For example, do not teach the spelling of *ie* words (believe) and *ei* words (perceive) on the same day.

- Highlight the important characteristics of new material. For example, underline or use bold letters to draw a stu-

dent's attention to the same sound pattern presented in a group of reading or spelling words (m<u>ou</u>se, h<u>ou</u>se, r<u>ou</u>nd).

deficit with hyperactivity disorder (ADHD), in addition to their diagnosis of learning disabilities.

Students with learning disabilities quite often experience difficulties in attention. In fact, attention deficits are probably the disorder most frequently associated with individuals with learning disabilities. Many teachers have described their students with learning disabilities as "distractible," "never with the class," "in his own world," and "always looking at everything except what she's supposed to be looking at." These teachers are talking about kids who have trouble coming to attention and maintaining attention—something appears to be interfering with their ability to get on task and stay focused. Sometimes they are distracted by things in the classroom; other times they are subject to internal distractions—random thoughts or ideas.

Teachers are also perplexed or frustrated because a child seems to be paying attention but doesn't follow directions or can't summarize the main idea of a story. These problems may be a result of difficulties with *selective attention*, the ability to zero in on the most important part of a piece of information (see Chapter 4). For example, given the directions "<u>Circle</u> the correct answer," Linda focuses on the fact that the word *circle* is underlined and proceeds to underline her answer. She attends to an inappropriate cue.

Again, once we understand the types of difficulties that can result from attention deficits, we can begin to restructure our teaching presentations to circumvent some of these problems or to teach some new attention skills. When children have difficulty attending to a task for a long period of time, it helps to break down the task into smaller segments. If Tom has difficulty maintaining attention, his assignment might be modified so he has to read two pages each night instead of twelve pages on Thursday evening. By gradually requiring a little more work each day, we can sometimes help children increase their attention span.

Problems with selective attention can first be addressed by making sure that the student attends to the *important* information. Use a variety of prompts and cues—written, verbal, and instructional—as shown in the accompanying box, "Teaching Strategies for Students with Attention Deficits."

Another technique is to teach students how to identify the important information in a task. As students become older, they are expected to do increasing amounts of independent work, including reading and writing. It is critical that they learn how to identify key material on their own.

■ **Memory** If perception and attention are the skills that form a foundation for learning, then memory is the major vehicle for acquiring and recalling information. Memory involves many different skills and processes. Some of these

～ Teaching Strategies for Students with Attention Difficulties

Maintaining Attention

- Break long tasks or assignments into smaller segments. Administer the smaller segments throughout the day, if a shorter assignment isn't acceptable.
- Present limited amounts of information on a page.
- Gradually increase the amount of time a student must attend to a task or lecture.

Selective Attention

- Use prompts and cues to draw attention to important information. Types of cues include:

1. Written cues, such as highlighting directions on tests or activity sheets.

2. Verbal cues, such as using signal words to let students know they are about to hear important information.

3. Instructional cues, such as having students paraphrase directions or other information to you.

- Teach students a plan for identifying and highlighting important information themselves.

Encoding processes organize information so it can be learned.

processes are used to organize information for learning; these are called **encoding processes.** When individuals encode information, they use visual, auditory, or verbal cues to arrange material; thus encoding relies heavily on skills such as perception and selective attention. Students with learning disabilities who experience difficulty in perception and attention are also likely to have problems remembering correctly, because they may be encoding partial, incorrect, or unimportant information.

Students with learning disabilities often show deficits in working memory—the ability to store and retrieve information.

Students with learning disabilities may experience many of the same problems with memory strategies that students with mild mental retardation do, including significant deficits in **working memory**—the ability to store new information and to retrieve previously processed information from long-term memory (Swanson, Cochran & Ewers, 1990). Deficits in working memory translate into difficulties in the classroom. Students who don't use memory strategies try to learn information that is not broken down into manageable parts or that is unconnected to any previous knowledge. This makes it difficult for them to transfer the information into long-term memory and to retrieve it later on.

It is important to teach students memory strategies. For example, allowing extended opportunities for practice—including active rehearsal of information—may be helpful. Sometimes teachers try to associate materials with pictures, key words, or context clues to help students remember a number of facts or the relationships between them. Remember that many students with learning disabilities do not use tools for remembering, but you can teach them some of these tools. The accompanying box, "Memory Strategies," describes some common ones.

■ **Metacognition** Metacognition, the ability to monitor and evaluate performance, is another area in which students with learning disabilities often experience difficulty (Hallahan, Kauffman & Lloyd, 1985; Wong, 1982, 1991). Metacognition requires the ability to identify and select learning skills and techniques to facilitate the acquisition of information; to choose or create the setting in which you are most likely to receive material accurately; to identify the most effective and efficient way to process and present information; and to evaluate and adapt your techniques for different materials and situations. Thus metacognitive skills are critical to all aspects of learning. These skills supply many of the keys to

Lack of metacognitive skills may hinder competent learning.

～ Memory Strategies

Remember this number: 380741529

Look quickly at the number written above, then cover it completely with your finger. Wait one minute, and try to say the number out loud. Check your accuracy, but then ask yourself a more important question: What did I do to try to remember that long string of digits?

If that experiment didn't work, think of this situation. You are in a telephone booth, without a pencil and paper. You call Directory Assistance to get the number you need to call. How do you remember the number?

In either one of those situations, you probably used one of the following memory strategies:

- *Chunking* is the grouping of large strings of information into smaller, more manageable "chunks." Telephone numbers, for example, are "chunked" into small segments for easier recall; remembering 2125060595 is much harder than remembering (212) 506-0595.

- *Rehearsal* is the repetition, either oral or silent, of the information to be remembered.

- *Elaboration* is the weaving of the material to be remembered into a meaningful context. The numbers above, for example, could be related to birthdays, ages, or other telephone numbers.

Another useful memory strategy is *categorization*, in which the information to be remembered is organized by the category to which it belongs. All the animals in a list, for example, could be grouped together for remembering.

learning from experience, generalizing information and strategies, and applying what you have learned.

The student who does not demonstrate metacognitive skills may experience difficulty developing into a competent learner (Kluwe, 1987). Because most of these skills focus on planning, monitoring, and evaluation, students without them may appear to plunge into tasks without thinking about them and never look back once they're done. Practicing a book report before delivering it to the class, making an outline of a paper before you begin writing, and jotting down the key points you want to make on an essay question before you begin writing all illustrate how metacognition can affect performance. As you probably know from personal experience, the students who practice, outline, and make notes are more likely to have coherent presentations or answers.

Fortunately, metacognitive skills can be taught. One technique that helps students plan, monitor, and evaluate, **self-monitoring,** is described in the accompanying box, "Teaching Self-Monitoring." Self-monitoring teaches students to evaluate and record their own performance periodically. Written or auditory cues are provided for students, which prompt them to check their behavior.

Self-monitoring teaches students to evaluate and record their own performance.

■ **Organization** If we look at the many behaviors we consider to be characteristic of individuals with learning disabilities and examine the processes we have just discussed, we can see the underlying thread—difficulty in **organization.** Because *organization* is a term we all use often, it is a useful and familiar framework to apply to learning disabilities

Difficulties in organization can affect the most superficial tasks or the most complex cognitive activities. The simple acts required to come to class with a paper, pencil, and books; to get a homework assignment home and then back to school; and to copy math problems on a piece of notebook paper all rely on organizational skills. These may seem minor problems that can be easily addressed. Next to attention deficits, however, these simple organization problems are mentioned most often by classroom teachers as sources of difficulty. Teachers often become frustrated at what appears to be a student's careless and

〜 Teaching Self-Monitoring

The following procedure teaches self-monitoring of attention, defined as attention to task, but the same technique can be used for a variety of skills.

- Teach students the difference between on-task and off-task behavior. Model the different behaviors and have students demonstrate them to you.

- Provide students with written or auditory cues (a timer, an audiotape with a tone or beep) that prompt them to check their behavior.

- Have students stop what they are doing when they hear the cue, ask themselves if they are paying attention, and record their response.

- Gradually fade the cues, then the recording sheets, as students learn to self-monitor independently.

thoughtless approach to class preparation. It is important to recognize, however, that many students with learning disabilities cannot plan effectively. To some extent, metacognitive skills play a role in organization. Students must be able to understand the need to have a system of organization and develop a plan for carrying it out.

Another factor that may interact with metacognitive activity to produce organizational problems is **cognitive style,** the cognitive activity that takes place between the time a student recognizes the need to respond to something and actually does respond. Students are often categorized along a continuum that ranges from impulsive to reflective. An *impulsive* cognitive style refers to rapid response, without engaging in activities that allow the learner to consider alternatives, consequences, or accuracy. A *reflective* cognitive style describes a slower rate of response that includes an examination of the response and its alternatives or consequences. Many students with learning disabilities possess an impulsive cognitive style (Walker, 1985). This means that they are likely to respond without thinking. A student with an impulsive cognitive style may wave her hand vigorously to answer a question before you have even finished asking it. The tendency to jump the gun precludes the opportunity for engaging in organizational activity regardless of the type of task or its complexity.

Individuals with learning disabilities often are described as passive learners; they don't take the initiative in the learning process.

Individuals with learning disabilities are also often described as inactive or passive learners (Torgesen, 1977). This characterization reflects behavior rather than the attitude we usually ascribe to the word *passive*. It suggests that students with learning disabilities often do not take the initiative in the learning process. This passive role may contribute to deficits in organizational skills, since organization requires the individual to recognize the need to take action and to develop and carry out a plan.

Classroom interventions designed to improve organizational skills usually provide students with specific actions or guidelines for organized behavior. Examples include strategies such as having a single notebook with designated places for homework, paper, and pencils; developing a list for students' lockers that identifies what is needed for each class; and preparing a standard end-of-the-day checklist for students to use to ensure they have all required materials. Strategies like these have helped counteract the day-to-day organizational problems of many students with learning disabilities. We will look more closely at complex organizational problems involving writing and thinking skills when we discuss academic interventions.

Learning Disabilities and Academic Performance

Before we look at the effects of learning disabilities on academic performance, let's review the key processes involved in cognition. If we keep these processes in mind, it becomes easier to understand and even anticipate the types of difficulties students with learning disabilities can experience. Perception, attention, memory, metacognition, and organization are the five key processes. Together, they enable us to receive information correctly, arrange it for easier learning, identify similarities and differences with other knowledge we have, select a way to learn the information effectively, and evaluate the effectiveness of our learning process. If a student has problems doing any or all of these things, it is easy to see how all learning can be affected. We will look at three basic skill areas—reading, language arts, and math—and give some ideas about how difficulties in these areas can affect other types of learning as well.

Reading

Reading is the most difficult skill area for the majority of students with learning disabilities. Because reading is necessary for almost all learning, the student with a reading disability often experiences difficulty in many other subjects as well. In addition, the emphasis on oral reading in the early school years may make the child with a reading disability reluctant to read, so he or she may fall progressively further behind in reading skills. Teachers are often faced not only with the challenge of trying to teach a child *to* read but also with motivating the child to *try* to read. The term *dyslexia* is often associated with reading difficulties in students with learning disabilities. Although this term was initially used

Reading is the most difficult skill area for most students with learning disabilities.

Assistive technology makes writing more enjoyable for students who struggle with difficulties in handwriting or spelling. (Kindra Clineff / The Picture Cube, Inc.)

many years ago to refer to a severe reading disability caused by neurological impairment, the word is often used today, by some educators, to refer to more general reading problems of students with learning disabilities (Wallace & McLoughlin, 1988).

If you think about everything you do when you read, you realize that it is a very complex process. To examine the potential effects of learning disabilities on reading, let's look at two of the major skills involved in the reading process: word analysis (identifying a word) and comprehension (understanding what is read).

■ **Word Analysis** In order to identify written words, we use a number of different skills. Some of the most important **word-analysis** skills include the ability to associate sounds with the various letters and letter combinations used to write them (phonic analysis), to immediately recognize and remember words (sight-word reading), and to use the surrounding text to help figure out a specific word (context clues). These skills rely heavily on perception, selective attention, memory, and metacognitive skills. Thus, word analysis is dependent almost entirely on the cognitive skills that are most problematic for individuals with learning disabilities.

In order to use phonic analysis, for example, the student must be able to remember all of the different associations between letters and sounds, learn the rules that govern different letter and sound patterns, remember the many exceptions to each rule, and blend sounds together. This process is the basic stumbling block to reading for most students who have difficulty reading. The extensive and rapid presentation of memory requirements simply overloads children with learning disabilities, especially those who have difficulty identifying and discriminating specific sounds and letters.

Without basic phonics skills, students are very limited in the number of words they can read. This is particularly true given that many of these same skills are required in other word-analysis strategies, such as reading sight words. The most frequently recommended approaches to teaching reading to students with learning disabilities, therefore, include a structured presentation of phonics skills and rules (Carnine, Silbert & Kameenui, 1990). These approaches are called *code-emphasis approaches.* Because the students cannot identify sound/letter associations and patterns on their own, it is necessary to present these associations in a very clear way and provide students with lots of opportunities to practice and remember them.

Many students with learning disabilities also run into obstacles when they try to use the sight-word approach to word analysis. Teachers often report spending an entire period working on a few sight words, only to find, the next day, that the child behaves as if he's never seen the word before. Learning most sight words, unless they are always in a specific context (such as the word *stop* on a stop sign), requires being able to identify and recall the aspects of the word that make it unique and to associate the correct sounds with the word. Children with learning disabilities may focus on only part of the characteristics of a letter or word, therefore increasing the probability of poor recall and confusion. In addition, active memory strategies are required for students to transfer words into their long-term memory, and we have seen that many students with learning disabilities do not use those strategies. There are many specific strategies for teaching sight words (see the accompanying box, "Teaching Word-Analysis Skills").

Teaching reading to students with learning disabilities involves a structured presentation of phonics skills and rules.

~ Teaching Word-Analysis Skills

Phonics
Use structured phonics programs that:

- Teach most common sounds first.
- Stress specific phonics rules and patterns.
- Expose the beginning reader only to words that contain sounds he or she has already learned.

Sight Words
During instruction:

- Require the student to focus on all important aspects of the word (all letters, not just the first and last ones).
- Have the student discriminate between the new word and frequently confused words (for example, if you are intro-

ducing the word *what* as a sight word, make sure the child can read the word when it is presented with words such as *that*, *which*, and *wait*).

- Help the student devise strategies for remembering a particular word.

Context Clues

- Control the reading level of materials used so that students are presented with few unfamiliar words.
- For beginning readers, present illustrations *after* the text selection has been read.
- Teach students to use context clues as a decoding strategy after they are adept at beginning phonics analysis.

Poor readers tend to use context clues as their major word-analysis strategy. Although context can be helpful when you come across one or two words that are difficult to decode, using context to figure out 50 or 60 percent of the words in a passage is ineffective. At the early elementary level, children may achieve some success with this method because of the many pictures in the story, and because they may hear the story read several times. Many students, therefore, develop patterns of guessing words. Of course, as stories become more complex, and students are required to read the words in other contexts, this strategy becomes useless. Yet, because students feel that their guessing method helps them read faster—more like other students—they continue to use it. This is the most common reading pattern we see in students with learning disabilities, and it is the most difficult to break. Some students try to guess their way through an entire story. Reading programs used for students with learning disabilities often try to prevent or eliminate this pattern by controlling the words students are expected to read so that only words the child knows how to decode are presented in stories and by eliminating pictures and other cues from initial reading passages. Once the child gains confidence in her ability to use other word-attack skills, and uses them effectively, then the use of context clues—which will become quite valuable when the student begins reading complex material—can be encouraged.

> Many students with learning disabilities depend heavily on context clues for guessing words.

■ **Reading Comprehension** Students with learning disabilities may experience difficulties in **reading comprehension** because they lack the skills required for understanding text and have poor word-analysis skills. The child who has difficulty reading words will have trouble understanding the gist of sentences and passages. It is important to adjust your expectations for comprehension if the child has difficulty in the actual reading of material. It is better to teach or assess reading comprehension skills on material the students can decode fluently or that is presented orally.

In addition to word-analysis skills, a number of other factors can affect a child's ability to comprehend text. Literal comprehension of material—the ability to identify specifically stated information—requires the ability to select important information from unimportant details, to organize or sequence this information, and to recall it. Again, you can see the need for cognitive skills that frequently pose problems for students with learning disabilities. The ability to select and categorize information is also necessary for organizational comprehension, which includes identifying main ideas.

For more advanced comprehension activities, such as interpreting text, evaluating actions in a story, predicting consequences, and relating text to personal experience, students with learning disabilities can experience difficulty because of the role-taking skills required in some of these tasks and a reluctance to go beyond what is specifically stated in the text. Being able to put yourself in another's place (Why was hitting Joe a poor choice? What would you do if that happened to you?) requires seeing the similarities and differences between yourself and the character. Some students with learning disabilities cannot put themselves in another person's shoes and see things from another perspective, and this can interfere with projective or evaluative types of comprehension activities.

Many difficulties in reading comprehension can also be traced to the lack of specific strategies used to help remember material or to self-check understanding (Malone & Mastropieri, 1992). If you are reading a book that is not particularly interesting, you may find, after you've read a few pages, that you haven't actually taken in anything you've read. If you are reading this book to prepare for a test, you may go back and reread the material, perhaps stopping every so often to paraphrase what you've read, rehearse the important points, or ask yourself questions to see if you really do understand it. All of these learning strategies, which are essentially memory and metacognitive skills, help you to comprehend the text, and they become increasingly important as reading material becomes denser and more complex. Because students with learning disabilities do not use these active strategies, good comprehension is unlikely.

Many teaching strategies that focus on reading comprehension emphasize the use of specific plans or behaviors for students to engage in to help them review material and check their comprehension periodically (Gajria & Salvia, 1992). Other techniques involve identifying and highlighting key information in the text. Usually the teacher will do this initially and then teach the student how to pull out the key information necessary for good comprehension. Similar techniques are used to help students at the secondary level identify important information from textbooks, which are frequently several grade levels above their reading level. By using specific comprehension strategies and the conventions of the text (headings, vocabulary words, questions in text) students can find and retrieve essential information.

Students need to develop strategies that will help them remember material and self-check their understanding of it.

Reading continues to be the biggest obstacle faced by most students with learning disabilities. Because of the specific difficulties experienced by these students, the type of reading instruction used is critical. Snider (1997) found that students with learning disabilities who received thirty to forty-five minutes of instruction in the vocabulary-controlled, code-emphasis reading programs Reading Mastery Fast Cycle (Englemann & Bruner, 1988) and Corrective Reading Decoding B1 (Englemann, Carnine & Johnson, 1988) acquired necessary decoding skills and transferred those skills to the material they read in their classrooms. Because more and more students with learning disabilities are served in general education classrooms, teachers must investigate ways to provide reading skill instruction, particularly for young children, in the classroom setting (see the accompanying box, "Suggestions for Teaching Reading Comprehension").

Predictions: Predictions can be based on pictures, headings, subtitles, or graphs. They can be used to activate students' prior knowledge before reading and to increase attention to sequencing, during reading, and they can be evaluated after reading to help summarize content.

Questions: Questions can be asked before reading to help students attend to important information, or students can be taught to transform subtitles or headings into questions to ask themselves as they read. Having students make up questions to ask each other after reading is a good alternative to the typical question-answer period and helps students develop study skills as well.

Advance organizers or outlines: You can prepare an advance organizer on the text to help focus students' atten-

tion on key material in the text. Students can review the organizer before reading and take notes on it while reading. When it is completed, the students have a study sheet to review.

Self-monitoring or self-evaluation: When students begin reading longer text selections, they can learn to stop periodically and paraphrase the text or check their understanding. This can be done using an auditory self-monitoring tape or by randomly placing stickers or other markers throughout the text. When the student reaches the sticker, it is time to think about what he or she just read.

Language Arts

In this section, we will look at three general areas: spelling, spoken language, and written language. Because of the close ties of some of these skills to reading ability, they tend to be areas of great difficulty for many students with learning disabilities.

■ **Spelling** Spelling requires all of the essential skills used in the word-analysis strategies of phonics and sight-word reading. The student must either know specific sound and letter relationships or be able to memorize words. Spelling, for some students, may be even more difficult than reading because there are no context cues and because spelling requires recall rather than the simpler recognition skills used in reading. The difficulty students with learning disabilities have in learning and applying rules of phonics, visualizing the word correctly, and evaluating spellings results in frequent misspellings, even as they become more adept at reading. It is not uncommon to find the same word spelled five or six different ways on the same paper regardless of whether the student is in the fifth grade or in college (for example, *ther, there, thare,* and *theyre* for *their*).

This pattern illustrates the procedure used by many students with learning disabilities when spelling a word: each word is spelled as if it were being approached for the first time, without reference to an image of the word held in memory or the consistent use of a most probable spelling. The majority of errors are phonetically acceptable, meaning that a reader can sound them out to read the word (Hom, O'Donnell & Leicht, 1988). Other common errors include errors made in the middle of the word (vowel combinations are the most variable and confusing), scrambled words, and, in younger children, carryover from just-learned letter combinations. An example of carryover would be a child who has been spelling words such as *cake* and *late* correctly until she has a spelling lesson that contains the words *rain* and *pain.* The next time the child writes *cake* she may spell it *caik,* and *rain* may sometimes turn into *rane.* When a number of spelling patterns are presented to a child at one time, or if she doesn't have

It is best to combine spelling lessons with reading lessons.

enough time to practice and recall individual patterns, the likelihood of confusion increases.

Many students with learning disabilities are in spelling programs that contain many words they cannot yet read. When this occurs, the students cannot be expected to succeed. If at all possible, it is best to combine spelling lessons with reading lessons. Use the sounds and words involved in reading as the sounds and words worked on in spelling lessons. This will increase the probability that students will learn to spell with more confidence, because they will have the necessary prior knowledge to apply to spelling, and because of the repeated opportunities to practice sounds and words. For students of all ages, learning to evaluate spellings and developing a consistent mental representation of the word are critical skills. Recommended spelling strategies include teaching students to visualize the whole word while studying. Common spelling activities used by many classroom teachers, such as writing the words five times each, are useless if the student is copying the word one letter at a time. If students are encouraged to write the word, spell the word out loud, visualize the word, spell the word aloud without looking at it, check the word's spelling, write the word without looking, and then compare their word to the original, the task will help develop needed memory and metacognitive skills.

Spoken Language Many students with learning disabilities experience difficulties in spoken or oral language, which can affect academic as well as social performance. These may include problems identifying and using appropriate speech sounds, using appropriate words and understanding word meanings, using and understanding various sentence structures, and using appropriate grammar and language conventions. Other problem areas include understanding underlying meanings, such as irony or figurative language, and adjusting language for different uses and purposes, called **pragmatic language skills** (Gibbs & Cooper, 1989; Henley, Ramsey & Algozzine, 1993).

Although you may not think of oral language as an academic skill, the effects of language difficulties on academic as well as social performance can be significant. For example, a student who has difficulty identifying and discriminating speech sounds may have difficulty reading and spelling. Many other difficulties with oral language may translate into problems understanding not only spoken directions or lectures but written language as well. A student who can only use or understand simple sentences (for example, "The dog licked the cat") will interpret the information incorrectly if given a more complex sentence ("The cat was licked by the dog"). Instead of realizing that these two sentences mean the same thing, the child may impose the simple subject-verb-object order on the second sentence and be convinced that the cat licked the dog.

Another area of spoken language that has an impact on academic performance is pragmatic language, or the ability to use language effectively in different settings and for different purposes. This includes **functional flexibility,** or the ability to move easily from one form of language to another to accommodate various settings or audiences (Simon, 1991). Functional flexibility requires the individual to identify the type of language appropriate to the setting, to anticipate the needs of the audience, and then to adjust language structure, content, and vocabulary to meet these needs. It also requires an understanding that different types of language are used for different purposes. Individuals with learning disabilities may have difficulty with pragmatic language because they have difficulty attending to the cues of various settings—the expected tone or type of language used by others, for example. In addition, anticipating an audience's needs requires putting yourself in other people's positions and being aware of, for example, their prior knowledge about a subject, or their desire for clarity or brevity when asking for directions or making a request. Students with learning disabilities may not monitor their effectiveness in communicating and, therefore, may not adjust their language to the setting.

It is important to provide students with many models of different language structures; however, it also is important to understand that using and interpreting oral language require instruction. Interpreting oral language correctly involves reading nonverbal cues, such as raised eyebrows or posture, and understanding vocal cues, such as inflection and emphasis. The sentence "Just turn in your paper whenever you feel like it" can mean two entirely different things, depending on the emphasis and inflection used. Because the identification and use of these conventions requires good perceptive and selective attention skills, many students with learning disabilities miss them.

Interpreting oral language correctly involves reading nonverbal cues, which can be difficult for students with learning disabilities.

■ **Written Language** Students with learning disabilities often experience great difficulty in written language or composition. Specific problems include inadequate planning, structure, and organization; immature or limited sentence structure; limited and repetitive vocabulary; limited consideration of audience; unnecessary or unrelated information or details; and errors in spelling, punctuation, grammar, and handwriting (Carnine, 1991; Mercer & Mercer, 1993a; Newcomer & Barenbaum, 1991). Students with learning disabilities are also found to be lacking in motivation and in the monitoring and evaluation skills often considered necessary for good writing (Newcomer & Barenbaum, 1991). When we look at the skills necessary for good writing and consider the characteristics of students with learning disabilities, the types of difficulties we have identified are not surprising.

Students with learning disabilities may have difficulty planning, organizing, and writing their papers.

Some students who are adept in oral language may show restricted syntax and vocabulary in written language. If a student has difficulty reading and spelling and is fearful of making errors, these written language problems may reflect fear of failure rather than actual limitations in language ability. It is important to encourage these students to work on transferring oral to written language, to have plenty of opportunities to write without fear of failing, and to have access to word or vocabulary banks if necessary, in order to encourage and broaden written language skills.

For most students with learning disabilities, the educational emphasis for written language is on the development and use of organizational and metacognitive skills. From the first paragraph a child writes to a major paper written by a college student, the ability to organize and sequence thoughts; present a logical, cohesive text; and review and edit writing are critical. Word processors and spell-check programs are used often by students with learning disabilities to address mechanical and handwriting problems, but the words chosen and the structure of the writing still must come from the students themselves.

Because many students with learning disabilities approach writing tasks without a plan, instructional techniques often include providing students with a series of steps to follow as guidelines for writing. Some techniques may be quite specific; for example, students may be taught to develop a graphic representation of their thoughts and ideas to assist them in organization before they begin writing. One example is an activity called *webbing*. In this activity, students write their main topic in the middle of their paper—for example, cats. They then draw lines from the main topic that represent different subtopics (what cats look like, what they like to eat, and how they move). Under each subtopic, the student writes notes or words related directly to it (for example, soft, furry, long or short hair, different colors). Now the student can use this web to help write the paper: Each subtopic can represent a paragraph and only related information will be included in the text (see Figure 5.1). Other techniques may be more general, so that they can be used in a variety of writing contexts, and include steps for planning, checking, and revising writing. As we will see when we discuss strategy instruction, a number of commercial strategies have been developed specifically to address the organizational skills of students with learning disabilities.

Mathematics

Although, in general, difficulties in math do not receive the same attention as problems in reading and language arts, students with learning disabilities often experience a number of problems in this area. Specific problem areas include difficulty understanding size and spatial relationships and concepts related to direction, place value, decimals, fractions, and time and difficulty remembering math facts (Lerner, 1993; McLeod & Armstrong, 1982; Wallace & McLoughlin, 1988). Remembering and correctly applying the steps to mathematical algorithms (for example, how to divide) and reading and solving word problems are significant problem areas (Cawley et al., 1996; Harris, Miller & Mercer, 1995). Students with learning disabilities, like all students, may also make simple computational errors due to inattention to the operation sign, incorrect alignment of problems, omission of steps in the algorithm, or not checking or reviewing work.

Many students with learning disabilities approach math skills as a series of unrelated memory tasks (Engelmann, Carnine & Steely, 1991). Because of the

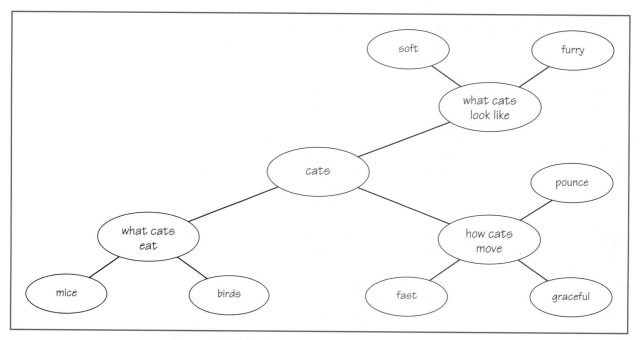

Figure 5.1 Webbing

Hands-on learning experiences are important and enjoyable additions to arithmetic instruction.
(Jill Fineberg/Photo Researchers, Inc.)

rapid presentation of skills in most math curricula, and the early and extensive memory requirements, students who experience difficulty conceptualizing the process or learning the facts just try to get through whatever skill is being worked on at the time. We are not suggesting that the rate of presentation results in the disability, only that if sufficient and appropriate instruction is not provided, these students probably will not absorb the material they need on their own.

Let's look at an elementary classroom for a typical example of a problem a student with learning disabilities might have in math. The teacher, Mr. Hernandez, has been teaching the students single-digit subtraction for two weeks. Jimmy, the little boy with a learning disability, knows what they are doing—they are putting out markers for the big number and then taking away the same number of markers as the smaller number. Mr. Hernandez gives a test, and Jimmy completes only five of the twenty problems, but he gets them correct. Now Mr. Hernandez decides it's time for review, and he gives the students a worksheet with addition and subtraction facts on it. What do you think Jimmy does with all of his problems? He puts out markers for the big numbers and takes away the same number of markers as the smaller numbers. Perhaps Jimmy didn't attend to the signs. Mr. Hernandez points out to Jimmy that some of the signs are addition signs. Jimmy looks at him in confusion. Addition? What is that?

Many students, like Jimmy, are just following the pattern of the week. It is important to review and assess constantly concepts and strategies for students with learning disabilities. It is likely that unless Mr. Hernandez reviews, has Jimmy practice, and encourages him to discriminate between operations, subtraction will become as vague a concept to Jimmy as addition is now. Even more important, teachers must actually instruct children in the concept behind the procedure they are doing. Without this connecting knowledge, math will become increasingly difficult because students will not be able to build on previous skills.

When teaching students with learning disabilities, teachers should always keep in mind the learning characteristics of their students and try to tailor instruction accordingly. Instruction in word problems, for example, should begin early with very simple problems; key words or information should be highlighted to help students identify what they need to solve the problem. Later, students can be taught to identify this information themselves. Consider also the importance of certain memory tasks. Students may be able to remember some math facts and may learn all of them if they are not forced into a time frame—most students with learning disabilities aren't going to be able to learn the first three multiplication tables overnight.

Current recommendations for instruction in mathematics include beginning your teaching, even of complex concepts, at the concrete level (materials that can be held and moved) and then gradually moving to the semiconcrete level (pictures or graphics), and finally to the abstract level (numbers only) (Harris, Miller & Mercer, 1995; Mercer & Mercer, 1993b). For instruction in algorithms, word problems, and complex functions, the use of step-by-step written plans for students to follow in order to assist them in organization, memory, and evaluation skills proves very helpful (Mercer & Miller, 1992; Miller & Mercer, 1991).

> It is important to review and assess math concepts and strategies constantly so that students can build on previous skills.

Learning Disabilities and Social and Emotional Development

> Students with learning disabilities may have difficulty acquiring and interpreting social behaviors.

Although you may typically think of students with learning disabilities as individuals who experience difficulty in academic tasks, it is important to realize that most social behaviors also involve learning. The characteristics that interfere with a student's acquisition of reading or writing skills can also interfere with his or her ability to acquire or interpret social behaviors (Carlson, 1987). Often these problems are related to difficulties in correctly interpreting or responding to social situations and in reading social cues, including nonverbal cues, and to acting impulsively without identifying the consequences of behavior or recognizing the feelings and concerns of others (Bryan, 1991; Carlson, 1987; Schumaker & Hazel, 1984). The individual who has difficulty identifying important information in academic work may also experience difficulty identifying important information in social situations. If a student has problems monitoring and evaluating his performance in spelling, he may also experience problems evaluating and adjusting his behavior on a date, in the classroom, or in the library.

Certainly, not *all* students with learning disabilities have problems with social behavior; however, many students with learning disabilities have problems relating to others and behaving acceptably at school. It is important to note that although some difficulties in social behavior may be related to learning characteristics, still others may be tied more directly to academic failure. The 16-year-old reading on the second-grade level may search for attention, acceptance, and control by engaging in inappropriate or even antisocial behavior. The search for a peer group, susceptibility to peer pressure, and problems anticipating consequences of actions may all contribute to the fact that adolescents with learning disabilities are often considered at risk for juvenile delinquency (Larson & Gerber, 1987).

The consequences of difficulty in academic work also include the possibility of emotional distress. The area of most concern is the self-esteem of students with learning disabilities. Research suggests that students with learning disabilities may not perceive themselves in a positive way—their self-esteem is lower that those of children without disabilities (Bryan, 1991; Vaughn, 1991). Rosenthal (1992) asserts that young adults and late adolescents with learning disabilities may have a poor sense of self as a result of the many pressures that arise from decisions related to education, career, and family. Again, not all students with learning disabilities have low self-esteem, but it certainly is understandable that an individual who must confront his or her disability on a daily basis would have difficulty feeling good about himself or herself, particularly in the area of personal competence.

Think for a moment about something you do not do well. Perhaps it is singing. If you really don't sing well, you may just avoid singing in public and it presents no real problem for you. What if, however, you had to sing every day, in front of all your friends? Not only do you have to sing in front of them, but you will receive a grade in singing. You've really tried, but you just can't carry a tune. Soon, all of your friends are singing Mozart and you are still trying to get the scales right. Can you imagine how you would behave or feel in that situation? Perhaps you would begin to look for ways to avoid singing (lots of sore throats) or skip school altogether. You also might think of ways to avoid interacting with your friends, since you are so obviously different, and try to find other, nonsinging friends. Or, maybe, you would say you just didn't care—you never really wanted to sing anyway.

If we substitute reading or math for singing in the preceding story, you may understand how students with learning disabilities often feel. As a teacher, it may also help you recognize the need to identify and develop your students' strengths as well as work on remediating their skill deficits. It also may inspire you to think of ways to make school a positive experience for students, including ways to facilitate enjoyable and constructive interactions between the student or students with a learning disability and other students in the class. Seidel and Vaughn (1991) found that students with learning disabilities who had dropped out of school reported strong feelings of social alienation and an absence of attachment to either teachers or classmates. By demonstrating positive attitudes and encouraging positive interaction in the classroom, teachers may not only be helping students with learning disabilities feel better about themselves, they may be helping to keep them in school as well.

It is important to make school a positive experience for students with learning disabilities.

Effects on the Family

Most families do not realize that their child has a learning disability until he or she reaches school age and begins to fail at a school-related task. For these families, the major challenge may be finding the appropriate special education services for their child, and helping the child deal with any stigma associated with the label "learning disabled" or with placement in special education services.

Learning that their child has a learning disability can have a number of different effects on a family, including increased family stress and conflict (Ehrlich, 1983). With all children with disabilities, parents are often put in the position of making educational decisions based on very little information, and this can result in conflicts between parents, and between parents and the child. Extra time may now need to be devoted to tutoring, homework, or conferences, which may mean taking time away from other children in the family. Usually, competition exists between children in a family, and this natural interaction may be either exacerbated or extinguished when one sibling has a learning disability. The child without a disability may be anxious for attention and promote his skills as a way of obtaining it. Parents, on the other hand, may want to protect the child with the disability and forbid overt competition. Any unnatural structuring of normal sibling interaction may serve only to add to stress within the family.

Observing the difficulties that a student with learning disabilities may have in academic skills and in social relationships with others can be very painful for parents; they may tend to be overprotective of the child in order to try to save him or her from pain. Ideally, parents will help the child develop strategies to cope with rejection from peers, but doing so may tax the emotional strength of even the strongest parent. Parents of learning-disabled students can derive both practical suggestions and emotional support from belonging to groups that include other parents of children with similar problems.

In spite of the many challenges they face, some families are relieved to find there is a reason for their child's poor school performance—and that the reason is a learning disability. As we mentioned earlier in the chapter, the label *learning disability* is much more acceptable to parents than some of the other labels. Others, however, may be ashamed or deny the existence of a disability.

Support groups can help parents of children with learning disabilities by providing both suggestions and support.

Educational Issues and Teaching Strategies

How to assess and teach students with learning disabilities is a question that has been asked and debated for the past three decades. Many different philosophies can be found in the variety of educational programs for students with learning disabilities. In this section, we present assessment and teaching procedures that reflect what research has suggested to be best practice in the field.

Early Identification

Deciding if a child is at risk for learning disabilities is a difficult task.

By virtue of the definition, a learning disability does not exist until a student has experienced an academic problem in school. Typically, that happens in the early elementary years. Some preschool-aged children, though, seem more likely than others to develop learning disabilities at a later age; they are generally considered to be "at risk" for the development of school problems. Some of the factors that place a child at risk are medical in nature, such as low birthweight. Other factors are related to the child's parent or environment—for example, a mother who drinks during pregnancy. Remember, though, that no one of these factors is enough to qualify a child for special services; it is more likely that children who have a *cluster* of risk factors will be candidates for evaluation for special programming.

There are many problems for professionals in deciding whether or not a child is at risk for learning problems in school. Those of you who have young children or work with them will know that there is tremendous variation in the characteristics of 2-, 3-, and 4-year-olds. In any class of "normal" preschoolers there will be those who are talkative and articulate and those who are relatively silent, some who are daring and able climbers and runners and some who are hesitant and awkward with those skills. How different must a child be before we become concerned? There are no concrete answers to that question. Many of the relative "weaknesses" of these children will have disappeared by the time they reach elementary school.

Even when a cluster of risk factors can be identified in a child, it is often difficult to determine what the precise nature of the child's problem will be. Will the child have mental retardation, or will the profile change to the point where he or she will ultimately have learning disabilities or a language disorder? Or is the child's behavior or emotional status the primary problem? Sorting these issues out at later ages is difficult enough; at 2, 3, or 4, there are simply too many possibilities for error.

Another difficulty in determining whether a young child needs special services lies with the assessment process. It is possible that many of the assessment instruments used with young children have poor **predictive validity** (McLoughlin & Lewis, 1986). That simply means that these tests may not predict accurately whether or not a young child actually *will* have later problems in school. With poor predictive validity, there will be too many "false positives"—children who will be targeted as having potential learning problems who will not end up having them—and too many "false negatives"—children who actually *will* have problems who will not be identified.

It is also important to ask whether the benefits of early identification and intervention outweigh the possible liabilities. An early label, or even a nonlabeled special class placement, may have stigmatizing effects on a child and set up a "self-fulfilling prophecy" for the child in which teachers' expectations for performance are lowered (Lerner, 1989).

Because of these problems, there are few, if any, preschool programs specifically for children with suspected learning disabilities. The programs that do exist serve children who have been given the generic descriptor of developmental disabilities and those with a variety of problems. Most professionals believe strongly in the effectiveness of early intervention, and their beliefs are backed up by research findings (see Chapter 3). Their hope would be that children who are identified early and who participate in early intervention programs could avoid the need for special education by the time they reach elementary school.

Assessment for Teaching

There are two major purposes for assessment of students with learning disabilities. First, we assess in order to *identify* students who need special services and to determine the placement that best suits each child. Recall that we discussed this process and its implications in the Framework section that preceded Chapter 4. Next we assess in order to *plan* the student's instructional program—to answer the question "What do I teach?" Assessment can also help us evaluate the effectiveness of the program and the progress that the student is making; in fact, it can serve a variety of purposes.

first person

For any student with a learning disability, school often provides overwhelming challenges, which must be faced. The struggles come from both internal and external sources. The impacts of the disability vary and evolve, compounding the student's difficulty. Teachers, friends, and parents often add to the stress, in spite of their best intentions. Although as a student with a learning disability, I myself have experienced a great deal of pain and frustration, there are several survival techniques that help me cope. To be a student with a learning disability is to be a member of a minority, and as such, each of us should share our experiences so that others may develop strategies to help them through their struggles.

I believe one key idea is to find one's own definition of the dual identity within oneself as a learner and as a student. The learner is the one who makes an effort to be curious, involved, and motivated. The student is the one who determines how you cope in school. Not all knowledge is taught in school. It is the student identity that gets labeled as disabled. The "learning disability" should not be allowed to overwhelm one's desire to attain knowledge. The learner in you must prevent it.

Another piece of advice besides developing a personal definition is developing one's self-esteem, to learn to have no fear of oneself. I felt like there was something wrong with me before I found out I had a disability; when I finally was diagnosed, it took me years to believe that I was not stupid or limited. However I now understand that "to be categorized is, simply, to be enslaved," as Gore Vidal expressed. The label of learning disability should not be allowed to determine one's identity, character, or self-image, nor one's potential.

Support from friends who can be trusted is crucial. It is destructive to believe that if you have a learning disability and your friends do not, you are too different from them to talk about your problems. I know from experience that the only result is self-imposed isolation. Asking for support from friends with whom you are comfortable will help maintain your self-esteem. Everyone wants to feel normal, not different, not disabled. The challenge is to accept yourself as who you are and believe in your own self-definition. Although there may be differences on some levels, you may also find friendships with those with whom you have something else in common. I have come to trust and value those similarities.

Getting help or asking for support in the areas that present hurdles is essential. What is equally important is choosing carefully which voices or people have influence over you, your goals, your self-esteem, and your successes. Well-meaning or good-intentioned professionals or teachers can be just as hurtful to you as those who speak with prejudice and ignorance about learning disabilities. It is not a kindness to limit opportunities in education when a student experiences difficulty. As a member of a minority group that frequently cannot be detected from behavior or external clues, a student with a "hidden" learning disability ought to be able to acknowledge his or her vulnerability without being overpowered by negative and condescending opinions. No one should determine what you can and cannot do because he or she thinks that having a learning disability automatically makes you less capable. "The power to exceed is not the same as the desire to exceed" (T.P. Gore). A student with a learning disability can have just as much desire for success as a student without a disability.

But most of all, a student with a learning disability should always ask questions—of herself, teachers, evaluators, and tutors. The reason is that only when there is knowledge about your disability can there be the opportunity for self-advocacy. Being able to speak for yourself is crucial for getting the accommodations needed for your education and for full inclusion in the class by the teacher. The children's storybook character Winnie the Pooh said appropriately that "rivers know this. There is no hurry. We shall get there someday." The fact is that every student can learn in school, even with a learning disability; we all will get there someday.

Caitlin Norah Callahan

Source: Caitlin Norah Callahan, "Advice about being an LD student." Reprinted by permission. LD OnLine is a service of The Learning Disabilities Project at WETA, Washington, D.C., in association with The *Coordinated Campaign for Learning Disabilities*. School partners include The Lab School of Washington and Arlington (VA) Public Schools. © 1997 WETA.

■ **Formal Assessment** Formal assessment, as you learned in the Framework, involves the use of standardized tests, the results of which can be used to compare the student's performance with that of his or her same-age peers. Three tests commonly used at schools and diagnostic clinics are the Keymath Diagnostic Arithmetic Test, the Woodcock Reading Mastery Test—Revised, and the Peabody Individual Achievement Test—Revised (PIAT-R). These tests assess the student's performance in math, reading, and several basic skill areas, respectively, and provide scores that reveal grade level and standing relative to other students. The tests are examples of those used to document grade of academic performance for use in determining if a discrepancy exists between achievement and ability.

Although the information yielded by these tests may be useful in diagnostic contexts, it is not detailed or specific enough to provide a foundation for instructional planning (Guerin & Maier, 1983). For that purpose, many teachers rely on informal measures.

■ **Informal Assessment** Informal assessment refers to direct measures of student performance and student progress in academic or behavioral tasks. These measures are the tools used to help the teacher identify what needs to be taught and how it should best be presented (McLoughlin & Lewis, 1986).

There are many ways for a teacher to get information using informal assessment. Among them are *observations* of the student's work habits—for example, identifying the amount of time a child is able to pay attention to a task or activity. Observing how a child performs his work can be very helpful to the teacher because of the particular difficulties experienced by many students with learning disabilities. Observations can provide some information about why the child is unable to do well in certain tasks. For example, you might notice that a child works very rapidly on certain tasks and never reflects on or checks his work. You may notice that the child spends large amounts of time playing with the buttons on his shirt, or writing, erasing, and rewriting his words. This information may help you target specific areas for intervention.

Another use for observations is to help prepare students to move into regular classroom settings. Because classroom teachers may have specific behavioral or learning requirements, the special education teacher or another professional can conduct an informal observation of the regular classroom into which the child will be placed. By noting specific requirements, such as length of seatwork time, types of tests, and behavior rules and requirements, the special education teacher can prepare the student for his move in a more effective manner. If Les is used to sitting in his seat for a maximum of five minutes, and the classroom teacher usually has the students doing twenty minutes of seatwork at a time, it may be important to target longer in-seat behavior and increased sustained attention for instruction before Les makes the move. Figure 5.2 provides an example of an interview form used by a special education resource teacher to help her plan instruction for one of her students. Teachers can also use an observation form like this to target suggestions for the regular classroom teacher to use. Once differences between the classroom requirements and the abilities of the student have been identified, the special education teacher can suggest modifications to the classroom teacher to help the student gradually learn the behaviors necessary for successful classroom performance.

A teacher can also analyze a students' work for error patterns by using **informal inventories** of reading and mathematics skills and teacher-made tests based on the classroom curriculum (Lerner, 1993). Informal inventories consist

Using informal inventories, teachers observe how children approach classroom tasks.

ASSESSMENT OF MAINSTREAMED ENVIRONMENT
TEACHER INTERVIEW

Teacher Sara Walker

Class Science 6th Grade

How much time are students required to listen to lecture or general instruction?

Generally the first 10-15 minutes of class is lecture or instruction.

How much in-class reading is required? What is the nature of the reading material?

A textbook is not used. In class reading would consist of worksheets, dictionary, and encyclopedias (research materials). This is done daily for most of the class period—around 30 minutes.

What is the nature of classroom activities? (cooperative learning, independent work, discussion, pairs)

Mainly independent work and some discussion. Once a week there is a special speaker—students are required to take notes on speakers. Definitions or notes for science are often given during Lang. Arts period. Question: How much assistance do you give? Whatever is needed—I can meet with students at recess and before school.

How much homework is required and what is the nature of it?

At the beginning of the 4-week unit, a packet of assignments is given to students with a list of due dates. What is not completed in class should be completed for homework. Assignments are explained <u>all</u> on the first day of the 4 weeks. Assignments consist of wordfinds with unit vocab, research projects, essays or papers, labeling diagrams, answering questions. Students find answers from resources in room.

Do you assign projects or long-term assignments, and if so, how much structure or guidance is given?

(see above) In the beginning, teacher gives dates and explains expectations. Students are left on their own to complete them throughout the 4 weeks. (Some time is spent working in class.) On the day the assignment is done, students present them in class or teacher leads a discussion.

Do you give a final test at the end of the four-week unit?

No – grades are based on accuracy, punctuality, etc. of all assignments.

What are your behavioral expectations?

That students are responsible and can work independently. Students should turn in assignments on time. Students work on tasks during class and participate in discussion. Students can move freely about the room without disrupting others.

Figure 5.2 Assessment of Mainstreamed Environment: Teacher Interview
Source: Kim Phillips, "Assessment of Mainstreamed Environment" (Columbia, SC: Rosewood Elementary School, 1993) (unpublished materials). Used by permission of the author.

of a series of sequential passages or excerpts, on different grade levels, usually taken from several curricula (Wallace, Larsen & Elksnin, 1992). By using the informal inventory to assess the child's reading, writing, or math skills, the teacher can observe how the child approaches the task as well as the specific types of difficulties he or she is experiencing. For example, the teacher may note that a child misreads all words with a double vowel combination in the middle or never regroups when a zero is in the subtrahend. If teachers construct their own informal inventories, they can determine how well the child interacts with the specific curriculum in areas such as vocabulary, interest, and sentence structure.

Ysseldyke, Thurlow, Graden, Wesson, Algozzine, and Deno (1983) caution teachers that too much time is spent on assessment, collecting information of dubious validity and usefulness. Nonetheless, appropriate assessment is necessary for valid instruction. Although informal assessment methods for determining what to teach are subject to error, they at least provide the teacher with concrete information about where the gaps exist in each student's repertoire of skills and abilities. Assessment provides the groundwork for direct instruction of the skills and knowledge that the student is lacking.

Approaches and Strategies

Ideas about how to teach students with learning disabilities are usually based on a professional's beliefs, explicit or assumed, about causes of learning disabilities and characteristics of students with learning disabilities. Thus, a wide variety of approaches for teaching students with learning disabilities has been presented over the years. Many of these approaches have been based on a hypothesized cause of learning disabilities (for example, brain damage, diet) and influenced by the professional affiliation and orientation of the developer (for example, physician, language therapist, optometrist). In our section on instructional approaches, we will focus on the most current and often-used procedures for teaching students with learning disabilities. Realize, however, that the field virtually abounds with instructional approaches and techniques, many of which are here today and gone tomorrow.

We will look at two major instructional approaches to academic skills: direct instruction of specific skills and strategy training. These approaches are integrated to a certain extent and reflect a similar philosophy about how students with learning disabilities should be taught as well as what types of skills should be taught. We also will review some of the approaches used to teach specialized skill areas, such as social or study skills.

In direct instruction, specific academic skills are taught using proven techniques.

■ **Direct Instruction** The term **direct instruction** may be interpreted several ways; however, as a philosophy and approach to teaching students with learning disabilities, direct instruction commonly refers to (1) the identification and instruction of specific academic skills and (2) the use of teaching techniques that have been empirically demonstrated to be effective with students with learning difficulties. The identification and instruction of specific skills may seem to be a fairly obvious approach to teaching, but it represents a departure from some of the instructional procedures used in the past for students with learning disabilities, in which the emphasis was on training sensory-processing abilities, such as visual or auditory discrimination. The philosophy behind direct instruction is that any specific processing disabilities the child demonstrates can be managed through effective teaching procedures and that the most efficient use of instructional time is to focus on the academic skills in need of remediation (see the accompanying box, "Designing Direct Instruction Programs in Reading").

The teaching techniques commonly identified in the direct instruction approach address the organization and presentation of instruction. The approach is very teacher-directed and includes an initial presentation based on the teacher first *modeling* the skill or response, then providing guided practice (*leading*), and,

⚊ Designing Direct Instruction Programs in Reading

The following six steps may be used for designing direct instruction programs in reading:

1. Identify specific objectives based on importance of skills.

2. Whenever possible, develop strategies or plans for students to follow to accomplish specific objectives (such as a strategy for decoding specific types of words).

3. Develop teaching formats and procedures *before* instruction begins; present only one concept at a time during each lesson.

4. Select examples for instruction; the role of examples is critical in direct instruction. If a concept is being taught, examples are used to teach students the critical attributes of the concept (for example, what makes a sentence a sentence); if a skill or strategy is being taught, examples are used to teach when and how to use the skill and provide practice and demonstration of skill application.

5. Sequence skills carefully before instruction; when presented with a new skill, students must know needed preskills. Other sequencing guidelines are based on the importance of the skill and difficulty of the skill and on reducing the potential for confusion between the new skill and other skills.

6. Provide sufficient opportunities for skill practice and continually review previous learning.

Source: *Direct Instruction Reading,* Third Edition by Carnine/Silbert/Kameenui, Copyright © 1990. Adapted by permission of Prentice-Hall, Inc. Upper Saddle River, NJ.

finally, eliciting independent student responses (*testing*). This process is designed to provide students with positive examples of the response or strategy. Exposure to positive examples promotes the probability of correct responding and helps to eliminate the possibility of confusion related to poor directions or student misinterpretation of the task. The modeling and leading steps of the process are part of initial instruction and are eliminated as instruction in a specific skill progresses (Engelmann & Hanner, 1982).

Presentation Techniques for Direct Instruction The direct instruction approach includes a number of presentation techniques designed to maximize student attention and involvement in learning (Lewis, 1983). Some of these presentation techniques include:

1. *Small-group instruction* Recommendations include seating students in a small semicircle, facing the teacher.

2. *Using response signals* The teacher chooses a signal that indicates it is time to respond (this could be a slight tap on the board or table or a snap of the fingers). The signal allows the teacher to delay the students' responses for a few seconds to encourage time to think about or reflect on the response. This delay or pause is called *wait time*.

3. *Choral or unison responding* When using the model–lead–test format, the teacher can have the whole group answer together during guided practice and independent student response time. Individuals' responses would then follow unison responses. Unison responding helps to maintain students' attention, allows for more opportunities for practice, and provides numerous models of correct responding.

4. *Providing corrective feedback* During instruction, errors are corrected immediately by modeling and then retesting responses; students also are praised when making correct responses.

5. *Pacing* Lessons are presented at a fairly rapid pace—this helps to maintain students' attention and interest in the lesson (Carnine, Silbert & Kameenui, 1990; Engelmann & Carnine, 1982; Engelmann & Hanner, 1982).

Evidence from research studies supports the effectiveness of direct instruction. Right now, it appears to be the most effective means of teaching students with learning disabilities (Darch, 1990; Rosenshine & Stevens, 1986). Some of the commercial programs based on this approach include Corrective Reading: Decoding Strategies (Engelmann, Carnine & Johnson, 1988), Corrective Mathematics (Engelmann & Carnine, 1982), and Reading Mastery (Engelmann & Bruner, 1988). Figure 5.3 is an excerpt from Word Attack Basics, a direct instruction program (Engelmann, Carnine & Johnson, 1988). All of the commercial direct instruction programs contain specific scripted lessons for teachers and incorporate the teaching techniques just described. Other materials that contain direct instruction techniques include a variety of computer software and multimedia and videodisk programs. These programs use direct instruction to involve students in more active learning (Hayden, Gersten & Carnine, 1992).

■ **Strategy Instruction** A strategy can be defined as a set of responses that are organized to perform an activity or solve a problem (Swanson, 1993). Although the current knowledge base about the relationship between learning disabilities, strategy deficits, and strategy instruction consists of contributions from a number of psychological and educational theories and research, in this section we will focus primarily on the strategy approaches used most often by teachers of students with learning disabilities. In addition to academic skills instruction, we will see that strategies are also used to teach specialized skills, adaptive skills, and life skills.

A **strategy instruction** approach to teaching students with learning disabilities involves first breaking down the skills involved in a task or problem—usually a procedure such as writing a paper—into a set of sequential steps. The steps are prepared so that the student may read or, later, memorize them in order to perform the skill correctly. Some strategies are developed so that the first letters of all the steps form an acronym to help students remember the purpose of the strategy and the steps involved (see the accompanying box, "Steps for Notetaking"). Many strategies also include decision-making or evaluative components designed to assist students in the use of metacognitive skills (Deshler, Warner, Schumaker & Alley, 1983).

Strategy training involves more than just the presentation of steps, however. Careful assessment and direct instruction, including sufficient opportunities to practice the strategy, are considered essential in most strategy instruction. Students should see how to use the strategy, practice, and receive feedback before attempting to use it on their own. Deshler et al. (1983) suggest that it is very important for students to be interested in learning the strategy. Consequently, instruction often begins by establishing a need for the strategy and getting a commitment from students to learn.

Strategies have been developed to address the needs of students with learning disabilities in a wide range of areas. Test-taking skills, study skills, reading comprehension, written composition, anger control, and math problem solving are all possible target areas for strategies. Some research suggests that the use of strategy instruction can be an important learning tool for students with learning disabilities. For example, elementary and secondary students with learning disabilities are found to write more reflective, complex, and well-written essays

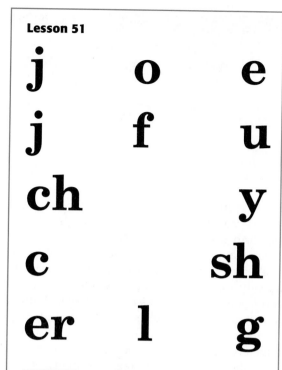

Lesson 51

j	**o**	**e**
j	**f**	**u**
ch		**y**
c		**sh**
er	**l**	**g**

EXERCISE 1: Sound Introduction

1. Point to **j. This letter makes the sound j. What sound?** Touch. j.

2. Point to **o. One sound you learned for this letter is the same as the letter name. Everybody, what's that sound?** Touch. ōōō. **Yes, ōōō. What's the other sound?** Touch. ŏŏŏ. **Yes, ŏŏŏ.**

3. Point to **e. One sound you learned for this letter is the same as the letter name. Everybody, what's that sound?** Touch. ēēē. **Yes, ēēē. What's the other sound?** Touch ĕĕĕ. **Yes, ĕĕĕ.**

4. Point to **j. What sound?** Touch. j. **Yes, j.**

5. Repeat step 4 for **f, u, ch, y, c, sh, er, l, g.**

Individual Test

Call on two or three students. Touch under each sound. Each student says all the sounds.

Figure 5.3 Word Attack Basics

Source: From S. Engelmann, L. Carnine, and G. Johnson, *Word-Attack Basics: Decoding A* p. 225, 251. Copyright © 1978. Reprinted by permission of the McGraw-Hill Companies, Inc.

～ Steps for Notetaking

Step 1 **N**ame the main point you've read
Step 2 **O**pen your learning journal
Step 3 **T**ake down the main point in the journal
Step 4 **E**xtend the main point with your own thoughts

Source: J.B. Schumaker and J. Sheldon, *The Sentence-Writing Strategy Instructor's Manual* (Lawrence: University of Kansas, 1985), p. 150.

Strategy instruction teaches specific skills by organizing steps, providing prompts, and focusing on metacognitive skills.

when using writing strategies (De La Paz & Graham, 1997; Graham, MacArthur, Schwartz & Page-Voth, 1992; Hallenbeck, 1996). Learning strategies have even been integrated successfully with some computer software to assist in the decision-making and problem-solving skills of older students with reading disabilities (Hollingsworth & Woodward, 1993).

Given what you have read about the learning characteristics of students with learning disabilities, you may be able to see why the strategy instruction approach is intuitively appealing to educators. It teaches specific skills in a manner that controls for potential problems in a student's ability to identify important information or steps, organizes the steps for the student, provides a continual prompt for remembering, breaks the task into its component parts, and often focuses on metacognitive skills. In addition, we know that many students with learning disabilities do not use strategies or plans when approaching academic tasks (Stone & Conca, 1993; Torgesen & Greenstein, 1982). An important question, however, is whether or not students with disabilities can learn and apply strategies in general education classrooms. Concerns about the students' abilities to generalize learning from one classroom to the next and the general education teachers' willingness to devote time to teaching learning strategies suggest the need for continued research on effective implementation of strategy instruction in general education classrooms (Scanlon, Deshler & Schumaker, 1996).

Although teachers often develop their own strategies, a number of commercially developed strategies and curricula based on strategies are available. One of the most well-known curricula designed for students with learning disabilities is the Learning Strategies Curriculum, which was developed at the University of Kansas Institute for Research in Learning Disabilities. This curriculum, which continues to expand, contains elaborate strategies and comprehensive procedures for teaching students ways to acquire information through skills such as paraphrasing, ways to store information through skills such as listening and notetaking, and ways to demonstrate knowledge through skills such as writing paragraphs and taking tests (Schumaker & Lyerla, 1991). Each component of the Learning Strategies Curriculum contains a sequence of steps for learners to follow and practice so they can perform the tasks. Teachers are provided with a series of specific guidelines for teaching students how to perform these strategies. As we usually see with strategy instruction, students are taught not only specific behaviors but also how to evaluate and monitor their performance.

■ **Special Skills Instruction** Many students with learning disabilities, especially older ones, may receive instruction in specialized skills such as study skills or social skills. Instruction in these skills may be the only type of service required by some students with learning disabilities; for others it may be one component of a more comprehensive set of support services. Sometimes special skills instruction is incorporated into the regular classroom curriculum; other times, these skills are taught in special education settings—for example, in a resource class. This section gives an overview of instructional approaches to teaching study and social skills.

Study Skills As we have seen throughout this chapter, the difficulties experienced by many students with learning disabilities revolve around the ability to receive, process, and express information effectively. Study skills instruction addresses these areas as they relate directly to classroom activities. The purpose of teaching study skills is to give the student a set of tools for performing required classroom activities, not to teach the content of a specific course. Because of the need for students to apply these skills in high school and college coursework, study skills instruction is increasingly considered a necessary component of the educational program for students with learning disabilities at both secondary and postsecondary levels (Ellis, Sabornie & Marshall, 1989; Smith & Dowdy, 1989).

Study skills instruction for students with learning disabilities might include teaching techniques for reading and remembering material in content-area texts, taking and reviewing notes, taking essay or multiple-choice tests, and preparing reports or projects. Students learn and practice these skills on materials from a variety of content areas. Study skills are frequently taught through the use of strategy training. The strategies are usually general enough so that they can be applied to many different types of tasks and content areas. For example, a strategy taught for taking an essay exam should work in any type of essay exam (English, history, science, or psychology). Other instructional techniques include teaching students to use graphic aids, such as semantic mapping; to apply time management and general organization aids to study behavior; to use structure or content outlines for taking notes; and to use alternative tools, such as tape recorders and computers, to assist them (Smith, Finn & Dowdy, 1993).

Study skills instruction provides practice on different types of work so that students can use the skills in many classes.

As you learned in the previous section, curricula such as the Learning Strategies Curriculum include strategies for teaching study skills. Other curricula, designed specifically to teach study skills, are currently available, such as Independent Strategies for Efficient Study (Rooney, 1988) and Future Success: Strategies for Success (McCandrew & Warner, 1991). Of course, a commercial curriculum is not necessary to teach study skills. If students are receiving a special course or series of classes in study skills, however, it is definitely helpful for the teacher to have an organized plan of instruction. Many teachers of students with learning disabilities develop original study skills curricula by drawing on existing programs and research and then adapting and applying those objectives and instructional techniques to the specific needs of their students. One of the most important goals of study skills instruction, regardless of the specific technique being taught, is to provide extensive practice on different types of work and to prompt the students to use the skills in other classes (Smith, Finn & Dowdy, 1993). These activities help to ensure that students will actually use the skills to do their coursework, which, of course, is the purpose of study skills instruction.

■ **Social Skills** As we've seen, some students with learning disabilities experience difficulties in emotional and social adjustment. Educators are concerned about the effects of these difficulties on the behavior and adjustment of young adults with learning disabilities.

Normal variation makes it hard to tell which children will develop learning disabilities. (Tom Prettyman/ PhotoEdit)

Although differences in the social behavior and social skills of students with learning disabilities have been documented over the years, instruction or training in social skills is often neglected. It is hard enough to find the time needed in a school day to provide all of the academic instruction, and it may be difficult to justify teaching social skills in lieu of reading or biology. In addition to finding time for instruction, another barrier to social skills instruction is the equivocal empirical support for its effectiveness. Recent reviews of social skills training programs suggest that few programs have resulted in any positive change in students' social performance or social acceptance (McIntosh, Vaughn & Zaragoza, 1991). Although students with learning disabilities certainly have been taught some skills, such as maintaining eye contact when talking to someone or using statements to help them resist peer pressure, the skill learning often has limited effects on a student's self-perception or others' perceptions of him or her. Because of the perceived need to teach social skills to students with learning disabilities, however, research continues in two major areas: what skills should be taught and how to teach the skills so students will generalize them to real-life situations.

Many commercial curricula include or focus on social skills. It is important, however, for teachers to observe the student and his surroundings carefully before selecting skills for instruction. Skills necessary for success in a certain peer group or work setting may not be identified in a certain curriculum. For example, certain terms, forms of address, postures, and verbal skills will differ across

Teachers must tailor the social skills curriculum to their students' particular environment.

～ Social Skills and Their Components

Social Skill	Component Skills	Social Skill	Component Skills
Conversation skills	Joining a conversation	Self-help skills	Good grooming (clean, neat)
	Interrupting a conversation		Good dressing (wearing clothes that fit)
	Starting a conversation		Good table manners
	Maintaining a conversation		Good eating behaviors
	Ending a conversation		
	Use of appropriate tone of voice	Classroom task-related behaviors	On-task behavior
	Use of appropriate distance and eye contact		Attending to tasks
			Completing tasks
Assertiveness skills	Asking for clarifications		Following directions
	Making requests		Trying your best
	Denying requests	Self-related behaviors	Giving positive feedback to self
	Negotiating requests		Expressing feelings
	Exhibiting politeness		Accepting negative feedback
"Play" interaction skills (e.g., making friends)	Sharing with others		Accepting consequences
	Inviting others to play	Job interview skills	Being prepared (dress, attitude, etc.)
	Encouraging others		
	Praising others		Being attentive
Problem-solving and coping skills	Staying calm and relaxed		Listening skills
	Listing possible solutions		Asking for clarification
	Choosing the best solution		Thinking prior to speaking
	Taking responsibility for self		
	Handling name calling and teasing		
	Staying out of trouble		

Source: M.A. Mastropieri and T.E. Scruggs, *Effective Instruction for Special Education* (Boston: MIT Press, 1987), p. 319. Copyright © 1987. Used by permission of PRO-ED, Austin, TX.

regions, ages, and settings. If these particular skills are not identified and incorporated into the curriculum, the program may not be as successful as anticipated. It is helpful to conduct informal observations that allow a comparison to be made between the skills required in the target setting and the skills displayed by the students. The differences can then be identified and additional skills or adaptations integrated into the curriculum selected. The accompanying box, "Social Skills and Their Components," contains a list of possible social skills for instruction.

Social skills may be taught in a separate class, like you would teach history or math, or integrated into the regular curriculum as needed. For example, a teacher may notice that Antonio is always standing by the fence during recess and decide that he might benefit from learning to play with other children. Another teacher might learn through experience that Sheila becomes very sullen and noncompliant whenever she receives any negative feedback or correction. The teacher may decide to teach Sheila some alternative ways to deal with criticism.

Generally, social skills programs involving multiple aspects of peer and adult interaction are taught in the classroom setting. However, social skills are difficult to transfer or generalize to other settings, and there is concern that the child who learns how to take turns and respond to questions in the classroom

Social skills instruction is difficult to transfer to other settings.

will not perform those behaviors in other classes or in the home and community. Nonetheless, Clement-Heist, Siegel, and Gaylord-Ross (1992) found that teaching job-related social skills in the classroom environment (for example, conversation skills, giving instructions) did result in behavior change in the actual work setting; even more change was noted when students were given additional instruction on the work site. The results of this study support the importance of teaching in the actual setting, yet also provide evidence that change can be achieved when community-based instruction is not possible. The social skills program, as do many others, includes a "homework" component that encourages students to practice the skills in real situations or settings. Most homework activities involve a recording sheet for students to identify when and how they use the skill.

Effective social skills training programs have a number of components in common, including small-group or individual instruction, long-term training programs, and procedures that show students how to guide, monitor, or evaluate their own behavior (McIntosh, Vaughn & Zaragoza, 1991). A number of social skills training programs are available commercially. One respected curriculum is the Walker Social Skills Curriculum: The ACCESS Program (Walker, Todis, Holmes & Horton, 1988). The procedures used in this curriculum to teach social skills related to peers, adults, and self are based on principles of direct instruction and include training in a general learning strategy. This program, as do many others, also includes extensive role-playing opportunities, feedback sessions, and self-evaluation or assessment activities. As you can see, social skills are taught essentially the same way as academic skills: students are taught the skills directly; when appropriate, they learn a problem-solving or learning strategy; and numerous opportunities are provided for them to practice and evaluate their performance.

Adapting Classroom Materials

One of the best ways for teachers to address the needs of students with learning disabilities is to adapt instruction and materials. Although the way a textbook or worksheet looks may seem relatively inconsequential, students with learning disabilities face many unnecessary obstacles because of the way material is presented—in terms of both content and format. Adaptation of materials may entail something as simple as redoing a skill sheet or as complex as restructuring a curriculum. An understanding of the basic approaches to learning by students with learning disabilities is necessary, as are time, motivation, and a knowledge of course content. As we look at some basic guidelines, remember that you can make a number of different adaptations. If you keep in mind that students with learning disabilities often have difficulty perceiving, attending to, and organizing important information, you can go a long way in identifying what adaptations are needed. Couple this knowledge with the basic concepts of direct instruction discussed earlier, and you will be able to teach students with learning disabilities in a more effective manner. Our focus in this section is mainly on adapting written materials typically used in regular class instruction, which are not developed with students with learning disabilities in mind. We will look at organizing lessons from textbooks, preparations for lecture and reading activities in content areas, and general ideas for worksheet and test construction.

■ **Modifications for Lesson Planning** Many textbooks include teachers' manuals to assist in the presentation of instruction. Too often, however, the lessons

～ Strategies for Lesson Planning

1. *Identify all of the new skills being taught in the lesson.* More than one is too many. Sequence the skills according to the hierarchy of content, and choose the first one in the sequence.

2. *Identify the preskills the student needs.* If the text does not provide a review of the preskills, prepare one.

3. *Review the introduction and actual teaching part of the lesson.* A surprising number of textbooks include very little instruction.

   - Is the skill or concept clearly identified and described at the begining of the lesson? In most cases, you should avoid open-ended questions at the beginning of the lesson (for example, "Who thinks they know what a pronoun is?"). You are likely to get incorrect answers and guesses that will create confusion.

   - Are there plenty of positive examples of the skill or concept being taught? Are there negative or incorrect examples that require the student to discriminate and actually identify the fundamental parts of the skill? If not, prepare additional examples in advance. Try to begin all instruction with positive or correct examples—too many texts begin with examples of errors. The first example students see is the one they will remember!

   - Think of a rule or cue to help the student learn the skill more efficiently.

4. *Look at the opportunities for practice presented in the manual and student text.*

   - Is there a lot of guided practice and opportunity for response before the student has to work alone? Prac-

tice with the teacher gives the student a chance to learn the skill and allows the teacher to correct any errors right away. You may have to develop some practice examples.

5. *Examine application exercises or "written practice" activities.*

   - Do the independent activities reflect the skill that was taught? Sometimes the independent activities require students to perform tasks that were not done during oral practice. Do not assume the student will know how to do this task, just because he or she could do the oral practice tasks. For example, if a language arts lesson revolves around identifying the parts of a sentence, the student should be expected only to identify the parts of a sentence, not write a complete sentence.

   - Are the language and reading requirements appropriate for your student? If the purpose of the activity is to assess the acquisition of a new skill, make sure other skills aren't interfering. You can always rewrite a practice sentence or substitute an alternative example.

   - Is the right amount of independent work provided? Is there enough practice to show you the student has mastered the skill, but not so much that the amount is overwhelming? No one needs to find the least common denominator for a hundred pairs of fractions to show that she knows how to do it.

presented in the manuals are brief and potentially confusing because of the amount and structure of the content. These lessons may need to be modified by you before presentation to the class.

The accompanying box, "Strategies for Lesson Planning," offers specific suggestions for modifying your lessons for students with learning disabilities. Keep them in mind as you review manuals before planning your lessons.

Lesson plans from a teacher's manual often have to be modified.

■ **Modifications for Lectures and Reading Assignments** In many content courses, particularly at the middle and high school level, the teaching format may be limited to lecturing by the teacher and independent reading by the student. Even if projects or other activities are a regular part of the class, much of the material essential for tests and passing the course comes from the student's ability to identify and organize important information from what is presented

Advance organizers or outlines can help students identify important information in lectures and take organized notes.

orally or in the textbook. Adaptations, therefore, focus on clarifying important information and providing a clear organizational structure.

Adaptations for lectures involve helping students with learning disabilities identify important information and take notes in an organized way. Some ways to help students do this include:

- Providing students with an advanced organizer, such as an outline of the lecture, or with some questions to read before the lecture begins. The students can review the organizer and be better prepared to listen for key information.

- Preparing a simple outline that includes major topics but has room for the students to take notes under the different headings. This will help students organize and see the relationship between various pieces of information.

- Reviewing key vocabulary before the lecture begins or writing critical information on the board or on an overhead. Tell students specifically that information written on the board is important.

- Teaching students to recognize and identify clues used most frequently to identify important information.

- Stopping every so often and ask students to paraphrase or talk about the topic.

Reading Assignments   Adaptations for written texts include many of the same ideas just listed. Suggestions include:

- Providing advance organizers before reading, including both outlines and questions about the materials to help students read for important content. A number of content textbooks present questions or "what you will learn" guidelines at the beginning of chapters. If these exist in your text, remember to show students how to use them.

- Reviewing, highlighting, or boxing critical vocabulary or facts prior to reading.

- Cueing students to stop reading after every paragraph or every few paragraphs to review the material. The review could consist of written or oral paraphrasing or answering questions prepared for the different sections of the text.

- Teaching students to develop questions about the text themselves for use during or after reading.

- Having students answer questions reviewed at the beginning of the passage, paraphrase, and fill in outlines or other advance organizers after they finish reading the text.

- Using other activities, such as the webbing technique discussed in the section on written language, or developing pictures or other graphic representations of content.

For students who are able to understand grade-level content but who read at a far lower grade level, interaction with the regular classroom text may be quite difficult. For these students, adaptations of content area texts may include simplifying instructional content so that the reading requirements are reduced and only key information is presented. Classroom teachers or special education consultants or resource teachers may want to prepare annotated outlines that present only essential information. In some instances, this technique may be very difficult because of the density of the text (U.S. history or chemistry, for example). Alternatives include taping the lectures, persuading someone to record the text on tape, attempting to find a simpler version of the text (some programs have two levels of textbooks), or using a peer or adult tutor to read the text.

Figures 5.4–5.6 show how one teacher adapted some material from an upper-elementary-level textbook. Figure 5.4 is an excerpt from the textbook, Figure 5.5 shows the material adapted as a review, and Figure 5.6 shows how the material has been adapted yet again for use as an advance organizer.

■ **Modifications of Worksheets and Tests**   Much evaluation and practice in the classroom takes place through written performance. The content, structure, and appearance of worksheets and tests is important because they affect the ability of students with learning disabilities to perform as well as they can. The guidelines we provide in this section are simple ones designed to call the students' attention to relevant information and to remove confusing or distracting information. They may be used when creating your own material or when adapting existing material.

Directions should be simple and clear.

Directions on tests and worksheets should be simple and clear.

- Use bold print, capital letters, or other means of highlighting important words in the directions.
- If more than one type of direction is necessary for different sections on the worksheet or test, make certain the sections are clearly separated from each other. Each set of directions should be clearly identifiable and immediately precede the related section.

The *appearance* of the material should be organized and uncluttered.

THE IMPORTANCE OF PLACE IN HISTORY

History contains four elements: place, time, people, and story. Place comes first. Place is the scene of the action, like the scenery for a play or a movie. But place is more than scenery. Place also shapes the story. Place changes over time, and it interacts with the people who create the story. The planet Earth is the major place of our history, though the Earth is affected by other parts of the solar system. The weather and the seasons affect all of history, and more recently, outer space and space travel are a part of the story.

Most of our attention will focus on the Western Hemisphere and on North America, in particular. The two areas we will study most thoroughly are the United States and the state of South Carolina.

Figure 5.4 Modifications of Material from an Elementary Textbook

Source: Archive Vernon Huff, Jr., "The History of South Carolina," in *The Building of the Nation* (Greenville, SC: Furma, 1991). Copyright © 1991. Reprinted by permission.

South Carolina History	Name: _____
Chapter 1: The Land	Date: _____
Lesson 1A	

1. The importance of place in history

    A. History contains four elements. _____ , time, _____ , and story.

Elements of History

place   time   people   story

    1. **Place.** Place tells where the action or event happened. Place is important because it can affect how the action or event occurs. Place is also important because it changes over time and it can affect the people who are a part of the event.

    2. **Time.** Time tells when something happened.

    3. **People.** The people are involved in the action or event.

    4. **Story.** The story tells about the action or event and sometimes what caused it to occur.

Review what you have learned

1. What are the four elements that make up history? (1A)

    a. _____   b. _____

    c. _____   d. _____

2. Name one way that place is important when we learn about history. (A1)

_____

Figure 5.5 Textbook excerpt adapted as an advance organizer.
Source: Archive Vernon Huff, Jr., "The History of South Carolina," in *The Building of the Nation* (Greenville, SC: Furma, 1991). Copyright © 1991. Reprinted by permission.

- Avoid unnecessary pictures. If a picture or graphic is necessary to answer a question (for example, a map or a graph), make sure that the questions related to the graphic are on the same page and adjacent to the questions if possible.

- Make sure all writing is clear and legible and that adequate space is provided for responses.

- Break up long tests or exams into different sections to help students organize responses (and possibly to prevent them from skipping or omitting questions). If possible, allow room for answers directly under the questions. Try to minimize the amount of page flipping the students have to do. Students do need experience in standardized test formats (for mini-

---

<table>
<tr><td>
South Carolina History
Chapter 1: The Land
Lesson 1A
</td><td>
Name: _____

Date: _____
</td></tr>
</table>

1. The importance of place in history

   A. History contains four elements: _____ , time, _____ , and story.

Elements of History

```
                    Elements of History
            ┌───────────────┴───────────────┐
          time                            story
```

1. **Place.** Place tells where the action or event happened. Place is important because it can affect how the action or event occurs. Place is also important because it changes over time and it can affect the people who are a part of the event.

2. _____ tells when something happened.

3. **People.** The people are involved in the action or event.

4. _____ tells about the action or event and sometimes what caused it to occur.

WORLD BANK: Lesson 1A

continental drift   story   people   time   place

Figure 5.6 Textbook excerpt adapted as a review.
Source: Archive Vernon Huff, Jr., "The History of South Carolina," in *The Building of the Nation* (Greenville, SC: Furma, 1991). Copyright © 1991. Reprinted by permission.

mum competency tests, basic skills tests, or SAT exams), so specific practice in these types of tests must be provided. Understand, however, that these formats are difficult for students with learning disabilities and may need to be introduced carefully.

Although types of questions or written activities will vary depending on grade level or subject area, the *format* of the presentation is always important.

- Avoid long columns of matching items—the ones that require drawing all of those lines between the items on both sides of the paper. Either use another format or break the list into sections.

- Essay questions will create problems for many students with disabilities, and some guidelines may be necessary (outline, approximate number of sentences, strategy for answering essay questions).

- Some students with poor reading skills may need to have the test read to them or have the whole test or worksheet on tape so that reading and writing is not necessary.

When preparing tests or other written assignments, it is important to remember that the goal of the assessment is to evaluate the students' knowledge in the subject matter. You don't want other skill difficulties to interfere with your understanding of what each student has actually learned.

■ **Curriculum** It is beyond the scope of this chapter to discuss curriculum in any detail; however, many educators have suggested the need to restructure the organization of curricula in order to present content effectively to students with learning disabilities and to encourage the development of higher-order thinking skills (Carnine 1991; Kameenui, 1991). Researchers have found that by organizing curriculum around the concept of "sameness," students were able to learn more effectively (Engelmann, Carnine & Steely, 1991; Woodward & Noell, 1991). The underlying principle here revolves around the idea of using the same strategy or conceptual model for approaching all tasks in a skill or content area. For example, Kinder and Bursuck (1991) suggest that a model based on organizing knowledge into a "problem–solution–effect" structure should be applied to all social studies content. The box "Summary of Sameness Analysis" shows examples of how this sameness concept can be applied in various content areas.

Placement and Program Options

Mercer (1987) reminds us there is a range of abilities and disabilities within the group of students with learning disabilities. Consequently, the range of program options discussed in the Framework preceding Chapter 4 should be available within most school districts so that the unique needs of each student can be met. Decisions about how best to serve a student with a learning disability involve considerations related to more than just where those services will be received. The type of instruction the student requires, as well as the eventual academic and professional goals of the student must be considered as well.

Although some students with learning disabilities have always received all their instruction in regular classroom settings, the stage is set for increased numbers of students to be served in this way. The national education reforms of the early 1990s calling for a restructuring and reorganization of educational programs, an increased emphasis on inclusion of all students in the regular classroom, and ongoing controversy about the effectiveness of resource or pullout programs have contributed to this movement. Although these factors are strongly disputed by a number of professionals, the overall effect has been an emphasis on serving students with learning disabilities in the regular classroom (Friend & Cook, 1990; Kauffman, 1989; Reynolds, Wang & Walberg, 1987; Wood, 1993)

Students with learning disabilities who are served in regular classroom settings receive the same basic curriculum as other students in the classroom. However, this type of program does not imply that special services are not provided. As we've mentioned earlier, regular curricula may present obstacles for students with learning disabilities and make service in the regular classroom more challenging (Pugach & Warger, 1993). A number of alternatives have been developed to allow these students to receive specialized services and still remain in the classroom setting. Chief among them are consultation, collaboration, co-teaching, and classroom tutoring, all of which provide for the teacher who has expertise in special education or learning disabilities to come into the regular classroom and work with the regular classroom teacher or the student.

Increasing numbers of students with learning disabilities are being taught in the regular classroom.

∼ Summary of Sameness Analysis

Topic	Greatly Different Examples	Surface Features	Structural Sameness
Earth science	a. Pot of boiling water: When heated, molecules of water flow in roughly a circular pattern. b. Earthquake: Molten sections between earth's crust and core move in constant circulation.	Small-scale example–stove; element, water Large-scale example–earth's core, molten rock	Convection cell: The circular movement of heat is away from a hot object, and the flow of cooler air is toward the object.
Social studies	a. Invention of cotton gin: It was difficult to remove seeds from short staple cotton. The cotton gin removed the seeds efficiently and created a greater market for cotton. b. Mormon practive of polygamy: Because of persecution over practice of polygamy, the Mormons moved west to Salt Lake and developed a successful farm community.	Economic context–cotton, demands of market Human rights context–Mormons, Salt Lake, development of a community	Problem-solution-effects analysis: The sameness is not in the events but in the nature and sequence of events that involve identifying a social, political, economical *problem,* its *solution,* and the *effects* of the solution.
Spelling	a. Three morphographs: *re cover -ed* *(prefix) (base) (suffix)* *recovered, recover, covered* b. Four morphographs: *un/dis -pute -able* *(prefix) (base) (suffix)*	Three different morphemes Four different morphemes	Morphonemics: By using the same morphemes in selected combinations, the following words are spelled: *recoverable, repute, reputable, reputed, disreputable, disrepute, coverable, discover, discoverable, discovered, undiscoverable, undiscovered, disputed.*
Mathematics: word-problem solving	a. Subtraction word problem: Mark can get some money from his mother to help pay for a school trip. He has earned $57. He needs $112. How much more money will his mother give him? b. Multiplication word problem: If each shirt requires 2 yards of material, how much material will be needed to make 5 shirts?	Subtraction–linguistic features, numerical features, syntactic structure Multiplication–different linguistic features, numerical features, syntactic structure	Number-family analyses: The sameness is in mapping what is known and not known in a problem by determining if the "big" number and a "small" number are given, or if just the small numbers are given.
Writing: text structure	a. Writing stories: Develop the setting of the story (characters, time, place), problem, response, outcome, and conclusion. b. Writing expositions: Identify what is being compared/contrasted, on what, and how they are alike and different.	Story grammar–characters, setting, problem, actions Topic–compare and contrast	Text structure analysis: Elements are used to map ideas.

Source: From "Toward a Scientific Pedagogy of Learning Disabilities: A Sameness in the Message," by E.J. Kameenui, *Journal of Learning Disabilities* 24 (1991), pp. 364–372. Copyright © 1991 by PRO-ED, Inc. Reprinted by permission of the McGraw-Hill Companies, Inc.

A closer look

Collaboration: Setting Them Up for Success

Here are some basic instructional adaptations for special needs students, prepared by a special educator who collaborates frequently in inclusion classrooms.

A. Adjust type, difficulty, amount, or sequence of material.

1. Break assignments into short tasks.

2. Give fewer problems.

3. Assign only necessary material.

4. Underline text passages for important facts or organization.

5. Give specific questions to guide reading.

6. Make sure the child's desk is free of unnecessary materials.

7. Establish a small number of realistic goals.

8. Take up the student's work as soon as it is completed.

9. Provide a written copy of notes and/or a study guide.

10. Provide a textbook that has important information highlighted.

11. Have frequent individual conferences with students to ensure mutual understanding of goals and to assess progress.

B. Adjust space.

1. Place the student close to you.

2. Place the student next to another student who can provide assistance.

3. Separate the student from others likely to distract him or her.

4. Let the student choose the area of the room where he or she can concentrate best.

5. Permit him or her to work alone, but do not isolate him or her against his or her will.

Some schools employ all of these models, while others select one or two depending on the needs of the students and regular classroom teacher.

In **consultation,** the special education teacher observes the student in the regular classroom and provides suggestions concerning how the regular classroom teacher can adapt instruction or materials to meet the specific needs of the student with learning disabilities in her class. "A Closer Look: Collaboration: Setting Them Up for Success" shows the first two pages of a manual on instructional adaptations developed by a consulting teacher for the regular classroom. **Collaboration** describes the process in which both regular and special education teachers identify the problems or difficulties a child is experiencing and work equally to find intervention strategies (Dettmer, Thurston & Dyck, 1993). Sometimes the special education teacher will come into the regular classroom and provide instruction. This method, called **co-teaching,** has many different forms. Co-teaching could involve the special educator teaching a specific subject area to the entire class (math, social skills) or teaching a group of students, which includes the student with a learning disability (often a subject such as reading, or a content area requiring reading skills). See the accompanying box, "Co-Teaching Models," for a description of the various co-teaching formats. A final alternative is the individual tutoring of the student with a learning disability within the classroom setting, by a teacher, peer, or older student.

In spite of the emphasis on serving students with learning disabilities in the classroom setting, the resource room continues to be an often-used placement in many schools. The resource model allows students to receive the special instruc-

C. Adjust work time.

1. Give extra time to complete assignments.
2. Allow short breaks after fifteen minutes of on-task reading or writing.
3. Set up a specific schedule so the student knows what to expect.
4. Alternate quiet and active time.
5. Give shorter assignments and more frequent tests.
6. For long-term assignments, provide structured short-term deadlines.
7. Provide extra time for teaching a new skill.

D. Adjust grouping.

1. Match a special needs student with a peer helper who can help by:

    a. making certain directions are understood;
    b. reading important directions and essential material;
    c. drilling orally on various skills;
    d. summarizing orally important textbook passages;
    e. writing down answers to tests and assignments;
    f. working on a joint assignment;
    g. making suggestions for improvement.

2. Formulate a small work group of three or four students, including one special needs student. Hold all members of the group responsible for making certain that each group member completes assignments successfully.

Source: Kim Phillips, "Setting Them Up for Success: Instructional and Behavioral Adaptations for Special Education Students in Regular Classrooms" (Columbia, SC: Rosewood Elementary School, 1993) (unpublished materials, pp. 1–11). Reprinted by permission of the author.

tion and support that they need but still maintain both academic and social contact with their nondisabled peers and continue, for the most part, in the general education curriculum. Generally, three types of instruction are provided in the resource setting: remedial academic, adaptive, or specialized skills instruction. Academic instruction is often provided in the areas of reading or math because these skills are so important and will be used in other subject areas throughout students' academic careers. Adaptive skills instruction may include studying for or taking tests, preparing reports, or reviewing textbook material. Finally, some resource classes are used to teach specialized skills such as study skills or social skills.

The resource room may include three types of instruction—remedial, tutorial, and special skills instruction.

Students who experience severe learning disabilities may still receive instruction in self-contained classes or alternative programs. Young children in self-contained programs may receive intensive remedial academic instruction in an attempt to bring them to grade level and eventually reintegrate them into the general education classroom. Because evidence suggests that many students with severe learning disabilities experience postschool adjustment difficulties, the content of the curriculum for older students in self-contained programs is often more functional in nature, emphasizing career and vocational instruction (Cline & Billingsley, 1991). A functional curriculum for students with learning disabilities is likely to be found at the middle school or high school level. For many students, this includes training and preparation for work activities, as well as social interaction skills and exposure to adult activities such as managing money, making major purchases (cars), and identifying community and legal resources.

∼ Co-Teaching Models

One Person Teaching in Classroom

1. One teacher prepares materials and offers strategies but does not actually teach in the classroom. This model frequently coexists with all of the other models.

2. One teach–one observe: One teacher observes a student in the classroom and perhaps takes data, evaluates student responses to instruction, etc. Could be occasional or structured.

Two Teachers in Classroom–One Supplementing General Instruction.

1. One teach–one drift: One teacher circulates around the room helping students with particular needs, and the co-teacher instructs the whole group. Can be most beneficial when roles are reversed regularly.

2. Alternative teaching: One teacher provides remediation, enrichment, or specialized instruction for students who need it while the other provides instruction for the rest of the group. This may be done occasionally, on an as-needed basis, or regularly–alternative reading instruction, for example.

Two Teachers in Classroom–Both Delivering General Instruction.

1. Station teaching: Curriculum content is broken into components; each teacher teaches one part of content to a group of children, then students switch. Could also include a cooperative learning or independent group station.

2. Parallel teaching: Class is broken into two groups of students; each teacher teaches the same content material to one group of students. (Don't put all special education students in one group.)

3. Team teaching: Both teachers deliver the instruction together at the same time–share leadership in the classroom. This may be done for one class a day or more, but it should be consistent across time, so that students perceive both teachers as the teachers.

Source: Adapted from M. Friend, *The Power of 2: Making a Difference Through Co-Teaching* (Bloomington, IN: Indiana University Press, 1996).

Many students with learning disabilities will graduate from high school with a diploma, and perhaps go on to postsecondary education. The adaptive and social skills addressed throughout elementary and secondary school are important for those students who plan to continue their education. Social and interpersonal skills training, college preparatory coursework, and the use of accommodations such as taped lectures or untimed tests are examples of skills that should be addressed before and after students begin postsecondary school (Aune, 1991; Gajar, 1992).

Because learning disabilities are defined within the context of school, some people may wonder if they persist into adulthood. Current research supports the conclusion that learning disabilities do continue throughout life. This is not too surprising if we look at learning disabilities as a collection of different ways of learning. Although a learning disability can be a significant challenge, it is not necessarily an obstacle to great success and accomplishments in adult life.

Why are some individuals with learning disabilities highly successful in their professional and personal lives? Gerber, Ginsberg, and Reiff (1992) talked to people with learning disabilities themselves to get the answers. The researchers interviewed a large number of adults who were considered highly or moderately successful (success was defined in terms of income, education level, prominence in field, job classification, and job satisfaction). Through their interviews, they tried to see if any factors were common to the individuals who achieved high degrees of success. Although they did find a number of self-described factors among successful adults, the one that was most strongly represented was the desire to take control of one's life. At one point or another, the successful adults with learning disabilities decided that they needed to take control of what was happening to them—and then they began to look for ways to achieve some control.

Many secondary programs for students with learning disabilities emphasize job instruction, but more students are attending college.

Learning disabilities usually persist into adulthood.

Highly successful individuals with learning disabilities credit their desire to take control of their lives for their success.

As you may remember, we described students with learning disabilities as inactive or passive learners—they often were not taking the actions necessary to participate in the learning process. When these adults decided to achieve some control, they changed not only their general approach to learning but to their lives as well. This study suggests that showing students how to use learning tools to create change and facilitate self-reliance may be a good framework for increasing their probability for success by fostering the concept that each student can do things that affect the outcomes of his or her life.

SUMMARY

■ Students with learning disabilities demonstrate a discrepancy between potential and achievement that cannot be attributed to other disabilities or to environmental or cultural factors. Although there is no single known cause of learning disabilities, internal and external factors may be involved.

■ Learning disabilities affect five major cognitive processes: perception, attention, memory, metacognition, and organization. Difficulties with each of these processes can lead to problems in academic areas such as reading, language arts, and mathematics.

■ The social difficulties often caused by learning disabilities may stem from problems learning appropriate behavior or from repeated failures in school that lead to low self-esteem, helplessness, or acting out. Families are a vital source of support, encouragement, and motivation for these students.

■ Students with learning disabilities are assessed formally and informally to determine their academic skills.

■ The most widely used instructional techniques for students with learning disabilities are direct instruction, strategy instruction, and special instruction in study and social skills.

■ Many classroom materials and presentations can be modified for students with learning disabilities. When students with learning disabilities are included in regular classrooms, general and special educators must collaborate on making the necessary modifications and providing instruction.

KEY TERMS

learning disabilities
word analysis
discrepancy
reading comprehension
exclusion clause
pragmatic language
Feingold diet
functional flexibility
perinatal stress
predictive validity
learning style
formal assessment

perception
informal assessment
attention
informal inventories
direct instruction
attention deficit
   disorder (ADD)
strategy instruction
attention deficit with
   hyperactivity disorder
   (ADHD)
consultation

selective attention
memory
encoding processes
collaboration
working memory
co-teaching
metacognition
self-monitoring
organization
cognitive style

MULTIMEDIA RESOURCES

Assis-TECH Inc.: http://www.irsc.org/learn_db.htm. This site is a source for assistive technology devices for students with learning disabilities.

Association for Direct Instruction: http://darkwing.uoregon.edu/~adiep/. This organization provides information, assistance, and support for educators interested in using direct instruction and/or ordering related materials.

National Center for Learning Disabilities (NCLD): 381 Park Avenue South, New York, NY 10016, (212) 545-7510.

Clayton, Lawrence. *Coping with a Learning Disability* (New York: Rosen Publishing Group, 1992). A book for families and teens that demonstrates that being a teen with a learning disability can be a positive experience. It discusses family, personal, and peer emotional reactions and provides biographies of famous people with learning disabilities as positive role models.

Cummings, Rhonda Woods, Garry L. Fisher, Pamela Espeland, and Rhonda Cummings. *The School Survival Guide for Kids with Learning Differences* (Minneapolis: Free Spirit, 1991). Practical advice for kids about organizing time, setting goals, and building confidence. Also discusses handling conflict, coping with testing, and getting help from adults.

Farnham-Diggory, Sylvia. *The Learning-Disabled Child* (Cambridge, MA: Harvard University Press, 1992). This is an intelligent, easy-to-read introduction to characteristics of students with learning disabilities.

The Gram. Newsletter of the Learning Disabilities Association (formerly ACLD), 4156 Library Road, Pittsburgh, PA 15234, (412) 341-1515. This newsletter provides information about current legislation, educational programs, and research in the area of learning disabilities.

Learning Disability Resources: http://www.as.wvu.edu/~scidis/ld_resources.html. This site has information and resources from the Research and Training Division of the Learning Disabilities Center at the University of Georgia.

National Center to Improve the Tools of Educators (NCITE): 805 Lincoln Street, Eugene, OR 97403-1211, (541) 346-1646, http: darkwing.uoregon.edu/~ncite/index.html. Numerous publications are available on academic skill instruction, a curriculum, and related research.

National Institute of Child Health and Human Development (NICHD). Contact: Dr. G. Reid Lyon, National Institutes of Health, 6100 Executive Boulevard, Room 4B05, Bethesda, MD 20892, (301) 496-6591. Publications related to understanding learning disabilities, reading and learning disabilities, and other research areas are available at this location.

Reading and Learning Disabilities, NICHCY briefing paper, National Information Center for Youth with Disabilities, 1995, (800) 695-0285, http://www.ldonline.org/ld_indepth/general_info/general.html. This paper includes a look at learning disabilities in children and youth, suggestions for parents on how to help their school-age children learn, and issues for adults with reading and learning problems.

USING YOUR KNOWLEDGE

 Can Do: How do successful adults with learning disabilities cope with the demands of their jobs and lives? Try to locate an adult with a learning disability. Invite him or her to talk to your class about the strategies he or she has used to succeed in life. What types of strategies are described? How might they be used by your future students?

 Collaboration: How do the different types of co-teaching models work? Would you be interested in co-teaching? Visit some classes in a local school district that employ co-teaching. Discuss benefits and concerns of the models with the teachers. Develop some strategies for co-teaching in your own classroom.

 Commonalities: Why are content, presentation, and classroom placement all vital to consider when planning a class that welcomes a student with learning disabilities? Based on what you've read in this chapter, and your own experience, list classroom modifications in each of these areas that would be effective for all students. Be sure to consider social aspects of the class as well as academic ones.

 Commonalities: Think back to Chapter 2 and the discussion of resilience. Which of the factors that promote resilience also apply to supporting and encouraging students with learning disabilities?

WHAT YOU CAN DO NOW

1. Contact the Learning Disabilities Association or the Orton Dyslexia Society to obtain information about resources available to parents of students with learning disabilities. What support groups are in your area? What kinds of materials are available to parents through these societies or through local school systems?

2. Select a lesson from a textbook in your content area. Adapt the material along the lines suggested in the text. What specific changes did you make? Who is the intended audience for your revised version of the lesson? Can you envision making these types of modifications in your classroom?

3. If possible, interview a school psychologist about the process used to identify students with learning disabilities. Ask the psychologist to identify the most common tests and the specific diagnostic criteria used in your geographic region.

4. Participate in a tutoring or support-skill program for students with learning disabilities at your college or university. Many postsecondary schools provide services for college students with learning disabilities that include notetaking, test administration, tutoring, and reading course material.

5. Review some curricula that are used for students with learning disabilities. Visit your university curriculum library or the curriculm resource center at a local school district. Look for curricula that address basic academic skills as well as those that address special areas such as study skills and social skills. Determine if direct instruction, strategy instruction, or other methods are included in the lessons.

Children with Behavioral and Emotional Disorders

6

IN this chapter, you will learn how behavioral disorders are identified and defined, the effects of these disorders on students and their families, and strategies that you can use to work with students who have them. We will also discuss some of the questions and problems surrounding the definition and identification of these disorders. As you read, think about how you would answer the following questions:

■ **How are behavioral disorders defined and classified?**

■ **Why is the federal definition a source of controversy?**

■ **What techniques are used to identify and assess children with behavioral disorders?**

Collaboration: Why is collaboration between teachers and parents so important when it comes to teaching children new behaviors?

Can Do: What strategies can you use to help students learn to manage their own behavior?

Commonalities: How can behavior-management strategies suggested for students with behavioral disorders be used to prevent or manage inappropriate behavior in other children?

If you were asked to describe yourself, you might say things such as, "I'm very outgoing," "I'm shy around strangers," or "I have a short temper and worry about everything." In other words, you would probably generalize about the way you behave. We tend to define ourselves—our personalities, our characters, and our temperaments—by our overall patterns of behavior.

There are many differences in the way people react to certain situations, act around other people, follow rules and regulations, and conform to society's expectations for behavior. A wide range of behavior patterns is considered "normal" and accepted as a reflection of individual differences. This is particularly true among adults, for we accept the fact that people choose their own lifestyles and behave in ways that are most comfortable to them. Concern is voiced only when there appears to be a chance that someone will harm others or himself or herself, or does not appear able to cope with the daily activities of life.

Our outlook on conformity and acceptable patterns of behavior is different when we look at children, particularly children in school settings. The range of behaviors considered acceptable in school settings is narrow. Our expectations, as adults, of how children should feel and act is also much more narrowly defined than are our expectations of acceptable adult behavior. In part, these expectations help ensure that children learn how to behave appropriately in a variety of situations and benefit from educational programming. Many children do, from time to time, behave in ways that appear to be out of bounds—beyond our typical standards of normal behavior. These children are not the focus of this chapter. As educators, we are concerned when inappropriate behavior persists, interferes with school performance, and appears harmful to the child or others.

Definitions and Terms

The children identified in this category of special education can be referred to in a number of ways. The terms used include *behavior disorders*, *severe emotional disturbance*, *emotional disturbance*, *emotionally handicapped*, and *behaviorally handicapped*. Professionals have many different opinions about which term is most appropriate (Forness, 1988). The differences result from whether educators focus on the causes of the behavior children exhibit or on the behavior alone.

The Federal Definition

At the present time, the federal definition in IDEA uses the term **emotional disturbance** and includes five major criteria used for identification:

Federal law cites five major criteria for determining whether a child has an emotional disturbance.

i. The term means a condition exhibiting one or more of the following characteristics over a long period of time and to a marked degree, which adversely affects educational performance.

    a. An inability to learn which cannot be explained by intellectual, sensory, and health factors;

    b. An inability to build or maintain satisfactory interpersonal relationships with peers and teachers;

    c. Inappropriate types of behavior or feelings under normal circumstances;

    d. A general pervasive mood of unhappiness or depression; or

    e. A tendency to develop physical symptoms or fears associated with personal or school problems.

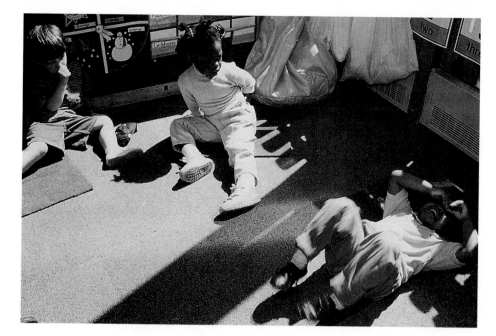

Typical behaviors may be considered to be problem behaviors if they are performed with unusual frequency or intensity. (Laura Dwight)

ii. The term includes children who are schizophrenic. The term does not include children who are socially maladjusted unless it is determined that they are emotionally disturbed. (*Federal Register* 42 [163], August 23, 1977, p. 42,478)

This definition, as is the case with most definitions in special education, is the source of much debate and discussion, and the term *emotional disturbance* is being challenged at the federal level. A number of professionals are urging that the term *emotional* or *behavior disorder* be used instead and are proposing several changes in the existing definition as well (Forness & Knitzer, 1990). Some states have adopted the term **behavior disordered** because of its more direct relationship to assessment and identification procedures (Smith, 1985).

Much of the controversy revolves around the ambiguity of the terms used as diagnostic markers and concern that this ambiguity excludes children who require services. For example, phrases such as *inappropriate types of behavior* or *satisfactory interpersonal relationships* are difficult to translate into clear-cut measures of performance. It is not too difficult to imagine that different people would interpret these terms in different ways. There is also much concern over the exclusion of children identified as "socially maladjusted"—the term is considered difficult to define, particularly in view of the possible overlap with behaviors (such as aggression, poor peer relationships) that *would* qualify a child for special education services.

> The ambiguities of the federal definition subject it to much controversy.

It does seem likely that changes are imminent in the definition of emotional and behavioral disorders, because the definition is less effective than it could be in providing guidelines for identification, assessment, and treatment.

Rate, Intensity, Duration, Age Appropriateness

Behaviors can differ in frequency or rate, intensity, duration, and age appropriateness. Often these factors determine whether behavior is considered normal

> A single episode of abnormal behavior does not mean that a child has a behavioral disorder.

or abnormal. In other words, abnormal behavior can be normal behavior that is performed to such a degree that it becomes atypical.

■ **Rate**   **Rate** refers to how often a behavior occurs in a given time period. Most children occasionally get out of their seats without asking permission or get into fights. A child who gets into a fight every day, however, or who gets out of his seat every two minutes would be demonstrating an unusually high rate of these behaviors.

■ **Intensity**   **Intensity** refers to the strength or magnitude of the behavior. For example, if a child hit his fist against the desk because he became frustrated, he might just hit it loud enough to make a noise, or he could hit it so hard he breaks either his hand or the desk. One instance would be considered a normal response; the other, more intense behavior would be considered problematic.

■ **Duration**   The length of time a behavior lasts is referred to as its **duration.** Any child might have an occasional temper tantrum or cry if his or her feelings are hurt. But a tantrum or crying spell that goes on for an hour or two will be considered differently than a ten-minute outburst.

■ **Age Appropriateness**   **Age-appropriate behavior** refers to the fact that some behaviors are considered quite normal in children of a certain age but are considered problematic when they persist as the child ages or occur before they are expected. For example, clinging to a parent, throwing tantrums, or being afraid of monsters in the closet are behaviors we might expect from a 5- or 6-year-old but not from a preteen.

Some children with emotional or behavior disorders exhibit *unusual* behaviors—behaviors we do not typically see at any level in other children. Most of these children have a more severe level of behavior disorders. Examples of this type of behavior include unusual patterns of language, distinctive hand movements and walking patterns, and behaviors directed at harming the child or others. We will look at these behaviors more closely when we discuss severe emotional or behavioral disabilities later in the chapter.

An important point to keep in mind is that a single episode of what appears to be abnormal behavior does not mean that the child has a behavioral disorder. Events within the child's life, as well as the changes and pressures of growing up, can result in an incidence of problem behavior, or perhaps even a few weeks in which the child seems to be exhibiting new and difficult behaviors. Typically, look for behavior that persists over several months and does not seem to have a readily identifiable cause (such as parents going through a divorce, death in the family). Another important factor to keep in mind is the degree to which you, or any other teacher who evaluates behavior, may respond to certain behaviors differently. Although we try to be as objective as possible when rating or counting behaviors, we must always keep in mind that our experiences or temperament can affect the way we judge or react to behavior.

Classifying Behavioral Disorders

Behaviors are usually classified into groups or categories. Sometimes this is done for the purpose of diagnosis, sometimes for assessment, and other times (though rarely) for placement and educational treatment. For the most part, be-

Teachers are more likely to focus on children who exhibit disruptive behavior than on those who are depressed or withdrawn. (Elizabeth Crews)

haviors that seem related in some way are grouped together. Often children exhibiting one type of behavior in a group or cluster will exhibit others found in that same cluster. Those children may be identified as having a specific type of syndrome or disorder. Other children display behaviors from a number of different groups. A number of classification systems are used with children having behavioral or emotional disorders. In addition to the various behaviors described in this section, we have included a separate section on attention deficit/hyperactivity disorder (ADHD) later in this chapter. Although ADHD is not technically a behavioral disorder, it has been considered a disorder of behavior due its historical relationship with hyperactive behavior. ADHD is not a separate category of special education under IDEA; however, it is a common diagnosis for students in general education classrooms and warrants a clear and thorough discussion (see pages 210–212).

The DSM-IV System

One classification system is presented in *The Diagnostic and Statistical Manual of Mental Disorders of the American Psychiatric Association* (fourth edition, 1993), known as **DSM-IV.** This manual groups behaviors in diagnostic categories. In other words, the manual lists specific behaviors and other criteria that must be present before a disorder can be diagnosed. Because many behavioral and psychiatric disorders are diagnosed on the basis of behavior alone, rather than a specific test or medical diagnosis, these behavioral descriptions can assist in the diagnosis of specific disabilities. Thus, a psychologist may collect observations and reports of a child's behavior in a number of settings over time and compare those behaviors to the categories in DSM-IV to assist in making a diagnosis.

The DSM-IV classifies behavior by diagnostic categories.

In some schools, the school or clinical psychologist makes the diagnosis of behavior disorders. In other schools a psychiatrist or pediatrician may diagnose the disability. This is particularly important when severe problems are exhibited or when therapy or medication are part of the remediation process. An example of diagnostic criteria from DSM-IV is found in the section of this chapter on ADHD.

Educational Classification Systems

Other systems of classifying behavior are more informal and based on groupings of a more general nature. Rather than looking for specific disorders, broad patterns of behavior or disorders are described. This type of classification system is used for educational placement, service delivery, and program development.

Kerr and Nelson (1989) grouped behaviors into the following categories based on the similarity of the instructional procedures or interventions that would be used to address them: disruptive behavior, socially inadequate and immature behaviors, social withdrawal, stereotypic behaviors, and aggressive behaviors.

Quay and Peterson (1983) devised a classification system based on extensive observations of children and the patterns of behavior that surfaced. They used six types of behavior as the basis for their classification scheme: conduct disorder, socialized aggression, attention problems-immaturity, anxiety-withdrawal, psychotic behavior, and motor excess.

Achenbach and Edelbrock (1979) classified behavior in even broader terms, as either externalizing or internalizing.

Externalizing behaviors, also known as acting out or aggressive behaviors, encompass all of those behaviors that are expressed overtly and that appear, in some way, to be directed toward others or the environment. These outwardly directed behaviors may represent impulsivity or a lack of self-control and can often be confrontational, aggressive, or disruptive.

Children with externalizing behavior disorders typically stand out in a classroom because of the impact their behavior has on others. The child who throws tantrums or teases his or her neighbor will interfere with others' abilities to listen or participate in class; aggressive actions may result in more than one child on the floor or in tears.

Internalizing behaviors are self-directed behaviors, such as withdrawal, avoidance, or compulsiveness. A child with an internalizing behavior disorder may be sad or depressed, withdrawn or shy, or focused on disturbing fears or fantasies.

Because of the nature of internalizing behavior disorders, a child's problems may not be recognized immediately, if at all. This child, typically, will not be a disruptive influence in the class and will not exhibit behaviors that draw attention from peers or the teacher. The student's avoidance of social interaction and the presence of fears or interfering thoughts, however, can affect his or her ability to perform in school and to establish social relationships. Recently, in light of the publicity given to adolescent suicides, more attention has been directed toward the identification of children with this type of disorder. Interestingly, females who have been identified as learning disabled or seriously emotionally disturbed appear to be up to three times more at risk than males for developing symptoms of depression (Maag & Behrens, 1989).

Table 6.1 **Systems of Categorization**

Externalizing behaviors	Internalizing behaviors
Conduct disorder	Attention problems, immaturity
Socialized aggression	Anxiety-withdrawal
Motor excess	Psychotic behavior
Aggressive behaviors	Socially inadequate and immature behaviors
Disruptive behaviors	Social withdrawal
	Stereotypic behaviors

Again, it is important to examine the extent and appearance of the behavior as well as the effects on the child when trying to identify internalizing behavior disorders. Many young children will exhibit excessively shy behavior when encountering new experiences or people (such as the first day of school). We might also expect a period of depressed or withdrawn behavior when a traumatic event such as death, divorce, or a move has occurred in a child's life.

Table 6.1 depicts the relationships among the different systems of categorization.

Classification and the Teacher

In the rest of this chapter, we will be using the Achenbach and Edelbrock classification system of externalizing and internalizing behaviors to look at the effects of behavioral or emotional disorders on children and their educational needs. This system is the least complicated, encompasses all behaviors, and focuses on the fundamental difference in children's behavior patterns.

From the teacher's perspective, the system helps to emphasize the relevance of *both* types of behavior. Unfortunately, the behaviors found in the internalizing dimension are not recognized as easily or as often as problematic even though these behaviors can have a profound effect on a child. As you might expect, teachers are more motivated to identify problems that disrupt the classroom and cause daily conflict than to recognize problems like depressed or withdrawn behavior that affect only the child in question.

Prevalence

The prevalence rate of behavioral disorders is estimated to be about 8.6 percent of the school-aged population with disabilities, although estimates have reached as high as 20 to 30 percent. In the United States and territories, 382,570 students were identfied as having a serious emotional disturbance during the 1994–1995 school year (U.S. Department of Education, 1996).

Although these numbers may seem large, they actually represent a figure far lower than most estimates of the true number of students with behavioral disorders. The vague criteria in the definition and the subjective nature of assessment often make a definitive diagnosis difficult. For example, the percentage of students identified with emotional disturbance in one state could be very different from the percentage of children identified in another. Wright, Pillard,

Some feel that many children with emotional or behavioral disorders are not receiving needed attention.

and Cleven (1990), however, determined that only about one-third of the variance in prevalence rates for students with behavior disorders could be attributed to the federal definition. They suggest that other factors, such as state definition, school district identification practices, and the frequency or type of prereferral interventions, could account for portions of the variance. Whatever the sources of variance, we know that there are important questions about the applicability of the definition. There are probably many students who are not receiving needed special education services.

Causes

The causes of most behavioral and emotional disorders are difficult to pinpoint. We often see children with very similar behavior patterns yet very different learning and family histories. Sometimes it is easy to pinpoint factors or situations that possibly contribute to behavioral and emotional disorders; sometimes there are no readily identifiable causal factors. Let's look at the following two examples of students with externalizing behavior disorders.

It is difficult to pinpoint the causes of most behavioral and emotional disorders.

Sandy, age 10, was identified as behavior disordered at age 7. At that time, she began demonstrating a number of problematic behaviors: She used extremely violent and obscene language toward her teachers and classmates; threw loud and long temper tantrums; hit her teacher and threw things when she was denied a request; and said cruel things to the other children in the class. She was failing the second grade. About two years later, it was discovered that Sandy had been the victim of sexual abuse by her mother's boyfriend. Although the abusive situation had ended, Sandy's behavior persisted. The identification of the specific cause could not, by itself, heal Sandy's emotional distress or end the behaviors that she had acquired and practiced over time.

Bill, age 13, has been identified as having emotional or behavioral disorders for five years. He is very active, always out of his seat and moving around. Although he can be compliant and cooperative, he flares up easily, becoming resistant and confrontational with teachers and principals. Bill constantly fights with other children. He seems to see every interaction as a challenge and responds with anger and aggression. He failed fourth grade and is barely passing his classes now. Most of the students in school dislike and avoid him. Bill lives with his mother and they apparently have a good relationship. Although Bill's behavior has improved some during the past few years, he is socially rejected and behind academically, and he still resorts to violent interactions when frustrated or when he feels challenged in any way.

Although Sandy's inappropriate behavior had a clear time of onset, Bill is an example of a child with a long history of problem behavior. He has trouble interacting with adults and peers and is not doing well in school. Bill seems to see things somewhat differently than other children; he feels others are out to get him, he can't control his temper, and he always uses aggression to respond.

∿ Factors Associated with Behavioral Disorders

Environmental Factors
- Family factors
- Cultural factors
- School factors

Physiological Factors
- Organic factors
- Genetic factors
- Specific syndromes with behavioral correlates

Why does Bill act this way? Does he live in a violent home or neighborhood? Does he have problems dealing with reality; is he just a bad kid? There are no simple answers to these questions for many students with behavior disorders. Sometimes we (as teachers) can speculate or make assumptions about the role of parents, peers, or temperament, but often this is all we can do. It is very difficult to determine why one child has a behavior disorder and another child in the same situation does not.

In spite of numerous theories and hypotheses about the causes of behavioral disorders, all we can do with certainty is identify factors that seem to coincide with the occurrence of behavioral differences. These factors can be grouped into two major categories: environmental and physiological. Environmental factors focus on the child's interactions with people and things external to him or her; physiological factors focus on the inner biology or psychology of the child. The accompanying box, "Factors Associated with Behavioral Disorders," summarizes these points.

Environmental Factors

Environmental factors that may contribute to behavioral disorders include family factors, cultural factors, and school factors. Family factors often revolve around the level and consistency of discipline; the history of violence and arrests in the family; and the way parents and siblings deal with feelings and each other. For example, Ramsey and Walker (1988) found that children who exhibit antisocial behaviors were more likely to live in homes with more negative and less competent family management styles. As you might expect, children who have experienced consistent behavior management practices, including positive as well as negative consequences for behavior, have a clearer idea of appropriate and inappropriate behavior. In other words, just as in the classroom, it is important for children at home to know the rules and be expected to follow them. Some other possible contributors to children's behavior can be the modeling of aggressive behavior by family members, neglect, or traumatic events such as death or divorce. Remember, however, that the way individual children respond to factors like these can vary considerably. Also, many children with externalizing or internalizing behavioral disorders seem to have very supportive and loving family environments.

Cultural factors may include the cultural norms for accepted levels of deviant behavior, and, some people suspect, the level of violence in the media. Schools themselves may foster the perception of behavioral disorders by requiring a different level and type of behavior than a child may typically exhibit in other environments. The personnel in a school also may promote inappropriate behaviors if school discipline is inconsistent or ineffective.

Physiological Factors

Physiological factors that may influence the development of behavioral disorders include organic factors, such as dysfunctions of the central nervous system; genetic factors, such as a family history of schizophrenia; or specific syndromes, such as Tourette's syndrome, which are accompanied by unusual behavior patterns. A child's temperament has also been identified as a possible source of behavioral differences. Again, with the exception of some syndromes with distinct behavior correlates, we must rely primarily on assumptions when dealing with physiological causes of behavioral disorders.

It is interesting to note that a number of students receive drug treatment for behavioral disorders. Although the cause of the behaviors may be unknown, certain drugs ameliorate symptoms for some people. Because drug treatments work on the symptoms rather than on the causes, drug therapy must be constant in order for the symptoms to stay suppressed. A prominent example is the use of drug therapy for attention deficit/hyperactivity disorder. Although the exact cause of this disorder is not known, certain drugs have been found to suppress its symptoms in some students. Young people with depression or who demonstrate psychotic behaviors may also receive medication. A medical model for treatment may be used with increasing frequency as we learn more about the role of physiological contributions to behavioral disorders. Professionals stress, however, that effective programs include medication in conjunction with behavioral and educational interventions (Forness, Sweeney & Toy, 1996).

Drug therapy can be an important component of a treatment plan for some students with behavioral disorders.

Effects of Behavioral and Emotional Disorders

Behavioral and emotional disorders, by definition, affect the way children interact with those around them as well as the performance abilities of the children themselves. In this section, we discuss some of the specific ways the child's life as well as the lives of those in his or her family can be affected by behavioral disorders.

Effects on the Child

To provide the appropriate support and intervention for students with behavioral disorders, we need to understand the effects the behavior can have on the child's academic performance and social interactions. Often, the extent and results of the behavior are more complex and difficult to remediate than the cause.

■ **School Achievement**   Most children with emotional or behavioral disorders are in the average range of intellectual functioning, yet do not do well in school. Although the extent to which behavior affects academic performance varies according to the individual child, poor schoolwork and underachievement in class are often cited as characteristics of children with behavioral disorders. Researchers have found a relationship between more difficult academic tasks and increased problem behavior and lower attention to task (DePaepe, Shores, Jack & Denny, 1996). Low achievement in school also may be associated with poor work habits, noncompliant behaviors, or poor attentional skills. Research suggests that students with behavioral disorders perform at approximately one standard deviation below the mean (Cullinan, Epstein & Kauffman, 1984; Luebke, Epstein & Cullinan, 1989). In other words, students with behavior dis-

Most children with emotional or behavioral disorders are in the normal range of intelligence but tend to do poorly in school.

orders may be close to one year behind their expected achievement level. Among adolescents, this effect is greater in math than in reading (Epstein, Kinder & Bursuck, 1989). The following profile of a student with an internalizing behavior disorder illustrates this effect.

Matthew is 8 years old and was identified early in the school year as having behavioral disorders. In spite of an IQ of 130, he is repeating second grade and is on his way to failing it again. Matthew's parents went through a divorce last year. His mother took Matthew and his younger brother to their father's apartment for a weekend visit and then left the state alone and never returned. Matthew never initiates conversations, plays by himself during free time, appears sad and listless, and is reluctant to participate in any class activities. His behavior has followed this pattern ever since his mother left him.

Although an apparent cause can be found for Matthew's behavior, the situation is not one that can be easily remedied. His reactions, although understandable, have persisted and intensified so that all aspects of his performace are suffering. Educational programs for Matthew and all children and adolescents with behavioral disorders must focus on remediating academic as well as behavioral skills. Addressing the behavioral or emotional disorders may not by itself improve academic achievement.

■ **Social Adjustment**   Children with emotional and behavioral disorders by definition exhibit behaviors that affect their social and emotional development. Externalizing behaviors such as violence and aggression may be directed toward classmates, and many children with externalizing behavior disorders do not have the skills for reflecting on and restricting their behavior. As these children grow into adolescence, their lack of control can often lead to serious conflicts. Internalized behaviors such as withdrawal or depression may result in the children being teased or rejected by classmates, and they may have great difficulty interacting with others. Research shows that children with behavior disorders are not accepted well by their regular classmates, even in adolescence—a time when some noncompliant behavior is the norm (Sabornie et al., 1988).

Without education and intervention, the behaviors that characterize a behavioral disorder will continue to affect the student after he or she leaves the school environment. What will happen when an aggressive child grows into an adult? Will he punch his coworkers or have a tantrum while driving or arguing with his girlfriend? If a student doesn't learn new ways to control and respond to anger or frustration as he or she grows older, the probability of encounters with the law increases.

High school classes for students with behavioral disorders often include students who have been in trouble with the law. The number of teens with behavioral disorders who have gone through the legal system at least once varies greatly from area to area; however, students with this diagnosis appear at higher risk for arrest both during and after the school years (Doren, Bullis & Benz, 1996). We certainly don't mean to imply that all or even most students with behavioral disorders are juvenile delinquents. We do know, however, that patterns of aggressive, rule-breaking, and risk-taking behavior are often found in students with behavioral disorders and that these behaviors set the stage for illegal activities.

Many adolescents with behavioral disorders have been in trouble with the law.

Social acceptance by class-mates is desired by every adolescent. The peer group can play an important role in identifying and supporting appropriate behaviors. (Brian Crites/Kansas City Star/SYGMA)

One study investigated the patterns of illegal drug use of junior and senior high school students with and without behavioral disorders (Devlin & Elliott, 1992). In the group of students with behavioral disorders, 51 percent were in the high-drug-use category, 20 percent were in the medium-drug-use category, and 28 percent were in the low- or negligible-drug-use category. Compare those figures with the ones for students without behavioral disorders: 14 percent in the high-use group, 10 percent in the medium-use group, and 74 percent in the low- or negligible-use group.

■ **Language and Communication**   As we look at the effects of emotional or behavioral disorders on communication, we must consider that in many ways behavior *is* communication. Some behaviors are learned as a way of responding to situations or events or of getting a response; some are developed because an individual has no other effective means of expression; and some are developed to enable an individual to control a situation. When we talk about teaching students appropriate behavior, or reducing inappropriate behavior, we are also teaching students alternative ways of communicating information, feelings, or needs.

Students with emotional or behavioral disorders may have great difficulty expressing themselves using verbal language, or they may experience much milder forms of language difficulty and delay. Some students with behavioral disorders are found to use fewer words per sentence, to have difficulty staying on a topic, and to have problems using language that is appropriate or meaningful in a given situation or conversation (McDonough, 1989). Students may also have difficulty organizing their thoughts to communicate effectively through oral or written language.

Language is crucial to academic performance, interactions with peers and adults, and the development of the sequential logical thought processes required in many self-management interventions, and it is an important component of the educational program. Communication, however, involves more than language. Teachers should always keep in mind the potential communicative

～ What Is a Functional Behavioral Assessment?

According to the IDEA amendments of 1997, all students with behavior problems served under IDEA must receive a functional behavioral assessment (Yell & Shriner, 1997). Brady and Halle (1997) describe a functional behavioral assessment as a way to determine the uses or functions of behavior. They identify the following components of a functional behavioral assessment:

1. Interviews: The student, parents, teachers, and other caregivers should be interviewed about the occurrence of the behavior and the surrounding circumstances.

2. Direct observation: The student should be observed in the setting or settings in which the behavior occurs. Observations should include what happens before, during, and after behavior occurrence.

3. Analog probes: The observer should manipulate specific variables such as the setting or the number of opportunities for interaction (for example, between the student and teacher) to get a better understanding of when and why the behavior occurs.

What Can We Learn from a Functional Behavioral Assessment?

1. When a behavior is most likely to occur: after lunch, during unstructured time, when the student is fatigued.

2. If something specific prompts the behavior: difficult seatwork, teacher correction, teasing.

3. What the student is trying to tell you: I want to be left alone, I want to get out of work, I am embarrassed, I love all this attention.

4. What usually happens after the behavior occurs: The student is ignored, put into time-out, or receives a lot of negative comments; the class laughs or works quietly; different consequences occur at different times of the day.

What Do We Do After a Functional Behavioral Assessment?

In the IEP meeting, the teachers, parents, student (if appropriate), and other relevant personnel develop an appropriate behavior management plan based on the information from the functional behavioral assessment. Answers to the following questions will be used to develop the plan:

1. Can changes in the student's environment (seating, method of teacher questioning, shortening assignments) help to prevent the occurrence of behavior?

2. What new behaviors (requesting, self-removal from setting) can the student use to satisfy the same communicative intent of the problem behaviors?

3. How can we prompt use of the alternative behavior (signals, self-monitoring, modeling)?

4. What consequences shall we provide for (a) demonstration of new behavior and (b) demonstration of problem behavior?

5. How can we evaluate behavior change?

---

intent of the *behaviors* students are exhibiting and be ready to provide appropriate alternatives—new ways of expressing how they feel or what they want—so they can successfully overcome their existing communication behaviors. This philosophy is reflected in the 1997 IDEA amendments, which require that a **functional behavioral assessment** be administered to students with behavior problems, in order to identify strategies that are positive and replacement behaviors that can serve the same communicative function as the problem behaviors (IDEA amendments, 1997). See the accompanying box, "What Is a Functional Behavioral Assessment?" for more information about this type of assessment.

Severe Disorders

In the case studies presented earlier, we saw the great impact behavioral disorders can have on a child's life. Yet the continuum of emotional or behavioral disorders extends even further than what has been already described. Some individuals exhibit severe disorders of behavior—behaviors that require even

Children with Behavioral
and Emotional Disorders

Some emotional and behavioral disorders are so severe that children
require assistance outside of school.

more specialized attention and intervention, some of which are provided outside of the regular school setting. Others have unusual patterns of behavior,
such as those found in autism (see Chapter 11), or a combination of disabilities
that also require specialized interventions and can have profound effects on the
individual's behavior in all areas of life.

■ **Severe Emotional or Behavior Disorders**   The children we refer to in this
section may either have externalizing or internalizing behavioral disorders, but
they exhibit behaviors that are markedly severe and intended to harm others or
themselves. Other children in this category may be so withdrawn as to resist
any semblance of normal social interaction. Their functioning may be severely
inhibited due to withdrawal, disoriented thoughts, or depression. In general,
these children require extensive and intensive educational assistance. Some children with severe disabilities receive educational services in public school settings, while others still are served, at least for a time, in segregated or residential
facilities.

> John, who is barely 8 years old, lives in a residential facility for children
> with severe behavioral disorders. He is exceptionally bright yet works at a
> primer level. By the age of 7, John had stabbed his mother twice with a
> knife, pushed his younger brother down the stairs and off a high chair, and
> tried to set fire to his room on three separate occasions. Although most of
> the time John seemed to be a friendly, outgoing child, his behaviors were
> determined to be so potentially harmful that he was placed in the residen-
> tial setting.

Behavior patterns similar to John's are among the most difficult for professionals and parents to handle. The child seems to be normal or above average in
so many respects, yet exhibits incredibly hurtful behavior without any warning
or apparent reason. Treatment for John will need to be very complex, and most
likely it is outside of the realm of school personnel. Teaching him to recognize
and control his impulses will be a key focus.

Other students with severe behavior disorders may be the target of their
own destructive behavior.

> Rhonda is 17 years old. Although she has always been moody and aggres-
> sive, she was identified as having behavioral disorders only a few years
> ago. At that time, her behaviors became increasingly self-destructive and
> violent. She broke her hand by slamming it against her locker, gave herself
> cigarette burns on her arms, and, in the last year, made two suicide at-
> tempts. Although Rhonda was placed in a public school resource class ini-
> tially, she was later placed in a residential setting for more intensive inter-
> ventions and close supervision.

Such violent, self-destructive behavior is often interpreted as a plea for attention or a cry for help. Interventions for suicidal students include counseling,
medication (when appropriate), helping them think more positively about
themselves, teaching new and more positive ways to communicate anger, fear,
or frustration, focusing on activities designed to demonstrate and accentuate
their skills and abilities, and developing positive friendships.

The specific instructional strategies and therapies used for children with severe disabilities will vary widely and must be tailored to the specific needs of
the individual. In a number of instances, drug therapy will be a component of
the treatment plan. In part, drug treatment is a response to recent discoveries
that some disorders, such as certain types of schizophrenia or depression, appear to have a strong physiological component.

Lewis (1988) suggests that successful movement of children with severe
emotional or behavioral disorders from residential treatment facilities to their
home and school environments must be accompanied by extensive liaison work
between the facility and the home and receiving school. In order for these children to continue to improve and function independently, they must be able to
cope with life in their everyday environments, not just in the residential facility.
The more teachers understand about the environments into which children will
be returning, the more they can prepare the students to handle those emotional
and behavioral requirements.

■ **Childhood Schizophrenia**   Childhood schizophrenia is classified as a behavioral disorder. The primary characteristics of childhood schizophrenia are:
(1) disorders in speech and language: Children's speech may take on peculiar
pitch and intonation and language may be self-directed or meaningless; (2) disorders in the ability to relate to other people or the environment: Children may
be extremely clingy or virtually ignore other people; and (3) emotional disorders: Children may be extremely anxious and nervous and experience extreme
mood swings that are often unpredictable and violent (Rosenberg, Wilson, Maheady & Sindelar, 1992). Childhood schizophrenia is rare. In the classroom, the
child with this disorder may experience great difficulty attending to work and
interacting with others. The unusual and unpredictable behavior patterns may
work against succesful social integration or group activities.

■ **Dual Diagnosis**   Behavioral or emotional disorders can be present in children who are also identified as having mental retardation, learning disabilities,
and other conditions. The term **dual diagnosis** refers to the coexisting conditions of mental retardation and behavioral disorders because both disabilities
can be clearly identified and can have equal impact on the overall functioning
of the individual. Individuals with severe mental retardation, for example,
are likely to exhibit self-abusive behaviors, problems with anger control, and
deficits in appropriate social interaction. The interventions used to address the
behavioral disorders of an individual with mental retardation are no different
from any other behavioral interventions, but they may need to be adapted to
meet the cognitive level and learning patterns of the individual. For example,
specific social skills may need to be broken down into smaller steps before instruction.

Effects on the Family

■ **Family Interaction**   The effects on the family of a child with behavioral disorders can be significant. Some parents struggle with the feeling that they contributed to the problem; others find dealing with the child's behavior emotionally and physically exhausting. Some parents, and siblings as well, feel they
have to focus all of their attention on a child with behavior disorders; others try
to ignore the behaviors. Because a child's behavior is often taken to be a reflection of parenting skill, a child with behavioral disorders may cause a parent to

Children with Behavioral
and Emotional Disorders

Some children experience difficulty adjusting to the behavioral requirements of social situations. A low level of tolerance or the misinterpretation of others' actions can result in inappropriate or aggressive behavior. (Owen Franken/Stock, Boston, Inc.)

feel embarrassed and guilty. Parents may try to "make it up" to the child or become angry with him or her—sometimes to the point of abuse. Try to remember this the next time you stare angrily at a parent whose child is crying in the grocery store. Parents may be faced continually with fear of what their child will do next or with feelings of helplessness.

A child with a behavioral or emotional disorder may become a victim of abuse. Zirpoli (1986) found that children with behavioral disorders are at increased risk for parental abuse. It is not clear whether abuse is more likely to cause behavioral disorders or whether behavioral disorders are more likely to cause abuse. Zirpoli, however, discusses the fact that the incidence of child abuse of children with all types of disabilities does not decrease after the age of 6, as it does with children without disabilities. One reason for this sad statistic may be that the presence of a lifelong disability is a continuing stressor to the family. (See the accompanying box, "A Closer Look: Commonalities: Charting the Aftermath of Child Abuse.")

Because of specific stress factors and other individual needs of families, educational plans must take the family's needs into account. Some of the feelings of helplessness can be addressed when parents are given strategies to implement and carry over to the home, particularly in the area of dealing with crises—a need frequently requested by parents of children with behavioral disorders (Simpson, 1988). For example, a family may be concerned about the tantrums their 10-year-old displays in public places when he is unable to get his way. Embarrassed by their child, the parents typically give in to him so that he will stop creating a public scene. The parents feel manipulated by their child and helpless. The teacher may come up with a set of techniques for the parents to try. These may include a checklist for the child to keep for himself while out in public. If all of the appropriate behaviors are checked off, the child could be

A closer look

Commonalities: Schoolwide Behavior Management: Programs for All Students

Most schools are faced with the challenge of designing programs or plans for school discipline. Increasingly, these plans focus on the prevention of discipline problems as well as on teaching students and teachers new strategies for dealing with inappropriate behavior when it does occur. An example of a program that focuses on both prevention and remediation is the schoolwide discipline plan developed by Nelson, Crabtree, Marchand-Martella, and Martella (1998). These educators and researchers describe their discipline program as a multilevel plan for all students, with greater levels of services and more comprehensive services provided to students who exhibit more pervasive patterns of disruptive behavior. Some characteristics of their program are as follows:

1. *Prevention* The schoolwide intervention includes adjustments in ecological or environmental factors that could contribute to inappropriate behaviors (such as reducing congestion), the development of specific behavioral expectations for students in common areas (such as hallways), and the supervision of students in common areas.

2. *Prevention and remediation* The school establishes a schoolwide discipline plan and a schoolwide strategy for classroom management. The strategy for classroom management is called the Think Time Strategy. In the Think Time Strategy, students engaging in problem behavior move to a Think Time classroom and meet with a designated teacher. The student and teacher engage in a debriefing process that consists of several steps, including having the student identify his or her inappropriate behavior, the motivation and consequence of the behavior, and appropriate alternative behaviors before he or she returns to the classroom. Students who are at-risk for disruptive behavior also receive more intensive instruction in behavior management skills, as well as academic and/or behavioral interventions designed just for them.

3. *Remediation* The continuum of services includes "wrap around services" for children with consistent disruptive behavior patterns. Wrap around services include the involvement of social service agencies and parents or other caregivers, so that interventions are comprehensive and consistent across environments.

Source: Nelson, J.R., Crabtree, M., Marchand-Martella, N., & Martella, R. (1998), Teaching good behavior in the whole school, *Teaching Exceptional Children 30*(4), 4–9.

eligible for some privilege or allowed to choose where to eat lunch. Other strategies include helping the parents develop consistent and firm consequences to implement if a tantrum should occur and taking the child on a number of short trips to places that usually do not result in problems (for example, the post office as opposed to the toy store) so that lots of praise and encouragement can be given when no tantrums occur.

■ **Parents and the Schools** The family of the child with emotional or behavioral disorders plays a critical role in the development and implementation of effective educational programs. Many educators try to involve the parents as much as possible in the establishment of consistent behavior-management strategies across settings. Programs with a home-based component that includes the delivery by parents of positive and negative consequences for behavior have resulted in decreases in noncompliance as well as in symptoms of depression in children (Johnston & Zemitzsch, 1988; Rosen, Gadardi, Miller & Miller, 1990).

Families of children with emotional or behavioral disorders play crucial roles in developing and implementing effective educational programs.

Teachers often involve parents in programs designed to teach behavior.

A key factor in consistent behavior management is communication between teacher and parent.

One major factor in consistent behavior management is the degree of communication between the teacher and the parent. Parents of a child with behavioral disorders should keep in close contact with their child's teachers so they can be aware of how he or she is progressing and how they can stress the same behavior patterns at home. Many teachers have devised daily or weekly forms that are sent home to let parents know how the child behaved that day and what the parents can do to help reinforce good behavior. Parents may provide consequences for good school behavior, such as taking the child to a movie on Saturday afternoon after a week of good reports. This type of teacher-parent alliance may be particularly helpful with older children who value their weekend and afterschool time.

Attention Deficit/Hyperactivity Disorder

As mentioned earler, **attention deficit/hyperactivity disorder (ADHD)** refers to a disorder that affects an individual's ability to attend to or focus on tasks and may involve high levels of motoric activity. As you can see in the accompanying diagnostic criteria from DSM-IV, the symptoms of ADHD are grouped into two major categories: (1) inattention and (2) hyperactivity-impulsivity. The number of symptoms a child displays in each category will determine if the child has primarily an attention disorder (ADHD, predominantly inattention type), a hyperactivity disorder (ADHD, predominantly hyperactive-impulsive type), or a combination (ADHD, combined type) (DSM-IV, 1994). You may hear the term *attention deficit disorder (ADD)* used by teachers or parents to refer to the inattention type of ADHD, or as a general description of attention problems.

Assessment and Diagnosis

Between 3 and 5 percent of children in the United States are identified as having ADHD (Lerner, Lowenthal & Lerner, 1995). The methods used to determine if a student has ADHD include interviews of the child, parents, and teachers, and behavior checklists. If you look at the DSM-IV diagnostic criteria in the accompanying box, you will note that all children display some of these behaviors at one time or another. As with all behavior disorders, the clinicians look at the degree to which these behaviors are performed and how the behaviors affect academic and social performance before reaching a diagnosis. ADHD is diagnosed in individuals of all ages; however, the symptoms must have been present before 7 years of age (DSM-IV, 1993). Lerner, Lowenthal, and Lerner (1995) summarize research that indicates that approximately 25 percent of students with ADHD have an additional diagnosis—for example, learning disabilities or conduct-related behavior disorders. Although assessment and diagnosis can be done by psychologists in the school setting, many children are referred to pediatricians for evaluation. A pediatrician's evaluation is preferred by some parents because the doctor can rule out other possible causes for the behavior and because drug therapy is often used, which must be prescribed by a physician.

Characteristics

The characteristics of children with ADHD will vary both across and within types of the disorder. When a child has inattention symptoms, his work may

~ Diagnostic Criteria for Attention Deficit/Hyperactivity Disorder

A. Either (1) or (2):

(1) six (or more) of the following symptoms of *inattention* have persisted for at least 6 months to a degree that is maladaptive and inconsistent with developmental level:

Inattention

(a) often fails to give close attention to details or makes careless mistakes in schoolwork, work, or other activities

(b) often has difficulty sustaining attention in tasks or play activities

(c) often does not seem to listen when spoken to directly

(d) often does not follow through on instructions and fails to finish schoolwork, chores, or duties in the workplace (not due to oppositional behavior or failure to understand instructions)

(e) often has difficulty organizing tasks and activities

(f) often avoids, dislikes, or is reluctant to engage in tasks that require sustained mental effort (such as schoolwork or homework)

(g) often loses things necessary for tasks or activities (e.g., toys, school assignments, pencils, books, or tools)

(h) is often easily distracted by extraneous stimuli

(i) is often forgetful in daily activities

(2) six (or more) of the following symptoms of *hyperactivity-impulsivity* have persisted for at least 6 months to a degree that is maladaptive and inconsistent with developmental level:

Hyperactivity

(a) often fidgets with hands or feet or squirms in seat

(b) often leaves seat in classroom or in other situations in which remaining seated is expected

(c) often runs about or climbs excessively in situations in which it is inappropriate (in adolescents or adults, may be limited to subjective feelings of restlessness)

(d) often has difficulty playing or engaging in leisure activities quietly

(e) is often "on the go" or often acts as if "driven by a motor"

(f) often talks excessively

Impulsivity

(g) often blurts out answers before questions have been completed

(h) often has difficulty awaiting turn

(i) often interrupts or intrudes on others (e.g., butts into conversations or games)

B. Some hyperactive-impulsive or inattentive symptoms that caused impairment were present before age 7 years.

C. Some impairment from the symptoms is present in two or more settings (e.g., at school [or work] and at home).

D. There must be clear evidence of clinically significant impairment in social, academic, or occupational functioning.

E. The symptoms do not occur exclusively during the course of a Pervasive Developmental Disorder, Schizophrenia, or other Psychotic Disorder and are not better accounted for by another mental disorder (e.g., Mood Disorder, Anxiety Disorder, Dissociative Disorder, or a Personality Disorder).

be messy, incomplete, and disorganized; directions may be forgotten or only partially followed; and he may be easily distracted and forgetful. The student with ADHD is likely to forget to bring pencils, paper, books, and lunch tickets to school—every day. Essentially, any activity that requires voluntary, sustained attention can be disrupted. For example, while you are giving directions for a test, the student may interrupt you to ask what is being served for lunch today. Long tasks or activities are particularly difficult, and the student may try to avoid them altogether. Your request for a student with ADHD to write a two-page essay in class could be met with (a) frequent trips to the bathroom, pencil sharpener, etc.; (b) a half-written sentence with the student gazing out the window; (c) a "completed" essay consisting of three sentences and written in less than five minutes; or (d) the student attempting the task, crumpling up the paper, and sulking with his head on his desk. A student's attention deficits can eventually result in learning deficits, because of difficulty attending to material long enough to learn and practice it. The behavior of students who experience impulsivity/hyperactivity symptoms reflects high and constant levels of activity. The characteristics of impulsive cognitive style that we discussed in Chapter 5 apply to students with ADHD. They may react quickly to situations, without considering the consequences, or they may shout out answers to questions without waiting for recognition or reflecting on their responses. The activity level demonstrated by many students with ADHD is much higher than that of other children, and it is constant. The child with hyperactivity symptoms is always moving—running, twitching, tapping, shifting, jumping, etc. Parents of young children with hyperactivity report that their children have trouble sleeping or eating (Fowler, 1995). The constant motion, combined with impulsivity, obviously is at odds with the behavioral requirements of school settings and often puts kids with ADHD at risk for accidents and social altercations.

Educational Programs for Students with ADHD

Although ADHD is not a category of special education identified in IDEA, many students with the disorder do receive special education or other educational support services. Students with ADHD who do not have another identified disability may receive services under the IDEA category "Other Health Impaired" or, more typically, under Section 504 of the Rehabilitation Act of 1973. It is likely, therefore, that if you have a student with ADHD in your classroom, he or she will have an IEP that identifies specific accommodations and educational needs. Educational strategies for students with ADHD focus on attention, organization, behavior management, and self-management. The specific interventions used with students with ADHD overlap considerably with the strategies we discuss in each of these areas in both Chapter 5 and this chapter. Students with ADHD need structure, consistency, and clear consequences for behavior. It is important for teachers and parents to remember that students with ADHD need to learn specific skills for organizing, attending, and self-management. Drug therapy is frequently a part of educational programs of students with ADHD. It is successfully used in many, but not all, cases to allow students time to think, reflect, and learn. Approximately 70 to 80 percent of students with ADHD respond to medication (DuPaul & Barkley, 1990). However, drug therapy does not *teach* students necessary skills, although it may give the students the time needed to learn them. If you have a student in your class who is receiving drug therapy for ADHD, it is important for you to provide feedback to the parents and the physician about the effects of the drug. Often, physicians must experiment with dosages before finding the correct one; your input will be important. The most common drugs used are psychostimulants, particularly Ritalin, Dexedrine, and Cylert (DuPaul & Barkley, 1990). Each child will react differently, and some side effects are indicated, so it is important to learn as much about each student's drug therapy regime as possible.

Educational Issues and Teaching Strategies

Educational planning and programming for students with emotional or behavioral disorders involve several interrelated issues: early intervention, assessment, placing children with behavioral disorders within the school system, choosing a philosophical approach, designing curriculum and instructional strategies to enhance learning, and handling discipline in the school.

Early Intervention

There is so much variation in what behaviors and emotional reactions are considered developmentally appropriate among young children that it is difficult to identify emotional or behavior disorders in the early years. Many educators, however, believe that early intervention is critical, particularly for antisocial or noncompliant behaviors (Kamps & Tankersley, 1996). Young children with behaviors that greatly concern parents may be eligible for services under Public Law 99-457, as we discussed earlier, without being labeled behavior disordered.

Identification and Assessment: The Classroom Teacher's Role

Identifying and assessing behavior disorders is not easy because of the ambiguity of the definition and the subjectivity involved in judging the appropriateness of behavior. For example, suppose I like my classroom busy and bustling, with chatter going on at all times, while you like your class perfectly still and quiet—no one moves without raising a hand. Further, suppose that little Bobby likes to roam around the class and talk. You and I will rate Bobby's behavior very differently. This point is important to keep in mind, because although there are many ways to assess behavior differences, including screening, rating scales, and psychological testing, the primary method of identifying students with emotional or behavior disorders is, increasingly, observations of the child's behavior.

■ **Screening** The purpose of screening is to identify children who exhibit behaviors that interfere with their classroom performance and academic achievement. One instrument designed to integrate screening and possible assessment for identification is the Standardized Screening for Behavior Disorders (SSBD), developed by Walker and Severson (Williams & Haring, 1988).

Screening identifies children whose behavior interferes with academic achievement.

This instrument involves what the authors call a multiple-gating procedure. That is, there are three stages, or gates, of the screening and assessment process. In the first stage, teachers rank all of their students in two types of behavior patterns: externalizing behaviors (such as stealing, throwing tantrums, damaging property, using obscene language or physical aggression) or internalizing behaviors (such as shyness, sadness, thought disorders). This step requires teachers to look at all of their students, therefore increasing the teachers' awareness of and attention to specific behavior difficulties children might be experiencing. In the second stage the three children who rank highest in the class on each of the two behavioral dimensions are assessed using comprehensive behavior rating scales. If any of the children score beyond a certain point on the behavior-rating instruments, then the final stage, direct observation in various settings, occurs (Todis, Severson & Walker, 1990; Walker, Severson, Stiller, Williams, Haring, Shinn & Todis, 1988).

■ **Testing** In addition to the IQ and achievement tests that are a part of all special education evaluations, a few specific types of instruments are employed if emotional or behavioral disorders are suspected.

Behavior-Rating Scales After a child is referred, teachers, parents, and school psychologists observe him or her in school and home settings and complete **behavior-rating scales** designed to reflect patterns of behavior. Behavior-rating scales used frequently in the schools include the Conners' Behavior Ratings Scales and the Peterson-Quay Behavior Rating Scales. An example of the Abbreviated Conners' Rating Scale for Teachers is found in Figure 6.1.

Projective tests may also be used in assessment. These are open-ended tests that provide an opportunity for the child to express himself or herself and possibly reveal evidence of behavioral or emotional trauma. One example is the Draw-a-Family test in which the child simply draws a picture of himself or herself with his or her family. Administrators of this test examine the quality and sophistication of the drawing as well as identify what they consider to be revealing aspects of the picture.

It is important to understand that there is no standard or uniform battery of tests, checklists, or procedures to follow for the identification of children or adolescents with behavioral disorders. Each state education agency establishes its own guidelines and identifies the particular tests that can be used. Intelligence and achievement tests may be used to substantiate or rule out specific disability areas. Other assessment devices are largely subjective. All of the information is examined to determine if the child has a behavioral disorder. There is no specific test score, test average, or level of behavior agreed on by professionals as an appropriate criterion for identification.

■ **Assessment Issues** Because classroom teachers play an important role in the identification of students with behavioral or emotional disorders, it is important for them to understand the issues involved in defining and identifying children who fall into this category.

One issue that surfaces repeatedly when assessment is discussed is the problem of personal bias in the referral system. It is easy to see how the effects of personal bias and tolerance can influence behavior-rating scales. Each of the people involved in the rating process can have very different perceptions of what is normal or acceptable in terms of activity level or acting-out behavior; the raters may have different personal feelings toward the child, which could bias ratings; and the level of experience a rater has had with children can affect scoring—a parent with no other children might rate behavior differently than a parent with three or four other children.

Professionals urge that children be observed in a number of different settings, that ratings and observations be conducted by several different people, that observations be conducted over a period of time rather than during a single session, and that predisposing factors, including the influence of cultural differences and family expectations, be considered during assessment (Executive Committee of the Council for Children with Behavioral Disorders, 1989). Adherence to these suggestions will help reduce the influence of personal bias and episodic or situational behavior problems on the assessment and identification process.

A related issue is the importance of the classroom structure on the behavior of the child. In other words, the way a class is conducted may affect a child's performance and behavior (Skiba, 1989). Some teachers have a very traditional

Teachers' personal biases can affect the referral and assessment process.

Name of child _____ Grade _____

Sex of child _____ School _____

Age of child _____ Person filling out this scale _____

Please answer all questions. Beside each item below, indicate the degree of the problem by a check mark (√)	*Not at All Present*	*Just a Little Present*	*Pretty Much Present*	*Very Much Present*
1. Restless in the "squirming" sense				
2. Makes inappropriate noises when he shouldn't				
3. Demands must be met immediately				
4. Acts "smart" (impudent or sassy)				
5. Temper outbursts and unpredictable behavior				
6. Overly sensitive to criticism				
7. Distractibility or attention span a problem				
8. Disturbs other children				
9. Daydreams				
10. Pouts and sulks				
11. Mood changes quickly and drastically				
12. Quarrelsome				
13. Submissive attitude toward authority				
14. Restless, always up and on the go				
15. Excitable, impulsive				
16. Excessive demands for teacher's attention				
17. Appears to be unaccepted by group				
18. Appears to be easily led by other children				
19. Appears to lack leadership				
20. Fails to finish things he or she starts				
21. Childish and immature				
22. Denies mistakes or blames others				
23. Does not get along well with other children				
24. Uncooperative with classmates				
25. Easily frustrated in efforts				
26. Uncooperative with teacher				
27. Difficulty in learning				

Figure 6.1
Abbreviated Conners' Rating Scale for Teachers
Source: R. Sprague and E. Sleator, "Effects of Psychopharmacologic Agents on Learning Disorders." *Pediatric Clinics of North America,* 20 (1973), p. 726. Copyright © 1973 by W. B. Saunders Co. Reprinted by permission.

⌇ Issues in the Assessment of Behavior Disorders

All of the following factors may cause problems during the assessment process.

Problem

- Personal bias: For example, the referring teacher's bias in favor of talkative or quiet children.

Possible Solution

- A child should be observed by a variety of raters.

Problem

- Effect of the specific classroom environment

Solution

- Evaluate a child's behavior in the context of several classroom environments and other settings.

Problem

- Noticing students with withdrawn or depressed behavior

Solution

- Ask for information or training about all types of behavior that could indicate an emotional or behavior problem.

classroom with clear rules and strict requirements for behavior. Others have an open, unstructured classroom, in which children walk around to various learning or discovery centers. Still other teachers simply have ineffective classroom-management strategies. The important point is that children's behavior must be evaluated within the context of the classroom environment.

Although classroom teachers are in a good position to judge the appropriateness of the behavior children display during school, they seldom receive any training in conducting observations or using rating scales. Some studies comparing the ratings of different teachers on the same children found very little agreement (Simpson, 1989). For example, one teacher would rate a child as having a very high activity level while another teacher would rate the same child as having an average or low activity level. Teachers also seem less likely to pick up on the behaviors that indicate sadness or depression than on more aggressive or externalizing behaviors (Epanchin & Rennells, 1989). In spite of these problems, teachers are playing an ever-increasing role in the identification and assessment of children with behavioral problems. See the accompanying box, "Issues in the Assessment of Behavior Disorders," for a summary of these issues.

Instructional Setting

Children with behavioral disorders have the same placement options as other children with disabilities. These options, as described in the Framework that precedes Chapter 4, range from the residential school to the regular classroom. Because of the nature of certain types of behavioral disorders, such as aggressive and threatening behavior, some segregated service-delivery models have persisted in many school systems. These placement options are usually reserved as a last resort for students, usually adolescents, who are deemed unable to cope with the regular school environment. Most students with behavioral disorders, however, are served through a resource setting. In the resource room, students with behavioral disorders may receive instruction in academic skills, as well as interventions or programs designed to increase appropriate behavior.

Recent research suggests that the number of adolescents with behavioral disorders mainstreamed into regular classes has grown in recent years. There has been very little research, however, on interventions that are successful for students with behavioral disorders in general education settings (Cullinan, Epstein & Sabornie, 1992; Dunlap & Childs, 1996). The ability of the special education teacher and classroom teacher to work together is a critical factor in the successful adjustment of these students in general education classes. Specific social skills or behaviors need to be targeted for instruction, and all individuals involved in educational planning need to agree on them.

Downing, Simpson, and Myles (1990) found in their sample of special education teachers and regular education teachers, that these two groups looked at students' behavior quite differently. For example, the special education teachers rated students with behavioral disorders significantly higher than general education teachers in areas such as interacting appropriately with teachers and peers, avoiding fighting, and obeying rules. The possible problem here is that the special education teachers might not be doing any training in skill areas that are seen as significant problems in the other classes. The two groups of teachers may have different expectations or tolerance levels, or the students might behave differently in separate settings. Whatever the reason, we see again the importance of communication between general and special education teachers. Teachers who work specifically with children having emotional or behavioral disorders must be aware of the specific skills needed by the students in their classes; they can get this information only through observation or direct input from the other teachers. Classroom teachers, by the same token, might want to apply the instructional strategies used in the resource class in their class.

Philosophical Approaches to Instruction

There is disagreement about what types of interventions are most appropriate for children with emotional and behavioral disorders (Gardner, 1990; Long, 1990). There are a number of different educational approaches based on differing philosophies. Following are brief explanations of some of the major approaches to teaching students with emotional and behavioral disorders (Kauffman, 1993).

There are several approaches to teaching students with emotional and behavioral disorders.

1. *Biogenic or biological*   This approach is based on the concept that emotional or behavioral disorders have a physiological cause such as diet, chemical imbalance, or neurological disorder. Treatment follows a medical model, and interventions such as drugs are considered.

2. *Psychodynamic or psychoanalytic*   This approach focuses on the underlying cause of behavioral disorders, which is assumed to be due to an imbalance among the id, ego, and superego. The interventions used in this approach focus on helping the child to resolve and express the conflicts that are the root of the behavior problems.

3. *Psychoeducational*   This approach focuses on addressing the underlying cause of behavior as well as attending to the remediation of the behavior displayed, including educational problems. Treatment includes an emphasis on talking out problems and talking children through crisis situations.

4. *Humanistic*   This approach interprets behavior disorders as evidence that a child is unaware of or out of touch with his or her own feelings and cannot communicate them to others. Interventions focus on providing students with nondirective, nonstructured learning environments in which the teacher functions as co-learner, and children are allowed to discover their emotions.

5. *Ecological*   This approach considers behavioral disorders as a sign that the child's behaviors are not compatible with the requirements of the environment. Interventions focus not only on modifying the child's behavior

but also on modifying the child's environment to create a better fit between the two.

6. *Behavioral*   In this approach, behavioral disorders are viewed as the learning of inappropriate responses. This model does not address the cause of the behavior but focuses on the instruction of new and appropriate responses using interventions that involve the manipulation or arrangement of an individual's environment.

As you read over these different approaches, perhaps you thought, "I think a lot of these make sense." The fact is, it is common to use several of these approaches when designing educational programs. The interventions that teachers typically use are those from the behavioral model. Interventions based on the behavioral model are strongly supported by research—and often result in relatively rapid behavior change. Clearly, the physiological origin of some disorders will result in treatments using the biological model. As we discussed earlier, however, the use of drugs does not necessarily preclude the need for academic and behavioral remediation. In a review of various models and their effectiveness in promoting behavior change, Gable et al. (1988) suggest that a growing body of research supports the use of what they call an "ecobehavioral" approach—a combination of the behavioral and ecological approaches. Continued research is needed, however, to identify the best and most effective approach for dealing with the complex needs of children with behavioral or emotional disorders.

Most teachers base their interventions on the behavioral model.

Teaching Strategies

■ **Curriculum Focus**   The curriculum for students with behavior and emotional disorders must address behavioral as well as academic needs. The teacher must include curriculum components that remediate behavioral excesses or deficiencies as well as those that teach the regular school curriculum. To address both of these major curriculum areas is quite a challenge for any teacher. Although the responsibilities of the classroom teacher and the special education teacher will vary depending on placement options and class size, the importance of collaboration in instruction and planning cannot be overemphasized. Students in self-contained or resource settings in the public schools typically receive programs that address their behavioral performance in current settings. This curriculum, however, does not adequately prepare them for the challenges they will face in future environments.

The curriculum for students with emotional and behavioral disorders must address both behavioral and academic needs.

Behavioral goals for students with behavior and emotional disorders must be individualized to meet each student's needs. These goals can be described in terms of their intended effects. In the following sections, we examine three common curriculum goals and related instructional methodology: developing appropriate cognitions, teaching new behaviors, and eliminating inappropriate behavior.

Developing Appropriate Cognitions   One of the recurring problems experienced by children with behavioral disorders is difficulty interpreting events realistically and determining socially appropriate responses. Many children need instruction in skills to help them identify and cope with both real and exaggerated concerns and thoughts. Regardless of the cause, children who have retreated from social activities and relationships usually receive instruction that will enable them to make slow and nonthreatening steps toward appropriate social behavior.

Educational programs should include components designed to teach students how to monitor their own behavior (Maag, 1988). Because of the possible role of a child's thoughts in behavioral disorders, it is difficult for the teacher, who cannot observe these thoughts, to manage the behavior without student participation. One way to address this issue is through the use of **self-management instruction.**

Instruction in self-management skills involves teaching children to pay attention to and record their performance (McLaughlin, Krappman & Welsh, 1985). For example, children record on a piece of paper every time they talk without raising their hand. Alternatively, children can record a mark for every five minutes they exhibit appropriate behavior such as time-on-task or time without fighting. With very young children, calling their attention to the "rules" with contingency statements ("If you keep your hands to yourself, then you can go outside at recess") has been found to help reduce aggressive or violent play (Sherburne, Utley, McConnel & Gannon, 1988). Other self-management programs involve the use of videotapes (Falk, Dunlap & Kern, 1996) and role play to assist in self-evaluation. Students can observe and record behaviors and practice giving alternative responses.

Teaching New Behaviors   Other programs focus on the instruction of new behaviors to take the place of the inappropriate ones. Interventions of this nature may involve teaching students problem-solving strategies to use when they begin to feel angry or upset. For example, a problem teachers often face is a child throwing a tantrum in the classroom when he becomes frustrated. Simply telling the child to stop, or even punishing the child, will not necessarily address the problem, because the child who habitually has tantrums does not know what else to do when he gets frustrated. Therefore, the teacher can give him a signal when he starts to get angry. When he sees the signal, he has three choices: He can count to 10 and take a deep breath to calm down, he can raise his hand and ask the teacher for help, or he can get up and go sit in the reading corner for five minutes to relax. Now the child has options. Instead of throwing a book, he can choose an alternative behavior.

Viewing videotapes of appropriate behaviors, modeling, and practicing appropriate responses are other activities that have been used effectively to teach new behaviors (Amish et al., 1988; Knapczyk, 1988). McCoy, Maag, and Rucker (1989) used semantic mapping to help develop communication skills and intervene with a student with depression and suicidal tendencies. As you may recall from Chapter 5, **semantic mapping** involves brainstorming about a specific idea or thing and making a diagram of the ideas that shows how they relate to each other. It can be used to help students organize material when writing an essay question or paper, for example, or when identifying important information in material they have just read. McCoy, Maag, and Rucker used this procedure to provide the student with a means of organizing information related to her thoughts, feelings, and behavior. It gave her a vehicle to use to express that information.

Eliminating Inappropriate Behaviors   Some behaviors (such as stealing and using obscenities) may seem more deliberate and manipulative and less a result of lack of control. Usually, behavior-management techniques that involve the application of specific consequences for appropriate and inappropriate behavior are used to address these types of behaviors. Some programs also include curriculum components devoted to moral development, such as decision-making

> Instruction in self-management skills teaches students to attend to and record their own performance.

Level System Evaluation Checklist

Below is a level system evaluation checklist. The person who is most familiar with the level system being evaluated should complete the form.

Answer each of the following questions regarding your level system.

I. Access to LRE [least restrictive environment]

A. Are mainstreaming decisions made by each student's IEP committee, regardless of the student's status within the level system?   YES   NO

If no, check below:

____ 1. Students are required to attain a predetermined level before they can attend a mainstream class.

____ 2. Mainstream classes are predetermined (e.g., P.E. for students on Level 2, P.E. and music for students on Level 3, etc.)

II. Placement in the level system

A. Are students initially placed in the level system at the level that is commensurate with their needs and strengths?   YES   NO

B. Is initial placement in the level system based on current, valid assessment?   YES   NO

III. Curriculum

A. Does each student have individual target behaviors designated in addition to those designated for the whole group?   YES   NO

B. Are group expectations considered by each student's IEP committee to determine if those expectations are appropriate for each individual student?   YES   NO

C. Are criteria for mastery of target behaviors determined individually?   YES   NO

D. Is the sequence of target behaviors developed individually for each student, based on that student's needs and areas of strength?   YES   NO

E. Are target behaviors differentiated as skill deficits or performance deficits?   YES   NO

F. Are reinforcers individualized?   YES   NO

G. Do you avoid using access to less restrictive environments/activities and nondisabled peers as reinforcers?   YES   NO

IV. Procedures

A. Are advancement criteria (criteria for movement from one level to the next) individualized for each student?   YES   NO

B. Are advancement criteria based on recent, relevant assessment data as well as expectations for age peers in general education environments?   YES   NO

C. Does each student's IEP committee determine whether advancement criteria are developmentally appropriate for a particular student?   YES   NO

D. Are behavior reductive strategies used separately from the level system (i.e., downward movement is not used as a consequence for inappropriate behavior or for failure to meet minimum criteria for a given level)?   YES   NO

If no, check below:

____ 1. Downward movement is used as a consequence for inappropriate behavior.

____ 2. Downward movement is used as a consequence for failure to earn minimum points for a certain number of days.

V. Efficacy

A. Is each student's progress through the level system monitored?   YES   NO

B. Is there a problem-solving procedure if data indicate a lack of progress through the level system?   YES   NO

C. Do students consistently "graduate" from the level system?   YES   NO

D. Do behaviors that are addressed in the level system maintain over time and generalize across environments?   YES   NO

E. Do students who complete the level system maintain successfully in less restrictive environments?   YES   NO

F. Are self-management skills incorporated into the level system?   YES   NO

~ Checklist for Positive Classroom Management

1. The teacher interacts positively with the student. Y   N

2. The teacher communicates high expectations to the student. Y   N

3. Opportunities are provided for students to become acquainted. Y   N

4. Students are actively involved with peers through cooperative learning or peer tutoring. Y   N

5. Classroom procedures are taught to students, who demonstrate understanding of the procedures. Y   N

6. Students' instructional programs are appropriate to their needs, skill levels, learning styles. Y   N

7. The subject matter is relevant to the students' lives and they understand the connection. Y   N

8. Students understand the teacher's instructional goals and why teaching strategies are being used to achieve these goals. Y   N

9. Students have been involved in some form of academic goal setting and recording. Y   N

10. The assessment system motivates the student to make good effort. Y   N

11. Rules for managing student behavior are appropriate, succinct, stated positively, and applied to all. Y   N

12. Consequences for inappropriate behavior are clear to all students. Y   N

13. Consequences are educational, respectful, and implemented consistently. Y   N

14. Students demonstrate understanding of rules and consequences. Y   N

15. If a problem arises, the teacher meets privately with the student to discuss the problem and jointly develop a plan to help. Y   N

Source: Vern Jones, "Responding to Student Behavior Problems," *Beyond Behavior* (Winter 1990), p. 20. Published by the *Council for Children with Behavior Disorders, Council for Exceptional Children,* 1920 Association Dr., Reston, VA 22091.

and value judgment (Swarthout, 1988). A major goal of programs for children with behavioral or emotional disorders is to teach them a level of control that will enable them to perform appropriately in regular classes.

One example of this type of program is the **level system,** which involves a stepwise progression through a predetermined set of behavioral requirements, restrictions, and responsibilities. Through the demonstration of appropriate behavior over time, students can achieve higher levels of freedom and responsibility. Depending on the specific situation, the highest level reached could be eligibility for partial or full inclusion. This type of system has been shown to be effective even when the only consequence for appropriate behavior was increasing levels of independence and responsibility (Mastropieri, Jenne & Scruggs, 1988). Some, however, have expressed concerns about the level system. For example, Scheuermann and Webber (1996) suggest that the least restrictive environment is an educational right, not something that can be earned only by students reaching a high level on the program. In addition, they report that a level system might emphasize a group, rather than an individualized curriculum, as mandated by law. See the accompanying box, "Level System Evaluation Checklist," for an example of an evaluation checklist for level systems.

Regardless of your ultimate behavioral goal for an individual student, several factors, such as consistency and clear consequences, are required for all behavior-management programs. It is also important for you, the parent, and the student to see the program as positive and practical. See the accompanying box, "Checklist for Positive Classroom Management," for a sample checklist. Although many behavior-management systems include tangible rewards for appropriate behavior, some students with behavioral disorders have actually rated good grades as their most desired reward (Martens, Muir & Meller, 1988). This type of reward structure (independence, responsibility, grades) is likely to appeal more to regular classroom teachers than one dependent on tangible rewards (stickers, toys, food). Consequently, they may be more inclined to continue implementing the system in the regular classroom setting.

Discipline in the Schools

Most schools have established programs for the purpose of disciplining children who exhibit inappropriate behavior. These programs may include suspension, in-school suspension, time-out, corporal punishment, and expulsion. Children with externalizing behavioral disorders may seem to be prime candidates for experiencing some of these disciplinary actions, but federal law states that children cannot be punished for their disability. In other words, if a child's disability is considered responsible for the behavior, that child should not be punished for it. The IDEA amendments of 1997 present some guidelines for addressing the behavior problems of students with disabilities, including those with behavioral disorders. One requirement in the 1997 amendments is that a school review, called a **manifestation determination,** must be conducted after a school behavior problem has occurred to determine if the student's behavior is related to the disability. If the ruling is that the behavior is not related to the disability, the student may be disciplined like any other child (IDEA amendments of 1997; Yell & Shriner, 1997). In addition, children with behavioral disorders must have a specific behavior management plan, including disciplinary procedures in their individual educational programs. Any disciplinary actions, such as suspension, that change the student's placement are limited to 10 days. Exceptions include the possession of firearms or drugs in school or at school functions, which allows adminstrators to place the child in a temporary alternative educational setting for up to 45 days (IDEA amendments of 1997; Yell & Shriner, 1997).

According to federal law, children cannot be punished for behavior that is a result of their disability.

Schools must develop guidelines that enable them to implement discipline without violating students' rights.

Consistency, appropriateness, and effectiveness are important factors when applying behavior management techniques. (Laura Dwight)

SUMMARY

■ Federal law lists five criteria for identifying children who are seriously emotionally disturbed: unexplained inability to learn, inability to relate satisfactorily to peers and teachers, inappropriate behavior under normal circumstances, pervasive unhappiness or depression, and a tendency to develop physical symptoms or fears associated with school or personal problems.

■ Behavior can be evaluated in terms of rate, intensity, duration, and age appropriateness.

■ It is difficult to determine the prevalence of behavioral disorders because of differences in instruments used to measure behavior, in terminology and interpretation of definitions, and in the subjectivity of behavior-rating systems.

■ The causes of behavioral disorders are not known; however, certain environmental and physiological factors seem to relate to behavior differences.

■ The effects of behavioral disorders on the child include underachievement in school, difficulties with social adjustment, and difficulties in self-expression or communication. Effects on the family include parental anger, stress, and guilt; helplessness; and an increased risk of child abuse.

■ Assessment techniques include screening instruments, observation, behavior-rating scales, and IQ and projective tests. States establish their own guidelines for selecting and administering tests, and professionals interpret the results based on the nature of the specific case and their own expertise. A teacher's conscious or unconscious bias, the way a class is structured, and lack of teacher preparation in using assessment tools can cause problems in assessment.

■ The most commonly used approaches to working with children with emotional and behavioral disorders are biogenic, psychodynamic, psychoeducational, humanistic, ecological, and behavioral.

■ Regardless of a student's placement, regular and special education teachers should share the same expectations for appropriate behavior and use a consistent behavior-management system. The major strategies for working with students with behavior disorders involve developing appropriate cognitions, teaching new behavior, and eliminating inappropriate behavior.

KEY TERMS

emotional disturbance
behavior disordered
rate
intensity
duration
behavior-rating scale
age-appropriate
  behavior

manifestation
  determination
DSM-IV
externalizing behavior
internalizing behavior
functional behavioral
  assessment
dual diagnosis

self-management
  instruction
semantic mapping
level system
attention deficit/
  hyperactivity disorder
  (ADHD)

MULTIMEDIA RESOURCES

Barkley, Russel A. *ADHD: What Do We Know?* and *ADHD: What Can We Do?* (New York: Guilford Publications, Inc., 1992). Two comprehensive, informative, and practical videotapes on attention deficit hyperactivity disorder; the tapes are appropriate for teachers and parents.

Fowler, Mary. *Maybe You Know My Kid* (New York: Carol Publishing Group, 1995). A parents' guide to identifying, understanding, and helping your child with attention deficit/hyperactivity disorder.

Gordon, Michael. *ADHD/Hyperactivity: A Consumer's Guide for Parents and Teachers* (DeWitt, NY: GSI Publications, 1991). A guide to essential concepts of ADHD and hyperactivity that covers obtaining a comprehensive and relevant evaluation, effective educational programs, and decisions about medication.

Hershowitz, Joel. *Is Your Child Depressed?* (New York: Pharos Books, 1988). Practical information for recognizing depression or suicidal signs in children. Written by a pediatric neurologist, the book presents interesting case studies and useful aids to diagnosing these disorders.

Kameenui, Edward J., and Craig B. Darch. *Instructional Classroom Management: A Proactive Approach to Classroom Management* (White Plains, NY: Longman, 1995). A text for classroom teachers about managing behavior in the context of instruction.

The Law and Special Education: http://www.ed.sc.edu/spedlaw/lawpage.htm. This site provides access to the latest updates in special education legislation and case law.

Resources in Emotional/Behavioral Disabilities: http://www.gwu.edu/~ebdweb/index.html. George Washington University's site for teachers and preservice teachers who relate experiences from a psychoeducational perspective.

Rockwell, Sylvia. *Tough to Reach, Tough to Teach: Students with Behavior Problems* (Reston, VA: CEC, 1993). This resource, written for both regular and special education teachers, contains many effective management strategies as well as anecdotal vignettes that every teacher will recognize.

Walsh, Maryellen. *Schizophrenia: Straight Talk for Families and Friends* (New York: William Morrow, 1985). The author, who is also a parent, writes with compassion and humor about what it is really like to live with someone with schizophrenia and gives information about treatment, results, and further resources for investigation.

Zabel, Mary K. *Teaching Young Children with Behavioral Disorders* (Reston, VA: CEC, 1991). This book looks at a variety of program models and offers information on what works with young children.

USING YOUR KNOWLEDGE

 Can Do: How does your local school district define and identify children with behavioral disorders? Arrange to visit a local public school to discuss the challenges of implementing the federal definition of emotional disturbance. Get the perspective of regular and special educators and school psychologists. What definition is used? What tests and assessment instruments are used? After you've collected this information, work with other members of your class to come up with your own realistic program for defining and identifying children with behavior and emotional disorders.

 Collaboration: How can the family be included in interventions for students with behavioral disorders? See if you can attend an IEP meeting for a student with a behavioral disorder. Observe how the teacher/specialist interacts with the family. What types of questions are asked? How are problems managed? How are the behavioral goals of both the parents and teachers addressed?

 Can Do: How does a general education teacher work with students with behavioral disorders? Arrange to visit a class in a local public school that contains several inclusion students. Observe how the teacher implements behavior-management strategies. What types of strategies are used? Discuss the needs of the students with the teacher, if he or she has time. Share your findings with your classmates. Can you identify any general goals for teachers who work with students with behavioral disorders?

 Commonalities: How do your expectations of classroom performance affect the ways you perceive students' behavior? Using a behavior checklist, visit several classrooms at various grade levels. Observe and record the behavior of a few children. Afterward, discuss your observations and ratings with the classroom teachers. Are your perceptions and observations similar to those of the classroom teacher? Evaluate your own biases and their effect on your ratings. Make a list of behaviors that are important to you in your own classroom.

WHAT YOU CAN DO NOW

1. **Plan some academic activities that involve students' social skills, such as field trips, sports, or projects based on science experiments. Write at least one behavioral objective related to behavior or social skills for each activity you plan. How could you structure the activities (a) to facilitate interaction with a withdrawn student or (b) to reduce the probability of conflict with an aggressive student?**

2. **Ask school guidance counselors or conflict-management specialists for suggestions of strategies and programs that teach self-control and problem solving. Ask them for some examples of curricula related to self-management, social skills training, and affective development. Could you integrate these curricula into a general education classroom?**

3. **Select a behavior you might observe in your college classroom setting, such as pencil tapping, stretching, and hair twirling. Decide how to measure the behavior (rate, duration, intensity) and observe and record your peers' performance. Examine the range of behavior in your classroom. What level of behavior performance would be a problem?**

4. **Interview a local pediatrician about the methods he or she uses to identify children with ADHD. Ask about classroom observations,**

behavioral checklists, and parent interviews. What criteria does the doctor use? If possible, interview several pediatricians and compare their diagnostic methods.

5. Create a general behavior-management plan for your present or prospective classroom. Identify some sample classroom rules and develop a list of positive and negative consequences you would consider using in your classroom. Try to list the rules in a positive way.

Children with Communication Disorders

CHILDREN with communication disorders may have subtle difficulties—or more obvious problems in speaking, understanding, or hearing. Because communication is central to the educational experience, teachers play a key role in recognizing students who are at risk for a language disorder or who are experiencing speech problems. Teachers also play a key role in providing communication strategies for these students in the classroom. As you read this chapter, think about the following questions:

- How do *you* define successful communication in the classroom?

- Can you think of any area of schooling in which communication is *not* important?

Commonalities: How are language, speech, and communication crucial to classroom success for all children?

Can Do: How can the classroom teacher help children communicate more successfully?

Collaboration: How can the classroom teacher and the speech-language pathologist work together to ensure the success of children with communication disorders—and those at risk for developing problems?

Most of you reading this book are highly verbal individuals. You know how to change your communicative style to talk in different ways to different people in different situations—talking to a toddler and talking to the school principal require distinct communicative styles. You can express a wide range of meanings, often in subtle ways; take your turn at speaking in all the many different situations you experience in a day; manage the flow and direction of conversations with both familiar and less familiar conversational partners; and fix breakdowns in understanding when they happen—for example, by asking for clarification. When it comes to reading and writing, you know how to read differently for different purposes—you can skim the newspaper versus reading a textbook—and you know what to do when you don't understand what you have read. You also know how to write for different purposes and audiences, how to adjust your style and form of writing for the occasion, and how to revise your meanings when you think they may not be clear for the reader. You are effective communicators. For you, communicating with others, either orally or through print, is relatively easy—at least in your native language.

Yet you have probably experienced difficulty in communication—the "fear and trembling" that can happen when a professor calls on you in class to answer a question, the frustration of having your speaking turn taken away when someone interrupts you, the inability to make sense of what you are reading, or the essay returned with a poor grade because the main ideas have not been communicated well.

Those who have experienced some disruption in the development and use of oral communication can experience similar difficulties every day, difficulties also reflected in their reading, writing, and spelling. Communication problems are common to many exceptional students studied in this book, such as those with mental retardation, learning disabilities, or behavioral and emotional disorders. For example, communication issues are at the core of autism; and students with a severe hearing loss or a physical disability may have difficulty acquiring effective oral communication skills.

The group of students emphasized in this chapter are different. Most of them have normal sensory and motor functioning and normal intellectual potential. Their primary disability involves the communication process; however, their problems with communication are often subtle. In the following sections we'll examine the components of communication, language, and speech, and their development, and then look at how teachers work with students with communication disorders.

Definitions and Terms

Communication, language, and speech are related terms. Since they constitute the foundation for teaching and learning in school, we will examine their meaning more closely.

Communication

Communication is the exchange of ideas, information, thoughts, and feelings (McCormick, Loeb & Schiefelbusch, 1997). It involves two or more people interactively sending and receiving messages. Communication has many purposes, and its power cannot be overestimated:

Communication comes more easily when there is something meaningful to communicate about—as well as joy in the moment. (Elizabeth Crews)

"No matter how one may try, one cannot *not* communicate. Activity or inactivity, words or silence all have message value: they influence others and these others, in turn, cannot *not* respond to these communications and are thus themselves communicating" (Watlawick, Beavin & Jackson, 1967, p. 49). It's important to think of communication as more than words—don't people communicate with their clothing, their movement, their facial expressions? Don't pets communicate to their owners when they are hungry or hurt? Even students with disabilities who lack the ability to speak express themselves in some way, as we will see in Chapter 10. Figure 7.1 displays some of the types of communication.

Communication can occur in many forms.

Language

Language is the system by which human beings communicate. According to Bloom and Lahey (1978), it is "a code whereby ideas about the world are expressed through a conventional system of arbitrary signals for communication" (p. 2). Let's look at each component of this definition. A *code* is a symbolic means we use to represent one thing by another in order to think about it, store it, or share it with others (Bloom, 1988). For example, the word *cat* is a symbol we use to represent a small, furry animal. The linguistic code provides the form through which the speech sounds of spoken language (or the signs of a manual language) combine to represent objects and ideas. Each spoken language has its own sound code. For example, in English the sound combination /k/ /â/ /t/ means *cat*, but in Russian this meaning is expressed through the sound combination *koshka* and in French, *chat*. This linguistic code

We communicate verbally through language.

Children with Communication
Disorders

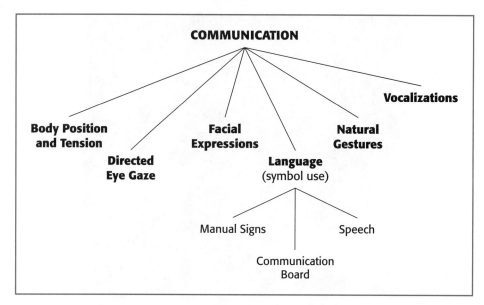

Figure 7.1
Types of Communication

Source: M. Diane Klein, Division of Special Education, California State University, Los Angeles. Used with permission.

is designed to communicate meaning, which is expressed through the *content*, or semantic component, of language. When we speak of vocabulary, we are actually referring to the meaning of words, or their dictionary meaning. Of course, most words do not have a single meaning; rather, they have multiple meanings, including nonliteral meanings, depending on the social context in which they are used.

The linguistic code is rule-governed. This means that patterns of regularity exist in the form or structure of language, or what is often called its *grammar*. For example, if you were asked to complete the following sentence: "Here is a bik; here are two ————," you would most likely respond *biks*, demonstrating your knowledge of language as ordered by rules (Berko, 1958). Linguists describe five interrelated components of language, each having a rule system: (1) **phonology:** phonological rules govern how we combine **phonemes,** or sounds, in permissible ways to form words; (2) **morphology:** morphological rules tell us how word meaning may be changed by adding or deleting **morphemes**—prefixes, suffixes, and other forms that specifically indicate tense and number, such as *-ed* to mark the past tense (miss*ed*) and *-s* to mark the plural form (dog*s*); (3) **syntax:** syntactic rules govern how words may be combined to form sentences; (4) **semantics:** semantic rules specify how language users create and understand the meaning of words and word combinations (McCormick, Loeb & Schiefelbusch, 1997); and (5) **pragmatics,** the component that involves knowing how to use language appropriately in a social context in order to achieve some goal desired by the speaker. Pragmatic goals might include finding information, fulfilling a need, or sharing a thought. All speakers of a language share the knowledge of how to use language in accord with the social rules of their speech community. Shared communication, called conversation, or **discourse,** has specific rules for taking turns, responding appropriately, and managing topics. Figure 7.2 depicts the interrelationship of the primary components of language: they can be addressed separately but are interrelated.

The form or structure of language is its grammar.

Phonemes are the smallest units of speech in a language.

Each component of language is rule-governed.

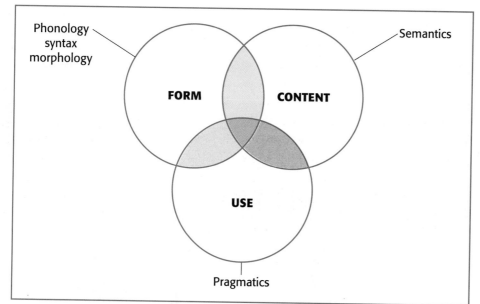

Figure 7.2
The Intersection of Content,
Form, and Use in Language

Source: L. Bloom & M. Lahey, *Language development and language disorders* (New York: Wiley, 1978),
p. 22.

Speech

Speech involves the physical action of orally producing words. It is a product of complex, well-coordinated muscular activity from respiration to phonation to articulation. Just to say "pop," for example, requires a hundred muscles coordinating their work at a speed of fifteen speech sounds per second (Haynes, Moran & Pindzola, 1990). Figure 7.3 shows the structures of the speech mechanism. Every language uses a set of sounds, or phonemes, from a larger set of all possible sounds. Languages do not all have the same number of phonemes. English uses approximately forty to forty-five phonemes.

Speech is a complex physical act.

Language Development

In about a thousand days, from birth to age 3, most children develop initial competence as oral communicators. How do children acquire communication skills so rapidly? What do they have to know about the world and about language? How is this knowledge organized? How and why does this knowledge change during the school-age years? Theories of communication acquisition attempt to address these vital questions.

Language Acquisition

The oral communication process is complex, and there is not agreement on a single theory of communication development. Rather, there are competing perspectives that attempt to explain the most probable ways children learn to communicate. Two of these major perspectives on communication acquisition are outlined in Table 7.1.

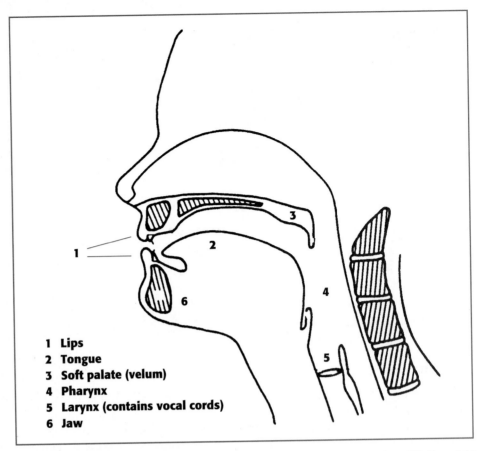

Figure 7.3
Structures of the Speech Mechanism

Source: M.L. Edwards, *Introduction to Applied Phonetics* (Austin, TX: Pro-Ed, 1986), p. 177. Copyright © 1986 by Allyn & Bacon.

Psycholinguistic and social interaction theories attempt to describe the language-acquisition process.

Most theories reflect a psycholinguistic or social interactional perspective, or a combination of both. Both perspectives stress the active, constructive nature of learning and the interrelationships among biological, cognitive, social, and linguistic systems (Kamhi, 1992).

Psycholinguistic theories are primarily concerned with mental processes within the child—what goes on inside the child's head. Often, the child is studied alone. *Social interactional theories* assume that mental processes originate as social processes and are progressively internalized by the child through interactions with a caregiver or teacher. This conceptual framework emphasizes the interpersonal context in which the child participates—how adults support the child as they collaborate to accomplish goals.

Although we do not know exactly how language is acquired, we can observe when most children reach milestones as language develops. There is variation in the age when individuals achieve these stages, but the process has a pattern and pace common among all languages and cultures. Table 7.2 summarizes five stages of language and communicative development from birth to age 12.

The age boundaries between phases, as well as the ages for the appearance of particular behaviors, represent data that have been compiled from many children and then averaged. In working with individual children, therefore, teachers should use this information only as a general guideline. Use caution when

Children learn language through interaction with others during meaningful experiences. (Elizabeth Crews)

applying milestones to children from cultural minority groups, because they have not typically been included in research studies.

You can see from the information in Table 7.2 how swiftly development proceeds during the first three to five years of life. For example, by approximately 12 months, the infant has become a highly social individual and has begun the transition to conventional first words. The child of 24 months has

Table 7.1 Two Perspectives on Communication Acquisition

Perspective	Focus	Main Assumptions
Psycholinguistic	Child is an explorer.	"You're basically taking this trip alone, but I'm here when you need me." Child is an active language processor whose task is to discover underlying rules based on adult input.
Social interactional	Child is a collaborator.	"I'm always with you for support, so don't worry about getting lost." Child and adult actively participate together to create communicative events; these events form the communicative contexts through which the child progressively discovers and applies underlying rules.

Source: J.N. Bohannan & A. Warren-Lenbecker, "Theoretical Approach to Language Acquisition," in J.B. Gleason, ed., *The Development of Language,* 2d ed. (Columbus, OH: Merrill, 1989), pp. 167–223. Copyright © 1989 by Allyn & Bacon. Reprinted/adapted by permission.

Table 7.2   **Overview of Communicative Development: Birth to 12 Years**

Age (Months)	Appearances
The examiner (1–6 mos.)	Responds to human voice; makes pleasure sounds (1 mo.)
	Produces strings of consonant-vowel or vowel-only syllables; vocally responds to speech of others (3 mo.)
	Smiles at person speaking to him/her (4 mo.)
	Responds to name; smiles and vocalizes to image in mirror (5 mo.)
	Prefers people games, e.g., peek-a-boo, I'm going to get you; explores face of person holding him/her (6 mo.)
The experimenter (7–12 mos.)	Recognizes some words; repeats emphasized syllables (8 mo.)
	"Performs" for family; imitates coughs, hisses, raspberries, etc. (9 mo.)
	Obeys some directives (10 mo.)
	Anticipates caregiver's goal and attempts to change it via persuasion/protest (11 mo.)
	Recognizes own name; engages in familiar routines having visual cues (e.g., bye-bye); uses one or more words (12 mo.)
The explorer (12–24 mos.)	Points to toys, persons, animals named; pushes toys; plays alone; begins some make-believe; has 4- to 6-word vocabulary (15 mo.)
	Begins to use 2-word utterances (combines); refers to self by name; has about 20-word vocabulary; pretends to feed doll, etc. (18 mo.)
	Enjoys rhyming games; tries to "tell" experiences; understands some personal pronouns; engages in parallel play (21 mo.)
	Has 200- to 300-word vocabulary; names most common everyday objects; uses some prepositions (*in, on*) and pronouns (*I, me*) but not always accurately; engages in object-specific pretend play and parallel play; can role-play in limited way; orders other around; communicates feelings, desires, interests (24 mo.)
The exhibitor (3–5 yrs.)	Has 900- to 1,000-word vocabulary; creates 3- to 4-word utterances; talks about the "here and now"; talks while playing and takes turns in play; "swears" (3 yrs.)
	Has 1,500- to 1,600-word vocabulary; asks many questions; uses increasingly complex sentence constructions; still relies on word order for interpretation; plays cooperatively with others; role-plays; recounts stories about recent experiences (narrative recounts); has some difficulty answering *how* and *why* (4 yrs.)
	Has vocabulary of 2,100–2,200 words; discusses feelings; understands *before* and *after* regardless of word order; play is purposeful and constructive; shows interest in group activities (5 yrs.)
The expert (6–12 yrs.)	Has expressive vocabulary of 2600 words while understands 20,000–24,000 word meanings; defines by function; has many well-formed, complex sentences; enjoys active games and is competitive; identifies with same sex peers in groups (6 yrs.)
	Verbalizes ideas and problems readily; enjoys an audience; knows that others have different perspectives; has allegiance to group, but also needs adult support (8 yrs.)
	Talks a lot; has good comprehension; discovers he or she may be the object of someone else's perspective; plans future actions; enjoys games, sports, hobbies (10 yrs.)
	Understands about 50,000 word meanings; constructs adultlike definitions; engages in higher-order thinking and communicating (12 yrs.)

Source: R.E. Owens, *Language Development: An Introduction,* 3d ed. (New York: Merrill, 1992), pp. 76–111. Copyright © 1992 by Allyn & Bacon. Reprinted/adapted by permission.

begun to combine two words, and at 48 months is using complex utterances. Such rapid learning is possible, in part, because of the typical child's communicative environment. It is estimated that by age 4, in the course of everyday interaction, the average child has been exposed to 20 to 40 million words and has spoken 10 to 20 million words (Chapman et al., 1992). By age 5, the basic system of oral communication has been acquired. This basic system continues to grow in more sophisticated ways during the school years because it is influenced by two new tools the child learns for thinking and communicating: reading and writing.

> We acquire the basic system of oral communication by age 5, and it forms the foundation for reading and writing.

Speech Production

Table 7.3 shows the path from vocalization to speech. During the first six months of life, infants primarily produce vowel-like sounds with some glottal and back consonant-like sounds. At about 6 months of age their vocalizations begin to include more consonant-like sounds ("ba-ba-ba"). This stage is called "babbling." These sounds tend to follow rather predictable patterns of development in all languages (Oller, Doyle & Ross, 1976; Oller & Eilers, 1982). Researchers have debated the relationship between babbling and subsequent

Table 7.3   The Path from Vocalization to Speech

Stage	Characteristic Behavior
Phonation (0–2 mos.)	Produces vowel-like sounds with vocal tract at rest.
	Produces reflexive sounds such as cries, grunts, hiccoughs, sneezes, which may sound consonantal.
Primitive articulation (1–4 mos.)	Produces coos and gurgles, which are primitive syllables using vowel sounds and some velar (back) sounds.
Expansion (3–8 mos.)	Produces more vowel sounds.
	Explores pitch through squeals, growls, yells, whispers, raspberries.
	Repeats particular sound types in vocal play.
Canonical syllable (5–10 mos.)	Produces babbling, which consists of well-formed syllables with combinations of consonants and vowels.
	Reduplicates sequences of these syllables, such as "ba-ba-ba."
Integrative (9–18 mos.)	Produces variegated sequences of babbling syllables.
	Mixes babbling and speech.
	Begins transition to meaningful speech (first words).

Note: These stages are based on age ranges. One infant may enter a new stage earlier or later than another infant.
Source: D.K. Oller and M.P. Lynch, "Infant Vocalizations and Innovations in Infraphonology," in C.A. Ferguson, L. Menn, and C. Stoel-Gammon, eds., *Phonological Development: Models, Research, Implications* (Timonium, MD: York Press, 1992), pp. 509–536. Used by permission.

speech production, but it seems clear that, as babbling becomes similar to speech, and as the infant and caretakers become aware of the similarities, the transition from babbling to speech occurs (Locke, 1986). Social interactions with caretakers involving imitative vocal play and turn taking, along with developing cognitive capabilities, such as increased memory span, play a role in this transition, along with the increasing fine motor control necessary for phoneme differentiation.

Types of Communication Disorders

The focus of this chapter is on the disruption of communication as the primary condition needing attention in a child. The IDEA definition of **communication disorder** is "a . . . disorder such as stuttering, impaired articulation, a language impairment, or a voice impairment that adversely affects a child's educational performance" (Federal Register, 1992). Disruptions can occur in any part of the communication process, including language, speech, or hearing. **Language disorders** involve disruptions in the form, content, or function of language. **Speech disorders** include phonological, fluency, and voice impairments. Figure 7.4 shows the relationship among communication disorders, language disorders, and speech disorders. Hearing loss, discussed in depth in the next chapter, also results in difficulties in acquiring and using language and speech.

Language Disorders

A language disorder is the impaired comprehension or use of spoken or written language.

The American Speech-Language-Hearing Association (ASHA), the national professional organization for speech-language pathologists and audiologists, defines language disorder as

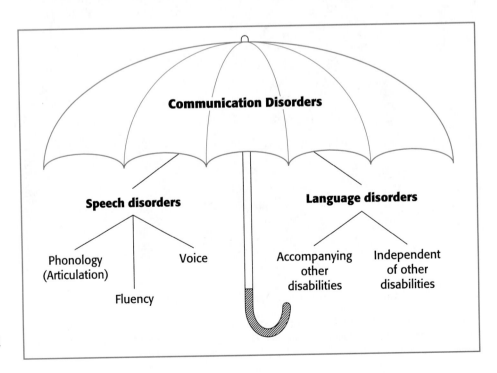

Figure 7.4
The Relationship of Communication, Language, and Speech Disorders

the abnormal acquisition, comprehension, or expression of spoken or written language. The disorder may involve all, one, or some of the phonologic, morphologic, semantic, syntactic, or pragmatic components of the linguistic system. Individuals with language disorders frequently have trouble in sentence processing or in abstracting information meaningfully for storage and retrieval from long-term memory. (ASHA, 1980, pp. 317–318)

Think about the five components of language described earlier. The ASHA definition tells us that a language disorder can occur as a result of a problem with one or more of those components. Since they are interrelated, difficulties often occur in combination.

There has been considerable debate among professionals about how to classify children with language disorders (Kamhi, 1998). Should it be by the primary label of disability, such as learning disability, autism, or motor disabilities? Certainly, many children who qualify for special education services in those specific disability areas have significant problems with language, spoken and written. Or should professionals describe children by the specific area of language that they have difficulty with—children with syntactical difficulties, for example? These descriptions would cut across traditional disability areas, but many children do have problems with language that involve more than one specific area.

Professionals use different classification criteria for children with language problems.

For this discussion, we refer to children whose *primary* difficulty is in learning and using language. (The language problems of children with other disabilities will be described in the chapters that focus on specific disabilities.) These children are sometimes referred to as those with **specific language impairment** (McCormick, Loeb & Schiefelbusch, 1997). Their problems learning and using language cannot be attributed to another disability—they have no other apparent problems. Later in their school careers, however, they are much more likely to have difficulties with reading and writing and, therefore, with school achievement—so they may end up with the label of *learning disability*. Table 7.4 describes some of the language problems associated with specific language impairment. Remember, in real life children do not appear in neat little chapters as they do in this book—their characteristics and needs are much more complex and challenging than the "categorical approach" we use here might suggest (see the "Framework" preceding Chapter 4).

Most current evidence supports the concept that students with language disorders follow the normal pattern of development but more slowly and over a longer period of time (Bashir & Scavuzzo, 1992). Longitudinal studies of preschool children with language delay have found that 28 to 75 percent of these children continue to have speech and language problems during the school-age years (Scarborough & Dobrich, 1990). More than 50 percent of these children manifest significant problems with academic achievement over the course of their school careers (Nelson, 1993). This evidence suggests that, despite special education services, a substantial number of children will not catch up with their peers. In other words, a language disorder is usually a chronic condition that persists into adulthood (Bashir & Scavuzzo, 1992; Snyder & Downey, 1991).

Most children with language disorders experience a delay in acquiring language, which often causes academic problems.

Speech Disorders

■ **Phonological Disorders**   Children with speech disorders may have difficulties performing the neuromuscular movements of speech as well as problems in

Table 7.4 **Language Difficulties Associated with Specific Language Impairment**

Language Dimension	Difficulties
Phonology	Failure to capitalize on regularities across words
	Slow development of phonological processes
	Unusual errors across sound categories
Morphology/syntax	Co-occurrence of more mature and less mature forms
	Fewer lexical categories per sentence than peers
	More grammatical errors than peers
	Slow development of grammatical morphemes
	Many pronoun errors
Semantics	Delayed acquisition of first words
	Slower rate of vocabulary acquisition
	Less diverse repertoire of verb types
Pragmatics	Intent not signaled through linguistic means
	Difficulty gaining access into conversations
	Less effective at negotiating disputes
	Less use of the naming function
	Difficulty tailoring the message to the listener
	Difficulty repairing communication breakdowns

Source: L. McCormick and D.F. Loeb, "Characteristics of Students with Language and Communication Difficulties," in L. McCormick, D.F. Loeb, and R.L. Schiefelbusch, *Supporting Children with Communication Difficulties in Inclusive Settings*, p. 85. Copyright © 1997. All rights reserved. Reprinted/adapted by permission of Allyn & Bacon.

Phonological or articulation disorders are the most common communication problems of the elementary years.

the underlying conceptual knowledge of the sound system and the rules for its use. Educators would probably identify **phonological disorders** (also referred to as articulation disorders), which are problems in understanding and using the sound system, as the most common communication problem seen during the elementary years. It is important to realize, though, that what appears to be a disorder may just be a normal difference in a child's rate of mastering certain phonological processes, particularly in young children (Haynes et al., 1990).

Normally developing children simplify adult speech so that they may acquire it. For example, they often simplify the production of a multisyllabic word (such as *nana* for *banana*). Another common process is simplifying two consonants produced together (such as *pin* for *spin*). Other pronunciation errors include addition, omission, substitution, and distortion of phonemes.

These processes are developmentally natural and are eventually discarded as the child becomes more skilled with the phonological system of the language. Whether a child has a phonological disorder is determined by two factors: (1) whether these phonological processes are being used far longer than they would normally be expected to be operating, and (2) whether the processes themselves are unusual; that is, they are not seen in normally developing children at any age. If a child's speech characteristics are embarrassing or lead to teasing from classmates, or if you are uncertain about whether a child has a phonological disorder, consulting with your school speech-language pathologist will help you come to a decision about whether to take action.

Listening to a child's language or speech with a speech-language pathologist can clarify whether a problem exists.

This student is working with a speech-language pathologist to improve his articulation. (Hattie Young/Science Photo Library/Photo Researchers)

■ **Dialects and Language Differences** Other kinds of pronunciation differences may be dialect-related. A **dialect** is:

> a variation of a symbol system used by a group of individuals that reflects and is determined by shared regional, social, or cultural/ethnic factors. A regional, social, or cultural/ethnic variation of a symbol system should not be considered a disorder of speech or language. (American Speech-Language-Hearing Association, 1993, p. 41)

A dialect is *not* a communication disorder, but teachers need to be aware of how dialects are used in their students' communities to prevent misidentifying a language difference as a disorder. Teachers also need to be aware of dialects in order to recognize when a speech or language problem coexists with a dialect. Children's use of English will reflect the characteristics of their cultural and ethnic communities. Table 7.5 describes some of those differences in the use of English.

A dialect is a regional, social, or cultural variation of a symbol system; it is not a speech disorder.

■ **Fluency Disorders** **Fluency disorder** is a broad term that describes interruptions in the flow of speaking (American Speech-Language-Hearing Association, 1993). The most familiar fluency disorder is **stuttering.** The primary symptoms of stuttering are excessive sound, syllable, and word repetitions, and sound prolongations and pauses. A child who stutters may also display a visible or audible struggle when talking.

In the past, it was believed that stuttering was a learned behavior: Children were conditioned to stutter because of stress in their environment. Today that explanation has been largely abandoned, for two reasons. First, there is substantial evidence of genetic transmission (Pauls, 1990). Second, for many children who stutter, their fluent productions of speech, as well as their disfluent

Table 7.5 **Contrasting Cultural Conventions in the Use of English**

	Black English	Asian Speakers of English	Standard American English	Hispanic English
Morphological and Syntactical Components				
Plural *s* Marker	Nonobligatory use of marker *s* with numerical quantifier. *I see two dog playing. I need ten dollar. Look at the dogs.*	Omission of plural marker *s* or overregulation. *I see two dog. I need ten dollar. I have two sheeps.*	Obligatory use of marker *s* with a few exceptions. *I see two dogs. I need ten dollars. I have two sheep.*	Nonobligatory use of marker *s*. *I see two dog playing. I have two sheep.*
Past Tense	Nonobligatory use of *ed* marker. *Yesterday, I talk to her.*	Omission of *ed* marker or overregulation. *I talk to her yesterday. I sawed her yesterday.*	Obligatory use of *ed* marker. *I talked to her yesterday.*	Nonobligatory use of marker *ed*. *I talk to her yesterday.*
Pragmatic Components				
Rules of Conversation	Interruption is tolerated. The most assertive person has the floor.	Children are expected to be passive; are discouraged from interrupting teachers; are considered impolite if they talk during dinner.	Appropriate to interrupt in certain circumstances. One person has the floor until point is made.	Official or business conversations may be preceded by lengthy introductions.
Eye Contact	Indirect eye contact during listening. Direct eye contact during speaking denotes attentiveness and respect.	May not maintain eye contact with authority figure but may make eye contact with strangers. May avert direct eye contact and giggle to express embarrassment.	Indirect eye contact during speaking. Direct eye contact during listening denotes attentiveness and respect.	Avoidance of direct eye contact is sometimes a sign of respect and attentiveness. Maintaining eye contact may be considered a challenge to authority.

Source: Adapted from Owens (1991) and Cheng (1987), in Ratner & Harris (1994).

productions, are characterized by brief but subtle malfunctioning of the laryngeal muscles (Conture, 1990). Some children go on to develop more severe forms of stuttering and clearly need treatment, while the stuttering of others may not progress in severity and resolves with or without treatment.

Because the onset of stuttering most typically occurs in the preschool to early elementary years, teachers need to know that referral to a speech-language pathologist is essential for appropriate diagnosis and the development of an intervention plan. Conture (1990) recommends that therapy begin immediately when: (1) two or more sound prolongations are produced per every ten instances of stuttering; (2) eye gaze is averted more than 50 percent of the time when the child is in the speaker role; and (3) delayed phonological development is also present (see the accompanying box, "Strategies for Children Who Are Beginning to Stutter").

Stuttering usually starts in the preschool or early elementary years.

Young children who stutter should be referred to a speech-language pathologist for evaluation and possible treatment.

∼ Strategies for Children Who Are Beginning to Stutter

1. Reduce the pressure to communicate.
2. Slow down your own rate of speech.
3. Avoid watching the child's effort to speak in obvious ways.
4. Avoid reacting with anger, shock, or distaste to speech blocks or repetitions.
5. Avoid suggesting by word or touch that "you know she has a problem, but you love her anyway."

6. Do not make comments such as "stop and start over" to a stuttering child.
7. Refuse to feel anxious yourself. It won't help.

Source: R.E. Cook, A. Tessier, and M.D. Klein, *Adapting Early Childhood Curricula for Children in Inclusive Settings* (4th ed.) (Englewood Cliffs, NJ: Merrill, 1996), p. 329.

■ **Voice Disorders**   **Voice disorders** may result from difficulties in breathing, abnormalities in the structure or function of the larynx, and/or certain dysfunctions in the oral and nasal cavities. These disorders can affect the pitch, loudness, and/or quality of a voice, all of which can have important social and emotional ramifications for a child. Whenever you become concerned that a child's voice is very unusual or abnormal, it's important to consult with the school nurse to rule out the possibility of a medical problem, then with the speech-language pathologist for suggestions about treatment.

> Voice disorders can affect the pitch, loudness, or quality of a voice.

Hearing Loss

The normal processing of spoken language is through hearing. Children with hearing loss frequently have significant communication problems; we will discuss hearing loss in greater detail in Chapter 8.

Causes of Communication Disorders

A number of communication disorders have known causes. In some cases, they are associated with genetic disorders such as congenital hearing impairment, fragile X syndrome, or cleft palate and other structural malformations (Gerber, 1990).

> Some communication disorders may have a genetic or an environmental cause.

Other communication disorders appear to be caused by biological and environmental factors. For example, maternal substance abuse affects fetal brain development and can result in delayed speech and language development. Multiple factors may play a role in conditions such as autism, stuttering, and language disabilities, which "run in families, affect more boys than girls, and are found in identical twins" (American Speech-Language-Hearing Association, 1991, p. 21). However, specific genes for language or speech have not been identified (Pembrey, 1992), and in many cases, the causes of children's speech and language disorders are not clear or are unknown.

> It is often difficult to pinpoint the cause of a language disorder.

Prevalence

The federal government uses the label "speech or language impairments" to describe the students we are discussing in this chapter. The Eighteenth Annual *Report to Congress on the Implementation of the Individuals with Disabilities Education Act* (1996) reported that 1,023,665 children were served by federally funded

A closer look

Can Do: Language Delay in Young Children

Jesy Moreno started school last fall, a lucky recipient of one of the limited public preschool spots in Los Angeles. But one thing immediately set the small boy apart from most of his classmates: At age 4½, Jesy hardly spoke.

He could utter a few words—mostly names of family members—and he understood some of what was said to him. But carrying on a conversation was impossible, and he could not follow the simplest instructions.

There are thousands of youngsters like Jesy in Southern California—children who are not mentally retarded yet enter school lacking rudimentary communication skills in both their home language and English.

Expressed simply: The less children speak, the more limited their comprehension and vocabulary and the harder it is for them to learn to read and write, not to mention navigate the social complexities of school.

Even now, after a year of concentrated effort by his teachers, Jesy cannot count to 10 or name the colors in the classroom's crayon box. When

another boy stole the wheels from a truck he had built, Jesy could not find the words to tell the teacher what had happened.

"Tell me, Jesy, what's wrong?" Maria Dolinsky asked in Spanish, crouching to his level and overenunciating her words, a practice everyone in the classroom follows with him.

"Ah, ah, *toda llanta,*" he answered haltingly. Um, um, all tire.

A classroom for children with language delays like Jesy's places new demands on a kindergarten teacher accustomed to teaching boisterous youngsters to raise their hands and wait their turn before speaking.

While the kindergartners next door were sitting in a neat circle and talking about their families and pets, Jesy's teacher, Toby Tilles, faced a clump of youngsters who ignored her and interacted with each other in grunts and baby talk and by hitting and "rolling around like puppies" on the classroom rug.

Slowly, she began coaxing words out of them, using techniques ranging from songs to sign lan-

---

Children with communication disorders are the second-largest group receiving special education services.

programs in this category during the 1994–1995 school year. Students with speech or language impairments constituted 20.8 percent of all students with disabilities between the ages of 6 and 11 in that school year, making this the second-largest group of students served in special education programs. Only the category of specific learning disabilities is larger.

Recognizing Risk for a Language Disorder

Teachers are often the first professionals to encounter children whose patterns of language development place them at risk for subsequent academic and social failure. Because you, as a future teacher, will have this unique "gatekeeping" role, it is important to know what patterns may indicate risk at different points in a child's school career. In the next sections, we discuss significant stages in language development and identifiable risk indicators.

Preschool Years

Children who are late talkers should be differentiated from children who are at risk for a language disorder.

Under Public Law 99-457, many states now provide programs for infants and toddlers who are at risk developmentally. If you are an early childhood education teacher, you will encounter very young children who appear to have significant delays in the development of language and communication. Some of these children may be late talkers, and some may have a language delay. By defini-

guage. When she talks, she pronounces each word carefully, repeats frequently, then urges the students to answer questions with more than a nod. Every lesson has a hands-on component, every response is recognized.

"I reward every approximation of a word. I started the year with very concrete rewards—stickers on hands—and now I can use mostly verbal rewards," Tilles said.

After they make Lego models during a free play period one morning, Tilles draws them together on the floor and has each describe what they have made.

"What is this?" she prompts one boy. "*Que es esto?*"

"*Un ah-oh,*" he says, clutching an airplane-like structure.

"*Un aeroplano?* Say '*aeroplano.*'"

He tries.

"Good, good. *Muy bien!*"

Although nearly all the students are from Spanish-speaking families, Tilles teaches mostly in English—with translation support from an aide—so the children do not have the added burden of trying to learn two languages.

It is unclear whether children like Jesy can "catch up" to others their age through an intensive language-emphasis program. Most researchers agree that there are windows of language acquisition opportunity that, once missed, cannot be recreated.

Yet for Jesy's teachers, such deep concerns evaporated in one moment this spring:

He stood at the phonics board in front of his preschool classmates and, with help from the teacher's aide, he slowly pieced together two sound cards—*ta* and *sa*. He stepped back for a moment, considered his creation, then said in a clear voice: "*ta sa . . . tasa*"—cup in Spanish.

"Jesy!" the aide and his teacher shouted simultaneously.

Source: Adapted from Amy Pyle, "Teaching the Silent Student," *Los Angeles Times*, June 11, 1996, p. 1. Copyright © 1996, Los Angeles Times. Reprinted by permission.

---

tion, "late talker" refers to delayed onset of speech, while **language delay** refers to delayed development in all areas of language.

The age of 30 months appears to be a critical time for determining whether a real problem exists. We know now there are links between preverbal and increasingly sophisticated verbal development (Stoel-Gammon, 1992). The "good babbler" tends to become a "good talker," even if an articulation problem is present. The "good talker" most likely becomes a good reader and writer. The opposite may also be true: The less adept babbler culminates in a less adept talker, reader, and writer unless appropriate early intervention is initiated. The child with language delay may have greater difficulties describing events, having conversations, and articulating sounds, and may be less likely to use meaningful gestures for communicating (Owens, 1995). As a teacher who may serve young children and their families, your understanding of risk for language delay becomes essential for effective early identification and intervention.

The age of 30 months appears to be critical for determining whether a language delay exists.

Kindergarten and the Early School Years

The profile of a language disorder changes over time. As children reach school age, patterns of difficulty can emerge that often involve learning to read and write. At this point, children with language disorders are often "relabeled" as learning disabled, or even as having emotional or behavioral disorders (Wallach & Miller, 1988). Again, teacher awareness of who may now be at risk is vital to assist children to remain in the regular education setting whenever possible.

Characteristics of language disorders change as the demands of the classroom change.

Children with Communication
Disorders

Observing students in classrooms provides a rich and
practical assessment of their
communication strengths
and needs. (Elizabeth
Crews)

Phonological awareness is the ability to recognize the sounds contained in words.

The best predictor of a child's ability
to learn to read is his or her phonological awareness.

■ **Phonological Awareness as a Risk Indicator**   How does a teacher recognize
risk in these early school years? One important indicator is **phonological awareness,** or the ability to recognize and analyze the sounds contained in words.
This ability is critical to emerging literacy.

Phonological awareness is the degree to which children's level of linguistic
development has allowed them to develop the explicit awareness that words
consist of sounds, or phonemes (Catts, 1991a; Chaney, 1992). Phonological
awareness is an aspect of metalinguistic awareness. When we consciously analyze and compare the sound structure of words or the meaning of words and
sentences in either oral or written language, we are using metalinguistic strategies for thinking critically about language. A strong connection exists between
aspects of oral language development and the word-recognition skills necessary
for learning to read (decode) and spell. In fact, in kindergarten, the best predictor of learning to read in first grade is a child's level of phonological awareness
(Catts, 1991a).

Children less sensitive to the sound structure of their language may also
have a less well-developed vocabulary, because words consist of phonemes.
During the early school years, despite experience with reading, these same children may encounter persistent problems in learning new vocabulary words.
Most likely, they will also have serious difficulties with phonics approaches that
require breaking words into their phonemic parts (for example, "What sound
does *dish* begin with?" or "How many sounds does *fish* have?") and blending
the parts into a whole. Difficulty with phonemic segmentation and blending
will also affect the ability to engage in more advanced manipulations of the
phonological code, such as deleting, adding, or reversing phonemes, and in
managing conventional spellings (Catts, 1991b; Ehri, 1989).

~ Developing Phonological Awareness

- Beginning at the preschool level, teachers can integrate phonological awareness activities in meaningful ways by using good literature that plays with the sounds in language, for example, through nursery rhymes and word games, and only then moving to judgments about sound similarities and differences (Catts, 1991b; Blachman, 1991a, 1991b; Griffith & Olson, 1992).

- A variety of writing experiences offers children rich opportunities to pay attention in a deliberate way to each letter in a word as they or the teacher actually writes words (Treiman, 1993).

- All children need to show the developmental evidence that they can consistently engage in these earlier phonological awareness activities before explicit instruction in phoneme segmentation and blending is introduced.

- Finally, following mastery of segmentation and blending, children should be introduced to letter-sound correspondences.

Research findings support the need for all students to have explicit instruction in phonological awareness in order to maximize success with word recognition in both reading and spelling (Blachman, 1991b; Snow, Burns & Griffin, 1998). Some forms of reading failure may be avoided if students are given explicit instruction in phonological awareness, and the instruction follows a developmental sequence. See the accompanying box, "Developing Phonological Awareness," for some teaching tips.

> Phonological awareness helps all students maximize success with word recognition in reading and spelling.

Once the phonological awareness of sound-letter correspondences becomes automatic, children do not need to pay as much deliberate attention to phonemic segmentation and blending of words. At that point, phonological awareness probably begins to play a lesser role in reading and spelling (Kamhi, 1989). However, many students with language disorders have persistent problems with word recognition well into adolescence. They may learn to compensate by relying more on comprehension strategies, such as guessing meaning from the context (Snyder & Downey, 1991).

> Many students with language disorders have problems with word recognition well into adolescence.

Educational Issues and Teaching Strategies

Identification

In most educational settings, the speech-language pathologist has primary responsibility for the identification, assessment, and treatment of students with communication disorders. When classroom teachers and speech-language pathologists work collaboratively, the best interests of children with speech and language problems can be met. (For more information about a career in speech-language pathology, see "A Closer Look: Collaboration: Who Is the Speech-Language Pathologist?").

> The speech-language pathologist identifies, assesses, and treats students with communication disorders.

Speech-language pathologists do not engage in medical or psychological diagnoses. However, they do have the professional and ethical responsibility to: (1) determine what may have caused the onset and development of the problem; (2) interpret whether other causal factors, such as the language demands of the classroom, may contribute to the maintenance of a speech or language problem; and (3) clarify the problem for a student and the family and counsel them appropriately (Lund & Duchan, 1993; Nation & Aram, 1991).

> The speech-language pathologist determines causal factors and counsels the student and the family.

 closer look

Collaboration: Who Is the Speech-Language Pathologist?

Speech-language pathologists in the schools are members of the educational team. Their traditional role has been to be the "expert" specialist who serves students in special education with speech, language, or hearing problems. This service has typically been provided outside of the classroom in a pullout model of service delivery. Today, the speech-language pathologist's role is changing from one of outside expert to a truer educational partnership with both regular and special education teachers. Because you are likely to work with these professionals, it's helpful to know about their background and training.

Speech-language pathologist is a professional title. Individuals holding this title must meet a number of academic and clinical requirements established by the American Speech-Language-Hearing Association (ASHA). This national organization is the professional, scientific, and credentialing body for more than 74,000 speech-language pathologists and audiologists. Approximately 45 percent of speech-language pathologists work in schools.

The professional credential is the Certificate of Clinical Competence (CCC). To be eligible for the CCC in either speech-language pathology (CCC-SLP) or audiology (CCC-A), individuals must have a master's or doctoral degree from an academic institution with an educational program accredited by ASHA.

In addition to these ASHA requirements for certification, forty-three states currently require licensing of speech-language pathologists and audiologists, similar to licensing for physicians and nurses. Licensure laws vary from state to state and are different from teacher certification. Many states have continuing education requirements as well to maintain the professional license.

The ASHA code of ethics states that only individuals who have the CCC, or are in the process of obtaining this certificate by working under an ASHA-certified supervisor, should practice speech-language pathology or audiology. However, to work in the public schools, a number of states require only a bachelor's degree in communication disorders, combined in some instances with teacher certification. Most states also require that, to continue working in the schools, a master's degree in communication disorders be obtained within a prescribed number of years. In all other settings, such as health-care facilities, the master's degree is the entry-level degree. Continuous efforts are being expended by ASHA and state professional organizations to have the master's degree also be the entry-level degree for school services.

Source: American Speech-Language-Hearing Association (1993). Implementation procedures for the standards for the certificates of clinical competence, *ASHA*, 35 (3), 76–83. Reprinted by permission of the American Speech-Language-Hearing Association.

Identifying causes may not be possible given the many factors that can influence the changing profile of a language disorder. Moreover, knowing that an initial cause, such as a birth injury or fetal alcohol syndrome, is related to the communication problem is not always useful for planning meaningful intervention for individual students (Lahey, 1988).

Assessment is an ongoing process.

Regardless of the emphasis given to causal factors in assessment, there is common agreement that assessment is not a one-time snapshot of a student at a particular point in time. Rather, it is a portrait that continuously evolves because it incorporates diagnostic information with new information obtained from the ongoing monitoring of progress.

Assessment

Identification of students who are at educational risk for a language disorder often begins with screening. Some states use standardized screening measures with large groups of students in order to determine whether students who do not meet the age-level criteria for language and speech should be formally referred to special education for a full assessment. In other states, mass screening of students is not used because it is not seen as cost effective. Instead, speech-language pathologists develop prereferral criteria for regular education teachers to document prior to the formal referral of a specific student for a suspected language disorder.

As a prospective teacher, it is important for you to be aware that referral criteria can sometimes result in overreferral. A major study on teacher decision-making about who should be referred to special education showed that the very existence of these referral criteria influenced teacher selection of students (Mehan, Hertweck & Meihls, 1986). Teachers discovered in their students previously undetected symptoms of "disability," which then tended to be confirmed by the traditional assessment process. Although the primary purpose of referral criteria is to identify students for special education who might otherwise go unnoticed, the researchers found that in many cases, students' behavior in the classroom was not the real rationale for referral. Videotapes of the classroom, for example, showed that the same behavior in two different students resulted in one student being referred for a learning disability or behavioral disorder while the other student was not referred. The referred student may have been described as having "poor language skills and acting out," while the student not referred might be described as "less talkative and shy" (even though this student can be seen on a videotape to "act out" also).

This inconsistent pattern seemed to derive from expectations about communicative competence that teachers hold about different students. These expectations influence how teachers interpret certain behaviors and may often result in unnecessary referrals to special education, particularly for students from cultural minority groups. The referrals may lead to the confirmation of disability when none actually exists.

The example of Jesy in "A Closer Look" (see pages 242–243) suggests how complicated the identification, assessment, and intervention of a language problem is when a child comes from a non-English-speaking background. A bilingual professional must conduct a careful assessment with such children in order to determine whether a language problem exists in the child's native language as well as in English. Only when the problem crosses both languages is it considered a language delay or disorder; otherwise, the child may simply be a nonfluent user of English. Professionals must take great care not to identify such children with a disability label. There is considerable evidence that this occurs with some frequency (Figueroa, Fradd & Correa, 1989).

Research makes the strongest possible case that you as a teacher must have good working knowledge of the language and communication system and its many normal developmental and cultural variations in order to know who should be referred. A delicate balance exists between failing to refer a child who needs assessment and referring a child who may be wrongly classified as disabled by the referral itself. The accompanying box, "Questions Asked in Traditional Assessment," presents the goals of assessment in greater detail.

Some states screen students for language disorders; in other states, general education teachers refer students.

Referral criteria may lead to overreferral.

Differentiating a child with a language disorder from a child with second-language acquisition difficulties can be challenging.

～ Questions Asked in Traditional Assessment

1. *Screening:* Are any students at risk for a communication disorder? Might a language learning disability exist? Screening is generally a brief and efficient assessment strategy performed on large numbers of individuals.

2. *Evaluation/diagnosis:* What are the student's strengths and weaknesses? What is the severity of the problem and how may it vary in different situations? Does the student or family view the problem as a handicap? What factors may be causing or contributing to the problem? An individualized in-depth assessment of communication abilities must be performed for these questions to be answered.

3. *Intervention/treatment:* Consistent with evaluation results, what specific recommendations can be made for an intervention plan that will best meet the student's needs (what goals, procedures, settings, and so forth)?

4. *Prognosis:* What is the student's potential for improvement with and without appropriate intervention?

5. *Progress:* What is the student's current level of performance when intervention is initiated? What is the student's level of performance after a period of intervention? Ongoing observation and informal assessment supply the answers to these questions.

6. *Effectiveness:* Does an intervention program result in the desired effects, both short term and long term, in communication and learning? Formal tests can be readministered or informal assessment can be used to answer this question.

Sources: B.S. Cornett and S.S. Chabon, *The Clinical Practice of Speech-Language Pathology* (Columbus, OH: Merrill, 1988); and N.J. Lund and J.F. Duchen, *Assessing Children's Language in Naturalistic Contexts,* 3d ed. (Englewood Cliffs, NJ: Prentice-Hall, 1993).

■ **Approaches to Assessment**   The specific approaches used in traditional language assessment may be determined by special education policies at state or local levels. However, speech-language pathologists generally use a combination of four approaches, or tools, for information-gathering: the interview, or case history report; norm-referenced measures; criterion-referenced measures; and observation. These tools will be discussed next.

Case History Report   Information for the case history report is obtained from direct interviews with parents, teachers, and, where appropriate, the student. Other sources of information may also be included, such as reports from the family physician, other medical specialists, teachers, or psychologists. The purpose of the case history report is to understand background information in order to be able to draw as complete a picture as possible of the student's current status and needs. The actual format and content of the case history will vary according to the requirements of individual school systems.

Direct interviews with the student and family are a source for the case history report.

Norm-Referenced Measures   Standardized tests are norm-referenced measures. Normal performance on a standardized test is defined according to a range of scores on the normal curve (Peterson & Marquardt, 1990), against which an individual student's score is compared. Norm-referenced tests are usually required to determine a student's eligibility for speech and language services. Many school systems also designate which tests should be used.

At the outset, three points should be made about language tests, which, in reality are achievement tests: (1) "Normal" generally means proficient; however, there is a lack of agreement on what constitutes proficiency in a native or first language; (2) language tests tend to reduce the complexity of communication into isolated parts, such as syntax, semantics, or pragmatics; these isolated parts are unrepresentative of how language and communication work as a

Language tests have several drawbacks and are currently being debated by regular and special educators.

whole in and out of school; and (3) because language tests reduce complex behaviors that in real life cannot be reduced, tests create the illusion that they are
objective (Oller & Damico, 1991; Stallman & Pearson, 1990; Weaver, 1991).

Because of these issues, it is critical to remember that "the blind use of a 'test
battery' is not language assessment" (Damico & Simon, 1993, p. 279), even when
testing is understood as one method of information collection. Teachers and
speech-language pathologists have a professional obligation to be informed test
consumers.

Criterion-Referenced Measures   Criterion referencing is a third method of information gathering. Criterion-referenced measures judge the student's performance according to some predetermined standard. The standard of comparison
is related to the student's own performance on specific tasks rather than the performance of a normative group. When a criterion-referenced approach is linked
to language assessment, the focus shifts to whether the student is using specific
kinds of language knowledge and strategies effectively to learn academic content (Nelson, 1993).

Criterion-referenced measures
judge performance according to the
student's performance on specific
tasks.

One advantage of the criterion-referenced approach over the norm refer-
enced approach is its clearer relationship to educational and intervention objectives. Also, the student's current level of performance is a primary emphasis,
not what the student might be capable of with assistance.

Observation   The fourth method for gathering information about students'
performance is direct observation. In fact, all of the assessment methods mentioned so far involve various degrees of direct observation. All consist of looking at and listening to what students and teachers actually do and say in order
to interpret the meaning of their behaviors. There is a difference among them,
however. The other methods focus on end results, which, sometimes, are far removed from the life of the classroom. Direct observation can provide information on teaching and learning as these actually happen in the classroom.

For observation to be useful for teachers, it must be *planned*. This means that
observation should be a systematic process with a clear purpose, one that involves a collaboration among teachers, speech-language pathologists, and other
educational staff. Becoming a skilled observer also requires experience with this
process in order for educators to have a shared frame of reference about classroom events.

Direct, planned, and purposeful observation in the classroom can provide important information on
teaching and learning.

The assessment process functions to determine whether a speech or language disorder exists, and, if present, its severity and variability. Eligibility for
special education and service options depends on how this evaluation question
is answered and whether a diagnostic category, or label, can be assigned, such
as speech impairment or language disorder. Although these categories may be
global and imprecise, they allow us to understand the commonalities that make
up a particular disability and to design assessment and intervention approaches
for students who share common symptoms (Nelson, 1993).

Placement and Service Options

The placement and service options for students with communication disorders
are similar to those already discussed in previous chapters, with one exception:
an emphasis on the pullout mode of service delivery. Students with speech impairments or language disorders are often removed from the regular or special
education classroom for one-to-one or small-group treatment.

～ Advantages of Integrated Classroom-Based Speech and Language Intervention

- The student gains and maintains access to "regular" educational opportunities and learning outcomes.

- Opportunities for team collaboration are maximized, and fragmentation (gaps, overlaps, and/or contradictions) in services are avoided.

- The input and methods of all team members are synthesized as they address a shared vision for the student's participation in social, educational, and vocational settings.

- Skills taught through integrated intervention are likely to generalize because they were learned and practiced in the integrated, natural environments where they need to be used.

The thinking behind this service option for language intervention has had a practical basis. In a smaller group setting, the speech-language pathologist can control some of the many variables that affect a student's successful performance in the classroom. On another level, many children can be served, which gives the appearance of cost-effective services but in reality often results in caseloads exceeding 75 to 100 students per week.

The pullout model may not be "best practice" and has been criticized for several reasons (Kamhi, 1993; McCormick, 1997). First, students' language learning may become increasingly isolated from the natural communication context of the classroom. Second, students tend to be stigmatized even further through their removal from the classroom and may suffer academically from missing important curricular content. Last, because speech-language pathologists were themselves isolated from the classroom and curriculum, teachers too often developed the unrealistic view that pulling students out was a way to "make them better and put them back" (Nelson, 1993).

In recent years, the trend has been toward integrated classroom-based services, in which language and communication instruction is provided in the context of daily activities in the classroom. When speech and language intervention is provided in the classroom, the general education or special education teacher can collaborate with the speech-language pathologist to provide the most effective intervention program for the child, in the natural setting in which the child will use the skills learned (see the accompanying box, "Advantages of Integrated Classroom-Based Speech and Language Intervention").

Although integrated intervention may be desirable, in many school districts across the country, students are still being "pulled out" of the classroom for speech and language services. There are many obstacles to changes in practice, such as (1) the evidence that accommodation to individual student needs within the regular classroom rarely occurs with ease; (2) the challenges presented by students with severe behavioral and emotional disorders; (3) the lack of adequate funding for an integrated system; and (4) the changes that must occur in teacher education as well as in the education of speech-language pathologists (Hoffman, 1993).

Pullout classes for students with communication disorders are coming under increasing criticism.

Obstacles to changes in practice must be overcome before integrated intervention can operate successfully.

The terms whole language and communication-centered learning refer to a holistic view that teaching and learning are communication processes.

Teaching Strategies

Whether or not you believe in integrated classroom-based speech and language services, many of its tenets are consistent with a holistic view of children and learning. Sometimes, the term *whole language* is used to describe the belief that teaching and learning are communication processes. To some extent, the term *whole language* is redundant. Since language works as a system, it is always whole; otherwise, we would not be able to communicate with one another. Others talk of communication-centered learning or the communication process model, meaning that listening, speaking, reading, writing, and spelling all share communication as their fundamental purpose.

■ **Integrating Language and Literacy Learning**   Several principles about language and literacy learning emerge from this philosophy, which is consistent with the earlier description of language and communication:

1. All children naturally learn language through social interaction with adults and peers.
2. Children learn best when they are guided by a "big picture" or theme and when they understand the reasons for learning.
3. Real learning is functional; it is also "messy" because active choice and risk-taking are required.
4. Real learning is challenging and involves cooperating with others.
5. All children are capable of learning; the guiding premise is that the learner's ability to be successful is always the focus of assessment and instruction.

For students with language disorders, these principles mean that the goal for instruction remains one of enabling communicative competence. Guided by these principles, the focus of instruction is twofold: to support the student's abilities through facilitation of active learning-how-to-learn strategies and to help the student develop more effective communication.

Supportive Discourse Scaffolding   The instructional strategies teachers use to help students achieve their goals are connected to the holistic view of language and learning. **Instructional discourse strategies** are the ways in which teachers communicate to students expectations for learning, how they are to learn, how they know they are learning, and, most importantly, the meaning of learning.

Another way of thinking about these discourse strategies is to consider them as a scaffold, or support for learning. **Scaffolding** refers to supporting a child so that she can understand or use language that is more complex than she could understand or use independently. Scaffolding occurs when a teacher asks questions about the elements of a story, or elaborates on the themes or vocabulary of a story, asks "thought" questions, or restates or summarizes concepts or themes. As the child is able to use the language independently, scaffolding is gradually withdrawn.

Supportive discourse scaffolding can provide a kind of "communication safety net" for students who need help in learning to communicate effectively (Silliman & Wilkinson, 1994). As the student becomes more capable, the discourse support is progressively removed. Thus, the transfer of responsibility for learning from the teacher to the student is built into the concept of supportive discourse scaffolding. Supportive discourse scaffolding provides opportunities for teachers and speech-language pathologists, as well as students, to act as working models in helping students to elaborate their own thinking (Shuy, 1988). At the same time, many opportunities are present to engage in *dynamic assessment*, which links assessment with instruction. Through dynamic assessment, we can observe the actual process of learning as it is happening and adjust discourse strategies accordingly. This can give us important information

Teachers use discourse strategies to communicate to students their expectations for learning.

Scaffolding is the guidance an adult or peer provides for students who cannot yet do a task alone.

Through dynamic assessment, teachers observe the process of learning and adjust their discourse strategies accordingly.

first person

For twelve and a half years I couldn't talk. I used a speechboard, a typewriter, and my hands to communicate with my family, friends and teachers. Before I learned to spell, it was very hard for them to know what I wanted.

When I was twelve, I saw a machine called a Handi-Voice, which is a precision electronic speech synthesizer for people who can't talk. It has a voice kind of like a robot. It will speak, save, recall or repeat any message. Now I could talk with my family. I called my sister a turkey. She said that the Handi-Voice said that, not me.

A new world has opened up for me since I got the machine. I use it in school and at home. The one thing I really very much appreciate is if people give me time to talk. For example, when a teacher asks the class a question, and I know the answer. She or he will see that I'm pushing in the answer in the Handi-Voice. When I'm ready I push a button and it talks for me. Some people, like my family, friends and teachers can make out what the voice is saying. But others can't make out a darn word.

Jason J. Homyshin, 13

Source: Helen Exley, ed., *What It's Like to Be Me* (Watford, U.K.: Exley, 1981), p. 112. Reprinted with permission of Exley Publications, Ltd.

about what a student is capable of when given support and moves us beyond just looking at the student's current status.

■ **Collaboration with the Speech-Language Pathologist** A collaborative approach requires the willingness to cross disciplinary boundaries. Members of an educational team must be willing to maintain their existing roles, or expertise, and also to expand their roles, or even relinquish them, when appropriate, to meet students' needs. Classroom-based instruction and intervention means that speech-language pathologists and regular and special education teachers will work together in new ways to achieve the goals of an integrated curriculum.

New roles for the speech-language pathologist are emerging.

There are at least seven new roles for the speech-language pathologist in language and literacy-based classrooms (Gerber, 1993; Miller, 1989; Nelson, 1993). None of these roles are exclusive—they can overlap in any combination—and all are compatible with inclusive schooling, an educational continuum, or other collaborative approaches. These new roles include:

- Teaching in a self-contained classroom for students with language disorders

Personal computers can be
effectively used to supplement classroom literacy experiences for students with
language disorders, who
need a great deal of practice
and redundancy in the de-
velopment of their reading,
writing, and speaking.
(Spencer Grant/
Monkmeyer Press Service)

- Teaching in a regularly scheduled class for these students, for example, at
  the secondary level
- Team teaching with the regular education teacher
- Team teaching in the self-contained classroom with another specialist
- Team teaching in a combination of resource and regular education
  modules
- Providing collaborative consultation to regular and special education
  teachers
- Providing staff, curriculum, or program development

The first five roles have in common direct service to students, while the last two
roles involve acting as a resource for classroom teachers, other specialists, administrators, and parents.

Role expansion in a collaborative approach also means that regular education teachers, with the support of speech-language pathologists, can learn to incorporate communication goals and strategies for individual students into
everyday classroom activities. Most importantly, effective role expansion depends on continuous planning and communication among all team members, as
well as on changes in attitudes and expectations.

In shifting toward more collaborative and integrated models of education,
including inclusive models, we need to start with the basics: challenging our

Jessie Alpaugh left school during her sophomore year, when she contracted a form of encephalitis which left her unable to speak and using a wheelchair. She returned to school at the beginning of her senior year. Here Jessie reminds us that we may take the ability to communicate freely for granted.

In the early stages of my illness, after I had started to recover from the initial shock of my new physical condition, I vowed that sometime in the future I would return to school and rejoin my class. It soon became evident, though, that if I did return, it would certainly not be under the same conditions as before my illness.

My first day back was tumultuous. After that, I calmed down a little. I came to realize that however uncomfortable and self-conscious I felt, this was the same school with the same friends and teachers I had known before I got sick. But overcoming my personal inhibition was problematic. While I recognized that this was the same school environment I had known two years ago, I did not feel at all like the same person inside. The way I interacted with the other students and my friends made me feel completely different. Just by the way countless strangers greeted me in the halls set me apart from everyone, and this was a daily reminder that I was different. It was a struggle to reconnect with my class

existing beliefs about how we work together, and what students are capable of when given appropriate support.

Technology

Technology can provide support for literacy learning and a voice for those without speech.

There are two major applications for technology for students with communication disorders. First, computer software in the area of literacy development can be effectively used to supplement classroom literacy experiences for students with language disorders, who need a great deal of practice and redundancy in the development of their reading, writing, and speaking. But more dramatically, students with severe language and speech impairments, such as those that accompany some physical disabilities, can benefit from augmentative and alternative communication systems such as electronic communication boards and computerized speech synthesizers. These systems can provide a system of communication for students who cannot speak for themselves. They will be described in more detail in Chapter 10. Developing useful communication skills can be challenging, but it is not impossible—even for students with the most significant communication disorders.

members and other peers, and I often felt quite lonely or trapped because of my speech impairment. I desperately hoped that the enthusiastic support from everyone was not only out of pity, but I think for some people it was. In the classroom I had to adjust to being solely a listener and not being able to participate in the discussions. While I have never been an outgoing ringleader in class discussions, this was nevertheless hard for me.

I have made it through my first semester back at school. Really, not a day goes by that I don't stop to think about what my life was like here before my illness. Some days I feel more nostalgic than others. It is a constant struggle to let go of the past and not become imprisoned within myself. I realize that I have set strong goals for the future, and I can educate myself. I know it is going to take a lot of strength, courage, and determination to become the person who I want and need to become. This frightens me because I often question whether I hold enough of these qualities. Sometimes I know I don't, but I try to be optimistic and remind myself that only I have the power to control my own future.

Jessie Alpaugh

SUMMARY

- Communication is the exchange of ideas. Language is one type of symbolic communication; its code expresses ideas or content. Language is functional, or pragmatic. A community of language users agrees on the appropriate ways to behave as speakers and listeners.

- Speech is one component of the total language system. It involves the physical actions needed to produce meaningful spoken words.

- Language develops very rapidly and in generally the same sequence in all children, although the ages at which children reach particular developmental milestones can vary significantly. Several theories have been proposed to explain the acquisition of language and communication. It is likely that social interaction with others in the language community plays a vital role in speech and language development. By 5 years of age, the basic system of oral communication has been acquired.

- Language disorders involve difficulties in the comprehension and expression of the meaning and content of language. Speech disorders include phonological, fluency, and voice impairments. *Communication disorders* is a more general term used to include difficulties with speech and hearing, as well as language and speech disorders.

■ Identification and assessment of students with communication disorders are typically the tasks of the speech-language pathologist. Approaches to assessment include case histories, norm-referenced tests, criterion-referenced tests, and observation.

■ Placement options for students with communication disorders are increasingly focusing on inclusion in the integrated classroom. This has led to a shift in the philosophy, principles, and practices of educators. Instructional strategies focus on integrating language and literacy develoment and supporting the use of oral communication for a variety of functional purposes.

KeY TeRMS

communication	discourse	dialect
language	speech	fluency disorder
phonology	communication	stuttering
phoneme	disorders	voice disorder
morphology	language disorders	language delay
morphemes	speech disorders	phonological awareness
syntax	specific language	instructional discourse
semantics	impairment	strategies
pragmatics	phonological disorders	scaffolding

MULTiMEDiA RESOURCeS

American Speech-Language-Hearing Association website: http://www.ASHA. org. The ASHA website offers information and resources to professionals in the field and others interested in speech and language.

Communication Disorders Health Guide website: www.speechpathology.com/. This is a source for information on communications disorders.

Kamhi, A. G., K. E. Pollock, & J. L. Harris, eds., *Communication Development and Disorders in African-American Children* (Baltimore: Paul H. Brookes, 1996). This scholarly book focuses on the nature and needs of African-American children with communication disorders.

National Institute on Deafness and Other Communication Disorders website: www.nih.gov/nidcd. This arm of the National Institutes of Health supports research on communication disorders and serves as a resource in the field.

USiNG YOUR KNOWLEDGe

 Commonalities: Do you agree that it is not possible *not* to communicate? Describe how you would communicate a specific idea through the following communication systems: music, gestures, dance, facial expressions, drawing.

 Collaboration: What is the role of the speech-language pathologist and how is it changing? Invite a speech-language pathologist to your class to talk about his or her daily activities and responsibilities. After the presentation, draw a diagram showing the relationships among service professionals and teachers who work with students with communication disorders.

 Can Do: How can teachers encourage oral communication in their classrooms? Using the suggestions in the chapter about literacy learning, develop ideas for encouraging communication in a fully inclusive classroom. Why is it important for teachers to be aware of milestones in language development and the risk factors that can indicate language learning problems? If possible, visit a kindergarten class or an early childhood education program. Watch teachers working with the children and talk with the children yourself, if allowed. Based on your reading of this chapter, would you recommend further evaluation for any of the students?

WHAT YOU CAN DO NOW

1. Talk to a school speech-language pathologist.

- Ask her to describe the students she sees: How many are there on her caseload? What are the speech and language needs that the students have?
- Ask her about her training. Does she have both a graduate and undergraduate degree in communication disorders? How many hours did she work with children before obtaining certification?
- Ask her about collaboration. Does she see children in their classrooms or in a pullout program? How does she find time to confer with their classroom teachers?
- Write an article for your school newsletter or newspaper describing your interview.

2. Many well-known and successful adults have overcome childhood stuttering.

- Visit the Stuttering Homepage (http://www.mankato.msus.edu/dept/comdis/kuster/stutter.html) on the World Wide Web.
- Read about famous people who have stuttered, from Moses (yes, Moses—see the Book of Exodus) to Christopher Robin Milne to novelist John Updike and actor James Earl Jones.
- How could you sensitively structure an assignment for a student who stutters using these resources?

3. Classrooms which include students with communication disorders should encourage multiple modes of communication. Students can express their ideas and feelings through painting, drawing, singing or using a musical instrument, creative writing, drama, email . . . the possibilities are vast. Can you design a classroom where multiple modes of communication will be encouraged? At the preschool level? At the secondary level?

Children Who Are Deaf and Hard of Hearing

STUDENTS who are deaf must be provided with a challenging academic curriculum. But first and foremost, schools must address their communication needs. They may learn to communicate through one of several communication methods. Deaf culture and the Deaf community are among the resources available to students who are deaf. The richness and complexity of Deaf culture provides a powerful context for learning and personal development for students with hearing loss and their families. As you read the chapter, think about the following questions:

■ **What is the relationship between hearing and language development?**

■ **What is Deaf culture, and what role does it play in education?**

 Can Do: What communication options are available for students who are deaf?

Commonalities: What are the technological advances and teaching strategies that can help a student with hearing loss be included in the general education classroom?

Collaboration: What professional resources are available to help the classroom teacher of children who are deaf or hard of hearing?

Many of us are fascinated by the world of deafness. We are touched by the beauty and expressiveness of sign language and by the animation of sign language users. We wonder how people who use sign language think. Do they dream in signs? We are surprised that many people who are deaf can speak. How can people speak if they cannot hear, we wonder—and how can they understand? Questions about our own ability to communicate successfully with students who are deaf may cause us to hesitate in our interactions with them. It's as if, we might think, they are people from another culture. Many people who are deaf would argue that indeed they are.

As you will see, students who are deaf or hard of hearing have much to offer to their hearing classmates. In many places, successful programs on regular school campuses encourage friendships between students who are hearing and those who are deaf. Many students who hear enjoy taking classes in sign language, which provide them with the means to communicate with their peers who are deaf. Your goal and challenge as a teacher will be to provide students who are deaf and hard of hearing with the academic and social skills they need in an environment that encourages open communication and frequent opportunities for interaction. In this chapter, you'll learn more about how to achieve these goals, as well as acquire important knowledge about hearing and the causes of hearing loss.

Definitions and Terms

Deafness is a hearing loss that precludes the learning of language through hearing.

Hard of hearing describes a loss less severe than deafness, while *hearing impairment* refers to all degrees of loss.

Deafness is usually defined as a hearing loss that precludes the learning of language through hearing (Northern & Downs, 1991). People who are deaf usually rely primarily on their vision both for their understanding of the world and for communication. **Hard of hearing** is a term used to describe a hearing loss that, although serious, is less severe than deafness and usually permits the understanding of spoken language with the use of hearing aids. **Hearing impairment** is an umbrella term that refers to all degrees of hearing loss, from slight to profound. Since many individuals in the **Deaf community**—those adults bound together by their deafness, the use of American Sign Language, and their culture, values, and attitudes—dislike the term *impairment*, we will avoid it in this chapter and instead use the term **hearing loss** when referring to individuals who are deaf and hard of hearing.

You may be confused about why the word *deaf* was sometimes capitalized and sometimes not in the preceding paragraph. It has become the convention to capitalize the word when referring to people who are deaf as a culturally different group, or to the culture of Deafness.

Residual hearing is the remaining hearing possessed by most people who are deaf.

Very few people with hearing loss are totally deaf—most have some remaining hearing, however slight. It is this remaining hearing, called **residual hearing,** that, with the help of a hearing aid, detects sounds within the environment and can be used to learn speech. Sometimes a baby is born with a hearing loss; then it is called a **congenital hearing loss**. A hearing loss can also be acquired at any time, in which case it is referred to as an **acquired hearing loss.** Most educators of students with hearing loss, however, consider it most important to know whether the child has **prelingual** or **postlingual** deafness—that is, whether the hearing loss occurred before or after the child developed spoken language.

Hearing and Hearing Loss

The human auditory system, as shown in Figure 8.1, is complicated and extremely delicate. Sound energy creates vibration, and the vibration travels in sound waves through a passageway called the ear canal to the eardrum, or tympanic membrane, a thin layer of tissue between the outer and middle ear. The vibration of the eardrum sets off a chain of vibrations in the three small bones of the middle ear, the malleus, incus, and stapes. The sound is transmitted through the cochlea, a tiny, spiral-shaped structure in the inner ear. Finally, it reaches the brain via the auditory nerve, where it is interpreted as meaningful.

Because hearing depends on the transmission of sound waves across numerous tiny structures throughout the auditory mechanism, malfunctions or damage to any part of the system can result in temporary or permanent hearing loss.

Damage or obstruction in the external or middle ear that disrupts the efficient passage or conduction of sound through those chambers results in a **conductive hearing loss**. Most conductive losses can be successfully treated medically, but research has shown that recurrent conductive hearing loss in young children can have serious long-term effects on their language development and school learning (Roberts, Wallace & Henderson, 1997).

Damage to the cochlea or the auditory nerve in the inner ear is called a **sensorineural hearing loss**. A sensorineural loss is permanent—at this time it cannot be medically treated (Northern & Downs, 1991). Most students with hearing loss in our schools have a sensorineural hearing loss, although some of them have a **mixed hearing loss**, with both conductive and sensorineural components.

Sound waves travel through the auditory canal to the eardrum, middle ear, cochlea, and (via the auditory nerve) the brain.

Damage or obstruction in the external or middle ear disrupts the passage of sound and causes conductive hearing loss.

Sensorineural hearing loss is usually caused by damage to the cochlea or auditory nerve.

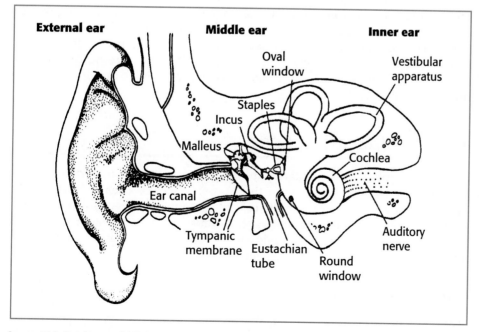

Figure 8.1
Structure of the Ear

Source: M.L. Batshaw and Y.M. Perret, *Children with Disabilities: A Medical Primer*, 3d ed. (Baltimore: Paul H. Brookes, 1992), p. 323. Used by permission of the authors.

Children with hearing loss can feel sound vibrations and watch lip movements, giving them an understanding of spoken language that can be supplemented by a hearing aid. (Michal Heron)

Researchers around the country have been surgically inserting **cochlear implants** in a relatively small number of profoundly deaf children with sensorineural hearing loss. Although the cochlear implant is not a cure for deafness, implants do appear to improve the perception of sound. The implants have become a source of controversy, however, as the accompanying box, "Cochlear Implants," explains.

Most school-age children who are deaf or hard of hearing have **bilateral hearing loss**; that is, they have a hearing loss in both ears (although one ear may have more hearing than the other). Some children, however, have normal hearing in one ear and a hearing loss in the other; they are said to have a **unilateral hearing loss**. Children with unilateral hearing losses may develop language normally, but some show evidence of problems in the classroom. They are at a disadvantage in noisy environments and may have difficulties picking out the most important source of sound, such as the teacher's voice. These children are more likely to repeat a grade in school, and many of them may require special education services, especially those provided through a resource specialist (Northern & Downs, 1991). See Table 8.1 for an overview of the effects of hearing loss on children.

Bilateral hearing loss is a loss in both ears; unilateral hearing loss is a loss in one.

Causes of Hearing Loss

Knowledge of the cause of hearing loss in young children is important for several reasons. In the case of conductive losses, which are usually treatable, the cause dictates the treatment; in the case of sensorineural loss, which is permanent, knowledge will help families gather information about the probability of hearing loss in any subsequent children and may help them master the feelings of stress related to their child's disability.

Causes of Conductive Hearing Loss

The most common cause of conductive hearing loss in children is middle ear infection, or **otitis media**. When, because of a cold or for some other reason, fluid gathers in the middle ear, it dampens or restricts the movement of the eardrum,

A cochlear implant is an electronic device designed to provide sound information for adults and children who have sensorineural hearing loss in both ears and obtain limited benefit from appropriate hearing aids. In the last thirty years, the technology has evolved from a device with a single electrode (or channel) to systems that transmit more sound information through multiple electrodes (or channels). The cochlear implant has been approved for use with children since 1990; a small but growing number of children with deafness are currently using cochlear implants.

Advocates such as Dr. Mary Jo Osberger, a researcher who has studied children with cochlear implants, assert that they can help children who do not benefit from hearing aids develop speech and language understanding and skills. She says that "no other sensory aid has had such a dramatic impact on improving the acquisition and use of spoken language by children with profound hearing impairments." The earlier the children received implants, the greater their chances of improvement.

However, the implant has been called "cultural genocide" by many in the Deaf community who believe American Sign Language is the linguistic base for a separate culture. Their response is built on a legacy of failed attempts to teach deaf children oral communication—in their view, to be more like hearing children.

In the view of Harlan Lane, a psychology professor at Northeastern University, "It's simply unethical to use force, surgery, or education to take children who would normally be members of a linguistic minority and try to make them into members of another linguistic group."

To many, the argument implies that deaf children belong to the Deaf community and not to their hearing parents, a view to which people like Donna Morere take exception. "There is a large segment within the community that identifies with Deaf culture and feels like hearing parents are not competent to make a decision like choosing a cochlear implant for their children," she says.

Morere is in a unique position to see both sides of the debate. As a psychology professor at Gallaudet University—the only liberal arts college for the deaf in the United States—she has taught at the heart of the Deaf culture movement. Morere has normal hearing, but when her son, Thomas, was diagnosed as profoundly deaf, she was suddenly faced not with the abstract arguments of ethicists and anthropologists, but with the hard reality that her child could not hear.

Initially, Morere says, she was persuaded by some of her colleagues at Gallaudet who cautioned her against opting for a cochlear implant. Her eventual decision to go ahead with the procedure is one she now says she wished she'd made earlier.

"When I saw what the CI could do, I really regretted the little over a year that he didn't have it," she says. "I'm so relieved when Thomas can ride his bicycle in the street with other kids and instead of having to run after him and drag him off the street when a car comes, I can yell 'Car!' and he will ride his bike off the street," Morere says. "If that was all the cochlear implant accomplished, that would have satisfied me, but it's gone way beyond that."

Sources: Adapted from Mary Jo Osberger and Harlan Lane, "The Debate: Cochlear Implants in Children," *Hearing Health 9* (2) (February–March 1993), pp. 19–22; "What Is a Cochlear Implant?" http://www.cochlear.com/pap/HearCI.htm; and "A Clash of Cultures," http://foxnews.com/health/features/cochlear/cultures.sml.

and hearing loss may result. Middle ear infection, or simply the presence of fluid in the middle ear, can have serious effects on hearing in children, and it should always be brought to the attention of the child's pediatrician. *Chronic* otitis media (ear infection that lasts for twelve weeks or longer), with long-term effects on hearing, can also delay the normal development of language and speech in young children (Friel-Patti & Finitzo, 1990). This language delay may, in turn, have adverse effects over time on a child's achievement in school, long after the ear infection has disappeared (Northern & Downs, 1991).

Children should be treated by a physician when warning signs of middle ear infection appear, and especially when they persist over time. Some of those signs are fever, redness of the ear, rubbing of the ear, or, in a young infant, rubbing the head against a mattress or blanket; reports of pain or itching; and, in extreme cases, dripping from the ear. Many middle ear infections can be

Otitis media is the most common cause of conductive hearing loss in children.

Table 8.1 Degrees of Hearing Loss

Average Hearing Level	Description	Possible Condition	What Can Be Heard Without Amplification	Handicapping Effects (If Not Treated in First Year of Life)	Probable Needs
0–15 dB*	Normal range		All speech sounds	None	None
15–25 dB	Slight hearing loss	Conductive hearing losses, some sensorineural hearing losses	Vowel sounds heard clearly; may miss unvoiced consonants sounds	Mild auditory dysfunction in language learning	Consideration of need for hearing aid; speech reading, auditory training, speech therapy, preferential seating
25–30 dB	Mild hearing loss	Conductive or sensorineural hearing loss	Only some speech sounds, the louder voiced sounds	Auditory learning dysfunction, mild language delay, mild speech problems	Hearing aid, speech reading, auditory training, speech therapy
30–50 dB	Moderate hearing loss	Conductive hearing loss from chronic middle ear disorders; sensorineural hearing losses	Almost no speech sounds at normal conversational level	Speech problems, language delay, learning difficulties	All of the above, plus consideration of other special education services
50–70 dB	Severe hearing loss	Sensorineural or mixed losses due to a combination of middle ear disease and sensorineural involvement	No speech sounds at normal conversational level	Severe speech problems, language delay, learning difficulties	All of the above; need for special education services
70+ dB	Profound hearing loss	Sensorineural or mixed losses due to a combination of middle ear disease and sensorineural involvement	No speech or other sounds	Severe speech problems, language delay, learning difficulties	All of the above; need for special education services

*dB stands for *decibels,* or units of loudness.
Source: Adapted from Jerry L. Northern and Marion P. Downs, *Hearing in Children,* 4th ed. (Baltimore: Williams & Wilkins, 1991). Copyright © 1991 by Williams & Wilkins. Used by permission of Waverly.

effectively treated with antibiotics, and chronic cases are often treated with the insertion of small tubes into the ear, through which the liquid in the middle ear will drain out naturally (Northern & Downs, 1991). Ear infections should always be treated promptly in babies and young children: their long-term effects can be very serious. You as a professional working with young children and families can play an important role in the prevention of conductive hearing loss by encouraging prompt medical treatment when an ear infection is suspected.

～ Causes of Sensorineural Hearing Loss

1. **Heredity.** We know that in a great number of cases, hearing loss is caused by heredity, or genetic factors. It is believed that hereditary deafness accounts for about 50 percent of the cases of congenital deafness in this country today (Moores, 1996).

2. **Meningitis.** Meningitis is a bacterial or viral infection that causes inflammation of the coverings of the brain and spinal cord. If the infection reaches the inner ear, it can destroy the delicate organs within, resulting in deafness. Meningitis is the major cause of acquired deafness occurring in children. It may also be associated with other neurological disabilities.

3. **Prematurity.** Prematurity and the traumatic medical events frequently associated with premature birth and low birthweight are sometimes associated with hearing loss. When infants are born early, sick, and small, they

are at considerably higher risk for hearing loss, but it is often difficult to isolate the factor that actually causes the deafness. With the increasing number of very low birthweight children who are surviving with the help of modern neonatal medicine, it is likely that the number of children with hearing loss in this category will increase.

4. **Other causes.** Other, less common causes of childhood hearing loss include mother-child blood incompatibility, or RH incompatibility. This is decreasing as a cause of deafness because of rhogam treatments and improvements in blood transfusion techniques. Cytomegalovirus (CMV) (see Chapter 2) accounts for a small but increasing number of cases of childhood hearing loss and is likely to cause additional handicaps as well (Schildroth, 1994).

Causes of Sensorineural Hearing Loss

Conductive hearing loss can often be successfully treated in young children, and it is not usually the major cause of hearing loss that places school-age children in special education services. Children with sensorineural hearing loss, though, usually have a permanent condition that cannot be medically treated and that makes special education services necessary.

Knowledge of the cause of a child's sensorineural hearing loss is often important for families. Parents may want to know if a child's hearing loss is hereditary. A genetic counselor can help a family know whether or not that determination can be made (Vernon & Andrews, 1990). Also, many parents feel a strong desire to know the cause of their child's disability. In fact, Kathryn Meadow (1968) found that parents who knew the probable cause of their child's hearing loss were better able to cope with the complex feelings associated with the diagnosis. Summers, Behr, and Turnbull (1989) suggest that identifying the cause of disability may be a positive process of adaptation for families.

The major causes of sensorineural hearing loss in children change over time, depending on the occurrence of epidemics, the development of new drugs and medical treatments, and public health conditions. For example, most of the children who lost their hearing as a result of maternal exposure to rubella during the 1960s rubella epidemic have by now left special education services, and since the rubella vaccine was introduced in 1969, rubella has become a less prominent cause of hearing loss. See the accompanying box, "Causes of "Sensorineural Hearing Loss," for a list of the current most common causes of sensorineural hearing loss in children.

Although there are benefits to be derived from knowing the cause of sensorineural hearing loss, that information is frequently unavailable. In at least one-third of the reported cases of hearing loss, despite the best efforts of parents and counselors to determine the cause, it remains unknown (Moores, 1996).

Children with sensorineural hearing loss usually require special education services.

Sensorineural hearing loss in children can be caused by hereditary factors, rubella, meningitis, and prematurity.

About 34 percent of children with hearing loss also have other disabilities.

Students with Hearing Loss and Additional Disabilities

About 34 percent of the children who are deaf and hard of hearing and enrolled in special education programs have been identified with a disability in addition to their hearing loss (Annual Survey of Deaf and Hard-of-Hearing Children and Youth, 1996–1997). Table 8.2 shows the numbers of children with hearing loss and additional disabilities. The most common additional disabilities are the cognitive-behavioral disabilities: mental retardation and specific learning disabilities. If 34 percent seems high to you, note that part of the explanation for this relationship comes from the linkage between the cause of hearing loss and the additional disability. Moores (1996) reminds us:

> All of the major contemporary known causes of early childhood deafness may be related to other conditions to some extent. These include maternal rubella, prematurity, cytomegalovirus, mother-child blood incompatibility, and meningitis. Even in the case of inherited deafness, whether dominant, recessive, or sex-linked, the hearing loss may be only one manifestation of a syndrome that includes a wide range of conditions. (p. 111)

Table 8.2   **Deaf and Hard-of-Hearing Students with Additional Disabilities, 1996 to 1997**

Additional Disabilities	Percentage
Legal blindness	1.5
Uncorrected visual problems	2.6
Brain damage or injury	1.2
Epilepsy/convulsive disorder	1.0
Orthopedic disabilities	2.7
Cerebral palsy	2.9
Heart disorder	1.1
Other health impaired	4.4
Mental retardation	8.3
Emotional or behavioral problem	3.9
Specific learning disability	9.3
Attention deficit disorder	3.7
Other	3.4
Totals:	
One or more additional disabilities[a]	34.3
No additional disabilities[a]	65.7

Note: Figures do not add up to 100 percent because some students have more than one disability.
Source: *1996–1997 Annual Survey of Deaf and Hard-of-Hearing Children and Youth* (Washington, DC: Gallaudet Research Institute, Gallaudet University). Used by permission of Gallaudet Research Institute.

   a. *Additional disabilities* refer to educationally significant disabilities reported in addition to hearing loss. For purposes of the annual survey, an educationally significant disability is regarded as one that places additional demands or requirements on instructional arrangements, causes modifications of teaching modes, or alters or restricts the student's activities or learning in ways additive to those occasioned by hearing loss alone.

There may also be social or environmental causes for an additional condition: An impoverished communication system, late entry to school, an inappropriate school program, and a lack of consistent behavioral limits, for example, could combine to allow the development of an additional disability.

Hearing loss is also frequently associated with other conditions that may be considered a student's primary disability, such as Down syndrome, cerebral palsy, and cleft palate (Northern & Downs, 1991). In addition, children who are both deaf and blind constitute a small but unique group of students who often have intensive communication and mobility needs and are best served by a multidisciplinary group of professionals (Chen & Dote-Kwan, 1995).

It is likely that the number of children who have hearing loss and multiple disabilities will increase over the coming years because of the improved survival rates of premature and medically at-risk infants and improved identification and diagnostic procedures. Effective strategies for teaching these children, always difficult to come by, must continue to be developed.

Prevalence

In comparison to other groups of children served in special education programs, the number of children who are deaf and hard of hearing is small. In fact, the number of children has declined slowly but steadily over the past three decades (Moores, 1997). Only 1.3 percent of the children served in special programs in the 1994 to 1995 school year were labeled hearing impaired (Eighteenth Annual *Report to Congress on the Implementation of the Individuals with Disabilities Education Act*, 1996). As many as 18.7 million Americans have some kind of hearing loss (Meadow-Orlans & Orlans, 1990), but the great majority of these are adults. Counting the number of children with hearing loss is made difficult by the fact that many children have such a mild loss that they are not receiving any special education services at all; in addition, some students with hearing loss are in programs designed for other disabilities and are not included in most counts.

A small percentage of all the children served in special education programs are deaf or hard of hearing.

Measurement of Hearing Loss

If you work with students with hearing loss, you will most likely come into contact with a number of other professionals who interact with the child and family. As you review your students' records, you will see their reports.

The **otologist** is a physician whose specialization is diseases of the ear. He or she may participate in the diagnosis of hearing loss and treat the child later for related problems. The otologist is also the specialist many children see for chronic middle ear infections.

The **audiologist** has special training in testing and measuring hearing. There are more than seven thousand professionally trained audiologists in the United States with the skills and equipment needed to evaluate the hearing of any child at any age with a high degree of accuracy (American Academy of Audiology, 1989). Many audiologists also participate in the process of rehabilitation, or treatment of the effects of hearing loss, and prescribe and evaluate the effectiveness of hearing aids.

The audiologist is trained to test and measure hearing.

The traditional first hearing test given by an audiologist is called a pure-tone test. You have probably had a test like this yourself, since hearing

The audiogram is the chart on
which the audiologist records the
individual's responses to sounds
presented.

screenings are common in schools. In a pure-tone test the individual, wearing headphones, is exposed to a series of tones or beeps measured in decibels (units of loudness). The tones vary in loudness, or intensity, from soft to loud, and in pitch, or frequency, from low to high. The **audiogram** is the chart on which the audiologist records the individual's responses to the tones. People with normal hearing generally respond to very soft sounds, whether they are high or low in frequency (pitch). Look at Figure 8.2 to see the responses of people with varying kinds of hearing loss. Note that each ear is tested separately.

There are a couple of simple principles that make interpreting an audiogram easier. First, the farther down on the audiogram that the responses are recorded, the less residual hearing a person has, or the louder the tones had to be before the person responded to them. Second, the most crucial sounds for a person to hear are those that fall between 500 and 2000 hertz, or cycles per second. Those are the "speech frequencies," the pitch range within which most speech sounds fall. Many professionals believe that it is more important that children with hearing loss hear speech than any other sounds. It is through amplification with hearing aids and the training of their residual hearing to respond to speech sounds that children can most efficiently learn to understand and express spoken language.

Effects of Hearing Loss

The impact of hearing loss on a person's ability to acquire naturally the spoken language of his or her community is often substantial. Those communication difficulties may then adversely influence school achievement, social and emotional development, and interaction with others. Relationships within families can be touched by these issues, too, as we will see.

Effects on the Child

Hearing loss has its most pervasive effect on the development of spoken language. It does not appear to affect cognitive or intellectual development, but it can have a significant impact on school achievement.

■ **Language Development** If you were to become deaf right now, your primary disability would be your inability to hear. Your relations with your family and friends might be strained by your inability to understand everything they say through lip reading. You would be particularly uncomfortable at parties and restaurants, where the noisy background would make it difficult for you to use your residual hearing to follow the conversation. Television and movies would be harder to follow, and listening to music would bring you less pleasure. Well, you might say, that's what deafness is all about, isn't it? Well, yes—for those of us who have already acquired language. For the prelingually deaf child, deafness is much more than that.

Kathryn Meadow-Orlans (1980) has said that for a child the primary disability of hearing loss is not the deprivation of sound, but the deprivation of *language*. Think about it. Young children with normal hearing learn how to talk by listening to the people around them use language meaningfully. They begin to understand and to say words. As they have more experiences listening and using language for different communicative purposes, and mature cognitively, their ability to communicate becomes much more sophisticated. But for the

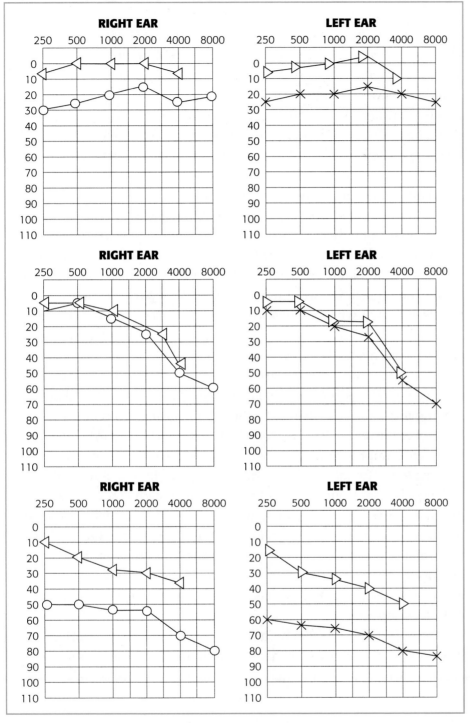

Figure 8.2
Three Examples of an Audiogram. Top: Bilateral conductive hearing loss. Center: Bilateral sensorineural hearing loss. Bottom: Bilateral mixed-type hearing loss.

Source: Jerry L. Northern and Marion P. Downs, *Hearing in Children,* 4th ed. (Baltimore: Williams & Wilkins, 1991), p. 11. Copyright © 1991 by Jerry L. Northern and Marion P. Downs. Used by permission of Waverly.

first person

Troy is 29 years old, deaf and does not use hearing aids. He lives in Mifflinburg, Pennsylvania. When he was 13, he lost his hearing.

I was born with normal hearing. In December of 1980, I lost my hearing suddenly (overnight) due to spinal meningitis (an illness affecting the brain). Up until this point in my life, I was very outgoing and sociable. After I lost my hearing, I felt inferior to others because I had known the enjoyments of hearing and felt I could no longer enjoy life like everyone else. I could have easily given up and taken the easy way out, but I didn't.

After I recovered from spinal meningitis and was released from the hospital, not only was I deaf, but I had to learn to walk all over again. (When the disease affected my inner ear, it affected my balance, too.) . . . I didn't know sign language and I couldn't read lips at all, so all my communication was through writing—on paper, napkins, towels, hands or whatever was available. . . . This was a total change in my life and I was only 13 years old. . . . My instinct told me to fight my way back and so I did.

I immediately set out to learn to walk, talk, and lip-read. I gave up my free period in school so that I could work with a speech and lip-reading instructor. This had to be the most helpful person in my life. I was never pushed so hard by someone to succeed. After four years, I made great improvements and was functioning well with everyone.

One of the first things I did after I went back to school was set some goals. I said, one day I will graduate with high grades, be a graduation speaker, play sports, graduate from college, get a good job and meet a woman who would love and understand me. Well, I immediately started getting very high grades. . . . I noticed that because I was deaf, I could concentrate better on what I was reading and I never got distracted by noises and things. It wasn't a handicap, but a blessing after all. . . .

When I graduated from high school, I was pleasantly surprised to be selected to be our class speaker at graduation. . . . This was an

Because hearing loss impedes the development of spoken language, most children with hearing loss begin school with a language deficit.

child who does not hear, or does not hear well, that listening experience does not occur, or occurs much less consistently. Unless sign language is used in the home, there are fewer occasions for practice using language to communicate. Many children who are deaf, particularly those who have not been involved in early intervention programs, come to school at age 3 (and sometimes much later) without any speech or signing skills at all. So, although there are exceptions, most children who are deaf or hard of hearing start school with a lan-

honor, but also a time for much nervousness. I still had some problems saying certain words, especially words with the letters *t* and *s*. Everyone said I sounded good. It probably helped that I could hear for 13 years because I knew what it felt like to talk.

After graduating from high school I attended . . . Bloomsburg University for computer and information science. After my second year, I hit a rough period in life. I was beginning to see a lot of discrimination against deaf people and I got discouraged. I dropped out of college and went through a number of jobs, none of which made me happy. Then, I met the woman I was to marry and things began changing for the better. I recently returned to Bloomsburg University and I'm currently studying for a degree in business management with a minor in marketing.

When I first lost my hearing, I was very nervous about the dark. When it is dark, you can't see or hear and it is quite an experience. I've found that the best thing for me for security at night was to have a dog. I have a black lab named Bear. Whenever anyone is around the house or even pulls into the driveway, he gets next to me and barks. . . . The companionship of a dog helped me get over the fact that I was deaf and gave me a buddy when I was 13.

I tend to look at life as a series of mountains. As I reach the zenith of a mountain, I cannot help but notice that there are other mountains nearby, all of which are taller, steeper, and more rugged than any mountain I've overcome. I believe as a deaf person, you must constantly strive to improve in life and communication. Nothing is handed to you and if you work for it, you will appreciate it a whole lot more.

Troy Bowerox

Source: Reprinted by permission of HiP magazine.

guage delay, and many of them never catch up to their hearing peers linguistically or academically while they are in school.

Genoval, for example, was a 15-year-old boy who was profoundly deaf. His family had recently moved from El Salvador to Los Angeles, and he had never been in school or had any communication development services. The language of his home was Spanish, but his family reported that he used no recognizable Spanish words. The language of the school was English (presented orally and accompanied by an English-order sign language system), but on entering school Genoval used no recognizable English vocabulary, either signed or spoken. This boy was very bright and sociable—he had developed his own gesture language, and through this pantomime could communicate simple needs and actions. But catching up to the other students who were deaf in his class presented a formidable challenge to Genoval and his teachers.

The first language of children who are deaf and hard of hearing depends to some extent on the language they are exposed to in the home. The more residual hearing a child has, the more likely it is that the child will learn to speak the language of the home. Children who have little usable residual hearing, however, may develop a relatively unique "first language" based on what they are exposed to—spoken words and formal sign, for example—and what they invent themselves—gestures and "home signs" that may be understood only by the child and family members (Luetke-Stahlman & Luckner, 1991). On the other hand, deaf children of deaf parents who use American Sign Language may begin school with communication abilities that are developmentally appropriate for their age—and continue to excel throughout their school careers.

For many children with hearing loss, learning *English* begins when they enter school. Research that has examined the acquisition of English literacy skills—speaking, reading, and writing—of children with hearing loss tells us that the English language of children who are deaf typically develops in the same order as that of hearing children, but at a considerably slower rate (Paul, 1998).

■ **Cognitive and Intellectual Development** The best information that we have today, based on the most recently conducted research, is that people who are deaf and hard of hearing as a group have normal cognitive and intellectual abilities (Paul & Jackson, 1993). However, that conclusion is a fairly recent one—for many years psychologists believed that the thinking and reasoning capacities of deaf people were "inferior" (Pintner & Patterson, 1917) or qualitatively different (Myklebust, 1964).

These earlier conclusions stemmed from the assessment process. People who are deaf or hard of hearing have, at times, been administered IQ tests that weigh verbal skills heavily; when they did not do well because of their limited understanding and use of English they were judged to be cognitively below normal—sometimes even mentally retarded (Moores, 1996). Even when a relatively "fair" test is used, the person with hearing loss may not understand the test directions given by a psychologist who does not have the skills necessary for communicating with him or her. Although psychologists and other test administrators have become more knowledgeable about testing people who are deaf and fewer abuses seem to occur today, great care should always be taken in interpreting test scores. As always, they are just one piece of the puzzle.

■ **School Achievement** Despite the normal cognitive and intellectual abilities of most children with hearing loss, their average school achievement is significantly below that of their hearing peers. Paul and Jackson (1993) report that "one of the most robust findings is that there is an inverse relationship between hearing impairment and achievement: the more severe the impairment, the lower the achievement" (p. 34).

Children who have a slight to moderate hearing loss, and therefore are considered hard of hearing, are more likely to be served in regular education classes or in self-contained classes where speech and hearing are emphasized. Despite their residual hearing, these children tend to lag one to three years be-

The more residual hearing children have, the more likely they will speak the language of their home.

Many children with hearing loss do not learn English until they begin school.

People with hearing loss have normal cognitive and intellectual abilities, although they may not score well on IQ tests.

hind their hearing peers in academic achievement (Ross, 1990). As for children with more severe hearing loss, Quigley and Paul (1986) found that there has been very little improvement in their academic achievement since the first study on the topic, published over seventy years ago. Although there has been some improvement in reading achievement scores in recent decades, the average deaf student finishing high school has reading and language abilities similar to a 9- or 10-year old hearing student, with math achievement scores a grade or two higher (Paul, 1998).

Why this discrepancy between ability and achievement? It hinges on the lack of mastery of the English language among students who are deaf. If a person can't comprehend and use the language fluently, then he or she can't read it—even basal reading materials incorporate sophisticated grammatical structures at preprimer and first-grade levels (King & Quigley, 1985). Reading ability is crucial for success in nearly all academic areas.

Students who are most successful in school are those who come from highly structured and comprehensive oral programs, where strong parental involvement and early education are integral. These students also have higher IQ scores than the average deaf student and come from higher socioeconomic levels (Quigley & Paul, 1986). Students with those advantages—intensive parent involvement, early diagnosis and intervention, high IQ scores, comfortable economic backgrounds, and school programs with committed professionals—would also be likely to succeed in a school program in which sign language was used. Educators of students with hearing loss must now find a way to improve the academic achievement of their students who do not have such advantages, as well as those from non-English-speaking families and those with other disabilities.

■ **Social and Emotional Development** Traditionally, psychologists and other professionals concerned with the social and emotional development of individuals who are deaf have concentrated on the differences in this group from the "norms" set by hearing subjects. From this approach has arisen what Donald Moores (1996) calls a "deviance model," which implies that there is something deficient in the psychological makeup of people who are deaf. Many of these conclusions have arisen because of the psychological assessment of students with hearing loss by examiners who are not trained in using sign language and who administer tests that are not appropriate.

Moores (1996) describes another view of the social and emotional development of individuals with hearing loss. This perspective focuses on the development of a healthy, whole, well-integrated person rather than concentrating on what is different or deficient. It assumes that all humans have similar basic needs, which must be met satisfactorily for healthy personal development—among them, the need to communicate with others. For people who are deaf, this need for basic human communication is not always met. Think about this example: Parents of young children who are deaf often feel they do not have the command of communication necessary to explain complicated events, such as a relative's death, a forthcoming move, or marital problems, and so do not fully communicate the meaning of these experiences to their child. As a result, the child's world may change drastically from one day to the next with no explanation—leaving him or her anxious, frightened, resentful, or confused (Meadow-Orlans, 1980). Thus the frustration that can arise from poor communication can spill over into the child's behavior, relationships, and motivation.

This is not to say that people who are deaf and hard of hearing, young and old, do not have problems like everyone else; only that those problems are not

Despite normal abilities, most children with hearing loss do not achieve at grade level.

Students with hearing loss who succeed in school often have many factors working in their favor.

Inadequate psychological assessment may label individuals with hearing loss as socially and emotionally deficient.

Frustration over inadequate communication may result in behavior or emotional problems for children who are deaf.

particular to hearing loss. Rather, they may arise from experiences within the family, school, and community where poor communication or no communication is the rule.

In summary, the primary effect of deafness on the developing child is to place the development of communication at risk. Because communication skills are so essential for school learning, when these skills are affected, school achievement is, too. But cognitive and social development need not be delayed in children with hearing loss when they are provided with a means and reason to communicate from an early age.

Effects on the Family

Hearing loss is not routinely screened for at birth, and many families do not begin to suspect that their child's hearing is impaired until the child's second year, when he or she does not begin to talk (see the accompanying box, "Speech and Hearing Checklist"). Even when parents have doubts about their child's hearing during the first year, they are frequently reassured by their pediatricians that the child is normal and that they are "overanxious." One mother, Elsa, told her story this way:

> I felt Pablo couldn't hear from the time he was about 6 months old. But my pediatrician clapped his hands behind Pablo's head and when he turned, the doctor told me he was fine, and I was worrying too much. I believed him for a while, but eventually I went to two more doctors before I found one who would listen to me and recommend a hearing test. Pablo wasn't diagnosed as deaf until he was 18 months old—one year after I first suggested there was a problem . . . and he is profoundly deaf!

Many parents do not begin to suspect a hearing loss until their child's second year.

This teacher and student are signing about the experience of blowing bubbles. The teacher wears a microphone, which sends a signal to the child's auditory trainer—his school hearing aid. (Ellen Senisi/The Image Works, Inc.)

～ Speech and Hearing Checklist

Average Speech and Hearing Behavior for the Child's Age Level

3–6 Months
The infant awakens or quiets to the sound of a voice. He typically turns eyes and head in the direction of the source of the sound.

7–10 Months
The baby turns her head toward familiar sounds, even when she cannot see what is happening:

- Dog barking or paper rustling
- Familiar footsteps
- Someone's voice

11–15 Months
The baby understands some words and makes appropriate responses or behavior:

- "Where's the cat?"
- "Find the truck."

She tries to imitate and match sounds with her own speech production (often nonsensical syllables), especially in response to human voices or loud noises.

1½ Years
The child identifies things in response to questions, such as parts of the body. He uses a few single words. Although not complete or perfectly pronounced, the words should be clearly meaningful.

2 Years
The child follows simple commands without visual clues from the speaker:

- "Get your book and give it to Daddy."
- "Bring me that ball."

She puts words together to make sentences, although they are not complete or grammatically correct:

- "Juice all gone."
- "Go bye-bye car."

The child uses everyday words heard at home or at day care or school. She enjoys being read to and shown pictures in books or magazines and points out pictures on request.

There is interest in the radio and television as shown by word or action.

2½ Years
The child says or sings rhymes and songs and enjoys music. When interesting sounds are heard, he responds by investigating the noise or telling someone what has been heard. For example:

- Car door slams.
- Telephone rings.

3 Years
The child understands and uses simple verbs, pronouns, and adjectives:

- Go, come, run, sing
- Me, you, him, her
- Big, green, sweet

She locates the source of a sound automatically. Complete sentences are often used.

4 Years
The child is able to give connected accounts of some recent experiences. He can carry out a sequence of two simple directions:

- "Find your sister and bring her here."
- "Get the ball and throw it to the dog."

5 Years
The child's speech should be intelligible, although some sounds may still be mispronounced. Neighbors and other adults outside the family can understand most of what the child says, and his grammatical patterns should match theirs most of the time. He can carry on a conversation, although vocabulary may be limited. Pronouns should be used correctly:

- "I" instead of "me"
- "He" instead of "him"

Source: Copyright © 1997 by Alexander Graham Bell Association for the Deaf, all rights reserved. 3417 Volta Place, N.W., Washington, DC 20007-2778, (202) 337-5220 Voice and TTY.

Once a family has had its child's hearing tested by an audiologist and a diagnosis of deafness has been given, reactions may range from shock to anger to depression. Most parents feel overwhelmed by helplessness and their own emotions and have a difficult time taking in the information that professionals—in this case usually the audiologist or teacher of the deaf—are eager to present to them. Involvement in an early intervention program is very important for the young child and the family, but it takes some time for the implications of hearing loss on language learning to become clear.

Most parents can and do learn to cope with their child's hearing loss. Here is Elsa again:

> I had to be able to cope with Pablo's deafness—at such a young age he had to get hearing aids and start school, and I had to be there to help him. I participated in the program with him, and began to learn sign language. Being with other parents in the same situation and having something to do really helped me, although sometimes at night I would get into bed by myself and cry. But for my husband it was much harder. He couldn't be as involved as I was, and for a long time he couldn't understand the deafness or accept it.

Koester and Meadow-Orlans (1990) describe the need of parents of young children who are deaf for social support from a network of family, friends, and professionals. But some reports indicate that families with young children who are deaf are less likely than others to have that social network; families report that unwanted advice-giving, misconceptions about the child, and underestimates of the child's ability often cause problems between parents and their family and friends.

The feelings that often accompany the diagnosis of hearing loss do not go away quickly. But sensitive professionals can do much to assist families through this period, by listening to them, by accepting the inevitability of their reactions, and by pointing out to them the strengths and beauties of their child. In addition, other parents with children who are deaf will provide significant support and models for successful coping for young families; meetings with groups that can enable experienced families and young families to share their feelings and experiences should be built into early intervention programs (Koester & Meadow-Orlans, 1990).

Some of the reactions that families experience may come as a result of not being familiar with positive images of adults who are deaf. The work that is being done to identify the cultural components of Deafness may someday change our society's perception of hearing loss.

Other parents with children who are deaf can provide significant support and models for successful coping.

Deafness and Culture

Our discussions so far in this chapter have centered around definitions and descriptions that place deafness in the context of *disability*—and that tend to measure people who are deaf by the yardstick of people who are hearing. We speak of deafness as hearing *loss* or hearing *impairment*—yet, as one deaf professional put it: "How would women like to be referred to as male-impaired, or whites like to be called black-impaired? I'm not impaired; I'm deaf!" Many professionals in the field of deafness, particularly those who are deaf themselves, have been urging teachers of deaf childen to drop the clinical perspective, in which deafness is seen as a pathology, a deviance from the "normal" condition of hear-

The clinical perspective of deafness views it as a disability; many prefer that a cultural perspective be adopted.

～ Deaf Culture and History

In March 1998 the Deaf community celebrated the tenth anniversary of the 1988 watershed political event at Gallaudet University, "Deaf President Now." Gallaudet students, faculty, and sympathetic deaf people from all over the country gathered to close down the university in protest because a hearing woman with little knowledge of deafness was named president. After a week of protests, the new president resigned and the university board of trustees named I. King Jordan, a man who became deaf early in life, president. In Jordan's first statement after he was named president, he stated, "We know that deaf people can do anything hearing people can do except hear" (Sacks, 1989). Many people who are deaf view that week at Gallaudet as a milestone in their history, and a powerful expression of the values of the Deaf community.

The Deaf President Now movement became a catalyst for a new study of the culture and history of deafness (Parasnis, 1996). If the values and culture of the Deaf community are to be integrated into the education of students who are deaf, then it is important to bring more teachers who are deaf into school programs. Deaf teachers can bring their own knowledge of Deaf culture and their own experiences to their students, as well as provide examples of successful adult life. In addition, many adults who are deaf are fluent ASL users but can also use manually coded English systems—they are bilingual.

Many professionals now believe that a knowledge and understanding of Deaf culture should be part of the school curriculum for students who are deaf, so that they are provided with opportunities to learn about other individuals with deafness and their achievements (Christensen, 1993; Schirmer, 1994).

ing, a condition that must be "cured" or "fixed." These deaf professionals are exhorting the field to adopt the *cultural* perspective, which describes people who are deaf as members of a different culture—a culture with its own language, social institutions, class structure, history, attitudes, values, and literature—that must be studied, understood, and respected (Crittenden, 1993).

Adoption of a cultural perspective on deafness demands a knowledge of **Deaf culture**, which Crittenden (1993) defines as "the view of life manifested by the mores, beliefs, artistic expression, understandings, and language particular to Deaf people" (p. 218). Deaf culture is the mainstay of the Deaf community, that group of people who share common goals deriving from Deaf cultural influences and work together toward achieving these goals. Crittenden (1993) describes the characteristics that members of the Deaf community share as follows:

Deaf culture unites those in the Deaf community who share common goals.

- "Attitudinal deafness," the desire to associate with other deaf people with whom values and experiences are shared
- The use of American Sign Language (ASL), considered by members of the Deaf community to be their native language
- The similar life experiences of many people who are deaf in relation to family, schooling, and interaction with "the hearing world"
- The bond between deaf people, the friendships and relationships that grow out of those shared experiences

Members of the Deaf community may not be physically deaf (that is, they may be hearing people), but they must actively support the goals of the Deaf community and work together with people who are deaf to achieve them (Padden, 1980). Padden and Humphries's book *Deaf in America: Voices from a Culture* (1988) portrays members of the Deaf community. These authors, deaf themselves, write:

In contrast to the long history of writings that treat [deaf people] as medical cases, or people with "disabilities," who "compensate" for their deafness by using sign language, we want to portray the lives they live, their art and performances, their everyday talk, their shared myths, and the lessons they teach one another. We have always felt that the attention given to the physical condition of not hearing has obscured far more interesting facets of Deaf people's lives. (p. 1)

Thomas Holcomb (1997) argues that it is important to offer deaf children opportunities to develop a deaf identity from a young age, so that they see themselves as bicultural in a diverse world (see the accompanying box, "Deaf Culture and History").

Educational Issues and Teaching Strategies

Students with hearing loss need the benefit of an interdisciplinary team of professionals who will cooperatively plan and implement their educational program, whether it is an individualized family service plan (IFSP) for the child from birth to age 3, the individualized education program (IEP) for the school-aged child, or an individualized transition plan (ITP) for the high school student. First we will discuss the implementation of programming for the youngest children.

Early Identification and Intervention

Because hearing loss affects language development so directly, and the years from birth to age 3 are so critical for language, the early diagnosis of hearing loss is essential so that work with the family and language intervention with the child with hearing loss can begin. LaVonne Bergstrom (1984) described the ideal: that all major losses be detected and rehabilitation begun by age 3 months so that the child has the opportunity to hear language and other sounds.

> The early diagnosis of hearing loss is essential.

The ideal, however, is far from being realized in everyday practice; in Dr. Bergstrom's large urban clinic, the average hearing loss was first suspected by the family at 10 months and detected by a professional at 21 months. Amplification and training did not typically begin until 27 months (Bergstrom, 1984). Many normally hearing children are speaking in sentences by that age, so the child who is deaf is at a disadvantage immediately; some feel that it is one from which the child never fully recovers.

> Parents need support and information so they can make key decisions about their child's education.

An early intervention program can serve many purposes for the family of a newly diagnosed child with hearing loss. Parents often need support from professionals in dealing with their reactions to the diagnosis of hearing loss; they also need information about the effects of hearing loss on language development. Families must make the important decision about how they will teach their child to communicate—will it be signs or speech? If signs are chosen, will it be American Sign Language (ASL) or manually coded English?

The early intervention teacher will help the family continue to communicate naturally to the child about everyday experiences, sometimes with the addition of sign language. She will help the family and the child understand how hearing aids are used and what they can and cannot do. Children with hearing loss do not automatically know where a sound comes from the first time they hear it

Approaches to Communication

Oral English Approaches   In educational programs designed to teach oral English, students are expected to understand English through speech reading and amplified residual hearing and to use spoken English to communicate. Oral approaches can be primarily auditory in emphasis or multisensory, also emphasizing speech reading and tactile input.

Manual Supplement to Speech   Cued speech provides visible cues for vowel and consonant sounds of speech in the form of hand and finger shapes.

Manually Coded English Approaches   Pidgin Sign English (PSE) is a mixture of structures and forms of ASL and English; it uses ASL signs in English order, usually without English tense markers, prefixes, suffixes, etc.

The following manually coded English systems are artificially created forms of a visual language and are not considered languages in themselves. These systems can be signed simultaneously with speech; they add word endings, tenses, and affixes (*-est, -ed, -ing,* etc.); they invent new signs; and they use initials in base signs to distinguish English synonyms.

Examples:
Signing Exact English (SEE II)
Signed English
Seeing Essential English (SEE I)

American Sign Language (ASL)   ASL is a natural manual language that has evolved over time through use by deaf individuals. ASL uses English vocabulary but has its own rules of order and meaning. Since ASL does not follow the same rules of word order as English, one cannot sign ASL and speak English at the same time. ASL is able to convey the same meanings, information, and complexities as English. ASL does not have a widely used written form. It is not frequently used by teachers but is used by students in schools whether it is officially condoned or not.

Fingerspelling   Fingerspelling is hand configurations of the manual alphabet associated with conventional alphabet symbols. It is not difficult to learn but is difficult to read. Fingerspelling is seldom used alone anymore, although it may be used with speech (the Rochester method). It serves as a useful supplement to a sign system to represent words that have a low frequency of use.

Simultaneous Communication   Simultaneous communication is the use of a manually coded English sign system with spoken English.

Total Communication   A philosophy incorporating appropriate aural, manual, and oral modes of communication.

Sources: H. Bornstein, "A Manual Communication Overview," in H. Bornstein, ed., *Manual Communication: Implications for Education* (Washington, DC: Gallaudet University Press, 1990); G. Gustason, "Signing Exact English," in H. Bornstein (1990); R.J. Hoffmeister, "ASL and Its Implications for Education," in H. Bornstein (1990); P.V. Paul and S.P. Quigley, *Education and Deafness* (New York: Longman, 1990).

with their hearing aids; they must be taught the association, for example, between the noise they hear and the airplane flying overhead. The child, the family, and the teacher must collaborate to maximize every communication opportunity during the child's waking hours.

Developing Communication Skills

Most educators of children who are deaf or hard of hearing agree that early diagnosis, amplification, and intervention are of paramount importance for their students, but there is no such unanimity on the topic of how these children should be taught to communicate. As the accompanying box, "Approaches to Communication," illustrates, there are many options. Should speech alone be emphasized, or signs be added? How much emphasis should there be on the use of residual hearing? Which sign language system should be used? What should be the role of the native language of the student, be it Spanish, Russian, or ASL, in school learning? Before we attempt to grapple with these thorny issues, let us discuss the communication methods or modalities that are currently used in classrooms with students who are deaf or hard of hearing.

Most teachers of students who are deaf or hard of hearing have as their ultimate goal that their students become fluent, competent users of English. Although the most intensive language teaching will take place in early intervention programs and in special schools and classes, the regular class teacher who works with the deaf or hard-of-hearing student will also play a role in introducing and expanding English vocabulary, structures, and use. Because of this emphasis, much of the training of teachers of students with hearing loss is on the development of skills related to language development, assessment, and teaching.

Traditionally, programs for students who are deaf and hard of hearing have differed in their approach to teaching communication skills. Some have emphasized the development of speech and auditory skills, while others have encouraged the growth of signs along with those skills. Let us take a closer look at these philosophies, the oral approach and the manual approach.

■ **The Oral Approach** The **oral communication approach** is built on the belief that children who are deaf and hard of hearing can learn to talk—and that speech should be their primary method of expression. Also, they should understand the speech of others through a combination of speech reading (lip reading) and residual hearing. The overall goal of oralism is that children with hearing loss learn intelligible speech and age-appropriate language (Connor, 1986). There are several different oral methods, but all high-quality oral programs share common goals:

The oral communication approach is based on the belief that children with hearing loss can speak.

- The earliest possible detection of hearing loss
- Amplification and intervention
- Intensive parent involvement in the child's education
- The use of residual hearing
- The exclusive use of speech, without sign language, for communication

Teaching speech and auditory skills are theoretically part of the educational program for the majority of children with hearing loss. Teaching speech is one of the teacher's most complicated and challenging responsibilities (Calvert, 1986; Wolk & Schildroth, 1986) and doing it well takes considerable training and skill.

Teaching speech takes considerable training and skill.

In many programs for students who are deaf and hard of hearing throughout the country, responsibility for teaching speech has been shifted to the school speech-language pathologist. This situation works best for students when the classroom teacher, whether a regular education teacher or a teacher of students with hearing loss, works collaboratively with the speech-language pathologist to help the students reach their speech goals and incorporate them into ongoing activities.

The teaching of listening skills, sometimes called **auditory training**, requires that the child be fitted with effective, appropriate hearing aids—preferably one in each ear (Ross, 1986). It begins with developing the child's awareness of all the sounds in the environment—doorbells ringing, dogs barking, people calling the child's name. The most important goal of training residual hearing, however, is to assist the child in understanding spoken language, and thereby support the development of oral language and speech (Flexer, 1994).

Auditory training itself does not enable the child to hear new sounds or words; it simply helps the child make sense of what is heard and use his or her residual hearing as well as possible. Attention to listening skills is important for the regular class teacher as well as the specialist, since there are safety issues involved for the student as well as language-learning issues. For example, attention to environmental sounds will help the student stay safe while riding a bike or crossing the street. Oral programs vary in the emphasis they give to speech reading and residual hearing. Those that emphasize speech reading are sometimes called *multisensory* or *visual-oral*, and those that emphasize residual hearing *auditory-oral* or *aural-oral*. Some professionals advocate a *unisensory* approach, which calls for total reliance on residual hearing to the exclusion of speech reading, and early mainstreaming of children with hearing loss into preschool programs.

■ **The Manual Approach** The use of the **manual communication approach** by and with people who are deaf has a long history. According to Baker and Cokely (1980), "Wherever there were deaf people who needed to communicate there have been signed languages that they and their ancestors have developed" (p. 48). The first to systematize a sign language for teaching purposes was the Abbé de l'Epée, a French monk who started the first school for deaf children in Paris in 1755 (Quigley & Paul, 1984).

Manual communication has two components: **fingerspelling**, in which words are spelled out letter by letter using a manual alphabet (see Figure 8.3) and **signs**, which are symbolic representations of words made with the hands.

The manual communication approach has two components—fingerspelling and signs.

The sign language considered by many deaf adults to be their "native language" is **American Sign Language (ASL)**. ASL uses the same lexicon, or vocabulary, as English, but its grammatical structure is different. Today, linguists consider ASL a legitimate language of its own, not simply a form of English (Hoffmeister, 1990; Stokoe, 1960). Because it does not correspond directly to English, and because there is no widely practiced method of writing in ASL, it has not traditionally been used as the primary language of instruction for children who are deaf. Instead, sign language systems that have been designed to represent English manually are usually used for educational purposes, since it is

American Sign Language uses the same vocabulary as English but has a different grammatical structure.

High school students who are deaf need the experience of communicating effectively with their peers. (© 1995 David Bacon/Impact Visuals)

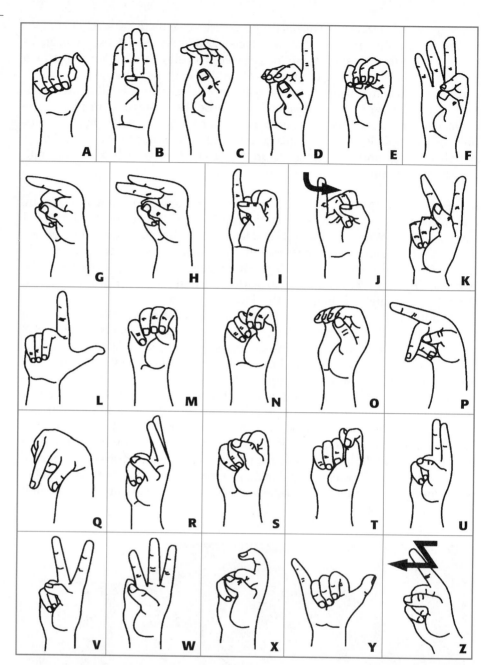

Figure 8.3
The Manual Alphabet

Source: T. Humphries, C. Padden, T.J. O'Rourke, *A Basic Course in American Sign Language* (Silver Spring, MD: T.J. Publishers, 1980). Reprinted by permission.

thought that their correspondence to reading and writing in English is closer. In these English-order systems, the intent is that every word and every inflection (for example, verb tense markers like *-ed* and *-ing*) of English are signed. The most commonly used of these systems are Signed English (Bornstein, 1990b) and Signing Exact English (SEE II) (Gustason, 1990).

Other terms are used to describe communication systems that incorporate elements of manual communication. The use of fingerspelling along with speech is called the *Rochester method*. Using an English-order sign system along with speech is *simultaneous communication. Cued speech* is a system that uses hand signals near the face (not signs or fingerspelling) to differentiate speech sounds that look alike in speech reading (Kipila & Williams-Scott, 1990). The philosophy that advocates the use of whatever communication system (ASL, English-order signs, speech, speech reading, fingerspelling, gestures, etc.) is appropriate for a given child at a given time is called **total communication**.

Total communication advocates the use of the communication system appropriate for a child at a given time.

■ **Communication Controversies** Since education of deaf children began in the sixteenth century, teachers have argued passionately about the best method of instruction. Advocates of the oral approach have maintained that teaching the child who is deaf to speak and to use residual hearing and speech reading to comprehend language provides the skills the individual needs to function both in the hearing world and in the community of deaf people. But teaching oral language and speech to a child who is profoundly deaf is an extremely difficult and laborious process.

The best results seem to occur when early diagnosis is combined with early amplification and early and consistent family involvement. Family involvement is the key. Typically, a preschool-aged child who is deaf speaks only a handful of words. Therefore, the family's commitment to teaching the child to talk is crucial in an oral program, and parents must be willing to experience the slow growth of communication skills in their child. For children who are hard of hearing, the growth of oral skills proceeds significantly faster; they frequently can learn oral language in the regular classroom, with support from a resource teacher or a speech-language specialist.

Children taught with the oral method do best when early diagnosis is combined with early amplification and family involvement.

However, for many children who are deaf—those whose hearing loss is diagnosed after age 2, those with additional handicapping conditions, or those whose families are unable to supply them with the complete support that they need, the oral approach is frequently not satisfactory. During the 1960s and 1970s, dissatisfaction with the oral approach grew, and school programs using total communication proliferated. By 1986, Jordan and Karchmer found that about two-thirds of the students included in the Annual Survey of Hearing-impaired Children and Youth attended schools in which some form of sign was used.

Total communication was designed to use any and all methods of communicating with students who are deaf—speech, fingerspelling, English-order sign language, American Sign Language—depending on the learning needs of the student at the moment (Garretson, 1976). In practice, however, most professionals equate total communication with the simultaneous method—using speech and manually coded English together.

Today the controversies in the field revolve not so much around whether speech or sign should be used but on which form of sign should be used in the classroom. Some professionals believe that advocates of the oral approach are operating under the clinical model of understanding deafness, where it is still seen as deviant; they believe that oralists want to turn children who are deaf into children who are hearing (Paul & Quigley, 1990). Proponents of viewing Deafness as a cultural difference rather than as a disability believe that American Sign Language should be the first language of all children who are deaf and that, therefore, it should be the first language taught in schools (Drasgow, 1998). These professionals, both deaf and hearing, use theories of first- and second-language acquisition of spoken language to support their argument that once fluency in the first language is acquired, second-language learning can and will follow (Drasgow, 1998). They propose teaching ASL first and then, when

Many in the Deaf community believe that ASL should be the first language of all children who are deaf.

children have a solid ASL base, introducing English as a second language (Newell, 1991). Other professionals object to this model, suggesting that since there is no widely accepted written form of ASL, reading and writing skills in English will be introduced too late. Also, since ASL is used without speech, young children may not be given the opportunity to develop speech skills through listening and observation.

Only research, study, and the introduction of model programs will demonstrate whether teaching ASL as a first language in a bilingual program will ultimately succeed in improving the English literacy of children who are deaf, and in the process make them fluent ASL users who are comfortable in their own culture as well as in the "hearing world." We must continue to try to improve services, and therefore opportunities, to children who are deaf, and new ideas and efforts to this end deserve our support.

Curriculum

There is evidence that students with hearing loss do not learn the same subject matter as their hearing peers.

Students who are deaf or hard of hearing should learn the same subject matter in school as their hearing peers, but there is some evidence that they do not. Donald Moores (1996) believes that the emphasis on teaching communication skills in most programs for students who are deaf or hard of hearing has resulted in the neglect of the traditional academic areas such as math, science, and social studies. Moores's own research (Kluwin & Moores, 1985) concludes that students with hearing loss who are mainstreamed for math at the secondary level have higher levels of math achievement than those who are in special classes. These researchers suggest that the more rigorous subject-area training of the secondary math teachers may be responsible for the superior achievement of their students with hearing loss. As Moores (1996) suggests, educators must pay more attention to the teaching of traditional content areas in order to prevent their students with hearing loss from experiencing a major "knowledge gap."

Many professionals advocate for the study of Deaf culture in the school curriculum.

In addition to the study of communication and the content areas, many professionals advocate for the study of Deaf culture in the school curriculum. There is hope that an understanding of the history and heritage of people who are deaf will help students "develop an appreciation for both their hearing and Deaf cultural and linguistic linkages with people throughout the world and . . . appreciate more fully the value and relevance of their educational experience" (Luetke-Stahlman & Luckner, 1991, p. 347).

Students from diverse cultural backgrounds can benefit from a curriculum that recognizes their personal experiences. Oscar Cohen (1993) recommends that minority cultures be identified and incorporated into the curriculum and that Deaf cultures within these cultures be recognized. Teachers should integrate ethnic and multicultural concerns into the curriculum as well.

Assessment

Tests often assess mastery of English rather than the content area.

Undertaking an educational assessment with a student who is deaf or hard of hearing is a difficult endeavor, because the typical student's English-language competency is often significantly delayed for his or her age (Paul & Quigley, 1990). As a result, each test, with directions and questions written (or spoken) in English, becomes a test not of its content but of the student's mastery of English. When a student does not do well on a test, it is often because he or she does not understand the language of the directions or the test items. Rephrasing or paraphrasing the language makes the test standardization invalid, so the results cannot be used comparatively (Salvia & Ysseldyke, 1998). Although it is possible to work around these complicating factors, it takes skill and considerable experience in communication to obtain valid assessment results with students with hearing loss, particularly those who are deaf.

■ **Formal Assessment** The school achievement test used most frequently with students who are deaf and hard of hearing is the Stanford Achievement Test, Hearing Impaired Version (SAT-HI) (1989, 8th ed.), which has been normed and standardized on students who are deaf by the Center for Assessment and Demographic Studies at Gallaudet University (Allen, 1986). The test is appropriate for students in the primary grades through high school, and it contains subtests in the areas of spelling, word meaning, paragraph meaning, arithmetic, word study skills, and vocabulary. There are prescreening tests available to determine the appropriate testing level for every child who is deaf, in order to ensure that the child can read at the level neccesary to respond to the test items (Paul & Jackson, 1993).

Bradley-Johnson and Evans (1991) reviewed and evaluated a selection of frequently used standardized tests and found that the majority are not reliable or valid for use with test-takers who are deaf. They also suggest that there are some tests that can be used with some confidence. As a rule, however, we suggest that the results of almost any standardized tests from students with hearing loss be reviewed with some skepticism. They will usually reflect an underestimate of the student's ability.

Most standardized tests are not reliable or valid for use with test-takers who are deaf.

■ **Communication Assessment** The foundation of educational planning for the student with hearing loss must be a comprehensive communication assessment (Kretschmer & Kretschmer, 1978). Although the content of such an assessment will vary according to the age and skill levels of the student, typically it should include a measure of English-language competence (Kretschmer & Kretschmer, 1978) and an evaluation of the student's speech skills (Ling, 1976) and sign language competencies (Hatfield, 1982).

Most important is to measure the student's use of his or her communication skills in a natural setting, and, whenever possible, both in school and at home. Frequently the classroom teacher and the speech-language therapist are responsible for gathering the information for this assessment. The results of the communication assessment become the base for all subsequent educational planning for the student.

It is important to measure a student's communication skills in a natural setting.

■ **Informal Assessment** The classroom teacher of students who are deaf or hard of hearing will obtain the most informative data from informal assessment. Language samples (Schirmer, 1994) and teacher-made or curriculum-based assessments (Luetke-Stahlman & Luckner, 1991) in subject areas can fill in some of the gaps in the teacher's information about the student's knowledge and functioning. See the discussion of informal assessment in Chapter 5 for ideas that also apply to students with hearing loss.

School Placement

Students who are deaf and hard of hearing can be found in a wide variety of educational settings, from the regular classroom to the residential school. According to the Eighteenth Annual *Report to Congress on the Implementation of the Individuals with Disabilities Education Act* (1996), about 50 percent of the children

Shared reading is crucial to literacy development for children with hearing loss. (David Young-Wolff/Photo Edit)

with hearing loss aged 6 to 21 were placed in the regular class or regular class with resource room, 31 percent were in separate classes on regular campuses, and 19 percent in special schools or residential schools. Let us discuss the variations on those three placement options.

■ **The Regular Classroom**   About half of all deaf or hard-of-hearing students are included in the regular classroom. From that classroom base they may receive a variety of specialized services. Their classroom amplification devices, whether they be personal hearing aids, cochlear implants, or classroom hearing aids connected to a teacher microphone, may be evaluated regularly by the school audiologist; they may receive direct services in speech, signs, or the development of auditory skills from the itinerant teacher with a specialization in hearing loss or from the speech-language therapist; perhaps they receive extra help with communication skills or academic subjects from the resource teacher, who is also a specialist in hearing loss. Students who participate in school programs with their hearing peers are likely to have more residual hearing than those who do not (Annual Survey of Deaf and Hard-of-Hearing Children and Youth, 1996–1997); they are also likely to have better communication skills.

Moores and Kluwin (1986) found that three factors—academic achievement or ability, communication skill, and personal or social adjustment—should be considered when deciding whether to mainstream a student with hearing loss. According to these authors, most mainstreaming is for nonacademic activities, followed by vocational education. Academic integration of students who are deaf and hard of hearing is less frequent and more selective. Integration occurs most frequently in mathematics classes and least often in English classes. It appears that in many school programs, although students with hearing loss enjoy proximity to their hearing peers, the amount of *meaningful* academic integration between the two groups is surprisingly low. Inclusion has sparked much debate among professionals, with many arguing that the regular classroom does not provide an optimal communication environment for students who are deaf (Stinson & Lang, 1995).

Not all professionals believe that inclusion is appropriate for children who are deaf.

Some students with hearing loss will be integrated in the regular classroom with a sign language interpreter (see the accompanying box, "A Closer Look: Collaboration: Get to Know Your Student's Interpreter"); others will rely on their speech-reading skills and residual hearing to gain information in the classroom. Most integrated students, whether they are in the regular classroom full time or part time, will need preferential seating so they are close enough to the teacher or other speaker to speech read. Remember that in a noisy setting students with hearing loss must rely heavily on vision to obtain information; often if they are not looking at the source of the sound, they are not "hearing" it or getting the information. The accompanying box, "Strategies for Enhancing Communication," outlines some common classroom problems and the strategies designed to eliminate them.

■ **Special Classes** A special class is composed of a group of students who are deaf and hard of hearing of similar age, taught on an elementary, middle school, or high school campus by a specialist teacher of deaf and hard-of-hearing students. More and more children with hearing loss are attending special classes on public school campuses, because this placement provides a home base for integrating these students with their hearing peers.

Some students in the special class are integrated with their hearing peers for academic subjects; others for subjects like art, music, or physical education; others may have contact with their hearing peers only at recess and lunch. The amount of time each student spends with hearing peers is specified on his or her individualized education program (IEP). Although characteristics of the student are obviously of prime importance in the decision whether or not to integrate, the availability of willing and competent regular education teachers to work with the students with hearing loss is often what makes or breaks the opportunity for the student.

■ **Residential Schools** The deinstitutionalization movement (see Chapter 1) has had an important influence on the education of children who are deaf. Twenty years ago, most children with hearing loss attended large residential schools, either as day students or as residents. These schools held a special place in the heart of the Deaf community. Many people who were deaf had left their homes to live at residential schools when they were very young; they learned to communicate there, made their lifelong friends there, met their spouses there, and settled in the surrounding area. They were anxious that their own deaf children attend these schools, too.

The nature of residential schools has changed dramatically since 1975, when P.L. 94-142 mandated a less segregated school setting.

The concept of the "least restrictive environment" in Public Law 94-142 has mandated a less segregated school setting for most children who are deaf, and the nature of residential schools has changed dramatically since the law was signed by President Ford in 1975, much to the dismay of many members of the Deaf community. Student enrollment has declined notably (Moores, 1996). Some of the schools have closed; many of them have become centers for students who are deaf with multiple disabilities; most have become day schools.

With a wider range of program options available in public schools, some professionals, often from outside the field of deafness, have seen very little justification for the removal of a child from his or her family in order to attend

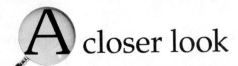

A closer look

Collaboration: Get to Know Your Student's Interpreter

Interpreters provide an essential service to both students and teachers in classrooms. Whether you are working with an *oral interpreter* or a *sign language interpreter*, it will be important to work collaboratively with that person to ensure that your student is receiving the kind of assistance you intend.

Oral interpreters silently repeat, with clear but unexaggerated lip movements, the message of another speaker. Why are they necessary? Try putting earplugs into your own ears. You will find that lipreading (also called speech reading) is extremely difficult, and some people are much easier to lipread than others. People who have mustaches and beards, who speak very quickly, or who move as they speak and turn their backs on the student (such as an instructor at a blackboard) are among those difficult to lipread. Many adults and students with hearing loss who use the oral method to communicate prefer to have the help of an oral interpreter in diffi-

cult communication circumstances (Northcott, 1984).

Sign language interpreters translate the spoken message into signs. Sometimes they provide a word-for-word translation, but if you have ever watched a fluent sign interpreter interpret a song, you will know that sometimes whole concepts can be communicated in a sign or two, and sometimes very beautifully. Since most sign interpreters in American classrooms are interpreting English, they usually sign in an English-order system. Often sign interpreters use Pidgin Sign English— ASL signs in English order—and sometimes they silently articulate the words they are signing. Teachers should know what form of sign system the interpreter is using, and whether that conforms to the expectations of the school district, the student, and the student's family. The most competent sign interpreters are certified by the National Registry of Interpreters for the Deaf; they have often undergone extensive and rigorous

school. Nonetheless, many members of the Deaf community and professionals in the field of deafness continue to fight for the right to choose a residential school for a child who is deaf. The schools are sometimes seen as the birthplace of Deaf culture in this country, places where students who are deaf can develop their own positive identity rather than being forced to accept the values and norms of the hearing world.

Residential schools, the birthplace of Deaf culture, are often places where students can develop positive identities.

Educational Quality for Deaf Students

In 1986, Congress established the Commission on the Education of the Deaf to assess the quality of all educational services provided to students who are deaf, from infancy and early childhood through postsecondary and adult education. Eight of the twelve commissioners were deaf or hard of hearing. The commission's 1988 report, *Toward Equality*, came to a strong and serious conclusion: The present status of education for persons who are deaf in the United States is unsatisfactory.

The Commission of the Education of the Deaf assessed the quality of educational services for students who are deaf.

The commission made fifty-two recommendations for the improvement of educational services to students who are deaf. The report, calling for significant changes in the focus of educational services, was supported nearly unanimously by adults who were deaf as well as by other professionals in the field.

One of the commission's major recommendations was that the federal government emphasize English language development among students who are deaf—including vocal, visual, and written language. It also called for recognition of the "unique needs" of students who are deaf when developing their

training in sign language and interpreting to prepare for their work (Frishberg, 1986).

Often educational interpreters are asked to perform additional duties within the school or classroom, such as tutoring, general classroom assistance, educational planning, and sign language instruction (Stuckless, Avery & Hurwitz, 1989). Teachers should consider two factors when asking the interpreter for this kind of assistance. First and foremost, will the additional responsibility interfere with interpreting for the student? This should be the absolute priority responsibility for the interpreter. Second, is the interpreter qualified to perform the additional responsibility? Most educational interpreters are not trained as teachers or teacher's aides; they should provide tutoring and educational planning only under the close supervision of the classroom teacher.

Leah Ilan is an interpreter in Los Angeles who has a busy career as both an oral and sign language interpreter. Leah believes that the most important factors in the relationship between the classroom teacher and the interpreter are communication and trust, and that the better the interpreter knows the teacher, the better work she does. Leah finds oral interpreting somewhat more difficult than sign interpreting. She describes the job as "sounding out every single sound and making it visible—with the mouth, jaw, eyes, and facial expression. I use it all." Leah finds the need for concentration greater with oral interpreting, since the oral "consumer"—the person with hearing loss—relies on small parts of speech and work endings for comprehension. She hastens to add that sign interpreting is not easy; in fact, the preference now is that sign interpreters work in teams of two on long assignments. This allows sign interpreters periods of rest and avoids the appearance of hand and arm injuries such as carpal-tunnel syndrome, which can limit or end their careers.

IEPs, including severity of hearing loss and the potential for using residual hearing; academic level and learning style; communicative needs and the preferred mode of communication; linguistic, cultural, social, and emotional needs; placement preference; individual motivation, and family support.

Another important recommendation urged that the federal Department of Education reconsider the emphasis of P.L. 94-142 on the least restrictive environment and instead focus on the *appropriateness* of the placement of each student who is deaf. In appropriate placements for students who are deaf, the commissioners believed, educators and other staff members must have the skills needed to communicate with the student. Bowe (1991) explained that these skills might include ASL fluency, Signed English ability, or clear enunciation. The Department of Education could look to the communication capabilities of the staff rather than the "least restrictive" nature of the setting.

> The commission focused on appropriate placement of students who are deaf rather than on the least restrictive environment.

In 1992 the federal government issued new policy guidelines relative to the education of students who are deaf in response to the commission report (Department of Education, 1992). The guidelines describe the current status of students who are deaf and identify the primacy of their needs for direct and meaningful communication with teachers and peers, which may be a primary consideration in making educational placement decisions. The accompanying box, "Improving Educational Quality," summarizes the priorities for developing an IEP for the student who is deaf.

The guidelines make a crucial point: "Any setting, *including a regular classroom* [italics added], that prevents a child who is deaf from receiving an appropriate education that meets his or her needs, including communication needs, is not the LRE [least restrictive environment] for that child" (Department of

∽ Strategies for Enhancing Communication

If the student has trouble understanding what you say, try the following strategies:

- Rephrase what you have said. Instead of "What's today's date?" try "What day is it today?"

- Slow down your rate of speaking. You may be speaking too quickly for speech reading to occur. (Don't exaggerate your lip movements, though; it won't make you any easier to understand.)

- Ask the student to repeat what you have said. This may help you to clarify the misunderstanding.

- Encourage the student to let you and the other students know when he or she has had difficulty understanding or needs a message repeated. Before this happens, though, the student must feel comfortable and secure in the classroom or any other setting.

If you have trouble understanding the student's communication, try these steps:

- Say or sign the phrase to yourself. Somehow silent repetition helps.

- Admit you don't understand. This will allow the person to come up with his or her own way to clarify the message.

- Ask the student to repeat the word, phrase, or sentence in question. Or ask, "Can you say/sign that a different way?"

- As a last resort, ask the student to write the message or draw a picture. At least you will let the student know that meaningful communication is important to you.

To arrange the classroom so that effective communication can occur:

- Seat the student so that he or she can see your face clearly, and, whenever possible, the other students, too. The student with a hearing loss will have difficulty following a group discussion unless the faces of all potential speakers can be seen clearly.

- The student with a hearing loss should be seated where lighting is adequate for reading signs and speech reading. It is difficult to do those things against the glare of a window.

- When the student with hearing loss is working with an interpreter, certain courtesies should be observed. For example, let the interpreter select his or her seat—he or she will be able to choose the spot where he or she will be seen best. Also, speak directly to the student, not to the interpreter. The student will then turn to the interpreter for the message.

- Encourage the student who is deaf or hard of hearing to participate in classroom and school activities involving music and drama. Many students with hearing loss have enough residual hearing to enjoy music—and they do. Participation in plays and dramatic speaking can also be fun and instructive. If the student's speech is not always intelligible, perhaps he or she could sign while a "reverse interpreter" speaks for him or her.

Consideration of appropriate placement must recognize the communication needs of the child.

Education, 1992, p. 49275). So the regular classroom may not always be the least restrictive environment for the child who is deaf; consideration of appropriate placement must include a priority placed on the communication needs of the child. The guidelines go further to conclude that, for some children, a special school may be the least restrictive environment in which their needs can be met.

Although it is too soon to measure the effect of these guidelines on educational decision-making for students who are deaf, there is little doubt that they will have a significant effect on placement decisions, as well as provide ammunition for the fight of the Deaf community against full inclusion.

Technological Advances

Many of the advances in services and opportunities for people who are deaf have occurred in the area of technology. Improved hearing aids, telecommunication devices and relay systems, and television captioning have made life more convenient and everyday experiences more accessible for many people with hearing loss.

～ Improving Educational Quality

Considerations for the IEP. When writing an IEP for a child with hearing loss, the team should consider the following:

- The child's communication needs and the family's preferred mode of communication
- Severity of hearing loss and potential for using residual hearing
- Academic level
- Social, emotional, and cultural needs, including opportunities for peer interactions and communication

Least Restrictive Environment. The least restrictive environment for the child who is deaf is the setting that best meets the child's needs, including communication needs. In some cases, the general education classroom may not be the least restrictive environment.

Source: U.S. Department of Education, "Guidelines for Educational Programs for Deaf Students," *Federal Register* (1992), pp. 49275–49276.

Improvements in Hearing Aids

Twenty-five years ago amplification was just emerging from the period in which it was viewed as an imposition by audiologists and other technocrats on helpless children (Ross, 1986). According to Mark Ross, at that time hearing aids were worn primarily by young children. Older children refused to wear the relatively cumbersome "body aids" that were widely used then, and most students did not wear their hearing aids outside the classroom.

A telecommunication device for the deaf (TDD) allows the deaf person to communicate with hearing people through a relay system or with other deaf people who use TDDs. (Michael Newman/PhotoEdit)

Modern hearing aids are much
more efficient and compact than
their predecessors.

Hearing aids today are considerably more efficient. They have been reduced in size, so they are more appealing cosmetically; the majority of children are now fitted with behind-the-ear aids (Northern & Downs, 1991). More important, their capabilities have improved, and they can be designed to match each individual's hearing loss. Most children can benefit from wearing two hearing aids, although Ross (1986) observes that only about 50 percent of them do so. New designs in hearing aids include those that have been miniaturized to the point that they fit completely in the ear. Although these tiny and lightweight in-the-ear hearing aids are just beginning to be recommended for young children or profoundly deaf users, they are prescribed more frequently for adolescents and adults, who often have great concerns about the visibility of their hearing aids. Today's cutting-edge hearing aids are programmable and can be customized to match an individual's hearing loss and characteristics of the environment. It is likely that the appearance and the functioning of hearing aids will continue to improve through the refinement of digital-based technology (Northern & Downs, 1991).

Assistive Listening Devices

Although a hearing aid makes all sounds in the environment louder, assistive listening devices increase the loudness of a desired sound—the teacher's voice, the actors on a stage, or the voice on the telephone. There are different types of assistive listening devices for different settings: Some are used with hearing aids, and some without. An audiologist can help a teacher or an individual determine which assistive listening device will be most helpful (American Speech-Language-Hearing Association, 1997).

Telecommunication Devices

Today most people with hearing
loss can use TDDs.

Until fairly recently, most people who were deaf did not have access to telephone services; when they wanted to send a message, they wrote a letter and waited for a response, or drove across town. This began to change in 1964 when Robert Weitbrecht, an American physicist who was profoundly deaf, discovered a way for two teletype machines to communicate with each other over a standard telephone line (Bellefleur, 1976). This device became the teletypewriter (TTY). Since then, the use of **telecommunication devices for the deaf (TDDs)** has slowly grown to the point where most adolescents and adults with hearing loss have access to this means of communication. TDDs are telephones with small screens that display the message of the sender. The system works like this: One person dials the number of a friend. The phone rings, and a light flashes in the home of the person receiving the call. When the receiver is picked up and placed in the cradle of the TDD, the two people can begin to type their communication into the TDD. The messages appear on paper, or, in the newest models, on a tiny screen on the TDD. Many agencies and businesses now routinely train their employees to use the TDD; they are used for business as well as social calls.

Since the passage of the Americans with Disabilities Act (1990), most states have developed telephone relay systems that allow a TDD user to communicate directly with a hearing person who does not have a TDD. The TDD user dials a relay operator, who also has a TDD. The relay operator then dials the number of the person with whom the TDD user wishes to communicate and reads the messages from the TDD user to the other person. That person responds orally, and the operator then types the oral message into the TDD for the TDD user. This goes on until the two people have finished their conversation, when they sign off. The ADA requires that all telephone companies offer relay systems to TDD users twenty-four hours a day, seven days a week. This national relay system allows TDD users access to every telephone in the United States.

Captioning

Television captioning for viewers with hearing loss began as a system of open captioning in which captions that paralleled the verbal content of the television program appeared on the bottom of every viewer's screen. Today, though, a system called **closed captioning** exists. Viewers with hearing loss can buy a decoder that, when connected to their television set, allows them to receive broadcasts carrying a coded signal that the decoder makes visible (Withrow, 1976). Since July 1, 1993, all TV sets thirteen inches or larger that are sold or built in the United States have been caption-chip-equipped (Bowe, 1991), allowing viewers to select captioning of all available programs.

The Commission on Education of the Deaf described the potential benefits of captioning for older Americans with hearing loss, as well as for people who are learning English, preschool children, and illiterate adults (Bowe, 1991). Captioning can thus potentially assist many more people than the relatively small number who were born deaf or acquired deafness early in life.

Not all television programs are closed captioned, but due to the rapidly expanding market for such services, television networks are making an increasing number of programs available to viewers with hearing loss. The Americans with Disabilities Act of 1990 requires that any television public service announcement that is produced with federal funds be captioned. Viewers with hearing loss and the National Captioning Institute are also working with television networks to increase the amount of real-time captioning on the screen (the immediate captioning of live television programs such as news broadcasts).

Technology for Instruction

Since many students who are deaf are dependent on their sight for processing information, visual representation of course content is highly important. Classroom computers can provide a crucial supplement to the school curriculum. Use of the classroom computer for instruction and curricular support, practicing literacy skills, access to content, research resources, and communication with others will enrich learning opportunities for students who are deaf or hard of hearing. These and other new forms of technology have shown promise of becoming an integral part of classroom instruction (Lang, 1996). Internet sites for users who are deaf are proliferating (see Multimedia Resources at the end of this chapter). Currently, advocates are focusing on ways to make the audio messages from the Internet accessible to users with hearing loss (McCollum, 1998).

SUMMARY

■ Deafness is hearing loss that prevents the learning of language through hearing. Conductive hearing loss results from damage to the outer or middle ear and can usually be corrected. Sensorineural loss involves damage to the cochlea or auditory nerve and as of now cannot be corrected.

■ The most common causes of hearing loss are otitis media, inherited genetic factors, rubella, meningitis, and premature birth. Approximately 34 percent of children with hearing loss have multiple disabilities.

■ Hearing loss is measured by an audiologist using a series of tests, including pure-tone tests. The results of these tests are illustrated by an audiogram.

■ Language is the most critical area affected by hearing loss, especially because hearing loss is usually not identified until after language normally appears.

■ The cognitive abilities of students who are deaf and hard of hearing as a group are the same as those of hearing individuals. Despite this, students with hearing loss frequently underachieve in school because of the heavy emphasis on English-language skills.

■ The Deaf community views deafness as a culture rather than a deficit and urges that understanding of Deaf culture be integrated into the curriculum for students.

■ Manual communication includes fingerspelling and signs. American Sign Language (ASL) is considered a language of its own and does not correspond directly to English. Total communication uses oral, aural, and manual modes of communication and advocates adopting whatever system seems most appropriate for a child at a given time.

■ Some standardized tests have been normed for students who are deaf; teachers can develop informal assessment instruments based on curriculum guides and other curricular material.

■ Many students with hearing loss attend regular classes and use amplification devices, special services provided by an audiologist or itinerant teacher, or an oral or sign language interpreter.

■ Hearing aids and telecommunication devices have greatly improved in recent years, and technological advances continue to provide opportunities for people with hearing loss to communicate freely across long distances.

KEY TERMS

deafness

hard of hearing

hearing impairment

Deaf community

hearing loss

residual hearing

congenital hearing loss

acquired hearing loss

prelingual deafness

postlingual deafness

conductive hearing loss

sensorineural hearing loss

mixed hearing loss

cochlear implants

bilateral hearing loss

unilateral hearing loss

otitis media

otologist

audiologist

audiogram

Deaf culture

oral communication approach

auditory training
manual communication approach
fingerspelling.

signs
American Sign Language (ASL)
total communication

telecommunication devices for the deaf (TDDs)
closed captioning

MULTIMEDIA RESOURCES

Cohen, Leah Hager (1994). *Train Go Sorry: Inside a Deaf World.* Boston: Houghton Mifflin. Leah Cohen, a hearing person with deaf family members, grew up in and around the Lexington School for the Deaf. Her insider/outsider view of her experiences conveys the world and the politics of Deafness with great vividness and warmth.

Gannon, Jack R. *The Week the World Heard Gallaudet* (Washington, DC: Gallaudet University Press, 1989). This book chronicles, in narrative and photographs, the history-making week of protest and the ultimate success of students, faculty, and staff in the choice of a new deaf president of Gallaudet University.

HiP Magazine Online website: http://www.hipmag.org. This is a magazine-style website designed for "deaf and hard-of-hearing kids and their pals."

Independence Through Telecommunications: A Guide for Parents of Deaf and Hard of Hearing Children (1994). This 18-minute videotape explains how visual telecommunications technology can provide deaf and hard-of-hearing children access to the telephone. The videotape focuses on TTYs, relay services, fax machines, and on-line services. It features easy-to-understand explanations and testimonials from parents of deaf and hard-of-hearing children who use visual telecommunications devices. On-screen explanations are in American Sign Language, with open captions and voice narration throughout. Order No. VT94-2; Price: $2.50. Available through the Gallaudet Research Institute, Center for Assessment and Demographic Studies, Gallaudet University, 800 Florida Avenue NE, Washington, DC 2002.

Jepson, Jill (Ed.). *No Walls of Stone: An Anthology of Literature by Deaf and Hard of Hearing Writers* (Washington, DC: Gallaudet Press, 1993). Full of wisdom, humor, and hope, this book contains plays, essays, poetry, and short stories contributed by writers with a variety of backgrounds, degrees of hearing loss, and writing styles.

The National Information Center on Deafness phone: (202) 651-5051; TTY: (202) 651-5052; fax: (202) 651-5054; e-mail: nicd@gallux.gallaudet.edu. NICD is a centralized source of accurate, up-to-date, objective information on topics dealing with deafness and hearing loss. NICD responds to a wide range of questions received from the general public, deaf and hard-of-hearing people, their families, and professionals who work with them. NICD collects, develops, and disseminates information on deafness, hearing loss, and services and programs related to people with hearing loss.

Padden, Carol, and Tom Humphries. *Deaf in America: Voices from a Culture* (Cambridge, MA: Harvard University Press, 1988). This book focuses on the stories of people who are deaf and offers intriguing insights into those who share the culture of American Sign Language.

Schleper, David R. *Reading to Deaf Children: Lessons from Deaf Adults* (Washington, DC: Pre-College National Mission Programs, Gallaudet University, 1997). This book and the accompanying videotapes present strategies for reading to children with hearing loss culled from observations of deaf adults.

Software to Go. This is a technology clearinghouse for those who work with students who are deaf or hard of hearing. Write to Software to Go, Gallaudet University, MSSD Box 77, 800 Florida Avenue NE, Washington, DC 20002, (202) 651-5705 (voice), (202) 651-5705 (TTY). Or visit them at http://www.gallaudet.edu/~precpweb/stgintro.html.

USING YOUR KNOWLEDGE

 Can Do: How can your classroom be arranged for maximum accessibility by a student with hearing loss? Try to take all possible factors into account, including ability to see the teacher; access to equipment such as computers, closed-captioned TV, projectors, cameras, and video; and use of literature and other materials in which deaf individuals are represented.

 Can Do: How do students with hearing loss communicate in the general education classroom? Have groups of students in your class visit several regular elementary schools in which students with hearing loss are included. Find out what communication approaches are used in the classroom and why those were chosen. Are teachers or support personnel available who can communicate with the deaf students? Write a brief summary of communication in the regular class and evaluate whether the class would be considered an appropriate placement.

 Commonalities: How does your college or university provide support services to students with hearing loss? In particular, find out what types of career counseling are offered. How might these services be improved? With others in your class, create a list of career services that could be used by students who are deaf.

 Collaboration: Find out what services are available to students with hearing loss in a local school district and how classroom teachers access these services. What types of professionals are available to assist classroom teachers meet the needs of these students? What structures exist to enhance collaboration?

WHAT YOU CAN DO NOW

1. Explore Deaf culture and interact with deaf individuals:

- Contact an adult service agency to find out how services are provided to deaf people.
- Volunteer to be a note-taker for a deaf student.
- Volunteer at a nursing home for elderly people who are deaf.

2. Get involved in education programs:

- Visit a community college and find out what programs are available for deaf students.
- Visit a residential school and investigate its curriculum. Many special schools provide courses on the history of Deaf culture. Ask the teacher to share course syllabi, notes, resources.
- Take a beginning course in American Sign Language.

3. Devise a unit on deafness and Deaf culture to include in your curriculum. Its components might include the following:

- What is sound; how is it made?
- What are the parts of the ear? What causes deafness?
- How does a cochlear implant work?
- What is Deaf culture and the Deaf community?
- Invite a mime group, signing song group, or Deaf theater group.
- Describe the types of manual languages and systems to transcribe them.
- What are the abilities, attitudes, accomplishments of deaf artists?
- Who are some famous deaf people and deaf history?
- Making communication work: What can deaf students tell their hearing friends so that they can improve their communication?
- Organize a Deaf Awareness Week at school.
- Explore jobs and higher education opportunities.
- Offer sign classes by hearing-impaired students for hearing students.
- Visit or host pen pal programs with hearing-impaired students in other programs, states, or countries. Source: Adapted from Barbara Luetke-Stahlman and John Luckner, *Effectively Educating Students with Hearing Impairments* (New York: Longman, 1991), p. 352. Copyright © 1991. Used by permission of the authors.

4. Investigate the community at Gallaudet:

- Request any literature available from the admissions or publications office.
- Invite a local graduate to visit the class. If several grads from different generations are available, have them in to discuss how Gallaudet has changed.

5. Visit some websites on the Internet to learn more about deafness and Deaf culture. For example:

- Deaf World Web: http://deafworldweb.org
- Gallaudet University: http://www.gallaudet.edu
- National Association for the Deaf: http://www.nad.org
- National Technical Institute for the Deaf: http://www.isc.rit.edu/~418www/
- National Information Center on Deafness: http://gallaudet.edu/~nicd/

Children Who Are Blind and Have Low Vision

IN this chapter we discuss how visual impairments can affect a child's education and development. Students with visual impairments experience difficulty seeing even with corrective measures such as glasses. Thus, educational goals such as learning to read, developing mobility, and planning for life after school are vital. As you read, think about the following questions:

Commonalities: How should education for children with visual impairments be different from that of sighted students—and how should it be the same?

Collaboration: Who are the school professionals who must work together to plan a high-quality educational program for students with visual impairments?

Can Do: What can we do to promote the social acceptance of students with visual impairment?

People who are sighted develop a concept of what it is like to be blind from experiences of maneuvering in the dark or wearing a blindfold during childhood games. As a result of these experiences, most of us believe that we understand what it is like to be blind.

We are probably wrong. In the first place, our experiences are based on the condition of total blindness. Most people who are visually impaired respond to some visual stimuli, such as shadows, light and darkness, or moving objects. The majority of people with visual impairments can read print, either regular print or print that is magnified or enlarged; only 10 percent of students meeting the requirements of legal blindness use Braille as their primary learning medium (American Printing House for the Blind, 1995).

Second, some of our early experiences of "blindness" may have been negative or frightening, due to a lack of preparation and skills. Most people rely on vision for protection and information. So, during the course of our childhood games we were usually tempted to peek or turn on the light for reassurance and confirmation. In contrast, people who are blind receive instruction in daily living skills and rely on their other senses to gain information about their world. Most people who are blind can move independently around their homes and travel in the community; they are productively employed and active in their communities (Scholl, 1986). Our negative or fearful concepts of blindness, therefore, do not reflect the real life of a person who is blind.

These common misconceptions about the ability of people who are visually impaired are important to remember when preparing to teach a child who is blind or visually impaired. We must look beyond our traditional view of blindness and our misconceptions to realize that with specialized instruction, children with visual impairments are capable of success in our classrooms.

Definitions and Terms

Like *hearing impairment*, **visual impairment** is an umbrella term that includes all levels of vision loss, from total blindness to uncorrectable visual limitations. A number of terms are used interchangeably to describe children whose vision is impaired, including *visually impaired, visually handicapped, visually disabled, blind, partially sighted*, and *low vision*.

The term visual impairment *covers all levels of vision loss.*

P.L. 94-142 (IDEA) defines children with visual impairments in the following way: "'Visually handicapped' means a visual impairment which, even with correction, adversely affects a child's educational performance. The term includes both partially seeing and blind children" (*Federal Register*, 1977, p. 42,474). It is helpful to think about the phrase *with correction* in this definition. Even with the best possible corrective lenses, these children have a vision problem that interferes with their learning at school. Many of us wear glasses or contact lenses that correct our vision. We are not considered visually impaired, since our learning is not adversely affected.

Legal blindness refers to visual acuity of 20/200 or less in the better eye after correction or a visual field of less than 20 degrees.

It is important to distinguish between legal definitions and educational definitions. A person is considered **legally blind** when his or her **visual acuity,** or sharpness of vision, is 20/200 or worse in the better eye *with* correction, or when he or she has a visual field no greater than 20 degrees. If vision can be corrected through glasses or contact lenses to 20/200 or better, the person is not considered legally blind. The term *legal blindness* describes visual impairments that qualify a person for a variety of legal and social services. This definition is used to determine eligibility for governmental funding, tax deductions, rehabilita-

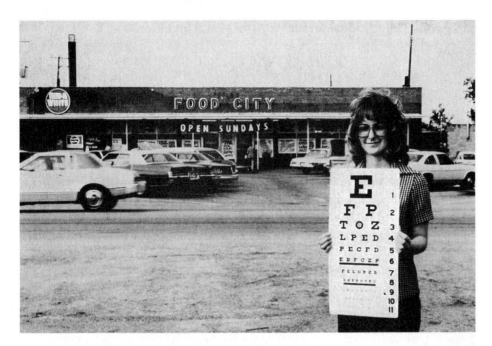

The top photograph shows a view as seen by a person with 20/20 vision; and the bottom photograph the same view as seen by a person with 20/200 vision. (From *Who is the Visually Impaired Child?*, Project MAVIS Sourcebook I, by M. Efron 1979, Boulder: Social Science Education Consortium. Copyright © 1980 by LINC Services. Reprinted by permission of publisher.)

tion, and other services. Although the legal definition is widely used, it is somewhat misleading, since many legally blind people have a good deal of useful vision.

For educators, actual measurements of visual acuity are less important than a description of how the student functions in school. **Educational definitions** are generally based on the way a student uses his or her vision in an educational setting—children who use Braille may be considered blind, and those who read large print may be designated "low vision." Table 9.1 lists the levels of visual

Educational definitions of visual acuity are based on functional vision— how well students use whatever vision they have.

Table 9.1 **Educational Implications of Visual Impairments**

Levels of Visual Impairment	Educational Implications
Total blindness	Students are totally blind or are able only to distinguish the presence or absence of light; they may learn best through tactile or auditory senses, although, if they do have some vision, they may use it effectively for orientation and mobility and other tasks.
Low vision	Students are severely visually impaired but may be able to see objects at near distances, sometimes under modified conditions, or may have limited use of vision under average circumstances.
Blindness in one eye	Students with vision in only one eye may or may not be considered visually impaired, depending on the vision in the sighted eye; they may have difficulty with depth perception and may need special consideration in physical education or other classroom activities.

impairment and their educational implications. These definitions rely less on visual acuity measurements and more on **functional vision** (how well a student uses his or her remaining vision). At times, students with exactly the same acuity will function very differently. In fact, professionals in the field of blindness and visual impairment often say that no two people see exactly alike (Augusto, 1996). While one student might respond visually to educational tasks, the other might rely more on hearing or sense of touch depending on his or her background, experience, type of visual impairment, and learning style. The real test of how well a student sees is how she accomplishes daily activities using her sight as well as her other senses. An assessment of functional vision will provide the most useful information on how much the student will use her vision in your classroom. You may be asked to participate on a functional vision assessment team, which will be spearheaded by a vision specialist or orientation and mobility specialist with unique training in this area.

Prevalence

The American Printing House for the Blind (APH) annually compiles data regarding the number of children, birth through age 21, who receive federal support for educational materials (American Printing House for the Blind, 1996) (see Table 9.2). In 1996, the APH reported that 56,275 students enrolled in residential schools, public schools, programs for the multihandicapped, and rehabilitation programs were registered to receive such assistance. The APH register includes only those students who are, by legal definition, blind; other students with less severe visual impairments are not included. As with many other handicapping conditions, accurate counts are difficult due to differences of definition and classification (Scholl, 1986). However, even when the highest estimates are used, visual impairments are still among the low-incidence (or least frequently occurring) handicapping conditions in children; only deaf-blindness is

The number of children with visual impairments is small.

Table 9.2 **Prevalence of Visual Impairments, Birth Through Age 21**

Reading Medium	Number of Children Reported	Percentage
Visual readers (print readers)	14,341	25%
Braille readers	5,449	10%
Auditory readers	4,428	8%
Prereaders	14,010	25%
Nonreaders	18,047	32%
Total	56,275	100%

Source: American Printing House for the Blind, *Distribution of Federal Quota* (Louisville, KY: American Printing House for the Blind, Inc., 1996). Used by permission.

lower. Visual impairment is much more common among people aged 65 and older.

How We See

The eye is a small but extremely complex structure that contains an immense network of nerves, blood vessels, cells, and specialized tissues (Ward, 1986). For most people, this complicated structure works quite efficiently—even if we need corrective lenses, most of us can see well. (Figure 9.1 shows the eye and its structures.) But impairments of vision can result from any interference with the passage of light as it travels from the outer surface of the eye, through the inner

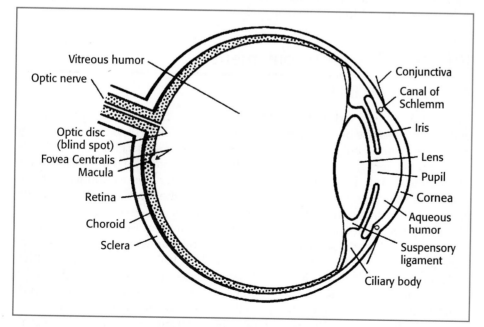

Figure 9.1   Structures of the Eye

Source: Used by permission of National Society to Prevent Blindness.

structures of the eye, and back through the visual pathways in the brain to the cortical brain centers.

When we look at an object, the light rays reflecting off it first pass through the outer membrane of the eye, the transparent, smooth **cornea,** through the **pupil** (the opening in the center of the eye), and through the **lens,** a transparent structure that lies between the iris and the tissue inside the eyeball, called the **vitreous humor.** The muscles in the **iris,** or colored part of the eye, expand or contract according to the amount of light available. The lens focuses the light rays so that they form clear images where they strike the **retina,** a layer of specialized cells at the back of the eye. The light rays activate the special cells on the the retina, which then transmit signals of the images through the fibers of the **optic nerve,** which connects the eye to the brain, where they are interpreted. Damage to any of these structures, or a breakdown in the processing of visual information, can result in visual impairment. In the next section, we discuss some of the more common causes of visual impairment and their implications for learning.

> Light rays pass through the cornea, pupil, and lens and are then projected onto the retina, which sends signals of the image via the optic nerve to the brain.

Causes of Visual Impairment

> Most visual impairments in children are congenital.

Most cases of visual impairment in school-age children are congenital in origin. Congenital conditions may be caused by heredity, maternal or fetal infection, or damage during fetal development or shortly after birth. Hereditary conditions include albinism, some forms of glaucoma, and retinitis pigmentosa. Other conditions, such as cataracts and underdevelopment or absence of parts of the eye structure, may be caused by damage during fetal development. It is important for classroom teachers to understand the eye conditions of their students, since the specific condition may affect what we expect for the child's visual functioning in the classroom. See the accompanying box, "Causes of Visual Impairment in Children," for additional details.

Effects of Visual Impairment

Effects on the Child

Kimberly is 9 years old and is in the fourth grade. She was born prematurely and is blind because of retinopathy of prematurity. Kimberly has above-average intelligence and is on grade level in every academic subject. In some subjects, she requires more time than the rest of the class to complete daily assignments. During the first and second grades, Kimberly's general education teachers decided that she should not be required to do all of the work that the rest of the class was required to do. When the rest of the class was assigned twenty addition problems, Kimberly was told to complete only ten. By the time Kimberly was in the third grade, she would complain that the assignments she was given were too hard, or that she couldn't complete them because she was blind. Kimberly's third-grade teacher, Ms. Charles, was concerned and contacted a vision specialist teacher and Kimberly's parents. They all agreed that this attitude could lead to a decline in Kimberly's self-esteem and confidence. At their meeting it was decided that Kimberly would benefit from completing all class assignments.

Causes of Visual Impairment in Children

- A **cataract** is a clouding of the lens of the eye. Congenital cataracts occur in about 1 in 250 births and account for about 15 percent of the cases of blindness in children (Ward, 1986). Children with cataracts will have difficulty seeing the board clearly and may need increased lighting or high-contrast educational materials.

- **Retinopathy of prematurity** (ROP) occurs most commonly in premature babies or even full-term babies suffering from respiratory distress syndrome (see Chapter 2) who require high levels of oxygen over an extended period of time for survival. With the advent of technology that allows very low birthweight babies to survive, new cases of ROP are becoming more frequent (Phelps, 1994).

- **Glaucoma** accounts for about 5 percent of cases of blindness in children and is a leading cause of blindness across all age groups (Ward, 1986). It occurs when fluid within the eye cannot drain properly, resulting in a gradual increase of pressure within the eye and damage to the optic nerve. Warning signs of glaucoma are often overlooked because they are subtle and develop slowly. In advanced stages, symptoms include painful pressure, hazy vision, discomfort around bright lights, and excessive tearing. When left untreated, glaucoma can cause blindness; if it is diagnosed and treated in time, vision can be saved.

- *Diabetes*, which can result in a condition known as **diabetic retinopathy,** is another major cause of blindness in this country. The circulation problems associated with diabetes can result in damage to the retinal blood vessels, resulting in loss of vision. Although diabetic retinopathy can occur in children, it is most common in older persons who have had diabetes for a long period of time.

- **Retinitis pigmentosa** is a hereditary condition that may be found in children but is more commonly diagnosed in young adults. It is a degeneration of the retina caused by a deposit of pigmentation in the back of the eye. Retinitis pigmentosa is a progressive disease that results in tunnel vision, or the loss of peripheral vision.

- **Cortical vision loss** results from damage to the brain rather than to the eye. The occipital lobes in the brain contain the visual cortex, which may be thought of as the screen on which the visual fields are projected (Bishop, 1996). If they are damaged, the brain cannot receive the images from the eye. Causes of cortical vision loss in infants and children are numerous; they include trauma and hydrocephaly.

- **Refractive errors** decrease the eye's ability to focus the sharpest image on the back of the retina and result in blurred vision. Most can be corrected with prescriptive glasses or contact lenses, but some children have refractive errors so severe they cannot be corrected. The three main types of refractive errors are *myopia* (nearsightedness), *hyperopia* (farsightedness), and *astigmatism* (an irregular shape of the surface of the cornea, which results in blurred vision).

- Other structural problems are associated with the muscles of the eye. The most common of these is **strabismus,** which is a deviation of one or both eyes resulting in the appearance of "crossed eyes" or "wall eyes." Untreated strabismus will result in *amblyopia*–severe, permanent vision loss in the unused eye. In order to avoid this condition, it is critical that treatment occur as quickly as possible–ideally during the earliest months and years of life (Bishop, 1996).

- **Nystagmus** is a "repetitive involuntary, rhythmic tremor-like oscillating movement of the eyes" (Goldberg, 1987, p. 42). This condition, which is common among children with visual impairments, is a result of decreased visual acuity. Children with nystagmus have blurred vision, but the objects in their view do not appear to move. This condition is more pronounced when the child is tired.

Ms. Charles re-examined the assignments she gave to her entire class, realizing that if ten addition problems were enough for her to determine mastery for Kimberly, they were enough for the other members of her class, as well. However, at this point in her education, it takes Kimberly longer to complete the assignment than her classmates, regardless of the amount of material. Ms. Charles, therefore, arranged her class schedule so that all students would have some time to complete assignments during school hours and could also take work home to complete.

It still takes Kimberly more time to accomplish these assignments, but when she is finished she is confident that she can compete with the other students in

The growth and development of
children with visual impairments are
similar to that of their nondisabled
peers.

Children with visual impairments
may be prone to verbalisms—using
words without firsthand knowledge
of their meanings.

Children with visual impairments
should have direct experiences with
complex concepts.

her class. At the same time, she is learning strategies to help her complete her work more efficiently.

In general, the growth and development of children with visual impairments is similar to that of their nondisabled peers (Scholl, 1986). Any differences may be a direct or indirect result of the visual impairment. For example, difficulty in the development of concepts involving colors is a direct result of the child's visual impairment. Society's lack of knowledge or negative attitudes may indirectly affect the child with a visual impairment by depriving her of opportunities or experiences important for development. As we saw with the example of Kimberly, it is a fairly common belief that people who are blind cannot accomplish certain tasks; unfortunately, this attitude deprives them of the opportunity to compete with people who are sighted.

Even when differences are caused directly by the visual impairment, the degree to which the person's development is affected depends on the severity and cause of the visual impairment, and whether the child has additional disabilities. Environmental factors, such as family background and the child's daily experience, are also significant. As you read the following sections, think about the ways in which the areas of development overlap and complement one another.

■ **Language and Concept Development** Although communication through babbling and early sound production is generally the same for children who are blind and children who are sighted (Warren, 1984), developmental differences arise when children begin to associate meaning with words. In a classic study, Thomas Cutsforth (1932) researched the use of words and the understanding of their meaning by children who were totally blind from birth. He discovered that children who are blind often use words for which they could not have firsthand knowledge through other senses, such as describing a blue sky. Cutsforth (1951) called this use of words without concrete knowledge of their meanings **verbalisms.**

Children who are blind may have other unusual language characteristics. For instance, they may ask frequent inappropriate or off-the-topic questions in order to maintain contact with partners or to respond to frightening or confusing situations (Finello, Hanson & Kekelis, 1992). They may also engage in **echolalia,** the repetition of statements used by other people. Interventions should be responsive to the content of the child's utterance, but teachers should not reinforce language behaviors that would not be acceptable in a sighted child.

Teachers working with children who are blind should be aware that even though a child may use verbal expressions that indicate an understanding of a concept, he may not really have the deeper understanding that comes with actual personal experience. If a child writes or reads a story about a big gray elephant and has had no firsthand experience with an elephant or the color gray, he is writing and/or reading about something that he does not truly understand. The teacher may want to work more closely with the child on these concepts, providing rich and meaningful experiences (see the accompanying box, "Promoting Language Development: Intervention Strategies"). By the way, this may also be true of children who are sighted; teachers can never assume that children's use of concepts in verbal or written communications indicates a clear understanding of those concepts. The challenge to educators, therefore, is to provide *all* children with a wealth of opportunities that increase their experiences through all senses, thus increasing their understanding of the language they use.

～ Promoting Language Development: Intervention Strategies

The following strategies will help promote language development in young children with visual impairments.

- *Maintain high expectations for the child's language.* Do not always guess the child's needs or wants; instead encourage the child to make her needs known.

- *Acknowledge the child's efforts to communicate.* A child's early attempts to communicate should be encouraged. When parents and professionals imitate and expand on children's language, children are encouraged to continue talking.

- *Provide opportunities for exploration and listening.* Children who are visually impaired learn by listening and by exploring the environment. However, too much input can be overwhelming and can cause a child to tune out sounds in his surroundings.

- *Try to provide extra information about things that are discussed.* Instead of merely labeling, describe the persons and objects that are of interest to the child.

- *Provide hands-on experiences.* The language spoken to a child who is visually impaired should be reinforced with firsthand experiences. When children with visual impairments understand language, they are less likely to be echolalic.

- *Respond to the ideas and feelings in the child's speech.* By paying careful attention to the child's actions and the events taking place around him, others will be able to respond to the child's underlying intentions.

- *Express your feelings and put the child's feelings into words.* Children with visual impairments cannot read feelings from the frowns, smiles, and expressions of others. Other persons' feelings should be explained, and the child should be taught to express feelings appropriately.

- *Assist the child in developing socially appropriate responses.* Attention should be paid to social skills. For instance, the child may be taught to listen to what other children are doing and to imitate their behavior when she wants to join in friends' play.

- *Be supportive and encouraging.* It is important that interactions be fun and that children talk about shared interests and enjoy interacting with one another. Respect the child's attempts to communicate.

Source: Adapted from K.M. Finello, N.H. Hanson, and L.S. Kekelis, "Cognitive Focus: Developing Cognition, Concepts, and Language in Young Blind and Visually Impaired Children," in R.L. Pogrund, D.L. Fazzi, and J.S. Lampert (eds.), *Early Focus: Working with Young Blind and Visually Impaired Children and Their Families* (New York: American Foundation for the Blind, 1992). Copyright © AFB Press, American Foundation for the Blind. Reproduced with permission from the American Foundation for the Blind, 11 Penn Plaza, Suite 300.

■ **Motor Development**   From infancy, motor development is stimulated by vision. An infant who sees a brightly colored object or her mother's face reaches out for it and thus begins the development of gross motor skills. Children who are blind have difficulty in this area. Movement, which people who are sighted take for granted, must be learned through observation of the movement of others (Ferrell, 1985). Children who are sighted learn how to move by watching the movement of others and imitating it. Then, they practice variations of this movement and observe their own movement, which gives them the feedback they need to change and modify their movements. Children who are blind, however, cannot observe others and imitate their movements.

P.L. 99-457, as you have learned, mandates that services be provided to children with disabilities from birth to 5 years. Under this law, children who are blind may receive instruction in **orientation and mobility,** a set of skills involved in establishing one's location in the environment and moving safely through it (Anthony, Fazzi, Lampert & Pogrund, 1992). When children who have visual impairments enter school, they should be able to move efficiently and safely through their environment.

The acquisition of motor development skills may be delayed by lack of vision.

Daily living skills are everyday activities, like making pudding, which need to be taught specifically to people with visual impairments. Mastering daily living skills will eventually lead to independent living. (Laura Dwight)

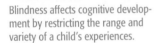

Blindness affects cognitive development by restricting the range and variety of a child's experiences.

■ **Cognitive and Intellectual Development**   Blindness affects cognitive development in young children in much the same way as it affects motor development, by restricting the range and variety of their experiences, by limiting their ability to move around, and by diminishing their control of the environment and their relationship to it (Lowenfeld, 1981).

With emerging research on newborns and infants we are discovering more and more about the importance of vision in early learning. In early infancy the eyes are the child's primary avenue for exploring the world. The newborn uses vision to follow objects with her eyes, for example, and can stick out her tongue after watching someone else do it (Freidrich, 1983). The visual sense motivates the infant to interact with people and objects, guides that interaction, and verifies the success of the interaction. Vision thus stimulates motor activity and exploration, forming the basis for cognitive growth.

Some research has suggested that there are critical periods for certain kinds of learning (Langley, 1980). If infants who are visually impaired miss out on those critical periods for reaching, crawling, or walking, for example, it may be difficult or impossible for them to "catch up" and develop at a normal rate later in life. School-aged children may continue to experience difficulties in their developmental progress. Thus, early intervention for infants with visual impairments is designed to use the child's intact senses to provide the kind of experiences that will promote cognitive growth (Finello, Hanson & Kekelis, 1992).

■ **Social and Emotional Development**   There is no unique psychology of blindness. The principles and issues related to social and emotional develop-

Activities for all Students

Study the anatomy of the eye through these activities:

- Let the students examine their own eyes in a mirror (place a magnifier on the mirror for students with low vision). Ask them to pay attention to the color and shape of their eyes and to any differences they observe.

- Let students compare and contrast their eyes with others.

- Use a pull-apart model to help students learn the location of different parts of the eye.

- Have students sketch their eyes with colored pencils, labeling the parts they have learned.

Simulating blindness and taking a walk with a sighted guide is a good way to sensitize students who are sighted to the importance of listening for students with visual impairments.

Opportunities for Students with Visual Impairments to Learn about Themselves

- Once students become familiar with the parts of the eye, have them name and identify the source of their visual impairments. (Use models or drawings.)

- Develop role-play scenarios in which students need to give information about their visual impairments to other children or to teachers.

- Provide opportunities for individual students to meet other children or adults with a similar visual impairment.

- Let students share information about their visual functioning—what they *do* see.

- Have students create a story depicting the main character as someone with low vision.

- Have students create television or radio commercials for adaptive equipment used by people with visual impairments.

Source: Adapted from S.Z. Sacks, "Psychological and Social Implications of Low Vision," in A.L.Corn and A.J. Koenig (eds.), *Foundations of Low Vision: Clinical and Functional Perspectives* (New York: AFB Press, 1996).

ment of people who are sighted are the same as those related to the social and emotional development of people who are blind (Tuttle, 1984). However, children who are blind do encounter unique difficulties in social situations. Primarily, the difficulties arise because of the way that the child is perceived by society and the way that the child perceives himself (Sacks, 1996).

For example, the child who completes class assignments develops a clear sense of accomplishment. Children who are visually impaired, however, are often allowed to turn in incomplete work or partial assignments, as in the case of Kimberly. As a result, such children may believe that they are not "smart enough" to do the same work that other children in the class do. The perception of other children in the class may also be that the child with a visual impairment cannot accomplish as much as the rest of the class. See the accompanying box, "Enhancing Understanding of Visual Impairment in School-Aged Children," for some suggestions on increasing understanding of visual impairments.

Children who are blind often encounter social difficulties because of how society perceives them and how they perceive themselves.

■ **School Achievement**   With appropriate assistance and placement, a student who is visually impaired and who has no additional disabilities should be able to participate actively in all aspects of school and compete with sighted peers in academic areas. If a student with visual impairment is having trouble achieving academic goals, the teacher and the vision specialist should work together to determine if he or she is receiving proper instruction and has the needed adapted materials. The sections later in this chapter on teaching strategies and technological aids will provide more information for this purpose.

Effects on the Family

The reaction of families to the fact that their infant or child is blind or has low vision depends on many factors. Most important, as we saw in Chapter 3, may be the degree of support available to the family through its informal network of relatives and friends and its formal network of helping agencies and professionals.

Several other characteristics of the family and the child may affect the parents' attitude toward their child's visual impairment (Ferrell, 1986):

Parents' attitudes toward their child's visual impairment are affected by its severity, age of onset, delivery of diagnosis, and the amount of medical and educational support they receive.

1. *The severity of the handicap* may be an important issue, because many children with visual impairments also have additional disabilities. Parents of children whose visual impairment is severe or is complicated by other disabilities must respond to a variety of physical and developmental issues; in some cases they must also cope with anxiety about life-threatening medical procedures.

2. *The age of onset of the visual impairment.* The later the diagnosis of disability, the more difficult the news is for the parents; they have had more time for their hopes and expectations for their child to develop. On the other hand, the development of bonding, that crucial early parent-child tie that is so important to social and emotional development, may be affected when the infant is congenitally blind. Babies who have visual impairments are less likely to make eye contact with their mothers, which can result in a lack of the "mutual gazing" that occurs between infants and mothers. In addition, these babies may smile less regularly and consistently at their parents. Smiling in infants is important to elicit social interactions with other people and serves as a means to include the infant in the social relationship (Warren, 1984).

3. *How the information or diagnosis concerning visual impairment was initially received.* Stotland (1984), the parent of a child who is blind, says, "Ask any five parents of visually impaired children how they first learned their child had vision problems and you will get five different horror stories. These stories will range from blatant misdiagnoses to inaccurate predictions of total blindness, to expressions of pity" (p. 69).

4. *Support from medical professionals and educators* is critical in the initial discovery of a child's visual impairment. Parents must feel comfortable asking questions and expressing concerns in order to accept their child's visual impairment.

A child with visual impairment creates a dynamic within the family that can affect it in many ways long after the initial diagnosis. These effects might include changes in daily routines, social interactions, and parent involvement at school.

Families of children with visual impairments are often able to incorporate their child into the family routine, ensuring that the child feels he or she is a vital member of the family. In some cases, caregivers allow more time for the child to complete a particular task, such as clearing the dishes from the table. Caregivers can also use special adapted materials for more complicated tasks; for example, Braille labels on the washing machine and dryer. Participation in family routines helps children learn to complete tasks that they have started, to perform as independently as possible, and to take responsibility for their actions.

Outside their daily routines, families often must deal with changes in their social relationships as an indirect result of their child's visual impairment. Parents, for example, may have difficulty coping with the attitudes and misconceptions of their friends. Deborah Barton (1984), the parent of a child who is blind, recalls, "When my child started walking and talking, my friends considered him a genius and thought of me as a saint. They misinterpreted what they saw, and I let them. They praised Jed for ordinary behavior ('he's walking,' 'he likes peanut butter,' 'he doesn't whine') and talked about me as if I was a cross between Madame Curie and the Flying Nun" (p. 67). Although at first this kind of acknowledgment might seem welcome, it is difficult for parents to endure misconceptions such as these over time since they indicate a lack of understanding of their child's needs and abilities.

Social interactions between the child who is visually impaired and children who are sighted may also require special attention and effort. Families of children with a visual impairment must be even more careful to provide social activities for that child outside of the family so that good social skills are established throughout the early years of a child's development. Unfortunately, some parents of sighted children may be reluctant to invite the child who is blind to participate in activities such as birthday parties or slumber parties because of their lack of understanding about blindness. Parents of children with visual impairments may need to initiate some of this social interaction and to educate the parents of their child's sighted peers. When inexperienced adults begin to learn about the abilities and needs of a child with visual impairment, they can model acceptance and understanding for their own children.

School is another area in which family participation and adaptation are important. Parents or caregivers should participate in the interdisciplinary team, which gathers as much information as possible concerning the child's abilities and needs, including the degree to which the child uses remaining vision. The family has a crucial role in providing the professionals with information on how the child uses his or her vision. Once decisions have been made regarding adaptive materials and curricular activities, parents become vital participants in their child's education. If, for example, a child is learning to travel independently with a cane, the parents can reinforce this skill by communicating closely with their child's teachers to monitor progress and to learn about the skill from them. In doing so, they encourage independence for their child. If a child is learning Braille, parents can learn it too. Close communication between parents and teachers and direct involvement of parents in the education of the child are critical to educational success.

Family participation in the child's education, especially in the interdisciplinary team, is crucial.

Educational Issues and Teaching Strategies

Understanding the following issues will help teachers and parents provide an appropriate education for children with vision loss, including necessary adaptations.

Early Intervention

Professionals have long recognized the need for intervention programs for infants and their parents as soon as a visual impairment is diagnosed. For babies with congenital blindness, this diagnosis comes at birth or soon after; for babies with lesser degrees of visual impairment, the diagnosis may occur later in

Tachers must expect children with visual impairments to follow the same routines as other students. There are benefits when friends stand in line together! (Ellen Senisi/The Image Works, Inc.)

Early intervention for infants with visual impairments may prevent the development of secondary handicaps.

infancy. Children with a moderate degree of impairment may receive a diagnosis only after they encounter difficulty in completing school tasks.

Kay Ferrell (1986) has described several reasons for early intervention with infants who are visually impaired. First, as discussed earlier, vision is an important component of early cognitive development, and there may be particular periods of early development when optimal learning occurs. Early intervention may also prevent the development of secondary disabilities. Failure to develop attachment to a significant adult, language, or ear-hand coordination may form the foundation for handicaps in addition to visual impairment that will emerge later in the child's life.

Early intervention can take numerous forms. Teachers of young children with visual handicaps will encourage parents to continue to talk to their baby, to "show" things to the baby by allowing her to touch and explore them, to teach the baby to listen for clues to what is happening around her, to play games that involve moving and identifying parts of the body—using the baby's hands to find her head, nose, ears, tummy, knees, and so on. Teachers can also help parents make the most of the learning opportunities that arise in daily life with their baby, so that he or she will grow into a healthy and well-adjusted child. This role is important, as parents sometimes alter their interactions with a child who is visually impaired. They may assume that a child who cannot see is less interested in his or her environment or does not need the stimulation of playing with household objects and toys or of playing baby games with parents.

Identification and Assessment

Assessment for students who are visually impaired is especially difficult for three reasons: the lack of standardized assessment instruments, the need for adaptations of existing assessment instruments to meet the needs of students with visual impairments, and the need for a fair interpretation of test results. The lack of standardized assessment instruments is a direct result of the small number of students with visual impairments. It has been impossible to standardize tests on this population because of the lack of homogeneity caused by differences in age of onset of visual impairment, degree of visual impairment, and differences in educational experiences.

Educational Issues
and Teaching Strategies

Assessment of students who are visually impaired is difficult, mostly due to lack of standardized tests for this population.

■ **Identification in School** Every state mandates vision screening in the schools to determine which students have visual problems that warrant further assessment. At least 25 percent of school-age children have eye problems that need professional attention (Harley & Lawrence, 1984), and that percentage is considerably higher among children with other disabilities.

The most common visual screening test is one you have probably taken yourself, although you may not know the name of it—the **Snellen Chart**. The person being examined is positioned twenty feet from the chart, on which eight rows of letters ranging from large to small are printed, and is asked to read the letters with each eye (while the other eye is covered). If there is difficulty reading any of the letters on the chart, the school nurse or other person conducting the screening usually makes a referral for a more comprehensive evaluation of vision.

The Snellen Chart is the most common visual screening test.

The Snellen Chart is used to screen for distance vision problems only. If you suspect that one of your students has a near vision problem (which would affect reading) or another kind of vision problem, then urge your school nurse to conduct or recommend a more complete visual evaluation for that student. (See the accompanying box, "Detection of Vision Problems.")

There are a number of ways to screen for visual impairments in very young children or those who do not know the letter names. The most common are the Snellen E Chart and the Apple/House/Umbrella Screening. There are also a variety of means for evaluating the vision of students with severe handicaps that the experienced examiner will be able to use (Harley & Lawrence, 1984). No student should be excluded from vision screening because he or she cannot provide traditional responses.

Ideally, vision screening should be the product of a team approach, with educational and medical staff working together (Harley & Lawrence, 1984). Continuous observation of the student in the classroom and in other natural settings should accompany the screening, plus referral of identified students for further visual evaluation and follow-up to ensure that the recommendations have been carried out.

■ **Functional Vision Assessment** In addition to the medical evaluations just discussed, it is critical to test students' functional vision—in other words, how well they use the vision that they do possess. If, for example, it is noted during a functional vision assessment that a student has difficulty moving and performing tasks in limited lighting, teachers will be more prepared to accommodate him or her in low-lighting situations.

In addition to medical evaluations of vision, it is critical to test a student's functional vision.

Functional vision assessments vary according to the type of information needed. Commercially produced functional vision assessments are available, such as the Program to Develop Efficiency in Visual Functioning (American Printing House for the Blind) and Project IVEY: Increasing Visual Efficiency in Young Children (Florida Department of Education), but most functional vision assessments are informal and may be a compilation of other assessments.

~ Detection of Vision Problems

Teachers are often the first to detect visual problems in their students. Symptoms of visual impairment may include:

- *Physical changes in or about the eyes and face.* Physical changes may include an eye that tends to wander or eyes that are bloodshot or show recurrent redness or watering. Children may complain that their eyes hurt or feel "dusty." Frequent rubbing of the eyes, facial distortions, frowning, and an abnormal amount of squinting or blinking may be other symptoms of trouble. Children may show a preference for using only one eye or for viewing only at a distance or only at close range, or they may tilt their heads or bring objects unusually close to their eyes.

- *Changes in vision.* Children may complain that objects look blurry or that they are unable to see something at a distance. Note also an inability to use vision in different situations or with different illumination.

- *Changes in behavior.* Children may become irritable when doing desk work or have a short attention span when watching an activity that takes place across the room. They may report headache or nausea after close work, hold books close to the eyes, or lean down close to the book.

If the teacher suspects a visual impairment, he or she should immediately notify the parents and refer the student to the school nurse or physician for evaluation.

Source: Adapted from I. Torres and A.L. Corn, *When You Have a Visually Handicapped Child in Your Classroom: Suggestions for Teachers* (2d ed.) (New York: American Foundation for the Blind, 1990), pp. 32–33.

Functional vision assessments are usually conducted by a vision specialist and an orientation and mobility specialist and may include the following (Erin & Paul, 1996; Roessing, 1982):

- Information on the student's visual disability and prognosis
- Classroom modifications for distance vision tasks
- Classroom modifications for near vision tasks
- Informal assessments of visual field and color vision
- Equipment adaptations for classes
- Travel skills

Functional vision assessments are individualized. By careful consideration of information provided by the assessment, teachers can make more informed decisions about educational programming.

■ **Assessment for Teaching** Students who are visually impaired must demonstrate knowledge through both informal classroom evaluations and formal standardized tests, just as their sighted peers do. They should be required to participate in evaluation activities along with their mainstreamed class; however, these students must be given every opportunity to take the test in such a way that their performance gives an accurate picture of their true abilities. In most cases students with visual impairments need modifications in the presentation of testing materials and in time requirements. Most commercially produced achievement tests are available in Braille and large-print versions. A vision specialist will be able to obtain copies of these tests.

Students who are visually impaired have difficulty completing tests with time limits since it generally takes longer to read material in Braille or in large print. Decisions regarding the testing time limit for a student who is visually impaired should be made by evaluating the student's needs and abilities.

Most commercially produced achievement tests are available in Braille and large print.

Students who use braille type their class notes on a braillewriter, a six-key device which produces the raised dots of braille. The student on the left is checking her work. (Amy Etra/PhotoEdit)

Finally, interpretation of test results should take into consideration the modification of test items and the testing situation as well as whether any test items rely heavily on visual experiences for correct answers. The scores of students who are visually impaired should not be compared with standardized scores since standardized scores do not reflect modifications for these students. Vision specialists can assist in the interpretation of test results for individual students.

Curriculum

Students who are visually impaired require instruction not only in academic areas but also in skills needed to compensate for their loss of vision. These skills are critical to students' success in life after school and so are an important part of the curriculum. In this section, we discuss skills such as using Braille and low-vision aids, low-vision training, listening, orientation and mobility, and daily living.

■ **Braille**   Learning Braille is essential for students who are so severely visually impaired that they cannot read print, and is recommended for students who are legally blind as well. Instruction in alternative methods of reading and writing is important in education, vocational opportunities, and daily living skills (Spungin, 1990).

Braille was devised by Louis Braille, a French musician and educator, in 1829. It is a code that uses raised dots instead of printed characters (letters). A unit in Braille is called a *cell*. Each cell consists of six dots, three dots high and two dots wide. The dots are numbered from 1 through 6, and the Braille alphabet is made of combinations of these six dots (Figure 9.2). The Braille alphabet is only a small part of the literary Braille code, which also consists of contractions

Some students who are blind read by using Braille—a tactile code of raised dots.

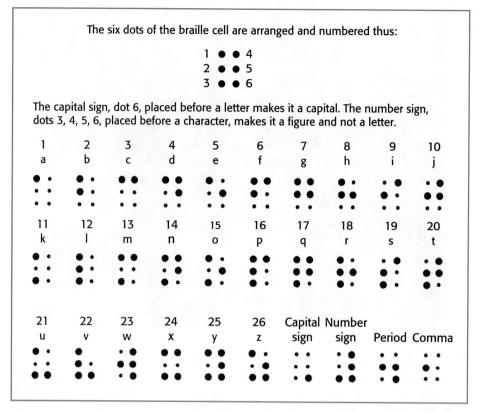

Figure 9.2   Braille Alphabet
and Numerals

Source: Division for the Blind and Physically Handicapped, Library of Congress, Washington, DC 20542.

(or combinations of letters). Braille is produced on a Braillewriter or on a hand-held slate and stylus. It can also be produced by a computer and Braille printer.

Learning to read Braille should begin long before a student enters school, just as learning to read print should (McComiskey, 1996). Sighted children begin the reading process by recognizing symbols in the environment. For example, children at an early age might learn to associate a hamburger and french fries with the golden arches of McDonald's. Children who are sighted have experience watching adults read books, looking at picture books, and having books read to them long before they know how to read. They also build background experiences through observation and participation.

In contrast, children who are severely visually impaired will not have experiences equating symbols with their meanings unless they are given tactile symbols. Children who are blind cannot watch adults read books, so they gain knowledge about books only if they have the opportunity to explore Braille books prior to school. Parents who give children opportunities to become familiar with Braille and tactile symbols help them achieve readiness for Braille reading. Without these experiences, it becomes necessary for the teacher to begin the process of developing an understanding of symbols. Children with visual impairments also need to be provided with the experiences that are described in basal reading series—usually the games and routines of sighted children (Koenig & Farrenkopf, 1997). All children need experiential background to understand fully what they read, but it is especially important to provide background experiences for children who are blind, for they may not have devel-

⌇ Aids for Students with Low Vision

- Optical aids, such as a hand-held magnifying glass
- Closed-circuit television sets that enlarge printed material onto a screen
- Computer software that varies type size and typeface
- Computer hardware such as large monitor screens and screen magnifiers
- Large-print textbooks

- Materials used to provide greater contrast in written and printed matter: yellow acetate, bold-line paper, felt-tip markers

Source: Adapted from G.J. Zimmerman, "Optics and Low Vision Devices," in A.L. Corn and A. J. Koenig (eds.), *Foundations of Low Vision: Clinical and Functional Perspectives* (New York: AFB Press, 1996).

oped symbolic meanings for themselves. Classroom teachers should request Braille copies of all classroom materials so that the student who is blind can be included in all activities.

■ **Low Vision Aids and Training**   Many students who are visually impaired do not use Braille as their primary learning medium; instead, they can learn to use large print or even regular print with magnification or low-vision aids (see the accompanying box, "Aids for Students with Low Vision").

Professionals in visual impairment no longer believe that using vision can damage it. In fact, professionals who work with students who are visually impaired now realize that instruction can actually help children develop better use of their vision.

Instruction in the use of low vision touches on three areas: environmental adaptations, which may involve making changes in distance, size, contrast, illumination, or time; enhancement of visual skills, such as attention, scanning, tracking, and reaching for objects, through integration of these skills into functional activities; and integration of vision into activities, or teaching skills within the actual activities where they are needed (Erin & Paul, 1996).

Many low-vision aids and systems of instruction are available for students with visual impairments.

■ **Developing Listening Skills**   Since students who are visually impaired receive a large percentage of information through their auditory sense, it is important to give them instruction and experience in using this sense to the fullest. Many people believe that people who are blind automatically have superior auditory skills, but this is not true.

Listening to recorded materials does not replace reading print or Braille as a means for developing literacy; however, it is important for students who are blind since it allows for efficient gathering of large amounts of materials over a short period of time. With instruction, a student can become more efficient in the use of listening for learning.

Students with visual impairments benefit from instruction in listening skills.

■ **Orientation and Mobility**   In addition to academic skills, students with visual impairment must develop skills to ensure that they can be independent adults, able to work and to move around in their environment with as little assistance as possible. For this reason, instruction in orientation and mobility is a critical component of the curriculum for students who are blind (see the accompanying box, "A Closer Look: Collaboration—Who Are the Professionals Interacting with the Student Who Is Visually Impaired?"). Ultimately, the goal of orientation and mobility is "to enable the student to enter any environment,

A closer look

Collaboration: Who Are the Professionals Interacting with the Student Who Is Visually Impaired?

A number of professionals with different educational backgrounds and specialized skills will likely work with the student who is visually impaired, and you as the teacher will have the opportunity to collaborate with some of them in order to provide services to the student. First, there are three groups of professionals involved with different aspects of evaluating vision and prescribing and fitting corrective lenses. An **ophthalmologist** is a physician who specializes in the treatment of eye diseases. This medical doctor can perform a complete eye examination, prescribe medicine, and perform surgery; the ophthalmologist should be consulted if there is any suspicion of eye disease. An **optometrist,** or doctor of optometry, although not a physician, undergoes postgraduate training enabling him or her to examine the eyes, evaluate visual problems, and prescribe corrective lenses. An **optician** grinds and fits corrective lenses that have been prescribed by an ophthalmologist or optometrist.

Next are the specialists working in school settings. The teacher of students with visual impairments has advanced training in providing specialized skills—reading skills, including Braille and large print; concept development; daily living skills; and so on. The teacher may provide direct services to students on an itinerant basis or in a special day class, resource room, or residential school; or may consult with the general education teacher. The teacher may work with students from infancy through transition to the workplace.

The orientation and mobility specialist teaches the skills for safe and independent travel, from toddlerhood through adulthood, as well as the use of specialized travel devices. Orientation and mobility instructors help students learn to detect obstacles and eventually to cross streets alone; they will be needed whenever a student needs to become familiar with a new setting, such as a new school.

The **vocational rehabilitation counselor,** usually associated with a state or private agency, assists adolescents with visual impairments making the transition from school to work by helping them and their families plan for post–high school education and training, as well as job placement.

Lisa Pruner, a teacher-consultant with students with visual impairments, developed these tips for working with a consultant:

1. Use the telephone! Your consultant won't know that you have questions or concerns unless *you* let her know. Don't try to "make do" until the next scheduled visit. That can be frustrating for everyone. When in doubt, call your consultant.

2. Set aside a block of time to talk to your consultant during her visit. It's important to be able to share observations and concerns immediately in a relatively distraction-free environment.

3. Let your consultant know what you need. If you need an observation, some suggestions for adaptations, or if you want to observe the consultant interacting directly with a student, tell your consultant. Every classroom has different needs, and every teacher has a different level of comfort with vision issues. Let your consultant know what she can do for you.

4. Make a list of questions to ask before each visit.

5. Contact therapists, specialists, administrators, and parents regarding the consultant's visit. Invite them to join you or submit questions through you if they can't attend.

6. Remember, the consultant's job is to provide technical assistance in an area in which classroom teachers aren't usually trained. Make good use of your consultant. I'm here to help!

Sources: Adapted from Appendix A: "Who Are the Professionals Who Work with Visually Impaired People?" in I. Torres and A.L. Corn, *When You Have a Visually Impaired Child in Your Classroom: Suggestions for Teachers* (New York: American Foundation for the Blind, 1990); and Lisa W. Pruner, "Tips for Working with a Consultant," *RE:view* 25(4) (1994), 174.

familiar or unfamiliar, and to function safely, efficiently, gracefully, and independently" (Hill & Ponder, 1976, p. 1).

Orientation and mobility consists of two equally important subparts: **orientation,** the ability to use one's senses to establish where one is in space and in relation to other objects and people, and **mobility,** the ability to move about in one's environment. Skill in orientation and mobility is crucial for several reasons:

- Psychological reasons, including the development of a positive self-concept
- Physical reasons, including the development of fitness
- Social reasons, including the increase of opportunities for social interactions through independent travel
- Economic reasons, including the increase of employment opportunities and options

There are four generally accepted orientation and mobility systems: **human guide, cane travel, dog guide,** and **electronic travel aids.** The first three systems will be discussed in this section, and electronic travel aids will be discussed in the section on technological advances. People who are blind often use a combination of these systems depending on the nature of the task they wish to accomplish.

Human Guide   In this system the person who is blind can travel safely through the environment, including maneuvering around stairs and obstacles, by holding lightly onto the elbow of a sighted person and following the movement of that person as he or she walks. Even though these techniques are relatively safe and efficient, and human guides are often able to assist the person who is blind in the development of kinesthetic awareness (awareness of movement), the continuous use of a human guide may also lead to a level of dependence instead of the independence that is the goal of instruction in orientation and mobility (Hill, 1986). It is also difficult to use human guide techniques properly, since few members of the general public are aware of them.

Cane Travel   One of the most common systems of orientation and mobility is the use of a cane for independent travel. Students who are visually impaired and use a cane must learn a variety of techniques in order to travel efficiently and safely. The canes used today are generally made from aluminum and vary in length according to a person's height, stride, and the time it takes him or her to respond to information gathered by moving the cane (Hill, 1986). Instruction in the use of the cane is very specialized and should be provided individually. This instruction is very important, since in many cases the safety of the student depends on the use of proper techniques. Instruction is most commonly given by an orientation and mobility specialist.

Dog Guides   The use of dog guides, though well publicized, is very limited. Only about 2 percent of people with visual impairments use a dog guide for travel (Hill, 1986). Dog guides are trained to assist people who are blind in safe travel; however, it is the person who is blind who makes decisions regarding travel route and destination. The use of a dog guide does not negate the need for a person who is blind to have good independent orientation and mobility skills.

> Orientation is the ability to use one's senses to establish one's relationship to objects and people; mobility is the ability to move about the environment.

> A human guide can help a person who is blind travel safely but may also lead to dependence.

> With proper training, students who are visually impaired can use a cane to travel independently.

> Dog guides are used only by a small percentage of people with visual impairments.

■ **Development of Daily Living Skills**   An important element in the curriculum is the development of daily living skills for students with visual impairments, which increases their ability to accomplish daily routines, such as selection and care of clothes, management (including identification) of money, independent preparation of food, shopping, and so on (Hill, 1986).

Children who are sighted learn most daily living skills through observation and imitation or instruction from parents or family members. Children who are blind may not be able to observe daily living activities with enough detail to imitate, and their parents may be unaware of adapted techniques for instruction. It is usually the responsibility of the vision specialist to provide this instruction. Consider, for example, Kelly's predicament:

> The vision specialist was unaware until Kelly was in the eighth grade that he was unable to tie his shoes. After investigating, the teacher found out that Kelly's parents had attempted several times to teach him, but he had difficulty accomplishing the task as it was described to him and consequently took a very long time to tie his shoes. As in most families, the mornings were hectic, so, two minutes before Kelly's bus arrived each morning, his mother gave in and tied his shoes. The problem came in junior high school, when Kelly had to get dressed and undressed for gym class, and no one was there to tie his shoes. Had instruction in daily living skills been a priority in earlier grades, this difficulty (and embarrassment for Kelly) might have been avoided. The vision specialist immediately began intensive instruction in daily living skills with Kelly. She taught him not only how to tie his shoes but also how to fold the bills in his wallet so that he could tell the difference between a $5 bill and a $10 bill and how to make healthy after-school snacks. As a result, Kelly is more confident and more independent.

One of the responsibilities of the vision specialist is to teach daily living skills.

See Table 9.3 for examples of daily living skills that can be taught to children who are visually impaired.

Placement for Students Who Are Visually Impaired

In the following sections, we will discuss the placement with the longest history, residential programs, as well as the range of options for more integrated education provided by public schools.

■ **Residential School Programs**   The first opportunity for students with visual impairments in the United States to receive an education was provided by residential schools, which were modeled after European residential schools for the blind. The first American residential schools were opened in New York and Massachusetts in 1832. By the end of the nineteenth century, thirty-six schools for the blind had been established throughout the United States. Residential schools have traditionally offered comprehensive services, providing instruction in academic skills, daily living skills, and vocational skills.

Residential schools have played a major role in the education of children with visual impairments.

Students attending residential schools go to classes and live on campus. There may be one residential school per state for students who are blind, so stu-

Table 9.3   **Typical Daily Living Activities for Children with Visual Impairments**

Preschool	Dressing Mealtime routines Toileting Use of eating utensils
Elementary years	Selection of clothes according to preference and weather Washing and caring for hair Household chores Handling small amounts of personal money
High school years	Grooming Self-care Organization of personal possessions Ordering and maintaining special devices and equipment Application of appropriate social skills

Source: N.C. Barraga and J.N. Erin, *Visual Handicaps and Learning* (Austin, TX: ProEd, 1992), pp. 152–153. Used by permission of Pro-Ed, Inc.

dents whose families live too far away from the school to commute every day live in the dormitory of the school.

The future of residential schools for students who are blind has been closely examined in recent years (McIntire, 1985; Miller, 1985). Hatlen and Curry (1987) believe that residential schools provide a strong educational foundation because they teach children who are visually impaired to succeed both in school and away from school. At the same time, however, these authors acknowledge the critical importance of interaction between children who are blind and their peers who are sighted (Hatlen & Curry, 1987).

Residential schools for students who are blind fill a continuing need that must not be ignored. It is clear, though, that residential schools must constantly re-evaluate their role and be willing to change to meet the changing needs and demands of their students (McIntire, 1985).

■ **Public School Programs**   Public school programs for students who are blind began as early as 1900. They are today the most popular service delivery model for students who are visually impaired. The three major educational models used within public, nonresidential schools are self-contained classrooms, resource rooms, and itinerant services, including consultative services.

Self-contained classrooms are classrooms within a public school in which only children with visual impairments are enrolled. The teacher of the class is certified in special education focusing on the needs of students with visual impairments. Self-contained classrooms are not necessarily uninvolved with the general education class: Sometimes both groups of students participate in the same activities. But the majority of instruction for students enrolled in a self-contained classroom is provided in that classroom by the certified teacher. Some students need additional instruction in adaptive learning techniques (such as Braille, listening skills, or use of adaptive technology) and, after such instruction, will be capable of entering the regular classroom and succeeding. Self-contained classrooms may be very useful in the education of very young

Most children with visual impairments are now educated in public schools.

~ What Specialized Instruction Do Students with Visual Impairments Need?

Specialized instruction from the resource teacher includes compensatory skills needed to allow full participation in a regular classroom, such as Braille, use of technology, keyboarding, and listening skills. Although instructing the student in academic skills is primarily the responsibility of the general education teacher, resource teachers who are fully qualified to teach students with visual impairments serve as a resource to both the classroom teacher and the student. The resource teacher can help students develop special skills and assist in teaching academic skills that may rely somewhat on vision for understanding (such as fractions, biology, and geography). The resource teacher will work with the classroom teacher to develop materials so that instruction in academic skill areas can occur within the regular classroom.

Itinerant teachers also provide instruction in special skills (such as use of technology, listening skills, daily living skills) to students who are visually impaired as well as consultation services to regular classroom teachers. In some cases the itinerant teacher will not provide the student with direct service but may assist the classroom teacher by giving adaptive materials or strategies for the presentation of academic material to a child who is visually impaired.

children who are blind in order to prepare them for full, successful inclusion in general education classrooms.

In resource room programs, the student who is visually impaired is enrolled in the general education classroom, where he or she receives most instruction. A resource teacher with special training provides assistance through direct instruction and consultation to the student and classroom teacher.

Some children are included in the general education classroom but get specialized instruction from the resource teacher.

Itinerant services, in which a trained teacher travels from school to school within a specific area, providing direct or indirect services to students with visual impairments, are available for students enrolled in public schools who need additional assistance. Itinerant teachers provide a variety of services to these students depending on their individual needs; for example, they may see one child every day of the week, and another one day each week or less. See the accompanying box, "What Specialized Instruction Do Students with Visual Impairments Need?" for further details on these service-delivery models.

Itinerant teachers travel from school to school to provide services to students with visual impairments.

One of the most critical decisions to be made for children with visual impairments and their families is placement. Following this initial placement decision, it is important that the appropriateness of the decision be reevaluated frequently so that the child will receive not only the best possible instruction, taking into account the need for adaptive skills, but also the social interactions and experiences that will prepare the child for adult life in a competitive world.

Students with Additional Disabilities

Many students with visual impairment have additional disabilities such as deafness, emotional disturbance, mental retardation, learning disabilities, and physical impairment. Regardless of additional handicapping conditions, students with visual impairments should be encouraged to make use of their functional vision as well as taught adaptive techniques for daily living and vocational skills. In most cases, special education teachers who have students with multiple disabilities in their classroom will receive consultation services from the vision teacher in order to provide them with adaptive instruction (Erin, 1996).

Children with visual impairments who have additional disabilities will also need specialized instruction.

This student with low vision is using a screen-enhancing software program which enlarges print to the size which is legible for her. (Robin L. Sachs/PhotoEdit)

Technological Advances

Technological changes have had a significant effect on the educational and vocational outlook for students with visual impairments. Many devices are now available to increase a student's ability to function independently in educational and employment settings. Teachers have a role to play, though, in making this technology accessible and understandable to their students (Mack, Koenig & Ashcroft, 1990). Teachers need to provide effective instruction, to maximize time management, and to advocate for purchase of equipment. There are four major categories of available technology:

Technological advances have allowed students with visual impairments to function more independently.

1. *Devices to increase visual access to print*, including closed circuit televisions (CCTV) that enlarge print size on a television screen. A student may use such devices to magnify all or some of her classwork. The CCTV should be available in a place where the student has easy access and is also still a part of the class. As soon as the student is introduced to the CCTV, she will receive instruction from the vision specialist on its use and should, within a short time, be able to use it independently. The student should then be allowed to use the CCTV whenever she believes it will help accomplish the classwork. Some students use the CCTV only for reading, preferring to complete written assignments without it, while other students use it for both reading and writing. If the student is just beginning to use the CCTV, a gentle reminder may be helpful when the student has an academic task that may be more efficiently completed with the device.

2. *Devices to increase auditory access to print*, including voice output for microcomputers and word processors and devices that convert print to auditory

Can Girls with Impaired Vision Be Mommies?

I was 26 the first time someone raised the question of whether I, who had been blind since age five, could have and raise children. I had three advanced degrees and three years of teaching to my credit and had lived on my own (first single, then married) since age 21. Now, here I sat in the hospital with a pink-blanketed bundle in my arms, awestruck, wondering what I would do next.

I wanted some hands-on experience in diapering. I told a nurse who was going off duty, and when her replacement came in, the experience was brutal. She pushed my hands away gruffly and impatiently, saying she could do it better. I felt inadequate and embarrassed. This episode shook my confidence in my ability to cope with this incredible responsibility of being a mother.

Of course, within hours, I learned that the problem was the nurse's ignorance about blindness—not my ability to fasten a baby's diaper! I would also learn that the attitudes of others would continue to be the most significant problem unique to parents with impaired vision.

Sure, I had to make adaptations along the way—just as I had to make certain adaptations in riding a bike, climbing a tree, or going to college as a kid who couldn't see. I read books, I talked to other mothers. I invented solutions as I went along.

Organizing objects and clearly defining spaces were two keys in the first three years. Toys, books, food—everything that needed a braille label got one. I pinned outfits together before laundering, so that my babies were color-coordinated, and I always put toys away in the same place. I carried my babies first in front carriers and later in backpacks, and when they became toddlers, I used child safety harnesses to keep them close to me in public places.

My children have all been extremely verbal, as I've noticed many children of parents with impaired vision to be. They have

output, such as the Kurzweil Reading Machine. A Kurzweil Reading Machine is quite expensive and will probably not be available in the classroom; however, this device may be available through the library or vision resource center in your school or region. In addition, voice output devices for microcomputers and word processors are becoming more and more available. For students who are unable to read the print on a computer screen, an output device may allow them to use the computer to complete assignments. Headphones are available, so that the student can use the output device without disturbing other students.

also been early avid readers, probably a consequence of all my talking out of necessity and my obsession with being sure there were plenty of opportunities for learning.

It always amuses me that sighted people are so particularly focused on the fact that I cared for my children as babies. That was, without doubt, the easy part. A baby stays where you put her. Even when crawling or early walking, a baby is easy to keep within a defined area. It's when they become truly mobile—and later, truly individualized with their own opinions—that parenting, with or without sight, gets most challenging.

Sure, there have been some things we couldn't do. Someone else has to kick a soccer ball around with my eight-year-old, and someone else had to teach my older kids to drive. But no parent can do it all. On the other hand, I have taught other kids to bake cookies, write stories, sing songs.

Over the years I have known many other parents who are blind and seen many styles of parenting. Why should we expect anything less? Vision impairment is an equal opportunity disability and affects people of all temperaments and leadership capabilities.

What I know for sure is that when it comes to parenting, the same rules apply for people with impaired vision as for all others. Anyone who wants to have children should do so and will figure out the logistics as they go along. We have loved, laughed, and lived family life to the fullest in my household, and there is no person, no professional accomplishment, no privilege I could ever cherish more than my three children.

Deborah Kendrick

Source: "Can Girls with Impaired Vision Be Mommies?" by Deborah Kendrick, *Envision*, August 1997, pp. 5–7. Copyright © 1997. Reprinted by permission of The Lighthouse, Inc.

3. *Devices to increase tactile access to print*, including Braille printers that can be attached to word processors for immediate access to print work and devices that convert print to a tactile output, such as the Optacon. In the past, students who were blind would complete assignments in Braille, but the classroom teacher who was unable to read Braille would have to wait for the vision specialist to transcribe the Braille into print before grading the assignment. With the introduction of devices that can convert print into Braille and Braille into print, students can print their assignments in both Braille and English.

4. *Devices to increase independent travel*, including electronic travel aids that are independent or attach to a long cane and provide supplementary information about the enviroment. Although these devices are not directly relevant to academic work, the classroom teacher should know as much as possible about any device the student is using, including how it works, when the student should use it, and how to reinforce the student's proper use of the device. An orientation and mobility specialist will be able to answer all of these questions.

SUMMARY

■ Students with visual impairments make up a relatively small percentage of school-age children. This low-incidence population includes children who are blind, who have low vision, and who are visually impaired and have additional disabilities. Although legal blindness is required for some services, educational services are also offered to students with less severe visual impairments. Each school district has its own policies regarding the provision of services to students who are visually impaired.

■ The process of seeing involves the passage of light through the eye and interpretation of the image by the brain. Damage to any of the eye structures, the nerves connecting them to the brain, or the brain itself can result in visual impairments.

■ Visual impairments may affect a child's development by limiting one source of sensory feedback from the environment. In language, children may use verbal expressions without understanding what they mean; in physical development, children may be less motivated to move and explore; in cognitive development, children may interact less with the environment, resulting in poorer concept development.

■ The family of a child with a visual impairment is affected by the severity of the impairment, the age of onset, the diagnosis, and the support received from family and professionals.

■ Early intervention involves allowing the child to explore and touch, and helping parents make the most of learning opportunities in daily life.

■ Teachers are often the first to recognize visual impairments. The most common screening test is the Snellen Chart. Ideally, vision screening is the product of a team approach, with continuous observation in the classroom, referral for evaluation, and follow-up provided by appropriate professionals.

■ A functional vision assessment is used to make decisions about the student's educational program. Interpretation of test results should take into account modifications to the test and items that rely heavily on visual experience.

■ A curriculum for students who are blind or have low vision usually includes one or more of the following: instruction in Braille, instruction in low-vision aids, development of listening skills, and orientation and mobility.

■ Placement options for students who have visual impairments were initially limited to residential schools; however, public schools now provide self-contained classrooms, as well as resource programs and itinerant services for students included in the general education classroom.

- Advances in technology have resulted in increasing visual, auditory, and tactile access to print; new technology for orientation and mobility has also been developed.

KEY TERMS

visual impairment	cataract	orientation and mobility
legal blindness	retinopathy of	Snellen Chart
visual acuity	prematurity (ROP)	Braille
educational definitions	glaucoma	ophthalmologist
functional vision	diabetic retinopathy	optometrist
cornea	retinitis pigmentosa	optician
pupil	cortical vision loss	vocational rehabilitation
lens	refractive errors	counselor
vitreous humor	strabismus	human guide
iris	nystagmus	cane travel
retina	verbalisms	dog guide
optic nerve	echolalia	electronic travel aids

MULTIMEDIA RESOURCES

American Foundation for the Blind. *AFB Directory of Services for Blind and Visually Impaired Persons in the United States and Canada*, 25th ed. (with accompanying CD-ROM) (New York: AFB Press, 1997). This directory, updated yearly, is a compilation of schools, agencies, organizations, and programs that serve individuals who are blind or have low vision and their families. The CD-ROM contains the same information, making it accessible to users with vision loss with adaptive equipment.

American Foundation for the Blind website: http://www.afb.org/afb/; AFB InfoLine: (800) 232-5463. The AFB InfoLine provides information about Talking Books, as well as other AFB services.

American Printing House for the Blind website: http://www.aph.org/. APH provides special media, tools, and material needed for education and daily life by people with visual impairments.

Blind Children's Center. This group publishes a series of booklets that are useful, inexpensive, and reader-friendly on topics such as communicating and encouraging movement with the young child with visual impairments. They are written with parents in mind but are helpful for early intervention specialists and teachers, too. Contact them at 4120 Marathon Street, Los Angeles, CA 90020, (800) 222-3566, http://www.blindcnter.org/.

Children's Braille Book Club. This group offers children's books with a Braille page inserted. Free membership provides a monthly catalog. Contact them at National Braille Press, 88 St. Stephen Street, Boston, MA 02115, (800) 548-7273, http://www.npb.org/.

Keller, Helen. *The Story of My Life* (Garden City, NY: Doubleday, 1954). This autobiography has inspired many a reader; for even more detail, read *Helen and Teacher* by Joseph Lash (republished in 1997 by the American Foundation for the Blind), or rent the movie version of *The Miracle Worker*, which tells the story of Helen's discovery of the meaning of language with Annie Sullivan.

Library of Congress National Library Service for the Blind and Physically Handicapped. A free library program of Braille and recorded materials circulated
to eligible borrowers through a network of cooperating libraries. Telephone:
(202) 707-9275; website: http://lcweb.loc.gov/nls.html/.

*The National Agenda for Children and Youths with Visual Impairments, Including
Those with Multiple Disabilities* (New York: American Foundation for the Blind,
1995). This resource lists the national priorities for children with visual impairments as identified by noted professionals in the field.

Swallow, Rose-Marie, and Kathleen Mary Huebner (eds). *How to Thrive, Not Just
Survive: A Guide to Developing Independent Life Skills for Blind and Visually Impaired Children and Youths* (New York: American Foundation for the Blind,
1987). This comprehensive guide, complete with photographs and resource
listings, offers an abundance of strategies for teaching daily living skills to
youngsters who are visually impaired or blind.

Torres, Iris, and Anne L. Corn. *When You Have a Visually Impaired Child in Your
Classroom: Suggestions for Teachers* (New York: American Foundation for the
Blind, 1990). This small book is available free from the American Foundation
for the Blind. It is a very straightforward and useful resource for teachers who
are including students with vision loss.

USING YOUR KNOWLEDGE

 Can Do: How does a person with a visual impairment carry out daily living tasks? Invite a person who is blind or visually impaired to visit the
class and speak about his or her life, daily routines, professional career,
and experiences.

 Collaboration: What are some adjustments made by parents of a child
who is blind or visually impaired? Interview parents to find out how
they make decisions regarding education, how their home has been
adapted to accommodate their child, and how they feel about their
child's friendships.

 Can Do: Is your classroom accessible for a blind student? Develop a set of
guidelines for access. Consider the arrangement of desks and chairs, location of the instructor, windows and light sources, and availability of
large-print books, tape recorders and cassettes, and computers or type-
writers with Braille keys. Also consider classroom attitudes—would a
person with a visual impairment feel welcome?

WHAT YOU CAN DO NOW

1. **Now that you've read the chapter, have your assumptions about what it
   is like to have a visual impairment changed? Try a simulation exercise:
   Wear a blindfold during the first half of class. Concentrate on orientation and mobility, using listening skills, and memorizing spatial relationships. What were your impressions?**

2. **What are the limitations of the simulation exercise you just experienced? Now that you've experienced the simulation, what are you**

going to do to improve the quality of life for people with visual impairments?

3. Find out what's involved in raising a dog guide puppy. Contact 4-H Clubs of America, Room 50355, U.S. Department of Agriculture, Washington, DC 20250.

4. Contact the Office for Students with Disabilities on your campus and ask if there is a need for readers for students who are blind. Some textbooks are not immediately available in Braille or large print, so listening to a book on audiotape is the only way students have access to text material.

5. Learn human guide techniques so that you can accompany and assist a person with vision loss.

   • Let the person take your elbow, and walk half a step in front of her.
   • Describe objects or obstacles.
   • If approaching a stairway, say whether the stairs are going up or down.
   • Describe a chair before placing a person's hand on the back of it; he can seat himself.
   • Make sure doors are fully closed or open.
   • Describe any changes in a familiar furniture arrangement.
   • Converse naturally; provide detailed descriptions; don't worry about using words like *see* or *look*; don't hesitate to ask if it's not apparent what kind of help to provide.

6. Plan a social studies or science lesson and modify it to meet the needs of students who are blind.

Children with Physical Disabilities and Health Impairments

10

CHILDREN with physical disabilities and health impairments are a diverse group. This category includes a wide range of individual differences. Because many students with physical disabilities and health impairments have acquired their disabilities after infancy or have short life expectancies, they face emotional stress that teachers and parents must address. As you read, think about these questions:

■ What are the differences between physical disabilities and health impairments?

■ How can knowing the cause and treatment of a student's condition help you work with the student most effectively?

■ How can age of onset and severity of a condition affect a child's social and emotional development?

✔ **Can Do:** How has legislation affected the accessibility of schools and other public buildings to individuals with physical disabilities?

Collaboration: What is the transdisciplinary approach? How is it implemented in the classroom?

Commonalities: How can technology facilitate communication and social interaction among all students in a classroom, including those with significant physical disabilities?

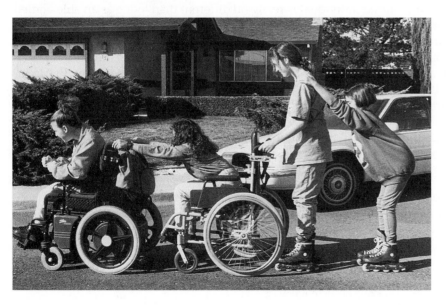

Although individuals with disabilities continue to battle for equal access to community and schools, their lives are also filled with many successes. You may already know many success stories. As a future teacher, you have the opportunity to learn from these successes as you work to make it easier for your students with physical disabilities to be part of rather than apart from your class.

Physical disabilities are frequently very visible. As a result, people ask questions. Imagine having to explain many times a day why you have no hair, why your hands are in splints, or why you have to rest a few seconds between words. In this chapter, we will rely frequently on the voices of persons with physical disabilities and health impairments as they answer these types of questions to help you learn more about them as people—friends, relatives, students.

Definitions and Terms

Probably more than any other disability, the presence of a physical disability makes us explore the meaning of such words as *disability*, *handicap*, and *severity*. This is because the degree of physical involvement and the degree to which the disability affects an individual's life are not necessarily correlated. You might consider paralysis from the neck down to be an extremely severe disability. Yet persons with this condition can lead fulfilling lives. They may not view themselves as "handicapped" at all. The individual adjusts, adapts, and contributes to the community. Disabilities become handicaps only when society uses them as a reason to discriminate against and segregate people.

Many people with physical disabilities prefer to use the term **physically challenged.** They view their physical conditions as a challenge to be faced rather than as a situation that disables or handicaps their existence. "Living as a spinal cord injured individual is really no different than living as an able bodied individual, except that you're doing it on wheels. Some of the technical aspects of living on wheels are different" (Corbet, 1980, p. 54).

Physical disability refers to a condition that incapacitates the skeletal, muscular, and/or neurological systems of the body to some degree. Many individuals with physical disabilities have no concurrent mental disability. This is an important point for us to keep in mind. Later in the chapter we will discuss conditions of coexisting mental and physical disabilities.

The Individuals with Disabilities Education Act (IDEA) identifies students who experience physical disabilities as "orthopedically impaired":

> "Orthopedically impaired" means having a severe orthopedic impairment. The term includes an impairment caused by a congenital anomaly (e.g., clubfoot, absence of some member, etc.), an impairment caused by disease (e.g., poliomyelitis, bone tuberculosis, etc.), and an impairment from any other cause (e.g., cerebral palsy, amputations, and fractures or burns which cause contractures). (Amendments to the Individuals with Disabilities Education Act, 1990, sec. 300.6[6])

The term **health impairment** also focuses on the physical condition of individuals. It includes conditions in which one or more of the body's systems are affected by diseases or conditions that are debilitating or life-threatening or that interfere with the student's ability to perform in a regular classroom setting. The definition of health impairment found in IDEA is as follows:

Many people with physical disabilities view their physical condition as a challenge rather than a handicapping condition.

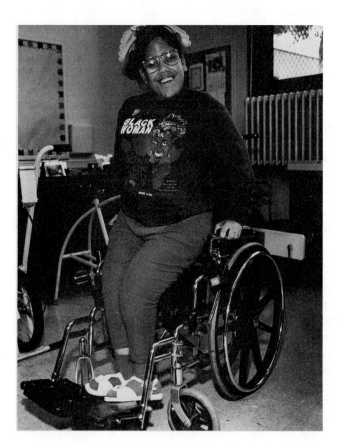

This teenager's face reflects independence, strength, and joy. (Pam Hasegawa/Impact Visuals)

"Other health impaired" means having limited strength, vitality, or alertness, due to chronic or acute health problems such as heart condition, tuberculosis, rheumatic fever, nephritis, asthma, sickle cell anemia, hemophilia, epilepsy, lead poisoning, leukemia, or diabetes. (Amendments to the Individuals with Disabilities Education Act, 1990, sec. 300.5[7])

Prevalence

Children with physical disabilities and other health impairments are among the smallest groups served under the federal laws known as IDEA. The Eighteenth Annual *Report to Congress on the Implementation of the Individuals with Disabilities Act* (1996) reported approximately 60,000 children from the ages of 6 to 21 with orthopedic impairments and 106,000 with other health impairments in the 1993–1994 school year.

Types of Physical Disabilities

In this section, we will look at the most prevalent types, causes, and treatments of physical disabilities in children. There are several reasons why you, as a prospective teacher, should know about particular disabilities. Understanding the cause may help you to know what to expect from a student, since certain causes lead to characteristic behavior. Understanding treatment requirements can also help you plan classroom time (for example, a student may need to miss class for dialysis) and become comfortable with helping the student with in-school treatment such as tube feeding. Once you know what to expect, you will be better able to plan instruction and to prepare the classroom from a physical perspective.

As we discussed in the Framework section preceding Chapter 4, there is a major disadvantage to grouping students into disability categories. The individual range of ability of students within each category varies widely. Resist stereotyping and base your expectations on the abilities and efforts of each individual student, regardless of the cause or apparent severity of the physical disability.

Within each disability category, the individual range of ability is very large.

Neurological Conditions

A neurological condition affects the nervous system—the brain, nerves, and spinal cord (Fraser, Hensinger & Phelps, 1990). The muscles and bones are healthy but the neurological messages sent to them are faulty or interrupted. Three of the more prevalent neurological conditions are cerebral palsy, spina bifida, and seizure disorders.

Cerebral palsy—caused by damage to the brain before birth or infancy—results in disabilities in movement and posture.

■ **Cerebral Palsy** **Cerebral palsy** is a condition involving disabilities in movement and posture that results from damage to the brain before or during birth or in infancy (Fraser, Hensinger & Phelps, 1990). The muscles and the nerves connecting the muscles to the brain are normal; the problem lies in the "communication" process between the brain and the muscles. Events like cerebral hemorrhages (bleeding in the brain), anoxia (lack of oxygen at birth), and fetal strokes can cause neurological damage that results in some type of cerebral palsy. However, in almost half of the instances of cerebral palsy, no specific cause can be identified (Healy, 1983).

The area and severity of brain injury, the cause of the injury, and when it occurs determine the type of cerebral palsy that appears and the extent of its effect on the body. Although incidence figures vary, it is estimated that 1.5 to 2 instances of cerebral palsy occur for every 1,000 live births (Batshaw & Perret, 1992).

Some children are identified as having cerebral palsy at birth, while others are not definitively diagnosed until they are a year old or even older. Young children are often identified as having cerebral palsy because of delay in meeting developmental milestones of motor development and the persistence of certain infant reflexes. Cerebral palsy also can be diagnosed in children up to age 6 who have brain damage due to external causes such as suffocation, near drowning, or encephalitis.

Cerebral palsy is often classified by type of motor dysfunction (see Figure 10.1). The most common type of dysfunction is *spasticity*, or hypertonia. Spasticity involves a mild to severe exaggerated contraction of muscles when the muscle is stretched (Denhoff, 1975). Spasticity is present in about 60 percent of all cases of cerebral palsy and occurs when the area injured is on the suface of the brain or on the nerves leading from the surface to the interior of the brain (Grove, Cusick & Bigge, 1991). Spasticity can involve the entire body or only some parts of the body.

Dyskenesia is a type of cerebral palsy characterized by involuntary extraneous motor activity, especially under stress (Blackburn, 1987). This type of cerebral palsy occurs in about 20 percent of all cases and is caused by injury to the

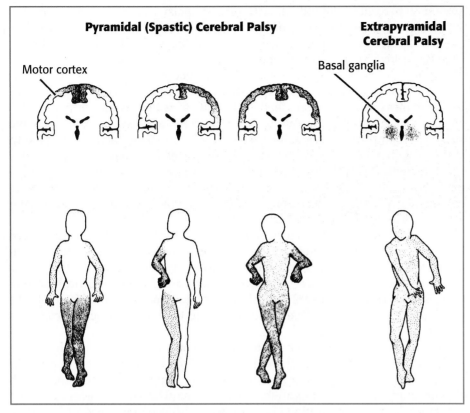

Pyramidal (Spastic) Cerebral Palsy

Extrapyramidal Cerebral Palsy

Motor cortex

Basal ganglia

Figure 10.1
Regions of the Brain Affected in Various Forms of Cerebral Palsy

Source: M.L. Batshaw and Y.M. Perret, *Children with Handicaps: A Medical Primer,* 3d ed. (Baltimore: Paul H. Brookes, 1992), p. 444. Copyright © 1992. Used by permission of the author. Note: The darker the shading, the more severe the involvement.

basal ganglia, the brain's motor switchboard (Healy, 1983). The involuntary movements sometimes accompany the individual's attempts at voluntary movement. One type of movement (*athetosis*) involves a slow, writhing type of movement. The person may appear to be repeatedly and slowly stretching his or her arms or legs when simply trying to reach for a book. *Choreoathetosis* refers to quick, jerky movements that may accompany the athetoid movements. Movements also may be slow and rhythmic and involve the entire limb or trunk (*distonia*).

Ataxia, a third type of cerebral palsy, is much less common. It occurs in about 1 percent of all cases, when the injury has occurred in the cerebellum. Ataxia refers to a lurching walking gait. People with ataxia also experience difficulty maintaining their balance.

About 30 percent of the individuals with cerebral palsy have a mixture of types (Healy, 1983). For example, a student might have spastic quadriplegia and ataxia. As we have already mentioned, the range of severity and involvement can be great. Some individuals may experience slight difficulty in muscle control—difficulty that may be undetectable by an observer. Others have almost no voluntary movement.

Some children with cerebral palsy also experience mental retardation, hyperactivity, or other disabilities such as visual impairment and hearing loss. The coexistence of other types of disabilities depends on the extent and location of brain injury as well as on early interventions. Some recent statistics suggest that around 30 percent of individuals with cerebral palsy have no coexisting mental retardation, and only 10 percent have moderate to severe mental retardation; others suggest that approximately 41 percent of individuals with cerebral palsy have IQs below 70 (Nelson & Ellenberg, 1986).

These statistics show quite a conflicting picture of mental ability among people with cerebral palsy. One explanation for this contradiction is the way the IQs were measured. For example, the use of IQ tests that require responses that are physical impossibilities for students with cerebral palsy (use of speech and language, manipulation of small objects) may underestimate ability. Most likely, students with cerebral palsy know more than IQ tests can measure. Speech that is slurred and difficult to understand due to cerebral palsy can initially prejudice a teacher to think that a student with cerebral palsy is "slow." New teachers like you will know more about cerebral palsy and will encourage all your students to learn to do their best.

Medical interventions such as braces, surgery, and prescribed therapies can help a student with cerebral palsy. For example, physical and occupational therapies exercise, strengthen, and position muscles, bones, and joints. Prevention of serious and painful contractures, dislocations, and rigidity is critical for individuals with cerebral palsy. Physical and occupational therapies facilitate the development of normal reflexes and maximize the control a person can have over the environment.

Positioning is a critical intervention for persons with limited mobility, especially in helping them meet the demands of the classroom. For example, although a physically capable individual can change positions when uncomfortable or fatigued, a student in a wheelchair or one who wears braces may need assistance for minor repositioning. A student with cerebral palsy may need an adult, such as the teacher, to provide physical assistance related to positioning, feeding, and other everyday needs. In the classroon, use of a tape recorder or a "note buddy" for writing notes are simple accommodations that teachers commonly arrange. Assistive technology, another significant intervention for students with cerebral palsy, will be discussed later in the chapter.

■ **Spina Bifida** **Spina bifida,** or open spine, and *neural tube defects (NTDs)* are general terms used to describe a midline defect of the skin, spinal column, and spinal cord that occurs during fetal development (Caldwell, Todaro & Gates, 1988). An estimated 1 out of every 2,000 births is affected (Grove, Cusick & Bigge, 1991). Spina bifida is most common in persons of Irish, Scotch, and English ancestry, and high-incidence regions in the United States, such as southern Appalachia, North and South Carolina, and Tennessee reflect this heritage (Greenberg, James & Oakley, 1983). Spina bifida and other NTDs have been correlated with a lack of folic acid, a vitamin found in green vegetables and fresh fruit, in the diet early in the pregnancy. Studies have found that minimal intakes of folic acid before and during pregnancy significantly decrease the incidence of spina bifida and other NTDs even in women who have had children with NTDs. Women of childbearing age should carefully evaluate their diets for proper amounts of folic acid or consult with a doctor about appropriate vitamin supplements.

In the margin:
In spina bifida, the spine does not close properly during fetal development, resulting in varying degrees of paralysis.

Children with spina bifida have spines that did not properly close during development, so the spinal cord protrudes from the weak point. As a result, nerves that control the lower parts of the body are not properly connected to the brain. Spina bifida usually results in limited or even no muscle control of the affected area. The extent of the defect depends on the location of the spinal cord damage (Grove, Cusick & Bigge, 1991). If the damage is at the base of the spine, the weakness may be limited to the muscles of the ankles and feet and the child may require only short leg braces for walking. A defect in the middle of the spine may result in paralysis below the waist, necessitating the use of a wheelchair. Bladder control problems and recurring kidney infections are also present (Caldwell, Todaro & Gates, 1988).

Hydrocephalus, a condition in which cerebrospinal fluid builds up in the skull and puts pressure on the brain, occurs in about 80 percent of cases of spina bifida. Untreated hydrocephalus may cause brain damage and mental retardation. Since spina bifida and other NTDs can now be detected early in pregnancy, children with this disability are likely candidates for prenatal surgery. Shunts (artificial openings) can be inserted while the fetus is still in the uterus to minimize damage to the brain from excess spinal fluid. Although the paralysis itself cannot be corrected, shunt implants, physical therapy, and surgery can help minimize the effects of the disability (Korabek & Cuvo, 1986).

In hydrocephalus, cerebrospinal fluid builds in the skull, sometimes causing brain damage and mental retardation.

■ **Seizure Disorders** Seizures occur when the normally ordered pattern of movement of electricity along the nerve pathways of the brain is disrupted by an unorganized burst of electric impulses. These bursts periodically disrupt the normal functioning of the brain. Seizure disorders occur in about 6 percent of the population (Batshaw & Perret, 1992). A condition of the nervous system that results in the recurrence of seizures is known as **epilepsy** (Wolraich, 1983b). There are a number of possible causes, including any direct injury to the brain, conditions such as cerebral palsy, or scarring of the brain as a result of infections or illness such as meningitis or rubella. In some instances, there appears to be a genetic component or predisposition. In many instances of epilepsy, however, there is no identifiable cause. It is important to know that not all seizures are epileptic in nature. For example, sometimes a young child with a high fever has an isolated seizure.

Epilepsy is a neurological condition characterized by recurrent seizures.

Two types of seizures found frequently in school-aged children are grand mal seizures and petit mal seizures. **Grand mal seizures,** also called generalized tonic-clonic seizures, are experienced by about 60 percent of all individuals with seizure disorders (Wolraich, 1983b). The seizures, which involve the whole body, usually last a few minutes and often result in a loss of consciousness. Most people experience a warning (called an *aura*) before the occurrence of a grand mal seizure. The aura may be characterized by unusual feelings or numbness. The seizure itself begins with a *tonic phase*, in which there is a stiffening of the body, often a loss of consciousness, heavy and irregular breathing, and drooling. In a few seconds, the seizure goes into the second, or *clonic phase*. At this time, the muscles alternately clench and relax. Finally, the seizure is followed by a period of fatigue or disorientation. (See the accompanying box, "What to Do If Someone Has a Tonic-Clonic Seizure.")

Petit mal seizures, also called absence seizures, occur most frequently in children between the ages of 4 and 12 (Wolraich, 1983b). Petit mal seizures often disappear as the child grows older; however, one-third to one-half of children with a history of petit mal seizures are likely also to have or eventually develop grand mal seizures. Petit mal seizures are very brief—usually lasting between 15 and 30 seconds. The episodes are sometimes difficult to recognize. The child will lose consciousness, but this is not accompanied by any observable physical changes. In other words, the child may appear to be just blinking his eyes or staring into space for a few seconds.

first
person

My Life

Hi! My name is Jessica Smallman. I am 14 years of age; I was born May 3, 1982, in Halifax, Nova Scotia. Before I was born my parents, Faye Smallman and John Smallman, Jr., were told that I had a birth defect called spina bifida. I also had something called hydrocephalus, which means I had water on and near the brain. After I was born the doctors did an operation on me to insert a shunt (a tube from my head to my stomach to drain the water from my head to my stomach). I was hospitalized for a little while after birth.

As I got older I needed special equipment to help me go to the washroom, stand, walk, and just for mobility reasons. Since my dad is in the navy, we move a lot and I went to several elementary schools and a new hospital in Montreal. When I went to new schools it was very hard because of the students at these schools. The kids didn't know what was wrong with me and they didn't know how to react around me. In class they would call me stupid. One day, I just could not take it anymore and I did a presentation in front of my grade five classmates on spina bifida. After the presentation they stopped bugging and teasing me. My parents pushed me to be more active and independent even though they saw how much I was hurting.

In the summer I went to the rehabilitation centre for four weeks. They taught me how to live on my own, how to keep fit, and how to protect myself. They also taught me not to be so upset about the way people treat me since the reason they act this way is because they don't understand me. They think they have to do everything for me, and if they move me a certain way I will break. This is not true because I'm very, very strong, and I'm not glass or something fragile or delicate.

I also have to say that I am not lazy and I don't like people saying that. People used to laugh because I couldn't do some of the things

Medications are used extensively in the treatment of seizure disorders. In most cases, appropriate medication can prevent seizures; some adjustment in prescription may be necessary as the child gets older or if different types of seizures begin to occur. A few children, who experience a number of different kinds of seizures or who have extensive brain damage, may have seizures that are difficult to keep under control. It is important for teachers to know when students are receiving medication for seizures, as medication can affect school

they could, but I try my best to do many things. I think I am almost the same as any kid I know. I think like everyone else and I talk like everyone else. The only things I don't do like everyone else is walk and go to the bathroom by myself. That is why I have to wear diapers and I do self-catheterizations every four hours, and I can't drink much after I do my catheters. If I do I will leak a lot more than I usually do. I also get infections a lot easier than other people. If I could tell people one thing, it is "please don't treat me like I'm fragile."

Life.....................

Life is like an elevator, some days are good some days are bad.
Life is like a book, some parts are boring and some are lots of fun.
Life is a bunch of songs, some are happy ones and some are sad ones.
Life is about heartaches and headaches and other different feelings.
Life is like school, you're always being educated
And some things you may not like, but you've got to continue.
Life is full of surprises that are waiting for us to discover them.
Some may cause pain and some may cause happiness
And life is having friends around you that care about you no matter
    what.
They won't do stuff behind your back or not believe you
    or the things you say,
And that's what life is all about (at least that's what my life is all
    about).

by Jessie Smallman

Jessie Smallman is a grade nine student at Gaetz Brook Junior High, Nova Scotia.

Source: "My Life" by Jessica Smallman, *Ability Network Magazine*, Vol. 5, Number 2. Winter 1996/97. Reprinted by permission of Ability Network Publishing Inc.

performance by causing changes in alertness and other school-related behaviors.

Musculoskeletal Conditions

In addition to physical disabilities caused by damage to the brain are conditions that directly affect muscles and bones. These musculoskeletal conditions

∼ What to Do If Someone Has a Tonic-Clonic Seizure

- Keep calm. Reassure the other children that the child will be fine in a minute.
- Ease the child gently to the floor and clear the area of anything that could hurt him.
- Put something flat and soft (like a folded jacket) under his head so it will not bang against the floor as his body jerks.
- Turn him gently onto his side. This keeps his airway clear and allows any fluid in his mouth to drain harmlessly away.

  Don't try to force his mouth open.

  Don't try to hold on to his tongue.

  Don't put anything in his mouth.

  Don't restrain his movements.
- When the jerking movements stop, let the child rest until full consciousness returns.

- Breathing may have been shallow during the seizure and may even have stopped briefly. This can give the child's lips or skin a bluish tinge, which corrects naturally as the seizure ends. In the unlikely event that breathing does not begin again, check the child's airway for any obstruction. It is rarely necessary to give artificial respiration.

Some children recover quickly after this type of seizure; others need more time. A short period of rest, depending on the child's alertness following the seizure, is usually advised. However, if the child is able to remain in the classroom afterward, he or she should be encouraged to do so.

Source: From *Children and Epilepsy: The Teacher's Role* (Landover, MD: Epilepsy Foundation of America, 1992), pp. 3–4. Copyright © 1992. Reprinted by permission of the Epilepsy Foundation of America.

debilitate the muscles, bones, or joints to such a degree that they cause limitations in their functional use.

■ Muscular Dystrophy

In muscular dystrophy, the voluntary muscles of the body progressively weaken.

Muscular dystrophy is a condition in which the voluntary muscles of the body are affected by progressive weakness. Although there are several types of muscular dystrophy, the most common in school-aged children is Duchenne's muscular dystrophy. This often hereditary condition, which affects boys, is usually diagnosed between the ages of 2 and 6. Neither the cause of Duchenne's muscular dystrophy nor a specific treatment has yet been discovered. The incidence is usually cited as one per 3,500 live male births (Grove, Cusick & Bigge, 1991).

Because muscular dystrophy is a progressive condition, the child becomes increasingly weak and less mobile with age. A young child with muscular dystrophy may have barely noticeable weakness; by the time the child reaches the age of 10 or 14, however, walking may no longer be possible. The muscle weakness usually begins in the shoulders and hips and then spreads to other areas. Secondary effects of muscular dystrophy include scoliosis (curvature of the spine) and a gradual loss of respiratory function. Respiratory disease is often a cause of death of individuals with muscular dystrophy, who frequently live only until adolescence or early adulthood (Grove, Cusick & Bigge, 1991).

Teachers must develop individualized modifications in the curriculum depending on the child's age and the condition's progress. It is important to be aware of the social and emotional effects muscular dystrophy may have on the child's understanding of his or her own mortality.

■ Juvenile Rheumatoid Arthritis

Juvenile rheumatoid arthritis affects the tissue lining of the joints, making them painful and stiff.

Juvenile rheumatoid arthritis (JRA) is a condition that affects the tissue lining of the joints, primarily the joints of the knees, ankles, elbows, hips, wrists, and feet, causing them to become painful

Musculoskeletal conditions vary widely; they may affect a child's ability to use his arms or legs or result in no visible limitations at all. (Bob Daemmrich/Stock, Boston, Inc.)

and stiff. JRA is found in children between the ages of 3 and adolescence and affects twice as many girls as boys. It is estimated that only three new cases per 100,000 children occur each year (Grove, Cusick & Bigge, 1991). Although the cause of JRA is unknown, it is suspected that infection or a defect in the body's immune system may be responsible (Caldwell, Todaro & Gates, 1988).

One complication of JRA is *iridocyclitis*, an inflammation of the eye that occurs without warning. If a student with JRA complains about bright lights or painful eyes, a teacher should help the student seek immediate medical attention.

■ **Congenital Malformations**   A **congenital malformation** is an incomplete or improperly formed part of the skeletal or muscular system that is present at birth. Congenital malformations occur in approximately 3 percent of all live births (Batshaw & Perret, 1992). Often, there is no known cause for these malformations, although many of the risk factors discussed in Chapter 2 have been partially implicated. In some instances, there may be a genetic component. In other cases, birth defects have been associated with medications or drugs taken during pregnancy, with illness, such as rubella, and with infections experienced by the mother during pregnancy. As discussed in Chapter 2, the use of the drug thalidomide by pregnant mothers during the 1950s resulted in a number of infants born with absent or shortened limbs (Batshaw & Perret, 1992).

Congenital malformations can take many forms; a few of them have particular implications for physical movement. One example is a clubfoot, in which the foot is structured so that the forefoot and heel are turned in and down toward the body and the toes are turned down and away from the body. A clubfoot is sometimes hereditary, with an incidence of 2 per every 1,000 live births. Surgery, physical therapy, and the use of casts are treatment options for children with this condition. Other malformations that can affect mobility are congenital hip dislocations, discrepancies of leg length, shortened or missing limbs, and scoliosis, or curvature of the spine. In some instances, treatment options include surgery, braces, special shoes, physical therapy, and the use of artificial limbs, or prostheses (Grove, 1982).

Many students with congenital physical malformations have no other accompanying disabilities. When the condition interferes with the student's regular education—because of surgery-related absences, for example—the student may qualify for special education and related services, such as physical or occupational therapy and transportation.

Traumatic Injury

Traumatic injury is damage to the brain or body that occurs after birth.

Traumatic injury refers to damage inflicted to the brain or body after birth. There are many possible causes of traumatic injury including child abuse and accidents, spinal cord injury, and closed-head injury.

■ **Spinal Cord Injuries** Spinal cord injuries, in which the spinal cord is damaged or severed, occur most frequently in adolescents and young adults. Diving, automobile, and motorcycle accidents are frequent causes of this injury in young people. As in spina bifida, the location of the injury determines its effects. A lower-spine injury may result in limited use or paralysis of the legs. An injury higher up the spine or to the neck may result in more extensive involvement, including the arms, trunk, and neck. In some cases, respiration is greatly affected and only facial muscles can be moved voluntarily.

Consider a student who falls from a tree or is involved in a car accident. The student recovers but must now use a wheelchair. The student has missed several months of school, his friends have moved on to the next grade, and he must adjust to a new perception of himself. A severe spinal cord injury may change how the student approaches all aspects of education. One very promising area for assisting students is technology. Technological advances have provided new opportunities for mobility of individuals with spinal cord injury. We will discuss these advances in more detail later on in this chapter.

Traumatic brain injuries are caused by an external physical force and may result in functional disability or psychosocial impairment.

■ **Traumatic Brain Injuries** Traumatic brain injury (TBI), or acquired brain injury, is a "traumatic insult to the brain capable of producing physical, intellectual, emotional, social, and vocational changes" (National Head Injury Foundation Task Force, 1985). TBI is now recognized as a separate diagnostic category by IDEA (1990).

Since the brain controls and processes how one acts, damage to the brain can cause serious disabilities. The student who survives an automobile accident but who suffers a moderate or severe brain injury may physically recover well, but changes in memory, problem solving, attention span, impulse control, and overall cognition are likely to persist. The student may look the same, but these behavior changes have a significant impact on school, home, and friends.

About 23 in 10,000 children sustain TBI each year (Grove, Cusick & Bigge, 1991). It is suspected that the actual incidence is much higher, but that less severe cases are not reported. Most cases involve individuals between the ages of 15 and 24, but the number of younger children affected is almost as high (Kraus, 1987). A small school district can anticipate having several children with traumatic brain injury. A large district can anticipate having over a hundred such students (Mira, Tucker & Tyler, 1992). Although the use of seat belts and bike and motorcycle helmets has reduced the rate of death and of severe brain injury, improvements in emergency medical services and technology have increased the number of students who become TBI survivors (Mira, Tucker & Tyler, 1992; Witte, 1998).

An individual who survives TBI will usually be in a coma for a period of time. The length of the coma indicates how severe the injury is. A mild brain injury usually results in loss of consciousness for less than an hour without skull fracture. A moderate injury results in one to twenty-four hours of unconsciousness and may be complicated by swelling of the brain and skull fractures. These symptoms persist for some time. A severe injury results in loss of consciousness for more than twenty-four hours. Bruising of the brain tissue (*contusion*) or bleeding in the brain (*intracranial hematoma*) is usually present. These serious conditions can result in lifelong cognitive deficits and difficulty with learning new information. Some deficits will be apparent immediately, and some will appear only after a period of time (Mira, Tucker & Tyler, 1992; Witte, 1998).

Brain injuries affect each individual differently.

Teachers should be aware that the student returning to school with a traumatic brain injury will fatigue quickly for the first few months. Adjustment to schedules, reduction in the amount of reading and writing, memory helpers, and organizers are strategies that will help the student who survives brain injury become adjusted to school.

■ **Child Abuse** According to Solomons (1983), a child who is battered may suffer burns, bruises, abrasions, and broken limbs—all injuries that could result from ordinary accidents. How, then, can abuse be detected? One key sign is the *number* of injuries a child exhibits. A discrepancy between the type of injury and how the injury occurred is also cause for concern.

The incidence of child abuse and neglect is not known, but a commonly accepted figure is one million cases per year. Each state has its own legal definition of child abuse. If all kinds of abuse and neglect are included, the figure would quadruple (Solomons, 1983). One-third of physical abuse cases involve children under 5. Sexual abuse of children is four to six times more common than physical abuse. Neglect is five to eight times more common (Solomons, 1983). It is estimated that 60 to 90 percent of abusers were abused themselves. Child abuse occurs in all socioeconomic levels and cultural backgrounds, and parents are not the only abusers. Friends, close family, neighbors, religious leaders, and trusted community members can also be abusers.

Child abuse is most likely to occur when there are high levels of stress in a family, when the parents' expectations for the child are too high, and when parents are emotionally and socially isolated. Children at high risk for abuse include low birthweight infants and children with disabilities (Beckwith, 1990).

～ Physical and Behavioral Indicators of Possible Neglect and Abuse

Physical indicators	Behavioral indicators
	Emotional abuse and neglect
• Height and weight significantly below age level	• Begging or stealing food
• Inappropriate clothing for weather	• Constant fatigue
• Scaly skin	• Poor school attendance
• Poor hygiene, lice, body odor	• Chronic hunger
• Child left unsupervised or abandoned	• Dull, apathetic appearance
• Lack of a safe and sanitary shelter	• Running away from home
• Unattended medical or dental needs	• Child reports that no one cares/looks after him/her
• Developmental lags	• Sudden onset of behavioral extremes (conduct problems, depression)
• Habit disorders	
	Physical abuse
• Frequent injuries such as cuts, bruises, or burns	• Poor school attendance
• Wearing long sleeves in warm weather	• Refusing to change clothes for physical education
• Pain despite lack of evident injury	• Finding reasons to stay at school and not go home
• Inability to perform fine motor skills because of injured hands	• Frequent complaints of harsh treatment by parents
• Difficulty walking or sitting	• Fear of adults
	Sexual abuse
• Bedwetting or soiling	• Excessive fears, clinging
• Stained or bloody underclothing	• Unusual, sophisticated sexual behavior/knowledge
• Venereal disease	• Sudden onset of behavioral extremes
• Blood or purulent discharge from genital or anal area	• Poor school attendance
• Difficulty walking or sitting	• Finding reasons to stay at school and not go home

Source: D. L. Cates, M. A. Markell, and S. Bettenhausen, "At Risk for Abuse: A Teacher's Guide to Recognizing and Reporting Child Neglect and Abuse," *Preventing School Failure,* 39 (2) (1995), 6–9, p. 7, Winter 1995, pp. 6–9. Copyright © 1995. Reprinted by permission of the author.

Teachers must report suspected child abuse.

Every state has laws that require teachers and health professionals to report child abuse when it is suspected. Penalties for not reporting suspected child abuse include loss of jobs and jail terms. An abused student may look to the teacher as a trusted individual. Remember that a student who tells you about abuse is seeking help. You must report these incidents to the proper authorities so that the student can be protected from the abuser. Perhaps a student will not tell you of abuse, but certain indicators may be present. See the accompanying box, "Physical and Behavioral Indicators of Possible Neglect and Abuse," for some of the signs that might suggest concern is warranted. It is important to look at the student's age and other historical information when evaluating these indicators (Sobsey, 1994). If you or one of your students seeks help for overcoming an abusive situation, confidentiality is guaranteed in counseling centers.

Types of Health Impairments

Many conditions and diseases can significantly affect a child's health and ability to function successfully in school. Most health impairments are chronic conditions, that is, they are always present, or they recur. Many of these conditions result in gradual deterioration of health and eventual death.

Students with health impairments typically receive their education in the regular classroom as long as their health allows. Some require home-based instruction for periods of time or support services when they must miss school for an extended time. Teachers will need to be sensitive to the obstacles to learning that can arise from the condition itself, the side effects of prescribed treatments, and the emotional challenges the student faces. Knowledge of the condition and the individual student's treatment regimen will help you plan and prepare appropriate educational programs.

Let's look at some conditions that can fall into the category of health impairment. In some cases, only some forms of the condition are severe enough to warrant special education or support services.

Students with health impairments should stay in the regular classroom for as long as possible.

Asthma

Asthma is a chronic obstructive lung condition characterized by an unusual reaction to a variety of stimuli that causes difficulty in breathing and coughing, wheezing, and shortness of breath (Caldwell, Todaro & Gates, 1988). As many as 11 percent of all children have a mild to severe form of the condition (Anderson et al., 1983). Many things can trigger an asthma attack. Some of the more common irritants are smoke, a cold or other infection, exercise, cold air, pollen, animal hair, and emotional stress.

Asthma can be managed. Special attention should be paid to the child's overall fitness (Mitchell, 1985). Allergens that cause the reactions can be removed or minimized wherever possible. Children can also receive *bronchodilators*, which are drugs that reverse the narrowing of the airways (Mitchell, 1985). Because there may be side effects to any drug treatment, parents and teachers should learn the possible side effects of the particular medications a child is receiving.

Some forms of exercise are better tolerated than others by children with asthma. Running may result in narrowing of the airways and severe wheezing. Swimming is less likely to cause wheezing, but the child should be carefully watched, for obvious reasons. Overall participation in regular games and activities is encouraged, and many students have little or no difficulty participating in active sports.

Much attention has been given to the psychosocial effects of asthma. Loss of sleep is a frequent problem when attacks flare up at night (Caldwell, Todaro & Gates, 1988), and it can be terrifying for a parent to watch a child fighting to breathe. Sometimes parents hesitate to discipline their child or to set limits for fear of triggering an asthmatic reaction. The child may also experience low self-esteem from a deformity in the chest cavity caused by the condition. Locker-room shyness may cause distress and anxiety (Mitchell, 1985). In general, however, the prognosis for future health is good for these children.

As a teacher you need to know the recommended physical activity levels for the student with asthma. Also, you should know what emergency procedures to take if the student has an asthma attack.

Juvenile Diabetes

Juvenile diabetes is a disorder of the metabolism caused by little or no insulin being produced by the body, which results in difficulties in digesting and obtaining energy from food. It is estimated that **juvenile onset diabetes** affects over 1.5 million children, and the overall prevalence appears to be increasing at the rate of 6 percent a year.

Juvenile onset diabetes can appear at any point between birth and the age of 30; it cannot be cured, but it can be controlled by daily intake of insulin, by exercise, and by a special diet (Verhaaren & Connor, 1981). Sometimes diabetes can also affect the eyes and the kidneys; unmanaged or severe diabetes may result in early blindness.

Even when children are receiving treatment for diabetes, teachers should be aware of two possible emergency conditions. The most severe of these is a *diabetic coma*, which results from insufficient insulin. Symptoms include fatigue, trouble breathing, skin that feels hot and dry to the touch, and excessive thirst.

A less serious condition is *diabetic shock*, which results from too much insulin. Its symptoms include dizziness, faintness, drowsiness, or irritability. Diabetic shock is most likely to occur if the child has gone without eating for a while or has been exerting himself or herself physically. Although parents should be informed of the reaction, certain foods, such as sugar, can be given to the child immediately to mitigate the condition. A tin of cake frosting is a good thing to keep on hand, as it not only contains sugar but is also easy to administer.

If you have a child with juvenile diabetes in your class, it is a good idea to have a complete list of symptoms and emergency actions ready; if the symptoms are present, a doctor or nurse should be contacted immediately.

Cystic Fibrosis

Cystic fibrosis is a progressive and usually fatal disorder characterized by lung damage, abnormal mucus production, and difficulties in the absorption of protein and fat. Damage to the lungs results in inadequate amounts of oxygen being delivered to the body, which stresses the heart. Children with cystic fibrosis are susceptible to lung infections, pneumonia, and collapsed lungs.

The disorder is an inherited recessive gene disorder, that is, both parents must be carriers in order for the child to have the condition. Parents who are carriers have a 25 percent chance per pregnancy of having a child with cystic fibrosis. The condition is most common in Caucasian populations and occurs in approximately one of every 2,000 births (Mitchell, 1985)—about 30,000 Americans each year (Angeter, 1992). Children with cystic fibrosis often die at a young age—the average lifespan is about 20 years. With early and continuous treatment, however, individuals with cystic fibrosis continue to live longer. In 1990, the gene carrying cystic fibrosis was identified; this is the crucial first step in finding a cure or treatment for this condition. This discovery led to the establishment of the first gene therapy centers. Although treatment is still in the earliest stages, it is apparent that a major breakthrough is at hand (Welsh & Smith, 1995).

Treatment for cystic fibrosis is extremely vigorous and often painful, including physical therapy (in some cases daily) to loosen the mucus secretions in the lungs. Because of problems in digestion, children must have dietary supplements of vitamins and enzymes, as well as antibiotics to fight off frequent infections. Hospitalization may be required because of bouts with pneumonia, other serious lung conditions, or lung collapse.

Teachers must be aware of the reduced energy level characteristic of children with cystic fibrosis and must understand that they may miss school due to therapy or hospitalization. Particularly difficult aspects, of course, are the child's awareness of the course of the disease, the fact that it is often a very painful condition, and the prospect of early death.

Acquired Immune Deficiency Syndrome (AIDS)

Acquired immune deficiency syndrome (AIDS) is a condition that has had a great impact on health concerns in recent years, and its effect on children has been recognized for some time (see the HIV/AIDS Fact Sheet in Chapter 2). AIDS is a viral disease that breaks down the body's immune system, destroying its ability to fight infections (Caldwell, Todaro & Gates, 1988). When a child gets even the slightest cold or infection, the symptoms linger as the child weakens. AIDS is progressive, resulting in increasingly greater weakness and illness, particularly lung disease and pneumonia, which are frequently the immediate cause of death. AIDS also can affect many areas of child development, including cognitive development as the infection attacks the central nervous system (Belman et al., 1988; Lesar, Gerber & Semmel, 1995).

AIDS is transmitted by the exchange of body fluids from an infected individual engaged in unprotected, high-risk behavior, such as unprotected sexual contact or sharing needles. AIDS has also been transmitted through blood transfusions and at birth from an infected mother to a newborn. Tragically, the number of children born with AIDS is increasing each year. Although much money and effort have been devoted to research on the virus that causes AIDS, no cure or vaccine is available yet.

AIDS is the only condition we have discussed that can be transmitted to others. So, in addition to the health maintenance procedures, hospitalization, and medication required for children with this condition, children often face the unwarranted prospect of social isolation. There have been many instances in which children with AIDS have been avoided or ostracized due to fear.

Children with AIDS often face social isolation.

Although transmission of AIDS in the normal course of school activities has never been documented, many parents—and therefore their children—have an extreme fear of this condition and sometimes fight the presence of the child with AIDS in the regular classroom. When a teacher is aware of a student with AIDS, he or she must work to facilitate appropriate and normal social interaction and to educate other children in the classroom. Children with AIDS and their families have the most difficult task of not only dealing with a painful and probably fatal illness but also of fighting for love and acceptance from the people around them.

Childhood Cancer

Although the prognosis for children with cancer is steadily improving, cancer continues to result in more fatalities among school-aged children than any other disease (Verhaaren & Connor, 1981). The extent to which childhood cancer will affect a child in school depends on whether the child is undergoing active treatment such as chemotherapy, the immediate state of the disease, and the general prognosis for the child.

Multiple Disabilities

This chapter focuses on individuals whose primary disability is a physical disability or health impairment. Some children born with mental retardation, hearing or visual impairments, communication disorders, and other categorized disabilities also experience physical disabilities or health impairments. For example, some children with Down syndrome experience congenital heart problems, and some children born with cerebral palsy have mental retardation. The Education of the Handicapped Act Amendments of 1990 (sec. 300.6[5]) define multiple disabilities as "concomitant impairments (such as mental retardation–blindness, mental retardation–orthopedic impairments, etc.) the combination of which causes such severe educational problems that they cannot be accommodated in special education programs solely for one of the impairments. The term does not include deaf-blindness."

Children whose multiple disabilities include physical or health disabilities need comprehensive treatment and educational programming. A child with both severe cerebral palsy and mental retardation, for example, requires an effective avenue for communication, mobility instruction, physical and occupational therapy, and a program that facilitates maximum physical, social, and intellectual development. Educational placement of the child whose multiple disabilities include physical or health impairments is likely to differ from that of other children with disabilities and is likely to include additional special education services.

Effects of Physical Disabilities and Health Impairments

The effects on the child and the child's family of a physical disability or health impairment vary, depending most of all on the severity of the disability and the threat to survival. The family roles and interactions are influenced by the child's condition and medical needs and by the planning needed to help the child participate fully in family life.

Effects on the Child

The severity of a disability is one gauge of its effect on the child. In some instances, mobility or communication may be the areas in which a child feels the greatest effect; in others, the child's overall energy and motivation for making it through a day may be his or her most difficult task. The visibility of the disability may also play a major role, but not always in the way you might think. A mild disability or condition such as infrequent asthma attacks may affect the child a great deal if unwanted attention during an attack makes the child feel embarrassed. A child with a visible orthopedic disability may adjust well to challenges. It's important for you as a teacher to understand that each child is an individual with unique needs and abilities, rather than a collection of characteristics of a particular condition.

In most cases, a physical disability has no direct effect on intellectual disability.

■ **Cognitive and Intellectual Development**   In most instances, a physical disability or illness has no direct effect on intellectual growth or development. The presence of a physical disability, even a severe physical disability, does not mean that the individual's intellectual ability has been affected. Sometimes, however, both physical and cognitive disabilities occur. Cerebral palsy, for example, may include mental retardation, and some children who experience extensive brain damage are affected in many areas of functioning, including intellectual ability. In some instances, a health impairment may actually affect the speed of mental processing or the ability to focus for long periods of time.

A health impairment can interfere directly with learning. Children with asthma, muscular dystrophy, or other chronic or progressive conditions may require extensive therapy or stays in the hospital, which may affect their academic progress. A serious illness or condition also might greatly affect the child's ability to concentrate on academics. As children tire more and more easily and lose energy, they may require school accommodations so that they can more readily handle academic work and attend to tasks.

Finally, cognitive development is closely dependent on communication abilities. This is particularly obvious in educational settings. Students with severe physical disabilities are most likely to succeed in academic subjects, particularly in regular classroom settings, if they are able to communicate visually, orally, or in writing. Students with physical disabilities who are able to speak and write may experience no exceptional difficulty with their academic tasks. We discuss communication further in the next section.

■ **Communication and Language Development** Communication is most frequently affected by a physical disability such as severe cerebral palsy or a brain injury. The effects of a congenital disability, however, are quite different from those of a condition with a gradual or sudden onset. Most persons with progressive conditions, or those who experienced a sudden onset of a disability, have had a number of years during which they could communicate using more conventional means. Their intellectual abilities were probably tested using standard assessment instruments, and there was time to plan for the future and teach alternative communication systems to the student and to others in his or her home, school, and social environments.

Children born with disabilities such as severe cerebral palsy face a different challenge, because they may not be able to communicate through conventional means. Their cognitive capabilities may remain hidden until they are old enough to use an alternative system, several of which we will decribe later in the chapter. People born with severe physical disabilities have faced extreme bias concerning their intellectual abilities, largely because of their inability to communicate with those around them. The assumption that severe physical disabilities were automatically associated with severe mental retardation resulted in the placement of many individuals in institutional settings with very little, if any, attempt to engage in reciprocal social interaction or communication. As you might imagine, this was not only a deplorable condition in its own right but extremely frustrating and painful for the people involved. One eloquent spokesperson, Ruth Sienkiewicz-Mercer, who lost bodily control and speech at age 5 due to encephalitis, describes her first communication breakthrough with her caretakers in a residential placement. At this point she had lived in the institution for three years without communicating with any of the adults present.

> As she brought the next spoonful of food to my mouth, she noticed that I was doing something funny with my eyes, obviously in reaction to what she had just said. I kept looking up at the ceiling, but Wessie couldn't figure

People with severe physical disabilities find their intellectual abilities underestimated because they communicate differently.

Don't Patronize Me—Communicate with Me

Jim Viggiano is a 37-year-old man who has cerebral palsy and spent 20 years in a state hospital in Massachusetts. Mr. Viggiano formerly used a word-board to communicate, but now uses an Autocom which will soon be configured with speech. He is an active advocate for nonverbal individuals and currently consults and lectures. The following is excerpted from a speech Mr. Viggiano gave at the Symposium on Nonverbal Communication in Boston, Massachusetts.

When I was young, I asked my mother, "Why did God make me like this?" She said to me, "God has His reasons." As time went on, I began to understand more and more of what she meant, especially in the past five years. In this time I have been able to help change things for other people and for myself. "We all get by with a little help from our friends" is my theme song. My goals are to work with people as a counselor and advocate and to help galvanize ideas as I was able to do for my friend Bob and his communication system.

Bob can only lay in bed and communicate by eye movements, since he cannot move his arms to spell. Some people talk to him like he is a three year old, even though he is 40 and very much "with it." I shudder when hearing some people say to him such patronizing things like, "Hi Babykins, here's your bunny!" Granted, to look at Bob you wouldn't think he is "with it," but he understands French just as well as English.

As I got to know Bob better, I got to know what he wanted just by his facial expressions and his eyes. I would tell a nurse what he wanted, that is, if they would listen to me. Often they wouldn't listen to me and would try to figure it out themselves. Five minutes later I would hear, "O.K. Viggiano, what does he want?" and Bob would be laughing his head off when I was right to start with.

When I first met Bob, I promised myself somehow he would get some way to communicate. I asked his brother many questions about Bob's education, because obviously he understands everything. I went to Tufts-New England Medical Center for a project they were working on. While there, I saw clear plastic sheets that had pictures on them (Etrans) and that is when it hit me that this was one way for Bob to communicate. I told one of the people there, Cheryl Goodenough-Trepagnier, about how I really wanted to help Bob and she agreed to see him. Meanwhile I wrote to Bob's brother to tell him about what we planned to do and he was so enthusiastic about it that he gave his full cooperation. But the staff at the state hospital gave me so much negativism and said things like, "Why don't you mind your business!" and "Bob isn't smart enough to do that." I asked, "How would you know by how you just baby him like he was three years old?"

Cheryl adapted the Etran, configuring it with one side in French for communication with his family. At first it just had pictures that Bob would fix his eyes on to tell what he wanted, like T.V. and drink. Now it has phonics on it with parts of words standing for sounds. He is doing great with it. But they said it couldn't be done.

However, only a handful of people use Bob's Etran. Most of the time it just sits there since most people aren't willing to take time to use it. They "cop-out" by saying that it's too complex for them. It's so paradoxical, because the same people who said that Bob was too retarded to learn are so befuddled, while Bob is doing so well! It's their loss, because he has so much to give if people take the time. It goes to show that all mountains aren't formed from stone, and all handicaps aren't physical.

I have problems with people accepting my communication system as well. Perfect strangers look at my spelling board and the first words out of their mouths are, "How do you play that game?!" or they say, "Can you spell cat?" or, "Where's the letter A?" Some people act like I am deaf, and some people just pat me on the head and say, "You are a good little boy!" I point to the sign on my board that says "I talk by spelling words," then I point to the sign on my board that says, "Don't Patronize Me!" That sign was inspired by one of my idols, Jill Kinmont, of "The Other Side of the Mountain" fame. The part of that movie that was especially good was when she applied for a teacher's job and the interviewer said to Jill, "You people really inspire me, Jill, but you are too handicapped to teach from a wheelchair." Jill replied, "Don't patronize me! Right now my handicap is your negativism that won't give me a chance!" Everybody at the movie heard a titillated yell from me as if to say, "Give 'em hell, Jill!" since so many people have said that I'm too handicapped to do things that I really wanted to do. One of my goals is to meet Jill, since she inspires me.

Even my own family had said things like I could not use an electric typewriter, and I would kill myself in a motorized wheelchair. They also said that I couldn't push play and record on my cassette recorder. Those things and more were mastered because nobody was about to tell me that I couldn't do it before having a fair chance to decide the facts for myself.

It seems that so-called free speech isn't for all Americans. Especially for people who can't verbalize their frustrations. Obviously the total answer to this acute communication problem isn't with building more complex equipment so nonverbal people can communicate with "normal" people who are so ill-bred and patronizing to start with. Maybe the answer to the problem is to teach people what it means to be handicapped and nonverbal. The most complex communication equipment is worthless if "normal people are not willing to let nonspeaking persons say their thoughts!" As the saying goes, "It takes two people to start a fight," it also takes two people to communicate rationally.

Jim Viggiano

Source: J. Viggiano (1982), "Don't Patronize Me—Communicate with Me," *Communication Outlook,* 3(4), 13. Copyright © 1982. Reprinted by permission.

Children with Physical Disabilities
and Health Impairments

Communication aids can be a tremendous asset to persons who have difficulty conveying information through speech, written language, or sign. Communication boards can vary in complexity and may be part of a system that includes synthesized speech. (Bob Daemmrich)

out why I was doing that. She put the spoon down and thought for a few seconds, then asked, "Ruthie, are you trying to tell me something?"

With a broad grin on my face, I looked at her squarely. Then I raised my eyes up to the ceiling again with such exaggeration that I thought my eyes would pop up through the top of my head.

Wessie knew she was onto something, but she wasn't sure just what. She pondered for a few more seconds . . . then it clicked! A silent conversation flashed between us as loud and clear as any spoken words. Even before she asked me a dozen times over, and before I exuberantly answered a dozen times with my eyes raised skyward, Wessie knew. And I knew that she knew.

I was raising my eyes to say yes.

We both started laughing. Then I started laughing really hard, and before I knew it I was crying so uncontrollably that I couldn't see because of the tears. They were tears of pure joy, the kind of tears a person sheds on being released from prison after serving three years of what she had feared would be a life sentence. (Sienkiewicz-Mercer & Kaplan, 1989, p. 110)

■ **Social and Emotional Development**   Children with physical disabilities and health impairments are faced with an incredible array of stressful emotions—both their own and the emotions of others. They must struggle with their own perceptions of themselves, the reactions of others to often obvious disabilities, and the impact on their families.

Many people avoid interacting with persons with physical disabilities not because they are insensitive or uncaring, but because they are confused about how to act. Sometimes it's difficult to judge whether or not you should provide assistance to someone, and often we become aware that we are noticing the disability—and this makes us uncomfortable with ourselves. Unfortunately, these concerns may result in the appearance of indifference or actual avoidance of persons with physical disabilities. Regardless of our reasons, the result is the same—a lack of communication and interaction with someone simply because of his or her physical appearance.

As you consider your reactions to persons with physical disabilities, past and future, remember our axiom of looking at the *person* first. We've alluded to the fact that sometimes our fear of acting patronizing or too helpful will insult or embarrass the individual with whom we are interacting. People with physical disabilities realize your apprehension (many may have experienced these feelings themselves if their disability is injury-related) and appreciate the fact that any meaningful social interaction must be reciprocal in nature. Syd Jacobs, a young woman who broke her back in a mountaineering accident, has the following to say about social perceptions:

> If people are going to have a good perception of people in wheelchairs and disabled people in general, it's up to us to make that perception good. And that's by being pleasant and teaching people what we can and can't do, instead of acting like we have a chip on our shoulder. If someone opens a door for me, fine. I'll say thank you. But I'll still open doors for other people too.
>
> I try to understand when people are trying to be helpful. If I'm pushing up a hill, got a rhythm going, I find it really aggravating when someone comes up behind me and just starts pushing me. It would be really easy to snap at them. I don't need your help! But I think it's really important to try to understand them. I think most people are pretty well-meaning, but you just have to be gentle with them—let them know. (Corbet, 1980, p. 47)

Growing up different often results in isolation. As children who develop normally are able to explore the world outside their home and community, the child with the disability is increasingly left out. The decision to send the child to a school out of the neighborhood that can meet his or her special needs further reduces opportunities for the child with a disability to grow with neighborhood friends.

Most of us are only too aware of the importance society places on appearance. As children get older, teasing of someone who looks different is, unfortunately, fairly common. Unkind and humiliating situations are encountered. The child with a disability must have the opportunity to cry, vent anger, and talk in order to learn to deal with these situations. A key factor in a child's ability to develop a positive self-image is the extent to which he or she can accept his or her physical differences.

A key factor in a child's development of a positive self-image is accepting his or her physical disability.

Another significant source of stress is the struggle for independence. For people with certain types of disabilities, such as seizure disorders or diabetes, it is very difficult to accept the fact that a certain level of dependence on others or on medications will be a continuing part of their lives (Bigge, 1982). The protectiveness of parents and other family members, and the possible adjusted expectations of others, may make the process of growing up very difficult.

Some children with progressive illness or deteriorating conditions must face the inevitable fact of an early death. Clearly, family, friends, and other support services and people can help children as they try to face this possibility. Experts advise teachers and other adults to be gentle, yet direct, with children who want to discuss death. Often, because children find it difficult to discuss this emotional topic with their parents, they may need to confide in another trusted adult. Although many children display incredible courage and consideration of others in the face of their disabilities, it is only natural for a part of this process to include the inevitable questions of "why me?" and "what if . . . ?" Sometimes these questions are directed at the condition itself, and sometimes at the pain or discomfort involved.

Effects on the Family

The impact of a child's physical disability or health impairment on a family can vary as greatly as the types of disabilities. The effects on the family of a child with cerebral palsy will be very different from the effects on the family of a child with muscular dystrophy, cancer, an amputated leg, or epilepsy. Yet parents of children with special needs do share many common experiences, such as dealing with medical professionals, educators, community prejudices, and the joys of loving a child.

Some families will be able to accept the child for who he is in spite of the child's condition and become strong while dealing with challenges and decisions that may overwhelm most of us. Other families will become frayed and severed as the child with the disability siphons all their emotional and physical energies. Some families face a potentially lifelong commitment to the education of their child; others must face daily the agony of watching their child's physical abilities and health deteriorate.

Children are often well aware of the impact of their disability on their families and may themselves feel a sense of guilt or responsibility for the ensuing emotional or financial strain. Sometimes, children will respond to this by avoiding discussion of their condition with their parents (Bigge, 1982) or by being careful of what they say or do. The child may focus on "taking care" of his or her parents. This unexpected interaction is illustrated in a touching passage from Frank Deford's book *Alex: The Life of a Child*, the story of his young daughter, who died of complications from cystic fibrosis.

> And so then Alex and I laughed. Unfortunately, at that point, late in her life, it was difficult for her to laugh without coughing and starting to choke. So she made sure she laughed gently, and I laughed extra hard, for both of us. Then she came over, sat in my lap, and this is what she said: "Oh, Daddy, wouldn't this have been great?"
>
> That is what she said, exactly. She didn't say, "Hasn't this been great?" She said, "Oh, Daddy, wouldn't this have been great?" Alex meant her whole life, if only she hadn't been sick.
>
> I just said, "Yes," and after we hugged each other, she left the room, because, I knew, she wanted to let me cry alone. Alex knew by then that, if I cried in front of her, I would worry about upsetting her, and she didn't want to burden me that way. She was the only one dying. (Deford, 1983, p. 9)

Because physical disabilities and deteriorating health are usually apparent to others, families also try to cope with the emotional pain faced by their children as they integrate into educational and social settings and deal with the countless questions about "what happened to you?" or "what's wrong with you?" Although it is important for families to encourage independence for their children, it is often difficult for them to let go of their desire to protect the child from more potentially painful situations (Haring, Lovett & Saren, 1991). One of the greatest tasks faced by families of children with physical or health disabilities is to encourage their children to experience life and take risks, just as they would with children without disabilities.

Practical issues faced by the family include treatment decisions. Families must make constant decisions about the type or extent of therapy they will select for the child involved. In some instances, these decisions may be relatively simple (selecting a type of medication, choosing a particular kind of prosthesis). When the child has a severe illness or disability, however, these decisions can be very complex and include considerations of time allocated to the child and other family members; finances; emotional stress on the part of the parents, siblings, and involved child; and sometimes the actual physical abilities of the family caretakers. Certainly one of the biggest decisions related to treatment is whether the child with severe physical involvement, particularly a child with multiple disabilities, should be at home or in a residential placement. Let's listen to the experiences of one parent, Helen Featherstone, the mother of a child with severe cerebral palsy, blindness, and mental retardation:

> Sometimes mothers and fathers of exceptional children face peculiar difficulties because they are divided internally as well as between themselves. Each partner feels deeply ambivalent—about the child, the future, the advice of experts, and many other problems. Ambivalence is, however, confusing and upsetting. Sometimes mixed feelings get swept under the rug, to be expressed in a conflict between husband and wife. This occurred with us. When Jody was around eighteen months old, Jay (and several other people) felt strongly that we should begin to make inquiries about residential placement. I felt equally strongly that we should wait. Although I expected that Jody might eventually live elsewhere, I wanted to care for him at home while he was still small. Without being unpleasant, I refused to budge from my position. Yet my feelings were, of course, profoundly divided. Jody exhausted both of us; his care consumed all my energy and most of my time. Residential placement would have offered unimaginable freedom. I am sure that a part of me yearned for a simple long-term solution to the problem. But another part—a part that I liked better, and therefore gave license to speak—wanted to give Jody everything I could. Jay's feelings were probably equally mixed, but after weighing the issues, he came down on the other side for a while. We survived what amounted to an undeclared war. (Featherstone, 1980, p. 119)

Although there may be some similarities in the ways families deal with the impact of a physical disability or health impairment, families are composed of individuals. The child with the disability and the other family members develop the pattern of interaction that works for them. Educators must be aware of the needs of individual families and the type of support services that might help them make informed decisions about the education and placement of their children.

Fortunately, the emphasis on parent services and training available through P.L. 99-457 enables greater education and support for parents of young children

Practical issues faced by the family include decisions about treatment and placement.

with physical disabilities and health impairments. Parents and families of older children who incur physical or health disabilities need immediate and continued information and assistance. Often, local, state, or national groups related to a specific disability area can be a great source of available services, information, and emotional support.

Educational Issues and Teaching Strategies

In the past, the diverse educational needs of children with physical disabilities and health impairments often kept them away from public education. Today's teacher needs to know, however, that in most cases these children can be part of the regular class with accommodations and support.

Early Intervention

For many children with physical disabilities or health impairments, the first educational issue to arise is the appropriate and early diagnosis of the condition and assessment of physical, cognitive, and language abilities. These diagnoses tend to be made by physicians rather than school personnel, and many diagnoses are made long before the child reaches school age.

As with other disabilities, early intervention services significantly affect the well-being of these children. For some of them, early intervention can mean the difference between life and death. For others, early intervention can mean the difference between a mild disability and a severe and long-term disability. Early and consistent therapy can help children to maximize their physical skills and sometimes prevent the occurrence of muscular atrophy and skeletal deformities.

Early intervention services that focus on family-centered service delivery models may have positive effects on the family as well as the child. Family-centered services can help parents establish a support network, as well as provide them with knowledge about their child's disability and a sense of empowerment (Thompson, Lobb, Elling, Herman, Jurkiewiez & Hulleza, 1997).

Identification and Assessment: The Classroom Teacher's Role

Most physical disabilities and health impairments are diagnosed before schooling begins, but some conditions will not be identified until later in the child's life. As a teacher you should be alert to gradual or sudden changes in children's physical abilities, energy level, and general behavior.

Regardless of the severity of any condition, it is your responsibility to assess and address continually the educational needs of the individual child. If you notice motor difficulties, a physical or occupational therapist may be called in to consult on the case or to provide assistance. See the accompanying box, "Some Considerations for Students with Mobility Impairments," for some general recommendations for interacting with students with physical disabilities or health impairments.

The Transdisciplinary Approach

Integrated, multidisciplinary planning is a requirement for appropriate education (York & Vandercook, 1991). IDEA requires that a multidisciplinary team

～ Some Considerations for Students with Mobility Impairments

- Many students with mobility impairments lead lives similar to those without impairments. Dependency and helplessness are not characteristics of physical disability.

- A physical disability is often separate from matters of cognition and general health; it does not imply that a student has other health problems or difficulty with intellectual functioning.

- People adjust to disabilities in myriad ways; students should not be assumed to be brave and courageous on the basis of disability.

- When talking with a wheelchair user, attempt to converse at eye level as opposed to standing and looking down. If a student has a communication impairment as well as a mobility impairment, take time to understand the person. Repeat what you understand, and when you don't understand, say so.

- A student with a physical disability may or may not want assistance in a particular situation. Ask before giving assistance, and wait for a response. Listen to any instructions the student may give; by virtue of experience, the student likely knows the safest and most efficient way to accomplish the task at hand.

- Be considerate of the extra time it might take a student with a disability to speak or act. Allow the student to set the pace walking or talking.

- A wheelchair should be viewed as a personal assistance device rather than something one is "confined to." It is also part of a student's personal space; do not lean on or touch the chair, and do not push the chair, unless asked.

- Mobility impairments vary over a wide range, from temporary to permanent. Other conditions, such as respiratory conditions, affect coordination and endurance; these can also affect a student's ability to perform in class.

- Physical access to a class is the first barrier a student with a mobility impairment may face, and this is not related only to the accessibility of a specific building or classroom. An unshoveled sidewalk, lack of reliable transportation, or mechanical problems with a wheelchair can easily cause a student to be late.

- Common accommodations for students with mobility impairments include priority registration, notetakers, accessible classroom/location/furniture, alternative ways of completing assignments, lab or library assistants, assistive computer technology, exam modifications, and conveniently located parking.

Source: Used by permission of Disability Services.

evaluate each student in special education programs. However, on a multidisciplinary team, professionals work independently with the child. According to Orelove and Sobsey (1991), this model lacks methods for coordinating assessment and prioritizing the student's educational needs. Instead of the multidisciplinary approach, then, Orelove and Sobsey recommend the **transdisciplinary model.**

The transdisciplinary model differs from the multidisciplinary approach because all interventions are delivered by one or two professionals. For example, a student who needs physical therapy to learn to walk is helped by his or her regular teacher to complete mobility exercises several times a day. This does not mean that the physical therapist never sees the student. It does mean that the physical therapist works closely with the teacher to carry out therapeutic activities properly and sees the student directly as needed. In a multidisciplinary or interdisciplinary team, the student would be pulled out of the class and given physical therapy once a week for thirty minutes. The teacher and parents would have little idea of how to help the student learn and practice mobility the rest of the week.

A transdisciplinary team of professionals, in conjunction with the family and, when appropriate, the child, works together to assess educational needs in a variety of areas and to determine appropriate program goals. For example,

In the transdisciplinary model, all interventions are delivered by one or two professionals to ensure continuity for the child.

this group would work together to determine what type of computer keyboard is most appropriate for a student with cerebral palsy who cannot use a regular keyboard.

The family's role on the transdisciplinary team is critical because family members are able to give insight into the child's demonstrated abilities, motivation, emotional adjustment, and goals. Whenever special therapy, communication systems, or adaptive equipment are suggested, the willingness and ability of the family members to accept and use them or to participate must be assessed and evaluated.

When interventions are integrated into the classroom, teachers better understand how to help students learn useful skills.

When interventions are integrated into the home and classroom setting, not only does the student learn meaningful and useful skills, but the teacher and parents get a better understanding of how to facilitate the development of those skills on a day-to-day basis.

Educational Setting

Special education services should be structured to support placement in the regular classroom.

In the past, children whose only disabilities were physical or health-related were placed in a variety of educational settings, ranging from a state hospital or institution to the regular classroom. Although there are still separate classes for children with "orthopedic handicaps," these classes are moving away from serving as the primary educational placement for children with physical disabilities and toward the role of a transition or support service. They provide a setting for initial instruction in skills such as mobility and language, which can then be used in regular class settings. Support or special education services are often provided in physical therapy, occupational therapy, speech or language therapy, counseling, and, in some instances, homebound instruction for periods of time.

Most placement options now focus on the regular classroom, and many general education teachers are responsible for educating students with physical or health impairments in their classrooms. In some instances, it is not necessary to make any specific instructional modifications for the student; in other cases, you will need assistance from special education teachers or other members of the student's education team to learn the best ways to encourage and facilitate communication, class participation, class interaction, and physical movement or activity. Salisbury, Evans, and Palombaro (1997) found that teachers in the primary grades used collaborative problem solving with all of their students to identify solutions to help students with significant disabilities participate more actively in the classroom. Sometimes, individuals with severe physical disabilities may have an aide who travels with them to assist in educational and health-care activities. It is important for the aide to step back whenever possible to allow full integration of the student and to encourage communication and other interactions with peers (Giangreco, Edelman, Luiselli & MacFarland, 1997). See the accompanying box, "Specific Strategies for Integrating Students with Physical Disabilities or Health Impairments in the Classroom."

When a student is too sick to attend school, he or she may receive a homebound program, either in the student's home or at a hospital. This homebound program should always include plans for the student to re-enter school as soon as possible. The teacher who visits the student at home or in the hospital coordinates with the student's regular teachers so that proper assignments, homework, tests, and other activities are completed.

Specific Strategies for Integrating Students with Physical Disabilities or Health Impairments in the Classroom

- Place students with limited physical movement front and center in a traditional classroom setting, to facilitate access to the teacher's presentation and material on the board. There are exceptions to this guideline; for example, a student with a traumatic brain injury might have a limited field of vision on one side and might follow the visual presentation of material more easily if seated at an angle.

- If students gather around small tables or learning centers, make sure the tables are at an appropriate height for the student who is in a wheelchair. If the students gather in groups on the floor, try to use chairs instead, so the child in a wheelchair is not sitting above and apart from the group. This is important for social integration as well as physical accessibility.

- Use bookshelves, material drawers, pencil sharpeners, and cubbies that are the appropriate height and can be reached by a student in a wheelchair. If a student cannot physically reach and grasp, make sure he or she has a trustworthy assistant for retrieving and putting away materials.

- Avoid the use of carpet squares or other floor materials, such as number lines, with raised sides or edges.

- Classrooms with fixed furnishings, such as science labs, can be particularly problematic for the student in a wheelchair. Creating an accessible work area may require significant changes in the classroom construction, so that the student will be truly integrated into the classroom setting.

- If a student requires assistive technology for communication, establish clear signals for typical classroom activities such as hand raising and asking a question. These signals should be clearly recognized by all students in the classroom, as well as the teacher. Provide training to all of the students in the classroom on how to communicate with the student using his specific assistive device. Always be careful to allow the student time to respond.

- Become an expert at identifying and creating learning experiences that allow all students in the classroom to participate fully.

Technology is quickly improving the quality of homebound programs. In some school districts, distance learning is now available, which permits the student to watch educational television programs along with classroom peers. For students with long-term homebound needs, telephones can be set up in the classroom that allow the student to listen to the teacher and respond to questions just like the other students. The homebound teacher makes sure the student has the necessary materials each week to follow along with the class. Fax machines are also used to connect the homebound student to the regular classroom.

Students Who Are Technologically Dependent

As a teacher, you may be required to assist students with physical disabilities in the use of equipment for moving, eating, breathing, and other bodily functions. These aspects of care are called physical handling and health maintenance.

Physical handling involves moving the student from one place to another or adjusting his or her placement in a fixed setting. For example, you might need to move a student from a wheelchair to another setting such as a group activity on the floor. There are very specific guidelines for picking up and carrying students with physical disabilities. It is important that you not try to lift or move students until you have received the information necessary to do it appropriately. In some instances, more than one person is needed to move a child, while in others, a specially trained aide or nurse will assist or do the lifting.

Children with Physical Disabilities
and Health Impairments

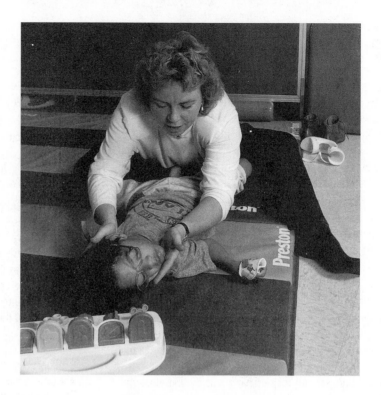

The skill areas addressed by this physical therapist can also be addressed by the classroom teachers if there is good communication among professionals. (Carol Palmer/The Picture Cube, Inc.)

Other aspects of physical handling include adjusting physical placement or using physical props to allow greater range of motion. If students have a tendency to lean to one side or have difficulty reaching needed materials, you can make simple adjustments such as using pillows to prevent leaning, having arm-rests or trays attached to wheelchairs to allow the closer placement of manipulative materials, or providing wedge-shaped props that children can lie on to allow greater range of arm movement (Kraemer, Cusick & Bigge, 1982; Lough, 1983). Again, the physical and occupational therapist can provide needed information and equipment.

Health maintenance involves assisting students in eating, drinking, and using the bathroom. A student with severe cerebral palsy, for example, might be unable to feed herself. Some students run the risk of choking when they eat or drink, so it is important that the person feeding the student be skilled in CPR. Often a nurse or trained aide will assist in this process, as they will when medically oriented processes such as catheterization are required. Students requiring medical technology for support, such a ventilators for breathing, are often placed in the general education class for instruction and require monitoring and additional health maintenance procedures (Levine, 1996).

Other health maintenance activities may include administration of medication, injections, and monitoring students for signs of distress such as diabetic shock. School nurses typically are responsible for the administration of any medical procedures, but as we mentioned previously, it is important for you to be aware of any particular signs or symptoms that signal a specific health problem. If you assist students with these activities, you must be taught correct procedures and be aware of potential risks. Federal guidelines and school district interpretations regulate who may or may not perform health-care services (Rapport, 1996). These guidelines should be reviewed by the evaluation team when decisions are being made about the delivery of these services in school.

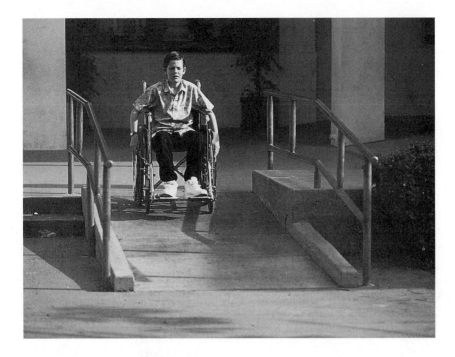

Ramps and other architectural changes remove the physical barriers to community inclusion for individuals with physical disabilities. (David Young-Woolf/PhotoEdit)

Classroom Accessibility

With the passage of the Americans with Disabilities Act in 1990, all public facilities and buildings were required to be barrier-free by 1994. Your classroom, therefore, will probably be adapted to the needs of students with physical disabilities.

Sometimes, however, schools may not take into account accessibility to such things as play equipment, furniture, or educational equipment. One potential problem area is the surface of floors and walls (Lewis & Doorlag, 1987). For example, carpeting, rugs, or uneven floor surfaces can cause difficulties for students using wheelchairs or other types of assistance for walking.

Although some of these areas should be addressed by working in conjunction with the student's therapists, you can take some simple precautions yourself to ensure optimum accessibility. Widening aisles between desks and placing equipment such as computers, tape recorders, and bookshelves appropriately are some tasks that teachers can attend to in their classes. When planning field trips, it is always a good idea to call ahead and check to ensure that the visiting site has been adapted to accommodate students with disabilities. Although adapted school buses are quite common, some public buses still cannot be used by persons in wheelchairs. The student then needs to be lifted onto the bus and the wheelchair folded up and carried along. This may present difficulties, particularly with an older student, so advance planning will be necessary.

Teachers should be sure that equipment and furniture are arranged for maximum accessibility.

Technology

We have alluded throughout this chapter to the importance of technology to many individuals with physical disabilities and health impairments. For individuals with physical disabilities, most of the technological assistance is either medical technology or assistive technology that is designed to help the individual perform life tasks. For school-age students with disabilities, assistive technology may be considered special education or a related service. Teachers, parents, students, and other members of the evaluation team must evaluate the student's needs and indicate the need for appropriate assistive technology on the student's IEP (Menlove, 1996). When selecting appropriate technology for a student, it is most important to look at the way the individual functions in his or her environment and to determine what specific pieces of equipment or training may help to support the student in various settings (Blackhurst, 1997).

Mobility

New designs in wheelchairs and controls for wheelchair movement have resulted in opportunities for independence for people who previously were dependent on others for even limited transportation. For example, individuals with very severe disabilities were unable to use conventionally designed wheelchairs to move because they had limited or no arm movement. A now-common mouth apparatus allows them to control wheelchair movement by blowing puffs of air through a tube.

Muscles that are not used because of injury (typically a spinal cord injury) can be given electronically stimulated "exercise" to prevent atrophy, contractions, and skeletal deformities. Some experiments using electrical stimulation and feedback have taken place that have allowed paralyzed individuals to walk a few steps (Dickey & Shealy, 1987).

Technology has also made it possible for people with physical disabilities to control some aspects of their home environment. Through the use of switches from a wheelchair panel or a voice-activated control device, it is possible to open doors or turn on lights from across the room (Bigge, 1991a). These devices provide an option for independent living that might not otherwise be available. Home accounting and banking software are examples of how technology has facilitated personal life-skills management for indiviuals with severe physical disabilities (Bigge, 1991b).

Communication

The most critical factor in using technology to meet communication needs is to identify processes that meet the individual's needs, allow and encourage intellectual and physical growth and development, and can be used by others in the environment. This last point is of the greatest importance. The latest high-tech system is useless if no one else takes the time to understand how it is used and to participate in the communication process. In this section we discuss some of the major developments in communication technology for people with physical disabilities.

Most advances in communication technology provide access to the symbols of written or oral language. The majority of these advances are associated with computer use. **Eye-gazing scanning systems** are a good example. As the individual scans a keyboard and focuses, a small and very sensitive camera detects the direction of the person's eyes and registers the letters, words, or phrases. A typed message can then be produced.

Augmentative communication aids are designed to be used in addition to the individual's existing speech or vocalizations (Bigge, 1991c). A person using an augmentative communication aid can directly select the desired message elements (such as words or pictures) from the display or can scan and then identify one of a series of potential message elements. In direct selection, the individual points to the desired message or message component using a finger, an adapted handpiece with a pointer attached, or a light beam attached to the head. In school settings, direct selection aids often take the form of alternative computer keyboards and overlays. These keyboards can look like an enlarged version of the typical keyboard, may contain numbers, pictures, or other symbols, and are designed to accommodate specific difficulties a person with limited motor control might encounter (such as difficulty pressing two keys at one time) (Intelli-tools, 1996).

In scanning, message elements are presented one at a time on flashcards, transparent charts, or a computer screen. As the potential messages are presented, the individual indicates which message(s) he or she wants to choose by making a sound, flexing a muscle, or fixing a visual gaze for a few seconds. This process eliminates the need for great mobility.

An adapted form of scanning is a multisignal process, in which the individual (a) scans groups (for example, fifteen groups of four messages), (b) selects a group (for example, group 9: I want to go see a movie. I want to see a television show. I want to turn the television off. Let's go to the video store.), and then (c) scans the message elements in that group to select the appropriate message (I want to see a television show.). This type of encoding allows the individual with limited movement and a large message vocabulary to cover a wide range of potential messages. Computers facilitate scanning because they can store and present many groups of messages quickly.

Another communication option available through advanced technology is synthesized and digitized speech. **Digitized speech** is the storage of words or phrases that can be recalled as needed; **synthesized speech** is the storage of speech sounds—a phonetic alphabet that can be put together to form any word using a sound-by-sound process similar to the spelling process (Bigge, 1991c). Synthesized speech allows greater variety of words and phrases but can be a much slower process. These devices can be designed in various sizes and can be portable or connected to a large computer screen. Digitized speech devices can be designed with customized keyboard overlays and can present language at various speeds (Breakthroughs, 1997).

Highly sophisticated communication programs include scanning, writing, and voice synthesizer systems. An example is the system used by British physicist Stephen Hawkings, who has amyotrophic lateral sclerosis, a progressive disease marked by nerve-cell degeneration. His computer, which contains 2,600 preprogrammed words for scanning, allows him to construct sentences at the rate of ten words per minute. It also has a synthesized speech system and a desk monitor for notetaking (Adler, Lubernow & Malone, 1988). Needless to say, this type of system can be quite expensive, and even the simpler computer-based systems will run several thousand dollars. Yet the value of these technological systems is often hard to measure in terms of dollars and cents. For some, they are the only option for fulfilling communication; for others they may be an important tool for education, eventual employment, and independent living.

Technological advances clearly have opened many new avenues for individuals with severe difficulties in communication. Not all procedures need to have a high-tech component; many augmentative communication processes can be integrated in very simple ways. The role of technology is to expand these options, particularly for individuals with limited movement or advanced cognitive capabilities.

Sophisticated technologies are expensive but offer priceless options to those who cannot otherwise communicate.

Advocacy

For the person with a physical disability or health impairment, life may sometimes seem an unending series of barriers that need to be overcome. Although we all face challenges in our lives, many individuals with physical disabilities are challenged every step of the way—telephones that can't be reached, doors that can't be opened, buildings that can't be entered, eye contact that doesn't take place, communication that isn't attempted, and assumptions that are made.

Educating people about the challenges faced by individuals with physical disabilities has an important purpose, far removed from emotional responses such as sympathy, pity, or even empathy. Rather, the purpose of awareness is to facilitate change. Although it's been a long time coming, public awareness and technology are combining to create a much more accessible environment for persons facing physical challenges. Change in interpersonal areas—efforts at communication, comfortable social exchanges, and acceptance—cannot be legislated and must be instigated at an individual level.

We hope that by listening to our words as well as to the words of children and adults who have experienced disabilities, you have gained some insight into their strength, optimism, struggles, and educational needs. The past decade has resulted in great strides in medical management and technology, which have dramatically increased the options for individuals with physical disabilities and health impairments. We look forward to the doors that will be opened in the future through continued advances in science, social awareness, and knowledge.

SUMMARY

■ Physical disabilities and health impairments as currently defined by IDEA include a wide range of conditions. Physical disabilities can be grouped into neurological conditions, musculoskeletal conditions, and traumatic injuries. Health impairments include debilitating or life-threatening diseases or conditions like cystic fibrosis and AIDS. Being familiar with what is known about the causes, prevalence, and treatment of these various conditions may help you to know what to expect from the student, plan time for the student's treatment, and become comfortable with helping the student with in-school treatment.

■ One of the most difficult aspects of physical disabilities and health impairments is the issue of mortality, since many conditions involve shortened life expectancy. Another issue is visibility and the continual need to educate others.

■ Educational issues to be aware of include transdisciplinary planning, the importance of early intervention, and the use of technology to increase access for students in the regular class as well as to provide opportunities to students at home.

■ New technologies for environmental control and communication have allowed people with physical disabilities and health impairments to participate more fully in many aspects of life.

KeY TeRMS

physically challenged

physical disability

health impairment

cerebral palsy

spina bifida

hydrocephalus

epilepsy

grand mal seizure

petit mal seizure

muscular dystrophy

juvenile rheumatoid
arthritis (JRA)

congenital malformation

traumatic brain injury
(TBI)

asthma

juvenile onset diabetes

cystic fibrosis

acquired immune
deficiency syndrome
(AIDS)

transdisciplinary model

physical handling

health maintenance

eye-gazing scanning
systems

augmentative
communication aid

digitized speech

synthesized speech

MULTiMeDiA ReSOURCeS

Adaptive Environments Center, Inc., 347 Congress Street, Suite 301, Boston, MA 02210; website: adaptive@adaptenv.org. This site provides sources and general information about adapting home and work environments.

Browne, Susan E., Debra Connors, and Nancy Stern. *With the Power of Each Breath: A Disabled Women's Anthology* (Pittsburgh: Cleis Press, 1985). Fifty-four women of all ages contribute powerful, poetic, and informational messages about their disabilities, both recent and lifelong.

Freedom Writer Software, Academics with Scanning: Language Arts and Math (World Communications, ACS Software). A source for software designed for students who use scanning techniques for communication.

Muscular Dystrophy Association, National Headquarters, 3300 East Sunrise Drive, Tucson, AZ 85738, (800) 572-1717. Information sources and resources for parents, professionals, and students interested in muscular dystrophy.

The National Organization for Rare Disorders (NORD). Website: http://www.pcnet.com/~orphan/. NORD is a unique federation of voluntary health organizations dedicated to helping people with rare "orphan" diseases and assisting the organizations that serve them. NORD is committed to the identification, treatment, and cure of rare disorders through programs of education, advocacy, research, and service. Since its inception in 1983, NORD has served as the primary nongovernmental clearinghouse for information on over 5,000 rare disorders. NORD also provides referrals to additional sources of assistance and ongoing support.

National Sports Center for the Disabled, P.O. Box 36, Winter Park, CO 80482, (303) 726-5514. Information and contacts for individuals with disabilities who wish to engage in a variety of sports.

Rehabilitation Robotics Research Program, Applied Science and Engineering Laboratories, DuPont Hospital for Children and the University of Delaware. Website: http://www.asel.udel.edu/robotics/. Updates and summaries of research involving robotics for individuals with physical disabilities.

Sienkiewicz-Mercer, Ruth, and Steven B. Kaplan. *I Raise My Eyes to Say Yes: A Memoir* (Boston: Houghton Mifflin, 1989). Now an advocate for all people with disabilities, Ruth Sienkiewicz tells the story of her loss of bodily control and speech due to encephalitis at the age of 5.

Thompson, Charlotte E. *Raising a Handicapped Child: A Helpful Guide for Parents of the Physically Disabled* (New York: Morrow, 1986). This is a great teacher resource guide that emphasizes the need for physical activity in the daily lives of people with physical disabilities. It describes specific activities and specific disabilities.

Trace Research and Developmental Center. Website: http://trace.wisc.edu/gofr_web/106.html. Information and resources on assistive and adaptive technology.

USiNG YOUR KNOWLEDGE

 Can Do: How accessible are your school's classrooms and other buildings? Design a checklist based on the criteria included in the chapter. After completing your survey, share the results with administrators and counselors, showing them which areas are accessible and what needs to be modified.

 Collaboration: What are the main sources of support for individuals with physical and health disabilities and their families? Talk with parents, counselors, social workers, teachers, and others to get an understanding of the support network that can be developed. What perspective does each individual bring to the support system?

 Collaboration: Why is the transdisciplinary approach so effective? Describe each of the team members and give an example of his or her contribution. If possible, visit a local school and watch members of a transdisciplinary team work with students.

 Commonalities: What are the important components of communication? Think about the messages you would select if you were creating your own communication board or scanning system. What messages would be most meaningful for you? For your friends? Have each student in your class make a communication board; compare similarities and differences in pictures, symbols, or messages. Have the students try to communicate with one another using the communication boards.

WHAT YOU CAN DO NOW

1. **Take an inventory of your college's or university's adaptations for individuals with physical disabilities. Visit your school's center for disability services to identify the support services available for students with severe physical disabilities.**

2. **Visit an elementary classroom and discuss attitudes toward and experiences with students with physical disabilities. Survey materials or curriculum elements designed to introduce elementary students to physical disabilities.**

3. **Make an appointment with a physical therapist or occupational therapist who serves your school district. Discuss with him or her the types of activities typically provided to the students he or she serves. If possible,**

accompany the therapist on a visit to a local school to observe individual service delivery.

4. Contact a local agency that helps AIDS patients. Obtain related literature and explore the possibility of attending an AIDS support group or doing volunteer work with children with AIDS.

5. Select a specific disability type, such as cystic fibrosis or muscular dystrophy. Read and record the newest research findings related to the disability type throughout the course of the semester.

Children with Severe Disabilities

11

STUDENTS with severe disabilities can benefit greatly from an educational program that prepares them for participation in the community. In this chapter, we introduce educational strategies designed to maximize these students' potential, and we raise questions about the protection of their rights. As you read, think about the following questions:

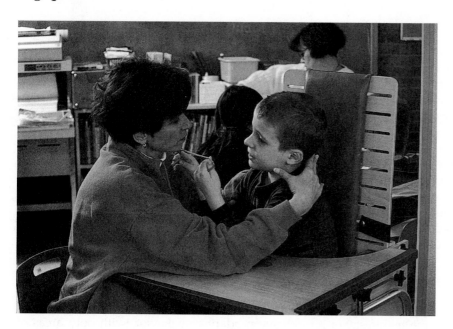

■ How has normalization affected the educational philosophies and options available to students with severe disabilities?

■ Why are physical and social integration both necessary for full inclusion, and how do they influence one another?

■ How does a teacher identify skills to be included in the life-skills curriculum?

✔ **Can Do:** What opportunities do technological aids provide to students with severe disabilities?

Collaboration: How can the educational team prepare a transition plan that will enable the student with severe disabilities to move to an integrated setting?

Commonalities: What key ethical issues are faced by parents, teachers, and others who work with students with severe disabilities?

The outlook and opportunities for individuals with severe and profound disabilities are now greater than many parents and professionals ever anticipated. Someone with severe mental retardation may be living in a home down the street from you. A person with autism may be working in your neighborhood grocery store. Unfortunately, however, many of us are not afforded, nor do we seek, the opportunity to interact in a meaningful way with people who have severe disabilities. Some school systems in the United States completely segregate these individuals from the mainstream of education. Although programs that prepare persons with severe disabilities to work, live, or interact with other members of the community are steadily increasing in both quantity and quality, there are still not enough of them. Through our selection of programs, curricula, and activities, we can promote and develop attitudes and procedures for facilitating knowledge, acceptance, and interaction among all individuals, including those who have severe disabilities.

Definitions and Terms

Individuals who are identified as having severe disabilities may display a variety of primary disabilities. In this section, we will look briefly at the definition of severe disabilities as well as at definitions of some disability areas that are included in the broader term.

Severe Disabilities

Individuals with severe disabilities require extensive support in major life activities.

According to the Association for Persons with Severe Handicapping Conditions (TASH), individuals with **severe disabilities** "require extensive ongoing support in more than one major life activity in order to participate in integrated community settings and to enjoy a quality of life that is available to citizens with fewer or no disabilities. Support may be required for life activities such as mobility, communication, self-care, and learning as necessary for independent living, employment, and self-sufficiency" (1989, p. 30). Although any of the disabilities we have discussed in this text can range in intensity from mild to severe (for example, learning disabilities, behavioral disorders), the term *severe disabilities* is used in this chapter to refer primarily to individuals who have severe or profound mental retardation, or to individuals with autism. The life supports and educational programs required by these individuals are typically more extensive than those required by individuals with other types of disabilities.

Severe and Profound Mental Retardation

The federal definition of **severe mental retardation** includes an IQ of less than 40 and the manifestation of deficits in adaptive behavior, with both areas of deficit originating during the developmental period. **Profound mental retardation** varies only in the range of the IQ score, which is 20 and below. It is sometimes very difficult to determine the extent of mental retardation in an infant. This is particularly true when the child also has severe health or sensory impairments. Thus the extent of mental retardation often cannot be determined until the child is much older. Even so, children thought to have severe or profound levels of mental retardation are often labeled as developmentally disabled (Gentry & Olson, 1985). Such labels must be regarded carefully and used only as a general indication of a person's abilities. This consideration may be critical for many individuals with the label of severe or profound mental retardation because of the effect these labels can have on expectations and educational programming (Blatt, 1977).

Autism

P.L. 101-476, the Education of the Handicapped Act Amendments of 1990, identifies autism as a specific category of special education. The term **autism** refers to a disability defined by the demonstration of certain types of behaviors and patterns of interaction and communication. We have included autism in this chapter because severe disabilities often coexist with autism. Because it is identified as a separate category in IDEA, you will find a special section in this chapter on autism.

Causes

There are numerous causes for severe and profound mental retardation, including genetic syndromes, physical trauma, and disease. Most disabilities considered to be severe or profound occur from similar causes. Some children are born with a cluster of disabilities, one of which is severe mental retardation.

Genetic syndromes, which result in a number of common physical, behavioral, and intellectual characteristics, include Down syndrome, Klinefelter's syndrome, Turner's syndrome, fragile X syndrome, and Tay-Sachs disease. One's probability of having a child with some of these conditions can be determined through genetic counseling. Others, such as Down syndrome, can be detected in utero.

Physical trauma to the head, caused by accidents or child abuse, can result in severe mental retardation. Medical abnormalities, such as brain tumors, can also cause severe disabilities.

In most cases, the ways we teach students with severe disabilities will be the same regardless of the cause. However, knowing the cause of a disability can be important—for example, certain physical disabilities or health concerns are associated with specific syndromes, such as Down syndrome and cerebral palsy. As a teacher, you should become familiar with the characteristics of these conditions to avoid exposing your students to injury or health risks. Sometimes knowing the cause of severe disabilities can help teachers know what to expect and to be better prepared for instruction. For example, if we know that children with some syndromes are likely to show extreme self-abusive behavior, we can be better prepared both emotionally and instructionally to deal with these difficult circumstances.

Prevalence

Neither social and economic status nor the general intellectual ability of the parents seem to be related to the incidence of severe or profound mental retardation, which is estimated to be .7 percent, or 7 per 1,000 births. Although medical technology has enabled many individuals with severe disabilities to live much longer than in previous years, infants born with severe and profound mental retardation have three times the mortality rate of nondisabled infants (Landesman-Dwyer & Butterfield, 1983).

Effects of Severe Disabilities

If you ask parents, siblings, and teachers of individuals with severe disabilities what the effects of those disabilities have been on them, you will get a wide range of answers—and they may be hard to understand. It is sometimes difficult to describe the effects of severe disabilities when you are personally involved. You keep thinking of the *person* with the disabilities—the person is wonderful and the interaction is rewarding even when the disabilities are very challenging and sometimes overwhelming.

Effects on the Child

■ **Cognitive Development**   The specific effects of mental retardation on cognitive development, which are discussed in detail in Chapter 4, include problems in such areas as selective attention, maintaining attention, short-term memory, metacognitive skills, and the maintenance, transfer, and generalization of skills. These problems may exist to an even greater degree in persons with severe and profound mental disabilities, although not always in a uniform or predictable way. Most people with severe or profound mental retardation experience disabilities across all cognitive skill areas.

The effects of severe disabilities on cognitive development are related partially to the learning experiences the person has throughout life, particularly in the early years. The frequent coexistence of physical or health impairments with severe cognitive disabilities often results in a reduction in the normal environmental interactions considered instrumental in the development of cognitive abilities. For example, an infant without severe disabilities, while lying in his crib, may accidentally hit the side of the crib with his hand and hear the noise it makes. After this happens a few times, the child will make the connection between his hand movement and the noise of it against the crib. This is called an understanding of cause and effect. The realization that something you do can have predictable consequences is an important tool for learning to control and interact with the environment. Another example, recognized immediately by parents and infants, is the connection between crying and parental attention. The child may begin to hit his hand against the crib for the purpose of making the noise or cry in order to be held. He intentionally does something to get a specific result. This purposeful behavior is referred to as a *means-end relationship*. The development of an understanding of cause and effect and of means-end relationships is critical for children to begin to explore their environments actively and with purpose; these skills are also considered important in language development (Iacono & Miller, 1989).

The child with severe and profound levels of disabilities may experience difficulty learning these early skills in the typical way. A child with severe physical disabilities or with very delayed motor development may not be aware that it is her foot or hand that is hitting the side of the crib—or she may not have sufficient motor control to direct it to happen again. A child with severe mental retardation may be unable to understand that her mother appears two or three minutes after she has started crying. As a result, the child may have difficulty making a connection between the things she does and the results of these ac-

Understanding cause and effect and means-ends relationships is critical for most cognitive skills.

tions or behaviors. The infant, therefore, may not acquire these important behaviors unassisted and may not attempt to interact with the world around her. The child simply may not know that what she does makes any difference.

The question of just how much a child with severe or profound mental retardation can learn has been much studied, and professionals primarily adhere to the principle that through careful modifications of the environment, people with severe disabilities can learn a range of complex behaviors and skills. A critical principle for teachers and parents to keep in mind is that there should be no inherent assumptions about what a child can or cannot learn as a consequence of an IQ score or a label of severe or profound mental retardation. Programs based on this principle have resulted in directed, functional teaching for students with severe disabilities, as discussed later in the chapter.

■ **Physical Development and Health** Children with severe and profound mental retardation are usually much below average in physical size (Landesman-Dwyer & Butterfield, 1983) and experience a wide range of physical and health-related difficulties. As we have mentioned, mental retardation of this degree of severity is typically accompanied by other disabilities.

Infants born with severe and profound mental retardation often experience significant delays in physical development. Because of this delay, the infant may have very limited physical movement at the beginning of life.

Sometimes physical disabilities and health risks are associated with the specific syndrome or condition responsible for the retardation. Children with

> Children with severe and profound mental retardation often experience health-related difficulties and severe delays in physical development.

Many types of recreational activities and environmental modifications can be used to teach complex behaviors and skills. (George Goodwin/Monkmeyer Press Photo Service)

Down syndrome, for example, often require heart surgery at a very young age because of congenital heart defects, and they are at risk for respiratory problems. Children with severe mental retardation and cerebral palsy may have varying degrees of motor impairment; sometimes the physical disabilities may affect mobility, speech, and regulated motor activity. A number of children will be prone to a seizure disorder such as epilepsy, although most types of seizures can be controlled or reduced by appropriate medication. Other syndromes or conditions may be degenerative in nature. In other words, the conditions will worsen over time, and the child's health will become progressively worse, until death occurs. An example we have already mentioned is Tay-Sachs disease.

In some instances, the physical development of the child with severe or profound mental retardation is compromised almost as a side effect of extreme developmental delay or physical complications. Intrusive procedures may need to be used on a regular basis in order to maintain comfort and sustain life. For example, a child who must be catheterized daily or fed through a stomach tube is exposed to more opportunities for infection. A number of children with profound mental retardation may not be independently mobile and thus may not use their limbs with any regularity. This can result in atrophy of the muscles. Quality care, therapy, and medical treatment can help to reduce the probability of problems like these.

■ **Language Development and Communication**   Severe and profound disabilities can have extensive effects on an individual's language development and communicative abilities. Some people with severe or profound retardation will have limited spontaneous oral language, others will have nonfunctional oral language, and some, no oral language at all. The presence or lack of spontaneous oral language does not, however, imply that no communication system can be taught. Sign language is one alternative. Because its use bypasses possible problems with speech production, involves tangible (hand) symbols, and provides a visible model for instruction, sign language has been considered a good choice for communication instruction. However, sign language is not without its own drawbacks, including limited use by others in the environment (Bryen, Goldman & Quinlisk-Gill, 1988).

Other types of nonverbal communication systems include language boards or communication boards: Words or symbols of needs and possible requests appropriate for a specific environment are placed on a lap board, and the person communicates by indicating the appropriate word or picture. Many people with severe and profound mental retardation do find ways of communicating their wishes and controlling their environment by using nonverbal means. Regardless of the method of communication selected, critical factors for effective communication include the preparation and interest of communication partners and an environment that supports individual interaction and communication (Butterfield & Arthur, 1995).

■ **Social Behaviors and Emotional Development**   By definition, students with severe and profound mental retardation will have deficits in adaptive behavior. The extent to which appropriate adaptive behaviors, such as self-help skills and general social skills, are acquired will vary according to the severity of the disability, the type and breadth of educational programming, and the environment in which the person lives, works, or goes to school. For example, positive changes in different areas of adaptive behavior have been found when persons with mental retardation live in group homes versus institutional settings and

Many people with severe or profound disabilities can use a verbal or nonverbal language system.

work in competitive employment versus sheltered workshops (Inge et al., 1988; Sullivan, Vitello & Foster, 1988). Because the labels *severe mental retardation* and *profound mental retardation* can encompass a wide range of ability and performance levels, it is difficult to characterize "typical" social behavior. For a few persons, social development may be very limited, and target skills may include establishing eye contact or acknowledging someone's presence. For others, social development goals may include appropriate social interaction in a community work setting. Often, a drawback to successful social interaction is the lack of a common communication system. Storey and Provost (1996) found that the use of communication books (essentially picture books) increased the amount of social interaction as well as interpersonal communication between individuals with severe disabilities and their nondisabled coworkers in a community work setting.

Although there is very little descriptive research available on the emotional development of persons with severe or profound mental disabilities, we know that all people experience an array of emotions. In some instances, we must learn to recognize the indicators of basic human emotions such as love, trust, fear, and happiness. More likely, we can observe emotional development and expression easily. The management or appropriate demonstration of emotions is an important aspect of adaptive behavior. The development and nurturing of many emotions rests with the significant others in the person's life, including the family.

Effects on the Family

In this section, we will look at the joys and struggles of families of children with severe disabilities. We also will discuss the multiple roles parents of children with severe disabilities must play.

■ **Family Attitudes and Reactions** Because most children with severe or profound mental retardation are diagnosed at birth, families must learn to deal immediately with the prospect of rearing a child with a severe disability (see the accompanying box, "A Family Perspective"). As you might expect, reactions to this diagnosis and the onslaught of ensuing emotions vary greatly. Parents have many questions about what the future holds for them and their other children: How can I care for this child? What will happen to her when I'm no longer around? How will my other children react to their brother? Some of these questions will be answered in time, some can be answered through education, and some can never be answered. The initial and continuing family experiences include acceptance, love, and joy in the child.

Most children with severe or profound mental retardation are diagnosed at birth.

You may see many differences in the lives of families that include an individual with severe disabilities. It is interesting to note, however, that mothers of youngsters with severe disabilities, like all mothers, hope and expect that their children will be able to achieve independence (Lehmann & Baker, 1995). Although there are more services than ever before to assist families, many parents are concerned about the lack of community support and related services available to them—services that are necessary for community inclusion and maximum independence for their child (Turnbull & Ruef, 1997).

Parents, of course, are not the only family members affected by the presence of a child with severe disabilities. Brothers and sisters will have their own reactions and ways of dealing with them. Reactions can range from resentment to extreme protectiveness; probably the whole spectrum of emotions will be

～ A Family Perspective

In the following excerpt from her book *A Difference in the Family*, Helen Featherstone (1980) describes her reactions to the discovery that her child had severe disabilities:

> When Jody was fifteen days old we learned that he was blind. We wept for the experiences he would miss—the changing colors of a New England autumn, the splendor of a clear night sky, the faces of the people he would love. Yet we realized how much remained—if he were "only" blind. Most of the activities that gave our lives meaning and importance would still be within his reach. He could read, write, teach, play, and enjoy the fellowship of friends. He could talk and think, give comfort and, in time, go about his own life independently, perhaps with some special understanding born of his disability. Anyway, that is what we hoped. The idea of blindness made us sad. It led us to examine our values: it did not shatter them. However, as the months went by, we learned that Jody was not "only" blind. He had cerebral palsy; he was probably severely retarded. During the first eighteen months of his life he cried almost continually from the pain that no one could diagnose or relieve. His days and nights were passed in misery; his future looked bleak and limited. Hardly a day passed without our asking ourselves whether his life was worth living. Each of us, separately and together, wished for an end to his ordeal: a peaceful, painless death.
>
> He did not die. He was remarkably tough. Unexpectedly, after the doctor removed an infected shunt, his pain went. He cried less during the day and slept longer at night. He smiled more often, even laughed. Liberated from his inner torments, he responded to us. We began to like him. He gave more: his smiles, his laughter, his delighted shrieks. He asked less. He still needed a lot of special care, but we no longer performed our family routines with one hand while patting a wretched baby with the other. Each of us began to feel that Jody's life was worth living, and that he made his own special contribution to the family.

Source: Helen Featherstone, *A Difference in the Family: Life with a Disabled Child* (New York: Basic Books, 1980). pp. 222–223.

experienced at some point during the sibling's lifetime. Although it is not unusual for siblings of children with mental retardation to experience high levels of stress, many children develop very close relationships with each other (Lindsey & Stewart, 1989).

■ **Family Roles in Education**   The family of an individual with severe or profound disabilities can play an active role in educational programming from the very beginning. The passage of P.L. 99-457 in 1986 provided the legislative impetus needed for the establishment of federal programs for infants and young children with disabilities and their families (Campbell, Bellamy & Bishop, 1988). The importance of early intervention and family responsiveness in the development of children with severe and profound mental retardation, as well as any type of disability, has been recognized and now legislated. Parents who learn how to encourage language or communication or who are trained to provide at-home occupational therapy will not only feel more competent in dealing with their child, they will be helping that child to build an important and perhaps critical learning foundation.

Early intervention programs provide crucial services for children with severe disabilities and their families.

Not everyone agrees with the present focus on early service provision in the home environment. Krauss (1990), for example, suggests that some families may resent the fact that they must be evaluated before their child can receive services and may feel that their privacy is threatened. Although you might think that most families would not feel this way, if you work with parents and families of infants or young children, it may be an important consideration to keep in mind.

Autism

Autism can be a lifelong developmental disability that typically appears during the first three years of life. Although autism has been recognized for many years, it was not identified as a separate category of special education until the IDEA reauthorization of 1990. Autism can best be described as a collection of behavioral symptoms. These symptoms include:

- Disturbance in the rate of appearance of physical, social, and language skills

- Abnormal responses to sensations

- Absent or delayed speech and language (although specific thinking capabilities may be present). Immature rhythms of speech, limited understanding of ideas, and the use of words without attaching the usual meanings to them are common.

- Abnormal ways of relating to people, objects, and events. Typically, children with autism do not respond appropriately to adults and other children. Objects and toys are not used as normally intended (Knoblock, 1982).

Causes and Prevalence

The specific psychological, physiological, or environmental factors that cause autism are unknown. Autism occurs by itself or in association with other disorders that affect the function of the brain, such as viral infections, metabolic disturbances, and epilepsy. Approximately 75 to 80 percent of individuals with autism also experience mental retardation (Knoblock, 1982).

About one of every 1,000 children is diagnosed with autism or as having autistic-like behaviors (Bryson, 1996). During the 1994–1995 school year, .5 percent of all students with disabilities ages 6 through 21, or 22,800 students, were served as students with autism (U.S. Department of Education, 1996).

Characteristics

Individuals with autism often demonstrate unusual patterns of learning, speech, and behavior. There is great variability in the amount and intensity of characteristics among children who are identified as having autism. Children described as having autistic-like behaviors usually have only a few of these characteristics.

Individuals with autism, even those with significant mental retardation, often have an unusual learning pattern. This uneven pattern may consist of a relative strength in one or two areas of learning. For example, a child with autism may demonstrate ability in auditory memory, organization, or telling time and yet have extreme difficulty in other learning skills such as reading or writing. Children with autism also may be very rigid in their demands for environmental sameness and dependent on exact routines during the day (Koegel et al., 1995). For example, a student who catches the school bus at 7:15 in the morning will always leave the house at 7:10 A.M. and walk the exact same number of steps each time. If the bus is early, the student will walk very slowly, so that he arrives and boards the bus at exactly 7:15.

first

person

Kevin

When Kevin was an infant my parents thought he was deaf because he was so detached. One of my earliest memories was my father firing a cap pistol near Kevin to see if he would respond. He didn't. My parents took Kevin to doctor after doctor before he was diagnosed as "autistic." I remember my mother saying she was happy to learn he wasn't deaf because "there are so many wonderful sounds to hear." I suspect as Kevin got older and his inappropriate behaviors began to emerge, she had second thoughts about her preference. Kevin's early years were difficult for our entire family. He would only drink milk and would not eat until age 4. Finally my grandmother, who was visiting from New York, got him to eat solid food. As a young child Kevin was quite destructive. I remember how distraught my mother was when Kevin used a lamp plug to scratch the surface of two new coffee tables she had recently brought home. From then on she realized she would never be able to keep beautiful things in our home. Kevin would wander the house at night, frequently falling asleep wherever he happened to be when he finally closed his eyes. My brothers, sister, and I would take turns being responsible for finding him and bringing him to bed. Kevin would frequently have night terrors and the only way my parents could calm him was to take him for a drive, often at 2:00 A.M. in the morning. As is true for so many other children with autism, he could not tolerate change and would frequently have tantrums when something familiar was moved from its usual spot. By trial and error we would try to figure out what was missing and put it back into place. Because Kevin did not have any outward signs of a disability, strangers didn't understand his bizarre outbursts. We were very defensive and protected him from annoyed stares and unkind comments.

Children with autism may have delayed speech or not acquire verbal language at all. Sign language or language boards are often used with nonverbal students. Often, even if oral speech is acquired, the speech patterns will take unusual forms. One example common to individuals with autism is **echolalia,** the repetition of speech sounds the child has heard. For example, if you asked a child, "What is your name?" the child would respond, "What is your name?" The child also may repeat certain words over and over—the jingle from a television advertisement or a sentence he or she has overheard. Some individuals with autism may speak telegraphically and may refer to themselves in the third

Despite all these problems, we loved Kevin very much. It became an early ritual that before any of us blew out our birthday candles, we would wish "for Kevin to get better." As Kevin got older his behavior began to improve. He attended a school for children with mental and emotional disabilities and later a sheltered workshop. Kevin learned to read simple phrases and add single digits. He became very close to me and would sit with me much of the time while I studied for school. He also loved to swim. Being in the water always seemed to make him relaxed and happy.

Kevin lived at home until his mid-thirties. I would frequently keep him overnight on the weekends. We would make our supper together and listen to music. We both enjoy music from the late 1960s. I don't think the Moody Blues have a more devoted fan than Kevin. Five years ago Kevin had a serious illness requiring hospitalization. I have never been so frightened in my entire life and realized just how much Kevin means to me. Fortunately, he recovered completely.

Kevin is now 42 and for the last three years has lived in an apartment with a caregiver and another man with autism. He continues to work and has become more self-sufficient. Kevin doesn't talk very much but does express all of his needs and preferences. He has become quite flexible when things are different from what he expects. Kevin and I always have lunch together on Sunday afternoons. Now that he lives independently, I have the opportunity to see how others view him. I recently read his quarterly service plan. As I read about Kevin's preferences and strengths, I realized that my "little" brother had become his own man. This year, my birthday wish will be for something else. Kevin is fine just the way he is.

Richard L. Sribnick, M.D.

Source: Reprinted by permission of the author.

person. Jim might say, "Jim watch TV" instead of "I want to watch TV." As you can probably see, many individuals with autism have a difficult time using reciprocal speech—using language to give and receive information. Much research is devoted to the observation and development of reciprocal speech in young children with autism (Savelle & Fox, 1988; Simpson & Souris, 1988).

Individuals with autism demonstrate patterns of social behavior that seem to reflect social withdrawal and avoidance of others. Many children with autism focus their attentions on objects instead of other people and simply do not react to or actively avoid other people's efforts at social interaction or communication. Not all individuals with autism are so completely withdrawn from social interaction with others, but most experience significant delays or deficits in social skills. For all individuals with autism, acquiring social skills and adaptive behaviors comprise a substantial portion of educational programs at any age.

An unusual behavioral tendency demonstrated by some individuals with severe mental retardation and autism is the performance of repetitive behaviors such as rocking, twirling objects, clapping hands, and flapping a hand in front of one's face. These repetitive, nonharmful behaviors are often referred to as **stereotypic behaviors.** A few individuals with autism exhibit self-injurious or self-abusive behavior ranging from hand biting or head slapping to life-threatening behaviors such as head banging. The individuals seem oblivious to the pain and damage caused by these behaviors. Research suggests many possible reasons for self-injurious behavior, including attempts at communication and efforts to manipulate the environment and avoid demanding or stressful situations (Durand & Carr, 1985; Wieseler et al., 1985). As teachers, our first instinct is to try to eliminate such behavior. We must, however, first assess the communicative intent on the part of the student and try to provide alternative behaviors or skills in language and communication when attempting to reduce inappropriate behaviors.

Interventions

The focus of curriculum and instruction for individuals with autism is essentially the same as it is for other students with severe disabilities. Although some individuals with autism are able to progress through a general education curriculum, the majority of students require extensive support and benefit from a functional, community-based curriculum. The areas of communication, socialization, and generalization or transfer of learning are particularly important in programs for individuals with autism.

The methodology used most successfully for individuals with autism and other severe disabilities is based on the principles of **applied behavior analysis.** Applied behavior analysis focuses on clearly defining the behavior in the context of the environment and arranging the environment to adjust the behavior by providing consequences for increasing or decreasing behaviors. For example, a specific disruptive or self-injurious behavior might be defined as an escape mechanism if a student's teacher removes the task from the student, or the student from the task when the behavior occurs. The consequences (removal) in the environment would be adjusted and new consequences presented to decrease the inappropriate behavior and increase the probability of an acceptable alternative response. The role or function the student's behavior plays in his environment is determined, and alternative behaviors that can serve the same function are identified. New behaviors are taught through reinforcement-based opportunities for response. Complex or multistep behaviors, such as some vocational tasks, may be taught in segments and then linked together. Other skills, such as getting dressed, are presented as a whole, with the student gradually increasing his or her participation. Students with autism may require many instructional trials and explicit training across environments.

Some intervention programs specifically designed for children with autism have been developed. The UCLA Young Autism Project, an intensive, three-year program for young children with autism, recently has received much attention by parents and some professionals. The project developers present data that support significant change in children's cognition, language, and behavior (Smith & Lovaas, 1997). The project is based on the principles of applied behavior analysis; however, some professionals question the curriculum context (what skills are taught and where they are taught) and criticize the quality and validity of the program's experimental research (Gresham & MacMillan, 1997).

Educational Issues

A term like *profound mental retardation* provides little information on how to understand or educate persons with extensive mental disabilities (Bricker & Filler, 1985). Explaining the term to educators by saying it means an IQ of 20 or below simply is an inadequate description of a population and does not address the educational or health-related issues of individual children. To help you understand the children identified as having severe and profound levels of mental retardation, the following description of a visit to a preschool program for children with developmental disabilities is presented. The setting and the children are real.

The school has two rooms, one for infants and toddlers, the other for 4- to 7-year-old children. Twelve children attend the school, and among them they exhibit a wide range of physical and cognitive differences. Six adults work with the children as either teachers or aides. When you first enter the school, you are struck by several aspects of the setting itself. There is a lot of equipment: mats, pads, wheelchairs, and so forth. The walls are covered with a few pieces of artwork and pictures of children, and prominently displayed are steps for CPR, the Heimlich maneuver, responding to failed heart or breathing monitors, and detailed assignments for any type of emergency occurrence. There are lots of diapers, blenders, and, of course, a wide variety of toys, books, records, and pictures.

As you meet the children, some of them run up to you and give you a hug, a few try to crawl in your direction or move their arms excitedly, others don't move and don't seem to know you are there. Some children begin talking to you, others give you big smiles, and still others make no noise at all.

William is 4 years old. He is sitting on a mat, propped up with pillows all around him. He seems to be staring into space. William is thought to have visual and hearing impairments, but no one is sure how severe they might be. Except for crying and some low moaning during one of his frequent seizures, William makes no noise at all. Although William takes a lot of medication, his seizures cannot be stopped. You cannot tell when he is having a seizure, but the teacher who works with him can tell by the angle of his body and the low noise he makes. She also has learned that rubbing his arms seems to make him relax. William receives lots of physical therapy because he makes little voluntary movement and his muscles need to be worked or they will atrophy.

Sandra is a little blonde girl with a ready smile. She is almost 8 years old but is the size of the average 4- or 5-year-old. Sandra's muscles are very tight, and she tends to curl up in a fetal position with her hands tightly clenched. Because of this, she is often propped up in a sitting position or lying on her side with pillows under and between her legs and arms to stretch out her muscles. Sandra has very limited voluntary movement, but she will stretch her arms out to reach objects and gets very excited about particular toys or dolls when they are directly in front of her. She doesn't speak, but her face is very expressive, and it is obvious when she is happy or upset. Sandra clearly recognizes faces and voices. She will turn her head toward your voice and is very particular about who is helping her eat her lunch.

James is 5 years old and very mobile but has no speech and makes very little eye contact with anyone. James wears thick glasses strapped to his head (or he'll take them off). He continually makes a low sound and engages in a lot of self-stimulation, including flapping his hands. James responds quickly to two things—food and music. He loves to eat and will finish a complete meal in about ten seconds. One of his favorite things to do is to listen to music while rocking in a rocking chair. When he is listening to music, the sound he makes all of the time becomes much louder; he seems to be trying to sing along.

These three children give you an idea of some of the educational challenges facing students with severe disabilities and their teachers. When you first enter a school or a class for children, adolescents, or adults with severe disabilities, the things that attract your attention are the differences. Puréed food, toilet training for people of all ages, unusual sounds, and strange equipment all stand out. When you meet the children, you may be overwhelmed by a sense of sadness because of their disabilities and by what is often perceived as their limited possibilities for normal life experiences. All of the implications of severe or profound mental retardation seem to be foremost in your mind as you begin to learn about and know the children themselves. Then an amazing thing happens. You spend time with the children, work with them, and begin to teach them. In a very short time, when you think of a particular child, the first things that come to mind are not the physical or cognitive limitations or the behavioral characteristics. Instead, you think of the skills the child has learned to perform, the look in his or her eyes when excited, the way the child responds to your voice, and the wealth of things that will be learned in the years to come. In short, you focus on *all* of the characteristics of the individual rather than only on the differences or the disabilities.

The future of these children will depend in part on the vision and commitment of their families, their teachers, and their peers—of people like you. The extent to which children with severe and profound levels of mental retardation will become adults who are accepted, valued, and integrated into the mainstream of society is our responsibility as well as theirs.

The nature and content of educational programming for individuals with severe and profound levels of mental retardation have changed significantly in recent years. Most of the changes have come about because of new or different educational philosophies and greater expectations and goals for children, adolescents, and adults with severe disabilities. Polloway, Smith, Patton, and Smith (1996) suggest that the most recent paradigm shift in the education of individuals with mental retardation and developmental disabilities is toward empower-

New educational philosophies and higher expectations have changed educational programming for people with severe and profound mental retardation.

ment. The importance of facilitating and planning for individuals with severe disabilities to have an important role in decisions regarding their lives is the underlying component of many educational programs.

Although there has been some disagreement among professionals about the rate or extent of some of the changes we will be discussing, the importance and need for programs that emphasize normalization, social and physical inclusion, and life-skills curricula are recognized as evident. Each of these areas will be discussed separately. As you will see, however, they are closely interrelated and, together, represent a continuing movement toward change for individuals with severe disabilities.

Normalization

One of the forces behind educational change for individuals with all levels of mental retardation is the movement toward normalization. The term **normalization,** or *social role valorization*, refers to an emphasis on conventional or normal behavior and attitudes in all aspects of education, socialization, and other life experiences (Wolfensberger, 1977, 1983). In other words, the focus of normalization is that all people should lead lives that are as normal as possible. For persons with mental retardation, this movement has great implications. Wolfensberger (1977) defines two dimensions of normalization: (a) direct contact or interaction with individuals and (b) the way an individual is described to others.

The first dimension involves the way we treat people with mental retardation and the things we decide to teach and encourage. It is important, for example, to consider a person's age and the usual criteria for normal behavior when we are interacting with someone or deciding what types of behaviors, skills, or recreational activities we will be teaching or doing. It may be easier and faster to feed a 10-year-old with severe disabilities, but it is not age-appropriate and, if at all possible, we should choose to implement a self-feeding program so that the child not only will become more independent but also will be expected to perform some of the skills of other children his age.

Sometimes it may be beyond a person's physical or cognitive abilities to perform some self-care skills (eating, toileting, dressing) or other types of tasks with complete independence. In these instances, we encourage partial participation. Partial participation refers to enabling the student to perform the parts of the skill or task that are within his or her ability range (Snell, 1988).

The second dimension of normalization refers to the way we portray or present persons with mental retardation to others. This dimension includes the way we may refer to a student in our class, the words or phrases we include in writing about or describing persons with mental retardation, the way we select clothing or hairstyles for our children or clients. The types of housing or educational environments in which we place persons with disabilities and the extent to which legislation protects and enforces basic human rights reflect our society's perceptions of individuals with disabilities. For example, most of us do not live with hundreds of other people in large housing facilities throughout our lives. Persons with mental retardation should live in environments and structures that approximate normal living arrangements and include a small group of friends, family, or caretakers (Taylor, Racino & Walker, 1992).

In general, the move toward a normalized existence for individuals with severe and profound mental retardation is dependent on the increased willingness of the public to recognize and accept the humanity, value, and contributions of persons with mental retardation. Normalization has served as a

The focus of normalization is that all people should lead lives that are as normal as possible.

foundation for many of the major social as well as educational changes that we have observed in the area of mental retardation over the past few decades.

Inclusion

One term you will hear or see repeatedly in any educational program description or curriculum for students with severe mental retardation is *inclusion*, the incorporation of all individuals into the mainstream of society. Examples of inclusion include attending a regular public school, working in a community establishment, and living in a home in the neighborhood. There are several reasons why inclusion has become an important facet of instructional programming for individuals with mental retardation. First, it is proposed that individuals are more likely to develop functional patterns of behavior and higher levels of functioning if they have the opportunity to interact with people without disabilities. Second, it is considered to be every individual's right to access the opportunities and facilities that the community has to offer to the greatest extent possible. Third, an emphasis on inclusion will provide many individuals with the direct training and experiences they will need in order to achieve full or partial independence (Stainback, Stainback & Ayres, 1996; Williams, Vogelsberg & Schutz, 1985).

Inclusion also involves the acceptance of individuals with mental retardation by the community. Of course, acceptance and social interaction cannot be dictated, but they can developed through encouragement, preparation, and the provision of opportunities for interaction (Shutz, Williams, Iverson & Duncan, 1984). Obviously, it is easier to develop friendships and good working relationships with people who are living and working in the same environment as you are. It is also possible that early physical integration will encourage the development of friendships that may persist during the school years.

> People with severe mental retardation may develop higher levels of functioning and independence when they interact with people without disabilities.

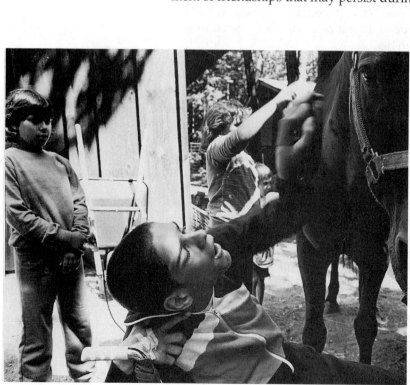

Students with severe disabilities can and do participate in age-appropriate activities with their friends and classmates. (Bob Kramer/The Picture Cube)

A key issue in inclusion is the extent to which people with severe mental re-tardation should be integrated into the school or community. Many professionals suggest that total inclusion should be the goal. An example of total inclusion in the public school setting would be the placement of students with severe disabilities in regular classes for part of the day in order to promote socialization experiences. Other professionals feel that inclusion to this extent may result in a reduced amount of needed educational programming for the students and that social integration can best be achieved in other settings. Some parents are concerned about their child's safety and emotional well-being in integrated environments and prefer, at least initially, less risky program options (Stetson, 1984).

The attitudes of the nondisabled persons in the community, school, or work setting are critical to successful inclusion. Some educational programs have been developed to give nondisabled persons some knowledge about individuals with disabilities, and many teachers do take the time to discuss individual differences and specific disabilities with their classes.

Curriculum

■ **Life Skills**   Most of the curricula currently used in instructional programs for individuals with severe and profound disabilities stress instruction in life skills and are designed to maximize independent functioning. A curriculum that emphasizes preparation for life and includes skills that will be used by the student in home, school, or work environments is called a **functional curriculum.** All types of instruction, including self-help skills, communication skills, mobility training, physical therapy, and occupational therapy are integrated so that they complement one another and focus on functional activities rather than isolated practice tasks (Snell & Drake, 1994).

■ **Designing a Functional Curriculum**   A functional curriculum includes instruction in all of the important areas of adult life, usually referred to as *domains.* Four major domains are typically addressed in the curriculum: domestic, community, recreation/leisure, and vocational. Each student must be taught the behaviors or tasks that are required in his or her home, work, or recreational setting (see the accompanying box, "Examples of Functional Curriculum Domains").

Communication skills are a vital component of the life-skills curriculum, so instruction in language is an important part of the curriculum for most persons with severe or profound mental retardation. This is especially true for individuals who will be going out to work or live in community settings. The first step in all language programs is to identify the type of oral, gestural, or physical means the students are currently using to convey information or desires to others. Once teachers, parents, or therapists have identified the types of behaviors and the motivation for them, instruction can focus on maximizing their use for purposes of communication. Caro and Snell (1989) have identified the following three major goals of programs designed to teach language or communication to persons with severe disabilities: to increase the frequency of communicative behavior, to enlarge the student's repertoire of communicative functions, and to promote the spontaneous and generalized use of communication skills in everyday life. Instructional programs in language and communication must occur in natural environments and focus on purposeful and meaningful communication (Caro & Snell, 1989; Reichle & Keogh, 1986).

⌇ Examples of Functional Curriculum Domains

Domestic

Areas or subdomains: kitchen, bathroom, laundry room, bedroom

Community

Areas or subdomains: grocery store, bank, post office, restaurants, school

Recreation/Leisure

Areas or subdomains: park, YMCA, movie theater, bowling alley, fishing pond

Vocational

Areas or subdomains: specific job sites (hotel, restaurant, landscape)

Skill areas to be addressed across all domains: communication, transportation, social skills, attire, behavioral expectations, word/sign/symbol recognition, area-specific skills (for example, using the stove, depositing money, bowling, greeting customers), decision-making skills.

The technique that is frequently used to identify skills for instruction is called an **environmental inventory,** or **environmental analysis** (Nietupski & Hamre-Nietupski, 1987). An environmental inventory involves a visit to the settings in which the student has to function. The environment might be a group home, the cafeteria in an elementary school, the local park, or the neighborhood bus station. A list is made of the specific skills needed by the average person to be successful in that environment. Then the skills of the individual student are compared to the needed skills, and specific behaviors or tasks are targeted for instruction. By using this procedure, the curriculum truly prepares the student to be successful in current or future life situations and channels valuable teaching time into meaningful instruction.

Integration is a natural outcome of community-based instruction.

■ **Community-Based Instruction** One way that integration is incorporated into educational plans is community-based instruction, which, as you learned in earlier chapters, involves actually conducting learning experiences in community settings. Students who are able to travel in the community will, for example, receive training on how to walk to their home or work site or how to take a bus. Instruction will take place on the very sidewalks or bus lines that the student will be using to travel. Community-based instruction not only provides students with direct training in skills they need to be integrated into society, it also allows them to experience integration during the instructional process (Voeltz, 1984). The accompanying box, "A Closer Look: Can Do: Scope and Sequence Chart for General Community Functioning," reflects the integration of community-based instruction in curriculum planning.

Technology

Technological advances in the areas of communication and cognitive development have contributed significantly to the quality of life of individuals with severe and profound levels of mental retardation. Technology has opened many avenues of communication not previously available to people with severe physical as well as cognitive disabilities. A description of these advances in communication is provided in Chapter 10. In this chapter, we will discuss the role of technology in the cognitive development of individuals, particularly infants. A few landmark studies have provided us with an increased awareness of the

A closer look

Can Do: Scope and Sequence Chart for General Community Functioning

Goal areas	Age and grade levels					
	Elementary school					
	Kindergarten (age 5)	Primary grades (ages 6–8)	Intermediate grades (ages 9–11)	Middle school (ages 12–14)	High school (ages 15–18)	Transition (ages 19–21)
Travel	Walk or ride bus to and from school	Walk or ride bus to and from school	Walk, ride bus, or ride bike to and from school	Walk, ride bus, or ride bike to and from school	Walk, ride bus, or ride bike to and from school	Walk, ride bus, or ride bike to and from home and community sites
	Walk to and from school bus and to points in school (classroom, office)	Walk to and from school bus and to points in school (classroom, cafeteria, office, music room)	Walk to various destinations in school and in the community (neighborhood grocery store, mailbox)	Walk to various destinations in school and in the community (store, restaurant, job site)	Walk to various destinations in school and in the community (store, restaurant, job site)	Walk to various destinations
	Cross street: stop at curb	Cross street: familiar, low-traffic intersections	Cross streets safely	Cross streets safely Use public bus/subway for general transportation	Cross streets safely Use public bus/subway for general transportation	Cross streets safely Use public bus/subway for general transportation
Community safety			Problem-solve if lost in new places Use caution with strangers	Problem-solve if lost in new places Use caution with strangers	Problem-solve if lost in new places Use caution with strangers	Problem-solve if lost in new places Use caution with strangers
Grocery shopping			Buy two to three items at neighborhood store for self (snack) or classroom snack activity	Buy items needed for specific planned menu	Buy items needed for specific meal or special event	Buy items needed for specific meal or special event
General shopping		Buy item at school store	Buy item at school store	Buy few items in store with limited money amount Purchase personal care items	Shop for desired items in shopping center Purchase personal care items	Shop for desired items in shopping center Purchase personal care items
Eating out	Carry milk/lunch money Follow school cafeteria routine	Carry milk/lunch money Follow school cafeteria routine	Carry milk/lunch money Follow school cafeteria routine Order and pay: familiar fast food restaurants, snack stand Buy snack/drinks from vending machine	Budget/carry money for lunch/snacks Eat in school cafeteria Order and eat in fast food restaurants Buy snack/drinks from vending machine	Budget/carry money for lunch/snacks Eat in school/public cafeteria Order and eat in fast food restaurants Buy snack/drinks from vending machines	Budget/carry money for meals and snacks Eat in public cafeteria Order and eat in fast food restaurants Buy snack/drinks from vending machines
Using services	Mail letter at corner mailbox	Mail letter at corner mailbox Use pay phone with help	Mail letters Use pay phone	Use post office Use pay phone Ask for assistance in stores	Use post office Use pay phone Ask for assistance in stores, information booths	Use post office Use pay phone Ask for assistance appropriately in stores, information booths

Source: From *The Syracuse Community-Referenced Curriculum Guide for Students with Moderate and Severe Disabilities*, edited by Alison Ford, Roberta Schnorr, Luanna Meyer, Linda Davern, Jim Black, and Patrick Dempsey, p. 78. Copyright © 1989. Reprinted by permission of Brookes Publishing and the author.

importance of early learning and the ways that modern technology can help to facilitate the educational process.

As we have mentioned already, the infant born with severe disabilities often experiences both cognitive and psychomotor developmental delays that can impede the acquisition of fundamental concepts such as personal control over the environment and the realization of cause and effect relationships. It is in the development of these initial and very important cognitive skills that technology can be instrumental.

One early example is the use of the microcomputer in the development of a contingency intervention curriculum (Brinker, 1984; Brinker & Lewis, 1982). Remember our discussion of the problems young infants might have in realizing that their kicks against the side of the crib made sounds or that their cries brought their mother to them? The results of their actions (the noise, the appearance of the mother) can be described as *contingencies*. The **contingency intervention curriculum** involves the immediate and distinct presentation of contingencies, or consequences, to children in order to help them understand the relationship between what they do and what happens in the environment. In these studies, a microcomputer was used to help provide infants with contingencies for even minimal movement. By setting up a very sensitive panel on a child's crib that was attached to a microcomputer, the child's random movements were picked up and recorded. The movement then triggered the computer to provide a consequence (or contingency). The consequences, which included things such as music and recordings of the mother's voice, were varied until ones were found to which the child would respond consistently. Because the child participating in this type of programming receives evidence of the effects her movement has on the environment, she is given the opportunity to develop purposeful behavior and interact with the environment in a meaningful way.

Software that teaches cause and effect relationships is also used frequently in the classroom for individuals with severe disabilities. Types of cause and effect software include programs that use abstract design, sound, graphics, and games (Lewis, 1993). The accompanying box, "Join the Circus," describes a commercial program designed to teach cause and effect relationships.

In addition to the program just described, some ways that technology is being used to develop these skills include biofeedback, corneal reflection monitoring, and even the development of small adapted cars for young children so that they can move around their homes or schools (Rostron & Sewell, 1984; Strain & Odom, 1986). In the near future, it is likely that technology will play an even greater role in providing individuals with severe and profound levels of mental retardation with the experiences necessary for the development of critical cognitive and communication skills.

Transition

As we've discussed throughout this text, *transition* refers to the process of preparing for and facilitating movement from one situation or place to another. In the area of severe and profound disabilities, the term usually refers to one of three types of movement: (1) movement from one level of school to another, (2) movement from a segregated school or home setting to an integrated or community-based school or residence, or (3) movement from school to a work setting, typically a work setting in the community. As we have seen already, the

~ Join the Circus

Join the Circus [Don Johnston Developmental Equipment, Inc.] is a cause-effect program for Apple II series computers. It requires a color monitor, a switch, and the Echo speech synthesizer; a printer is optional. Join the Circus contains three activities: The Juggling J's (jugglers), Magnificent Maggy (a magician), and Katy the Lion Tamer. In the lion tamer's act, . . . the lion jumps on the stand and roars. For the finale, Katy places her head in the lion's mouth. . . .

All the activities in Join the Circus require switch responses. However, each activity can be used on four different levels. In level 1, one switch press shows the entire circus act. In level 2, the student must press the switch twice, once to start the act and once to see the finale. In level 3, five switch presses are required. In level 4, two students work cooperatively and take turns pressing their switches.

One advantage of this and many other programs from Don Johnston is the amount of control that teachers have over instructional variables. At the teacher's menu (called the Parameters Menu), teachers can make decisions related to the timing of the program and the cues and feedback provided to the learner. Among the choices in the Cues/Feedback menu are whether or not the program uses speech and sound effects, whether the screen should go blank when it's time to press the switch, and whether the synthesizer prompts the student if he or she has not responded after a

set time limit. The Timing menu sets the level of the program (1, 2, 3, or 4), the amount of time the student has to respond, how long the switch must be held down, and the length of the action delay. The action delay is the amount of time between the switch press and the action on the screen; this is a useful feature for students who need time to shift their attention from the switch to the monitor. During the operation of the program, the teacher can press Control-W to change any of the Timing parameters. For example, the level of the program can be changed if it is too easy or too difficult for the student.

It is also possible to set the menu of Join the Circus to operate by switch or keyboard commands. With the menu in the switch mode, students can make their own decisions about which activity to work with. The program can be personalized to some extent by having the speech synthesizer address the student by name. To make this happen, the teacher chooses Names from the Parameters Menu and enters the phonetic spelling of the name of player 1 and, if level 4 of the program is being used, that of player 2.

Source: From Rena B. Lewis, *Special Education Technology: Classroom Applications* p. 199. Copyright © 1993 by Brooks/Cole Publishing Company. Used by permission of Wadsworth Publishing Company.

educational and philosophical movements in the field today have been directed toward the preparation of individuals with severe disabilities for integration in local communities. The need for advance planning and continual instruction in the skills and behaviors needed to maximize the potential for successful experiences in future environments has resulted in the development of specific programs and extensive research focused on the transition process.

Transition Between Levels of School

Transition programming in educational settings often begins immediately for the infant born with severe disabilities. As soon as the need for specialized services is recognized, interventions are put in place that are designed to prepare the child for success in future environments as well as the present one. Programs are available at day-care centers, through home-based instruction, and in preschools that are, in part, designed to help the infant or child move to an integrated setting or to prepare him or her for the next level of schooling.

The process of preparation for a new school situation will take place as long as the child is in the school system. If a child is already in an integrated setting, the change from elementary school to a middle school, or from junior high school to senior high school, will need to be addressed in the curriculum. All children must learn to cope with the new physical environment, the usually larger number of students, and the progressively greater freedoms that are present as they go from first through twelfth grade. The individual with severe mental retardation must be prepared to cope with these changes. If the student is also moving from a segregated school or a segregated classroom to an integrated one, additional challenges must be addressed through transition programming.

Transition from Segregated to Integrated Settings

The education of students with severe or profound levels of disabilities has, on the whole, been segregated. The recent movement to end the practice of segregating students with severe disabilities is reflected in the transition plans of students of all ages. Many transition plans, therefore, contain programming and educational goals intended to enable students to move to a partially or fully integrated school setting. In some instances, these goals may be to prepare students to move from a protective, residential school to a classroom in the local public school. For other students, the goals may be to move them from a separate lunch held in their classroom to a fully integrated lunch with all of the other students in the school, or for them to join the regular classroom for certain nonacademic or even academic subjects.

The individualized transition plan prepares the child with disabilities for new environments.

Transition plans that include a focus on inclusion will probably contain many skills and experiences that address different aspects of communication, socialization, and independent movement. A student who has little or no experience interacting with nondisabled peers will not have the skills needed to benefit from new school situations. The transition plans may thus include trial experiences in the new school to help the student gradually get accustomed to the change.

Successful transition into an integrated environment depends on appropriate educational programs and support.

As you might expect, the success of a student's transition into an integrated environment will depend not only on the appropriateness of the educational program the student receives before the move but on the support the student receives once he or she is in the school as well. Cooperative planning between the student's present and future teachers will help to facilitate a smooth transition.

Although many school personnel are becoming more receptive to the integration process (Stainback, Stainback & Stainback, 1988), those involved in transition plans should always anticipate possible resistance. Letting people know exactly what to expect and ways to deal with potential difficulties will help alleviate anxiety. Often, visits to schools with existing integrated programs for students with severe and profound disabilities, or films of such schools, can provide a demonstration of effective programming.

Another factor critical to the successful movement of students with severe disabilities from segregated to integrated facilities is the role of parents. When it comes to decisions related to integrated placements, particularly if they involve changes in schools, parents may be concerned about the quality of programming in a new school or class situation and about the safety of their child, or they may be worried that their child will be rejected in the new situation.

These feelings will be less pronounced if the parents have been planning for transitional placements during the course of the child's life. Parents may find support, encouragement, and strategies for helping to prepare themselves and their children through support groups composed of other parents of children with similar disabilities who have experienced the same concerns. Teachers and school administrators can help to get parents together if groups do not exist already in the community. Parents also might benefit from observing model pro-

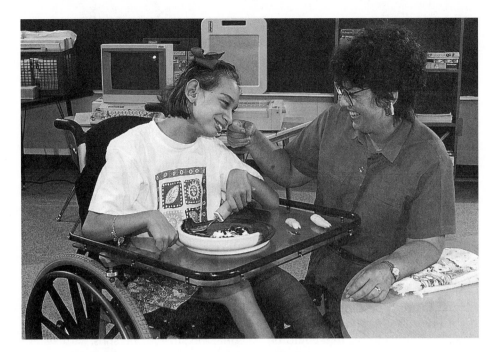

Instruction in life skills forms the core of the curriculum for many students. Adapted materials and equipment can facilitate the extent to which an individual can participate in important skills such as eating, dressing, and cooking. (Bob Daemmrich/The Image Works, Inc.)

grams that include integration and from communicating with personnel at the new school (Hanline & Halvorsen, 1989).

Transition from segregated to integrated settings can involve residential as well as school settings. Up until very recently, the vast majority of individuals of all ages who experienced severe or profound levels of mental retardation lived in segregated residential facilities. Most of these were institutional or private settings such as nursing homes. During the past two decades, however, many of these individuals have moved to smaller and more integrated residences, such as group homes, or to live with their families. According to Taylor, Lakin, and Hill (1989), the number of children and youth in long-term residential facilities decreased from 91,000 to 48,450 in the years from 1977 to 1986. Similarly, according to the U.S. Department of Education's Eighteenth Annual *Report to Congress on the Implementation of the Individuals with Disabilities Education Act* (1996) only 1.4 percent of students with disabilities, ages 3 to 21, were served in residential or hospital environments during the 1993–1994 school year.

Transition to an integrated setting focuses on helping families keep and support their child in the home and on enabling adults to live as independently as possible and to maximize interaction within the local community. Both the child who has been living at home and the child who has lived in a segregated facility must receive transition training for adult living. In many cases, it will be possible for individuals with autism or severe mental retardation to live in group homes or apartments in a community setting. People living in independent or semi-independent housing must be prepared emotionally and technically. Skills involved in cooking, cleaning, dressing, recreational activities, and transportation must be taught and will usually require extensive planning and instruction. Preparation in these skills and in related ones must begin early and then be extended to enable the individual to function in the specific home or apartment setting.

Transition from School to Work

Probably the most commonly perceived meaning of the term *transition* across the field of special education is the transition from school to work settings. Preparing students with severe disabilities to go into the work force, particularly the community work force, is a major educational goal.

Although it is suggested that transition programming from school to work begin at least five years before graduation from school, preparation is often a major component of the curriculum throughout the student's educational experience (Noonan & Kilgo, 1987; Wehman et al., 1987). The transition process will encompass not only skills directly related to a work situation but also the necessary skills involved in social interaction, self-help areas, and transportation.

An essential component of all school-to-work transition programs is community-based work experience. When possible, the student should try out several types of work experiences and have an important decision-making role in job selection (Brooke et al., 1995; Wehman et al., 1987). How receptive are business owners to training opportunities for students with severe disabilities? As you might expect, the receptivity will vary from person to person and from community to community. Aveno and Renzaglia (1988) approached sixty-one community businesses that could be potential job sites for persons with severe mental retardation (stores, restaurants, recreational facilities, etc.) and found that the business personnel had generally positive attitudes toward community integration of the students. Although the attitudes were generally supportive, Aveno and Renzaglia suggest that teachers recognize the need to develop strategies to help increase positive attitudes in the community. Examples they suggested included in-service training and opportunities for structured exposure to persons with severe disabilities.

Teaching in community-based settings involves some of the same processes and people discussed in Chapter 4. For example, job coaches go with students to the work site to provide on-the-job instruction. Supported employment is a desired goal for many young adults with severe disabilities. Continued business and community support is needed, however, to provide adequate opportunities for supported employment to interested individuals (Brooke et al., 1995).

Teachers also need to look at ways to teach students to work independently in the work situation. **Self-management procedures** have been taught to students with severe mental retardation to facilitate independent performance (Lagomarcino & Rusch, 1989). These procedures include self-monitoring or recording of completed tasks and giving praise or other reinforcement to yourself when a task or step of a task has been completed. For example, a student might have a series of five photographs that are used as prompts for the five steps needed to complete a task, such as setting a table in a restaurant. A self-recording procedure might involve putting a check or mark beside each picture as the task is completed. Students who can learn to monitor themselves accurately will require less direct supervision over time and, therefore, may be more likely candidates for permanent employment opportunities.

Permanent employment in community settings is the ultimate goal of transition programming from school to work; it requires not only effective instructional techniques but also extensive coordination among the school, family, employers, and adult service agencies. Remember that the primary service providers for people with severe and profound mental retardation will change from the school to adult agencies once the students reach the age of 22. Work-

Joining the community work force is a major educational goal for many students with severe disabilities.

Self-management procedures facilitate independent performance.

related goals that are intended to extend into the student's adult life must include the cooperation and participation of case managers from the community service agencies.

Ethical Issues

The ethical issues that have arisen in the area of severe and profound disabilities revolve around the basic rights of all individuals: the right to life, the right to education, and the right to freedom from persecution. Professionals in the areas of medicine, education, and law have become involved with children with severe disabilities and their parents in attempts to resolve some of these issues and to find answers to some very disturbing questions. The fact that questions are raised at all relative to the human and constitutional rights of individuals with severe or profound levels of disabilities is difficult for many of us to understand. As we present these issues, we will attempt to provide you with both sides of the controversies. It is inevitable, however, that our biases will be revealed through the discussion. We do not feel that it is appropriate for any professional in the field of special education to present noncommittal statements on issues that are so fundamental to the philosophy we espouse.

Ethical issues arising from severe disabilities concern the rights to life, education, and freedom from persecution.

The Right to Life

Do all newborn infants have the right to live? Should lifesaving surgery be performed on infants who have an assortment of potentially painful and disabling physical and mental disabilities? Should heroic measures be taken to save the life of an infant with suspected severe mental retardation? Do parents, doctors, lawyers, or the government have the right or responsibility to make life-and-death decisions for these children?

These questions are at the heart of the ethical issue of the right to life of children born with severe mental retardation and physical disabilities. In essence, the questions are asked because judgments are being made at the time of a child's birth about the prospective quality of life of that child. **Quality of life** refers to the extent to which an individual can participate in, enjoy, and be aware of the experience of living. When a child with severe mental and/or physical disabilities is born, assumptions are also made about his or her prospective quality of life. Sometimes these assumptions focus on whether or not the child's life is worth living, whether the mental or physical disabilities experienced by the child will enable him or her to have a meaningful life. Often these assumptions are accompanied by concern about the physical pain or discomfort the child is likely to experience, the prospect of a painful death later in life, or the likelihood of an existence filled with endless surgical procedures and medical treatment. In other instances, the presence of moderate, severe, or profound levels of mental retardation may lead to negative assumptions about the child's quality of life. All of these considerations have come into play when medical decisions are made about whether or not to treat children with severe disabilities when life-threatening conditions occur. In some cases, the decision is made that, due to the prospect of a poor quality of life, the infant should be allowed to die.

Although allowing any infant to die because of nontreatment is illegal (Orelove & Sobsey, 1987), such cases are rarely prosecuted. A major reason that

Quality of life refers to the extent to which an individual is aware of, participates in, and enjoys life.

many of the deaths of nontreated newborns are not investigated and do not result in litigation is the feeling by many individuals that these decisions can and should be made by the parents of the children and their physicians (Hentoff, 1985). When an investigation has occurred, it has usually resulted in extensive media coverage and publicity (Lyon, 1985), which has done little to encourage further prosecution. Certainly, any parent who chooses to withhold treatment, or, in some instances, nutrition from a child is making an incredibly difficult decision. Yet the fact remains that if this type of decision were made for an infant without a disability, the persons responsible for allowing the infant to die would unquestionably be punished.

Orelove and Sobsey (1987) present five basic alternatives for the right-to-life issue: (1) to treat all nondying newborns, (2) to terminate the lives of selected infants who are not determined to be viable individuals, (3) to withhold treatment according to parental discretion, (4) to withhold treatment according to a quality-of-life determination, and (5) to withhold treatment judged not to be in the child's best interest. All of these alternatives, with the exception of the first, involve subjective determinations that will result in the life or death of the child. Who, if anyone, has the right to determine if the child has the right to live? This, of course, is the root of the dilemma. Once this right has been placed in the hands of the parents or physicians, their personal criteria for the quality of life will serve as the basis for life-and-death decisions.

Smith (1989) points out that most of the individuals who make decisions about the potential quality of life for individuals with mental retardation, including parents, physicians, and lawyers, have had little, if any, experience living, working, or spending time with persons with any degree of mental retardation. This lack of familiarity results not only in fear for the child's future but often in misconceptions about the potential quality of life of individuals with varying levels of mental retardation.

The Right to Education

We may take it for granted that all children and adolescents have the right to receive an education. Legally, this was not the case for individuals with severe and profound levels of mental retardation until 1975, when P.L. 94-142, the Education for All Handicapped Children Act (now known as IDEA), was passed. Even now, although the law states specifically that all children have the right to a free and appropriate education, controversy persists. The source of the controversy lies in the extent to which education is actually possible in some individuals with profound mental retardation. If, as some contend, there are children or adolescents who cannot benefit from educational programs, there remains the question of whether these individuals would qualify for school-based programs.

Some people feel that not all children will profit meaningfully from educational programming.

There are a few students whose levels of disability are so severe as to limit greatly the amount of instruction to which they can respond. These students will receive educational programming that may be limited to sensory stimulation and efforts to establish some type of communication skill or preskill, such as eye contact. Questions have been raised by some people about the need to continue educational programming for individuals with such profound levels of mental retardation. Their feeling is that it is misleading to describe every child as educable and that it must be recognized that some students will not profit meaningfully from educational programming and should not be subjected to such programs. This point of view, when expressed by special educators, is supposedly applicable only to a very small number of children, and proponents stress that documented educational efforts must precede the label of ineducability.

Other special educators, however, feel that no child should be identified as unable to benefit from educational programming. There are a number of reasons for this point of view. Some express a fear that because such judgments are subjective and cannot be monitored across educational settings, a large number of students with profound levels of mental retardation will be labeled ineducable without receiving adequate or appropriate programming. Others have suggested that such determinations will undermine the progress made in the area of education for students with severe and profound levels of mental retardation by placing a limit on instructional efforts and expectations. Certainly, few individuals who taught several decades ago would have anticipated the amount of learning and skill now routinely acquired by individuals with all levels of mental retardation.

Other professionals feel that no limits should be placed on instructional efforts and expectations.

Perhaps the most important concern, however, involves the philosophy of education revealed when instructional effort is evaluated in terms of the amount or quality of student response. Ferguson (1987) proposes that education should be presented because of our commitment to individuals and should not be measured in terms of a cost-benefit standard. She suggests that it is our criteria for "meaningful" responses or functional skill acquisition that contribute to the constant delineation of a portion of the population as ineducable, or not capable of meaningful learning. In other words, she suggests that as long as we feel the need to justify education in terms of the types or amount of skills students are able to learn, we will always find a group of students who will be considered ineducable. According to Ferguson, the right to education does not have to be earned by the student; we should simply espouse the philosophy that we are committed to educating everyone.

The Right to Nonaversive Interventions

One of the pressing issues both within and without the community of special educators is the use of **aversive interventions** for reducing or eliminating inappropriate, abusive, or self-abusive behaviors. Aversive interventions are typically defined as those that involve the presentation of unpleasant consequences or stimuli as a means of modifying behavior. This issue applies to the educational programming of all students with disabilities, but it is strongest in the area of severe disabilities. Many students with severe and profound levels of mental retardation, severe behavior disorders, or autism exhibit some behaviors that may be self-destructive, injurious to others, or extremely inappropriate in any given setting or situation. Historically, a variety of interventions that could be considered aversive in nature have been used to reduce or eliminate these behaviors. These included the use of restraints, corporal punishment, and, in some cases, electric shock. Today, aversive treatments are used infrequently. Great care has been taken in special education planning procedures to avoid the use of aversive interventions. A specific protocol and guidelines have been established for teachers to follow if they want aversive procedures to be considered for a specific student's educational program.

Today, aversive treatments are used infrequently.

One area in which aversive procedures are still used to some extent, however, is the treatment of self-abusive behavior, particularly when that behavior could be considered life-threatening or could result in severe mutilation, as in a behavior such as head banging. Some teachers find aversive procedures to be an acceptable option because of the potential for rapid elimination of the behavior. Other special educators feel very strongly that no aversive consequences should be included in students' educational programs. The Association for Persons with Severe Handicapping Conditions (TASH) has issued several statements in support of a completely nonaversive philosophy of behavior management and education. This organization's statements reflect the feelings of many teachers and parents of individuals with severe and profound disabilities that any use of aversive or painful techniques is not necessary, obstructs the development of more efficient positive approaches to behavior management, and is contradictory to the individual's right to happiness and basic freedom from persecution.

SUMMARY

■ Severe mental retardation is defined as an IQ score of 40 or below, and profound mental retardation as an IQ score of 20 or below accompanied by deficits in adaptive behavior. Severe and profound disabilities are caused by a variety of genetic and environmental factors and are usually identified at birth.

■ The effects of a severe disability on the child include cognitive difficulty in making connections between the action and the environment, relatively small physical size and high risk of health problems, delays in or lack of oral communication, and limited social skills due to lack of interaction with others.

■ Educational issues include normalization, integration, and an appropriate life-skills curriculum. Normalization involves age-appropriate treatment and providing environments and representations of individuals that are as close to normal as possible. Integration refers to both physical and social integration. The functional curriculum emphasizes preparation for life and instruction in integrated skills useful in school, work, or home.

■ Transitional programming for children with severe and profound disabilities includes preparation for changes in schools, for movement from a segregated to an integrated setting, and for work after school.

■ Basic rights, including the right to life, to education, and to nonaversive interventions, have been questioned for people with severe disabilities. We have discussed both sides of the controversies while upholding our view that all individuals' rights should be protected.

KEY TERMS

severe disabilities
severe mental retardation
profound mental retardation
autism
echolalia
stereotypic behaviors

applied behavior analysis
normalization
functional curriculum
environmental inventory (environmental analysis)

contingency intervention curriculum
self-management procedures
quality of life
aversive interventions

MULTIMEDIA RESOURCES

The Association for Persons with Severe Handicaps (TASH), 26 West Susquehanna Avenue, Suite 210, Baltimore, MD 21204, (410) 828-8274, website: http://www.tash.org.

Autism Society of America, 7910 Woodmont Avenue, Suite 650, Bethesda, MD 20814-3015, (800) 3-Autism, website: http://www.autism-society.org/. This site provides information and resources for professionals and parents interested in autism.

Behavioral Disorders, Journal of the Council for Children with Behavioral Disorders (August 1997, Vol. 22, No. 4). The August 1997 issue contains a comprehensive critique of the Lovaas Early Intervention Project and a response to that critique.

Center for the Study of Autism, P.O. Box 4538, Salem, OR 97302, website: http://www.autism.org/. Research descriptions and updates related to interventions for individuals with autism.

Orelove, Fred P., and Dick Sobsey. *Educating Children with Multiple Disabilities: A Trandisciplinary Approach* (Baltimore: Brookes, 1987). This text gives a model for providing services that relies on cooperation among teachers, therapists, and parents and includes specific techniques and strategies for teaching children with severe mental retardation and motor or sensory impairments.

Wilcox, Barbara, and G. Thomas Bellamy. *The Activities Catalog: An Alternative Curriculum for Youth and Adults with Severe Disabilities* and *A Comprehensive Guide to the Activities Catalog* (Baltimore: Paul H. Brookes, 1987). Both the catalog and the accompanying guide offer hundreds of innovative approaches for designing meaningful curriculum for persons with severe disabilities.

Williams, Donna. *Nobody Nowhere: The Extraordinary Autobiography of an Autistic* (New York: Times Books, 1992). This fascinating autobiography tells of one woman's struggle to discover why she was different and how she learned to integrate the reality of the outside world with her inner world of perception.

USING YOUR KNOWLEDGE

 Commonalities: How do people with severe disabilities benefit from integrated school settings? Investigate several local schools, including preschools, elementary schools, and high schools. What accommodations have been made for students with severe disabilities? What goals have teachers with mainstreamed students set for their classes? How are these goals similar or different from the goals set for all students in the classroom?

 Collaboration: Why is a functional or life-skills curriculum of primary importance for people with severe disabilities? Obtain several curricula from local public and/or residential schools. What characteristics do all the curricula have in common? Are there any significant differences? To what extent are individuals in community or home settings involved in the curricula?

 Commonalities: What is your position on the issue of rights for people with severe disabilities? How did you develop your view?

Can Do: What are some specific strategies that classroom teachers can use to prepare their students for inclusion of a student with severe disabilities?

WHAT YOU CAN DO NOW

1. **Visit a teacher or transition coordinator in a local school who specializes in working with individuals with severe or profound mental retardation. Ask to observe the teacher working with students in community-based settings.**

2. **Identify a task you do frequently as part of your daily or weekly routine, such as doing laundry or preparing a meal. Carefully observe and write down all of the components of that task, including specific behaviors, and any decisions that must be made during the completion of the task. Prepare some ideas for how you could teach all of these task components.**

3. **Locate several grocery stores or fast food restaurants in your local community. Before visiting them, make a list of things you might need to know if you were teaching individuals with severe disabilities—for example, the location of specific food items, exits, and check-out lines in the grocery store; or methods of ordering, use of picture cues, and location of trays and condiments in the fast food restaurants. Then visit each location. Identify the similarities and differences at each location. Which would be the easiest location at which to begin instruction?**

4. **Go to a meeting or conference of the Autism Society or the local organization for individuals with autism in your community. Identify the local issues or concerns that are discussed by the parents and professionals.**

Children Who Are Gifted and Talented

T HIS chapter examines the category of students who are identified as gifted and talented. We cover changes in the definition of giftedness over time, the effects of giftedness on a student and his or her family, the teacher's role in identifying students who are gifted, and the influence of programs designed for gifted students on the education of *all* students. As you read, think about these questions:

■ **What does it mean to be gifted?**

■ **What is the teacher's responsibility toward students with high ability?**

■ **What can a teacher do to modify the curriculum for the needs of a student who is gifted?**

Commonalities: What teaching strategies and enrichment activities can you use to improve the thinking skills of *all* children in your classroom?

Collaboration: How can you include other teachers and members of the community in providing a challenging education for students who are gifted and talented?

Can Do: What specific strategies and techniques will be most helpful for students who have both intellectual gifts *and* learning disabilities?

When you hear the term *gifted* used to describe a child, what images come to mind? Often, the first one is of a 3-year-old who reads the encyclopedia or a 12-year-old who is graduating from Harvard with a straight-A average. These images are mostly false. Though gifted children such as these exist, they do so mostly in fictional books or made-for-TV movies. In reality, students who are gifted and talented are more similar to other students than they are different from them. They find some school subjects hard and others easy; they want friends to sit with them at lunch and play with them at recess; and they need the support of parents and teachers if they are to achieve academic and social success. Students who are gifted have special learning needs that, like all other categories of exceptionality, are best addressed by a curriculum that takes these special needs into account. You, as a classroom teacher, are in the best position to ensure that the gifted and talented students whom you teach will be able to take full advantage of their talents.

Definitions and Terms

Generally, it would be appropriate to begin a chapter on giftedness wih a definition of that term. However, that is easier said than done. Instead, in this section you will read about the various conceptions of giftedness that have evolved over the past hundred years or so. You will also read about some individuals who have devoted their lives to studying students with gifts and talents, as well as current ideas about intelligence and giftedness.

It's hard to find two "experts" who agree on a single definition of giftedness. For that matter, it is difficult to find two experts who agree on whether *giftedness* and *talent* are synonyms or merely related terms. **Giftedness** often refers to exceptional intelligence or academic ability, while **talent** is often used to indicate exceptional artistic or athletic ability. These distinctions are too simplistic, however, in a time when, as we shall see, new theory and research are challenging our traditional ideas about intelligence, giftedness, and talents.

Although the problem of defining giftedness has perplexed educators and psychologists for generations, everyone seems to agree on at least one thing: There is a universal fascination with people—especially children—who are intellectually very capable.

Giftedness is a complex and controversial subject.

Early Scholars and Their Thoughts on Giftedness

From the time of the earliest scholars to today's most influential theorists, debate has centered on whether abilities and talents are born or made. This question continues to be of interest to teachers, who have a considerable stake in the belief that experiences can make a difference! In the 1800s, giftedness was often considered a personality flaw. Lombroso, a nineteenth-century physician, proffered a popularly held view that genius was just a short step from insanity. Other nineteenth-century theorists believed that each individual had only so much brain power to expend and that if a person used up this intellect early in life, she or he could expect an adulthood filled with madness or imbecility. This "early ripe, early rot" theory, though scientifically groundless, was believed by many nineteenth-century scholars.

According to early views of giftedness, it is a step away from insanity, and environment plays no role in developing talent.

■ **Galton**   When Sir Francis Galton began his study of eminent scientists (*English Men of Science*, 1890), he concluded that "genius" (the nineteenth-century

Gardner's multiple intelligences theory identifies musical intelligence as an important characteristic in young people. (Cynthia Carris/Newsweek)

term for *giftedness*) was a natural talent composed of three traits: intellectual capacity, zeal, and the power of working. However, Galton believed fully in the idea that geniuses were born, not made. He dismissed the role of environment in the development of talent, even going so far as to suggest that "inferior specimens—for example, the mentally handicapped" (Kitano & Kirby, 1986, p. 36)— be sterilized to safeguard society from the further production of mental defectives.

■ **Terman** Using Galton's work as a cornerstone of his own, Lewis M. Terman is generally credited as being the "grandfather" of gifted education in the United States. Beginning with the publication of his article "Genius and Stupidity" (1906) and continuing until his death in the 1960s, Terman left his mark on all psychological research with his longitudinal study of over 1500 children determined to be gifted because of an IQ score of 140+ on the Stanford-Binet Intelligence Test. Today, this original group of 1500 "Termites" is still studied (Friedman, Tucker, Schwartz, Tomlinson, Keasy, Martin, Wingard & Criqui, 1995). The Terman legacy can be found in his five-volume series, *Genetic Studies of Genius* (Terman et al., 1925, 1926, 1930, 1947, 1959).

Terman's work did much to dispel the myths of the eventual mental breakdown of individuals with gifts or talents, for his picture of highly able children was one of absolute mental health—of children who were immune from social and emotional crises. As his career progressed and his knowledge of gifted persons deepened, Terman realized how complex the phenomenon of giftedness was. Near the end of his career, Terman acknowledged the powerful influence of family, marriage, self-confidence, work habits, and mental health in the

Terman's longitudinal study of 1500 gifted children dispelled many misconceptions about giftedness.

development of talent, for even among his 1500 high-IQ subjects, vast discrepancies existed in their contributions to society (Delisle, 1991).

■ **Hollingworth** Leta S. Hollingworth, a contemporary of Terman at Columbia University, added another dimension to the understanding of people with gifts and talents. A psychologist by training, she had tested thousands of children with mental disabilities before becoming interested in extreme intelligence. Hollingworth, who began a public school program for gifted elementary students in New York City, is best remembered for her recognition of the element of vulnerability that she knew to be a part of these very bright children.

Hollingworth's research and writing concentrated on the humanity of children with gifts and talents, and the idea that individual students had unique personalities in addition to their IQs. In effect, Hollingworth presented a middle ground: She identified specific social and emotional concerns that might affect the behavior of students with gifts and talents. A tribute to Hollingworth's continuing impact on the field is shown by renewed interest in her work (Silverman, 1990).

Hollingworth identified social and emotional concerns that might affect students who are gifted and talented.

Current Definitions of Giftedness

A complete history of ideas about giftedness, talent, or intelligence cannot be written in these few pages. More thorough analysis of these topics is available elsewhere (Thurstone, 1924; Gould, 1981), and you may wish to consult them once you have completed this book and this course. Now let us turn to the theorists who are influential today in the education of gifted children.

Contemporary views on the nature and scope of giftedness are still tied to concepts of that nebulous construct, **intelligence.** As you recall from Chapter 4, intelligence is the capacity to acquire, process, and use information. Terman's early work suggested that giftedness was limited to a select few who scored 140+ on an IQ test. One important contributor to contemporary understanding, Paul Witty, moved the thinking in a different direction. Witty suggested that anyone "whose performance is consistently remarkable in any potentially valuable area" (Witty, 1940, p. 516) should be considered gifted. He based this assertion less on statistical evidence and more on observation of the world around him. Thus, the poet whose words make you weep, the teacher who inspires you to learn, and the architect who causes you to look skyward in awe would be considered gifted, regardless of their IQ scores.

Taking this thought a few steps further, Joseph Renzulli (1978) elaborated on the idea that giftedness lies not so much in the traits you have as in the deeds you do. His conception of giftedness highlights the importance of **creativity** (the ability to generate original or imaginative ideas) and **task commitment** (the ability to stay focused on a task to its completion), in addition to above-average intellectual abilities, in the development of gifted behaviors (see Figure 12.1). Like Witty, Renzulli believed that IQ alone provides insufficient evidence of giftedness, and only after a student, an architect, or a poet creates a visible product can an analysis be made of that person's intellect. This product-based formula for giftedness fits right in with our own culture's current emphasis on performance and educational accountability. For these reasons, Renzulli's conception of giftedness has enjoyed wide popularity among educators.

According to Renzulli, giftedness includes creativity and task commitment as well as above-average intellectual ability.

Robert Sternberg and Howard Gardner, two psychologists whose work has revitalized the debate on intelligence, propose broader views of human capabilities. Gardner's **theory of multiple intelligences** (1983) postulates that there are

General Performance Areas

Mathematics	Visual arts	Physical sciences
Philosophy	Social sciences	Law
Religion	Language arts	Music
Life science		Movement arts

Specific Performance Areas

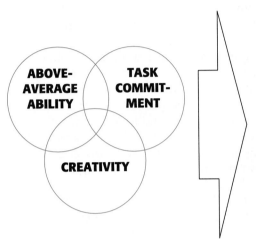

Cartooning	Demography	Electronic music
Astronomy	Microphotography	Child care
Public opinion polling	City planning	Consumer protection
Jewelry design	Pollution control	Cooking
Choreography	Fashion design	Furniture design
Biography	Weaving	Navigation
Film making	Play writing	Genealogy
Statistics	Advertising	Sculpture
Local history	Costume design	Wildlife management
Electronics	Meteorology	Set design
Musical composition	Puppetry	Agriculture research
Landscape architecture	Marketing	Animal learning
Chemistry	Game design	Film criticism
Etc.	Journalism	Etc.
	Etc.	

Figure 12.1
A Graphic Representation of Renzulli's Definition of Giftedness
Source: Joseph S. Renzulli, "What Makes Giftedness?" *Phi Delta Kappan 60* (1978): 180–184. Used by permission of the author.

at least seven distinct intelligences (see the accompanying box, "Gardner's Seven Intelligences"). An abundance of talent in any of these areas constitutes giftedness, according to Gardner, and although people can be capable in several different intelligences, one does not have to excel in every area to be considered gifted. (See "A Closer Look: Model Programs for Gifted Students" for a description of a program based on Gardner's theories.)

Sternberg adds yet another tile to this ever-expanding mosaic with his **triarchic theory,** which includes three kinds of intellectual giftedness: analytic, creative, and practical (Sternberg, 1997; Sternberg & Clinkenbeard, 1995). Students

Gardner postulates at least seven kinds of intelligence.

∼ Gardner's Seven Intelligences

- Linguistic intelligence (verbal facility)
- Logical-mathematical intelligence (symbolic reasoning)
- Musical intelligence (performance-based or the ability to *perceive* great music)
- Spatial intelligence (heightened awareness of structural components of ideas and objects)
- Bodily-kinesthetic intelligence (lithe movement and expression)
- Interpersonal intelligence (ability to lead or inspire others)
- Intrapersonal intelligence (deep self-knowledge and actualization)

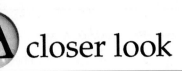

A closer look

Model Programs for Gifted Students

Like many other districts, the Baldwin Park schools, northeast of Los Angeles, relied on test scores to identify gifted students, and the result was "really lopsided," says coordinator Carol Kaylor. Hispanics made up 80 percent of the student body but only 30 percent of the gifted programs, while Asians, Filipinos, and whites were overrepresented. The mix has changed markedly since administration started asking teachers, parents, and even peers to help pick out the brightest children. One group of second-graders nominated a quiet, unassertive child who spoke only Spanish and had average test scores. The teacher began observing her more closely and noticed that she stayed inside during recess, drawing pictures and writing poems on her own. Her work included sketches of a rabbit from the front, side, and back perspectives, very unusual for a 7-year-old. A one-on-one test with a Spanish-speaking psychologist revealed that she had an IQ of 175. Overall, the gifted program is now 46 percent Hispanic, though Kaylor stresses that wasn't the goal of the reforms: "As far as we're concerned, the kids could have come from Mars . . ."

Educators are making a special effort to identify talented students from poor homes, the group least seen in gifted programs. Since 1988 the federal government has awarded some $10 million a year in demonstration grants for that purpose in a program named after the late U.S. Senator Jacob Javits of New York. Deep in Brooklyn, N.Y., one district is using a Javits grant to fund a gifted program based on Gardner's theories in four schools in Canarsie and East Flatbush, working-class communities with many West Indian immigrants.

Specially trained teachers spend months assessing every kindergartner, one-on-one, for strengths in all seven of Gardner's intelligences—linguistic, logical-mathematical, musical, spatial, bodily-kinesthetic, and intra- and interpersonal relationships. Kids who show special promise in one or more areas are grouped together, all day, from the first grade on, and taught with novel methods that capitalize on their widely varying skills.

Sternberg proposes knowledge-based skills, social/practical intelligence, and fluid abilities.

who are analytically gifted are effective at analyzing, evaluating, and critiquing; those who are creatively gifted are skillful at discovering, creating, and inventing; and those who are practically gifted are good at implementing, utilizing, and applying (see Figure 12.2). In Sternberg's view, "the big question is not how many things a person is good at, but how well a person can exploit whatever he or she is good at and find ways around the things that he or she is not good at" (1991, p. 51).

Finally, the federal government definition of giftedness states that gifted children are those

P.L. 97-35 defines giftedness as high performance in intellectual, creative, artistic, leadership, and academic areas.

who give evidence of high performance capability in areas such as intellectual, creative, artistic, leadership capacity, or specific academic fields, and who require services or activities not ordinarily provided by the school in order to fully develop such capabilities. (P.L. 97-35, Education Consolidation and Improvement Act, sec. 582, 1981)

The federal definition specifies areas of giftedness; it allows for gifted traits and gifted behaviors; and it ties in the definition of giftedness with the need to provide special educational programs for children identified as gifted. Overall, it is a comprehensive definition that has been adopted enthusiastically by many states.

One day, an all-black "Javits" first-grade class at P.S. 135 was crayoning pictures to Beethoven's Fifth Symphony and excitedly comparing it to works by Chopin, Mozart, and Prokofiev. "Tell me how it makes you feel and tell me *why*," teacher Lynn Rosen demanded. Hands flew up across the room.

Some kids who had learning or behavioral problems have flourished under teaching that allows them to use their bodies. Some parents were also surprised to learn that their kids had special talents. Says Joyce Rubin, the district's director of gifted programs: "It's like that song from *Carousel*—some said, 'If I have to beg or borrow or steal, I'll get this kid music lessons!'"

Rubin's program does stress hard work and rigorous academic achievement. But critics say that some reformers elsewhere misinterpret Gardner's work, using it as a rationale for mushy "self-esteem" programs that insist that everyone is special in some way. Instead, many top educators hope that Gardner's emphasis on individual tal-

ents will be used to encourage all students to move at their own pace in specific subjects, with more challenging curricula for some advanced students, rather than march in lock step with traditional grade levels. That's in sharp contrast to the old "tracking" system, where top kids were often grouped together for all subjects, and where those who tested below the cutoff were excluded and ignored. "We should be trying to meet the individual needs of every child," says [Carol] Mills [director of research at Johns Hopkins University's Center for Talented Youth]. "For one, it might mean an accelerated math class and an average reading class, or special education in written language. That makes more sense than saying you're either gifted or not."

Unlike P.L. 94-142 and P.L. 99-457, P.L. 97-35 does not *require* educational services for students identified as gifted, nor does it provide any funds for implementation of gifted programs. Since its enactment, however, many individual states have incorporated the federal definition into state legislation; and, since more than half the states now require special educational provisions for students identified as gifted or talented, this federal definition has encouraged a substantial increase in state-based initiatives for serving students with gifts or talents.

> Federal law does not require educational services for gifted students but encourages state initiatives for serving these students.

It is doubtful that one definition of giftedness will ever be written that satisfies every theorist, educator, and parent. Nor is it likely that all gifted children will ever be identified for the special education they require. Still, it is important for you to realize that if you are unsure about "exactly" who is gifted, you are joined in your lack of certainty by some of the world's experts on the theory and measurement of intelligence.

Criteria for Identification

If a child begins to read independently at the age of 3 or a 15-year-old graduates as high school valedictorian, it is quite apparent that you are observing atypical behavior—not "abnormal" behavior, but behavior that appears in advance of its usual developmental onset.

Figure 12.2
Sternberg's Triarchic Theory
of Intelligence
According to Robert Sternberg, intelligence comprises
analytic, creative, and practical abilities. In *analytical
thinking*, we try to solve familiar problems by using
strategies that manipulate
the elements of a problem or
the relationships among the
elements (e.g., comparing,
analyzing). In *creative thinking*, we try to solve new
kinds of problems that require us to think about the
problem and its elements in
a new way (e.g., inventing,
designing). In *practical thinking*, we try to solve problems that apply what we
know to everyday contexts
(e.g., applying, using).

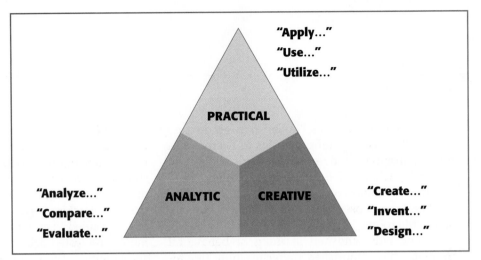

Source: Figure from *In Search of the Human Mind* by Robert J. Sternberg, p. 395. Copyright © 1995 by Harcourt Brace & Company, reproduced by permission of publisher.

Advanced development is one of the most commonly applied criteria in the identification of students with gifts and talents. Measurement of this advanced development historically has been through standardized tests commonly given by school psychologists or teachers.

Individual IQ tests, like the WISC-III or the Stanford-Binet (see Chapter 4), can be used to assess intellectual capacity. However, the extensive costs in terms of time and money needed to administer and score the tests have caused most school districts to forgo their use. Instead, standardized group intelligence tests are often used. When given as part of the annual battery of achievement tests administered to all students, these group tests provide a general assessment of how students compare intellectually with their classmates. Those students who score two or more standard deviations above the mean of the test (which gener- ally results in an IQ of 130–135) are often classified as gifted. Similarly, students who score at the 95th percentile or above on standardized achievement tests of reading, math, and other content areas are often identified as academically gifted.

Achievement and IQ tests, though, have been criticized as being too narrow in focus. Barbara Clark (1997) points out that tests do not give an accurate de- scription of a person's capacity or potential and Frasier (1987) cautions that standardized tests often ignore the special background and characteristics of culturally diverse populations. Many scholars have noted that using IQ tests as the primary means of identifying candidates for gifted programs inevitably leads to underrepresentation of children with disabilities as well as those from culturally and linguistically diverse backgrounds (Salvia & Ysseldyke, 1998).

Informal assessment by parents, teachers, peers, and community members who know the student can provide school personnel with non-test-based infor- mation about the range of a student's specific skills or talents. Beverly Parke (1989) suggests that people consider affective, cognitive, and creative character- istics (see the accompanying box, "Characteristics of Students with Gifts and Talents").

The yardsticks for measuring giftedness are many and varied. The teacher's role in identifying and assessing giftedness and talent is discussed later in the chapter.

Students scoring two or more stan- dard deviations above the mean on IQ tests are usually classified as gifted.

Standardized tests that determine giftedness are criticized because they may lead to underrepresenta- tion of children from minority groups.

Characteristics of Students with Gifts and Talents

Cognitive Characteristics	Affective Characteristics	Creative Characteristics
Early ability to manipulate symbols (e.g., alphabet, numerals)	Sensitivity to others' perceptions of them	Resourcefulness: able to come up with multiple solutions to a problem
Unusual ability to recall facts	Preference to be with adults or older children	Playful attitude toward work
Large storehouse of information on a variety of topics	Inner drive toward perfection	Unbridled curiosity to explore new ideas
Ability to generalize to larger concepts	Highly developed sense of right and wrong	Challenges the status quo and the conventional
Long attention span	Advanced sense and appreciation of humor	Preference for holistic (conceptual) thinking; sees the "big idea"
Rapid acquisition of information	Intensity, perseverance, and commitment to tasks of interest	Questions authority
Uneven cognitive and physical abilities		

Source: Beverly N. Parke, *Gifted Students in Regular Classrooms* (Boston: Allyn & Bacon, 1989), pp. 19–23. Copyright © 1989 by Allyn & Bacon. Reprinted/adapted by permission.

Factors Contributing to Giftedness

For as long as gifts and talents have been recognized and studied, the question of nature versus nurture has been pondered. Are individuals with gifts and talents endowed with a pool of superior genes, or is their environment responsible for the emergence of superior performance? The best answer seems to be "It depends."

Hereditary and Biological Factors

Scientists and educators agree that genes are but one element in the complex development of human intelligence. Vernon (1979), in arguing against overemphasizing any one element—genes, environment, or opportunity—in the development of intelligence, reminds us that since none of these factors occurs in total isolation from the others, it is impossible to tell where the effects of heredity end and the impact of environment takes over.

Both genetics and environment play crucial roles in determining giftedness.

Environmental Factors

The role played by the family in the development of gifts and talents has been studied extensively, and virtually every study has shown the importance of nurturance. Wendy Roedell (1989) points to the special importance of early identification "that begins with the child's earliest years and continues with appropriate educational experiences throughout the child's educational life" (p. 27). Benjamin Bloom (1985), in his study of Olympic athletes, musical prodigies, and others of exceptional achievement, points to the vital role played by the family (not just the parents) in channeling these remarkable talents and downplays the role of the school in the realization of noteworthy accomplishments.

Family encouragement of the child's talents is of critical importance.

The role played by peers, especially among economically disadvantaged children, has also been shown to have a significant impact on the desire to

Children Who Are Gifted
and Talented

Family members playing
games and puzzles with
young children are helping
to lay the foundation for the
development of strategies
and abilities. (Elizabeth
Crews)

achieve academically (Kulieke, 1985). In short, the debate over the development
of gifts and talents has grown far beyond the nature-nurture arguments of past
generations. Today, the emphasis is on the practical: designing structure and
strategies at home and at school that encourage these talents to bloom and
blossom.

Prevalence

Considering the variety of definitions of giftedness, it is not surprising that the
prevalence of gifts and talents in the population is also open to debate. For example, if you were to use the criterion of an IQ of 140 as the baseline for intellectual giftedness, you would exclude 99 percent of the population. If, however,
you were to use the federal definition of giftedness written in P.L. 97-35, 3 to 5
percent of the school-age population would qualify as having gifts or talents.
Renzulli's conception of giftedness (1986) identifies a set of behaviors that can
emerge in students who are above average (though not necessarily superior) in
ability. Thus, he suggests a figure of 15 to 20 percent of the population as capable of performing gifted behaviors. And Henry Levin (1996) believes that if we
take time to look, we will find that almost every student in a class is above average in some skill, ability, or knowledge area—everyone is gifted in some way.

Many theorists and researchers, although arguing about the exact prevalence of gifts and talents, do agree that for funding purposes the figure of 5 percent is useful. Thus, although experts may disagree philosophically on where
giftedness begins and ends, the prevalence figure of 5 percent is common in
most states.

In most states, the prevalence of
giftedness among the population is
placed at 5 percent.

Special Populations of Gifted Students

As much as we'd like to think otherwise, the term *gifted child* conjures up images of well-scrubbed, academically able youngsters who live on the right side of town. Certainly, this type of youngster represents one category of students who are gifted, but there are also others:

- Ryan Walter, a 13-year-old from a single-parent home, who lives in subsidized housing
- Allyson Matt, a 9-year-old who is legally blind
- Wayne Floyd, a cadet at the U.S. Air Force Academy who spent his high school years in Skwenta, Alaska (where he was in a graduating class of four)
- Maja North, an award-winning graphic designer, singled out for her excellence in vocational arts

These students give evidence that gifts and talents exist in varied cultures and contexts and that talents are sometimes accompanied by a disability.

Thanks to the broadened conceptions of giftedness addressed earlier in this chapter, these "atypical" gifted children do not seem as unusual as they would have seemed a generation ago. And recently, when funds were appropriated by the federal government to identify and serve gifted children (the first such funds in over a decade), the target populations were those gifted students who had been "historically underrepresented" by mainstream gifted programs.

The following sections address some special populations of gifted children and the special needs these young people have.

Gifted Girls

Until the impact of the women's movement began to be felt in American education in the 1970s and 1980s, little was done to identify and develop giftedness and talents in girls. Although it is now generally understood that it is illegal to discriminate on the basis of gender in any arena, unconscious biases may still prevent girls who are gifted and talented from being identified and from persevering through rigorous educational programs, particularly in middle and secondary school. It should be recognized that gifted girls often have a broader conception of what constitutes *achievement* than boys; it is not limited to degrees and career status, but is the successful balance of professional, personal, and relationship achievements in their lives (Hollinger & Fleming, 1992). Gifted girls should be encouraged to take the most challenging coursework available, to engage in play activities that are physically challenging and occasionally competitive, and to speak out and defend their opinions in groups (Kerr, 1991). See the accompanying box, "Profile of Gifted Females," which lists some distinguishing characteristics of girls who are gifted.

Gifted girls must be identified, supported, and challenged, particularly in the middle school years.

Gifted Students with Disabilities

As early as 1942, Hollingworth saw the possibility that disabilities could coexist with giftedness. But only recently have the needs of these "twice exceptional" students been addressed.

∼ Profile of Gifted Females

Regarding younger gifted girls

- Many gifted girls are superior physically, have more social knowledge, and are better adjusted than are average girls, although highly gifted girls may not seem as well adjusted.

- Highly gifted girls are often second-born females.

- Highly gifted girls have high academic achievement.

- In their interests, gifted girls may be more like gifted boys than they are like average girls.

- Gifted girls are often confident in their opinions and willing to argue for their point of view.

- By age 10, gifted girls express wishes and needs for self-esteem and are interested in fulfilling those needs through school and club achievements; highly gifted girls, though, may be loners without much need for recognition.

- Actual occupations of parents do not affect gifted girls' eventual career choices.

- Gifted girls have high career goals, although highly gifted girls aspire to careers having moderate rather than high status.

Regarding adolescent females

- Gifted girls' IQ scores drop in adolescence, perhaps as they begin to perceive their own giftedness as undesirable.

- Gifted girls are likely to continue to have high academic achievement as measured by grade point average.

- Gifted girls take less rigorous courses than gifted boys in high school.

- Gifted girls maintain a high involvement in extracurricular and social activities during adolescence.

- Highly gifted girls do very well academically in high school; however, they often do not receive recognition for their achievements.

- Highly gifted girls attend less prestigious colleges than do highly gifted boys, which may lead to lower-status careers.

Remember that, like any list of group characteristics, these are not hard-and-fast rules; there will be exceptions to all of them in gifted females.

Source: Adapted from *Smart Girls* (Revised Edition) by Barbara Kerr. Copyright © 1998. Used by permission of Gifted Psychology Press.

Some gifted students have learning disabilities, sensory impairments, or motor limitations.

June Maker (1977) was among the first to suggest that options should be provided in schools for highly able students who also had learning disabilities, sensory impairments, or physical disabilities. But she warned that her work was merely a beginning, serving to "identify issues and raise questions to a greater degree than it solves or answers them" (p. xi). Later, Whitmore and Maker (1985) combined their efforts and experiences to produce more specific suggestions for working with students who are gifted and disabled in school and community settings. Their suggestions appear in the accompanying box, "Strategies for Working with Students Who Are Gifted and Disabled."

Students with learning disabilities are a unique group. Reis, Neu, and McGuire (1997) conducted in-depth interviews with twelve young adults who were successful in college while receiving support services for their identified learning disabilities. All had been tested earlier in their schooling and found to have high IQs. The researchers found that these students uniformly reported negative experiences in elementary and secondary school. Their learning disabilities tended to be identified relatively late in their schooling, despite problems that had appeared early; they reported negative interactions with teachers, some of whom told the students they were lazy and could achieve if they worked harder; they felt isolated from peers and unaccepted by them. But be-

~ Strategies for Working with Students Who Are Gifted and Disabled

- Find alternate ways to help these students attain their goals rather than change (that is, lower) their aspirations.
- Locate specialized equipment and technology that can help students attain their objectives and share their talents with others.
- Allow students to explore their environments fully, rather than isolating them from others or making every activity a "safe" one.
- Plan activities and interventions that take advantage of the students' individual strengths.

cause these students developed compensation strategies, had parental support, and participated in a university learning disability program, they succeeded despite their early negative experiences (see the accompanying box, "Successful College Students with Learning Disabilities"). Sally Reis and her colleagues suggest that it was the combination of their high abilities and disabilities that set them up for problems in school such as the late referrals to special education and poor relationships with teachers.

These students had other advantages and a secret weapon: "Each person in this study had a mother who devoted herself to using different strategies to help her child succeed. This assistance was given regardless of whether the mother worked outside of the home and regardless of how many other children were in the family. One may ask, therefore, what happens to children who do not have a similar source of support?" (Reis, New & McGuire, 1997, p. 477).

Underlying all approaches to locating and serving gifted children with disabilities is a need to change society's attitudes and perceptions. There remains a need for each of us to see that *cap*ability is more important than *dis*ability.

High-ability students with learning disabilities can succeed in college with the right supports.

Underachieving Behaviors in Gifted Students

Think of someone you knew in school who was always told by teachers, "You're a smart kid; I know you could do better if you wanted to." Usually, this type of student frustrates teachers and parents, for they see a lot of talent going to waste. The technical term applied to students whose aptitude is high but whose performance is low (or mediocre) is **gifted underachiever,** but the less technical terms are the ones that sting—terms like *lazy, unmotivated,* or *disorganized.* Whatever you call these students, one thing is certain: When *you* get one in *your* classroom, you'll wish there was some magic elixir available that would cause this "underachievement" to disappear.

Some gifted students are underachievers.

What causes this disheartening underachievement? Hollingworth (1942) believed that students with an IQ of 140 spend half of each school day in activities that are unchallenging and monotonous, and Delisle and Berger (1991) state that students with academic gifts may learn to underachieve if the curriculum presented to them is not intellectually challenging. The result is often a poor attitude toward school ("school is boring") or even misbehavior, as shown by the comment of this 12-year-old girl: "I learned I was gifted in third grade. I would finish my work early and disturb others because I had nothing to do" (Delisle, 1984, p. 11).

Methods of modifying school curriculum and structure for students with gifts and talents are discussed later in this chapter. What is important to note here is the intimate link between school achievement and school attitude; for if intellectually able students perceive school as drudgery, it is unlikely that they will develop their talents fully (Whitmore, 1980).

Intellectually gifted students who dislike school may not develop their talents.

～ Successful College Students with Learning Disabilities

Students who had high ability levels and also had learning disabilities found that the following strategies and supports helped them succeed in college work.

Compensation strategies

- Use of computers and word processors, books on tape, self-advocacy skills

Learning strategies

- Methods of learning to study, notetaking, identifying key points

Planning techniques

- Time management, use of metacognitive skills such as mnemonic devices, setting work priorities

Parental support

- Parents, particularly mothers, were energetic advocates for their children.

Participation in a university learning disability program

- The students cited help with study skills, a network of support, and a consistent program director.

Self-perceived strength and future aspirations

- Students had a strong work ethic and the conviction that they could succeed.

Source: S.M. Reis, T.W. Neu, and J.M. McGuire, "Case Studies of High-Ability Students with Learning Disabilities Who Have Achieved," *Exceptional Children* 63:4 (1997), 463–479.

Researchers seem to be at a loss to offer effective solutions to the problem of underachievement. Some of the first educators to write about this dilemma were Raph, Goldberg, and Passow (1966), who offered school-based solutions to reversing patterns of underachievement. Joanne Whitmore (1980) has produced the definitive work on this topic, and her approach combines curricular changes (focusing on a child's strengths and interests), family involvement (parent conferences and "partnership" in rewarding even small improvements in performance), and self-concept education (based on the premise that students who feel good about themselves will choose to achieve).

Later efforts have suggested more mechanistic solutions—like behavioral contracts—and more coercive measures—like punishment (Rimm, 1986). These efforts, though possibly successful in the short term, tend to be less effective than the approaches described by Whitmore.

However, there is one point on which all researchers agree: The earlier the problem of underachievement is detected and addressed, the more hopeful is the prognosis for positive change. The problem of underachieving behaviors will not be easy to solve, but if you look toward making the gifted child's schooltime relevant, interesting, and intellectually stimulating, chances are good that the student's response will be positive. See the accompanying box, "Working with Gifted Underachieving Students," for some additional suggestions.

When underachievement is detected early, the prognosis for positive change is good.

Culturally Diverse Gifted Students

Gifts and talents exist in children of every race, culture, and socioeconomic group. However, gifted program planners have often been criticized for not looking hard enough to find talents in children who may not represent the majority culture or its values. Case in point: In Arizona, 16.7 percent of all school-age students use English as their second language, but a scant .14 percent of these students are involved in gifted programs (Maker, 1987). Indeed, blacks are overrepresented in all categories of special education except for one, gifted edu-

As you work with gifted children whose daily performance does not match their tested aptitude, keep these truths in mind:

- *Underachievement is often context specific.* Seldom do gifted children underachieve at *everything* they do. In fact, they may be *very* successful in particular subjects (in or out of school) that interest them.

- *Underachievement is in the eyes of the beholder.* The level that constitutes success is very much individually de-

termined. Thus, do not assume that your students or colleagues all agree on where underachievement stops and achievement begins.

- *Sometimes it is a child's curriculum that is underachieving, not the child.* If a gifted child must complete page after page of worksheets on topics he or she has already mastered, the child may refuse to complete the work or do so only intermittently. The problem here is not with the child but with the curriculum.

cation, where they are severely underrepresented (Baldwin, 1985). So, although every thinking person agrees that one's skin color or primary language are not intrinsic limitations to the expression of one's talents, many gifted programs are filled with students from the white, middle-class culture of our population.

Cohen (1990) saw this as a problem related to *misuse* and *nonuse:* misuse of assessment instruments (like IQ tests) that were normed on middle-class students with middle-class experiences and nonuse of alternative methods of non-test-based indicators of giftedness—like nominations from parents or community leaders or a portfolio of a student's work samples that indicate superior performance. Paul Torrance (1969), ever conscious of the fact that different cultures have different standards of appropriate behavior, reminded us to look for qualities like *expressive speech, enjoyment and leadership in group-based activities,* and *the ability to improvise with commonplace materials and objects* as indicators of giftedness in culturally diverse groups.

> Using non-test-based indicators, children with gifts and talents can be found in every race, culture, and socioeconomic group.

Identifying gifted children from diverse cultural backgrounds has become a major goal of professionals involved in gifted child education (Clark, 1997). Once the students are identified, the program itself must be tailored to suit the needs, interests, learning styles, and cultural values of its participants. Cohen (1990) encourages approaches that promote multiethnicity so that all students come to appreciate each other's cultures and backgrounds, while Eby and Smutny (1990) believe it important to establish links with the child's family, especially by someone who is familiar with the cultural heritage of the program's students.

> Programs for gifted children should help students learn about many cultures.

As the twenty-first century approaches, and our world becomes even smaller through the wonders of travel and technology, program planners for gifted students, and *all* educators, must look for new ways to identify and foster the talents of each child. The challenge is great, but the individual and societal benefits, should we succeed, are even greater.

Highly Gifted Students

Just as educators who work with students with developmental disabilities classify disabilities by level of severity—mild, severe, or profound, for example—gifted child educators sometimes do the same thing regarding the label of gifted. Often, an IQ score is used to define a population that has come to be called the **highly gifted.** Terman and Merrill (1973) and Whitmore (1980) use an

IQ score of 140 to classify a child as highly gifted, while McGuffog, Feiring, and Lewis (1987) call an IQ of 164 "extremely gifted." And Hollingworth (1942), in an early and classic study, used an IQ of 180 as the point at which giftedness is manifest in an extreme form.

Despite this apparent disagreement over the exact point where "regular" giftedness ends and "extreme" giftedness begins, most researchers agree on the distinctive characteristics of this population of students. For example, highly gifted children generally:

- Prefer adult company to that of their agemates
- Maintain an extraordinary energy level, even as infants, and frequently require less sleep than children their own age
- Exhibit marked discrepancies between intellectual abilities and social skills
- Display intense reactions regarding injustices and moral wrong. They perceive that "everything matters, and it matters that it matters." (Kline & Meckstroth, 1985, p. 25)

Most gifted children are placed in regular classrooms, which often don't meet their needs.

A regular classroom placement for a child whose intellect surpasses that of 99.99 percent of his or her classmates can pose problems. Yet Gaunt (1989) found that most highly gifted children are placed in regular school classes, and even though many of these students are involved in part-time enrichment programs, the majority of their time is spent in classes that take their extreme intelligence into account only minimally (Kearney, 1988).

The problems and solutions involving highly gifted students are complex and varied, but the extremely gifted child has been receiving increasing attention over the past decade. Advocates for this population of students point out that even the best school program that includes opportunities for **academic enrichment** (broadening the experience base of the students without changing the instructional objectives) and acceleration may fall far short of meeting the needs of highly gifted children. Radical acceleration (for example, skipping several grades), early entrance to college (some preteen students have attended university full time), and home schooling are some options that have been used effectively to meet the needs of this population.

Despite the abilities of these students, all advocates point out the continued need to treat these most-able youngsters as the children they are. Take, for example, David Huang, who graduated from high school at the age of 8 and began college the next year, maintaining an A- in such courses as organic chemistry and calculus. He began reading at age 2, and at age 4 taught his father the BASIC computer language. But after school David enjoyed riding his bike with friends and watching cartoons (especially Woody Woodpecker and Scooby-Doo). And David's mother drove him to school each day and helped him cross the street, because he sometimes forgot to look both ways (*Time*, Oct. 21, 1985).

Students with exceptional abilities have nonacademic needs that must be addressed.

If David were one of your students, what would you do? Ideally you would do the same thing you would for a child who has severe disabilities: Modify the environment and curriculum as best you could and demand help from others to ensure that his or her intellectual, social, and emotional needs were addressed fully.

Will you be intimidated by children like David? Perhaps, but once that initial reaction passes, you must take care to see that highly gifted children succeed both in school and in life—and you cannot accomplish this alone.

Effects of Giftedness and Talents

Students who are gifted and talented represent a cross-section of humanity: All races, cultures, sizes, and shapes are apparent. Yet as different as these individual students seem at first glance, their intelligence has affected their cognitive and social-emotional development in similar ways. The following sections highlight some of these effects, as well as the impact of the gifted/talented student on the family.

Effects on the Child

We will first look at how giftedness affects individuals in the areas of cognitive, social and emotional, and physical development.

■ **Cognitive Development** As discussed in the first part of the chapter, there are many perspectives on the nature of giftedness and cognitive development. In general, cognitive development is frequently accelerated, which can cause problems in the classroom. For example, a child who learned to read independently at the age of 3 may have difficulty in a kindergarten class where he or she is expected to learn the alphabet. A junior high student well versed in algebra may question the point of completing pages of long-division problems. A 10-year-old who perceives subtle distinctions in moral reasoning may be frustrated by agemates who see only cut-and-dried, right-and-wrong solutions.

■ **Social and Emotional Development** Very closely tied to the cognitive effects of giftedness and talents is the social and emotional impact of these talents on students' performance. Students may feel "different," misunderstood, and socially isolated. To address these issues, several authors (Adderholt-Elliot, 1987; Buescher, 1984; Colangelo, 1989) have recommended particular strategies:

Some gifted students experience social isolation.

These fourth-graders in a New York City public school are in an accelerated science class, working cooperatively on a soil absorbency project. (Elizabeth Crews/The Image Works, Inc.)

- Explaining their abilities to students so they can understand their specific areas of talent

- Reviewing expectations and setting them realistically, so that gifted students do not interpret any level other than perfection to be failure

- Establishing short-term, reachable goals and various ways of reaching these goals

- Concentrating on the idea that although they may be better at some activities and academic areas than other students, they are intrinsically no better than these students.

The interplay between intellect and emotion is clear to people who work with students with talents and gifts. An intellectually able 6-year-old may cry uncontrollably when confronted with inequity or injustice, either on the schoolyard or while watching the evening news.

A fastidious high school junior may consider herself a failure if she receives a grade of B+ in advanced physics. It is your job, as a teacher, to understand that intellectually capable students, whatever their ages, be appreciated for their strengths and their vulnerabilities; for even though these young people are smart, they are not small adults.

■ **Physical Development**   Early research by Terman (1954) showed students with gifts to be stronger, bigger, and healthier than their agemates. In fact, Terman's findings did much to dissolve the stereotype of the gifted student as a bespectacled weakling who carries a briefcase to school instead of a backpack. However, Terman's research included primarily children from advantaged backgrounds whose physical prowess was bolstered by nurturing and plentiful home environments. Today, as gifted programs expand to students from all cultures and socioeconomic backgrounds, we see an array of physical characteristics that defies any simple categorization. In effect, a gifted student has no certain look or appearance.

The gifted student cannot be identified by appearance.

One effect of giftedness that relates to physical development occurs frequently in young gifted children. Kitano and Kirby (1986) and Roedell, Jackson, and Robinson (1980) have researched situations in which a child with advanced cognitive development is able to visualize an idea or a picture but is unable to reproduce this thought in writing or drawing because his or her fine motor development is not as advanced. The ensuing frustration may cause the child to feel that he or she is "stupid." Teachers and parents can deal with these differences between levels of cognitive and physical development in several ways:

1. Become a scribe, transferring the child's ideas onto paper.

2. Explain that although it is frustrating not to be able to reproduce what their minds can see, this will change as their muscles become stronger.

3. Group this child with another student or peer who might be able to work as a partner in written or artistic projects.

Acceleration may have social implications for students, particularly in adolescence.

School-age students who are gifted may face another physical challenge if they are accelerated. **Acceleration** involves skipping several grades to provide a more appropriate curriculum; as a result, accelerated students are two or more years younger than classmates. Especially in junior high and high school, this becomes an important consideration, as few adolescents want to be left behind when growth spurts occur for everyone but them. This possibility, which can also have social side effects, should be reviewed before acceleration is undertaken.

■ **Gifted Adolescents** Struggling for social acceptance, experiencing physical changes, and conducting inner searches for meaning in one's life are some of the benchmarks of adolescence. Gifted adolescents are as concerned about these issues as are their agemates, but there may be unique implications for gifted adolescents. (See the accompanying "First Person" for examples.)

Birely and Genshaft (1991) point out that adolescence for gifted students involves special concerns in the social and emotional, educational, ethical and spiritual, and career and lifestyle domains. In the area of social and emotional issues, gifted females may struggle with decisions related to the often conflicting needs for social acceptance and the full expression of their talents (Kerr, 1985). In effect, gifted girls often feel they must suppress or disguise their abilities to be accepted by boys. Conversely, Alvino (1989) contended that most gifted males feel obligated to use their academic talents, often at the cost of the emotional aspects of their lives; the result may be increased stoicism and tendency to overwork. Teachers should be aware of these potential issues and be prepared to provide appropriate support.

> Gifted adolescent girls often feel they must suppress or disguise their abilities to be accepted.

Educationally, adolescents with gifts and talents tend to question how best to further their intellectual development. For example, if they are admitted to college after their junior year in high school, do they stay in high school and not miss the senior prom and varsity football, or do they go on to college and seek social outlets there? Or, given the opportunity to pursue intellectual challenges independently, do they choose this route and forgo other options? Chad Gervich, a 15-year-old gifted student, summarizes these issues when describing his difficult decision whether to attend a summer residential program for gifted students:

> The biggest problem I encountered was my friends. They never let me forget I was applying to "Nerd Camp," "Geek City," and "Dweebville." "It's summer; school's out," they'd say. "Why do you want to go back?" That was a question I couldn't easily answer. Even I didn't know. (Delisle, 1992).

Ethical and spiritual issues may become important to gifted students at an earlier age than is typically expected. Clark and Hankins (1985) posed twenty-five philosophical questions to children ages 6 to 10, who were matched on all variables except intellectual ability. They found that in response to such questions as "What is the worst thing that could happen in the world?" and "Who is the best person in the world, living or dead?" the gifted children were found to be more knowledgeable about their world and more pessimistic about their future.

> Ethical and spiritual issues may be especially important to gifted students during adolescence.

Career and lifestyle issues include a problem that many people see as a benefit: the ability to be successful in so many fields that selecting a career becomes problematic (Birely & Genshaft, 1991). The societal expectation that gifted students should become highly valued professionals (doctors, lawyers, professors) may intrude on an adolescent's personal choice if he or she wishes to enter a career such as artisan, laborer, or homemaker (Hollinger, 1991).

Through discussion of these issues with other adolescents with similar talents, or through academic and curricular programs that address intellectual and emotional growth, many of these issues can be addressed before they become problems (Silverman, 1991).

Perspectives from Gifted Adolescents

These are excerpts from essays written by eighth-graders at the Mirman School, a private school in Los Angeles for children who are gifted and talented.

When I was in first grade, I bought my own math book, because the rest of the class was still doing addition and subtraction, when I was on multiplying and dividing decimals. My teacher took my book away and told me I had to stay with the class. When I came home and told my mom, she went and talked to the teacher. The teacher said I could correct the other kids' papers. When I did this, the other children made me an outsider. For the rest of the school year . . . I'd come home from school and just cry, because I was so bored. The only place I felt like I could be myself and would be halfway accepted and not be teased was on the playground playing basketball, because we were all equal there.

Gifted children are very unique and are different from normal kids in many ways. They are also different among themselves, for some kids excel in certain areas where others don't. All I can say to teachers is, if you end up with a gifted child in your class or someone that excels in a specific subject, don't hold them back, give them whatever they want or need. Because if you don't they'll become disruptive or a problem at school. Most kids won't get the chance to come to a school like Mirman, and a gifted mind is a horrible thing to waste.

Slade Smith

Effects on the Family

The effects of a student's giftedness or talents on the family have received considerable attention, and much research has been conducted to determine the effect of labeling a gifted child, and on the transfer of values between parents and a gifted child.

Joyce Van Tassel-Baska (1989) investigated the variables attributed to the success of gifted students from economically disadvantaged families and found that genuine support and encouragement of talents predicted high achievement—a reaffirmation of the important role of parents in the full development of their children.

There are, unfortunately, cases where a gifted student is exploited by the family or put on public display for all to see. There is also the possibility that a

In all respects I consider myself to be a normal 14-year-old girl. I love horror movies, talking on the phone, and anything that has the word chocolate in it. I can't go a week without shopping, and I can never quite keep my room clean. Yet when I tell my cousins what school I go to, they reply, "Isn't that for gifted kids? Hey, do you think you can help me with my math homework?"

It bothers me that kids think I'm some kind of wonder, and that I spend eighteen hours a day studying, and use words like *preposterous* and *masticate* in everyday language. The truth is I find math difficult and I despise Latin. I would much rather be watching "Seinfeld" than studying for a science test. Instead of discussing quantum numbers with my friends, I'd much rather discuss the latest episode of the "X Files" (which happens to be my obsession, and I've seen every episode at least ten times).

I don't think that teachers should treat gifted children any differently from other children. My mom is a first-grade teacher, and she teaches each one with respect and trust. I think *that* is the key to becoming a successful teacher. Not how many chapters can you get through in a week, and not how well your students do on a test, but how much they *enjoy* learning.

Rachel Stone

gifted child's talents may be ridiculed by parents, although the parents in Roald Dahl's *Matilda* are not representative! In those instances, the underlying problem may be related to dysfunctional family dynamics rather than the direct result of the child's giftedness.

Educational Issues and Instructional Strategies

Educational options for students with gifts and talents are many and varied. Many strategies that are appropriate in school settings can also be used in a child's early years, before school placement occurs.

Children Who Are Gifted and Talented

Teachers and parents should gently encourage children to develop their talents. Adolescent girls, in particular, need to see that their academic gifts are valued. (Elizabeth Crews/The Image Works, Inc.)

Early Intervention

Children are often not formally identified as gifted or talented until sometime during their school career—usually in third or fourth grade. Due to particular advanced behaviors, though, many gifted young children show signs of high potential before they enter the classroom, and the people who identify these talents are often the child's parents.

Disagreement exists regarding the appropriateness of early identification of gifts and talents. On the one hand, there are educators who believe that it is imperative to identify and challenge talents at the youngest age possible. Eby and Smutny (1990) argue that such identification helps not only the child but also the child's caregivers; for if teachers, child-care workers, and parents are informed of a young child's strengths, they will be better able to provide academic and creative options that match these strengths. Joanne Whitmore (1980), in her classic study of underachieving gifted students, found that patterns of underachievement were developed during the primary school years, yet intervention seldom occurred until the intermediate grades. This unwillingness to address problems as they emerge means that much remediation will have to be done later, whereas preventive measures could have been less extreme yet equally effective.

Some professionals are concerned that early identification of gifts and talents creates the "superbaby syndrome."

On the other hand, critics of early identification of gifts and talents point to the "superbaby syndrome" as a problem that cannot be ignored. Parents who replace their gifted children's toys and free play with flash cards and classical concerts are, to the critics, misguided in their attempts to challenge their children. Eby and Smutny (1990), in critiquing these efforts, state that such "programs impose adult agendas on their young participants and forget that children learn best through experience" (p. 158).

The label of "gifted" tells us little about a child's specific unique talents. As parents and teachers work together to match a child's needs with appropriate services, they must keep in mind that the child's individual physical, emotional, and intellectual needs must be considered in order to provide a healthy balance of rigor and fun.

Identification and Assessment: The Teacher's Role

It was once considered easy to identify gifted students. An individual intelligence test on which a student scored 130 or higher qualified him or her as intellectually gifted. A student who scored 126 was summarily excluded.

Today, as the validity of standardized intelligence test scores has become more suspect, especially for students from minority cultures (Baldwin, 1991), and educators and parents have become more involved in the assessment of exceptional children, best practices call for multiple measures to be used to identify giftedness in students (Eby & Smutny, 1990). Most often, classroom teachers will be asked to supplement information about a child through the use of behavioral checklists. These checklists come in many varieties, but generally require the teacher to rate a child on a scale of 1 to 4 (1 = seldom; 4 = always) on how often he or she observes behaviors like these:

Today there is a greater likelihood that multiple measures will be used to identify giftedness.

- Learns rapidly, easily, efficiently
- Prefers to work alone
- Has a vocabulary above that of classmates
- Displays curiosity and imagination
- Goes beyond the minimum required with assignments
- Follows through on tasks
- Is original in oral and written expression

Essentially, teachers are being asked to select children who "go to school well" and whom teachers love to have in their classes. Yet if teachers are asked to consider only positive student traits and behaviors, they may not identify some gifted children who could surely benefit from advanced instruction.

Consider your own education. Were you ever in a class where you felt that your time was being wasted or your talents ignored? Perhaps it was a class that was repetitive to you, or one that provided few challenges or little outlet for creative expression. Whatever the reason for your dissatisfaction, do you recall how you acted in that class? It's unlikely that you led an animated discussion or that you were overly eager to answer the teacher's easy questions. In fact, if someone were to observe you in that class, he or she might find that you appeared bored, off-task, or looking for excitement in all the wrong places (like talking to your friends or passing notes). These would hardly seem to be behavioral indicators of giftedness but, in fact, they might be exactly that.

The point is this: When you, as a teacher, are asked to select children for gifted program services, remember that some indicators of giftedness in children are those very behaviors that teachers usually find distasteful—boredom, misbehavior, even incomplete assignments on easy tasks or worksheets. This is not to say that all gifted children display negative behaviors in class, but it is a reminder to you that some gifts are wrapped in packages (that is, "behaviors") that are not so pretty. Be aware of this possibility when you question why a seemingly bright child is responding negatively to a class assignment or lecture.

Some indicators of giftedness are behaviors that teachers find irritating.

The identification of gifted children is a complex, ongoing process (Davis & Rimm, 1989), and it sometimes appears that the main goal is not to locate talents in children but to find ways to exclude them from gifted program services. However, with the insights that can be provided by using a variety of standardized test scores (achievement and intelligence tests); parent, teacher, and peer nominations; and the inclusion of students' prior projects or portfolios as evidence of talent, we will do a better job of locating the variety of abilities that students display both inside and outside of school.

Curriculum Modifications in the General Education Classroom

Every classroom teacher has (or can develop) the skills to work with gifted students within a regular classroom structure. By adapting and modifying the basic curriculum through techniques such as curriculum telescoping and content acceleration, teachers can determine when students have mastered particular skills, allowing them to move on to explore new ideas. Effective use of options such as independent study, cluster grouping, and cooperative learning can help satisfy students' individual learning interests. Finally, the appropriate use of higher-level thinking strategies and creative thinking skills can benefit *all* students, including those who are highly able. We'll discuss each of these methods of modifying the regular classroom in further detail.

> Modifying the basic curriculum can make it more effective for gifted students in the regular classroom.

■ **Curriculum Telescoping**   **Curriculum telescoping,** or compacting, involves an analysis of the specific subject matter (for example, spelling, math, language arts) to determine which parts of those subjects are inappropriate for gifted students because they have already mastered them. Return for a minute to your fourth-grade class. It's math time, and let's assume you are a strong math student. As the teacher hands out worksheets, you have a sinking sense of *dèja vu,* for you are confronted with fifty problems like these: 26×247; 69×189; 24×790; $126 \div 4$; $4216 \div 57$. You think to yourself, "Didn't I see these yesterday? And the day before, too?" A conscientious math teacher would know that not all students in the class need extensive instruction in the basic math operations involved in these problems. In fact, a teacher who knew something about curriculum telescoping would probably not even require good math students like you to complete basic skill worksheets once you had mastered the concepts involved. What would be the point? If you already know how to multiply and divide large numbers, what possible benefit could there be to your completing more of these problems? There are dozens of more difficult concepts in math that you could probably work on instead of these basic skills.

That is the core of curriculum telescoping: determining what individual students already know and allowing them the chance to explore concepts, subjects, or topics that better tap into their talents (Renzulli & Reis, 1985, 1991). Several authors have addressed the logistical problems of curriculum telescoping. Starko (1986) recommends several management techniques, including **group telescoping,** in which the teacher uses preexisting "top groups" in reading or math as the core group to telescope a particular concept or content area (see the accompanying box, "Steps in Curriculum Telescoping"). Figure 12.3 shows documentation for curriculum telescoping.

> Curriculum telescoping allows students to explore new concepts or subjects.

■ **Content Area Acceleration**   Content area acceleration is another modification available to regular classroom teachers. Most often, educators equate *acceleration* with grade skipping, a practice that is not endorsed as enthusiastically

⌁ Steps in Curriculum Telescoping

1. Provide evidence of students' mastery (left column of Figure 12.3).

2. Describe how students may have their basic curriculum modified (center column of Figure 12.3).

3. List options for enrichment activities that take advantage of students' talents (right column of Figure 12.3).

Source: A.J. Starko, "Meeting the Needs of the Gifted Throughout the School Day: Techniques for Curriculum Compacting," *Roeper Review 9:11* (1986), 27–33.

today as in past generations (Pendarvis, Howley & Howley, 1990). However, **content area acceleration** can occur within regular classes at virtually every grade level and within virtually every subject area. It happens every time a teacher allows students to "jump ahead" at a faster pace than most of their classmates. Thus, the first-grade teacher who provides literature to a child who has outgrown a basal reader is accelerating curriculum content for that child; so is the high school science teacher who works with a tenth-grader on physics experiments, even though physics is generally taken by twelfth-graders.

> With content acceleration, students proceed at a faster pace than most of their classmates.

When you accelerate a student's curriculum in a basic skill area, there is always the possibility that other teachers (especially those in subsequent grades) will disapprove of this strategy. Some may prefer that students pursue areas of study that do not infringe on the content they will teach. Others may believe that content acceleration complicates their role as teachers since not all students are taught the same thing at the same time.

The most important consideration, however, remains the student's learning needs, even if fulfilling those needs complicates scheduling or planning. If teachers lose sight of this basic principle, students may be deprived of instruction or content that matches their level of ability. In extreme cases, students may adopt a negative attitude toward school.

> Content acceleration may create complications for teachers, but student learning needs are most important.

Content area acceleration can be a nonobtrusive way to modify the curriculum for gifted students, but like any other activity, it will take practice for you to perfect. See the accompanying box, "Guidelines for Modifying Curriculum," for some tips.

■ **Independent Study** Independent study is one of the more popular forms of classroom modification for gifted students. **Independent study** provides "a chance for students to inquire about topics of interest to them in a manner that allows extensive exploration" (Parke, 1989, pp. 99–100).

> In independent study, students pursue topics on their own, under teacher supervision.

Kaplan et al. (1980) suggest using a process called webbing to help focus a child's specific interests within a broad topic. **Webbing** is a graphic representation of ideas and the relationships among them. In Figure 12.4, the topic of magnets is subdivided into many smaller, manageable subtopics. Students should not be required to complete all of these subtopics, but rather only those aspects of magnets that interest them. A secondary benefit to webbing is that it allows students to see how various content areas relate. For example, students may explore geography ("magnetic poles of the Earth"), English ("famous attractions and repulsions in literature"), and social studies ("history of man's use of magnets"), in addition to the expected scientific aspects of magnets.

> Webbing focuses a child's specific interests within a broad topic by subdividing it into many smaller topics.

Once webbing has been done, students can decide what resources they will need to research their topic and how they will display the knowledge they have

IEP COMPACTOR

Name Wendy, Mike, Carol, Paul, Chris, Kurt   **Age** _____   **Teacher(s)** _____

School Smith _____   **Grade** _____   **Parent(s)** _____

Individual conference dates and persons participating in planning of IEP _____

_____

CURRICULUM AREAS TO BE CONSIDERED FOR COMPACTING: Describe basic material to be covered during this marking period and the assessment information or evidence that suggests the need for compacting.	PROCEDURES FOR COMPACTING BASIC MATERIAL: Describe activities that will be used to guarantee proficiency in basic curricular areas.	ACCELERATION AND/OR ENRICHMENT ACTIVITIES: Describe activities that will be used to provide advanced levels of learning experiences in each area of the regular curriculum.
Math: Houghton Mifflin Mathematics Level 6	Pre- and posttests will be used to check skill proficiency.	Selected enrichment masters
This group scored above 90% ile on CTBS math.	No assignment of math text examples or basic masters for skills already mastered.	Pre-algebra with Pizzaz and After-Math materials
		Logic puzzles: mind benders, logic box
	Students will be individually assigned student text pages and skill sheets as indicated by pretests.	Individual or small-group advanced-level independent study.

Figure 12.3
Individual Educational Programming Guide: The Compactor
Source: Alane J. Starko, "Meeting the Needs of the Gifted Throughout the School Day: Techniques for Curriculum Compacting," *Roeper Review* 9: 1 (1986): 27–33. Copyright © 1986. Reprinted by permission of *Roeper Review*, P.O. Box 329, Bloomfield, MI 48303, and the author.

gained. By following these steps and by putting a specific timeline on the student's efforts, you can use an independent study project to fill the time you have "bought" by telescoping the regular curriculum.

Like any strategy, independent study can be done improperly. Perhaps the most common mistake teachers make is to assume that since they're so smart, gifted students can succeed without any help. Teachers should introduce research skills such as library and computer information searching, generating hypotheses, and basic statistical analysis, which will give students tools for higher-level independent study. Unless a student selects a topic that is specific enough to be manageable, even a gifted student may wallow in a sea of confusion. As a teacher, you will need to provide appropriate direction through a technique such as webbing, as well as support for the independent work.

~ Guidelines for Modifying Curriculum

1. Assess the student's skill level accurately, making sure he or she understands *each* of the concepts involved in any material that might be replaced or skipped over.

2. Talk with the student's teachers from the previous year and the teacher(s) who may be receiving this student the following year. *Team planning can avoid many problems of miscommunication.*

3. Remember that an option other than accelerating content is enriching it. So, if a student skilled in reading and language arts wants something more complex to do, consider activities such as play writing, cartooning, interviewing, or designing posters for a schoolwide project. These projects increase the student's breadth and depth of understanding of a subject.

4. Speak with your school district's director of curriculum or assistant superintendent about materials, resources, and options about which you might be unaware.

■ **Cluster Grouping** In **cluster grouping,** students who are identified as gifted at a given grade level are grouped together in the same classroom with a teacher who has training in educating students who are gifted. The rest of the class is a diverse group of learners. The cluster arrangement allows the gifted learners to be grouped together for some activities and to be mixed with their age peers for others. Cluster grouping appears to be an increasingly popular option (Schuler, 1997).

■ **Cooperative Learning** **Cooperative learning** operates under the assumption that "all students are learners and teachers; all have an equal responsibility to explain to others and discuss with others. The pace of instruction is similar to what it would be in a traditional class, so high achievers are exposed to the same material they would have otherwise been taught" (Slavin, 1990, pp. 6–7). Thus, under cooperative learning strategies, students are grouped heterogeneously in clusters of five or six, and they learn a body of material by capitalizing on the strengths each member brings to the "team." Often, the same grades are awarded to all group members, which is meant to engender a team spirit in which everyone pulls his or her own weight.

In cooperative learning, groups of five or six learn material by capitalizing on the strengths of each member.

Johnson and Johnson (1989) report that "performance on daily assignments and . . . retention tests [show] high achievers working in heterogeneous cooperative groups have never done worse than their counterparts working competitively and individualistically" (p. 318). However, critics of cooperative learning contend that "not doing worse than their counterparts" is not a reason to adopt cooperative learning for gifted students. One opponent enumerates the objections:

> The disadvantages of cooperative learning for academically talented students are primarily those of limiting instruction to grade level materials, presented at the pace of a grade level group and evaluated primarily on basic skill measures. The corollary is that opportunities which can meet intellectual needs may be made unavailable to talented students because cooperative learning is assumed to be a substitute. (Robinson, 1990, p. 22)

Since there is no clear-cut agreement as to whether cooperative learning should be used with gifted students, and if so, how frequently, the new teacher should approach this technique cautiously.

Teachers should be cautious in using cooperative learning with highly able students.

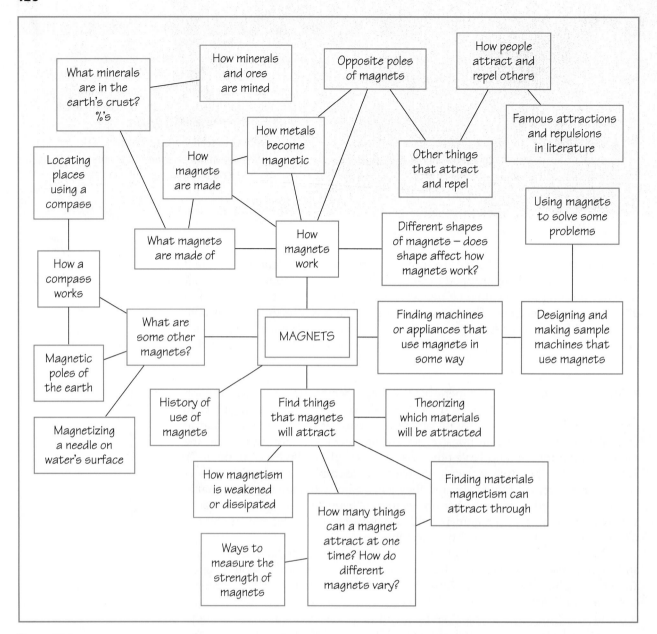

Figure 12.4
A Learning Web
Source: Sandra Kaplan, JoAnn Kaplan, Sheila Madsen, and Bette Gould, *Change for Children: Ideas and Activities for Individualizing Learning* (Santa Monica, CA: Goodyear, 1980), p. 179. Copyright © 1980 by Scott, Foresman and Company. Reprinted by permission.

■ **Creative and Higher-Level Thinking** Creative and higher-level thinking processes are another area in which the curriculum can be modified. Consider the following two questions, either of which could appear on an elementary-level geography test:

1. What is the capital of Massachusetts?
2. Considering the geography of the state of Massachusetts, why might Boston have been chosen to be the state's capital?

The first question requires little thought, merely a good memory. Students need to know nothing about Boston other than that it is the state capital. The second question, though, requires analytical thought and some comprehension of the role that geography, location, and politics may have played in choosing the site for a state's capital.

Gifted students often think naturally—with little direction from parents or teachers—about these "bigger questions," the ones that require the use of more complex levels of thinking. When they are in a classroom setting where the majority of time is spent on activities or questions that have one right answer requiring only rote memorization to deliver, they often feel stifled intellectually. To compound this problem, classroom materials and texts usually emphasize the acquisition of low-level thinking skills (like memorization) rather than the more sophisticated thinking patterns required to answer questions like the second one (Raths, Wasserman, Jones & Rothstein, 1986).

Higher-level thinking skills should be incorporated into the curriculum for gifted students.

There are, however, methods and systems for incorporating higher-level thinking skills into your curriculum. Benjamin Bloom (1956) developed a taxonomy of educational objectives to distinguish among the various ways that questions and teaching strategies can be designed to promote varied levels of thinking (see Table 12.1). Another scholar proposed that teachers should train their students to use three distinct types of critical thinking strategies, which are outlined in the accompanying box, "Critical Thinking Strategies" (Ennis, 1985).

Some problems, however, do not require analytical thinking as much as they require creative thinking. That is, rather than trying to find a *solution* to a problem, it is more important to first determine what the problem itself really is. **Brainstorming** (Osborn, 1963) is a basic creative problem-solving technique. In brainstorming, there are no right or wrong answers, students cannot criticize each others' responses, and "piggybacking" an idea on someone else's is encouraged. Group brainstorming can be the beginning step to positive problem solving.

In brainstorming, participants come up with many ideas on a specific subject.

Teaching materials for all these areas of higher-level thinking are available through such publishers as Good Apple (student workbooks and teacher guides), Cuisenaire Publications (manipulative and written materials), and Midwest Publications (critical and logical thinking). Also, many teacher's manuals to textbooks include "enrichment" questions or activities. Seek these out; your most highly able students will appreciate that you did.

Placement Alternatives

The majority of students who are gifted and talented students are served in the general education classroom—both those who have been identified and those who have not. Even though elementary and secondary classroom teachers can provide rich intellectual stimulation for gifted students, many school districts offer other options that take place outside of a regular classroom setting. Probably the most common service delivery model is **enrichment.** According to Barbara Clark (1997), "Enrichment can refer to adding disciplines or areas of learning not normally found in the regular curriculum, using more difficult or in-depth material to enhance the core curriculum, or enhancing the teaching strategies used to present instruction" (p. 204). Typically, students identified as gifted participate in pullout or afterschool enrichment activities. Clark believes that enrichment is the least desirable option for the gifted student, since it involves the least change in learning opportunities.

Enrichment activities supplement the core curriculum for students identified as gifted.

Table 12.1 Bloom's Taxonomy: Cognitive Domain

Area of Taxonomy	Definition	What Teacher Does	What Student Does	Process Verbs	
Knowledge	Recall or recognition of specific information	Directs, tells, shows, examines	Responds, absorbs, remembers, recognizes	define repeat list name label	memorize record recall relate
Comprehension	Understanding of information given	Demonstrates, listens, questions, compares, contrasts, examines	Explains, translates, demonstrates, interprets	restate describe explain identify report tell	discuss recognize express locate review
Application	Using methods, concepts, principles, and theories in new situations	Shows, facilitates, observes, criticizes	Solves problems, demonstrates use of knowledge, constructs	translate apply employ use practice shop	interpret demonstrate dramatize illustrate operate schedule
Analysis	Breaking information down into its constituent elements	Probes, guides, observes, acts as a resource	Discusses, uncovers, lists, dissects	distinguish calculate test contract criticize debate question solve analyze	appraise differentiate experience compare diagram inspect inventory relate examine
Synthesis	Putting together constituent elements or parts to form a whole requiring original, creative thinking	Reflects, extends, analyzes, evaluates	Discusses, generalizes, relates, compares, contrasts, abstracts	compose propose formulate assemble construct set up manage	plan design arrange collect create organize prepare
Evaluation	Judging the values of ideas, materials, and methods by developing and applying standards and criteria	Clarifies, accepts, harmonizes, guides	Judges, disputes, develops criteria	judge evaluate compare score choose estimate predict	appraise rate value select assess measure

Source: Bloom, Englehart, Furst, Hill, and Krathwohl (1956).

⌒ Critical Thinking Strategies

- *Defining and clarifying problems*, including the abilities to identify a problem's central issue, identify assumptions underlying a problem, and identify appropriate questions to ask to better understand a situation.

- *Judging information*, including the ability to determine the relevance of information and the credibility of sources and observations.

- *Inferring solutions*, including the abilities to make deductive and inductive conclusions and to predict probable consequences of particular actions.

Classroom strategies based on Ennis's theory will prompt independent and logical thinking in children, especially in problem-solving situations encountered in math, science, social studies, and interpersonal relationships.

————

Source: R.H. Ennis, "A Logical Basis for Measuring Thinking Skills," *Educational Leadership 43*:2 (1985), 44–48.

Some school districts have special schools or self-contained classes for students who are gifted and talented. In other locales, a resource room model is preferred. Just as there are a variety of ways to serve students with gifts and talents within a classroom setting, there are multiple options for meeting the needs of these students in other settings. Some of the more popular out-of-class methods are reviewed here.

■ **Resource Rooms** The most popular option at the elementary school level may be the resource room approach. Similar in design and structure to such programs for children with disabilities, the gifted education resource room allows gifted students to work together. Often, cross-age grouping is used, and it is not unusual to see third-grade students working alongside fifth-grade students. One pervasive problem with resource rooms is the consequences gifted students feel due to their participation, as expressed by a 10-year old girl:

> Last year I wasn't at school one day a week (my gifted program was in another school), so I didn't finish all my classwork. I would have finished, but my teacher wouldn't let me bring anything home as homework. When my mother asked her about my grade, the teacher said that "if I was smart enough to go to another school I should be smart enough to keep up with my own classwork." (Delisle, 1984, p. 75)

"Makeup work"—needing to complete worksheets and text assignments in addition to the work in the gifted program—can cause students to question the benefits of their resource room participation. The conscientious classroom teacher, by using pretesting and curriculum telescoping, can relieve many of these problems.

The resource room is a part-time solution to the full-time problem of educating gifted students.

Another problem occurs when the classroom teacher relinquishes responsibility for educating gifted students by assuming that "they're getting all they need in the resource room." Teachers must remember that the resource room presents only a part-time solution to the full-time problem of educating gifted students (Cox, Daniel & Boston, 1985). The resource room works best when its teachers communicate frequently with regular classroom teachers and both work together to benefit gifted students.

The self-contained gifted education classroom denies program services to students who may have talents only in one area.

Tracking, or academic ability grouping, has been criticized for its negative impact on children not in the highest tracks.

Magnet schools emphasize a specific content area to attract students with interests or talents in those areas.

Magnet schools attract a racial, ethnic, and economic mixture while meeting the needs of students with specialized talents.

■ **Self-Contained and Homogeneously Grouped Classes**   Often the option of choice a generation ago, the self-contained gifted classroom is still used today, but less frequently. In this type of class, gifted students are identified and placed together for instruction. This placement limits participation to a select group of gifted children—enough to fill one classroom—while denying gifted program services to those students who may have talents only in particular areas. An additional concern is more sociological in nature, "based upon the apprehension that such a grouping of the bright children will cause the nongifted to regard the gifted negatively, resentfully or hypercritically, and that the gifted, by virtue of being in separate groups, will come to look disdainfully or contemptuously upon the nongifted" (Newland, 1976, p. 271). Whether real or imagined, this fear goes back to our ambivalence about labeling children, especially when one group of students is selected because they have "more" of something than their classmates.

Homogeneously grouped classes are similar to those that are self-contained, with this one exception: Students are grouped according to content area or specialty, based on similar levels of aptitude or achievement. Thus, a student may be in a homogeneously grouped accelerated math class one hour and in a reading class for children of average reading ability the next. Most often used in middle and high schools, academic ability grouping, or tracking, has been criticized for its negative impact on children not in the highest tracks (Oakes, 1985), as it is believed that these children begin to see themselves as less capable, less smart. Others believe that the practice of academic tracking is still open to debate (George, 1988; Slavin, 1988) and in fact, "at the middle [grades] level, [tracking] may be the single most important unresolved issue in education" (George, 1988, p. 22).

■ **Magnet Schools and State-Sponsored Residential Schools**   Magnet schools are designed to place special emphasis on science, the arts, or some other content area and to attract students with interests or talents in that area. These students work with teachers who are specialists in the particular content area.

Often used in large school districts or urban settings, magnet schools can exist at both the elementary and secondary levels. In recent years, magnet schools have been heavily subsidized by federal government funds targeted toward racial desegregation. It was believed that if all students had the chance to attend the school of their choice because of the specialized focus of that school's curriculum, then each school would attract a mixture of racial, ethnic, and economic groups. This goal, as well as the goal of meeting the specific intellectual needs of students with specialized talents, has met with varying degrees of success.

In a magnet school, students receive accelerated and enriched instruction in their areas of greatest strength and interest. For example, if students attend a science magnet, they may spend a lot of time in laboratories conducting experiments. In a creative arts magnet, a portion of each school day will emphasize art, dance, or other creative endeavors. In magnet schools, other basic content areas (reading, language arts, math) are taught, but it is not assumed that students are highly capable in all areas. Thus, a student attending the science magnet may be enrolled in a basic English class as well as an advanced chemistry or biology class.

State-sponsored residential schools, often called "governor's schools," because they are established by an individual state's legislature and governor, have continued to increase in popularity in recent years. Highly competitive, these schools seek nominations from across the state's high schools for unusually talented juniors and seniors who will spend up to two years at the residential setting. The first governor's schools focused almost exclusively on math and science, but now many states have incorporated the arts and humanities into their stringent curricula. Among the states with well-established governor's schools are North Carolina, Louisiana, Indiana, and Illinois. Criticized by some as "hothousing" gifted students by surrounding them only with classmates who are similarly gifted, these residential schools still continue to flourish—as do their students.

State-sponsored residential schools for the gifted and talented have increased in popularity.

■ **Other Options**   Not all educational options for gifted students take place within the school building or, for that matter, within the school year. **Mentorships,** during which time secondary students work with a community member to learn, firsthand, a specific skill, trade, or craft, are common. Research on the effectiveness of mentorships shows the very positive results of these community-school interactions, as participating students learn from the mentor's skill and expertise, receive valued and substantive praise and encouragement, and have as a role model a person who loves his or her field of study as much as does the student (Torrance, 1984).

In mentorships, secondary students learn specific skills, trades, or crafts from community members.

Summer and weekend programs are also offered for gifted students at many colleges and universities. Purdue University's Super Saturday Program, for example, serves children from preschool through high school with a variety of accelerated and enrichment classes each semester (Feldhusen, 1991). The Purdue model has been replicated across the country.

Summer programs can be either day programs or residential in nature, depending on the student's age. In Ohio, each of the thirteen state universities and several private colleges offer one- to three-week "summer institutes," financially supported by the state. Michigan and Iowa also offer extensive summer programs for gifted students.

With summer and weekend programs gifted children remain with their peers; in other programs they progress rapidly through high school and college.

In addition, early entrance to college or dual enrollment programs allow gifted secondary students to progress through high school and college at a more rapid pace. In high schools, students enrolled in Advanced Placement courses may earn up to a year's worth of transferable college credit by taking rigorous courses and advanced placement tests, generally in their junior and senior years. Also, many colleges have an "honors college" component, which offers rigorous, and often accelerated, courses to highly able students. Some colleges encourage full-time enrollment by students as young as 15. Simon's Rock of Bard College in Great Barrington, Massachusetts, has been doing this for over twenty-five years, and Mary Baldwin College in Staunton, Virginia, has a similar program, PEG (Program for the Exceptionally Gifted), open only to young women; these students generally attain both a high school diploma and a college degree within five years.

Program Models

Acceleration and enrichment options for gifted students, as we have seen, have existed for generations. But only within the past fifteen years have organizational models been developed. These models serve to structure the activities in which gifted children participate to provide a "skeleton" format for teachers and gifted program planners.

Each of the models highlighted in this section was chosen from the many that have been proposed; they were selected because they provide, in the words of Joseph Renzulli, "guidelines without straitjackets" (1986, p. vii).

■ **The Classroom Enrichment Model (Grades K–3)**   Unique among the program options available for young gifted children, the **classroom enrichment model** (CEM) (Cohen, Burgess, & Busick, 1990) provides guidance for both identification and programming. After discussing several conceptions of giftedness and reviewing methods of identifying talents or potential in young children (with a heavy emphasis on parent involvement), the authors review ways in which teachers can differentiate their curriculum for able learners—for example, by focusing on higher-level thinking and research skills. The CEM is useful because it allows the flexibility to provide for gifted young children within a regular classroom setting. Because most gifted programs in the primary grades take place within this structure, the CEM, along with other resources that provide clues to curriculum differentiation (Kaplan et al., 1980; Roedell, Jackson & Robinson, 1980; Saunders & Espeland, 1986), is a useful program model for the developmentally appropriate education of young gifted children.

■ **The Enrichment Triad Model (Grades 4–6)**   The **enrichment triad model** (ETM) (Renzulli, 1977) is based on the following premises:

- Some types of academic and creative enrichment are good for all children.
- Students must master certain "process skills" (such as research skills and creative problem-solving) if they are to master curriculum content.
- Students should investigate problems of their own interest, rather than topics chosen by teachers, and they should share the results of their work with audiences outside of their school.

Enrichment models help teachers differentiate the curriculum.

The ETM model builds in the teaching strategies from gifted education for a wider group of students, and allows children to express their talents to others in visible ways.

■ **Schoolwide Models**   With so many interesting and innovative teaching strategies and models designed for students identified as gifted and talented, why not use them to benefit all children? Two school reform efforts attempt to do just that. The **Accelerated Schools Project** (Levin, 1996) operates on the principal that every child is a gifted child (Hopfenberg, Levin, and Associates, 1993). According to Levin,

all students are treated as gifted and talented students, because the gifts and talents of each child are sought out and recognized. Such strengths are used as a basis for providing enrichment and acceleration. As soon as one recognizes that all students have strengths and weaknesses, a simple stratification of students no longer makes sense. Strengths include not only the various areas of intelligence identified by Gardner (1983), but also areas of interest, curiosity, motivation, and knowledge that grow out of the culture, experiences, and personalities of all children" (1996, p. 17).

Accelerated Schools operate with the philosophy that building on the strengths of each student is more successful than identifying and remediating weaknesses. (For more information, visit the Accelerated Schools website at http://www.stanford.edu/group/ASP.)

Renzulli's **Schoolwide Enrichment Model** was originally developed for gifted education programs as the enrichment triad model (1977; see above). It is now being used on a schoolwide basis to improve the creative productivity and academic achievement of *all* students (Renzulli, 1996). The model serves as a framework for organizational and curricular changes and rests on specific curriculum modification techniques, enrichment learning and teaching, and the recognition and development of student talents. (For more information, visit the National Research Center for the Gifted and Talented website at http://www.ucc.uconn.edu/~wwwgt/nrcgt.html.)

Technology

It is difficult to overestimate the importance of technology as a tool for research and creative efforts for students who are gifted and talented. Access to various kinds of software and to the Internet is essential for students who can learn independently, and the computer skills of these students grow quickly—often they teach *us* in this arena. Vahidi (1998) notes that the Internet can be used for research, for expressing views, for teleconferencing and telementoring, and to plug into advanced online curriculum. Students may develop their future careers by pursuing a hobby or interest on the Internet. In this age of technology, the proliferation of information, and access to information in our "global village," the sky's the limit for our very capable students.

Today's technology can be a tool for independent study for gifted students.

SUMMARY

- The concept of giftedness has changed greatly over time, as has our view of students who are gifted. Giftedness has been described in terms of creativity and task commitment, multiple intelligences, successful manipulation of the environment, and heightened sensitivity and understanding.

- Standardized test scores are one criterion for identifying giftedness, but they should be supplemented by other measures, as well as by informal observations by teachers and parents.

- Although biological factors may play a role in giftedness, educators focus on environmental factors, especially the importance of family support, guidance, and encouragement that can contribute to the full expression of a student's gifts.

- The prevalence of giftedness varies because of differing definitions and criteria; for funding purposes many states use a figure of 5 percent. Gifted females, students who are gifted and disabled, gifted underachievers, culturally diverse students, and the highly gifted are often underrepresented.

- Teachers usually play a central role in identifying gifted students through multiple measures, including observations of behavior (which might include boredom with regular classwork) as well as test scores and grades.

- The curriculum can be modified through telescoping, content area acceleration, independent study, cluster grouping, and cooperative learning.

Modifications should be based on the student's needs and interests. Gifted students are usually served in the regular classroom and pulled out for resource-room time. If self-contained classes are used, the students may be grouped according to their level or type of ability. Magnet schools are another setting in which students can receive a special emphasis on a specific type of ability.

■ Many models for organizing gifted education have been proposed, including the classroom enrichment model and the enrichment triad model. These models help teachers plan curriculum modifications and activities to fulfill the social and emotional needs of gifted students.

KEY TERMS

giftedness	academic enrichment	enrichment
talent	acceleration	mentorships
intelligence	curriculum telescoping	classroom enrichment model
creativity	group telescoping	
task commitment	content area acceleration	enrichment triad model
theory of multiple intelligences	independent study	Accelerated Schools Project
	webbing	Schoolwide Enrichment Model
triarchic theory	cluster grouping	
gifted underachiever	cooperative learning	
highly gifted	brainstorming	

MULTIMEDIA RESOURCES

Selected Internet Resources for Gifted Education, ERIC Clearinghouse on Disabilities and Gifted Education. Website: http://www.cec.sped.org/faq/gt-urls.htm. The ERIC Clearinghouse has created and updates a list of links to research centers and organizations centered on gifted children.

Bireley, Marlene. *Crossover Children: A Sourcebook for Helping Children Who Are Gifted and Learning Disabled,* 2d ed. (Reston, VA: Council for Exceptional Children, 1995). This book provides specific strategies designed to help students who are gifted and learning disabled increase attention, enhance memory, and improve social skills, as well as recommendations for academic interventions and enrichment activities.

Delisle, James R. *Guiding the Social and Emotional Development of Gifted Youth: A Practical Guide for Educators and Counselors* (Reston, VA: Council for Exceptional Children, 1992). This research-based guide offers practical suggestions on how to understand, motivate, and respond to the affective needs of gifted students.

Parenting for High Potential. A publication of the National Association for Gifted Children, 1707 L Street NW, Suite 550, Washington, DC 20036. Telephone: (202) 785-4268. Website: http://www.nagc.org. This quarterly magazine is designed for parents who want to make a difference in their children's lives, who want to develop their children's gifts and talents, and who want to help them develop their potential to the fullest. Each issue includes special features, expert advice columns, software and book reviews, ideas from parents, and a pullout children's section.

Van Tassel-Baska, Joyce. *Planning Effective Curriculum for Gifted Learners* (Reston, VA: Council for Exceptional Children, 1992). This book provides specific ideas for designing and implementing a curriculum that works, including practical ideas and sample units for teaching gifted students.

Winebrenner, Susan. *Teaching Gifted Kids in the Regular Classroom* (Minneapolis: Free Spirit Publishing, 1992). An excellent source for teaching ideas.

USING YOUR KNOWLEDGE

 Commonalities: If possible, try to interview a student who is high in abilities or talented. Ask open questions, such as, What do you think about during class? Who are your best friends and why? What are your favorite parts of school? Least favorite parts of school? Do you have hobbies? Although this project will help you understand one student, it doesn't mean that all gifted individuals have the same or even similar characteristics. The goal is to help you develop your awareness of gifted students as complete individuals.

 Can Do: Using the information on curriculum modifications provided in this chapter and the recommended readings, develop some activities that would allow gifted students to enrich their learning in the regular class.

 Collaboration: Where are gifted students in your school district served? Arrange to visit a local public school and see what combination of regular class, resource room, and self-contained class instruction gifted students receive. If possible, observe students in each of these environments. How do the settings vary?

WHAT YOU CAN DO NOW

1. Commonalities: Explore the diversity of gifted students.

- Visit local schools and talk to teachers who work with students identified as gifted and talented.
- Talk with gifted students about their diverse backgrounds and their attitudes and aspirations.
- Select one or two books or articles about gifted students from the list in the Multimedia Resources section. Compare the authors' perspectives with your own knowledge and experiences.

2. Investigate popular culture and media images.

- How do films and television shows portray gifted children? How have those images changed?
- Interview a gifted student, classmate, or other person and note how that person differs from media stereotypes. Why might these stereotypes exist?
- Rent the video of the film *Little Man Tate.* Do you consider that portrait of a gifted child and his mother realistic? Write a review of the movie based on your analysis.

- Identify a public figure whom you consider gifted or talented. Using the characteristics described in this chapter, explain how this person fits the criteria for giftedness.

3. Can Do: Survey attitudes in your class.

- Find out what stereotypes or preconceptions students hold about gifted children.
- Have students write about one area in which they feel they are gifted. Does this ability shape their view of themselves, or is it just one characteristic?
- Compile the responses about individual areas of giftedness into a poster to show the range of gifts in the class.

Framework 2

Common Issues for All Developing Professionals in Special Education and Related Fields

Introduction

Framework: A structure for supporting or enclosing something else, especially a skeletal support used as the basis for something being constructed: a fundamental structure. (American Heritage Dictionary of the English Language, Third Edition)

You have just journeyed through our chapters describing the groups of students who receive special education services, and although you may have been enlightened, you may also be somewhat overwhelmed! There are lots of ideas, names, and facts to remember in this book . . . perhaps more than can be absorbed in one quarter or semester.

The amount of information covered in a "survey" of the field of special education is part of what inspired us to build these Frameworks into our textbook. We hope that they will serve as a structure on which you can construct and hang your own developing ideas about our field and your students. As a newcomer to the field of special education, you will build on the knowledge that you have acquired, and we want to provide you with some additional resources for your growth as a professional—or, as they say in schools, your "professional development."

Today schools and teachers are under considerable pressure from government, the media, and our society at large to improve the academic achievement of *all* students. Education is a national policy issue, and the status of teaching is frequently called into question. Yet we remain strongly committed to the concept of teaching as a profession. As professionals, it is our obligation to keep up with changes and issues in educational policies and practices—without, we hope, becoming slaves to every passing fad. For further discussion of these points, you may want to read "What Does It Mean to Be a Professional?" in Ryan and Cooper's *Those Who Can, Teach* (1998).

We hope that this second Framework will provide you with reassurance that your expertise will continue to grow. In fact, your learning has just begun!

Revisiting Framework 1: Common Issues for All Exceptional Children and Youth in Special Education

Because the issues raised in our book are many and complex, we have developed some organizational structures to help you understand and remember them. Among those structures are these Frameworks. You might think of them as a set of "bookends" framing the categorical chapters. Framework 1 provided an introduction to four topics that were common to each of the next nine chapters. These topics emerge and re-emerge in significant ways for all individuals in special education—students and professionals alike. As a result, these topics can become a frame for the larger picture of the issues prevalent in the entire field of special education.

The major topics in Framework 1 were as follows:

- *Categorical and noncategorical special education*   The labels and categories we use to identify and classify students (using the criteria spelled out in the Individuals with Disabilities Education Act) and determine their eligibility for services,

- *Evaluation and assessment of exceptional students*   The process of screening, referring, and assessing the nature, need, and eligibility of students for special education services,

- *Service-delivery models*   The places where students can receive special education services, such as the general education classroom, the resource class, the self-contained classroom, separate schools, and life settings, and

- *Instruction* in academic skills, specialized skills, adaptive skills, and life skills.

Posing Questions

Framework 1 describes these topics and related issues in detail. The nine categorical chapters then delve more deeply into these topics, adding background information and providing specific examples of the issues surrounding them. Now that you have had an opportunity to read about the topics, here are some questions to help you determine what *you* think about them.

- *Categorical and noncategorical special education*   Do the labels that we use to determine a student's eligibility for special education services—such as learning disability, low vision, developmental delay, autism—dictate how we teach them? Or should, for example, all students with reading difficulties be grouped together, regardless of their label?

- *Evaluation and assessment of exceptional students*   Are the lengthy and expensive evaluation and assessment procedures we use to determine a student's eligibility for special education services worth the time and expense? Are the characteristics of each categorical area so precise—like the symptoms of an illness—that we can recognize them through testing? Do current procedures qualify too many students—or too few? How do we explain the students who "fall between the cracks" and never receive the help they need?

- *Service-delivery models*   Special education services can be provided in a range of settings, from what is considered the most restrictive—a residential school, for example—to the least restrictive—the general education classroom. How much does it matter *where* services are provided? How important is a normal social experience of schooling for students with disabilities? We tell our students that "special education is *not a place* . . ." Do you agree?

- *Instruction*   In academic skills, specialized skills, adaptive skills, and life skills, this is "the heart of the matter." How important is it for students with disabilities to be exposed to the core curriculum? Will you be able to take the first step in making it accessible to them?

These and many other questions will continue to present themselves throughout your career. Learning to anticipate and identify the questions is in itself a professional process and skill. You are becoming an experienced professional when you begin to know what the questions are! Most important is the notion, however, that questions such as these are the stuff of sustained thought and experience in the context of the real world of schools. Learning to pose questions and live with them as a condition of being a professional is essential to your development as a reflective practitioner. (We will briefly discuss reflective thinking later in this Framework.)

Our Themes

As the authors of this book, we hope that you remember as much as humanly possible of what you have read . . . and the human brain is capable of a great deal! Most important, though, is the spirit of the book . . . the attitude of respect, interest, and determination to help that we hope is communicated.

That attitude is exemplified in our three themes:

- **Commonalities** Children with identified disabilities and children with special abilities and talents are much more like their age peers than the labels we apply to them might suggest.

- **Collaboration** As a colleague often says, "No one of us is as good as all of us." The best services for exceptional children emerge from the collected efforts of family members, teachers, and other professionals.

- **Can Do** We often ask our students in this course what the most interesting fact that they learned in the class was. Recently, one student responded: "I have learned many interesting facts in this course, but the most important thing that I have learned is that as a teacher I can teach all children—disabled or not. This idea scares me a little, but with good training, schooling, and a sincere desire to teach—I CAN DO IT!"

We have used these themes in several places throughout this book, particularly in the questions that open each chapter and in the Closer Look features. But even when they are not directly articulated, our themes are present implicitly throughout the book—particularly in the sections on teaching strategies.

We believe that these themes will continue to have meaning for you as you begin your career as a professional working with exceptional students. As you approach the end of our book (and your course), how do these themes jibe with your own personal philosophy and beliefs?

Using the Strategies

You may feel that you are near the end of your journey through our book, but in fact, this is just the beginning of your adventure with diversity in learning. We hope that this book will continue to serve as a resource and a reference for you as you travel into our schools and work with students with a wide range of talents, abilities, and challenges. We hope that you come back to the strategies that appear in each chapter and try them out with the students with whom you work.

Some of what we have presented in this book will make the most sense when you are actually faced with a student in a classroom. We hope that we have provided you with some of the tools you will need to serve all students well. But we know that the book cannot provide you with all you need to know, no matter how thick it is!

Lifelong Learning

Recently one of us had the occasion to listen to a group of professors from a university school of engineering discuss their undergraduate engineering major. The explosion of technology has added a great deal of necessary learning to the

already large knowledge base in engineering, and they had despaired of covering all that needs to be covered in an undergraduate engineering major. So they
have adopted a new philosophy. They just can't do it all—and they have recon-
ceptualized their approach to educating engineers. They now see their undergraduate major as just the beginning of a lifetime of learning that engineers
must engage in to be current in their field.

On reflection, we believe that teacher education can be thought of in a similar vein. We do not believe—along with the engineers—that lifelong learning is
code for "spare the content"! Rather, it is a realistic way to acknowledge the
information-explosion age in which we now live. We provide you with a set of
tools, but your toolbox must expand as you develop experiences with children
and schools. You will learn, as did Anna in *The King and I,* that "by your students you are taught." They may be your best teachers. But you will also learn
from your teaching colleagues, from specialists providing services in the school,
from family members. You are beginning what we hope will be a long and fruit-
ful lifetime of teaching children—and a lifetime of learning about them.

Resources for Lifelong Learning and Professional Development

Of course there are additional tools that you will use to implement your lifetime
of learning, and we'd next like to discuss some of them.

- *Writing as a means of understanding: keeping a reflective journal* John
  Dewey defined *reflective thinking* as "the kind of thinking that consists in
  turning a subject over in the mind and giving it serious and consecutive
  consideration" (Dewey, 1933, 1998, p. 3). *Reflection*, then, is careful thinking. As your teaching experience grows, you will find yourself reflecting
  over teaching challenges and successes. We suggest that you write in a
  journal in order to order and record your thoughts. Many novice teachers
  have found journal writing an effective tool for documenting their
  thoughts and experiences—and the expert teachers among you might be
  surprised at how helpful writing about a problem can be.

  There is no one way to develop teaching expertise. Expert teachers,
  however, have learned to "reflect in action" (Schon, 1990). They more easily recognize the essence of a problem, use their own experience, and
  focus on the learning environment. Although there is no royal road to expert teaching, reflective journal writing can help you cope with the pressures of teaching and become a significant tool in your professional
  development (Wolozin, 1998). The accompanying box contains some
  guidelines for reflective journal writing.

  As those of you who have ever kept a diary or personal journal know,
  writing can be a cathartic process—one that helps vent and settle your
  feelings and reflections. Try it.

- *Exploring the world through technology* Technology and the Internet are
  literally revolutionizing the way we teach—and the way we think. But
  technology is a tool for teachers—not a teacher in itself. It can't replace
  you. You can—and most likely will—help your students learn to explore
  our "global village" through the Internet; they can learn to research a
  topic, express their views, collaborate with others, find a "telementor" in

∿ Journal-Writing Guidelines

- **Write 15 minutes per day,** Monday through Thursday, while you are studying, doing student teaching, or working as a practicing classroom teacher.

- **Date each entry using a pen** rather than a pencil because it is easier to read.

- **Write from your own experience.** Describe a single event—a personal experience or a classroom experience.

- **Write in narrative form,** making sure your story has a beginning, middle, and end.

- **Write to apply, discover, or challenge principles or concepts** found in this book.

Source: J. Wakefield, *Using Learning Journals: A Guide for Instructors* (Boston: Houghton Mifflin, 1996).

their area of interest, start a hobby or develop lifelong interests, create their own Web pages—and on and on (Vahidi, 1998).

But technology is a tool for *your* professional development, as well. Some of you will have already made that discovery, and others may be uninitiated. Professional organizations are on the web, along with compendiums of information for teachers on commercial Internet service providers. There are listserves and "chat rooms" where teachers can exchange ideas. We have listed some of these sites for you at the end of each chapter of the book, in the section titled Multimedia Resources. Most of those sites have a section of links to related sites. As you explore the Internet, you will find other resources that are useful and interesting to you.

- *Taking an interest in global issues* As technology brings us closer to our neighbors around the world, there is the potential to learn from teachers everywhere. What are the teaching methods used with students in Japan? What kinds of services are provided to infants with disabilities in Sweden? How is culture incorporated into the curriculum in South Africa? We have much to learn from one another.

- *Developing your own teaching strategies through creativity and experimentation* Although the teaching strategies that we describe in this book provide a starting place for you, nothing can replace your own application of the "can-do" spirit. Be creative and open to new strategies and ideas as you work with students with disabilities in the schools.

- *Observing good teaching* Observing a good teacher is an even more meaningful experience when you have been a teacher for a while yourself. You can see how other teachers handle behavior, organize their classrooms, motivate students, ask questions, prepare lessons, and impart content. Some school districts provide their new teachers with a *mentor teacher* for this purpose. Take advantage of any opportunity you have to see a seasoned teacher in action—it will help you reflect on your own practices and improve them to your own satisfaction.

- *Joining professional organizations* Becoming a member of a national professional organization and attending its conferences and meetings can provide you with the means to continue your learning. Most likely your professors are active in their professional groups; that's one of the major ways that we continue to learn and keep up with what's new in our areas of interest. Most professional organizations are large, and have a variety of divisions or special interest groups, so you should be able to find a group of people who are interested in exactly what interests *you*.

The major professional organization in special education—but by no means the only one—is the Council for Exceptional Children (CEC). CEC has seventeen specialized divisions; each one provides additional focus and depth of information for a particular exceptionality or interest area in special education. Each publishes journals, newsletters, books, and monographs; sponsors conferences and other professional development programs; and provides networking opportunities. CEC's website is http://www.cec.sped.org.

There are many professional organizations for the general educator. Among the best is the Association for Supervision and Curriculum Development (ASCD). ASCD has a very informative website: http://www.ascd.org.

We have listed other professional organizations at the end of each chapter of our book. Visit their websites and give one or two organizations a try. Dues are usually lower for students, so now is a good time to investigate a group.

- *Continuing your formal education* Although some of you might feel you need a breather from school, others will be interested in continuing their education. Since most states require teachers to continue their professional development in order to renew their license or credential, some of you may decide to continue your schooling later in your career. If you are not already in a master's degree program, you may want to consider one. If you are interested in conducting your own research or teaching at a university, you may consider a doctoral degree—a Ph.D. or an Ed.D.

  The National Clearinghouse for the Professions in Special Education (NCPSE) is an information resource for professionals and potential students in the fields of special education and the related services professions. NCPSE gathers, develops, and disseminates information on recruitment, preservice preparation, employment opportunities, and attrition and retention issues. NCPSE also maintains data on personnel supply and demand. Look it up!

NCPSE
1920 Association Drive,
Reston, VA 20191-1589. Telephone:
(800) 641-7824 (toll free);
(703) 264-9476 (voice);
(703) 264-9480 (TTY);
(703) 264-1637(fax).
Website: http://www.cec.sped.org/cl/ncpseabo.htm.

What You Can Do Now

In each chapter of our book, we have provided you with a list of activities that allow you to learn more about the chapter's topic. But now, the list of activities is up to you. Choose from our suggestions in this Framework or come up with your own . . . it's time to put your knowledge to work on behalf of *all* children. We wish you and your students the very best as you continue your journey.

Considering Cultural Diversity and Lifespan Factors

Three

THE CHAPTERS in Part III discuss how issues of exceptionality are influenced by the cultural and age norms of individuals with and without disabilities. Each chapter looks at the accomplishments of people with disabilities in gaining rights and opportunities, as well as areas that continue to present challenges.

$\mathcal{E}$xceptional Children from Diverse Cultural Backgrounds

$\mathbf{A}$s we've discussed throughout this text, all children have differences that shape their learning needs and abilities. Cultural differences are one of many factors to consider when planning instruction and helping students reach their potential. This chapter touches on the meaning of cultural and linguistic diversity in terms of values, assessment issues, and teaching approaches. As you read, think about the following questions:

- How does linguistic diversity relate to exceptional students' learning and achievement?

- Why is cultural competence necessary for effective education?

- How can standard materials and practices be adapted for culturally diverse exceptional students?

Commonalities: Why have students from diverse cultural backgrounds been disproportionately represented in various types of special education?

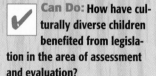 **Can Do:** How have culturally diverse children benefited from legislation in the area of assessment and evaluation?

 Collaboration: How can educators become aware of the cultural diversity of their students and their families?

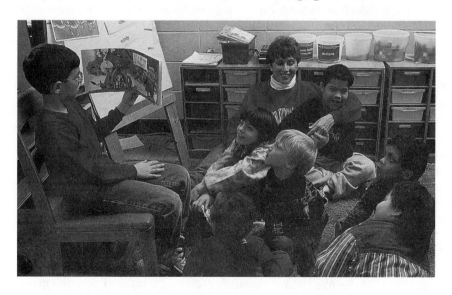

Kristin Roberts is a first-year third-grade teacher in the Los Angeles Unified School District. Recruited from the Midwest, Kristin was lured to southern California by its promise of warm weather, beaches, and good salaries. Now, looking over her class roll for the ninth time, Kristin tries to pronounce the names: "Aragon, Ayala, Gutierrez, Huang, Lee, Manufafoa, Morales, Munoz, Ng, Nguyen . . . Seau, Soriano . . . Wilkerson, Williams . . . Yamashita . . ." Kristin Roberts will discover that not only are most of her students from ethnic minority backgrounds, but several have limited proficiency in English.

One out of every eight Americans lives in California. Even more dramatic is the fact that over half of California's school-age children are from ethnic minority groups. California is not alone: Nearly half of Texas's school age population is ethnic minority. In the year 2010, close to 42 percent of the U.S. school-age population will be minority (National Center for Educational Statistics, 1996).

Religious diversity affects the classroom in much the same way as ethnic diversity, reflecting the pluralistic nature of religion in the United States. Close to 143 million individuals in this country have some religious affiliation, and immigrants are bringing with them their religions—Buddhism, Islam, Hinduism, Catholicism, and so on. The manner in which your students behave and respond to situations in your classroom may be as much related to their religion as to their ethnicity or other cultural identities.

In this chapter, we will first examine ethnic and cultural factors that affect the education of all students, such as linguistic diversity and parent-professional relationships. Then we will look at how multicultural factors affect the provision of special education services to exceptional students.

As you read this chapter, we ask you to keep in mind the principles that guided our previous discussions of the special education categories: All individuals are unique, regardless of group or category, and general descriptors reflect only tendencies or generalizations, not hard and fast rules that apply to all group members. As always, your own efforts to understand and address each student's needs will show you what information is most important for that student's education.

Definitions and Terms

Culture means different things to different people. Although many people equate "culture" with knowledge of good music, art, and the theater, most anthropologists define **culture** more broadly, as ways of perceiving, believing, evaluating, and behaving (Goodenough, 1987). Think of culture as a series of norms or tendencies that are shared, interpreted, and adapted by a group of people. The characteristics of a given culture may be described as specific behaviors or life patterns; however, keep in mind that every person is an individual, and groups of individuals within a culture represent a *range* of characteristics (Hanson, 1998). Culture, therefore, may guide the way you think, feel, behave, dress, and eat but it does not ensure that every member of a culture will do things in the same way. The word *culture* can also be used to describe many of the shared behaviors we experience in a number of different parts of our lives. For example, the shared language, dress, communication patterns, and food preferences of our ethnic background, as well as the behavioral, ethical, social, and dietary guidelines of our religion, reflect two aspects of culture.

As you read the following sections, think about your own cultural identities. Reflect on your participation in the macroculture and microcultures. Why

Culture is a way of perceiving, believing, evaluating, and behaving shared by a group of people.

The playground is like a world in miniature—where children from a variety of cultures and ethnic backgrounds get to know one another. (Laura Dwight)

is this important to you as a prospective teacher? A thorough knowledge of who you are, how your beliefs and actions are influenced, and how you relate to people who have different life experiences can lead not only to self-growth, but also to your ability to teach all children effectively.

Macroculture

Have you noticed how your classmates, roommates, and friends from different ethnic groups seem to have quite a lot in common with you? If so, it is because you all belong to the **macroculture,** the core, or universal, culture of this country. Our macroculture evolved from Western European traditions. No longer limited to white Anglo-Saxon Protestants, the macroculture comprises many different ethnic groups, primarily middle class. Traits such as individualism, industriousness, ambition, competitiveness, self-reliance, and independence are highly valued by the macroculture (Gollnick & Chinn, 1994). Most educators, regardless of their ethnic background, belong to the middle class and subscribe to the values of the macroculture.

Microcultures

The macroculture alone does not define our pluralistic society, however. In your classroom you will find that all of your students belong to subcultures, or **microcultures,** which have their own distinctive cultural patterns while at the same time sharing core values with the macroculture. There are many microcultures, and each of your students will belong to several. All of your students will belong to a microculture related to ethnicity. Some will be Chinese, Vietnamese, Cuban, or Haitian in national origin. All will also belong to a microculture related to socioeconomic status. Some may be middle class, others poor. All will belong to a language group. Probably all speak English to some extent. Some,

Different individuals identify with certain microcultures to a greater or lesser degree than others.

Exceptional Children from Diverse
Cultural Backgrounds

These children read from a book made in their bilingual classroom. Text is in both English and Spanish. (Elizabeth Crews/Stock, Boston, Inc.)

however, may speak Spanish or Korean as their primary language. All will belong to a microculture related to gender. You will find that the boys are socialized to behave differently than the girls. All will belong to a microculture related to geographic region. If you live and teach in the Midwest, it is likely that your students are socialized differently from American children living in Hawaii. Consequently, the way an African American gifted female in your classroom thinks, feels, perceives, and behaves may be related to the fact that she is African American, or it may be directly related to her middle-class background, her close relationship to and beliefs in the Roman Catholic church, or the fact that she is a female.

Assimilation and Acculturation

Why is it that some of us retain the habits, rituals, language, and dress of our native culture, while others do not? An obvious reason might be that some of us have ethnic backgrounds, appearances, religions, and languages that already closely resemble those of the macroculture. Another reason might be that a family or an individual wishes to blend in with the new culture and therefore decides to make changes. Of course, time is also an important factor. Newly arrived immigrants are more likely to reflect their native culture than those who are several generations removed from their immigrant forebears.

The ways in which an individual chooses to integrate into a new culture can be described by the terms *assimilation* and *acculturation*. **Assimilation** refers to the attempt to completely embrace all aspects of the new culture, thereby replacing characteristics of the native culture with those of the new. **Acculturation,** on the other hand, refers to learning and performing the characteristics of the new culture while still retaining and practicing those of the native culture. Assimilation and acculturation are illustrated in the following example.

Pepe Ortiz is an 11-year-old whose father is a graduate student in a relatively small midwestern college town. Pepe was born and raised in Colombia and speaks some English. He is in a third-grade class and is somewhat intimidated because this is his first experience in American schools.

Pepe is bright and very observant. He has readily identified the boys in the class who are viewed as leaders. He knows what type of clothing they wear and is learning what type of music they like and what foods they prefer. Pepe feels that the way he can be accepted by his classmates is to be like them. So, he dresses like them. He asks his parents to buy him specific brands and types of shoes. He says he loves pizza and hamburgers. He is saving his allowance to buy the same type of music the other children say they like. Although his speech is still heavily Spanish-accented, Pepe is trying very hard to improve his English. He is using many of the same terms his classmates use. This is Pepe's assimilation process. He is allowing the cultural patterns he has followed all his life to disappear or to become subordinate to the values of the dominant group in his class.

If, however, Pepe chooses to develop and maintain his participation in both cultures, he is choosing acculturation. He may, for example, work on improving his English while still speaking Spanish in his home and with other Spanish-speaking students. Pepe may dress like his classmates at school and listen to the same music they do, yet celebrate the holidays and festivals of his native culture with traditional dress, music, and dancing.

It is critical for us as educators to understand that although Pepe (as a subordinate group member) can choose to a great extent the degree of his acculturation or assimilation, the students in the "in group" (the dominant group) control the extent to which he will be allowed to participate. No matter how proficient linguistically and socially Pepe becomes, full access into the innermost social settings of the class (being invited to the really important parties, etc.) could be denied, as it could be to any child.

Minority and Ethnic Groups

Minority and *minority group* are terms often used in discussions about certain groups in this country. Although **minority** usually denotes a numerical minority, it may also be used to suggest a subordinate power position in society (Gollnick & Chinn, 1994). **Minority groups** may be categorized according to ethnicity, gender, language, religion, disability, or socioeconomic status.

Often the members of minority groups are stereotyped and may be viewed negatively by some members of the majority group (Eitzen & Zinn, 1989). Members of minority groups may be targets of discrimination and are often relegated to a low status in society (Yetman, 1985). This is particularly true in parts of the country where African Americans, American Indians, or Latinos are numerically dominant but have minimal political, economic, or social status.

Ethnicity—common history, values,
attitudes, and behavior—binds people together.

Ethnicity denotes the common history, values, attitudes, and behaviors that bind a group of people together (Yetman, 1985). Examples of ethnic groups in this country include Irish Americans, Chinese Americans, Latinos, and German Americans. Ethnic groups may be *ethnocentric:* they view their own traits as natural, correct, and superior to that of other ethnic groups, whom they tend to view as odd, amusing, inferior, or immoral (Yetman, 1985). Used in a broader context, the term *ethnocentrism* describes the narrow perspective of individuals from various microcultures. An example of this might include the ethnocentric, or intolerant, view of a particular Protestant group toward Roman Catholics. Although ethnicity is often the benchmark factor we think of when we use the term *culture,* remember that culture and ethnicity are not the same, and that many different microcultures interact with a person's ethnicity to form his or her cultural heritage (Keogh, Gallimore & Weisner, 1997).

Cultural Diversity

The United States is characterized
by cultural diversity—a wide range
of cultural characteristics and
norms.

For the remainder of this chapter, ethnic minority groups will be referred to as *culturally diverse groups.* This designation is primarily a recognition of the pluralistic nature of the United States and the numerous contributions diverse groups have made to the development of this country. Using the term **cultural diversity** does not place or rank groups in relation to one another; rather, it acknowledges that a wide range of cultural characteristics and norms exists within our society.

Linguistic Diversity

The complex interaction between
language and culture makes it difficult for immigrant children to master English.

Linguistic diversity refers to the variety of languages spoken in the homes of schoolchildren. There are over three thousand known languages spoken in the world, with over one thousand in Africa alone. Hundreds of languages are spoken in the United States, although it is unlikely that you as a teacher will have children from more than a few different language groups. It is likely, though, that during your teaching career you will have students who are **limited English proficient (LEP).** It is also likely that some of your students will have a primary language other than English, one with which you have no skills.

When you are in your own classroom, observe your students carefully. Notice how culturally diverse children who have the same primary language tend to bond with one another. Language is a focal point for cultural identity. Individuals who share the same language often share similar values, beliefs, and behaviors. Thus a Puerto Rican child in your class may be initially drawn to a Guatemalan child when she hears the other speaking Spanish.

The subtle but complex nature of the interaction between language and culture makes it difficult for immigrant children to master English usage fully in the schools. Cultural conventions related to communication patterns and nonverbal communication styles, for example, may be different in the child's home and school environment. The task is even more complex for culturally and linguistically diverse exceptional children. Many haven't even grasped the fundamentals of their primary language when the task of learning English is imposed on them. Learning a second language is a difficult challenge for the brightest students. For those who have cognitive deficits, the task is even more complex.

Many of the children we teach will come from cultures very different from our own. This boy is participating in a foot washing ceremony in his church. (Chester Higgins, Jr.)

One of the characteristics of language is that it is dynamic. Like everything else in our society, language changes constantly. Although some changes are gradual, others take place more rapidly. For language minority children, learning a language that changes in "midstream" is an added challenge.

Dialects

Not only will you find that your students come from different language backgrounds, but you will also find that your English-speaking students have different **dialects.** Your student from Hawaii may speak pidgin English, your African American students Black English; those from the South may have a drawl.

Dialects differ from one another in a variety of ways. Differences in vowels tend to distinguish regional dialects (see the accompanying box, "A Southern Vowel Pronounciation"), while differences in consonants are more likely to distinguish social differences. Dialects that have a lower socioeconomic class basis tend to be viewed negatively and can have social consequences for the user.

One of the most controversial issues in American education is the use of **Black English,** the primary form of verbal communication for one of the largest

∿ A Southern Vowel Pronunciation

In some Southern dialects of English, words such as *pin* and *pen* are pronounced the same. Usually, both words are pronounced as *pin*. This pattern of pronunciation is also found in other words. List A gives words in which the *i* or *e* are pronounced the same in these dialects.

List A: *I* and *E* Pronounced the Same

1. *tin* and *ten*
2. *kin* and *Ken*
3. *Lin* and *Len*
4. *Windy* and *Wendy*
5. *sinned* and *send*

Although *i* and *e* words in List A are pronounced the *same*, there are other words in which *i* and *e* are pronounced differently. List B gives word pairs in which the vowels are pronounced *differently*.

List B: *I* and *E* Pronounced Differently

1. *lit* and *let*
2. *pick* and *peck*
3. *pig* and *peg*
4. *rip* and *rep*
5. *litter* and *letter*

Compare the word pairs in List A with those in List B. Is there a pattern that can explain why the words in List A are pronounced the *same* and why the words in List B are pronounced *differently*? To answer this question, you have to look at the sounds that are next to the vowels. Look at the sounds that come after the vowel. What sound is found next to the vowel in all of the examples given in List A?

Use your knowledge of the pronunciation pattern to pick the word pairs in List C that are pronounced the *same* (S) and those that are pronounced *differently* (D) in this Southern dialect.

List C: Same or Different?

__ 1. *bit* and *bet*
__ 2. *pit* and *pet*
__ 3. *bin* and *Ben*
__ 4. *Nick* and *neck*
__ 5. *din* and *den*

How can you tell where *i* and *e* will be pronounced the same and where they will be pronounced differently?

Source: Carolyn Temple Adger, Walt Wolfman & Jennifer Detwyler (1993). Language differences: A new approach for special educators. *Teaching Exceptional Children*, 26, 44–47. (p. 46). Copyright © 1993 by The Council for Exceptional Children. Reprinted with permission.

ethnic groups in this country. Approximately 80 percent of African Americans use Black English regularly. Another 19 percent of African Americans use language that, with the exception of minor differences in vocal quality and pronunciation, is indistinguishable from standard English. The remaining 1 percent use standard English or another dialect. Considered a legitimate form of communication by most African Americans and most linguists, Black English is criticized by others, including some educators. Critics contend that it is a substandard dialect and a poor form of English.

Many African American children in special education classes speak Black English. Although there are vocational and social disadvantages for individuals who are unable to speak standard English, there are advantages for those who are *bidialectal*, able to speak both standard English and the local, regional, or community-based dialect. These individuals can choose the dialect that best meets their needs at a given time. Educators who realize this can foster in their culturally diverse students a desire to develop standard English skills and at the same time maintain the advantages of being bidialectal. Most of your limited English proficient students will likely be motivated to develop their English skills. In communities where there are high numbers of language minority students, the motivation could be less intense since it is socially easier to get along if there are many others for the individual to communicate with. However, in those communities and schools where the LEP student is a distinct minority, linguistic acculturation is a necessity to survive socially as well as academically.

People who are bidialectical can choose the dialect that best meets their needs at a given time.

Bilingual Education: Proceeding with Caution

The number of LEP children (also referred to as English learners) in U.S. schools now totals over 3 million, and this number should continue to increase. The challenge of teaching LEP children is being met, in part, through **bilingual education,** the use of two languages as mediums of instruction for part or all of the school curriculum. The primary goal of bilingual education is to teach children concepts, knowledge, and skills in the language they know best and to reinforce this through the use of English (Baca & Cervantes, 1989).

Although it is important for LEP students to develop their English skills, research suggests that too early immersion in English-only classrooms can have negative consequences. If a child's development in the first language is interrupted by instruction in the second language, there are a number of possible consequences: (1) There could be a loss of the child's first language (Lambert & Freed, 1982); (2) there could be a mixing or combining of the first and second languages, resulting in the child's own unique (idiosyncratic) communication system (Ortiz & Maldonado-Colon, 1986); (3) the child may develop only limited proficiency in both the first and second languages (Skutnabb-Kangas & Toukomaa, 1976); and (4) the result may be the inability to develop English language proficiency in the school years (Cummins, 1984). These research observations suggest that we should enable LEP children to develop a firm grasp of their home language prior to instruction in an English-only environment.

> Research suggests that interrupting development in one language by instruction in a second language may produce several negative consequences.

Another important research finding explains why many LEP children fail academically after they are placed in monolingual English class settings. Many LEP children are able in only two years to develop sufficient basic English communication skills to lead their teachers to believe that they are prepared for monolingual English class placement. However, a noted bilingual researcher, James Cummins (1984), found that these basic skills were not adequate for learning in a high-level academic setting. Cummins found that although two years was sufficient for everyday conversational usage, an additional five to seven years of school training was necessary to develop the level of skill needed to do well in academic settings. Therefore, it would be inappropriate for you as a teacher to assume that an LEP child has the necessary skills to function well academically in your English-only classroom because he or she can carry on an adequate conversation in English. If there is any doubt that your LEP student is able to grasp the concepts in highly structured academic settings, it would be wise for you to examine the student's records for evidence of appropriate language proficiency. If this information is not available, the next step might be to refer the child for assessment to determine proficiency level. The accompanying box, "A Closer Look: Commonalities: Project Aim for the Best," describes a program that has been very influential in developing strategies for improving the academic achievement of language minority students.

English as a Second Language

English as a Second Language (ESL) programs, also called English Language Development (ELD) programs, differ considerably from bilingual education. Both programs promote English proficiency for bilingual students. ESL programs, however, rely exclusively on English for teaching and learning. ESL programs are used as a primary medium to assimilate LEP students into the linguistic mainstream as quickly as possible. In ESL programs, the home language

> ESL programs rely exclusively on English for teaching and learning.

A closer look

Commonalities: Project Aim for the Best

A three-year federally funded project entitled "Aim for the Best" was awarded to the University of Texas at Austin from 1988 to 1991. The project sought to improve academic achievement and decrease the inappropriate referral of language minority students to special education programs.

Student/Teacher Assistance Teams The model used school-based problem-solving teams, termed Student/Teacher Assistance Teams (S/TAT), composed of teachers and other school resource personnel. The teams met to review areas of behavior and learning problems identified by teachers. The goal of the teams was to assist the teachers in developing approaches to resolving the problems. Only after all apparent alternatives for addressing the problems were exhausted were students referred and possibly placed in special education.

Curriculum-based Assessment Another major component of the model was curriculum-based assessment (CBA). CBA is a system for determining the instructional needs of students based on their ongoing performance in existing school course content and for delivering classroom instruction as effectively as possible to match those needs.

Instructional Approaches Two instructional approaches, Graves Writing Workshop and Shared Literature, were utilized in the model. These interactive approaches involve the students and teachers in collaborative work on a variety of literacy tasks. Shared Literature involves a story-reading approach in which students are exposed to a variety of award-winning literature to develop their oral language and reading comprehension and to familiarize them with a variety of writing styles. These experiences also provide support for the activities in the Graves Writing Workshop.

In the Graves Writing Workshop (Graves, 1983), children write every day, developing topics of their own choice with the consultation of the teacher. The emphasis is on reciprocal interaction, with students sharing and talking about their writing. An objective of this activity is to stimulate conversational and academic language skills. Revisions are based on the students' own research and feedback from both teachers and peers.

These two instructional programs allow for reciprocal interaction, cooperative learning, and the development of language skills critical for language minority students.

Initial Findings Findings suggested that the S/TATs were a valuable asset to the teachers. Teachers reported that the students involved in the interactive instructional approaches improved in reading, vocabulary, comprehension, and oral and written language proficiency. Students also demonstrated greater self-confidence and self-esteem. Project staff reported that the collaborative nature of the model offers opportunities for teachers and staff to share their knowledge and perspectives. In addition, the interaction between bilingual and regular staff leads to greater understanding of the students' language and home background, particularly with respect to planning for instruction and making assessments.

For further description of this project, see A. A. Ortiz and C.Y. Wilkinson, "Assessment and Intervention Model for the Bilingual Exceptional Student (AIM for the BEST)," *Teacher Education and Special Education*, 14 (1991): 35–42.

and culture are given less emphasis than the acquisition of the English language (Gollnick & Chinn, 1994).

Parent-Professional Relationships: Understanding the Values of the Home

Communicating effectively with the parents of your culturally diverse exceptional students is one of the more interesting challenges you will face as an educator. Communicating effectively involves, in part, being sensitive to the parents' cultural values and attitudes toward their family and child.

It would be a lot easier for you to understand culturally diverse parents if an accurate summary of each ethnic group's values could be provided. Some texts attempt to do this, but it often results in stereotyping. Asians are much too diverse a group to describe in a few paragraphs or pages. The same is true of Latinos and of all other groups.

It is impossible to provide generalized characteristics for members of any group without taking into consideration their level of acculturation into mainstream society, their socioeconomic level, their religious background, or even the region of the country in which they live. Remember, also, that the ways a family thinks, feels, perceives, and behaves are related to personality factors as well as to characteristics such as social class and ethnicity. The following generalizations are just that: broad generalizations subject to infinite individual variation.

Values and Perceptions

At the risk of some stereotyping, let's examine a few examples so that we can understand how some culturally diverse parents may perceive their children, including those with a disability, and the implications of these perceptions for special education services.

Asians, as we have already indicated, are an extremely diverse group. Among some Asians, however, there are some common values that transcend religion, social class, and level of acculturation. Approximately two-thirds of the Asians in the United States are Chinese, Japanese, Korean, or Vietnamese. These four groups are strongly influenced by Confucian philosophy. Parents who adhere to Confucian values view their children as "gifts from the gods." They are to be cherished, and parents often sacrifice financially and in other ways for their children. Children, in return, are expected to be obedient, to excel in school, and to enter an honorable profession. They are expected to bring honor to the family. Deviant behavior brings shame not only to the child but to the entire family. The shame extends to extended members of the family and even to ancestors who are deceased. This is a heavy burden to place on children.

Asian parents often pressure their children to excel. Some have been observed giving their children additional homework assignments beyond that required by the school. It is quite easy to see how an Asian child who is obedient and diligent in all of his or her assignments could quickly become one of your favored students. The work habits and high achievement levels of many Asian students may be a substantial reason these students tend to be overrepresented

Effective communication requires that teachers be sensitive to parents' cultural views.

Children enjoy learning
about the traditions of other
cultures. Here a student
teacher makes wonton soup
with her students. (Laura
Dwight)

in gifted classes. The implications for children with disabilities are obvious. Their failure to excel brings shame on the family. The problem is exacerbated by the belief of some Asians that the disability is retribution for parental wrong-doings. Guilt on the part of the parents may ensue, and refusal to acknowledge the child's disability is a possibility.

Another example of family values and parental influence is that which you may find in some Mexican American families. Surveys of Mexican Americans tell us that they express stronger feelings of family solidarity than do most Anglos. As such, some Mexicans may feel more attached and committed to their families than do Anglos. Interactions with extended family members are described as frequent, with exchanges of information, services, and support. Other characteristics include the greater level of protective behavior on the part of Mexican parents than Anglo parents of the same socioeconomic background (McClintock, Bayard & McClintock, 1983).

Again we have some implications for educators. Mexican American parents are more protective of their children than those from some other cultural groups and tend to receive support from the extended family. In addition, Roman Catholic parents may be more accepting of a child with a disability than some parents of other religious groups (Hutchinson, 1968; Zuk, 1959). Since many Mexican Americans have Catholic backgrounds, the church and the support from the extended family may provide them with a greater ability to cope with a child with a disability. At the same time, the cooperative values instilled in the Mexican child in the home may work against him or her in the typical American classroom and may result in borderline children being referred to special education or bright children not receiving referrals to classes for the gifted.

Developing Cultural Competence

To be able to work effectively with culturally diverse parents, it is important for teachers to be aware of their own attitudes toward people from diverse groups. Because of their different backgrounds, parents will often look different, speak differently, and dress differently than you do. Thus, you must begin to develop **cultural competence,** "respect for difference, eagerness to learn, and a willingness to accept that there are many ways of viewing the world" (Hanson, 1998, p. 493).

Cultural competence is a willingness to accept many ways of viewing the world.

Cultural competence is based on two key skills: awareness and communication. These skills become especially important when working with exceptional students and their families. See the accompanying box, "Questions About Cultural Competence," for questions that can be used to develop your awareness and communication skills and, ideally, to establish trust and rapport between you and the family.

According to Hanson (1998), "our cultural and ethnic identities help to shape our beliefs and practices, and who we are as individuals and family members. These identities are not the script for our behavior, but they do provide a texture and a richness—and they can bind us together in groups or separate us from one another. Knowledge and understanding, sensitivity, and respect for these cultural differences can significantly enhance the effectiveness of service providers in the helping professions" (p. 21).

Knowledge and respect for cultural differences can significantly enhance educators' effectiveness.

Regardless of their economic status, language skills, or educational level, parents are greatly concerned about the welfare of their children. They, better than anyone else, know the child's characteristics, strengths and weaknesses, and perceptions of the school. Cultivating a working relationship with culturally diverse parents requires mutual respect and trust.

In special education, our work with families begins early, particularly if a disability is discovered when the child is quite young. As we discussed in Chapter 3, the development of the Individualized Family Service Plan involves planning not only for the child but for the family as well. Therefore, our ability to communicate and relate to the family, to identify the information parents need, and to integrate our educational and social interventions with the participation preferences of the family are critical aspects of service delivery (Sontag & Schacht, 1994). Our knowledge of how a family perceives not only a disability but also special services can affect the type of programming permitted and the extent to which services such as assistive technology are used (Hourcade, Parette & Huer, 1997). Linan-Thompson and Jean (1997) suggest that when communicating with linguistically diverse parents of students with disabilities, it is important to use the method of communication preferred by the parent, to have interpreters who are knowledgeable about special education as well as bilingual, and to provide information to the family in a variety of formats (videos, text, etc.).

Representation of Culturally Diverse Children in Special Education Classes

Where do individuals with disabilities fit within the cultural framework? Although individuals with disabilities, like all people, are members of a variety of cultures, culture does influence the assessment, identification, and educational

⚬ Questions About Cultural Competence

- How is the family organized (extended or nuclear)? Who are the primary caregivers? What language is spoken at home? What is the family pattern of decision-making? Does the family wish to include traditional practitioners or other members of the community in program planning and/or implementation?

- What values are shared with the Anglo mainstream? What aspects of working with the Anglo mainstream may be difficult?

- What is the most comfortable way for the family to work with the service provision system?

- Is there any other information that is important for personnel to know regarding the family and child and/or that is important to the family to relate or to question?

Source: P.P. Anderson & E.S. Fenichel, *Serving Culturally Diverse Families of Infants and Toddlers with Disabilities* (Arlington, VA: National Center for Clinical Infant Programs, 1989), p. 16.

placement of children with disabilities. We know that children with disabilities must be identified before they can receive appropriate educational programming—because the general education curriculum is not appropriate, or alternative teaching methods must be used, or specific accommodations must be made. We also know that children from diverse cultures, particularly those with languages or communication patterns that differ from those of the macroculture, may need accommodations to adapt and perform successfully in the classroom. In addition, many teachers in all areas of education are not prepared to address the educational needs of students with varied cultural and/or linguistic backgrounds. On the surface, we might think that because both individuals with disabilities and individuals from diverse cultural backgrounds may require support, there might be a logical overlap between cultural diversity and special education—but there is not. There is a great distinction between (a) providing a native Spanish-speaking student with a Spanish version of a science textbook, and (b) referring the child for special education assessment because he can't do grade-level work in science when using the English text.

Historically, and currently, however, there is a relationship between cultural background and the extent to which children are identified as having disabilities. Obviously, cultural diversity is not a category of disability. We can turn it into a handicap, however, through our lack of knowledge and effort, bigotry, absence of cultural awareness, and inflexibility as educators. The overrepresentation and underrepresentation of individuals from certain ethnic cultures in categories of special education persists today. This suggests that we, as educators, must continue to examine this issue and ourselves.

Overrepresentation and Underrepresentation

The number of culturally diverse children in special education classes has been greater than their total population would suggest.

In an often-cited article in *Exceptional Children*, Dunn (1968) reported that a disproportionately high number of African American, American Indian, Mexican, and Puerto Rican children from low socioeconomic backgrounds were being placed in special education classes for students with mild mental retardation. Mercer (1973) provided support for Dunn's findings when she reported that three times as many African American and four times as many Mexican American children were being placed in classes for students with mild mental retardation as compared to their numbers in the general school population. This situation is referred to as **overrepresentation,** or a representation greater than would be expected based on the actual number of students from that group in school.

In 1968, the Office of Civil Rights (OCR) began surveying schools and school districts regarding student enrollment and placement in special education classes. Chinn and Hughes (1987) analyzed data from the 1978, 1980, 1982, and 1984 OCR surveys and found that the number of African Americans in classes for students with mild mental retardation was approximately twice as great as their representation in the general school population. In addition, African Americans were overrepresented in classes for students with moderate to severe mental retardation and severe emotional disabilities. They were underrepresented in classes for students labeled gifted and talented. **Underrepresentation** occurs when fewer students are receiving services than would be expected based on their representation in the general school population. Contrary to Dunn and Mercer's findings, Chinn and Hughes found that Mexican Americans were underrepresented in classes for students with mild mental retardation, severe emotional disturbance, and speech impairments, as well as gifted and talented. Some reasons for this will be discussed in the next section.

Asian and Pacific American children were underrepresented in all categories for children with disabilities and overrepresented in classes for the gifted and talented. American Indians were overrepresented in classes for students with mild mental retardation, in three of the four survey years, and overrepresented in classes for those with moderate or severe retardation in 1984. They were overrepresented in classes for students with learning disabilities all four survey years and underrepresented in classes for the gifted and talented. White students were underrepresented in classes for students with mild mental retardation and moderate or severe mental retardation and overrepresented in gifted and talented classes. The most recent OCR surveys report similar findings (*Eighteenth Annual Report to Congress on the Implementation of the Individuals with Disabilities Education Act*, 1996).

Factors Contributing to Over- and Underrepresentation

Why are some culturally diverse groups overrepresented in classes for children with disabilities and others not? Why is there underrepresentation in classes for students labeled gifted and talented among African Americans, American Indians, and Hispanics? Do the statistics accurately reflect the incidence of exceptionalities among culturally diverse students? In addressing these questions we must consider the referral, assessment, and placement process. We must also concern ourselves with the access these children have to educational services, along with environmental and poverty factors.

One factor in overrepresentation may be overreferral of culturally diverse children. Ysseldyke, Thurlow, Gruden, Wesson, Algozzine, and Deno (1983) suggest that a very high percentage of children referred to special education end up being placed. Therefore, if a child is referred to special education, chances are high that he or she will end up there. Who is making these referrals? They are made primarily by teachers, and most teachers are white, middle-class women. Most referrals to special education involve males from culturally diverse lower socioeconomic backgrounds. Even if the teachers themselves are from culturally diverse backgrounds, they are still typically from a different gender group and a different socioeconomic background. Different backgrounds may result in incongruent values for behaviors, and a lack of tolerance or understanding may lead to a predisposition toward referrals.

Teachers and the students they refer to special education often come from different cultural backgrounds.

Culturally diverse groups are disproportionately affected by poverty.

Another variable contributing to the overrepresentation of culturally diverse children in classes for students with mild mental retardation has been the
use of culturally biased assessment instruments. These assessment tools are
often used by psychologists, psychometrists, or diagnosticians who are inadequately trained and unprepared to test culturally and linguistically diverse children. The problem becomes even more acute when bias enters into the interpretation of test results and the placement process.

Poverty is a third factor that affects representation rates in special education
classes. When you have your own classroom, you will find that poverty tends to
affect some ethnic groups more than others. In 1995, 29.3 percent of African
Americans and 30.3 percent of Hispanics in this country were poor (U.S. Bureau
of the Census, 1995). Poverty contributes to poor nutrition, poor quality of medical care, and poor living conditions. Poor women must often work even when a
pregnancy is at risk. These factors can contribute to children being born preterm
or at risk. As you learned in Chapter 2, children born at risk are susceptible to
neurological trauma. In addition, poverty often contributes to stress, which affects the overall mental health of a family. Finally, studies have demonstrated
that children from poor environments are more likely to suffer from lead poisoning. In two California communities, over half the children had lead in their
blood at levels sufficient to affect cognitive functioning and behavior (Dolan &
Abramson, 1990).

Reasons for underrepresentation are as varied as the reasons for overrepresentation and may differ according to the type of cultural diversity. The low national prevalence figures for Hispanics in classes for students with mental retardation and emotional disturbance, for example, may be related in part to the
advent of bilingual education programs. These programs were only in their infancy at the time of the Dunn (1968) and Mercer (1973) studies but now provide
an alternative to special education programs. School districts with bilingual education programs have fewer problems with disproportionate representation of
students than those without bilingual programs (Finn, 1982). Aware that the
language of instruction in special education is primarily English, bilingual
teachers are sometimes reluctant to refer their students to special education, believing that their needs can better be met in a bilingual setting (Dew, 1984).

Additionally, there are more than 800,000 migrant students in this country—the children of the migrant workers who move from state to state to get
work in the fields. Many of these migrant families are Latino. Only 1 percent of
migrant students were identified as placed in special education in a recent study
(Interstate Migrant Council, 1984). This figure is only one-tenth the overall
prevalence rate in this country and suggests that migrant students are not being
identified and placed in special education.

A third reason for the underrepresentation of Latino children is that many
are now being declassified as having mental retardation. One study found that
many Latino students were reclassified from having mental retardation to having learning disabilities (Ortiz & Yates, 1983). Learning disabilities is a more socially acceptable classification than mental retardation, and parents tend to be
more willing to accept placement in a learning disabilities classroom (Chinn &
Harris, 1989).

As with Latinos, there are several reasons why Asians may be underrepresented in classes for the disabled. First, some Asian parents are reluctant to seek
external assistance for their child with disabilities (Chan, 1986). Parents may be
hesitant to grant permission to school personnel to test their child or to consider
special education placement. A second variable is the fact that, as a group (with

some exceptions), Asians in the United States enjoy a relatively high standard of living. With the exception of the second wave of Southeast Asian immigrants beginning in 1978, most of the Asian immigrants entering the country have middle- or upper-middle-class backgrounds with a relatively high educational level. The children from these families are at less risk of special education placement than many of the children from other culturally diverse groups who come from backgrounds of poverty. In addition, educators may also have a tendency to stereotype Asian children as being very quiet. Thus children who are seriously withdrawn may be passed off as having typical Asian behaviors rather than being referred for possible special education placement.

The disproportionately low placement of American Indian, African American, and Latino children in classes for students labeled gifted and talented is also an important issue. To be placed in such a class a child's potential must be recognized by someone, usually a teacher. He or she must then be referred, tested, and ultimately placed. A child will not be placed, however, if no one recognizes his or her abilities and makes a referral. Gifted children from culturally diverse backgrounds may go unnoticed because they express their talents in ways different from some white children (Kitano & Kirby, 1986). Negative teacher attitudes toward culturally diverse students may also affect their referral rates (High & Udell, 1983). Parents from culturally diverse low-income backgrounds may be less likely to recognize their child's giftedness and less likely to nominate their child for gifted class placement.

Since teachers often unwittingly contribute to the problems of disproportionate placement of culturally diverse children in special education classes, it is important for you as a teacher to be aware of your own attitudes toward diverse students and to develop greater insight and sensitivity toward cultural diversity. You can make a difference. Figures 13.1 through 13.5 outline special considerations for evaluating language minority children for placement in special education. The questions presented in the figures in the areas of teacher variables, student variables, exposure to curriculum, and instructional variables can serve as guidelines for critiquing the assessment process and for generating prereferral interventions. As you look at these figures, remember that the purpose of these guidelines is to prevent the *inappropriate* referral and placement of language minority students in special education.

> Teachers who are aware of their attitudes can develop greater insight and sensitivity toward culturally diverse students.

Litigation

In the past twenty years the education and services provided to culturally diverse exceptional children have changed dramatically, often for the better. Litigation frequently influences legislation, and as we examine the components of major legislation such as the Individuals with Disabilities Education Act, we can readily see how laws reflect the decisions made in the courts. As a teacher, it is important for you to remember that the law is fluid and dynamic. Each year, new laws are passed by state legislatures and the U.S. Congress, and the courts are called upon to interpret the law.

> IDEA reflects court decisions that tried to rectify inequities in our educational system.

A number of critical court cases have addressed the issues of overrepresentation in special education and the appropriate assessment and placement of students from culturally diverse backgrounds. Most of the key court cases were discussed in Chapter 1, including *Brown v. Board of Education* (1954), *Diana v. California State Board of Education* (1970), and *Larry P. v. Riles* (1979). As you may recall, these important cases addressed, respectively, equal access to education for students of all races; special education assessment administered in a

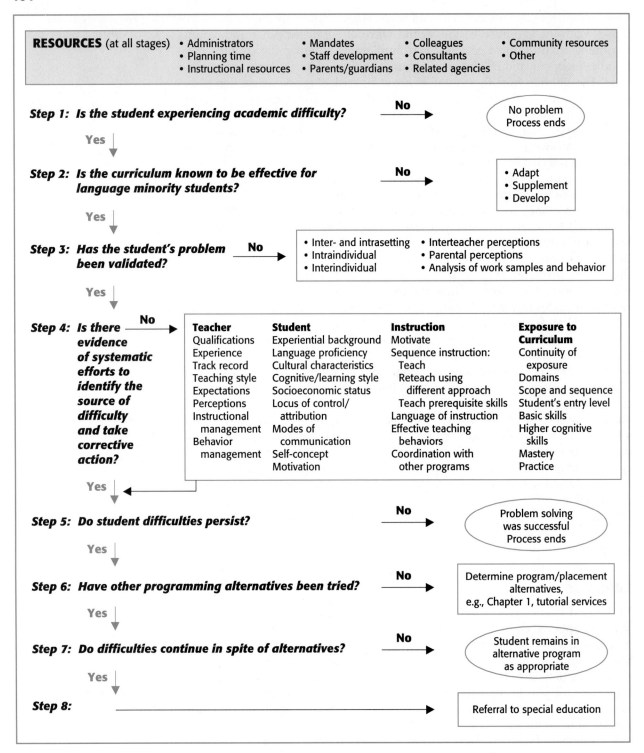

Figure 13.1

Preventing Inappropriate Placements of Language Minority Students in Special Education: A Prereferral Process

Source: Shemaz B. Garcia and Alba B. Ortiz, "Preventing Inappropriate Referrals of Language Minority Students to Special Education," *New Focus: National Clearinghouse for Bilingual Education,* 5 (June 1988): 3. Used by permission of National Clearinghouse for Bilingual Education.

Experiential background:
Does the teacher have the training and experience to work effectively with multicultural populations?

What resources has the teacher utilized in attempting to resolve the problem?
    District resources (instructional supervisors, in-service training, media and materials)
    Volunteers
    Community resources
    Colleagues
    External consultants
    Professional associations

Culture:
Has the teacher gathered cultural information specific to the student and his/her family?
    Native/traditional versus immigrant group
    Parent interviews
    Student interviews
    Home visits

Does the teacher incorporate aspects of the student's culture into the curriculum?
    Pluralistic goals, perspectives
    Integrating information across subject areas versus isolating units or presenting fragmented bits of information around holidays, festivals, etc.
    Accurate representation of culture and contributions of the group

Language proficiency:
Are the teacher's language skills adequate to deliver instruction in the student's native language?

If the student is not in bilingual education, what resources have been utilized to provide native language support?

Is the teacher adequately trained to provide dual language instruction? English-as-a-second-language intervention?

Were the student's linguistic characteristics addressed by the teacher in planning instruction?
    Comprehensible input is provided.
    Focus of instruction is on meaning rather than error correction.
    There are opportunities for English language acquisition.

Teaching style/learning style:
Is the teacher aware of his/her own preferred teaching style?

Is the teacher aware of the student's preferred learning style?

Does the teacher use a variety of styles to accommodate various learning styles of students? Is the student's style addressed?

Expectations/perceptions:
What are the teacher's perceptions of the student?

Are expectations and level of instruction geared to higher levels of thinking?

How does the teacher view cultural diversity in the classroom?

How do these views influence expectations as well as instructional planning?

Figure 13.2
Teacher Variables

Source: Shernaz B. Garcia and Alba B. Ortiz, "Preventing Inappropriate Referrals of Language Minority Students to Special Education," *New Focus: National Clearinghouse for Bilingual Education*, 5 (June 1988). Used by permission of National Clearinghouse for Bilingual Education.

student's native language; and the use of unbiased, nondiscriminatory standardized tests.

Another Supreme Court decision, *Lau v. Nichols* (1974), had a great impact on culturally and linguistically diverse children. A class action suit on behalf of 1800 Chinese students in the San Francisco Unified School District, *Lau* sought appropriate educational provisions for limited English proficient (LEP)

Experiential background:

Are any factors in the student's school history related to the current difficulty?
   Attendance/mobility
   Opportunities to learn
   Program placement(s)
   Quality of prior instruction

Have any variables related to family history affected school performance?
   Lifestyle
   Length of residence in the U.S.
   Stress (e.g., poverty, lack of emotional support)

Have any variables related to the student's medical history affected school performance?
   Vision
   Hearing
   Illness
   Nutrition
   Trauma or injury

Culture:

How is the student's cultural background different from the culture of the school and
larger society? (Mattes & Omark, 1984; Saville-Troike, 1978)
   Family (family size and structure, roles, responsibilities, expectations)
   Aspirations (success, goals)
   Language and communication (rules for adult, adult-child, child-child communica-
   tion, language use at home, non-verbal communication)
   Religion (dietary restrictions, role expectations)
   Traditions and history (contact with homeland, reason for immigration)
   Decorum and discipline (standards for acceptable behavior)

To what extent are the student's characteristics representative of the larger group?
   Continuum of culture (traditional, dualistic, atraditional [Ramirez & Castañeda, 1974])
   Degree of acculturation or assimilation

Is the student able to function successfully in more than one cultural setting?

Is the student's behavior culturally appropriate?

Language proficiency:

What is the student's dominant language? What is the preferred?
   Settings (school, playground, home, church, etc.)
   Topics (academic subjects, day-to-day interactions)
   Speakers (parents, teachers, siblings, peers, etc.)
   Aspects of each language (syntax, vocabulary, phonology, use)
   Expressive vs. receptive

Figure 13.3
Student Variables

children. The school's position was that it was the responsibility of the home to rectify children's linguistic limitations, since the district provided equal facilities and instruction for all children. The Court unanimously ruled in favor of the plaintiffs, stating that "there is no equality in treatment merely by providing students with the same facilities, textbooks, teachers, and curriculum, for students who do not understand English are effectively foreclosed from any meaningful education." The Court, which did not stipulate the method of instruction for these children, stated that special language programs were necessary if schools were to provide equal educational opportunity.

These cases are a small sample of the numerous court decisions rendered on behalf of culturally and linguistically diverse students. They illustrate the inequities inherent in our educational system, many of which are so institutionalized that it often requires the threat of litigation to inspire changes.

What is the student's level of proficiency in the primary language and in English? (Cummins, 1984)

   Interpersonal communication skills

   Cognitive/academic literacy-related skills

Are the styles of verbal interaction used in the primary language different from those most valued at school, in English? (Heath, 1986)

   Label questions (e.g., what's this? who?)

   Meaning questions (adult infers for child, interprets or asks for explanation)

   Accounts (generated by teller, information new to listener; e.g., show & tell, creative writing)

   Eventcasts (running narrative on events as they unfold, or forecast of events)

   Stories

If so, has the student been exposed to those that are unfamiliar to him/her?

What is the extent and nature of exposure to each language?

   What language(s) do the parents speak to each other?

   What language(s) do the parents speak to the child?

   What language(s) do the children use with each other?

   What television programs are seen in each language?

   Are stories read to the child? In what language(s)?

Are student behaviors characteristic of second language acquisition?

What types of language intervention has the student received?

   Bilingual v. monolingual instruction

   Language development, enrichment, remediation

   Additive v. subtractive bilingualism (transition versus maintenance)

Learning style:

Does the student's learning style require curricular/instructional accommodation?

   Perceptual style differences (e.g., visual v. auditory learner)

   Cognitive style differences (e.g., inductive v. deductive thinking)

   Preferred style of participation (e.g., teacher v. student directed, small v. large group)

If so, were these characteristics accommodated or were alternative styles taught?

Motivational influences:

Is the student's self-concept enhanced by school experiences?

   School environment communicates respect for culture and language

   Student experiences academic and social success

Do the student's family and community perceive schooling as relevant and necessary for success?

   Aspirations

   Realistic expectations based on community experience

   Culturally different criteria for success

   Education perceived by the community as a tool for assimilation

Figure 13.3
Student Variables
(continued)

Source: Shernaz B. Garcia and Alba B. Ortiz, "Preventing Inappropriate Referrals of Language Minority Students to Special Education," *New Focus: National Clearinghouse for Bilingual Education,* 5 (June 1988). Used by permission of National Clearinghouse for Bilingual Education.

As discussed in Chapter 1, IDEA reflects many of the decisions handed down by the courts through the years. The provisions in IDEA require testing in the native language by trained professionals, nondiscriminatory assessment, due process, least restrictive environment, appropriate education, individualization, and confidentiality. In addition, IDEA provides certain procedural safeguards for language minority students by requiring written or verbal communication to be provided to parents or guardians in the language of the home. All meetings or hearings must have a qualified translator.

Were skills in question taught?

Did the student receive adequate exposure to curriculum?
 In his or her dominant language
 Sufficient practice to achieve mastery

Was instruction sensitive to the student's level of performance?
 Instructional, frustrational, independent levels
 Higher-level cognitive skills vs. basic skills

Was adequate mastery of skills/concepts ensured prior to moving on to new material?

Figure 13.4
Exposure to the Curriculum

Source: Shernaz B. Garcia and Alba B. Ortiz, "Preventing Inappropriate Referrals of Language Minority Students to Special Education," *New Focus: National Clearinghouse for Bilingual Education,* 5 (June 1988). Used by permission of National Clearinghouse for Bilingual Education.

Assessment of Culturally and Linguistically Diverse Students

We use educational assessment to obtain information that helps us make informed, valid educational decisions. This information (1) helps in determining eligibility for special education, (2) identifies academic, linguistic, or cognitive

Does the learning environment promote intrinsic motivation?
 Relevant activities
 Incorporation of student's interests
 Addressing student needs
 Sensitivity to experiential background

Does the teacher use alternative approaches when there is evidence of a learning difficulty?
 Teach
 Reteach using significantly different approaches
 Teach prerequisite skills

Does the teacher use strategies that are known to be effective for language minority students?
 Native language and ESL instruction
 Genuine dialogue with students
 Contextualized instruction
 Collaborative learning
 Self-regulated learning

Does the teacher use current approaches to the teaching of ESL?
 Total physical response approach (Asher, 1979)
 The natural approach (Terrell, 1983)
 Sheltered English teaching (Northcutt & Watson, 1986)

Does the teacher use approaches to literacy development with focus on meaningful communication?
 Shared book experiences (Holdaway, 1979)
 Graves's writing workshop (Graves, 1983)
 Language experience stories
 Dialogue journals (Staton, 1987)
 Journals

Figure 13.5
Instruction

Source: Shernaz B. Garcia and Alba B. Ortiz, "Preventing Inappropriate Referrals of Language Minority Students to Special Education," *New Focus: National Clearinghouse for Bilingual Education,* 5 (June 1988). Used by permission of National Clearinghouse for Bilingual Education.

At PS 217 in Brooklyn, parents who speak Urdu, Russian, Chinese, Haitian-Creole, or Spanish do everything from acting as interpreters at parent-teacher conferences to helping families find city services. (Jacques Chenet/Newsweek)

strengths and deficits and facilitates the development of Individualized Educational Programs (IEPs) for the student, and (3) helps to determine appropriate interventions to facilitate the student's learning and progress. For culturally diverse children, particularly language minority children, it is essential that we first determine if a child has had an appropriate opportunity to learn before we engage him or her in the formal assessment process (Leung, 1996). Again, Figures 13.1 to 13.5 give us guidance in prereferral evaluation.

Once a child has been referred, the major assessment tool is tests—and herein lies a problem. If you want to develop and write a test, you must first decide what you wish to test. What do you want to learn from the test results? Who is the person or group of persons you want information about? Let us say you want to know how well the average Japanese child in the fourth grade in Japan can multiply. Your test would probably begin with easy questions and then become progressively more difficult. However, Japan is quite far away. What if you developed your test, gave the test to fourth-grade children in Iowa, found out what their average score was, and then announced that this would be the average by which all Japanese fourth-graders would be judged? Your sample of children in Iowa is the group on which your test is *normed*. But, since the test is really to be used for Japanese students in Japan, the Iowa norming sample is inappropriate. Seem obvious? Maybe, but this is exactly the problem with many of the tests that have been used with culturally and linguistically diverse students. In the past, tests were normed primarily on white, middle-class children. Culturally diverse students were excluded or used only sparingly in the norming sample. Today, many of tests used in educational assessment and intelligence testing have been normed on diverse populations. As a teacher, you will administer tests and interpret test scores. It is important, therefore, for you to be able to evaluate the norming procedures of individual tests and to take the norming procedures into account during interpretation. A good resource on assessment procedures can assist you in evaluating and interpreting the norms of frequently administered tests (see Salvia & Ysseldyke, 1998, in the Multimedia Resources section).

Would it be fair to show a 4-year-old child in Hawaii a picture of a snake and one of a squirrel and expect the child to respond as well as a 4-year-old child in rural west Texas? There are no snakes or squirrels in Hawaii, and the child in all likelihood would never have seen one. Conversely, would it be fair to show a 4-year-old in west Texas a picture of a mongoose and one of a coconut and expect the Texas child to do as well as the child in Hawaii, who has grown up seeing both from a very early age? This is the problem with bias. Tests are seldom, if ever, unbiased. However, some tests are more biased than others and tend to place culturally diverse students at a disadvantage compared to white students. At times the questions are written in a manner that tends to favor a certain socioeconomic group (assuming, for example, that everyone has a checking account or has seen a tennis match). Then there is the issue of the examiner. If the person doing the testing is white, male, and speaks only English, there could be some very real disadvantages for the student from a different background. If the student is young, female, Asian, Hispanic, American Indian, or African American, and limited English proficient, this could be an extremely intimidating and frightening experience.

Types of Assessment

According to IDEA, students must be assessed by a multidisciplinary team, and placement cannot be based on the results of one test.

IDEA mandates assessment guidelines to minimize abuses in the assessment process. Students must be assessed by a multidisciplinary team of trained individuals, and placement in a special education class cannot be based on a single test result. It is the responsibility of the multidisciplinary team to provide a culture-fair process for culturally diverse students. There are four fairly common options used in testing language minority students: (1) translating the existing tests, (2) using interpreters in testing, (3) using tests normed or renormed in a primary language, and (4) using a bilingual school psychologist or psychometrist (Cheng, 1987).

Despite these attempts at improvement, the assessment process is still one of the most controversial issues in special education and will continue to be the center of controversy since the various efforts and methods used to reduce bias are still badly flawed. First, translating the tests does not fix the inherent problem of content bias. Second, often the child is proficient neither in English nor in the language of the home, and the translations are often in a more "pure" form of a language, such as Castilian Spanish as compared to the border Mexican many Mexican American children speak. This factor also may result in the misdiagnosis of a communication disorder, because of a child's bilingual delay in language development (Schiff-Myers, Djikie, McGovern, Lawler & Perez, 1993). Third, interpreters are not always proficient, and some are unable to translate technical terms.

As you may remember from earlier chapters, adaptive behavior assessments and functional assessments have found new importance in recent years for both identification of students with disabilities and educational planning (Artiles & Trent, 1994). These types of assessments have helped to widen the focus of evaluations of students' performance to the context of their home environment and therefore include reference to cultural norms.

The assessment system is still flawed, but it is slowly improving.

In summary, when assessing a child from a culturally diverse background, the multidisciplinary team, clinical judgment, and multiple sources of information are important (Leung, 1996). Standardized tests will be used in most evaluations, but also trust your and others' knowledge of the culturally diverse child and his or her academic skills. Although the system is still flawed, we are aware today of problems we were either unaware of thirty years ago or ignored. Today the laws mandate that we pay attention to these problems, and test developers continue to strive to create culture-fair tests. We now have the knowledge, the alternative means, and the safeguards that minimize or eliminate many of the abuses of the past.

Educational Implications and Teaching Strategies

As a teacher, your responsibility in the classroom is to assist your students in reaching their academic, vocational, and social potentials. Given the large size of many classrooms and the diversity of your students, this will be a challenging but exciting task.

Knowing Yourself

As we have suggested throughout this chapter, one of your first steps should be self-examination. Self-examination is not particularly difficult, but doing it honestly and objectively may be a little harder than you think. Begin by asking yourself who you are. Get a sheet of paper and provide information on your:

- ethnicity
- social class
- gender
- geographical background
- language background
- age
- religion
- teaching style

After you have completed the initial exercise, examine the importance you place on each of these items. Now go down your class roll and ask yourself where each of your students fits in each of these areas. How important is ethnicity to them? How important is language and dialect? How congruent are your values with those of your students? Your values don't have to be congruent, but it is important to know who you are with respect to your students. Do you have biases and prejudices? Almost everyone does. You should be suspicious of the teacher who says, "I don't have a prejudiced bone in my body!" What is important is that we recognize these biases and not let them cause us to be unfair or insensitive to students, their parents, our colleagues, and others who are associated with the school.

Educational Issues

As increasingly large numbers of culturally and linguistically diverse children enter the schools, there are among them increasing numbers with disabilities. One of the greatest challenges in special education has been to provide appropriate services to these children, because of the interaction among variables such as disability type, primary and secondary language development, and cultural norms. A major issue in this field is bilingual special education services.

■ Bilingual Special Education When students receive resource or self-contained programs, one approach is to place these children in classrooms with special education teachers who are bilingual. There are two basic problems with this approach: There are too few special education teachers who are bilingual, and those who are may have only limited skills in the language other than English. In addition, few of these teachers have adequate preparation in bilingual education methodology.

Because there are such extreme shortages of trained personnel, a common approach has been to place the LEP children in a special education class with an English-speaking teacher. A bilingual aide is often placed in the classroom to assist in instruction. Because of the communication limitations between the teacher and LEP student, the aide often ends up providing most of the instruction. These aides typically have insufficient training, particularly in special education techniques, resulting in an educational process that is lacking.

A new breed of teachers is currently being prepared in either bilingual/special education or ESL/special education programs. These individuals also have specialized preparation in developing their cultural sensitivity and awareness.

Even when language minority students are placed with appropriate teachers in appropriate settings, there are still adjustments to make to the typical methodologies we might use to teach other students with disabilities. Some modifications in material presentation, as well as integration of various instructional strategies, will be necessary during basic academic instruction.

■ Basic Skills Instruction If students in your classroom are not native English speakers, they may speak and understand at different levels of proficiency. Obviously, it is important for you to know each student's level of proficiency. The way you present information to students can help to facilitate their understanding. Many of the suggestions discussed in earlier chapters, such as Chapter 5, also will help students who are not native English speakers. Examples include using clear, simple instructions or sentences; providing examples; and using response signals or clues. In addition, the use of contextual support or context-embedded information may be very helpful. For example, holding and pointing to the material and demonstrating the response format provide a context by giving the listener cues about what is required (Fueyo, 1997).

The specific difficulties encountered in reading and writing by students who are learning two languages also may require adjustments in how we teach basic skills. In fact, many bilingual special educators advocate the use of the whole language method of instruction, or direct instruction in a literature-based context, for students who are not native English speakers. This type of instruction allows students to use relevant books in their native language and helps the teacher to evaluate the student's performance in higher-level thinking, planning, and conversational skills (Lopez-Reyna, 1996). The specific skill instruction characteristic of most special education programs, therefore, may need to be supported or integrated with the use of motivating literature and with extensive opportunities to read, write, and discuss content in both native and new languages in order to facilitate development in both (Gersten & Woodward, 1994). The accompanying box, "Cultural and Linguistic Considerations Related to IEP Development," provides examples of specific strategies for planning instruction for culturally diverse students with disabilities.

■ Awareness of Behavioral Norms Awareness of differences in cultural behavioral norms and receptivity to treatments is also a critical concern for

～ Cultural and Linguistic Considerations Related to IEP Development

Selection of IEP Goals and Objectives

Considerations for IEP Development

IEP goals and objectives accommodate the student's current level of performance.

Classroom Implications

- At the student's instructional level
- Instructional level based on student's cognitive level, not the language proficiency level
- Focus on development of higher-level cognitive skills as well as basic skills

Goals and objectives are responsive to cultural and linguistic variables.

- Accommodates goals and expectations of the family
- Is sensitive to culturally based response to the disability
- Includes a language use plan
- Addresses language development and ESL needs

Selection of Instructional Strategies

Considerations for IEP Development

Interventions provide adequate exposure to curriculum.

Classroom Implications

- Instruction in student's dominant language
- Responsiveness to learning and communication styles
- Sufficient practice to achieve mastery

IEP provides for curricular/instructional accommodation of learning styles and locus of control.

- Accommodates perceptual style differences (e.g., visual vs. auditory)
- Accommodates cognitive style differences (e.g., inductive vs. deductive)
- Accommodates preferred style of participation (e.g., teacher- vs. student-directed, small vs. large group)
- Reduces feelings of learned helplessness

Selected strategies are likely to be effective for language minority students.

- Native language and ESL instruction
- Teacher as facilitator of learning (vs. transmission)
- Genuine dialogue with students
- Contextualized instruction
- Collaborative learning
- Self-regulated learning
- Learning-to-learn strategies

English as a second language (ESL) strategies are used.

- Modifications to address the student's disability
- Use of current ESL approaches
- Focus on meaningful communication

Strategies for literacy are included.

- Holistic approaches to literacy development
- Language teaching that is integrated across the curriculum
- Thematic literature units
- Language experience approach
- Journals

Source: Garcia, Shemaz B., & Malkin Diana H. (1993). "Toward Defining Programs and Services for Culturally and Linguistically Diverse Learners in Special Education," *Teaching Exceptional Children, 26,* 52–58. Copyright © 1993 by The Council for Exceptional Children. Reprinted with permission.

teachers of students with behavior and emotional disorders. Teachers must adjust behavior management programs so that they work with the behavioral traits of students from diverse cultural or family backgrounds, rather than challenging them (McIntyre, 1996). Although it is important to be sensitive to cultural variation in behavioral patterns, it also is important to maintain high levels of school behavioral expectations for your students. The last thing you want to do is assume that Malcolm's, Juan's, and Lisa's behaviors, however problematic, must be culturally generated and therefore are not amenable to change.

Using Textbooks and Instructional Materials

Traditional classroom activity revolves around textbooks. Nearly half of the states have state adoptions, which means that every school in the state uses the same textbooks. In those states where there are no state adoptions, there may be districtwide adoptions. Hence, you as a classroom teacher may not have a voice in determining which textbooks or material will be used in your classroom. Nonetheless, there are certain issues of which you should be aware, so you can use your textbooks as effectively as possible.

A number of biases may be found in textbooks and other materials, although in recent years, publishers and authors have devoted considerable effort to eliminate them. Although the problems with bias are improving, they still exist. See the accompanying box, "Checklist for Selecting and Evaluating Materials," for some guidelines to use in your classroom.

Invisibility, one type of bias, means that groups of individuals, particularly women and culturally and ethnically diverse groups, are either neglected or underrepresented. This omission suggests that these groups have less value and less importance than the dominant group. Look through your text. If it fails to include ethnically diverse groups, women, individuals with disabilities, and the aged adequately, you may either choose not to adopt the text (if you have a choice) or be prepared to point out these errors of bias to your students.

Stereotyping is another type of bias in which traditional and rigid roles are ascribed to women, various cultural and ethnic groups, the aged, and so on. For example, some books may show Mexican Americans only as farm or ranch hands or as domestics, not as physicians, teachers, lawyers, and police officers.

Textbooks that consistently present issues and situations from the perspective of only one group (usually the dominant group) show biases of *selectivity and balance* (Gollnick & Chinn, 1994). Thus, texts often fail to discuss adequately the role of African Americans, Hispanics, Asians, and American Indians in developing this country. Too often the history of this country is told only from the perspective of the Western European.

We can find *linguistic bias* in many of our instructional materials, particularly in older editions. At times only masculine pronouns are used, such as *he* or *him*. At other times we can find materials that use only Anglo names—there are no names like Juan, Margarita, or Yong Sook. This again tells the reader that only Anglo children are important and the value of other cultures is minimal at best (Gollnick & Chinn, 1994). One way to counteract this is to develop worksheets using the names of your students or culturally diverse names familiar to them.

You as a teacher need not sit back and allow biased material to affect your students negatively. If you must use biased texts, you can point out omissions. You and the students can together examine the author's perspective and compare it to your own and that of your students. One instructional technique is to fill in the omissions. Another technique is to rewrite portions of the text, as a

Teachers should point out textbook biases to their students and work with them to provide missing information.

～ Checklist for Selecting and Evaluating Materials

- Are the perspectives and contributions of people from diverse cultural and linguistic groups—both men and women, as well as people with disabilities—included in the curriculum?

- Are there activities in the curriculum that will assist students in analyzing the various forms of the mass media for ethnocentrism, sexism, "handicapism," and stereotyping?

- Are men and women, diverse cultural/racial groups, and people with varying abilities shown in both active and passive roles?

- Are men and women, diverse cultural/racial groups, and people with disabilities shown in positions of power (i.e., the materials do not rely on the mainstream culture's character to achieve goals)?

- Do the materials identify strengths possessed by so-called "underachieving" diverse populations? Do they diminish the attention given to deficits, to reinforce positive behaviors that are desired and valued?

- Are members of diverse racial/cultural groups, men and women, and people with disabilities shown engaged in a broad range of social and professional activities?

- Are members of a particular culture or group depicted as having a range of physical features (e.g., hair color, hair texture, variations in facial characteristics and body build)?

- Do the materials represent historical events from the perspectives of the various groups involved or solely from the male, middle-class, and/or Western European perspective?

- Are the materials free of ethnocentric or sexist language patterns that may make implications about persons or groups based solely on their culture, race, gender, or disability?

- Will students from different ethnic and cultural backgrounds find the materials personally meaningful to their life experiences?

- Are a wide variety of culturally different examples, situations, scenarios, and anecdotes used throughout the curriculum design to illustrate major intellectual concepts and principles?

- Are culturally diverse content, examples, and experiences comparable in kind, significance, magnitude, and function to those selected from mainstream culture?

Source: Garcia, Shemaz B., & Malkin Diana H. (1993). "Toward Defining Programs and Services for Culturally and Linguistically Diverse Learners in Special Education," *Teaching Exceptional Children, 26,* 55. Copyright © 1993 by The Council for Exceptional Children. Reprinted with permission.

class assignment, from a more culturally diverse and accurate perspective using women, older individuals, individuals with disabilities, and non-Anglos. You can also make use of your school or local library to supplement this text with more wide-ranging and authentic materials (Gollnick & Chinn, 1994).

Understanding Your Community

If you are to be an effective teacher, you need to understand your community. More specifically, you need to know the community in which your students live. If you live in a large city such as Los Angeles, you may live in one community and teach in another. If your students live in a housing project in the inner city, they will have difficulty relating to a reader with a story about a girl named Lori who lives in a single-family home in the suburbs and whose father is an airline pilot. Knowing the community will enable you to relate learning to relevant aspects of the students' lives and will also permit you to develop and/or use materials specific to their interests and needs.

Teachers must know the community in which their students live.

Utilizing Community Resources

Utilizing community resources can often be an effective instructional strategy. There are individuals from the community who enjoy the respect of your

People from the community can help teachers convey messages about important issues to their students.

students who can occasionally be asked to come into your school to speak about important issues such as drugs, AIDS, race relations, completing school, and so on. These individuals—college or professional athletes, politicians, business/community leaders—may have more credibility than you do. Even though you may say the same thing in the same manner, the community resource people may simply be more believable to the students.

SUMMARY

■ The United States is one of the most pluralistic nations in the world. Individuals from every ethnic background and nearly every linguistic group make up the mosaic of our country. This chapter has reviewed some basic concepts related to culture and has examined how culture can affect exceptionality and special class placement. Educators who are sensitive to their own cultural identity as well as that of the children they teach can better understand and modify their own behaviors so that the negative impact of incongruent values can be minimized.

■ By examining the inherent problems in the assessment process, the concomitant problems associated with bias in the special class placement of culturally diverse children, and the problems related to language acquisition and assimilation of culturally diverse children, we can better and more appropriately provide for their needs.

■ The legal battles waged to assure fair treatment of these children in our schools provide us with a historical perspective of what has been and what can be in terms of providing an adequate education for *all* our children. As we strive to make the adjustments necessary to accommodate the dramatic changes in the schools, we are in many ways privileged to be a part of one of the most exciting eras in American education. History will some day tell us how we fared. The commitments we as educators make today and the actions we take tomorrow will help to shape this history.

KEY TERMS

culture	minority group	dialect
macroculture	ethnicity	Black English
microculture	cultural diversity	bilingual education
assimilation	linguistic diversity	cultural competence
acculturation	limited English	overrepresentation
minority	proficient (LEP)	underrepresentation

MULTIMEDIA RESOURCES

Baca, Leonard M. *Language Minority Students with Disabilities* (Reston, VA: Council for Exceptional Children, 1991). Helps teachers understand how proper prereferral, assessment, and instruction can help these at-risk students succeed in school. Includes several resources for further investigation.

Derman-Sparks, Louise. *Anti-Bias Curriculum: Tools for Empowering Young Children* (Washington, DC: National Association for the Education of Young Children, 1989). This important resource helps teachers make their classrooms inclusive environments—providing activities, methodology, anecdotes, and photographs to help even the youngest children learn about diversity.

Division for Culturally and Linguistically Diverse Exceptional Learners. The Council for Exceptional Children, 1920 Association Drive, Reston, VA 20191-1589. This organization provides information about services, conferences, programs, and publications for teachers, parents, and other professionals.

Hollins, Etta R. *Culture in School Learning: Revealing the Deep Meaning* (Mahwah, NJ: Lawrence Erlbaum, 1996). This text is designed to provide teachers with a deeper understanding of culture and its role in education.

Lynch, Eleanor W., and Marci J. Hanson. *Developing Cross-Cultural Competence* (Baltimore, MD: Paul H. Brookes, 1992). A text that explores a wide range of cultural perspectives and implications for interventions.

Multicultural and Bilingual Special Education. Website: http://aznet.net/~zatyko/html/mc.html/. A variety of educational material related to multicultural and bilingual special education, such as books and thematic units, can be found here.

Optimal Learning Environment Project (Bilingual Special Education). Website: http://edweb.educ.csus.edu/Projects/ole/G.Info.html. Information and materials about a research-based project on reading instruction for culturally and linguistically diverse students.

Ortiz, Alba A., and B. Ramirez. *Schools and the Culturally Diverse Exceptional Students: Promising Practices and Future Directions* (Reston, VA: Council for Exceptional Children, 1988). A collection of papers that answer questions on how to nurture potential giftedness, commonalities, and diversities among Asian Americans, and how to improve education for American Indian exceptional children.

Salvia, John, and Ysseldyke, James E. *Assessment*, 7th ed. (Boston: Houghton Mifflin, 1998). An overview of a variety of assessment tools. Includes in-depth discussion of bias in assessment.

USING YOUR KNOWLEDGE

Commonalities: What are the cultural and linguistic backgrounds of students in your local school district? What is the cultural or ethnic background of teachers in your local school district? Collect data from your school district's central office if it is available. What does the data reveal?

Can Do: What types of assessment methods might be used with a student who speaks Spanish as her first language and has a physical disability? Identify the appropriate tests and assessment procedures you would need to ensure that this student receives a fair and appropriate evaluation. Are these options available in your school district?

Commonalities: Throughout this text, we have discussed the differences among students, while also presenting their similarities or commonalities. As a teacher, you must take into account the diversity of your students, yet make all students feel as if they belong. Discuss some ways to accomplish this in the classroom. What strategies are most appropriate for you?

Collaboration: What do you know about your community and its resources? Identify the different cultures that are clearly represented in your community. Talk to people and gather materials from cultures with which you are unfamiliar. How can you use that knowledge to create a culturally sensitive classroom?

WHAT YOU CAN DO

1. **Create a student-centered classroom.** Identify and incorporate learning materials and situations into your teaching that are familiar to the culturally diverse students in your class. Identify and provide support for culturally diverse gifted students.

2. **Develop a plan and model script for a meeting with a non–English-speaking parent and an interpreter.** If possible, interview an interpreter to identify important information and considerations. Make sure that your plan includes attention to cultural issues and factors such as seating arrangements, order of speaking, and protocols for asking questions.

3. **Using the sources of bias in instructional materials given in this chapter, collect samples of instructional materials used in a classroom (perhaps your own) and prepare a descriptive evaluation of cultural bias.** Make sure you collect teacher-made materials, textbooks, and supplemental books or activities.

4. **Research the testing methods used in a local district or at the state department of education.** Identify the range of possible tests and examine some of them to obtain norming data or for other potential sources of bias. A district school psychologist can give you information about which tests are used most frequently in a given district or state for special education evaluations.

$\mathcal{E}$xceptional Individuals Through the Lifespan

$\mathcal{E}$DUCATION is a lifelong experience. As we'll explore in this chapter, a lifespan perspective looks at the ongoing personal growth of exceptional individuals as well as their relationships and interactions with the surrounding community. Key areas for lifespan development include employment, living arrangements, personal relationships, and quality of life. As you read, look for answers to these questions:

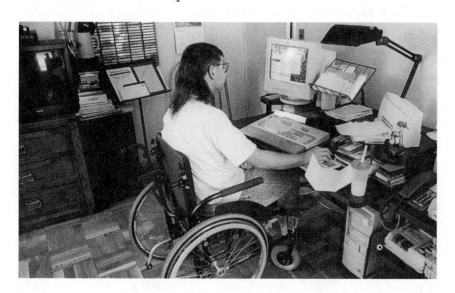

■ What factors influence an individual's successful transition to adulthood and independence?

■ How is transition programming related to (and developed from) a student's Individualized Education Program?

Commonalities: How do we use age and social norms to describe lifespan development?

Can Do: What employment options are available for individuals with disabilities, and what issues do they face in finding meaningful employment?

Collaboration: What are the effects of discrimination? What laws have been designed to counteract discrimination? What can we do?

How often have you thought eagerly about what lies ahead in your life? How much of what you do today is done in preparation for the next phase of your life? The 4-year-old child cannot wait until he is old enough to ride a "big boy's bike." The 13-year-old dreams of the day she will turn 16 and can get that driver's license. A 20-year-old studies intently so she can get the job of her choice after college graduation and begin a successful career. The 39-year-old works extra hours to put away money for his children's education and to prepare for retirement.

Each culture develops certain benchmarks of progress—activities, achievements, or acquisitions—that signal that an individual has reached independence and maturity. These benchmarks, which occur at all stages of the life cycle, reflect an individual's level of independence and social status. Most people are continually aware of their own performance relative to the achievements of those around them. Persons who are considered exceptional, however, frequently perform at levels that differ from those of others in their culture, *and these differences are expressed in every stage of development*, including adulthood. In this chapter, we will look at the changing roles and responsibilities of exceptional individuals as they grow and mature into adulthood. We will also explore their challenges and opportunities as they strive to achieve the universal human goals of meaningful work, independence, self-determination, and social acceptance.

Definitions and Terms

Although each of us aspires to unique individual goals, certain aspects of growing up are pretty much the same for all of us. Our lives can be perceived as a series of stages, or phases: infancy, early childhood, school-aged childhood, adolescence, and adulthood (young, middle-aged, and senior). Each stage is accompanied by new behaviors, roles, and responsibilities. As exceptional individuals move through the stages of life, they may face special challenges brought about by their disability, yet aspire to the same age-appropriate goals as anyone else. In this final chapter, we will look at the experiences of growing up and growing old. For persons with disabilities, these experiences may be as varied as those of any group of individuals. One common experience, however, may be the need to demonstrate their competence and to convince society to provide them with opportunities to grow.

Age and Social Norms

Both biological and social maturing occur as people move through the stages of life, and behaviors usually associated with the different stages of development are called **norms**—normal or typical ranges of expected behavior. Two types of norms are important to the developmental process: age norms and social norms (Sigelman & Shaffer, 1991; Vander Zanden, 1989).

Norms are normal or typical ranges of expected behavior.

Age norms are the behaviors considered appropriate or usual at a certain point in a person's biological life cycle. For example, many new parents anxiously read books on infant and child development to see if their child displays appropriate behavior for his or her age. Certain behaviors such as turning over, sitting up, and saying the first word are associated with specific age ranges. We use the term "the terrible twos" because we expect toddlers to try to take control—crying fits and tantrums are seen as the unfortunate norm. Parents and teachers of teenagers commiserate about the behaviors they expect from adolescents. As adolescents become young adults, age norms include increased responsibility for personal behavior.

Age norms for adults are more difficult to identify. Often, they include a rejection of the behaviors of youth and the assumption of a less egocentric view of the world. Being able to take care of yourself and others, and weighing the risks of what you do could be considered age-related norms for adults. Often, age norms in the adult stages are difficult to distinguish from social norms because our expectations of adults are so closely tied to social achievements.

Social norms are behaviors that reflect the typical patterns or standards of a particular group (Vander Zanden, 1989). Attending school, owning your own home, and having a family are examples of social norms in mainstream American culture. Social norms are age related; the social norms of elementary school children differ from those of middle-aged adults. They are, however, more variable than age norms because they reflect the surrounding culture or society.

We expect social norms to change gradually over time and to reflect the changing environment and needs of individuals. A good example of changing social norms is the role of women in the home and workplace. It has become socially acceptable—in fact, "normal"—for women with families to work outside of the home. The social and economic environment has resulted in changes in the expected roles of women as they mature into adulthood.

The Impact of Exceptional Characteristics on Age and Social Norms

There are no separate norms applied by society for individuals with exceptionalities. They are judged, and often judge themselves, according to achievements, behaviors, and activities associated with the age and social norms of our society.

Some individuals with disabilities do not demonstrate the behaviors associated with age and social norms. In fact, the discrepancy between age norms and the behavioral level of a specific child is frequently used as a means of determining the existence of a disability (for example, the term *developmental delay*). Other people may lose their previous ability to meet these norms through accident or the onset of a particular illness or condition. Because age and social norms play an important role in our perceptions of maturity and adulthood, the individual who has not achieved some of these milestones may be seen as unable to or not needing to progress through the social stages of human development.

Our widespread use of age and social norms for guiding interactions with others can have a negative impact on exceptional individuals. For example, some individuals may not be afforded the opportunity to demonstrate the age-appropriate behaviors they have acquired. A young adult with severe physical disabilities may not be given the opportunity or means for communication because his lack of speech or motor control gives rise to the assumption that he cannot participate in meaningful conversation. A young woman with Down syndrome may not be interviewed for a job she has trained for because of the employer's preconceived ideas about mental retardation.

This history of prejudging individuals with disabilities is, at long last, changing. Parents, teachers, caretakers, and, most important, persons with exceptionalities have recognized the importance of adult roles and responsibilities for *all* individuals. Assumptions of social and age norms change slowly, however, and require the participation of all members of society.

Some individuals may not have opportunities to demonstrate age-appropriate behaviors.

Factors Influencing Adult Performance

A number of factors influence the extent to which persons with exceptionalities have been able to participate in the usual roles of adulthood. Some of these factors involve discrimination and the recognition of basic human rights. Other factors are the same things that influence all of us and help to determine which of us will be successful, unemployed, homeless, wealthy, married, single, parents, unhappy, or contented. These common factors include family and social support as well as personal determination.

Legislation

Recent legislation has helped to refine the legal requirements for public services and places of employment as well as to put in place a system of preparation for work while individuals are still in the school system. For example, the **Education for Handicapped Children Amendments of 1984 (P.L. 98-199)** allocated educational funds for the purpose of facilitating the transition of adolescents to adult life. The **Education of the Handicapped Act Amendments of 1990 (P.L. 101-476)** required that a formal transition plan be developed for all secondary students identified as disabled. The **IDEA Amendments of 1997** required that transition services be included in a student's IEP when the student is 14 years old and that the transition services focus on the student's educational plan (Yell & Shriner, 1997).

The **Americans with Disabilities Act (ADA) of 1990 (P.L. 101-336)** extends civil rights protection to individuals with disabilities in private-sector employment. In addition, the law requires that public services such as telecommunication and transportation make accommodations for individuals with disabilities. For example, if a company offers telephone service to the general public, telecommunication services for the deaf must be provided. Transportation systems such as buses and railroads must include access for individuals with physical disabilities. Other public accommodations and facilities (stores, hotels, schools) must be accessible and must provide any support material necessary to allow individuals to use their services (Council for Exceptional Children, 1990).

Supportive legislation helps to ensure that integration will take place and normalized interpersonal relationships will develop. A less obvious benefit of this legislation is the implicit acceptance and recognized importance of all persons in our society. Legislation is one of the ways our nation has of conveying information important to our culture. The message sent by these laws is that our society should and will encourage participation by all people in the socially important roles of adulthood.

Legislation signals the increased acceptance of persons with disabilities in our society.

Appropriate and Continuous Services

Appropriate services for individuals with disabilities include all of the educational, social, physical, emotional, and support services that are now available from birth through adulthood. Some people will require extensive training and preparation to move into the world of independent work and community living; others require only minimal assistance.

Support services for individuals with disabilities go beyond vocational training and assistance and include counseling, family planning, and commu-

Individuals with disabilities are strong advocates for their own civil rights and have been instrumental in effecting legal and social change in this country. (Marilyn Humphries/Impact Visuals)

nity living services. Living in a community setting or living independently are life goals for many people with disabilities. The realization of these goals will depend on many things, including employment status, amount of money earned, and, for some people, appropriate training.

Societal Awareness: Acceptance or Discrimination

As our collective social conscience, understanding, and attention to human rights issues have grown, educational techniques and technology have become more refined and purposeful. This surge of growth in both social and technological areas has provided many of us with the understanding of what is needed to facilitate personal growth and development and has given educators and other professionals the means by which to accomplish change. The results have included related legislation and a number of community programs. Nonetheless, social awareness and acceptance are difficult areas to address and assess, and they continue to be obstacles for some individuals with disabilities.

Probably one of the most frustrating conditions that could occur for any of us is to know what we want, to know we can do or have it, and then to be denied access to the activity, job, situation, or setting because of discrimination. In this context, **discrimination** refers to a categorical denial of equal opportunity and equal access based on arbitrary personal characteristics, such as a disability.

Social acceptance continues to be
an obstacle for some individuals
with disabilities.

Individuals with disabilities may
need to demonstrate competence to
help create public respect and acceptance.

■ **The Origins of Discrimination** Each person has his or her own perceptions about disabilities and their effect on others. Sometimes these perceptions are based on material garnered from the media, early personal experience, or hearsay. Some people have difficulty accepting differences of any kind. We have discussed in earlier parts of this book the importance of attitude in the areas of social integration and normalization. Just because a person is able to secure a job in a major company, enroll in college, or live in a home within the community does not mean that the individual will experience the quality of social interaction or general treatment accorded other adults in similar settings.

Probably the greatest obstacles in terms of attitude and acceptance faced by adults with disabilities are not feelings of ridicule or dislike, but rather feelings of pity and sympathy. Although individuals with disabilities have been much more visible in stories and pictures in recent years, the media continue to focus on sentimentality. From the slow-motion tapes of a child with Down syndrome running in the Special Olympics to newspaper stories containing emotionally charged and inspirational stories of the "victims" of disabling conditions, we see many presentations designed to move us to tears. Sympathy is a more positive attitude than fear or avoidance, but it is no less of an obstacle to the individuals attempting to establish their rightful place in the world of adult life.

Many adults with disabilities are not only challenged by patronizing attitudes, they are offended by them (Keller, Hallahan, McShane, Crowley & Blandford, 1990). As these adults and others speak out, changes can be expected in the portrayals of exceptional people in the entertainment and news media. If the need for demonstrations of competence can be replaced by expectations of competence, we will have gone a long way toward addressing the problems of societal attitude and acceptance.

■ **The Effects of Discrimination** At the present time, many professionals in schools or adult services feel confident that demonstrations of competence will help to generate public respect and acceptance of individuals with disabilities. In other words, once the young computer programmer with severe cerebral palsy shows that she can perform at the same rate level as her coworkers, doubts will be dispelled and a more accepting attitude will result. There is, however, something disturbing in the concept that an individual with an exceptional characteristic must continuously prove his or her competence. It is true that we all have to do well at our job in order to keep it, and we all have to demonstrate competence in order to advance. But there is a big difference between starting the first day of work with everyone assuming you will be able to do well and starting the first day with everyone assuming you will not be able to succeed.

The effects of discrimination can be felt in other aspects of adult life as well. Because of the increase in community housing for many individuals with moderate or severe disabilities, community attitudes and acceptance are important factors that can affect social and physical integration. Although many communities welcome integrated housing, agencies that buy real estate to use as group homes or apartment residences sometimes face resistance from the surrounding community. In some cases, the source of this resistance is a lack of knowledge about people with disabilities. Because many people have had few interactions with persons with mental retardation or mental illness, for example, they may have fears or concerns that translate into housing discrimination. Other individuals exhibit resistance due to impressions that the property will not be maintained and, therefore, the surrounding property values will decrease. Although housing discrimination is illegal, one avenue of resistance communities sometimes use is to prohibit zoning changes that are necessary for multiple-person residences such as group homes. In places where multiple-person residences are already in existence, such as areas surrounding colleges and universities, legal avenues of resistance are limited to verbal protest or the selling of personal property. Such actions continue to be the biggest obstacles to successful community integration. How can we change these attitudes? Education and experience with persons with disabilities may be the most important factors in changing attitudes and preventing future discrimination. Again, however, we find people with disabilities in the position of having to prove that they are good neighbors before they can gain acceptance.

As we have seen, recent legislation and a greater social awareness help to expand the options and personal determination of people with disabilities. Prior to the Federal Fair Housing Amendment of 1988 and the Americans with Disabilities Act of 1990, many people had no legal recourse when their rights to equal opportunities for education, employment, and housing were denied. Because of this legislation, however, individuals with disabilities cannot be denied opportunities on the sole basis of their disability.

Experience with people with disabilities is an important factor in changing attitudes and preventing discrimination.

Family Support and Interaction

In Chapter 3, we discussed the importance of the family in providing support and opportunities to exceptional individuals. The role of the family continues to be important throughout the lives of individuals with disabilities. Often, families are faced with a number of decisions about their child's eventual preparation for life—decisions related to education, housing, and community involvement.

Although educational and life challenges increase with time, families are provided with progressively fewer support services as their children grow into adults. Once the school is no longer available to provide services and assistance, families often must seek out services on their own. Many parents, therefore, make decisions for their child based on their own ideas of what the child will be able to do or to achieve—sometimes without knowing what is actually possible. Without support services, a parent might be unaware of available assistance (such as temporary care providers) or of training for which their child is eligible (vocational preparation, training for independent living).

The decisions that parents of individuals with disabilities must make become increasingly difficult as their children grow up and as life becomes more complicated. The parents of a young woman with mental retardation, for example, may be reluctant to agree to a community living arrangement because they are afraid of how she will react and how she will be treated by others, and because they want to be able to care for her and protect her. For such parents, a visit to the work or home site may help to ease their fears. Professionals at adult service agencies may be able to offer trial arrangements, such as weekend visits or daytime living in the community setting, until the parents become more comfortable.

Decisions parents make throughout the lifespan have significant effects on the adult life of the child. Many young adults with disabilities cite parental support as a major contributor to their achievements in life (Liebert, Lutsky & Gottlieb, 1990; Malcom, Polatajko & Simons, 1990). Researchers have also found that parental support (or lack of it) is a significant factor in determining the successful placement of individuals with disabilities in community employment or

The love and support of family continues to be important to us throughout our adult years. (Will & Deni McIntyre/Photo Researchers, Inc.)

residential settings (Heal, Gonzalez, Rusch, Copher & Destefane 1990). Expectations for success, curriculum decisions, educational placement, living arrangements, community employment, college enrollment, and career aspirations are only some of the areas that can be influenced by the attitudes, knowledge, and support of parents. It also seems clear that parents need to have continuous access to information and support services so they feel confident when making decisions that can facilitate integration and normalization of their child as he or she becomes an adult.

Personal Determination

Self-confidence and self-determination are important factors in successful adjustment.

At each stage of an individual's life, personal characteristics seem to be the underlying factor in perceived success. Self-determination, the ability to make and carry out personal life decisions, is emerging as an increasingly important factor in the successful transition to adult life in areas such as employment for individuals with disabilities (Wehmeyer & Schwartz, 1997). You will see and hear much about educational programming related to self-determination as you examine outcome goals for adolescents and adults with disabilities. Some of the related terms are *self-advocacy*, *autonomy*, and *personal choice*.

Encouraging choice and providing options to individuals with disabilities may be one of the most important ways to provide opportunities for each person to exert his or her own personality and self-determination. The presence or absence of choice directly affects to what extent an individual can determine the course of his or her life in both major and relatively minor ways. When all life decisions are made by others, individual characteristics are buried; we become what others determine we should be and do what others determine we should do. Although it is often well intentioned, the removal of choice and risk reduces the ability of the individual to determine the direction of his or her life.

For example, the high school vocational program for persons with mental retardation may provide two training options: horticulture and gardening skills or training in housekeeping skills—and you may be interested in auto mechanics or caring for children. The mother of a young woman with severe physical disabilities does not want her to date, so the young adult is not given the opportunity to develop important personal relationships. For some people with disabilities, self-determination may be difficult to achieve. Many individuals with disabilities, however, do find ways to take their lives into their own hands and are able to achieve the goals they have set for themselves.

We have mentioned a number of factors that can influence adult achievement and independence. In the following sections, we will look at four of the most important aspects of preparation for and participation in adult life for individuals with disabilities. These are transition programming, employment, independent living, and the development of personal relationships and leisure activities.

Removing choice and risk reduces an individual's ability to determine the direction of his or her life.

Transition: Preparing for Options Beyond School

The transition movement attempts to provide opportunities and training for all people to participate fully in adult life. **Transition programs** are designed to facilitate movement from school to work, from segregated to integrated settings, and from isolated living to community living and employment. They address the issues of participation in society and adherence to social norms. Through educational programs that include life-skills curricula and encourage the modification of existing environmental and social structures, we may increase the range of employment and living options available to persons with disabilities. Transition programming has important implications for maximizing the quality of life and the potential achievements of individuals with disabilities.

Well-planned transition programs can maximize the quality of life of individuals with disabilities.

Transition Programming

The emphasis on successful transitions to postschool settings has significantly changed the educational emphasis for many students with disabilities. Educational programs for most exceptional individuals are now expected to lead to measurable results—to produce individuals who are capable of leading independent and productive lives. Because the Individuals with Disabilities Education Act now requires all students with disabilities over the age of 14 to have a transition plan, specific goals are established annually that indicate how the student's educational program will address his or her future needs as an adult. Transition programming is a lifelong activity—one that addresses the changing needs of individuals throughout the lifespan (Clark & Kolstoe, 1990). Specific strategies for transition can be found in the accompanying box, "Eight Transition Support Strategies."

Transition programs, in general, attempt to prepare the student in specific job skills or to teach work-related skills such as appropriate dress, attitudes, time management, and on-the-job behaviors (Malcom, Polatajko & Simons, 1990; Smith, Price & Marsh, 1986). These work-related skills have been

～ Eight Transition Support Strategies

These support strategies are validated by transition service providers.

- Promote acceptance in the environment.
- Identify environmental support and provide needed changes within the environment.
- Identify and provide social support from employers, coworkers, peers, and family.
- Teach self-management.
- Provide opportunities to learn and practice social skills.
- Provide opportunities for choice making.
- Identify student's strengths and areas needing support.
- Observe and identify student's opportunities for choice.

Source: C. Hughes et al., "Practitioner-Validated Secondary Transition Support Strategies," *Education and Training in Mental Retardation and Developmental Disabilities 32* (1997), 205.

identified as important factors in an individual's ability to get and maintain a job. Recent research suggests that secondary work-focused transition programs should include a one-year follow-up program, incorporate work experience, and infuse general academic skills in the curriculum in order to maximize the probability for successful student transition to the world of work (Benz, Yovanoff & Doren, 1997).

Although specific preparation in domestic living skills is a part of the curriculum for many students with moderate and severe disabilities, little attention has been given to this area in the curriculum of students with mild disabilities until recently. Many young adults with mild disabilities appear to be unprepared to face the challenges presented in securing and maintaining a home and an independent life. Malcom, Polatajko, and Simons (1990) reported that 83 per-

Teenagers can help identify the skills, including recreational activities, that they enjoy doing. (Richard Hutchings/Photo Researchers, Inc.)

cent of the young adults with learning disabilities in their study had at least one major difficulty in daily living or life skills.

Existing secondary school programs include a number of models designed to teach information and prepare adolescents for life as adults. The type of model used depends on the extent of the disability of the individual and the projected postsecondary school goals (Masters, Mori & Mori, 1993). For example, some students will be entering the world of work immediately after leaving school and may be placed in a work environment during high school and receive on-the-job training. Other students, those with more severe disabilities, may receive all of their instruction in the community, as they learn directly the job, transportation, and domestic living skills necessary for independent life. A list of these and other secondary curriculum options is presented in Table 14.1. As we mentioned earlier, the effectiveness of these models is continually being investigated through research. Many questions have yet to be answered about the most necessary content and most effective approaches for addressing the adult needs of individuals with a wide range of disabilities.

The appropriate curriculum options, as well as content targeting transition to adulthood, are identified on each student's transition plan. In order to provide the most realistic assessment of needs at the postsecondary level, schools now provide multidisciplinary transition plans. Representatives of adult service agencies participate in the actual writing of a transition program for high school students in order to encourage familiarity and future use of the adult programs. For example, a job trainer from the state department of mental retardation or a counselor from the state vocational rehabilitation agency can provide specific information on what types of skills are needed for certain jobs and what problems a student is likely to encounter as she enters the world of work or independent living. Transition programming and follow-up services can help students become aware of what assistance is available and how to secure it.

The format and content of transition plans vary greatly from school to school and from agency to agency. Figure 14.1 is one example of a transition plan for a secondary school student. As you can see, a number of individuals representing different services and agencies participated in its development.

Although transition programming has become an extremely important aspect of education, recent studies of adults with disabilities suggest that educators and adult service providers still have much to learn about how to prepare individuals for independent work and living. Research indicates that in spite of existing transition programs, many individuals with disabilities are still not socially or physically integrated into their community setting (Drew, Logan & Hardman, 1992; Hasazi, Johnson, Hasazi, Gordon & Hull, 1989). It may be that transition programs need to be tailored even more specifically to the individual's ability to perform in the particular environment and must emphasize subsequent or future environments rather than current ones, such as the regular classroom setting (Polloway, Patton, Smith & Roderique, 1991).

The recent emphasis on preparation for community employment for all individuals with disabilities should help to make transition programs more relevant. Input from the student may be a critical factor in achieving this goal of relevance. Currently, teachers often fail to include adolescents and young adults in planning and educational programming for their own lives (Cronin & Patton, 1993). Since many students receive job training for a position that is intended to be temporary (such as working in a fast-food restaurant), if the individual does not receive further training and employment later, he or she may have difficulty finding a job that is satisfying, as well as one that allows economic

Table 14.1   Overview of Curricular Options

Currriculum Theme with Specific Orientation	Major Features	Functional Relevance
Academic content coverage	General education content taught in special settings Materials can be those used in general education or alternative ones Concern about special teacher's background to teach some content areas	Need for same content acquisition as nondisabled peers Precursor to integration into general education classes
Remedial: Basic skills	Goal is to increase academic performance to desired levels Intensive programming in reading, math, language arts Generalization of skills needs to be programmed Some programs that focus too much on this orientation may neglect other areas	Increase literacy levels Can address deficit areas so that students can be integrated into general education classes
Social skills	Related to social skill development, affective needs, and behavior change needs Generalization of acquired behaviors can be a concern	Increase one's social competence Potential benefits for inclusive settings Importance of developing one's self-concept
Regular class support: Tutorial assistance	Teacher works with student on instructional topics that have immediate relevance in the general classroom Provides a short-term emphasis on needs but may not have long-term value	Addresses immediate needs (e.g., test) for the student Serves a diplomatic function—it helps the general education teacher with students who need ongoing assistance
Compensatory tactics	Idea is to circumvent areas of difficulty (e.g., using a calculator when significant problems arise in this area) Techniques may not be available for all situations Typically used in conjunction with other orientations	Provides an alternate way to achieve desired goals in spite of problems
Learning strategies	Cognitive-based techniques that teach students how to use their abilities and knowledge to solve problems, acquire information, deal with given situations May not be useful with all students Must be used in conjunction with other orientations if students are not in general education Important to program for transfer of skills from the training setting to others	Provides long-term tactics for dealing with similar situations Allows students to compete with peers who do not have difficulties
Cooperative teaching	Team approach to addressing the needs of students Special education teacher works in the general education classroom	Provides content learning and inclusion
Adult outcomes: Vocational training	Focus is on the acquisition of requisite skills in a specific vocational area Variety of vocational training options are available Addresses a major component of the transition service requirement of Individuals with Disabilities Education Act (IDEA)	Students acquire a specific vocation skill or skills before leaving school Motivates students by providing relevance to the curriculum Shifts focus away from past failure in academic domains
Life skill preparation	Acquisition of specific life skills to deal with the typical challenges of everyday life Content emphasis should be based on a realistic appraisal of what students will face when school is over Life skills can be taught in educational placement	Competency in dealing with major life demands is required of all individuals Motivates students and shifts focus away from previous failure experiences

Source: M.E. Cronin & J.R. Patton. *Life Skills Instruction for All Students with Special Needs: A Practical Guide for Integrating Real Life Content into Curriculum* (Austin, TX: PRO-ED, 1993), pp. 5–6. Copyright © 1993. Used by permission of PRO-ED.

Name DAVID RYAN   **Date** 7-1

Transition Service Areas	Person/Agency Responsible	Timeline	Comments
A. Employment/ education goal: Seek and secure a job	Transition coordinator, student	January of school year	Prepare career planning packet. Identify job sites.
B. Home and family goal: Prepare for marriage and family	Teacher	October of school year	Identify community resources.
C. Leisure pursuits goal: Attend special neighborhood events	Teacher, student	September of school year	Link interests with local options.
D. Community involvement goal: Know about wide range of services available in the community.	Teacher	December of school year	Use community-based experiences.
E. Emotional/physical health goal: Seek personal counseling	Counselor, Teacher	October of school year	Locate and contact community services.
F. Personal responsibility and relationship goal: Get along with others	Teacher, Transition Coordinator	January of school year	Identify interpersonal job skills required in warehouse setting.

Figure 14.1
Individualized Transition Plan
Scenario: David is a 16-year-old male who is tired of school and wants to get a job. He is interested in finding a job working in a warehouse. His reading skills are adequate, and his math skills are weak. He also has some problems relating appropriately to peers. His probable subsequent environment: working in a nearby community, living at home, and having a car.

Source: M.E. Cronin & J.R. Patton, *Life Skills Instruction for All Students with Special Needs: A Practical Guide for Integrating Real Life Content into Curriculum* (Austin, TX: PRO-ED, 1993), p. 57. Copyright © 1993. Used by permission of PRO-ED.

self-sufficiency. Increasingly, the importance of participation by persons with disabilities in the determination of their life goals and objectives is being recognized as a critical factor in a successful transition to adult life.

The movement from school to adult services must be effected quickly and smoothly so that there is no break in needed assistance. The types and levels of

adult services must be examined so that individuals with disabilities continue
to receive appropriate needed services after leaving the public school setting.
Many educational and support programs are being evaluated to determine the
key factors in postschool success, and teaching techniques and curriculum content are being assessed to identify the programs that result in successful performance (Westling & Floyd, 1990).

Transition Programs for Postsecondary Education

Another avenue to successful employment is further training through college or
other postsecondary training programs. Many high schools now offer programs
that help students prepare for college or university: courses or curriculum components in study skills, notetaking, time management, and organization. Many
students with disabilities are successful in postsecondary education programs.
Although Blackorby and Wagner (1996) reported that about 26.7 percent of all
students with disabilities had attended some type of postsecondary school after
being out of high school for three to five years, the percentages were higher for
students with some types of disabilities (for example, individuals who are deaf
or hard of hearing, 60 percent; students with visual impairments, 57 percent; individuals with other health impairments, 56 percent). Greenbaum, Graham, and
Scales (1995) found that about 90 percent of a sample population of students
with learning disabilities who enrolled in college went on to graduate.

A critical role of teachers is to help prepare interested students for postsecondary education. Part of a teacher's job is to encourage the development of
skills, abilities, independence, and positive self-concepts. Some important areas
of instruction for students with disabilities who will be entering postsecondary
educational settings include teaching students about their specific strengths
and weaknesses, providing them with instruction and practice in self-advocacy
skills, and providing instruction and practice in study skills and specific learning strategies, such as test taking. Students who plan to go on to college should
be integrated into college prep courses at the high school level and receive career and vocational counseling to help them identify appropriate career goals
and select supportive college or technical school programs (Aune, 1991; Gartin,
Rumrill & Serebreni, 1996; Seidenberg & Koenigsberg, 1990).

It is important for us to remember that students' needs don't end with high
school graduation. State-supported colleges and universities are required, by
the Americans with Disabilities Act of 1990, to have programs to assist students
with disabilities. It is often up to the student, however, to tap into these services.
Some procedures for identifying these services are found in the accompanying
box, "Strategies for Identifying College Support Services."

Although schools can tell you what types of services they offer, they do not
tell you which of these services are most effective for students at the postsecondary level. One school may offer tutoring and notetaking services but not
study-skills instruction. A second school may offer study-skills classes and individual counseling but not tutoring or notetaking services. Which school should
you advise your student to attend? Because many of these programs are so new,
there are very little data on the effectiveness of specific components. The few
empirical studies on postsecondary transition programs have evaluated model
programs and, therefore, assessed a number of combined components rather
than the effectiveness of individual ones. In one study, students with learning
disabilities reported that the most used and most effective services were academic and career counseling, adapted test taking, notetaking, tutoring, and

Transition programs are being assessed to determine what techniques and curricula result in successful postschool performance.

Strategies for Identifying College Support Services

- Call the college or university. Each college or university should have an office established specifically to provide information and assistance to students with disabilities. This office might be called the Office of Disabled Student Services. Usually the school's office of student services should be able to direct you if you cannot locate the correct office from the phone directory.

- Use the Internet. Locate the college's or university's home page on the Internet. You should be able to find a separate page on services for students with disabilities. Again, look under general student services if a separate section for students with disabilities doesn't exist. When using the Internet, check the date on which the page was updated. Sometimes the most recent services may not yet be listed.

- Locate a book on college services. Some national publications are available that outline college support services for students with learning disabilities. Examples of these are *Peterson's Colleges with Programs for Learning-Disabled Students* (Mangrum & Strichart, 1988) and *The K&W Guide to Colleges for the Learning Disabled* (Kravets & Wax, 1998). If you use publications like this with your students or recommend them to parents, remember to use the most recent editions.

study strategy instruction (Loveday, 1993). Much more research along this line needs to be done, however, before the most effective postsecondary programs can be identified for students with disabilities. Presently, the best plan may be to see what types of services benefit the student in the high school setting and look for similar services at the postsecondary level.

Making Connections to Adult Service Agencies

Transition programs help students establish initial contacts with the **adult service agencies** that can provide guidance and assistance once the students have graduated from high school. Adult service agencies can provide medical and psychological examinations and counseling, training and job placement, and financial assistance for adaptive equipment, prostheses, and basic living costs during training (Smith, Price & Marsh, 1986). The accompanying box, "Adult Services: Vocational Rehabilitation Department," illustrates one state department of vocational rehabilitation's eligibility requirements, financial considerations, and list of services. Although such services may be provided automatically for persons under the care of state-run facilities, individuals with mild disabilities, physical disabilities, or sensory impairments who are living on their own will need to seek and secure available services. Knowing what services are available and how to go about finding assistance may be important elements in the search for employment.

Adult service agencies provice medical, employment, and financial assistance.

The names of the agencies that provide transition or adult services and the nature of the service provided may differ from state to state. State departments of education have a **transition coordinator** or transition council responsible for developing, coordinating, and evaluating school-based transition programs. Teachers can get in touch with the transition coordinator at their state department of education to find out the agencies or groups that provide these services in their particular state.

Some studies have found that exposure to specific agencies or adult resources and a linkage between these programs and the high school program can influence the choices students make after graduation as well as their future success. For example, Hasazi et al. (1989) discovered that students with mild disabilities who engaged in vocational classes or in paid work during high school

∼ Adult Services: Vocational Rehabilitation Department

Eligibility

A. The individual must have an impediment to employment caused by a physical or mental impairment that substantially limits the ability to work.

B. The impaired individual must require vocational rehabilitation services to prepare for, enter, engage in, or retain gainful employment; and must benefit from these services in terms of an employment outcome.

Financial Considerations

In some states, clients are responsible for helping to pay for rehabilitation training and other services. A vocational rehabilitation counselor will help the client apply to funding sources such as educational grants, federal tuition grants, social services, and social security.

Services

Step 1 Referral and intake: Individuals must apply for services in person, in writing, or by phone.

Step 2 Evaluation: A medical examination, vocational evaluation, and, sometimes, a psychological evaluation may be required to determine eligibility for services and rehabilitation needs.

Step 3 Rehabilitation planning: An Individualized Written Rehabilitation Program is developed by the individual and his or her assigned counselor. Long-term and short-term employment goals are identified.

Step 4 Treatment: Medical or psychiatric care may be provided on a short-term basis along with specific therapies such as speech therapy or physical therapy. When necessary for job performance, equipment such as artificial limbs, hearing aids, and wheelchairs, and materials such as books, supplies, and licenses may be provided.

Step 5 Training: If needed, training in personal and social skills, work performance, and work adjustment is available. Vocational training may include education in technical schools or colleges.

Step 6 Placement: The counselor will assist in identifying job opportunities and helping to match the individual with the position of his or her choice.

Step 7 Closure: After an individual has been employed for a length of time, vocational rehabilitation services may be discontinued. Individuals may return for services if needed again; however, if more than a year has passed, reapplication may be necessary to reassess eligibility.

Source: *Your Handbook of Vocational Rehabilitation Services,* South Carolina Vocational Rehabilitation Department, 1991, pp. 1–11.

had a higher rate of employment than the students who did not have these experiences. In a study of young adults with learning disabilities, Miller, Rzonca, and Snider (1991) found that exposure to community college resources led to participation in the community college system, while exposure to other agencies was more likely to result in military or private training. Fairweather and Shaver (1991) also found that participation in community or four-year college programs seemed to have a long-lasting positive effect on the employment of students with disabilities. Studies such as these are being conducted to help us better understand how we can help students and adults become better prepared for adult life and be more successful in getting and maintaining jobs.

Employment Options

As you prepare for a career in teaching, you are probably well aware of the number of jobs available and the competition you will face in applying for those jobs. Will you be as prepared as the other job candidates? Will you be able to show how much you know and make a good impression at your interview? All of us experience a certain amount of apprehension and concern about finding a

John Yeh, President of Integrated Microcomputer Systems, found deafness to be no obstacle to success in the business world. (Andy Levin/Photo Researchers, Inc.)

job and pursuing a career. Persons with disabilities also face these concerns; often, however, their fears are compounded by an awareness that their disability may be all that the employer will see—that their abilities will be obscured by their physical disability, their learning disability, or their blindness.

Data from a national longitudinal transition study (Blackorby & Wagner, 1996) reveal that approximately 56.8 percent of individuals with disabilities were competitively employed three to five years after leaving secondary school. Competitive employment was higher for individuals with some disabilities (for example, individuals with learning disabilities, 70.8 percent; individuals with speech impairments, 65.4 percent). Although the national data indicated that deaf individuals were employed at a rate of 43.5 percent, Bullis, Bull, Johnson, and Peters (1995) found that deaf women from mainstream programs were employed at a rate of 83.3 percent. Other studies, however, suggest that between 66 and 90 percent of individuals with disabilities who graduate from public schools fail to find competitive employment (Harris & Associates, 1989; Stark, Kiernan, Goldsburg & McGee, 1986). Although there is some variability in the results of these studies, it is clear that many persons with disabilities encounter greater difficulty finding and keeping jobs than do individuals without disabilities.

The employment problem for individuals with disabilities includes not only unemployment but also underemployment—taking jobs that do not match their capabilities. Most of the employment figures do not separate full-time from part-time employment, and studies are just now beginning to look at salaries as indices of success. The information we do have, however, suggests that the majority of employed persons with disabilities do not make enough money to support themselves or to live independently (Affleck, Edgar, Levine & Kortering,

Unemployment and underemployment are problems faced by adults with disabilities.

1990). In fact, only about 39.8 percent of individuals with disabilities earn more than $6 an hour three to five years after graduation from high school (Blackorby & Wagner, 1996). Needless to say, the lack of substantial wages also has a negative effect on other aspects of adult life, such as owning or renting a home or having a family.

The fact that large numbers of adults with disabilities are unable to secure any employment continues to serve as an impetus for better transition programming during the school years and for continuous opportunities for services throughout the adult years. The range of employment options for persons with disabilities includes: (1) sheltered employment, (2) supported employment, (3) unskilled work in community settings, and (4) independent competitive employment in community settings. Although all these options are used as employment settings, employment in the community is a major vocational goal.

Sheltered Employment

Sheltered employment is the placement of individuals with disabilities in work settings, usually set up as assembly-line workshops, in which individuals work on assigned contracts. Typically these contracts involve activities such as assembling items or putting packets together. The adults who work in sheltered workshops receive payment on a piecework basis—that is, they get paid for each task or product that is finished. This type of employment, which not so long ago was the primary work opportunity for individuals with moderate and severe disabilities, persists even in the face of the strong movement toward community-based employment and integration. Some individuals suggest that sheltered workshops are a viable opportunity for individuals with severe disabilities to prepare for the larger work force and to gain skills and practice in work habits that might facilitate later community employment (Rosen, Rice, Walsh, Hartman & McCallion, 1992). Others argue that sheltered workshops are too often a final place of employment rather than a training placement. A strong feeling exists that sheltered employment works against the goals of integration into the community and that the low wages and repetitive work restrict the potential contributions of individuals with disabilities to society (Drew, Logan & Hardman, 1992). The future role of sheltered workshops will be largely determined by the extent to which individuals with more severe disabilities are employed and accepted in supported or competitive employment settings.

Supported Employment

Supported work is designed for individuals who have traditionally not found jobs in the community.

Supported employment is often used as a means of effecting the transition of individuals with disabilities into community employment settings. In supported work settings, people are placed in jobs that are either located in integrated settings or that facilitate social integration. The term *supported* refers to the training, supervision, and, sometimes, financial assistance that is provided to the individual and the employer in the work setting. Supported work is designed for individuals who traditionally have not found jobs in the community; therefore, comprehensive and long-term support may be necessary. Increasingly, supported work opportunities are initiated during high school so that students are placed in a job by the time they graduate or leave the secondary setting. There are a number of different models for supported employment, including the mobile work crew, the enclave, and supported jobs (Kiernan & Stark, 1986).

The **mobile work crew** is a group of individuals with disabilities who have learned a specific trade or set of skills that can be applied in the community. Gardening and catering are two examples of the type of work mobile crews do. Often, the mobile work crew functions like any other business—advertising its services, traveling to jobs, and incorporating profits into salaries, equipment, and materials. Typically, the work crew is managed by a trainer or trainers who help the workers solicit jobs and manage finances and provide on-the-job assistance and instruction. Advantages of this model include the ability to select desired, competitive, and appropriate work; the potential for individuals to learn skills in management and independent contracting; and the ability to earn good wages. The mobile work crew also offers an avenue for supported employment in locations that have few businesses or work opportunities, such as in rural farming communities. A major disadvantage, however, is the fact that the crew continues to work as a segregated unit—all of the workers have disabilities, and although the work is done in the community, social integration may be limited to lunch and breaks during the workday. In addition, individuals in a mobile work crew receive continuous supervision and support, which does not facilitate eventual independent work.

A second supported employment option is the **enclave.** An enclave is a small group of individuals with disabilities who are placed in a work setting, usually within a large business or corporation. Individuals in an enclave receive on-the-job training and support from job coaches, schools, or social service agencies and from within the corporation itself. Training within an enclave may begin with an expected level of partial or limited skill performance; as individuals become more adept and receive more training, more work is required. The financial responsibility for paying individuals within an enclave will be gradually assumed by the employer as the employees become more competitive and independent. Although individuals working in an enclave are placed as a group, the workers do not necessarily work as a unit and may be scattered and integrated throughout the business. The enclave provides an opportunity for maximizing personnel resources, as one supervisor can provide support to a number of individuals, particularly when the employer also provides support personnel. In addition, the employee has the opportunity to earn a standard wage in a setting that facilitates physical and social integration.

The final supported employment model we will look at is the **individual supported job model.** This model involves one-to-one coaching and teaching of a single individual in a job setting. Supported jobs are likely to be used when the agency or school has a number of job coaches or support personnel, when only a few students or clients are placed at a given time, or when the individuals placed require limited or only occasional support. In an individual supported job model, the job coach provides on-site training and ongoing problem solving. Typically, the level of support will gradually diminish until only occasional visits are provided. Supported job models may lead to independent competitive employment, as the need for support fades and the individual learns to perform effectively in the work setting. In addition to the obvious advantages of independent performance, regular wages, and constant opportunities for social integration and participation, this model also increases the probability that the individual may have some say in what type of job he or she gets. The role of choice in identifying an employment option cannot be underestimated in terms

closer look

Can Do: Matching People and Jobs

Some Boston-area employers are solving the perennial problem of finding highly motivated, reliable, productive workers for entry-level jobs. They hire people who meet all specifications and really want to do the work involved, but have been out of the labor market because of psychiatric, emotional, or developmental disabilities

Greater Boston Rehabilitation Services, a non-profit vocational training and placement agency, is the source for applicants. Employers interview, check references, and use the same screening applied to other candidates. If they hire a referral, the agency offers staff for on-the-job guidance in the first week or so and contacts employer and employee frequently on how things are going. All services to employers are free.

Leo Ladas, a manager of Applied Image Reprographics, hired a GBRS referral full time to assist with photocopying. He gets full benefits and earns more than twice the minimum wage. Lader says the hire "is definitely a plus; he fits in very well. His disability is not obvious; I never asked what it is. You get tax credits for employing full time, but that wasn't the biggest reason I hired him. I had used GBRS before for temporary employees. They offer a low-cost approach to getting good people and will present four or five candidates already in job training and working in a production atmosphere under their supervision.

They stay in touch after you hire, and you can call them any time. I haven't needed them."

Hiring job developers with employment agency and outplacement agency experience in business instead of staff with background in human services plays a major role, says Susan Able, GBRS vice president for marketing and development. Costs to the agency for placements are no higher, possibly slightly lower. Job developers and vocational staff work together as a team.

Staff training also helped to boost placement, she says. Brian Gerry, president of Results: Training for Success, ran about eight workshops and one-to-one sessions. Helping clients improve their résumés and interviewing skills, finding out what a prospective employer really wants, and presenting an applicant's work achievements rather than job titles and responsibilities, was the focus.

Successful transition to the workplace is a first step, not a permanent move. Most placements last six months, longer for some, says Terry Ann Lunt, GBRS president and chief executive. "We encourage people to think about their work and future like anybody else." Matching what an employer wants to what a GBRS referral wants is crucial.

Source: Juliet F. Brudnoy, "Living with Work," *Boston Globe*, June 29, 1993.

of maintaining motivation and performance; people who like their work are much more likely to do well.

Independent Competitive Employment

Most students with mild disabilities, physical disabilities, or sensory disabilities will find independent competitive employment. Agencies such as vocational rehabilitation may be tapped, but often individuals seek and get jobs independently. As we mentioned earlier in this chapter, transitional programming can help students become equipped vocationally and socially to develop into productive and successful workers. In addition, factors such as gender, socioeconomic status, and general academic and living skills also seem to affect the probability of employment (Heal & Rusch, 1995). We do know, however, that many individuals with disabilities who find competitive employment independently work in low-paying jobs and are unsatisfied with their work (Edgar, 1988; Neel, Meadows, Levine & Edgar, 1988). These people may be more likely to quit their jobs or to continue to depend on their families for housing or support. We hope that continued research on needed skills for adult employment, the requirements for transition planning at the secondary school level, and a wider recognition by persons with disabilities of the training and support services available to them will help to address these difficulties and result in more employment options and increased job satisfaction. For one successful program, see "A Closer Look: Can Do: Matching People and Jobs."

Living Settings

Individuals with disabilities often want to live in independent, community-based homes. For many people, these goals are realized through independent living arrangements. For others, the goals are adapted to include the most independent and normalized setting possible.

Unfortunately, limited resources in living sites, trained personnel, and income level still stand in the way of normalized or independent living settings for many adults with disabilities. Studies suggest that most young adults with mild disabilities live in dependent settings, typically a parent's home (Hasazi et al., 1989). In a study comparing the independent living status of young adults with and without disabilities at thirty months after high school graduation, Affleck et al. (1990) found that approximately 57 percent of the adults without disabilities were living independently, compared to 39 percent of the adults with learning disabilities and 21 percent of the adults with mild mental retardation.

The results of these and other studies suggest the need for more attention during educational programming to the future living needs of individuals with both mild and severe disabilities. In addition, we must continue to advocate for more and better jobs and vocational preparation programs for adults with disabilities so that the possibility of financial independence can be increased.

Institutions

Large, segregated residential buildings known as **institutions** were used for years to house thousands of individuals with mental retardation, mental illness, sensory impairments, or physical disabilities. After numerous revelations of the neglect and abuse that often took place in institutions, a social and legal movement began in the 1960s and 1970s to take people out of the institutional setting and relocate them in smaller, community-based settings. This movement, as you learned in an earlier chapter, is called *deinstitutionalization*. Although this movement led to the development of many good community-based residential programs, the results were not all positive. In some instances, deinstitutionalization resulted in the transfer of individuals from large institutions to smaller but still segregated settings such as nursing homes. In other places, deinstitutionalization led to the release of individuals from institutions without the benefit of a support structure that would enable them to obtain appropriate housing or, in some cases, any housing at all (Taylor, Racino & Walker, 1992). Although the intentions behind deinstitutionalization may have been good, the lack of existing support networks and community-based housing resulted in many displaced and homeless persons. Community living options must become much more

The deinstitutionalization movement resulted in community-based residential programs.

commonplace and accepted in order to provide viable residential alternatives, especially for those with severe disabilities.

Although institutions still exist, they are less frequently chosen as a residential placement of choice, and in some states are not considered at all. Interesting recent research suggests the possible power of residential settings on individuals' hopes and aspirations. LoConto and Dodder (1997) found that the wishes of individuals with developmental disabilities in a variety of residential settings varied according to placement, reflecting their knowledge of possible "worlds to explore."

Community-Based Residential Settings

Some individuals who in times past lived in segregated settings have moved directly and successfully into the community. Individuals with visual or hearing impairments and many individuals with physical disabilities or health impairments live independently in homes within the community. Sometimes adaptive equipment is necessary or a personal attendant is required, so financial resources may be the factor that determines independent living for some people.

People with other types of disabilities, such as moderate or severe mental retardation, may live in settings that range from nursing homes to community-based homes or facilities. Because of the present trend toward normalization, we find that opportunities for community-based residences are continuing to increase for all individuals. The more complex an individual's health-care and personal maintenance needs, however, the more likely it is that the person continues to live in one of the more segregated settings. Often, these settings are able to employ support personnel, such as nurses and therapists, and have available more elaborate medical equipment than a group home or apartment. As federal and state agencies become more experienced in integrated service delivery, however, it is likely that soon all individuals with disabilities will have service options that include integrated community placement.

■ **Intermediate-Care Facility**   An **intermediate-care facility (ICF)** is composed of a number of individuals with disabilities living together in a supervised setting. Some large ICFs do not provide for community integration, however, and may serve as permanent, segregated living settings for individuals with disabilities. These facilities may include cottage living or other congregated living options.

Individuals living in group homes benefit from a receptive community.

■ **Group Home**   Small **group homes** house several adults with disabilities who live with a nondisabled person responsible for general supervision and coordination of activities. As we've mentioned previously, such living situations require not only financial resources and trained personnel but also a receptive community. The resistance of some communities to the placement of group homes adds one more obstacle to be overcome in the move toward normalized and independent living. In addition to the problem of actually securing a home, a resistant attitude suggests that the road to normalized socialization and integration within the community will not be an easy one.

■ **Apartment Living**   Another housing option for many individuals with disabilities is apartment living. A variety of living situations may be found in apartment settings. For example, one or more individuals with disabilities may live independently in the apartment, with only periodic visits from a counselor or case manager. Another option may be a person with a disability living with a roommate without a disability. (The roommate may be a residential care provider—or just a friend!) As you can see, apartment living is one step closer to an independent, normal living arrangement for many young adults.

■ **Living with Family**   Another living option is the family home. Many individuals with mild disabilities and a number of people with more severe disabilities continue to live in the family home during their adult years. Financial dependence, emotional dependence on the part of the family as well as the individual, and a lack of alternative living options may contribute to adults living in this setting.

The Challenge of Independent Living

Living with parents or in a group home is no assurance, however, that community involvement and normalized living experiences will occur. The skills of people involved in managing and running group homes may influence greatly the extent of actual community participation and integration (Burchard, Gordon & Pine, 1990). Alternative housing options or financing opportunities may remain untapped unless individuals know what resources are available to them and whom to contact. Parents, teachers, and case managers can explore these options by contacting social service agencies, state agencies, and councils on specific disabilities, or parent groups. Groups such as a developmental disabilities council, the department or board on mental retardation, or the Society for Individuals with Autism are good sources of community and adult living program options.

Personal Relationships

A very important aspect of adult life is the development of personal relationships like friendships and intimate relationships that may lead to marriage and children. Our personal lives are very important to us—many of us consider our roles as spouse or parent to be the most important facet of our adult lives. Exceptional individuals benefit as well from participating in the social and personal relationships so important to self-determination and personal satisfaction.

The personal relationships of people with disabilities are, of course, as varied as the individuals themselves. Forming friendships, falling in love, and having children are a part of the lives of many adults with disabilities. In the past, the segregation and close supervision of many adults with disabilities impinged on their ability to meet people and become involved with them. Overprotectiveness on the part of parents or caretakers and restricted mobility may still limit the extent and type of social relationships that a person can develop.

The questions of who should or should not engage in sexual activity, marry, or have children are with us still. They are mostly directed toward persons with mental retardation, whom some still consider incapable of forming lasting relationships with a partner, unable to act responsibly, and incapable of rearing a child. Dickerson (1988) asserts that the two civil rights most difficult to protect for persons with mental retardation are the right to informed, voluntary sterilization and the right to marry. Although the idea of sterilizing people with mental retardation may seem arcane and unethical to us, it was a common practice

Segregation and close supervision of adults with disabilities can interfere with the development of close personal relationships.

The development of satisfying personal relationships is a crucial part of adult life. (R.M. Collins, III/The Image Works, Inc.)

not too long ago and is still used as a means of birth control at the request of either residential institutions or parents. Related information about these rights should be shared with adolescents and their parents at the onset of sexual maturity and the coming of legal age of consent. For individuals with mental retardation to make clear decisions regarding marriage and childbearing, they need not only basic information but also an understanding of the consequences of their actions.

Because parents may continue in the role of guardian for some persons with mental retardation, they may have a strong influence on the extent to which their adult child participates in the development of relationships. Teachers of adolescents with mental retardation acknowledge that their students want to get married and have children (Brantlinger, 1988). Advocates for persons with mental retardation will argue for the right of all individuals to participate in all aspects of adult life. Often, of course, sexual relationships and childbearing occur regardless of parental permission or the feelings of society. Whether by accident or design, increasing numbers of people with mental retardation are getting married and raising children.

Programs have been and continue to be developed that focus on working with young mothers and fathers with mental retardation and teaching basic child-rearing practices and safety measures (Tymchuk, Hamada, Andron & Anderson, 1990). One example is the Parents Learning Together (PLT) program that was developed in St. Louis, Missouri. This program, funded by a grant from the city, teaches parents with mental retardation specific parenting skills, such as how to set limits for a child, how to bathe an infant safely, and how parents can manage their own frustration or anger (Futterman, 1984). Programs like these can help to ensure infant safety and competence in parenting.

Many educators feel strongly about the need for frank and clear school courses in human sexuality and the responsibilities of marriage and parenting (Brantlinger, 1988). Although controversial, these courses could be extremely important to the successful adjustment to adult life for persons with disabilities. Sparks and Caster (1989) suggest that sex education and related issues be taught to individuals with disabilities throughout the school years. They suggest that the curriculum include biological information, health and hygiene, emotions and feelings, self-protection, and social skills. Numerous opportunities for discussion and questions should be provided to ensure understanding and application of related information.

A number of specialized curricula are available for individuals with developmental disabilities that deal with sexuality, health, abuse, and social development. A list of these curricula can be obtained from the Sex Information and Education Council of the United States (SIECUS Report, 1988).

Recreation and Leisure Activities

One of the most enjoyable aspects of adult living is the ability to choose recreational activities that interest you. Many individuals with disabilities enjoy diverse recreational and leisure activities, which they choose, as we all do, on the basis of what relaxes and challenges them. A number of community recreational centers and athletic competitions include specific programs for individuals with disabilities, while others simply integrate individuals with disabilities into their existing programs (see "A Closer Look: Can Do: Able to Compete"). Programs that require specialized supervision and training, such as skiing for individuals who are blind or horseback riding for individuals with physical disabilities, can also be found across the country.

Still, there are a number of individuals with disabilities who do not have access to desired recreational activities because of physical barriers or who have difficulty identifying and finding a way to participate in recreational opportunities. Many adults with mental retardation who live at home, for example, may spend much of their free time alone, engaged in relatively monotonous daily routines that may consist of watching television or just sitting around (Drew, Logan & Hardman, 1992). Because many individuals with disabilities have social skill deficits that make it difficult to find and maintain a peer group for social activities, social isolation may be a common phenomenon in the adult years if recreation and leisure activities are not facilitated. In addition, participation in sports or physically oriented recreational activities may be important for health reasons, as many individuals with mental retardation, for example, tend to have lower levels of physical fitness than individuals without disabilities and are more likely to experience problems related to general health and weight management (Kelly, 1989). As we plan for successful transition into adult life and look for appropriate support services for adults with disabilities, it is important to keep in mind the domain of recreation and leisure. Helping individuals experience and identify a range of leisure options, providing necessary training or adaptations to facilitate independent participation in the activities, and

Many individuals with disabilities enjoy diverse recreational and leisure activities, but others have difficulty participating.

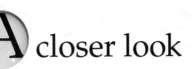

A closer look

Can Do: Able to Compete

Jean Driscoll has been disabled [by spina bifida] since birth and uses a wheelchair to provide the mobility her legs cannot. . . . But Driscoll is a world record holder, a three-time defending champion in the Boston Marathon, and a fierce competitor who scorns sympathy as vehemently as she does the obstacles to victory.

Driscoll's focus is using victory to reinforce the point that there is more ability than disability in the [handicapping condition]. It's a sentiment shared across the sport. "When I was growing up, sports were never an option for me," says Driscoll, 26, "This chair has brought me a lot of opportunities."

Opportunities such as representing the United States in the Barcelona Summer Olympics, traveling worldwide to compete against the sport's elite, and building on the respect that the wheelchair division now enjoys at such premier events as the Boston Marathon.

"The wheelchair division has grown in both numbers and stature," says Boston Marathon director Guy Morse, "because the BAA feels, and I personally feel, that the wheelchair athletes are as viable as the able-bodied athletes."

That sentiment has helped attract more and more wheelchair racers, and increasing quality, to Boston. . . .

"We don't treat the wheelchair athletes any different in terms of what we do for them and don't do for them," Morse says. Which is exactly the way the athletes want it. Gone, at least along the Boston course, are hordes of spectators who gawk at the wheelchair racers as valiant invalids struggling against mighty odds to reach the finish. The crowds in Boston are knowledgeable, says Driscoll, and regard the wheelchair race as a legitimate contest among elite athletes. That's not always the case, she adds. "When I went to the Summer Olympics, people would say, 'Special Olympics?' and I'd say, 'No, Summer Olympics, just like Jackie Joyner-Kersee.'"

For wheelchair athletes, the sport is a joy but it is also the medium for a message about equal opportunity. Bob Hall, the first person to race the Boston Marathon in a wheelchair, says, "Because of wheelchair races, the norm for many people is that maybe we should be active, that we should be competing in marathons. When people ask someone in a wheelchair, 'Have you ever done a marathon,' that's a positive social statement."

Driscoll revels in the independence that wheelchair racing has brought her and the opportunities that she has to educate others about the abilities of the disabled. "Growing up, being disabled was the center of my life," she says. "Now, with school and athletics as a focus, you don't even remember that you have a disability."

Especially on race day, Driscoll says, when you push toward Boston and everybody seems to know your name.

Source: Brian McQuarrie, "They're Able to Compete," *Boston Globe*, April 16, 1993, p. 33. Reprinted by permission.

providing support services such as transportation and social interaction skills are important transition goals.

Quality of Life: Evaluating Outcomes

Transition programs and adult services are designed to facilitate the successful adjustment of individuals with disabilities to adult life. Figure 14.2 illustrates

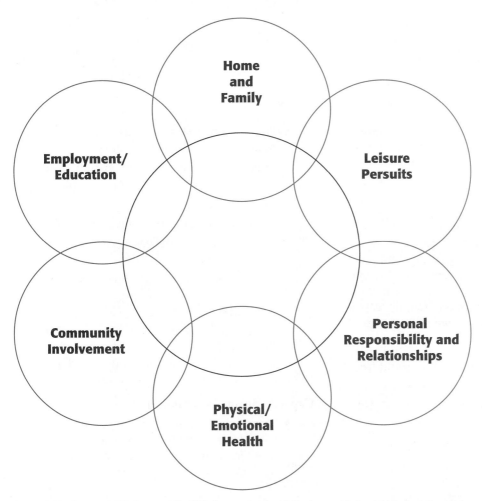

Figure 14.2
Domains of Adulthood

Source: M.E. Cronin & J.R. Patton, *Life Skills Instruction for All Students with Special Needs: A Practical Guide for Integrating Real Life Content into Curriculum* (Austin, TX: PRO-ED, 1993), p. 13. Copyright © 1993. Used by permission of PRO-ED.

the six areas of adult life that should be addressed by transition programs. How do we know if our programs have been successful in these areas? How can we determine if someone is productive, happy, and healthy? A number of research investigations are conducted to determine such things as employment rates, graduation rates, and living arrangements of individuals with disabilities. Many educators, however, look to a more holistic evaluation—quality of life—as an index of successful adjustment and happiness. We have seen the term *quality of life* before, in our overview of special education (Chapter 1) and in reference to evaluating the potential of life in newborns with disabilities (Chapter 11). This time the term is used as a measure of successful adult performance.

Quality of life is defined many different ways when used to measure adult outcomes. Halpern (1993) suggests that the major criteria for quality of life are (1) physical and material well-being, (2) performance of adult roles, and (3) personal fulfillment. These domains are supported not by group evaluations or placement statistics but by assessment of the individual in the context of home,

A closer look

Can Do: Focus on the Future

All people bring important gifts to community life. Too often, however, the positive characteristics and qualities of many people with disabilities have been denied or ignored. Many human services focus on deficits and negative characteristics.

A positive alternative approach to planning for the future is called the "capacity search," which helps others see how competent people can be when they have the opportunity to express their gifts. The following profile contrasts the traditional "deficiency description" with a "capacity search description" for a woman named Alma.

Deficiency Description

- She is a physically large 18-year-old female.
- She is enrolled in an education program for children with moderate mental handicaps.
- She is physically handicapped.
- Her right side and arm seem partially paralyzed.

- Her speech is slow and considered related to brain dysfunction and injury.
- There are signs of scars on her right arm.
- She has speech deficits and lags in developmental speech.
- She has epilepsy and delayed mobility.
- There is left hemiparesis associated with brain damage.
- She scores at first-grade level on information, spelling, and reading, and at second grade in math.
- She has a full-scale IQ of 58, a verbal quotient of 62, which indicates functioning within mild mental retardation, and an age equivalent of 10 years, 8 months.

Capacity Search Description

- Home: She could live independently if something were to happen to her grandmother. Alma wants to have her own apartment.

work, and community environments. Objective, quantitative evaluations are important tools for identifying target instructional skills in the environment that may lead to successful performance—specific job requirements, for example. Qualitative or descriptive analyses of an individual's performance and personal fulfillment are considered necessary, however, for an accurate picture of that person's quality of life. Dennis, Williams, Giangreco, and Cloninger (1993) suggest that there is no single definition of quality of life. They, too, recommend that an individual's performance be evaluated in the context of his or her environment, using indices that reflect that person's culture, family or support system, and personal preferences. These indices may be different for each person, reflecting those facets of life that are important to the individual and his or her significant others (see "A Closer Look: Can Do: Focus on the Future"). Storey (1997) asserts the need for broad, generally accepted operational definitions of quality of life, acknowledging that definitions might change according to the age and population.

It may be some time before we understand how best to evaluate outcomes of transition programs and apply the concept of quality of life to the evaluation process. It is evident, however, that many educators feel that a single set of objective criteria is not the most effective way to evaluate personal success and ad-

- Health: She is generally healthy, although she has chronic allergies.

- People: She has fifteen significant people in her network. They include her teacher, friends from school, and family members. Her friendships with nonhandicapped peers have decreased over time.

- Places: Alma goes all over town on her own. She walks to the grocery store and other shops. She goes to the Freewill Baptist Church. She visits a lot of people. She would like to be able to get out of town more.

- Choices: Alma decorates her room. She chooses to visit her father. Her grandmother makes many choices for her and decides how her check is spent.

- Respect: Alma is congenial and helpful and has a pleasant personality. She is in the "trainable mentally retarded class" and likes to tell other people what to do.

- Personal preferences: Alma cooks simple meals. She gets up at 6 A.M. every day and cooks breakfast for everyone. She is a good babysitter for Maria, her little sister. She shows leadership ability. She likes to travel. She likes music and dancing. She likes "circle a word" and math exercises. She likes to help clean. She likes to watch TV. She doesn't like to wash dishes, tend to babies, or read.

- Personal images of the future: Alma wants to acquire a skill through the vocational technical school. She wants her own apartment and a job. She would like to be able to drive. She wants to have more friends.

Source: Beth Mount and Kay Zwernick, *It's Never Too Early, It's Never Too Late* (St. Paul, MN: Metropolitan Council, 1988), pp. 918–919. Copyright © 1988. Reprinted by permission of Metropolitan Council Offices.

justment. The importance of individual differences, personal preferences, and the surrounding social and behavioral norms should be given more consideration when determining quality of life than the expectations of the majority culture or predetermined indicators of success such as amount of money earned, job status, and the level of functional independence.

Because many of us view a disability as an adverse condition, we ascribe certain characteristics to the person who has been able to get a successful job and conduct a relatively normal existence. We speak frequently of the bravery of people who must deal with sensory impairments, debilitating illnesses, or physical conditions. Sometimes we wonder if we would be able to exhibit the same strength if we were in similar situations. There is no doubt that many people with disabilities are engaged in mighty struggles and exhibit courage and tenacity.

It is important for us to realize, however, that these struggles are often due to the physical and social barriers imposed by others—they are not a necessary consequence of disability. As in all historical battles for human and civil rights, ordinary people must become heroes in order to gain their rightful place in society. Although we admire the risks heroes take and the strength they show, it is unfortunate that we still live in a society in which heroic acts are necessary before basic rights and acceptance can be obtained.

People with disabilities may struggle more with physical and social barriers imposed by others than with their own disabilities.

SUMMARY

- Adults with disabilities have in the past been subjected to inappropriate judgments of their abilities and needs when they do not conform to age and social norms. Changing society's perceptions takes concerted effort by all people, including those with disabilities.

- Legislation prohibits discrimination and mandates support services for adults with disabilities, making integration and normalization more readily achieved. People with disabilities continue to face discrimination, though, particularly in being denied self-determination or in being treated with pity rather than respect.

- Families often continue to make decisions regarding the well-being of a family member with disabilities throughout the lifespan and so need to have continuous access to information and support services.

- Transition programs can facilitate movement from school to work and from segregated to integrated settings. Most are designed to produce measurable results in areas such as work-related skills. Transition programs also establish contacts to adult service agencies that provide a variety of supports.

- Employment options include sheltered employment, supported employment, and independent competitive employment. Employment in community settings is a major vocational goal. Supported employment involves job coaches, who provide on-the-job training and support.

- Living settings range from institutions to community-based residences such as intermediate-care facilities, group homes, and apartments to living with family. Independent living and maximum integration in the community are important goals.

- Personal relationships vary with individuals, whether they are disabled or not. Exceptional individuals need access to information about human sexuality and the responsibilities of marriage and parenting. Programs have been developed to teach basic child-rearing practices and safety measures.

- A holistic assessment of quality of life looks at the individual in the context of home, work, and community environments and reflects the person's culture, family or support system, and personal preferences.

KEY TERMS

lifespan
norms
age norms
social norms
Education for Handicapped Children Amendments of 1984 (P.L. 98-199)
Education of the Handicapped Act Amendments of 1990 (P.L. 101-476)

IDEA Amendments of 1997
Americans with Disabilities Act of 1990 (P.L. 101-336)
discrimination
transition program
adult service agency
transition coordinator
sheltered employment
supported employment

mobile work crew
enclave
individual supported job model
institution
intermediate-care facility (ICF)
group home

MULTIMEDIA RESOURCES

Brolin, Donn E. *Lifecentered Career Education: A Competency Based Approach*, 3d ed. (Reston, VA: Council for Exceptional Children, 1989). This book helps teachers integrate life skills into traditional subject areas. Activities and strategies for daily living skills, personal/social skills, and occupational guidance are included.

The Capitol Connection Policy Newsletter. Published by the Division on Career Development and Transition and George Washington University. The Division on Career Development and Transition, The Council for Exceptional Children, 1920 Association Drive Reston, VA 20191. This newsletter addresses interdisciplinary policy and practice in career preparation and transition to postsecondary education, employment, and responsible citizenship for special learners.

The Disability Rights Activist. Website: http://www.disrights.org. This site provides information to individuals with disabilities and their parents and advocates about legal rights and courses of political action.

President's Committee on Employment of People with Disabilities. Website: http://www.pcepd.gov/. Provides information in many areas related to the employment of individuals with disabilities, including laws, benefits, publications, federal programs, and special projects.

Scheiber, Barbara, and Jeanne Talpers. *Unlocking Potential: College and Other Choices for Learning Disabled People: A Step-by-Step Guide* (Bethesda, MD: Adler & Adler, 1987). Good information for learning-disabled students to help explore higher education options and ways to find career counseling. Lists of organizations are provided.

School Based Sexuality Education Programs (SIECUS). Website: http://www.siecus.org. Provides an overview of SIECUS's educational programs, research, material, and technical assistance concerning sexuality education.

Taylor, Steven, Robert Bogdan, and Julie Ann Racino. *Life in the Community: Case Studies of Organizations Supporting People with Disabilities* (Baltimore: Brookes, 1991). This text reports on innovative community integration efforts from twenty-one states. Case studies are organized around three themes: families and children, housing and support for adults, and the community's role in integration.

Turnbull, H. Rutherford, III, et al. *Disability and the Family: A Guide to Decisions for Adulthood* (Baltimore: Brookes, 1989). The authors provide answers to the questions that parents face by using guidelines and exercises for adult decision making.

USING YOUR KNOWLEDGE

 Commonalities: What are your rights to education and housing? What legislation exists to protect the rights of adults with disabilities? Consider why legislation is necessary in this country to identify and protect the rights of individuals with disabilities and others. Find out what legislation currently is under consideration at the state or national level.

 Collaboration: Consider all of the possible areas of adult life that transition plans should address (for example, employment, recreation). What are some possible goals of transition programs in each of these areas?

What individuals or agencies outside of the school system would need to be involved with a student's transition plan in order to accomplish these goals?

 Can Do: Does your school or university employ individuals with disabilities? What types of support services are available at the school site or in your community to support individuals with disabilities in the workplace?

 Commonalities: What does quality of life mean? How do you define it for yourself? What reasons might you give for setting a different standard for another individual or group?

WHAT YOU CAN DO NOW

1. **Identify a job in your community often held by high school students (working in a fast-food restaurant or grocery store). Observe and identify the specific skills that are required. What adaptations would be needed for a student who is in wheelchair to do that job?**

2. **Talk to local business owners about the procedures they follow to ensure compliance with the ADA. Discuss hiring practices, personal perspectives, and issues related to accessibility and accommodations.**

3. **Invite an adult with a disability to visit your class and talk about work, living, social opportunities, challenges to acceptance, and achievement. Perhaps an adult with a disability is in your class and would also be interested in sharing his or her experiences.**

4. **Talk to a secondary teacher of students with moderate or severe disabilities. Ask the teacher to discuss the process he or she goes through to identify appropriate transition goals for his or her students. Also ask the teacher to describe the range of living and work settings for which he or she must prepare his or her students.**

5. **Visit an adult service agency for individuals with disabilities in your area (Vocational Rehabilitation Services, Commission for the Blind, State Department of Mental Health, etc.). Ask questions about the specific services they provide, the challenges they face in providing services, and the recommendations they would offer to teachers.**

Glossary

AAMR Adaptive Behavior Scale one of the most widely used instruments for measuring adaptive behavior.

academic enrichment broadening the experience base of the students in an academic content area without changing the instructional objectives.

Accelerated Schools Project school reform model that extends the expectations and strategies used in gifted education to all students in the school.

acceleration providing a more appropriate program for a gifted student by moving the student ahead in the curriculum; the most common example is grade-skipping.

acculturation refers to learning the characteristics of the new culture while retaining the characteristics of the native culture.

acquired hearing loss a hearing loss acquired at any time after birth.

acquired immune deficiency syndrome (AIDS) a viral disease that breaks down the body's immune system, destroying its ability to fight infections; AIDS is transmitted by the exchange of body fluids which can occur through sexual contact or sharing contaminated needles to inject intravenous drugs.

adaptive behaviors the age- and situation-specific social, maturational, self-help, and communicative acts that assist each individual in adapting to the demands of his or her environment.

adult service agencies agencies that provide medical and psychological examinations and counseling, training and job placement, and financial assistance for adaptive equipment, prostheses, and basic living costs during training to adults with disabilities.

age-appropriate behavior behavior considered normal for a particular age.

age norms the behaviors considered appropriate or usual at a certain point in a person's biological life cycle.

American Sign Language (ASL) the sign language considered by many deaf adults to be their "native language"; it has the same vocabulary as English but a different grammatical structure.

Americans with Disabilities Act of 1990 (P.L. 101-336) a law that extends civil rights protection to individuals with disabilities in private-sector employment and requires that public services like telecommunications and transportation make accommodations for individuals with disabilities.

amniocentesis a prenatal testing technique that analyzes amniotic fluid to identify certain chromosomal and neural tube abnormalities.

anxiety-withdrawal behaviors, such as extreme sensitivity or depression, that reflect fear of performance and avoidance.

assimilation the process of subordinating old cultural patterns to the patterns of the dominant culture.

asthma a chronic obstructive lung condition characterized by an unusual reaction to a variety of stimuli that causes difficulty in breathing, coughing, wheezing, and shortness of breath.

at-risk infants and young children who have a higher

likelihood of developing a disability because of factors like extreme prematurity, chronic poverty, or medical problems.

attention the ability to focus on information.

attentional deficits the inability to come to attention, to maintain attention, or to pay attention selectively.

attention deficit disorder (ADD) a condition determined by difficulty in focusing on information and in sustaining attention.

attention deficit with hyperactivity disorder (ADHD) a condition determined by difficulty in focusing on information, sustaining attention, and hyperactive behavior.

audiogram the chart on which the audiologist records an individual's responses to a hearing test.

audiologist the professional who tests and measures hearing.

auditory training enhancing the residual hearing of a student with hearing loss by teaching listening skills.

augmentative communication aid a system designed to give individuals assistance in communication, such as a scanning system or communication board.

autism a severely incapacitating lifelong developmental disability characterized by certain types of behaviors and patterns of interaction and communication. Symptoms include disturbance in the rate of appearance of physical, social, and language skills; abnormal response to sensation; delayed or absent speech and language; and abnormal ways of relating to people, objects, and events. It usually appears during the first three years of life.

behavior disordered a term used by some states instead of "serious emotional disturbance" to classify children with behavior and emotional disorders.

behavior-rating scale an observation form that allows teachers, parents, and psychologists to rate patterns of behavior.

Bell, Alexander Graham the well-known inventor of the telephone, who also had a strong interest in enhancing speech and residual hearing in deaf children.

bilateral hearing loss hearing loss in both ears.

bilingual education the use of two languages as mediums of instruction for part or all of the school curriculum; its goal is to teach children literacy skills in their first language as a foundation for literacy in English.

biological aging the physiological changes that occur over the lifespan.

biological risk the risk associated with damage to a child's developing systems before, during, or after birth.

Black English a dialect used by many African Americans.

Board of Education of Hendrick Hudson School District v. Rowley a 1982 Supreme Court decision that an "appropriate" education does not mean that a student must reach his or her maximum potential, only that the student have access to educational opportunity.

Braille a system of reading that uses raised dots to signify numbers and letters.

brainstorming a basic creative thinking technique used in problem solving; participants are asked to come up with as many ideas as possible relative to a certain topic—there are no right or wrong answers; responses cannot be criticized; and piggybacking an idea onto someone else's is encouraged.

Brown v. Board of Education of Topeka, Kansas a 1954 Supreme Court ruling prohibiting the use of "separate but equal" schools for African American and white students.

cane travel using a long white cane to scan the environment while walking.

caregiver any person who takes care of or raises a child.

cataract a clouding of the lens of the eye.

cerebral palsy a neurological condition resulting from damage to the brain before or during birth or in infancy; it is characterized by disabilities in movement and posture.

chorionic villous sampling (CVS) a prenatal testing technique that analyzes cells from the chorion to determine if certain genetic abnormalities are present.

civil rights movement the 1960s movement for social and political equality for African Americans; it provided a model for activists seeking similar rights for people with disabilities.

classroom discourse strategies ways in which teachers communicate their expectations for learning to students.

Clerc, Laurent a deaf teacher who trained many of the teachers at the early schools for deaf children in the United States.

closed captioning captions that parallel the verbal content of a television show; they are made visible through decoders built into all television sets manufactured after July 1, 1993, which allow viewers to select captioning of all available programs.

cluster grouping students who are identified as gifted at a given grade level are grouped together in the same classroom with a teacher who has training in educating students who are gifted. The rest of the class is a diverse group of learners.

cochlear implants tiny processors that are surgically implanted in the cochlea and serve to electrically stimulate the auditory nerve fibers.

cognitive style the cognitive activity that takes place between the time a student recognizes the need to respond to something and actually does respond; cognitive styles are categorized along a continuum ranging from impulsive to reflective.

collaboration professionals working together with a shared purpose in a supportive, mutually beneficial relationship.

collaborative consultation teachers and other school

professionals working together on an equal footing to solve students' problems.

communication the exchange of ideas.

communication disorders a language or speech disorder that adversely affects a child's educational performance.

community-based employment the placing of students in jobs for which they receive on-site training while still in school.

community-based instruction working on a student's instructional goals in the community setting in which they would naturally be used.

conduct disorder individual disruptive, aggressive, non-compliant behaviors.

conductive hearing loss hearing loss resulting from damage or blockage to the outer or middle ear that disrupts the efficient passage or conduction of sound; most conductive losses can be treated medically.

congenital a condition present at birth.

congenital hearing loss a hearing loss present at birth.

congenital malformation an incomplete or improperly formed part of the skeletal or muscular system that is present at birth.

consultation a means of providing specialized services in the regular classroom whereby the special education teacher observes students with disabilities in the regular classroom and provides suggestions to the teacher about adapting instruction or materials to meet students' needs.

consultation model special education resource teacher meets with classroom teachers to plan instructional adaptations for students and provides direct services in the classroom.

content area acceleration a curriculum modification for gifted students that allows students to proceed at a faster pace than their classmates.

contingency intervention curriculum the immediate and distinct presentation of consequences in order to facilitate an understanding of the relationship between actions and their results; this curriculum is used to give infants with severe disabilities the opportunity to develop purposeful behavior and interact with the environment in a meaningful way.

cooperative learning a learning strategy that involves providing small groups of children of various skill levels with a task to complete so that each child makes a significant contribution.

coping strategies things people do to enhance a sense of well-being and avoid being upset by stressful demands.

cornea the transparent outer membrane of the eye.

cortical vision loss vision loss resulting from damage to the brain rather than the eye.

cultural competence a respect for and knowledge of cultural differences and a willingness to accept that there are many ways of viewing the world.

cultural diversity the wide range of cultural characteristics and norms that exist within our society.

culture a way of perceiving, believing, evaluating, and behaving shared by a group of people.

curriculum-based assessment (CBA) a method of assessment based on materials in the child's curriculum rather than on a general achievement test.

curriculum telescoping a curriculum modification for gifted students that involves determining what the students already know and allowing them the chance to explore concepts, subjects, or topics that better tap into their talents.

cystic fibrosis a progressive and usually fatal disorder characterized by lung damage, abnormal mucus production, and difficulties in the absorption of protein and fat.

cytomegalovirus (CMV) a relatively common infection that if contracted by a pregnant woman can cause microcephaly, mental retardation, neurological impairments, and hearing loss in the surviving infant.

Deaf community those adults bound together by their deafness, the use of American Sign Language, and their culture, values, and attitudes.

Deaf culture the view of life manifested by the mores, beliefs, artistic expression, and language particular to Deaf people.

deafness a hearing loss that precludes the learning of language through hearing.

deinstitutionalization the movement away from housing people with mental retardation in residential institutions and toward integrating them more fully into the community.

diabetic retinopathy a condition of the eye that can cause blindness; it occurs when the circulation problems associated with diabetes result in damage to the blood vessels of the retina.

diagnostic assessment the gathering of information about a child's developmental levels, usually through observation, interview, and formal testing, to determine whether the child has a disability.

dialect a variation of a spoken language used by a group of individuals that reflects and is determined by shared regional, social, or cultural/ethnic factors.

Diana* v. *Board of Education a 1970 California decision that children must be tested in their primary language when special education placement is being considered.

direct instruction the identification and instruction of specific academic skills and the use of teaching techniques that have been empirically demonstrated to be effective with students with learning difficulties.

disability a limitation, such as difficulty learning to read or inability to see.

discourse shared communication or conversation.

discrepancy the gap between a student's performance in school and his or her intellectual potential.

discrimination the denial of equal opportunity and equal access based on arbitrary physical or personal characteristics.

dog guide a trained dog used to identify obstacles to safe travel.

Down syndrome a condition caused by an extra twenty-first chromosome that results in mental retardation and physical anomalies.

DSM-IV *The Diagnostic and Statistical Manual of Mental Disorders of the American Psychiatric Association,* fourth edition. A classification system for behavior and emotional disorders.

dual diagnosis the coexisting conditions of mental retardation and behavioral disorders.

due process the right of families and school districts to resort to mediation and appeal procedures when they do not agree with each other concerning a child's education.

due process hearing a procedure to resolve a conflict between a school and family over the evaluation, placement, or program of a child with a disability.

duration the length of time a behavior lasts.

early intervention a comprehensive set of services provided to children from birth to 3 years and their families designed to minimize the effects of risk status or disability.

echolalia the immediate or delayed repetition of someone else's utterance.

Education of the Handicapped Act Amendments of 1990 (P.L. 101-476) amendments to IDEA that require that a formal transition plan be developed for all secondary students identified as having a disability.

educational definitions those definitions of degrees of vision loss focusing on academic functioning and reading medium.

electronic travel devices devices that use sonic waves to detect obstacles in the environment.

enclave a small group of individuals with disabilities who are placed in a work setting, usually within a large business or corporation, and receive on-the-job training from job coaches or social service agencies and from the business itself.

encoding processes processes used to organize information so it can be learned.

enrichment adding disciplines or areas of learning not normally found in the regular curriculum, using more difficult or in-depth material to enhance the core curriculum, or enhancing the teaching strategies used to present instruction.

enrichment triad model (ETM) a program option for upper-elementary gifted children that exposes students to new curricular areas they might wish to explore in greater depth.

environmental analysis *see* environmental inventory.

environmental inventory (environmental analysis) a technique used to identify skills for instruction; it involves a visit to the settings in which the student lives or works so a list can be made of the specific skills needed to be successful in that environment.

environmental risk risk factors related to the environment in which a child develops.

epilepsy a condition of the nervous system that results in seizures that disrupt the normal functioning of the brain.

ethnic minority group an ethnic group that holds a subordinate power position to the majority group.

ethnicity the common history, values, attitudes, and behaviors that bind a group of people.

exceptional the label used to describe the range of students who receive special education services in the school.

exclusion clause the sentence in the federal definition of learning disabilities that excludes from the definition learning problems that are primarily the result of visual, hearing, or motor handicaps, mental retardation, emotional disturbance, or environmental, cultural, or economic disadvantage.

expert consultation the special educator advises the regular educator about the management and instruction of students with special needs.

extended family grandparents, aunts, uncles, cousins, and other relations who may or may not live with a child and parent(s).

externalizing behavior overtly expressed behavior directed toward others or the environment.

eye-gazing scanning system a system that allows an individual to select letters, words, and phrases from a display by simply focusing his or her eyes on the display; a small, sensitive camera detects the direction of the person's eyes and registers the selected elements so a typed message can be produced.

family characteristics the traits, such as size, socioeconomic status, cultural background, and geographic location, that give each family its unique identity.

family configuration the adults present in a family.

family functions all the life tasks of the family necessary for meeting family needs, including economic, daily care, recreation, socialization, self-identity, affection, and educational/vocational functions.

family interaction the relationships among family members.

family life cycle the lifespan of a family, starting with the marriage of a man and a woman and evolving through the birth and growth of their children.

family size the number of children in a family.

family systems approach a framework for understanding the family as an interrelated social system with unique characteristics and needs.

Feingold diet an attempt to eliminate hyperactivity and

learning disabilities by removing artificial colors and flavorings from a child's diet.

fetal alcohol effects the cognitive and behavioral characteristics associated with fetal alcohol syndrome (FAS) without the characteristic physical abnormalities.

fetal alcohol syndrome (FAS) a syndrome resulting from maternal alcohol intake during pregnancy; it is characterized by altered facial features, developmental delays in language and cognition, and behavior problems.

field independent student a student who does well on independent projects and on analytical tests.

field independent teacher a teacher who prefers to use the lecture approach, with limited interactions with students, and who encourages student achievement and competition among students.

field sensitive student a student who performs well in group work and cooperative learning situations.

field sensitive teacher a teacher who prefers to use interpersonal teaching methods, such as personal conversations.

fingerspelling spelling the manual alphabet with the fingers.

first trimester the first three months of pregnancy.

fluency disorder an interruption in the flow of speaking which significantly interferes with communication.

formal assessment using standardized tests to compare a student's performance with that of his or her peers.

functional academics basic academic skills taught in the context of real-life activities; a curricular emphasis on academic skills that are meaningful and useful for daily living.

functional curriculum a curriculum that emphasizes preparation for life and includes only skills that will be useful to the student in home, community, school, or work environments.

functional vision how well a student uses whatever vision he or she may possess.

Gallaudet, Thomas Hopkins a teacher who became the principal of the first school for the deaf in the United States; Gallaudet University is named after him.

generalization *see* skill transfer.

genetic counseling the process of discussing with a trained counselor the likelihood that a child will inherit a genetic condition.

giftedness high performance capability in intellectual, creative, artistic, leadership, or academic areas.

gifted underachiever the term applied to students whose aptitude is high but whose performance is low.

glaucoma a disease of the eye that can lead to blindness if untreated; it occurs when fluid within the eye cannot drain properly, resulting in a gradual increase of pressure within the eye.

grand mal seizure an epileptic seizure that involves the whole body, usually lasts a few minutes, and often results in a loss of consciousness.

group home a community residence shared by people with disabilities under the guidance of a trained supervisor.

handicap the limitations imposed by the environment of a person with a disability or by people's attitudes toward disability.

hard of hearing a term that describes a hearing loss less severe than deafness that usually permits the understanding of oral speech through the use of hearing aids.

health impairment a term used to describe a condition in which one or more of the body's systems are affected by debilitating or life-threatening conditions or diseases.

health maintenance the assisting of or instruction of a student with a physical disability or health impairment in eating, drinking, or using the bathroom.

hearing impairment a term that refers to all degrees of hearing loss from slight to profound.

hearing loss a term used to describe hearing problems.

highly gifted a term used to designate someone whose IQ score is in the 140+ range. Highly gifted children generally prefer adult company, maintain a very high energy level, exhibit marked discrepancies between intellectual abilities and social skills, and display intense reactions regarding injustices and moral wrongs.

home- or hospital-based instruction instruction provided by a special education teacher to students with chronic illness or other medical needs; it is usually temporary.

Howe, Samuel Gridley an American teacher who created the teaching techniques used at the Perkins School for the Blind.

human guide a person, usually sighted, accompanying someone with vision loss while walking.

hydrocephalus a condition in which cerebrospinal fluid builds up in the skull and puts pressure on the brain; if untreated, it can cause brain damage and mental retardation.

hypoxia decreased availability of oxygen during pregnancy, labor, delivery, or newborn life; it can result in death or brain damage.

immature behavior behavior that exhibits a low level of frustration tolerance and the inability to say and do socially appropriate things.

inclusion the provision of services to students with disabilities in the general education classroom.

independent study a curriculum modification for gifted students that allows them to explore topics of interest to them; the student does require teacher guidance to be sure a manageable topic is selected.

individual supported job model a form of supported employment in which a job coach provides on-site training and problem solving for a single individual; the goal is to gradually decrease the level of support until the individual is ready for independent competitive employment.

individualized education the concept that each student should have a program tailored to his or her unique learning needs.

individualized education program (IEP) the written plan for each student's individual education program.

individualized family service plan (IFSP) a written account of the personal and social services needed to promote and support the child and family for the first three years of an exceptional child's life.

Individuals with Disabilities Education Act (IDEA) the name given in 1990 to what was formerly known as the Education for All Handicapped Children Act, P.L. 94-142 and its amendments.

informal assessment measures of student performance and progress in academic or behavior tasks; focuses on individual growth and skill acquisition rather than on a comparison of one child's performance with that of others.

informal inventories a series of sequential passages or tasks, on different grade levels, used to assess the specific difficulties a student is having with reading, writing, or math skills.

inoculation vaccination against such infectious diseases as rubella, pertussis, measles, mumps, and polio.

institution a large, segregated, residential building used to house individuals with mental retardation, mental illness, or physical disabilities.

intensity the strength or magnitude of a behavior.

interdisciplinary team a group of professionals from a variety of disciplines who work with a family to plan, coordinate, and deliver services.

intermediate-care facility (ICF) a community-based residential placement comprised of a number of individuals with disabilities living together in a supervised setting.

internalizing behavior self-directed behavior, such as withdrawal, avoidance, or compulsiveness.

iris the colored part of the eye.

Irving Independent School District* v. *Tatro a 1984 U.S. Supreme Court decision that schools must provide medical services that a nonphysician can perform if a child needs them to remain in school.

Itard, Jean-Marc-Gaspard a young French physician who attempted to teach the "wild boy of Aveyron" to talk.

job coach a person trained in special education who trains people on the job and works with on-site supervisors to help integrate the person with disabilities into the employment setting.

juvenile onset diabetes a metabolic disorder caused by an insufficient amount of insulin produced by the body, which results in difficulties in digesting and ob-

taining energy from food; it can appear at any point between birth and age 30.

juvenile rheumatoid arthritis a condition that affects the tissue lining of the joints.

Kennedy, John F. a president with a strong personal interest in improving the quality of life for people with mental retardation.

language the verbal means by which humans communicate.

language delay a delay in the acquisition of normal language milestones.

language disorders the impaired comprehension and/or use of spoken, written, and/or other symbol systems that may involve the form, content, or function of language.

Larry P.* v. *Riles a 1979 California state court decision that IQ tests not be used in placing African American students in classes for students with mental retardation.

learning disability a disorder in one or more of the basic psychological processes involved in understanding or using language. A student who has a learning disability does not achieve at the expected age and ability level in one or more academic areas and shows a severe discrepancy between achievement and intellectual ability.

learning style the way a student approaches learning.

Learning Strategies Curriculum a well-known curriculum developed at the University of Kansas Institute for Research in Learning Disabilities that focuses on strategy instruction.

least restrictive environment the setting that allows each child to be educated with his or her nondisabled peers to the maximum extent appropriate.

legal blindness a visual acuity of 20/200 or worse in the better eye after correction or a visual field of no greater than 20 degrees; this level of visual impairment qualifies a person for a variety of legal and social services.

lens the clear structure between the iris and the tissue inside the eyeball, which focuses light on the retina.

level system an educational program that involves a stepwise progression through a predetermined set of behavioral requirements, restrictions, and responsibilities that allow students to achieve higher levels of freedom and responsibility once they demonstrate appropriate behavior.

life-skills curriculum a course of study intended to provide the skills necessary to enable a student to live and work independently.

lifespan the time between birth and death.

limited English proficient (LEP) a student with a first language other than English who is not yet fluent in English.

linguistic diversity the variety of languages spoken in the homes of schoolchildren.

low birthweight a weight less than five and a half pounds at birth.

macroculture the core, or universal, culture of a country; in the United States it is characterized by traits such as individualism, industriousness, ambition, competitiveness, self-reliance, and independence.

Macy, Anne Sullivan Helen Keller's legendary teacher.

mainstreaming the practice of providing children with disabilities an education with their nondisabled peers.

maladaptive behavior behavior that obstructs the development of socially appropriate behaviors and social acceptance.

manual communication approach an approach to the teaching of students who are deaf or hard-of-hearing that emphasizes the use of signs and sign language; its basic components are finger spelling and signs.

mediation discussion between families and school districts over a point of disagreement, for the purpose of resolving the disagreement before a due process hearing must be held.

meningitis a serious illness that can cause brain damage and result in a range of disabling conditions such as hearing and vision loss and mental retardation.

mental retardation a mild, moderate, or severe condition that is manifested in childhood and characterized by subaverage intellectual functioning and impairments in adaptive behavior.

mentorship an arrangement whereby a secondary-level student works with a community member to learn a specific skill, trade, or craft.

metacognition "thinking about thinking"; the ability to identify how one learns and to evaluate, monitor, and adapt the learning process.

microculture a subsociety, or subculture, that has its own distinctive cultural patterns while at the same time sharing core values with the macroculture.

Mills v. Washington, D.C. Board of Education a 1972 decision that required the District of Columbia to provide a free, appropriate public education for students with disabilities.

minority a numerical minority; it also suggests a subordinate position in society.

minority group a group that can be categorized by ethnicity, gender, language, religion, handicap, or socioeconomic status.

mixed hearing loss a hearing loss with both conductive and sensorineural components.

mobile work crew a group of individuals with disabilities who have learned a specific trade or set of skills that can be applied in the community.

mobility the ability to move about in one's environment.

Montessori, Maria an Italian physician who founded the Montessori method of teaching based on the work of Itard and Seguin.

morphemes the smallest units of meaning in a language.

morphology the rules that govern how word meanings may be changed by adding prefixes, suffixes, and other forms that specifically indicate tense and number.

multiple intelligences Howard Gardner's theory that there are at least seven distinct intelligences. An abundance of talent in any of these areas constitutes giftedness, according to Gardner.

muscular dystrophy a condition in which the voluntary muscles of the body are affected by progressive weakness.

neonatal intensive care unit a specialized unit of the hospital for the care of high-risk newborns.

neonatology the study of high-risk newborns.

nondiscriminatory evaluation evaluation procedures must be conducted with fairness in the child's native language.

normalization an emphasis on conventional or normal behavior and attitudes in all aspects of education, socialization, and other life experiences for people with disabilities.

norms normal or typical ranges of expected behavior.

nystagmus a repetitive, involuntary, rhythmic movement of the eyes common among children with visual impairments.

ophthalmologist a physician who specializes in the treatment of eye diseases.

optic nerve the nerve that connects the eye to the brain.

optician someone who grinds and fits corrective lenses.

optometrist a professional trained to examine eyes, evaluate visual problems, and prescribe corrective lenses.

oral communication approach an approach to the teaching of students who are deaf and hard-of-hearing that emphasizes the development of speech and auditory skills through a combination of speech reading and residual hearing.

organization a cognitive skill that involves the ability to see and use similarities and differences and to categorize, arrange, and plan.

orientation the ability to use one's senses to establish where one is in space and in relation to other objects and people.

otitis media middle ear infection; the most common cause of conductive hearing loss in children.

otologist a physician who specializes in diseases of the ear.

overrepresentation a representation in a specific group or class that is greater than would be expected based on actual numbers.

parent-to-parent model a model for parent support that links experienced parents of children with disabilities to parents who are new to the programs and processes.

Pennsylvania Association for Retarded Citizens (PARC) **v.** *Commonwealth of Pennsylvania* a 1972 state decision that required Pennsylvania to provide a free, appropriate public education for students with mental retardation.

people-first language language that concentrates on describing the person first, then the disability.

perception the ability to organize and interpret what one experiences through the senses.

perinatal period the period from the twelfth week of pregnancy to the twenty-eighth day of life.

perinatal stress traumatic events such as difficult or prolonged labor and delivery, hypoxia, low birthweight, or illness that occur during birth or the first twenty-eight days after birth.

petit mal seizure an epileptic seizure that occurs most frequently in children between the ages of 4 and 12; these seizures are very brief—usually only a few seconds—and although the child may lose consciousness, there may be no observable physical changes.

phoneme the smallest unit of speech.

phonological awareness the ability to recognize the sounds contained in words.

phonological disorders problems with the consistent articulation of phonemes, the individual sounds of speech.

phonology the rules for combining sounds in permissible ways to form words.

physical disability a condition that incapacitates to some degree the skeletal, muscular, and/or neurological systems of the body.

physical handling the moving of a student with a physical disability from place to place.

physically challenged the descriptive term preferred by many people with a physical disability; it describes their physical condition as a challenge to be faced rather than as a handicap.

polydrug user someone who uses a combination of illegal drugs, plus alcohol.

postlingual deafness deafness that occurs after language is acquired.

postnatal period the period from the twenty-eighth day of life on.

pragmatic language the ability to use language effectively in different settings and for different purposes.

pragmatics the rules governing language use in differing situations.

predictive validity how accurately a test can predict academic performance.

prelingual deafness deafness that occurs before language is acquired.

premature a baby born before thirty-seven weeks' gestation.

prenatal care the care provided to an expectant mother during pregnancy by her physician, usually an obstetrician.

prenatal period the period from conception to birth.

prereferral intervention team a team of teachers and other professionals that works to keep children in the regular classroom instead of referring them to special education.

preterm *see* premature.

prevalence the number of students within a given category.

profound mental retardation a level of retardation characterized by an IQ of less than 20 and deficits in adaptive behavior.

projective test an open-ended test that provides an opportunity for a child to express himself or herself and perhaps reveal evidence of behavioral or emotional trauma.

prompt a cue or guide that helps a student attend to or learn the appropriate material.

Public Law 94-142 a 1975 federal law that requires that every child between the ages of 3 and 21 with a disability be provided a free, appropriate public education in the least restrictive environment.

pullout program a service that involves the student leaving the classroom to receive specialized instruction.

pupil the opening in the center of the eye.

quality of life an index of adult performance, adjustment, and happiness.

rate how often a behavior occurs in a given time period.

reading comprehension the ability to understand the meaning of sentences and passages.

refractive errors myopia, hyperopia, and astigmatism resulting from differences in the shape of the eye.

relational meaning the meaning that goes beyond the individual meanings of words and links word meanings together into topics.

remedial instruction teaching the basic skill or content subject in which a student is having difficulty.

residential school a special school where students live during the school year.

residual hearing the remaining hearing most people with hearing loss possess.

resilient the ability to resist stress, to overcome risk factors and develop well.

resource room a service that involves students leaving the regular classroom for specialized instruction in academic areas of need.

respite care care given to a family member with a disability by a trained substitute caregiver.

retina a layer of specialized cells at the back of the eye that are highly sensitive to light.

retinitis pigmentosa a hereditary condition of the eye characterized by degeneration of the retina caused by a deposit of pigment in the back of the eye; it is a progressive disease that results in tunnel vision.

retinopathy of prematurity damage to the eye that can cause vision loss in premature infants.

risk factors biological and environmental conditions associated with the increased probability of developmental problems.

rubella also known as German measles; a highly contagious virus that can cause severe damage to the fetus if contracted by a mother in the first sixteen weeks of pregnancy.

scaffolding the guidance an adult or peer provides through verbal communication as a way of doing for the student what the student cannot yet do alone.

screening quick evaluation of large numbers of children for developmental and health problems.

Schoolwide Enrichment Model Joseph Renzulli's model for school change that is based on curriculum modifications and enrichment strategies used with gifted students.

Section 504 of the Rehabilitation Act of 1973 a law requiring that all facilities that receive federal funds be accessible to people with disabilities and prohibiting discrimination against people who are disabled.

Seguin, Edouard a French teacher who built on Itard's methods to form his own approach to teaching students with mental retardation.

self-management procedures procedures such as self-monitoring and recording of completed tasks taught to students to facilitate their independent performance.

semantic mapping a graphic representation of related words, topics, or ideas, used to facilitate organization for producing (writing) or understanding (reading) information.

semantics the rules used to create and understand meaning in words and word combinations.

sensorineural hearing loss permanent hearing loss that usually results from damage to the cochlea or auditory nerve.

serious emotional disturbance a condition including one or more of the following characteristics over a long period of time and to a marked degree, which adversely affects educational performance: an inability to learn, an inability to build satisfactory interpersonal relationships, inappropriate types of behavior, a general mood of unhappiness or depression, and a tendency to develop fears associated with personal or school problems.

severe disabilities disabilities that require ongoing support in one or more major life activity, such as mobility, communication, self-care, and learning, in order to participate in integrated community settings and enjoy a quality of life available to people with fewer or no disabilities.

severe mental retardation a level of retardation characterized by an IQ of less than 40 and deficits in adaptive behavior.

sexually transmitted diseases (STDs) diseases spread by sexual intercourse.

sheltered employment contract work conducted in settings designed for individuals with disabilities—usually assembly-line workshops.

sheltered workshops large facilities for people with disabilities that provide simple contract work.

signs manual symbols for a word or concept.

skill transfer (generalization) the ability to apply a specific skill learned in one context to a different context.

Snellen Chart the most common visual screening test; it consists of eight rows of letters, each row smaller in size than the previous one; the person being tested is asked to read the letters with each eye while the other eye is covered. Each row represents the distance at which a person with normal vision can see the letters.

social aging the different roles a person acquires and abandons over the course of the lifespan.

social norms age-related behaviors that reflect the typical patterns or standards of a particular group.

socialized aggression aggressive and disruptive behaviors on the part of a group.

socioeconomic status a measure of a family's social and economic standing based on family income and education and employment of the parents.

special class a class within a regular elementary or high school that groups children by exceptionality; a specialist teacher instructs these students together.

special education the educational program designed to meet the unique learning and developmental needs of an exceptional student.

special school a school designed exclusively for students with exceptionalities.

specific language impairment primary difficulty in learning and using language which cannot be attributed to another disability.

speech the spoken part of the language system; it is produced by complex, well-coordinated activity from respiration to phonation to articulation.

speech disorders impairments of articulation, fluency, or voice.

speech-language pathologist the specialist concerned with the identification, assessment, and treatment of students with communication disorders.

spina bifida a midline defect of the skin, spinal column, and spinal cord that occurs during fetal development; it is characterized by varying degrees of paralysis.

stage theory an assumption that changes occur in a predictable order and that movement to the next stage depends on successful resolution of the prior stage.

Stanford-Binet a widely used standardized test of intelligence that places great emphasis on verbal judgments and reasoning.

stereotypic behaviors repetitive, nonharmful behaviors sometimes exhibited by people with severe mental retardation and autism; examples include rocking, twirling of objects, clapping of hands.

strabismus a structural defect associated with the muscles of the eye resulting in the appearance of crossed eyes or wall eyes; the result of this deviation is that the eyes focus on two different things at the same time, leading the brain to suppress one of the images.

strategy instruction an approach to teaching students with learning disabilities that involves first breaking down the skills involved in a task or problem into a set of sequential steps and then preparing the steps so that students may read and later memorize them in order to perform the task correctly.

stuttering the habit of repeating a sound, syllable, or word while speaking, which significantly interferes with communication.

supported employment an employment setting in which a job coach trains a student at the job site, and a support system is established to help the student maintain the job and adjust to new job requirements over time.

syntax rules governing how words may be combined to form sentences.

synthesized speech the storage of words or phrases that can be recalled as needed, or the storage of speech sounds that can be put together to form words using a sound-by-sound process.

talent a mental or physical aptitude or ability.

task analysis the process of breaking down a task or skill into its component parts.

teacher assistance team (intervention assistance team) a group of teachers and other professionals who work together to assist the regular classroom teacher.

team teaching shared instruction of a lesson, a subject area, or an entire instructional program.

telecommunication devices for the deaf (TDDs) telephones with screens and keyboards that allow people who are deaf to communicate with others.

teratogen a substance that can cause birth defects.

Thalidomide a drug prescribed to pregnant women in the 1950s that caused severe birth defects.

total communication the philosophy that advocates the use of whatever communication system is appropriate for a given child with a hearing loss at a given time.

transdisciplinary model an approach to assessment and planning in which professionals with differing specializations work together on an equal footing.

transition coordinator a person designated by the state, school district, or school to plan, coordinate, and supervise transition services.

transition programs programs designed to facilitate movement from school to work, from segregated to integrated settings, and from isolated living to community living and employment.

traumatic brain injury an acquired injury to the brain caused by an external physical force resulting in total or partial functional disability or psychosocial impairment.

triarchic theory Robert Sternberg's theory which describes three kinds of intellectual giftedness: analytic, creative, and practical.

tutorial instruction helping the student in the specific subject in which he or she is having difficulty; usually occurs at the secondary level.

underrepresentation a representation in a specific group or class that is less than would be expected based on actual numbers in the population.

unilateral hearing loss normal hearing in one ear and hearing loss in the other.

verbalism the use of words without concrete knowledge of their meanings.

Vineland Adaptive Behavior Scale one of the most widely used instruments for measuring adaptive behavior.

visual acuity sharpness of vision.

visual impairment a term that describes all levels of vision loss, from total blindness to uncorrectable visual limitations.

vitreous humor liquid-filled "eyeball."

vocational rehabilitation counselor person who assists adolescents and adults with disabilities in making the transition from school to work by helping them plan for post high school education and training, and job placement.

voice disorder any disorder resulting from difficulties in breathing, abnormalities of the larynx, or dysfunctions in the oral and nasal cavities that can affect the pitch, loudness, and/or quality of a voice.

webbing a process that can help focus a child's specific interests within a broad topic by subdividing it into many smaller, manageable subtopics.

Wechsler Intelligence Scale for Children, Third Edition (WISC-III) a test frequently used to predict academic achievement in school-age children.

word analysis the process of identifying written words; it involves the use of phonics, sight words, and context clues.

zero reject the principle that no child with a disability shall be refused an appropriate education by the schools.

References

Achenbach, T., & Edelbrock, C. (1979). The child behavior profile II: Boys aged 12–16 and girls aged 6–11 and 12–16. *Journal of Consulting and Clinical Psychology, 47,* 223–233.

Adderhold-Elliott, M. (1987). *Perfectionism: What's bad about being too good?* Minneapolis: Free Spirit.

Adelman, H.S. (1996). Appreciating the classification dilemma. In W. Stainback & S. Stainback (Eds.), *Controversial issues confronting special education: Divergent perspectives* (2d ed.) (pp. 96–111). Boston: Allyn & Bacon.

Adler, J., Lubenow, G.C., & Malone, M. (1988). Reading God's mind. *Newsweek, 111*(24), 56–59.

Affleck, J.Q., Edgar, E., Levine, P., & Kortering, L. (1990). Postschool status of students classified as mildly mentally retarded, learning disabled, or nonhandicapped: Does it get better with time? *Education and Training in Mental Retardation, 25,* 315–324.

Agency for Toxic Substances and Disease Registry (1988). *The nature and extent of lead poisoning in children in the United States: A report to Congress.* Washington, DC: U.S. Department of Health and Human Services.

Agran, M., Salzberg, C.L., & Stowitchek, J. (1987). An analysis of the effects of a social skills training program using self-instructions on the acquisition and generalization of two social behaviors in a work setting. *Journal of the Association for Persons with Severe Handicaps, 12*(2), 131–139.

Albert, R.S. (1978). Observations and suggestions regarding giftedness: Familial influences and the achievement of eminence. *Gifted Child Quarterly, 28*(3), 201–211.

Alberto, P.A., & Troutman, A.C. (1990). *Applied behavior analysis for teachers* (3d ed.). Columbus, OH: Merrill.

Allen, R., & Petr, C.G. (1996). Toward developing standards and measurements for family-centered practice in family support programs. In G.H.S. Singer, L.E. Powers & A.L. Olson (Eds.), *Redefining family support: Innovations in public-private partnerships* (pp. 57–86). Baltimore: Brookes.

Allen, T. (1986). Patterns of academic achievement among hearing impaired students: 1974 and 1983. In A.N. Schildroth & M.A. Karchmer (Eds.), *Deaf children in America* (pp. 161–206). San Diego: College-Hill.

Alvino, J. (1989). From the editor. *Gifted Children Monthly, 10*(2), 23.

American Academy of Audiology. (1989). Position statement on early identification of hearing loss in infants and children. Houston, TX: American Academy of Audiology.

American College of Medical Genetics. (1996). Statement on guidance for genetic counseling in advanced paternal age. http://www.faseb.org/genetics/acmg/pol-20.htm.

American Printing House for the Blind (1996). *Annual Report.* Louisville, KY: American Printing House for the Blind.

American Speech-Language-Hearing Association. (1991). The prevention of communication disorders tutorial. *ASHA, 33* (Suppl. 6), 15–41.

———. (1993). Definitions of communication disorders and variations. *ASHA, 35* (Suppl. 10), 40–41.

———. (1997). *Assistive listening devices.* Rockville, MD: American Speech-Language-Hearing Association.

Amish, P.L., Gesten, E.L., Smith, J.K., Clark, H.B., & Stark, C. (1988). Social problem-solving training for severely emotionally and behaviorally disturbed children. *Behavioral Disorders, 13,* 175–186.

Anastasiow, N.J. (1986). The research base for early intervention. *Journal of the Division for Early Childhood, 10,* 99–105.

Anderson, H.R., Bailey, P.A., Cooper, J.S., Palmer, J.C., & West, S. (1983). Morbidity and school absence caused by asthma and wheezing illness. *Archives of Disabled Children, 58,* 777–784.

Anderson, P.P., & Fenichel, E.S. (1989). *Serving culturally diverse families of infants and toddlers with disabilities.* Arlington, VA: National Center for Clinical Infant Programs.

Angier, N. (1992). *New York Times,* Friday, Dec. 4.

Annual Survey of Deaf and Hard-of-Hearing Children and Youth. (1996–1997). Washington, DC: Center for Assessment and Demographic Studies, Gallaudet University.

Anthony, T.L., Fazzi, D.L., Lampert, J.S., & Pogrund, R.L. (1992). Movement focus: Orientation and mobility for young blind and visually impaired students. In R.L. Pogrund, D.L. Fazzi & J.S. Lampert (Eds.), *Early focus: Working with young blind and visually impaired children and their families* (pp. 80–111). New York: American Foundation for the Blind.

Arnold, L., Christopher, J., & Huestis, R. (1978). Megavitamins for minimal brain dysfunction: A placebo-controlled study. *Journal of the American Medical Association, 240,* 2642.

Artiles, A.J., & Trent, S.C. (1994). Overrepresentation of minority students in special education: A continuing debate. *Journal of Special Education, 27,* 410–437.

ASHA Committee on Language Speech and Hearing Services in the Schools. (1980, April). Definitions for communicative disorders and differences. *ASHA, 22,* 317–318.

Association for Persons with Severe Handicaps. (1989). *TASH resolutions and policy statements.* Seattle, WA: TASH.

Augusto, C. (1996). Foreword. In A.L. Corn & A.J. Koenig (Eds.), *Foundations of low vision: Clinical and functional perspectives* (p. v). New York: AFB Press.

Aune, E. (1991). A transition model for postsecondary-bound students with learning disabilities. *Learning Disabilities Research and Practice, 6,* 177–187.

Aveno, A., & Renzaglia, A. (1988). A survey of attitudes of potential community training site staff toward persons with severe handicaps. *Education and Training in Mental Retardation, 23,* 213–223.

Baca, L.M., & Cervantes, H.T. (1989). *The bilingual special education interface* (2d ed.). Columbus, OH: Merrill.

Baker, C., & Cokely, D. (1980). *American Sign Language: A teacher's resource on grammar and culture.* Silver Spring, MD: T.J. Publishers.

Baker, R.L., Mednick, B.R., & Hunt, N.A. (1987). Academic and social characteristics of low-birth-weight adolescents. *Social Biology, 34*(1–2), 94–109.

Baldwin, A.Y. (1985). Programs for the gifted and talented: Issues concerning minority populations. In F.D. Horowitz & M. O'Brien (Eds.), *The gifted and the talented: Developmental perspectives.* Washington, DC: American Psychological Association.

———. (1991). Ethnic and cultural issues. In N. Colangelo & G.A. Davis, *Handbook of gifted education.* Boston: Allyn & Bacon.

Barnard, K.E., & Kelly, J.F. (1990). Assessment of parent-child interaction. In S.J. Meisels & J.P. Shonkoff (Eds.), *Handbook of early childhood intervention* (pp. 278–302). New York: Cambridge University Press.

Barton, D.D. (1984). Uncharted course: Mothering the blind child. *Journal of Visual Impairment and Blindness, 78*(2), 66–69.

Bashir, A.S., & Scavuzzo, A. (1992). Children with language disorders: Natural history and academic success. *Journal of Learning Disabilities, 25,* 53–64.

Batshaw, M.L., & Conlin, C.J. (1997). Substance abuse: A preventable threat to development. In M.L. Batshaw (Ed.), *Children with disabilities* (pp. 143–162). Baltimore: Brookes.

Batshaw, M.L., & Rose, N.C. (1997). Birth defects, prenatal diagnosis, and prenatal therapy. In M.L. Batshaw (Ed.), *Children with disabilities* (pp. 35–52). Baltimore: Brookes.

Beckwith, L. (1990). Adaptive and maladaptive parenting: Implications for intervention. In S.J. Meisels & J.P. Shonkoff (Eds.), *Handbook of early childhood intervention.* New York: Cambridge University Press.

Bellefleur, P.A. (1976). TTY communication: Its history and future. *Volta Review, 78*(4), 107–112.

Belman, A.L., Diamond, G., Dickson, D., Horoupian, D., Llena, J., Lantos, G., & Rubenstein, S. (1988). Pediatric acquired immunodeficiency syndrome. *American Journal of Diseases in Children, 142,* 29–35.

Belsky, J., Lang, M.E., & Rovine, M. (1985). Stability and change in marriage across the transition to parenthood: A second study. *Journal of Marriage and the Family, 47,* 855–865.

Benson, H.A. (1989). An investigation of respite care as a mediator of stress in families with members with developmental disabilities. Doctoral dissertation, University of Kansas.

Benz, M.R., Yovanoff, P., & Doren, B. (1997). School-to-work components that predict postschool success for students with and without disabilities. *Exceptional Children, 63,* 151–165.

Bergstrom, L. (1984). Congenital hearing loss. In J.L. Northern (Ed.), *Hearing disorders* (2d ed.). Boston: Little, Brown.

Berko, J. (1958). The child's learning of English morphology. *Word, 14*, 150–177.

Bernbaum, J.C., & Batshaw, M.L. (1997). Born too soon, born too small. In M.L. Batshaw (Ed.), *Children with disabilities* (pp. 115–139). Baltimore: Brookes.

Berry, J.O., & Hardman, M.L. (1998). *Lifespan perspectives on the family and disability.* Boston: Allyn & Bacon.

Bigge, J. (1991a). Self care. In J. Bigge, *Teaching individuals with physical and multiple disabilities* (3d ed.) (pp. 379–398). New York: Merrill.

———. (1991b). Life management. In J. Bigge, *Teaching individuals with physical and multiple disabilities* (3d ed.) (pp. 399–427). New York: Merrill.

———. (1991c). Augmentative communication. In J. Bigge, *Teaching individuals with physical and multiple disabilities* (3d ed.) (pp. 199–246). New York: Merrill.

———. (1982). *Teaching individuals with physical and multiple disabilities* (2d ed.). Columbus, OH: Merrill.

Bigler, E.D. (1992). The neurobiology and neuropsychology of adult learning disorders. *Journal of Learning Disabilities, 25*, 488–506.

Bireley, M., & Genshaft, J. (1991). *Understanding the gifted adolescent.* New York: Teachers College Press.

Bishop, V.E. (1996). Causes and functional implications of visual impairment. In A.L. Corn & A.J. Koenig (Eds.), *Foundations of low vision: Clinical and functional perspectives* (pp. 86–114). New York: AFB Press.

Blacher, J. (Ed.). (1984a). *Severely handicapped young children and their families: Research in review.* Orlando, FL: Academic Press.

———. (Ed.). (1984b). Sequential stages to parental adjustment to the birth of a child with handicaps: Fact or artifact? *Mental Retardation, 22*, 55–68.

Blachman, B.A. (1991a). Getting ready to read: Learning how to print maps of speech. In J.F. Kavanagh (Ed.), *The language continuum: From infancy to literacy* (pp. 41–62). Parkton, MD: York Press.

———. (1991b). Early intervention for children's reading problems: Clinical applications of the research in phonological awareness. *Topics in Language Disorders, 12*(1), 51–65.

Blackburn, J.A. (1987). In M.L. Wolraich (Ed.), *The practical assessment and management of children with disorders of development and learning* (pp. 164–193). Chicago: Yearbook.

Blackhurst, A.E. (1997). Perspectives on technology in special education (1997). *Teaching Exceptional Children, 29*(5), 41–48.

Blackorby, J., & Wagner, M. (1996). Longitudinal postschool outcomes of youth with disabilities: Findings from the National Longitudinal Transition Study. *Exceptional Children, 62*, 399–413.

Blatt, B. (1966). *Christmas in purgatory.* Boston: Allyn and Bacon.

———. (1977). Issues and values. In B. Blatt, D. Bilken & R. Bogdan (Eds.), *An alternative textbook in special education* (pp. 3–28). Denver: Love.

Bloom, B. (Ed.). (1956). *Taxonomy of educational objectives, Handbook I: Cognitive domain.* New York: David McKay.

———. (1985). *Developing talent in young people.* New York: Ballantine.

Bloom, B., Englehart, M., Furst, E., Hill, W., & Krathwohl, D., (1956). *Taxonomy of educational objectives, Handbook 1: Cognitive domain.* New York: McKay.

Bloom, L. (1988). What is language? In M. Lahey (Ed.), *Language disorders and language development* (pp. 1–19). New York: Macmillan.

Bloom, L., & Lahey, M. (1978). *Language development and language disorders.* New York: John Wiley.

Bonnet, K.A. (1989). Learning disabilities: A neurobiological perspective in humans. *Remedial and Special Education, 10*, 8–19.

Bornstein, H. (1990a). A manual communication overview. In H. Bornstein (Ed.), *Manual communication: Implications for education.* Washington, DC: Gallaudet University Press.

———. (1990b). Signed English. In H. Bornstein (Ed.), *Manual communication: Implications for education.* Washington, DC: Gallaudet University Press.

Bowe, F. (1991). *Approaching equality: Education of the deaf.* Silver Springs, MD: TJ Publications.

Brady, N.C., & Halle, J.W. (1997). Functional analysis of communicative behaviors. *Focus on Autism and Other Developmental Disabilities, 12*, 95–104.

Bradley-Johnson, S., & Evans, L. (1991). *Psychoeducational assessment of hearing impaired students.* Austin, TX: Pro-Ed.

Brantlinger, E.A. (1988). Teachers' perceptions of the parenting abilities of their secondary students with mild mental retardation. *Remedial and Special Education, 9*(4), 31–43.

Breakthroughs. (1997). Augmentative communication product catalog. Pittsburgh, PA: Sentient Systems Technology, Inc.

Breslau, N., Staruch, K.S., & Mortimer, E.A. (1982). Psychological distress in mothers of disabled children *American Journal of the Disabled Child, 136*, 682–686.

Bricker, D., & Filler, J. (1985). The severely mentally retarded individual: Philosophical and implementation dilemmas. In D. Bricker & J. Filler (Eds.), *Severe mental retardation: From theory to practice* (pp. 2–10). Reston, VA: Division for Mental Retardation of the Council for Exceptional Children.

Brinckerhoff, J.L., & Vincent, L.J. (1986). Increasing parental decision-making at their child's individualized education program meeting. *Journal of the Division for Early Childhood, 11*(1), 46–58.

Brinker, R.P. (1984). The microcomputer as a perceptual tool: Searching for systematic learning strategies with handicapped infants. In R.E. Bennet & C.A. Maher (Eds.), *Microcomputers and exceptional children* (pp. 21–36). New York: Haworth Press.

Brinker, R.P., & Lewis, M. (1982). Making the world work with microcomputers: A learning prosthesis for handicapped infants. *Exceptional Children, 49*, 163–170.

Bronfenbrenner, U. (1979). *The ecology of human development.* Cambridge, MA: Harvard University Press.

Brooke, V., Wehman, P., Inge, K., & Parent, W. (1995). Toward a customer-driven approach of supported employment. *Education and Training in Mental Retardation and Developmental Disabilities, 30*, 308–320.

Brooks, P.H., & McCauley, C. (1984). Cognitive research in mental retardation. *American Journal of Mental Deficiency, 88*, 479–486.

Browder, D.M., & Snell, M.E. (1987). Functional academics. In M.E. Snell (Ed.), *Systematic instruction of persons with severe handicaps* (3d ed.) (pp. 436–468). Columbus, OH: Merrill.

Bruder, M.B. (1995). The challenge of pediatric AIDS: A framework for early childhood special education. *Topics in early childhood special education, 15*(1), 83–89.

Bryan, T. (1991). Social problems and learning disabilities. In B. Wong (Ed.), *Learning about learning disabilities* (pp. 196–231). San Diego: Academic Press.

Bryen, D.N., Goldman, A.S. & Quinlisk-Gill, S. (1988). Sign language with students with severe/profound mental retardation: How effective is it? *Education and Training in Mental Retardation, 23*, 129–137.

Bryson, S. (1996). Brief report: Epidemiology of autism. *Journal of Autism and Developmental Disorders, 26*, 165–167.

Buescher, T.M. (1984). Gifted and talented adolescents: Challenging perspectives. *Journal for the Education of the Gifted, 8*(1), 1–8.

Bufkin, L.J., & Altman, R. (1995). A developmental study of nonverbal pragmatic communication in students with and without mild mental retardation. *Education and Training in Mental Retardation and Developmental Disabilities, 30*, 199–207.

Bullis, M., Bull, B., Johnson, B., & Peters, P. (1995). The school-to-community transition experiences of hearing young adults and young adults who are deaf. *Journal of Special Education, 28*, 405–423.

Burchard, S.N., Gordon, L.R., & Pine, J. (1990). Manager competence, program normalization, and client satisfaction in group homes. *Education and Training in Mental Retardation, 25*, 277–285.

Burton, B.K., Schulz, C.J., & Burd, L.I. (1992). Limb anomalies associated with chorionic villus sampling. *Obstetrics and Gynecology, 79*, 726–730.

Butterfield, N., & Arthur, M. (1995). Shifting the focus: Emerging priorities in communication programming for students with a severe intellectual disability. *Education and Training in Mental Retardation and Developmental Disabilities, 31*, 41–50.

Caldwell, T., Todaro, A.W., & Gates, A.J. (Eds.). (1988). *Community provider's guide: An information outline for working with children with special needs.* Children's Hospital, New Orleans, LA.

Calvert, D.R. (1986). *Physician's guide to the education of hearing-impaired children.* Washington, DC: Alexander Graham Bell Association for the Deaf.

Campbell, P.H., Bellamy, G.T., & Bishop, K.K. (1988). Statewide intervention systems: An overview of the new federal program for infants and toddlers with handicaps. *Journal of Special Education, 22*, 25–40.

Carlson, C.I. (1987). Social interaction goals and strategies of children with learning disabilities. *Journal of Learning Disabilities, 20*, 306–311.

Carnine, D. (1991). Curricular interventions for teaching higher order thinking to all students: Introduction to the special series. *Journal of Learning Disabilities, 24*, 261–269.

Carnine, D., Silbert, J., & Kameenui, E.J. (1990). *Direct instruction reading* (2d ed.). New York: Merrill/Macmillan.

Caro P., & Snell, M.E. (1989). Characteristics of teaching communication to people with moderate and severe disabilities. *Education and Training in Mental Retardation, 24*, 63–77.

Cates, D.L., Markell, M.A., & Bettenhausen, S. (1995). At risk for abuse: A teacher's guide for recognizing and reporting child neglect and abuse. *Preventing School Failure, 39*(2), 6–9.

Catts, H.W. (1991a). Early identification of reading disabilities. *Topics in Language Disorders, 12*(1), 1–16.

———. (1991b). Facilitating phonological awareness: Role of speech-language pathologists. *Language, Speech, and Hearing Services in Schools, 22*, 196–203.

Cawley, J.F., Parmar, R.S., Yan, W.F., & Miller, J.H. (1996). Arithmetic computation abilities of students with learning disabilities: Implications for instruction. *Learning Disabilities Research and Practice, 1*, 230–237.

Cazden, C.B. (1988). *Classroom discourse: The language of teaching and learning.* Portsmouth, NH: Heinemann.

Cegelka, P.T., & Prehm, H.J. (1982). *Mental retardation: From categories to people.* Columbus, OH: Merrill.

Chan, S. (1986). Parents of exceptional Asian children. In M.K. Kitano & P.C. Chinn (Eds.), *Exceptional Asian children and youth* (pp. 36–53). Reston, VA: The Council for Exceptional Children.

Chaney, C. (1992). Language development, metalinguistic skills, and print awareness in 3-year-old children. *Applied Psycholinguistics, 13*, 485–514.

Chapman, R.S., Streim, N.W., Crais, E.R., Salmon, D., Strand, C.A., & Negri, N.A. (1992). Child talk: Assumptions of a developmental process model for early language learning. In R.S. Chapman (Ed.), *Processes in language acquisition and disorders* (pp. 3–19). St. Louis: Mosby Year-Book.

Chedd, N.A. (1995). Genetic counseling. *Exceptional Parent, 25*(8), 26–27.

Chen, D., & Dote-Kwan, J. (1995). *Starting points: Instructional practices for young children whose multiple disabili-*

ties include visual impairment. Los Angeles: Blind Children's Center.

Cheng, I. (1987). Cross-cultural and linguistic considerations in working with Asian populations, *ASHA 29*(6), 33–38.

Cheng, L.L. (1987). *Assessing Asian language performance: Guidelines for evaluating limited-English-proficient students.* Rockville, MD: Aspen.

Children's Defense Fund. (1997). *The state of America's children yearbook.* Washington, DC: Children's Defense Fund.

Chinn, P.C., & Hughes, S.E. (1987). Representation of minority students in special education classes. *Remedial and Special Education, 8*(4), 41–46.

Christensen, K.M. (1993). A multicultural approach to education of children who are deaf. In K.M. Christensen & G.L. Delgado (Eds.), *Multicultural issues in deafness.* White Plains, NY: Longman.

Clark, B. (1997). *Growing up gifted* (5th ed.). Upper Saddle River, NJ: Merrill.

Clark, G., & Kolstoe, O. (1990). *Career development and transition education for adolescents with disabilities.* Boston: Allyn & Bacon.

Clark, W., & Hankins, N. (1985). Giftedness and conflict. *Roeper Review, 8,* 50–53.

Clement-Heist, K., Siegel, S., & Gaylord-Ross, R. (1992). Simulated and in-situ vocational social skills training for youths with learning disabilities. *Exceptional Children, 58,* 336–345.

Cline, B.V., & Billingsley, B.S. (1991). Teachers' and supervisors' perceptions of secondary learning disabilities programs: A multi-state survey. *Learning Disabilities Research and Practice, 6,* 158–165.

Cohen, H.J., Grosz, J., Ayoob, K.T., & Schoen, S. (1997). Early intervention for children with HIV infection. In M.J. Guralnick (Ed.), *The effectiveness of early intervention.* Baltimore: Brookes.

Cohen, L.M., Burgess, A.C., & Busick, T.K. (1990). *Teaching gifted kindergarten and primary children in the regular classroom.* Eugene, OR: Oregon School Study Council.

Cohen, O. (1993). Educational needs of African American and Hispanic Deaf Children and youth. In K.M. Christensen & G.L. Delgado (Eds.), *Multicultural issues in deafness* (pp. 45–68). White Plains, NY: Longman.

———. (1994). Replacing myths about deafness. In R.C. Johnson & O.P. Cohen (Eds.), *Implications and complications for deaf students of the full inclusion movement* (Gallaudet Research Institute Occasional Paper 94-2). Washington, DC: Gallaudet University.

———. (1995). The adverse implications of full inclusion for deaf students. Paper presented at the 18th International Congress on Education of the Deaf (Tel Aviv, Israel, July 16–20).

Cohen, S.E., & Parmalee, A.H. (1983). Prediction of five-year Stanford-Binet scores in preterm infants. *Child Development, 54,* 1242–1253.

Colangelo, N. (1989). Moral dilemmas as formulated by gifted students. *Understanding Our Gifted, 1*(6), 10–12.

Coles, R. (1977). *Children of crisis: Vol. IV. Eskimos, Chicanos, Indians.* Boston: Little, Brown.

Connor, L.E. (1986). Oralism in perspective. In D.M. Luterman (Ed.), *Deafness in perspective* (pp. 117–129). San Diego: College-Hill.

Conture, E.G. (1990). *Stuttering* (2d ed.). Englewood Cliffs, NJ: Prentice-Hall.

Cook, P.S., Petersen, R.C., & Moore, D.T. (1990). *Alcohol, tobacco, and other drugs may harm the unborn.* Rockville, MD: Office for Substance Abuse Prevention, U.S. Department of Health and Human Services.

Cook, R.E., Tessier, A., & Klein, M.D. (1996). *Adapting early childhood curricula for children in inclusive settings* (4th ed.). Englewood Cliffs, NJ: Merrill.

Corbet, E.B. (1980). Elmer Bartels. *Options: Spinal cord injury and the future* (pp. 145–147). Denver: Hirschfield Press.

Cott, A. (1972). Megavitamins: The orthomolecular approach to behavioral disorders and learning disabilities. *Academic Therapy, 7,* 245–257.

———. (1977). *The orthomolecular approach to learning disabilities.* San Rafael, CA: Academic Therapy.

Council for Exceptional Children. (1990). Americans with Disabilities Act of 1990: What should you know? *Exceptional Children, 57,* Supplement.

———. (1997). *CEC policy manual: Basic commitments and responsibilities to exceptional children.* http://www.cec.specl.org/pp/policies/ch3. htm#35.

Cox, J., Daniel, N., & Boston, B. (1985). *Educating able learners: Programs and promising practices.* Austin: University of Texas Press.

Crittenden, J.B. (1993). The culture and identity of deafness. In P.V. Paul & D.W. Jackson, *Toward a psychology of deafness.* Boston: Allyn & Bacon.

Cronin, M.G., & Patton, J.R. (1993). *Life skills instruction for all students with special needs: A practical guide for integrating real-life content into curriculum* (pp. 5–6, 57, 63–65). Austin, TX: Pro-Ed.

Cullinan, D., Epstein, M.H., & Kauffman, J.M. (1984). Teachers' ratings of students' behaviors: What constitutes behavior disorders in school? *Behavioral Disorders, 10,* 9–19.

Cullinan, D., Epstein, M.H. & Sabornie, E.J. (1992). Selected characteristics of a national sample of seriously emotionally disturbed adolescents. *Behavioral Disorders, 17,* 273–280.

Cummins, J. (1984). *Bilingualism and special education: Issues in assessment and pedagogy.* San Diego: College-Hill.

Cutsforth, T.D. (1932). The unreality of words to the blind. *Teachers Forum, 4,* 86–89.

———. (1951). *The blind in school and society.* New York: American Foundation for the Blind.

Damico, J.S., & Simon, C.S. (1993). Assessing language abilities in school-age children. In A. Gerber (Ed.), *Language-related learning disabilities: Their nature and treatment* (pp. 279–299). Baltimore: Brookes.

Davis, G.A., & Rimm, S.G. (1989). *Education of the gifted and talented* (2d ed.). Englewood Cliffs, NJ: Prentice-Hall.

Deford, F. (1983). *Alex: The life of a child.* New York: Viking Press.

De La Paz, S., & Graham, S. (1997). Strategy instruction in planning: Effects on the writing performance and behavior of students with learning difficulties. *Exceptional Children, 63,* 167–181.

Delisle, J.R. (1984). *Gifted children speak out.* New York: Walker.

———. (1991). *Guiding the social and emotional development of gifted students: A practical guide for educators and counselors.* New York: Longman.

———. (1992). *Kidstories: Biographies of twenty young people you'd like to know.* Minneapolis: Free Spirit.

Delisle, J.R., & Berger, S. (1991). Underachieving gifted students. In S. Berger (Ed.), *Flyer files for the gifted and talented.* Reston, VA: Council for Exceptional Children.

Denhoff, E. (1976). Medical aspects. In W.M. Cruickshank (Ed.), *Cerebral palsy, a developmental disability* (3d ed.) (pp. 29–72). Syracuse: Syracuse University Press.

Dennis, R.E., Williams, W., Giangreco, M.F., & Cloninger, C.J. (1993). Quality of life as context for planning and evaluation of services for people with disabilities. *Exceptional Children, 59,* 499–512.

DePaepe, P.A., Shores, R.E., Jack, S.L., & Denny, R.K. (1996). Effects of task difficulty on the disruptive and on-task behavior of students with severe behavior disorders. *Behavioral Disorders, 21,* 216–225.

Department of Education. (1992). Deaf students education services: Policy guidance. *Federal Register, 57*(211). (Friday, October 30, 1992): 49274–49276.

Deshler, D.D., Warner, M.M., Schumaker, J.B., & Alley, G.R. (1983). Learning strategies intervention model: Key components and current status. In J.D. McKinney & L. Feagans (Eds.), *Current topics in learning disabilities.* Norwood, NJ: Ablex.

Dettmer, P., Thurston, L.P., & Dyck, N. (1993). *Consultation, collaboration, and teamwork for students with special needs* (pp. 1–35). Boston: Allyn & Bacon.

Devlin, S.D., & Elliot, R.N. (1992). Drug use patterns of adolescents with behavioral disorders. *Behavioral Disorders, 17,* 264–272.

Dew, N. (1984). The exceptional bilingual child: Demography. In P. Chinn (Ed.), *Education of culturally and linguistically different exceptional children* (pp. 1–41). Reston, VA: The Council for Exceptional Children.

Diagnostic and Statistical Manual of Mental Disorders (4th ed.) (1994). Washington, DC: American Psychiatric Association.

Dickerson, M.U. (1988). Adulthood and maturity. In E.W. Lynch & R.B. Lewis (Eds.), *Exceptional children and adults* (pp. 619–648). Boston: Scott, Foresman & Co.

Dickey, R., & Shealy, S.H. (1987). Using technology to control the environment. *American Journal of Occupational Therapy, 41*(11), 717–721.

Disability Services: webmaster@disserv.stu.umn.edu.

Dixson, B. (1989). *Environmental effects on fetal development.* Sacramento: California State Department of Education.

Doren, B., Bullis, M., & Benz, M.R. (1996). Predicting the arrest status of adolescents with disabilities in transition. *Journal of Special Education, 29,* 363–380.

Dorris, M. (1989). *The broken cord.* New York: Harper Perennial.

Downing, J.A., Simpson, R.L., & Myles, B.S. (1990). Regular and special educator perceptions of nonacademic skills needed by mainstreamed students with behavioral disorders and learning disabilities. *Behavioral Disorders, 15,* 217–226.

Drasgow, E. (1998). American sign language as a pathway to linguistic competence. *Exceptional Children, 64*(3).

Drew, C.J., Logan, D.R., & Hardman, M. (1992). *Mental retardation: A life cycle approach* (5th ed.) (pp. 233–341). New York: Macmillan.

Dunlap, G., & Childs, K.E. (1996). Intervention research in emotional and behavioral disorders: An analysis of studies from 1980–1993. *Behavioral Disorders, 21,* 125–136.

Dunn, L.M. (1968). Special education for the mildly retarded: Is much of it justifiable? *Exceptional Children, 35,* 5–22.

Dunst, C.J. (1993). Implication of risk and opportunity factors for assessment and intervention practices. *Topics in Early Childhood Education, 13*(2), 143–153.

DuPaul, G.J., & Barkley, R.A. (1990). Medication therapy. In R.A. Barkley, *Attention deficit hyperactivity disorder: A handbook for diagnosis and treatment* (pp. 573–612). New York: Guilford Press.

Durand, V.M., & Carr, E.G. (1985). Self-injurious behavior: Motivating conditions and guidelines for treatment. *School Psychology Review, 14,* 171–176.

Eby, J.W., & Smutny, J.F. (1990). *A thoughtful overview of gifted education.* New York: Longman.

Edgar, E. (1987). Secondary programs in special education: Are many of them justifiable? *Exceptional Children, 53,* 555–561.

———. (1988). Employment as an outcome for mildly handicapped students: Current status and future directions. *Focus on Exceptional Children, 2*(1), 1–8.

Edgerton, R.B. (1967). *The cloak of competence: Stigma in the lives of mentally retarded.* Berkeley: University of California Press.

Edgerton, R.B., Bollinger, M., & Herr, B. (1984). The cloak of competence: After two decades. *American Journal of Mental Deficiency, 88,* 345–351.

Ehri, L.C. (1989). Movement into word reading and spelling. In J.M. Mason (Ed.), *Reading and writing connections* (pp. 65–81). Boston: Allyn & Bacon.

Ehrlich, M.I. (1983). Psychofamilial correlates of school disorders. *Journal of School Psychology, 21,* 191–199.

Eighteenth Annual Report to Congress on the Implementation of the Individuals with Disabilities Education Act. (1996). Washington, DC: U.S. Department of Education.

Eitzen, D.S., & Zinn, M.B. (1989). *Social problems* (4th ed.). Boston: Allyn & Bacon.

Ellis, E.S., Sabornie, E.J., & Marshall, K.J. (1989). Teaching learning strategies to learning disabled students in postsecondary settings. *Academic Therapy, 24,* 491–501.

Englemann, S., & Bruner, E. (1988). *Reading Mastery Fast Cycle.* Chicago: Science Research Associates.

Englemann, S., & Carnine, D. (1982). *Corrective mathematics program.* Chicago: Science Research Associates.

Englemann, S., Carnine, D., & Steely, D.G. (1991). Making connections in mathematics. *Journal of Learning Disabilities, 24,* 292–303.

Englemann, S., Carnine, L., & Johnson, G. (1988). *Word-Attack Basics: Decoding A.* Chicago: Science Research Associates.

Englemann, S., & Hanner, S. (1982). *Reading mastery, level III: A direct instruction program.* Chicago: Science Research Associates.

Englemann, S., Johnson, G., Hanner, S., Carnine, L., Meyers, S., Becker, W., & Eisele, J. (1988). *Corrective reading: Decoding strategies.* Chicago: Science Research Associates.

Ennis, R.H. (1985). A logical basis for measuring critical thinking skills. *Educational Leadership, 43*(2), 44–48.

Epanchin, B.C., & Rennels, M.S. (1989). Parents' and teachers' sensitivity to unhappiness reported by undercontrolled children. *Behavioral Disorders, 14,* 166–174.

Epstein, M.H., Kinder, D., & Bursuck, B. (1989). The academic status of adolescents with behavioral disorders. *Behavioral Disorders, 14,* 157–165.

Epstein, M.H., Polloway, E.A., Patton, J.R., & Foley, R. (1989). Mild retardation: Student characteristics and services. *Education and Training in Mental Retardation, 24,* 7–16.

Erikson, E.H. (1968). *Identity: Youth and crisis.* New York: Norton.

Erin, J.N. (1996). Functional vision assessment and instruction of children and youths with multiple disabilities. In A.L. Corn & A.J. Koenig (Eds.), *Foundations of low vision: Clinical and functional perspectives* (pp. 221–245). New York: AFB Press.

Erin, J.N., & Paul, B. (1996). Functional vision assessment and instruction of children and youths in academic programs. In A.L. Corn & A.J. Koenig (Eds.), *Foundations of low vision: Clinical and functional perspectives* (pp. 185–220). New York: AFB Press.

Executive Committee of the Council for Children with Behavioral Disorders. (1989). White paper on best assessment practices for students with behavioral disorders: Accommodation to cultural diversity and individual differences. *Behavioral Disorders, 14,* 263–278.

Fairweather, J.S., & Shaver, D.M. (1991). Making the transition to postsecondary education and training. *Exceptional Children, 57,* 264–270.

Falk, G.D., Dunlap, G., & Kern, L. (1996). An analysis of self-evaluation and videotape feedback for improving the peer interactions of students with externalizing and internalizing behavior problems. *Behavioral Disorders, 21,* 261–276.

Falvey, M. (1995). *Inclusive and heterogeneous schooling.* Baltimore: Brookes.

Featherstone, H. (1980). *A difference in the family: Life with a disabled child.* New York: Basic Books.

Federal Register. (1977). Implementation of part B of the Education of the Handicapped Act, *42*(163), Aug. 23, 1977.

Federal Register. (1992). Washington, DC: U.S. Government Printing Office, September 29.

Feingold, B.F. (1975). Hyperkinesis and learning disabilities linked to artificial food flavors and colors. *American Journal of Nursing, 75,* 797–803.

Feldhusen, J.F. (1991). Saturday and summer programs. In N. Colangelo & G.A. Davis (Eds.), *Handbook of gifted education* (pp. 197–208). Boston: Allyn & Bacon.

Ferguson, D.L. (1987). *Curriculum decision making for students with severe handicaps: Policy and practice.* New York: Teachers College Press.

Ferrell, K.A. (1985). *Reach out and teach.* New York: American Foundation for the Blind.

———. (1986). Infancy and early childhood. In G.T. Scholl (Ed.), *Foundations of education for blind and visually handicapped children and youth: Theory and practice.* New York: American Foundation for the Blind.

Figueroa, R.A., Fradd, S.H., & Correa, V.I. (1989). Bilingual special education and this special issue. *Exceptional Children, 56*(2), 174–178.

Finello, K.M., Hanson, N.H., & Kekelis, L.S. (1992). Cognitive focus: Developing cognition, concepts, and language in young blind and visually impaired children. In R.L. Pogrund, D.L. Fazzi & J.S. Lampert (Eds.), *Early focus: Working with young blind and visually impaired children and their families* (pp. 34–49). New York: American Foundation for the Blind.

Flexer, C. (1994). *Facilitating hearing and listening in young children.* San Diego: Singular.

Ford, A., Schnorr, R., Meyer, L., Davern, L., Black, J., & Dempsey, P. (1989). General community functioning. In A. Ford, R. Schnorr, L. Meyer, L. Davern, J. Black, & P. Dempsey (Eds.), *The Syracuse community-referenced curriculum guide for students with moderate and severe disabilities* (pp. 77–88). Baltimore: Brookes.

Forness, S.R. (1988). Planning for the needs of children with serious emotional disturbance: The national special education and mental health coalition. *Behavioral Disorders, 13,* 127–139.

Forness, S.R., & Knitzer, J. (1990). A new proposed definition and terminology to replace 'Serious Emotional Disturbance' in Education of the Handicapped Act. Workgroup on Definition, the National Mental Health and Special Education Coalition, National Mental Health Association.

Forness, S.R., Sweeney, D.P., & Toy, K. (1996). Psychopharmacologic medication: What teachers need to know. *Beyond Behavior, 7*(2), 4–11.

Fowler, M. (1995). *Maybe you know my kid.* New York: Carol Publishing Group.

Frankenberger, W., & Fronzaglio, K. (1991). A review of states' criteria and procedures for identifying children with learning disabilities. *Journal of Learning Disabilities, 24,* 495–500.

Fraser, B., Hensinger, R.N., & Phelps, J. (1990). *Physical management of multiple handicaps.* Baltimore: Brookes.

———. (1987). The identification of gifted black students: Developing new perspectives. *Journal for the Education of the Gifted, 10*(3), 155–180.

Friedman, H.S., Tucker, J.S., Schwartz, J.E., Tomlinson-Keasey, C., Martin, L.R., Wingard, D.L., & Criqui, M.H. (1995). Psychosocial and behavioral predictors of longevity: The aging and death of the "Termites." *American Psychologist, 50*(2), 69–78.

Friedrich, O. (1983, August). What do babies know? *Time,* pp. 70–76.

Friel-Patti, S., & Finitzo, T. (1990). Language learning in a prospective study of otitis media with effusion in the first two years of life. *Journal of Speech and Hearing Research, 33,* 188–194.

Friend, M. (1996). *The Power of 2: Making a difference through co-teaching.* Bloomington, IN: Indiana University Press.

Friend, M., & Cook, L. (1996). Collaboration as a predictor for success in school reform. *Journal of Educational and Psychological Consultation, 1*(1), 69–86.

Friend, M., & Cook, L. (1996). *Interactions: Collaboration skills for school professionals.* White Plains, NY: Longman.

Frishberg, N. (1986). *Interpreting: An introduction.* Silver Spring, MD: RID Publications.

Fueyo, V. (1997). Below the tip of the iceberg: Teaching language-minority students. *Teaching Exceptional Children, 30*(1), 61–65.

Futterman, E. (June 3, 1984). The right to bear children: Can mentally retarded adults make good parents? *St. Louis Post-Dispatch,* pp. 6–7, 9–10.

Gable, R.A., Hendrickson, J.M., Warren, S.F., Evans, W.H., & Evans, S.S. (1988). The promise and pitfalls of an ecological perspective on children's behavioral disorders. In R.B. Rutherford, Jr. & J.W. Maag (Eds.), *Monograph in Behavioral Disorders: Severe Behavioral Disorders of Children and Youth, 11,* 156–166.

Gajar, A. (1992). Adults with learning disabilities: Current and future research priorities. *Journal of Learning Disabilities, 25,* 507–519.

Gajira, M., & Salvia, J. (1992). The effects of summarization instruction on text comprehension of students with learning disabilities. *Exceptional Children, 58,* 508–516.

Gallagher, J.J. (1992). The role of values and facts in policy development for infants and toddlers with disabilities and their families. *Journal of Early Intervention, 16*(1), 1–10.

Garbarino, J. (1990). The human ecology of early risk. In S.J. Meisels & J.P. Shonkoff (Eds.), *Handbook of early childhood intervention.* Cambridge: Cambridge University Press.

Garbarino, James. (1997). Educating children in a socially toxic environment. *Educational Leadership, 54*(7), 12–16.

Gardener, R. (1990). Life-space interviewing: It can be effective, but don't . . . *Behavioral Disorders, 15,* 110–126.

Gardner, H. (1983). *Frames of mind.* New York: Basic Books.

Garretson, M.D. (1976). Total communication. *Volta Review, 78*(4), 107–112.

Gartin, B.C., Rumrill, P., & Serebreni, R. (1996). The higher education transition model: Guidelines for facilitating college transition among college-bound students with disabilities. *Teaching Exceptional Children, 29*(1), 30–33.

Gath, A. (1977). The impact of an abnormal child upon the parents. *British Journal of Psychology, 130,* 405–420.

Gaunt, R.I. (1989). A comparison of the perceptions of parents of highly and moderately gifted children. Doctoral dissertation, Kent State University. *Dissertation Abstracts International, 50,* A.

Gelfand, D.M., Jenson, W.R., & Drew, C.J. (1988). *Understanding child behavior disorders* (2d ed.). New York: Holt, Rinehart & Winston.

Gentry, D., & Olson, J. (1985). Severely mentally retarded young children. In D. Bricker & J. Fuller (Eds.), *Severe mental retardation: From theory to practice* (pp. 50–75). Reston, VA: Division on Mental Retardation of the Council for Exceptional Children.

George, P.S. (1988). Tracking and ability grouping—which way for the middle school? *Middle School Journal* (Sept.), 21–28.

Gerber, A. (1993). Interdisciplinary language intervention in education. In A. Gerber (Ed.), *Language-related learning disabilities: Their nature and treatment* (pp. 301–322). Baltimore: Brookes.

Gerber, P.J., Ginsberg, R., & Reiff, H.B. (1992). Identifying alterable patterns in employment success for highly successful adults with learning disabilities. *Journal of Learning Disabilities, 25,* 475–487.

Gerber, S.E. (1990). *Prevention: The etiology of communicative disorders in children.* Englewood Cliffs, NJ: Prentice-Hall.

Gersten, R., & Woodward, J. (1994). The language-minority student and special education: Issues, trends, and paradoxes. *Exceptional Children, 60,* 310–322.

Giangreco, M.F., Edelman, S.W., Luiselli, T.E., & MacFarland, S.Z.C. (1997). Helping or hovering? Effects of instructional assistant proximity on students with disabilities. *Exceptional Children, 64*, 7–18.

Gibbs, D.P., & Cooper, E.B. (1989). Prevalence of communication disorders in students with learning disabilities. *Journal of Learning Disabilities, 22*, 60–63.

Goldberg, S. (1987). *Ophthalmology made ridiculously simple.* Miami, FL: MedMaster.

Gollnick, D.M., & Chinn, P.C. (1994). *Multicultural education in a pluralistic society* (4th ed.). Columbus, OH: Macmillan.

Goodenough, N. (1987). Multi-culturalism as the normal human experience. In E.M. Eddy & W.L. Partridge (Eds.), *Applied anthropology in America* (2d ed.). New York: Columbia University Press.

Gorski, P.A., & VandenBerg, K.A. (1996). Infants born at risk. In M.J. Hanson (Ed.), *Atypical infant development* (2d ed.) (pp. 85–114). Austin, TX: Pro-Ed.

Gould, S.J. (1981). *The mismeasure of man.* New York: Norton.

Graden, J.L. (1989). Redefining 'prereferral' intervention as intervention assistance: Collaboration between general and special education. *Exceptional Children, 56*(3), 227–231.

Graham, E.M., & Morgan, M.A. (1997). Growth before birth. In M.L. Batshaw (Ed.), *Children with disabilities* (pp. 53–69). Baltimore: Brookes.

Graham, S., MacArthur, C., Schwartz, S., & Page-Voth, V. (1992). Improving the composition of students with learning disabilities using a strategy involving product and process goal setting. *Exceptional Children, 58*, 322–335.

Graves, D.H. (1983). *Writing: Teachers and children at work.* Exeter, NH: Heinemann.

Greenbaum, B., Graham, S., & Scales, W. (1995). Adults with learning disabilities: Educational and social experiences during college. *Exceptional Children, 61*, 460–471.

Greenberg, F., James, L.M., & Oakley, Jr., G.P. (1983). Estimates of birth prevalence rates of spina bifida in the United States from computer generated maps. *American Journal of Obstetrics and Gynecology, 145*, 570–573.

Gresham, F.M., & MacMillan, D.L. (1997). Autistic recovery? An analysis and critique of the empirical evidence on the Early Intervention Project. *Behavioral Disorders, 22*, 185–201.

Griffin, D.K., Rosenberg, H., Cheyney, W., & Greenburg, B. (1996). A comparison of self-esteem and job satisfaction of adults with mild mental retardation in sheltered workshops and supported employment. *Education and Training in Mental Retardation and Developmental Disabilities, 31*, 142–150.

Griffith, D.R. (1992). Prenatal exposure to cocaine and other drugs: Developmental and educational prognoses. *Phi Delta Kappan, 74*(1), 30–34.

Griffith, P.L., & Olson, M.W. (1992). Phonemic awareness helps beginning readers to break the code. *The Reading Teacher, 45*, 516–523.

Grigorenko, E.L., & Sternberg, R.J. (1997). Styles of thinking, abilities, and academic performance. *Exceptional Children, 63*(3), 295–312.

Grove, N., Cusick, B., & Bigge, J. (1991). Conditions resulting in physical disabilities. In J. Bigge, *Teaching individuals with physical and multiple disabilities* (3d ed.) (pp. 1–15). New York: Merrill.

Guerin, G.R., & Maier, A.S. (1983). *Informal assessment in education.* Palo Alto, CA: Mayfield.

Guralnick, M.J. (1997). *The effectiveness of early intervention.* Baltimore: Brookes.

Gustason, G. (1990). Signing exact English. In H. Bornstein (Ed.), *Manual communication: Implications for education.* Washington, DC: Gallaudet University Press.

Hack, M., Klein, N.K., & Taylor, H.G. (1995). Long-term developmental outcomes of low birth weight infants. *Future of Children, 5*(3), 176–196.

Hall, R.J. (1980). Cognitive behavior modification and information processing skills of exceptional children. *Exceptional Education Quarterly, 1*, 9–15.

Hallahan, D.P. (1992). Some thoughts on why the prevalence of learning disabilities has increased. *Journal of Learning Disabilities, 25*, 523–528.

Hallahan, D.P., & Cruikshank, W. (1973). *Psychoeducational foundations of learning disabilities.* Englewood Cliffs, NJ: Prentice-Hall.

Hallahan, D.P., Kauffman, J.M., & Lloyd, J.W. (1985). *Introduction to learning disabilities* (2d ed.). Englewood Cliffs, NJ: Prentice-Hall.

Halpern, A.S. (1993). Quality of life as a conceptual framework for evaluating transition outcomes. *Exceptional Children, 59*, 486–498.

Halvorsen, A.T., Doering, K., Farron-Davis, P., Usilton, R., & Sailor, W. (1989). The role of parents and family members in planning severely disabled students' transitions from school. In G.H.S. Singer and L.K. Irwin (Eds.), *Support for caregiving families* (pp. 253–268). Baltimore: Brookes.

Hanline, M.F., & Halvorsen, A. (1989). Parent perceptions of the integration transition process: Overcoming artificial barriers. *Exceptional Children, 55*, 487–492.

Hanson, M.J. (1996). Early intervention goals and outcomes. In M.J. Hanson (Ed.), *Atypical infant development* (2d ed.) (pp. 477–513). Austin, TX: Pro-Ed.

———. (1998). Ethnic, cultural, and language diversity in intervention settings. In E.W. Lynch & M.J. Hanson (Eds.), *Developing cross-cultural competence* (2d ed.) (pp. 3–22). Baltimore: Brookes.

Hanson, M.J., & Carta, J.J. (1996). Addressing the challenges of families with multiple risks. *Exceptional Children, 62*(3), 201–212.

Hanson, M.J., Ellis, L., & Deppe, J. (1989). Support for families during infancy. In G.H.S. Singer & L.K. Irvin (Eds.), *Support for caregiving families* (pp. 207–219). Baltimore: Brookes.

Haring, K.A., Lovett, D.L., & Saren, D. (1991). Parent perceptions of their adult offspring with disabilities. *Teaching Exceptional Children, 23*(2), 6–11.

Harkness, S., Super, C., & Keefer, C. (1994). Learning to be an American parent. In R. D'Andrade & C. Strauss (Eds.), *Human motives and cultural models.* Cambridge, UK: Cambridge University Press.

Harley, R.K., & Lawrence, G.A. (1984). *Visual impairment in the schools.* Springfield, IL: Thomas.

Harris, C.A., Miller, S.P., & Mercer, C.D. (1995). Teaching initial multiplication skills to students with disabilities in general education classrooms. *Learning Disabilities Research and Practice, 10,* 180–195.

Harris, L., & Associates. (1989). *International Center for the Disabled Survey III: Employing disabled Americans.* New York: L. Harris & Associates.

Harry, B. (1992a). Making sense of disability: Low-income, Puerto Rican parents' theories of the problem. *Exceptional Children, 59*(1), 27–40.

———. (1992b). Restructuring the participation of African-American parents in special education. *Exceptional Children, 59*(2), 123–131.

Harry, B., Allen, A., & McLaughlin, M. (1995). Communication versus compliance: African-American parents' involvement in special education. *Exceptional Children, 64*(4), 364–377.

Hasazi, S.B., Gordon, L.R., & Roe, C.A. (1985). Factors associated with the employment status of handicapped youth exiting high school from 1979–1983. *Exceptional Children, 51,* 455–469.

Hasazi, S.B., Johnson, R.E., Hasazi, J.E., Gordon, L.R., & Hull, M. (1989). Employment of youth with and without handicaps following high school: Outcomes and correlates. *Journal of Special Education, 23,* 243–255.

Hasselbring, T.S., & Goin, L.I. (1989). Use of computers. In G.A. Robinson, J.R. Patton, E.A. Polloway & L.R. Sargent (Eds.), *Best practices in mild mental disabilities* (pp. 395–412). Reston, VA: The Division on Mental Retardation of the Council for Exceptional Children.

Hatfield, N. (1982). Sign language assessment. In D.G. Sims, G.G. Walter & R.L. Whitehead (Eds.), *Deafness and communication: Assessment and training.* Baltimore: Williams & Wilkins.

Hatlen, P.H., & Curry, S.A. (1987). In support of specialized programs for blind and visually impaired children: The impact of vision loss on learning. *Journal of Visual Impairment and Blindness, 81*(1), 7–13.

Hayden, M., Gersten, R., & Carnine, D. (1992). Using computer networking to increase active teaching in general education math classes containing students with mild disabilities. *Journal of Special Education Technology, 11,* 167–177.

Haynes, W.O., Moran, M.J., & Pindzola, R.H. (1990). *Communication disorders in the classroom.* Dubuque, IA: Kendall/Hunt Publishing.

Heal, L.W., Gonzalez, P., Rusch, F.R., Copher, J.I., & DeStefano, L. (1990). A comparison of successful and unsuccessful placements of youths with mental handicaps into competitive employment. *Exceptionality, 1,* 181–195.

Heal, L.W., & Rusch, F.R. (1995). Predicting employment for students who leave special education high school programs. *Exceptional Children, 61,* 472–487.

Healy, A. (1983). Cerebral palsy. In J.A. Blackman (Ed.), *Medical aspects of developmental disabilities in children birth to three* (pp. 31–37). Iowa City: University of Iowa.

Henley, M., Ramsey, R.S., & Algozzine, R. (1993). *Characteristics of and strategies for teaching students with mild disabilities* (pp. 69–110). Boston: Allyn & Bacon.

———. (1984). *Education of exceptional learners.* (3d ed.). Boston: Allyn & Bacon.

High, M.H., & Udall, A.I. (1983). Teacher ratings of students in relation to ethnicity of students and school ethnic balance. *Journal of Education and the Gifted, 6,* 154–166.

Hill, E., & Ponder, P. (1976). *Orientation and mobility techniques.* New York: American Foundation for the Blind.

Hill, E.W. (1986). Orientation and mobility. In G.T. Scholl (Ed.), *Foundations of education for blind and visually handicapped children and youth: Theory and practice.* New York: American Foundation for the Blind.

Hobbs, N. (1975). *The futures of children: Categories, labels, and their consequences.* Nashville: Vanderbilt Institute for Policy Studies.

Hoffman, L.P. (1993). Language in the school context: What is least restrictive? *Proceedings of contemporary issues in language and learning: Toward the year 2000, point and counterpoint* (pp. 16–18). Rockville, MD: American Speech-Language-Hearing Association, Division 10, Language Learning and Education.

Hoffmeister, R.J. (1990). ASL and its implications for education. In H. Bornstein (Ed.), *Manual communication: Implications for education.* Washington, DC: Gallaudet University Press.

Hollinger, C.L. (1991). Career choices for gifted adolescents: Overcoming stereotypes. In M. Bireley & J. Genshaft (Eds.), *Understanding the gifted adolescent* (pp. 201–214). New York: Teachers College Press.

Hollinger, C., & Fleming, E.S. (1992). A longitudinal examination of life choices of gifted and talented young women. *Gifted Child Quarterly, 36*(4), pp. 207–212.

Hollingsworth, M., & Woodward, J. (1993). Integrated learning: Explicit strategies and their role in problem-solving instruction for students with learning disabilities. *Exceptional Children, 59,* 444–455.

Hollingworth, L.A. (1942). *Children above 180 I.Q. Stanford-Binet: Origin and development.* Yonkers-on-Hudson, NY: World Book Company.

Hom, J.L., O'Donnell, J.P., & Leicht, D.J. (1988). Phonetically inaccurate spelling among learning-disabled, head-injured, and nondisabled young adults. *Brain and Language 33,* 55–64.

Hopfenberg, W.S., Levin, H.M., Chase, C., Christensen, S.G., Moore, M., Soler, P., Brunner, I., Keller, B., & Rodriguez, G. (1993). The Accelerated Schools resource guide. San Francisco: Jossey-Bass.

Hourcade, J.J., Parette, H.P., Jr., & Huer, M.B. (1997). Family and cultural alert! Considerations in assistive technology assessment. *Teaching Exceptional Children, 30*(1), 40–44.

Houston, W.R. (Ed.). *Handbook of research on teacher education* (pp. 826–857).

Hughes, C., Kim, J., Hwang, B., Killian, D.J., Fischer, G.M., Brock, M.L., Godshall, J.C., & Houser, B. (1997). Practitioner-validated secondary transition support strategies. *Education and Training in Mental Retardation and Developmental Disabilities, 32,* 201–212.

Hunt, N.A. (1982). The relationship of medical, social, and familial variables with school-related performance of adolescents born at low weight. Doctoral dissertation, University of Southern California.

Hutchinson, G. (1968). Theological implications of having a handicapped child. Panel discussion, East Texas State University.

Hutchinson, M.K., & Sandall, S.R. (1995). Congenital TORCH infections in infants and young children: Neurodevelopmental sequelae and implications for intervention. *Topics in Early Childhood Special Education, 15*(1), 65–82.

Iacono, T.A., & Miller, J.F. (1989). Can microcomputers be used to teach communication skills to students with mental retardation? *Education and Training in Mental Retardation, 24,* 32–44.

Individuals with Disabilities Education Act Amendments of 1997. (1997). P.L. 105-17, 105th Cong., 1st sess.

Inge, K.J., Banks, P.D., Wehman, P., Hill, J.W., & Shafer, M.S. (1988). Quality of life for individuals who are labeled mentally retarded: Evaluating competitive employment versus sheltered workshop employment. *Education and Training in Mental Retardation, 23,* 97–104.

Intellitools. (1996). Spring Catalog. Novato, CA: Intellitools.

Joe, J.R., & Malach, R.S. (1998). Families with Native-American roots. In E.W. Lynch & M.J. Hanson (Eds.), *Developing cross-cultural competence* (2d ed.). Baltimore: Brookes.

Johnson, D.W., & Johnson, R.T. (1989). The high achieving student in cooperative learning groups. *Cooperative Link, 5*(2), 317–321.

Johnston, J.C., & Zemitzsch, A. (1988). Family power: An intervention beyond the classroom. *Behavioral Disorders, 14,* 69–79.

Jordan, I.K., & Karchmer, M.A. (1986). Patterns of sign use among hearing impaired students. In A.N. Schildroth & M.A. Karchmer (Eds.), *Deaf children in America.* San Diego: College-Hill.

Kamhi, A.G. (1989). Causes and consequences of reading disabilities. In A.G. Kamhi & H.W. Catts (Eds.), *Reading disabilities: A developmental language perspective* (pp. 67–99). Boston: College-Hill.

———. (1992). Three perspectives on language processing: Interactionism, modularity, and holism. In R.S. Chapman (Ed.), *Processes in language acquisition and disorders* (pp. 45–64). St. Louis: Mosby Year-Book.

———. (1993). Some problems with the marriage between theory and clinical practice. *Language, Speech, and Hearing Services in the Schools, 24,* 57–60.

———. (1998). Trying to make sense of developmental language disorders. *Language, Speech, and Hearing in the Schools,* January, 35–44.

Kamps, D.M., & Tankersley, M. (1996). Prevention of behavioral and conduct disorders: Trends and research issues. *Behavioral Disorders, 22,* 41–48.

Kaplan, S.N., Kaplan, J.A.B., Madsen, S.K., & Gould, B.T. (1980). *Change for children.* Santa Monica, CA: Goodyear.

Kauffman, J.M. (1989). The regular education initiative as Reagan-Bush education policy: A trickle-down theory of education of the hard-to-teach. *Journal of Special Education, 23,* 256–278.

———. (1993). *Characteristics of emotional and behavioral disorders in children and youth* (5th ed.). New York: Merrill/Macmillan.

Kavale, K.A., & Forness, S.R. (1983). Hyperactivity and diet treatment: A meta-analysis of the Feingold hypothesis. *Journal of Learning Disabilities, 16,* 324–330.

Kearney, K. (1988). The highly gifted. *Understanding Our Gifted, 1*(1), 13.

Keller, C.E., Hallahan, D.P., McShane, E.A., Crowley, E.P., & Blandford, B.J. (1990). The coverage of persons with disabilities in American newspapers. *Journal of Special Education, 24,* 271–282.

Kelly, L.E. (1989). Physical education. In Robinson, G.A., Patton, J.R., Polloway, E.A., & Sargent L.R. (Eds.). *Best practices in mild mental disabilities* (pp. 243–262). Reston, VA: Division on Mental Retardation of the Council for Exceptional Children.

Keogh, B.K., Gallimore, R., & Weisner, T. (1997). A sociocultural perspective on learning and learning disabilities. *Learning Disabilities Research and Practice, 12,* 107–113.

Keogh, B.K., Wilcoxen, A.G., & Bernheimer, L. (1986). Prevention services for high risk children: Evidence for policy and practice. In D.C. Farran & J.D. McKinney (Eds.), *Risk in intellectual and psychosocial development* (pp. 287–315). New York: Academic Press.

Kerr, B.A. (1985). *Smart girls, gifted women.* Columbus: Ohio Psychology Publishing.

———. (1997). Smart girls two: A new psychology of girls, women, and giftedness. In B. Clark, *Growing up gifted* (5th ed.). Upper Saddle River, NJ: Merrill.

Kerr, M.M., & Nelson, C.M. (1989). *Strategies for managing behavior problems in the classroom* (2d ed.). New York: Merrill/Macmillan.

Kiernan, W.E., & Stark, J.A. (1986). *Pathways to employment for adults with developmental disabilities.* Baltimore: Brookes.

King, C., & Quigley, S. (1985). *Reading and deafness.* San Diego: College-Hill.

Kipila, E.L., & Williams-Scott, B. (1990). Cued speech. In H. Bornstein (Ed.), *Manual communication: Implications for education.* Washington, DC: Gallaudet University Press.

Kitano, M.K., & Kirby, D.F. (1986). *Gifted education: A comprehensive view.* Boston: Little, Brown.

Klein, M.D., & Briggs, M.H. (1987). Facilitating mother-infant communicative interaction in mothers of high-risk infants. *Journal of Childhood Communication Disorders, X,* 91–106.

Kline, B.E., & Meckstroth, E.A. (1985). Understanding and encouraging the exceptionally gifted. *Roeper Review, 8*(1), 24–30.

Kluwe, R. (1987). Executive decisions and regulation of problem-solving behavior. In F. Weinert & R. Kluwe (Eds.), *Metacognition, motivation and understanding* (pp. 31–64). Hillsdale, NJ: Erlbaum.

Kluwin, T., & Moores, D.F. (1985). The effects of integration on the mathematics achievement of hearing-impaired adolescents. *Exceptional Children, 52,* 153–160.

Knapczyk, D.R. (1988). Reducing aggressive behaviors in special and regular class settings by training alternative social responses. *Behavioral Disorders, 14,* 27–39.

Knoblock, P. (1982). *Teaching and mainstreaming autistic children.* Denver: Love.

Koegel, R.L., Koegel, L.K., Frea, W.D., & Smith, A.E. (1995). Emerging interventions for children with autism: Longitudinal and lifestyle implications. In R.L. Koegel & L.K. Koegel (Eds.), *Teaching children with autism: Strategies for initiating positive interactions and improving learning opportunities* (pp. 1–16). Baltimore: Brookes.

Koenig, A.J., & Farrenkopf, C. (1997). Essential experiences to undergird the early development of literacy. *Journal of Visual Impairment and Blindness, 91*(1), 14–24.

Koester, L.S., & Meadow-Orlans, K.P. (1990). Parenting a deaf child: Stress, strength, and support. In D.F. Moores & K.P. Meadow-Orlans (Eds.), *Educational and developmental aspects of deafness* (pp. 299–320). Washington, DC: Gallaudet University Press.

Kopp, C.B. (1983). Risk factors in development. In M. Haith & J. Campos (Eds.), *Infancy and the biology of development* (Vol. II). In P. Mussen (Ed.), *Manual of child psychology.* New York: Wiley.

Korabek, C.A., & Cuvo, A.J. (1986). Children with spina bifida: Educational implications of their medical characteristics. *Education and Treatment of Children, 9,* 142–152.

Kraemer, K., Cusick, B., & Bigge, J. (1982). Motor development, deviations, and physical rehabilitation. In J. Bigge, *Teaching individuals with physical and multiple disabilities* (2d ed.) (pp. 12–14). Columbus, OH: Merrill.

Krauss, M.W. (1990). New precedent in family policy: Individualized family service plan. *Exceptional Children, 56*(5), 388–395.

Kravets, M., & Wax, I.F. (1998). *K & W Guide to Colleges for the Learning Disabled 1998* (4th ed.). Princeton.

Kretschmer, R.R., & Kretschmer, L.W. (1978). *Language development and intervention with the hearing impaired.* Baltimore: University Park Press.

Kulieke, M. (1985). The effects of residential integration on children's school and neighborhood environments, social interactions, and school outcomes. Doctoral dissertation, Northwestern University.

Lagomarcino, T.R., & Rusch, F.R. (1989). Utilizing self-management procedures to teach independent performance. *Education and Training in Mental Retardation, 24,* 297–323.

Lahey, M. (1988). *Language disorders and language development.* New York: Macmillan.

Lambert, P., & Freed, B. (Eds.). (1982). *Loss of language skills.* Rowley, MA: Newbury House.

Landesman-Dwyer, S., & Butterfield, E.C. (1983). Mental retardation: Developmental issues in cognitive and social adaptation. In M. Lewis (Ed.), *Origins of intelligence: Infancy and early childhood* (2d ed.) (pp. 479–519). New York: Plenum Press.

Lane, H. (1976). *The wild boy of Aveyron.* Cambridge: Harvard University Press.

Lang, H.G. (1996). Teaching science, engineering, and mathematics to deaf students: The role of technology in instruction and teacher preparation. *Proceedings of the Symposium on Technology for Persons with Disabilities.* Northridge: California State University.

Langley, M.B. (1980). *Assessment of multihandicapped visually impaired children.* Chicago, IL: Stoelting.

Larson, K.A., & Gerber, M.M. (1987). Effects of social metacognitive training for enhancing overt behavior in learning disabled and low achieving delinquents. *Exceptional Children, 54,* 201–211.

Le Grice, B., & Blampied, N.M. (1994). Training pupils with intellectual disability to operate educational technology using video prompting. *Education and Training in Mental Retardation and Developmental Disabilities, 29,* 321–330.

Lehmann, J.P., & Baker, C. (1995). Mothers' expectations for their adolescent children: A comparison between families with disabled adolescents and those with non-labeled adolescents. *Education and Training in Mental Retardation and Developmental Disabilities, 31,* 27–40.

Leiberman, L.M. (1996). Preserving special education . . . for those who need it. In W. Stainback & S. Stainback (Eds.), *Controversial issues confronting special education: Divergent perspectives* (2d ed.) (pp. 16–27). Boston: Allyn and Bacon.

Lerner, J. (1993). Young children with disabilities. *Learning disabilities: Theories, diagnosis, and teaching strategies* (6th ed.) (pp. 245–271). Boston: Houghton Mifflin.

Lerner, J.W., Lowenthal, B., & Lerner, S. (1995). *Attention deficit disorders: Assessment and teaching.* Pacific Grove, CA: Brooks/Cole.

Lesar, S., Gerber, M.M., & Semmel, M.I. (1995). HIV infection in children: Family stress, social support, and adaptation. *Exceptional Children, 62,* 224–236.

Leung, B.P. (1996). Quality assessment practices in a diverse society. *Teaching Exceptional Children, 28*(3), 42–45.

Levin, H.M. (1996). Accelerated schools: The background. In C. Finnan, E.P. St. John, J. McCarthy & S.P. Slovacek (Eds.), *Accelerated schools in action: Lessons from the field* (pp. 3–23). Thousand Oaks, CA: Corwin Press.

Levine, J.M. (1996). Including children dependent on ventilators in school. *Teaching Exceptional Children, 28*(3), 24–29.

Lewis, B.A. (1992). Pedigree analysis of children with phonology disorders. *Journal of Learning Disabilities, 25,* 586–597.

Lewis, R.B. (1993). *Special education technology: Classroom applications* (pp. 176–219). Pacific Grove, CA: Brooks/Cole.

Lewis, R.B., & Doorlag, D.H. (1987). *Teaching special students in the mainstream* (2d ed.). Columbus, OH: Merrill.

Lewis, W.W. (1988). The role of ecological variables in residential treatment. *Behavioral Disorders, 13,* 98–107.

Liebert, D., Lutsky, L., & Gottlieb, A. (1990). Post-secondary experiences of young adults with severe physical disabilities. *Exceptional Children, 57,* 56–63.

Linan-Thompson, S., & Jean, R.E. (1997). Completing the parent participation puzzle: Accepting diversity. *Teaching Exceptional Children, 30*(2), 46–50.

Lindsey, J.D., & Stewart, D.A. (1989). The guardian minority: Siblings of children with mental retardation. *Education and Training in Mental Retardation, 24,* 291–296.

Ling, D. (1976). *Speech and the hearing impaired child: Theory and practice.* Washington, DC: Alexander Graham Bell Association for the Deaf.

———. (Ed.). (1984). *Early intervention for hearing-impaired children: Oral options.* San Diego: College-Hill.

Locke, J.L. (1986). The linguistic significance of babbling. In B. Lindblom & R. Zetterstrom (Eds.), *Precursors of early speech* (pp. 143–157). New York: Stockton Press.

LoConto, D.G., & Dodder, R.A. (1997). The right to be human: Deinstitutionalization and wishes of people with developmental disabilities. *Education and Training in Mental Retardation and Developmental Disabilities, 32,* 77–84.

Long, N.J. (1990). Comments in Ralph Gardner's article 'Life-space interviewing: It can be effective, but don't . . .'. *Behavioral Disorders, 15,* 119–125.

Lopez-Reyna, N.A. (1996). The importance of meaningful contexts in bilingual special education: Moving to whole language. *Learning Disabilities Research and Practice, 11,* 120–131.

Lorsbach, T.C., & Frymier, J. (1992). A comparison of learning disabled and nondisabled students on five at-risk factors. *Learning Disabilities Research and Practice, 7,* 137–141.

Lough, L.K. (1983). Positioning and handling. In J.A. Blackman (Ed.), *Medical aspects of developmental disabilities in children birth to three* (pp. 203–206). Iowa City: University of Iowa.

Loveday, E.B. (1993). Postsecondary transition services for students with learning disabilities within South Carolina. Doctoral dissertation. Columbia, SC: University of South Carolina.

Lowenfeld, B. (1981). *On blindness and blind people.* New York: American Foundation for the Blind.

Luebke, J., Epstein, M.H., & Cullinan, D. (1989). Comparison of teacher-rated achievement levels of behaviorally disordered, learning disabled, and nonhandicapped adolescents. *Behavioral Disorders, 15,* 1–8.

Luetke-Stahlman, B., & Luckner, J. (1991). *Effectively educating students with hearing impairments.* New York: Longman.

Lund, N.J., & Duchan, J.F. (1993). *Assessing children's language in naturalistic contexts* (3d ed.). Englewood Cliffs, NJ: Prentice-Hall.

Luterman, D. (1979). *Counseling parents of hearing-impaired children.* Boston: Little, Brown.

Lyon, J.S. (1985). *Playing God in the nursery.* New York: Norton.

Maag, J.W. (1988). Treatment of childhood and adolescent depression: Review and recommendations. In R.B. Rutherford, Jr. & J.W. Maag (Eds.), *Monograph in Behavioral Disorders: Severe Behavior Disorders of Children and Youth, 11,* 11–21.

Maag, J.W., & Behrens, J.T. (1989). Epidemiologic data on seriously emotionally disturbed and learning disabled adolescents: Reporting extreme depressive symptomatology. *Behavioral Disorders, 15,* 21–27.

Mack, C.G., Koenig, A.J., & Ashcroft, S.C. (1990). Microcomputers and access technology in programs for teachers of visually impaired students. *Journal of Visual Impairment and Blindness, 84*(10), 526–530.

MacMillan, D. (1989). Mild mental retardation: Emerging issues. In G.A. Robinson, J.R. Patton, E.A. Polloway & L.R. Sargent (Eds.), *Best practices in mild mental disabilities* (pp. 1–20). Reston, VA: Division on Mental Retardation of the Council for Exceptional Children.

MacMillan, D.L. (1982). *Mental retardation in school and society* (2d ed.). Boston: Little, Brown.

MacMillan, D.L., & Hendrick, I.G. (1993). Evolution and legacies. In J.I. Goodlad & T.C. Lovitt (Eds.), *Integrating general and special education.* New York: Macmillan.

MacMillan, D.L., Semmel, M.I., & Gerber, M.M. (1994). The social context of Dunn: Then and now. *Journal of Special Education, 27,* 466–480.

MacMillan, D.L., & Turnbull, A.P. (1983). Parent involvement with special education: Respecting individual differences. *Education and Training of the Mentally Retarded, 18*, 4–9.

Magnusson, D. (1994). Human ontogeny: Longitudinal perspectives. In D. Magnusson & P. Casaer (Eds.), *Longitudinal research on individual development: Present status and future perspectives.* Cambridge, UK: Cambridge University Press.

Maker, C.J. (1977). *Providing programs for the gifted handicapped.* Reston, VA: Council for Exceptional Children.

———. (1987). *Project DISCOVER: Discovering intellectual skills and capabilities while providing opportunities for varied ethnic responses.* Tucson, AZ: University of Arizona, Special Education and Rehabilitation.

Malcom, C.B., Polatajko, H.J., & Simons, J. (1990). A descriptive study of adults with suspected learning disabilities. *Journal of Learning Disabilities, 23*, 518–520.

Malone, L.D., & Mastropieri, M.A. (1992). Reading comprehension instruction: Summarization and self-monitoring training for students with learning disabilities. *Exceptional Children, 58*, 270–279.

Mangrum, C., & Strichart, S. (Eds.). (1988). *Colleges with programs for learning disabled students.* New Jersey: Peterson's Guides, Inc.

Maratens, B.K., Muir, K.A., & Meller, P.J. (1988). Rewards common to the classroom setting: A comparison of regular and self-contained room student ratings. *Behavioral Disorders, 13*, 169–174.

Masters, L.F., Mori, B.A., & Mori, A.A. (1993). Program administration: Organization and operation. *Teaching secondary students with mild learning and behavior problems* (2d ed.) (pp. 29–67). Austin, TX: Pro-Ed.

Mastropieri, M.A., Jenne, T., & Scruggs, T.E. (1988). A level system for managing problem behaviors in a high school resource program. *Behavioral Disorders, 13*, 202–208.

McClintock, E., Bayard, M.P., & McClintock, C.G. (1983). The socialization of social motivation in Mexican American families. In E.E. Garcia (Ed.), *The Mexican American child.* Tempe, AZ: Center for Bilingual Education.

McCollum, K. (1998). Web-standards group releases draft rules to help the disabled explore cyberspace. *Chronicle of Higher Education,* February 4, p. 1.

McComiskey, A.V. (1996). The Braille readiness skills grid: A guide to building a foundation for literacy. *Journal of Visual Impairment and Blindness, 90*(3), 190–193.

McCormick, L. (1997). Policies and practices. In L. McCormick, D.F. Loeb & R.L. Schiefelbusch, *Supporting children with communication difficulties in inclusive settings: School-based language intervention* (pp. 149–178). Boston: Allyn & Bacon.

McCoy, K.M., Maag, J.W., & Rucker, S. (1989). Semantic mapping as a communication tool in classrooms for the seriously emotionally handicapped. *Behavioral Disorders, 14*, 226–235.

McDonnell, A., & Hardman, M. (1988). A synthesis of "best practice" for early childhood services. *Journal of the Division for Early Childhood, 12*, 32–341.

McDonough, K.M. (1989). Analysis of the expressive language characteristics of emotionally handicapped students in social interactions. *Behavioral Disorders, 14*, 127–139.

McGuffog, C., Feiring, C., & Lewis, M. (1987). The diverse profile of the extremely gifted child. *Roeper Review, 10*(2), 82–89.

McIntire, J.C. (1985). The future role of residential schools for visually impaired students. *Journal of Visual Impairment and Blindness, 79*(4), 160–161.

McIntosh, R., Vaughn, S., & Zaragoza, N. (1991). A review of social interventions for students with learning disabilities. *Journal of Learning Disabilities, 24*, 451–458.

McIntyre, T. (1996). Guidelines for providing appropriate services to culturally diverse students with emotional and/or behavioral disorders. *Behavioral Disorders, 21*, 137–144.

McLaren, J., & Bryson, S.E. (1987). Review of recent epidemiological studies of mental retardation: Prevalence, associated disorders, and etiology. *American Journal of Mental Retardation, 92*, 243–254.

McLaughlin, T.F., Krappman, V.F., & Welsh, J.M. (1985). The effects of self-recording for on-task behavior of behaviorally disordered special education students. *Remedial and Special Education, 6*(4), 42–45.

McLeod, T., & Armstrong, S. (1982). Learning disabilities in mathematics: Skill deficits and remedial approaches at the intermediate and secondary level. *Learning Disabilities Quarterly, 5*, 305–311.

McLoughlin, J.A., & Lewis, R.B. (1986). *Assessing special students* (2d ed.). Columbus, OH: Merrill.

Meadow, K. (1968). Parental responses to the medical ambiguities of deafness. *Journal of Health and Social Behavior, 9*, 299–309.

Meadow-Orlans, K.P. (1980). *Deafness and child development.* Berkeley: University of California Press.

Meadow-Orlans, K.P., & Orlans, H. (1990). Responses to loss of hearing in later life. In D.F. Moores & K.P. Meadow-Orlans (Eds.), *Educational and developmental aspects of deafness* (pp. 417–429). Washington, DC: Gallaudet University Press.

Mechaty, I.R., & Thompson, J.E. (Eds.). (1990). *New perspectives on prenatal care.* New York: Elsevier.

Mechling, L.C., & Gast, D.L. (1997). Combination audio/visual self-prompting system for teaching chained tasks to students with intellectual disabilities. *Education and Training in Mental Retardation and Developmental Disabilities, 32*, 138–153.

Medley, L.P., Roberts, J.E., & Zeisel, S.A. (1995). At-risk children and otitis media with effusion: Management issues for the early childhood special educator. *Topics in Early Childhood Special Education, 15*(1), 44–64.

Mehan, H., Hertweck, A., & Meihls, J.L. (1986). *Handicapping the handicapped: Decision making in students' ed-*

ucational careers. Stanford, CA: Stanford University Press.

Meisels, S.J., & Provence, S. (1989). *Screening and assessment: Guidelines for identifying young disabled and developmentally vulnerable children and their families.* Washington, DC: National Center for Clinical Infant Programs.

Meisels, S.J., & Wasik, B.A. (1990). Who should be served? Identifying children in need of early intervention. In S.J. Meisels & J.P. Shonkoff (Eds.), *Handbook of early childhood intervention.* Cambridge: Cambridge University Press.

Menlove, M. (1996). A checklist for identifying funding sources for assistive technology. *Teaching Exceptional Children, 28*(3), 20–24.

Mercer, C.D. (1987). Definitions and characteristics. *Students with learning disabilities* (3d ed.) (pp. 28–51). Columbus, OH: Merrill.

Mercer, C.D., & Mercer, A.R. (1993a). Assessing and teaching handwriting and written expression skills. *Teaching students with learning problems* (4th ed.) (pp. 533–581). New York: Merrill.

———. (1993b). Teaching math skills. In *Teaching students with learning problems* (4th ed.) (pp. 273–342). New York: Merrill.

Mercer, C.D., & Miller, S.P. (1992). *Multiplication facts 0 to 81.* Lawrence, KS: Edge Enterprises.

Mercer, J. (1973). *Labeling the mentally retarded.* Berkeley: University of California Press.

Miller, L. (1989). Classroom-based language intervention. *Language, Speech, and Hearing Services in Schools, 20,* 153–169.

Miller, R.J., Rzonca, C., & Snider, B. (1991). Variables related to the type of postsecondary education experience chosen by young adults with learning disabilities. *Journal of Learning Disabilities, 24,* 188–191.

Miller, S.P., & Mercer, C.D. (1991). *Addition facts 0 to 9.* Lawrence, KS: Edge Enterprises.

Miller, W.H. (1985). The role of residential schools for the blind in educating visually impaired students. *Journal of Visual Impairment and Blindness, 79*(4), 161–164.

Milstead, S. (1988). Siblings are people, too! *Academic Therapy, 23,* 537–540.

Mira, M., Tucker, B.F., & Tyler, J.S. (1992). *Traumatic brain injury in children and adolescents: A source book for teachers and other school personnel.* Austin, TX: Pro-Ed.

Mitchell, I. (1985). The child with chronic illness. In H.A. Haslam & P. Balletutti (Eds.), *Medical problems in the classroom.* Austin, TX: Pro-Ed.

Moores, D.F. (1969). The vocational status of young deaf adults in New England. *Journal of Rehabilitation of the Deaf, 2*(1), 29–41.

———. (1987). *Educating the deaf: Psychology, principles, and practices* (3d ed.). Boston: Houghton Mifflin.

———. (1996). *Educating the deaf: Psychology, principles, and practices* (4th ed.). Boston, MA: Houghton Mifflin.

Moores, D.F., & Kluwin, T.N. (1986). Issues in school placement. In A.N. Schildroth & M.A. Karchmer (Eds.), *Deaf children in America* (pp. 105–123). San Diego: College-Hill.

Morgan, R.L., Moore, S.C., McSweyn, C., & Salzberg, C.L. (1992). Transition from school to work: Views of secondary special educators. *Education and Training in Mental Retardation, 27,* 315–323.

Morsink, C.A. (1984). *Teaching special needs students in regular classrooms.* Boston: Little, Brown.

Morton, K. (1985). Identifying the enemy: A parent's complaint. In H.R. Turnbull & A.P. Turnbull. *Parents speak out: Then and now* (pp. 143–147). Columbus, OH: Merrill.

Myers, B.J., Olson, H.C., & Kaltenbach, K. (1992). Cocaine-exposed infants: Myths and misunderstandings. *Zero to Three, 13*(1), 1–5.

Myklebust, H. (1964). *The psychology of deafness* (2d ed.). New York: Grune & Stratton.

Nation, J.E., & Aram, D.M. (1991). *Diagnosis of speech and language disorders* (2d ed.). San Diego: Singular Publishing.

National Center for Educational Statistics (1996). *Youth indicators.* Washington, DC: U.S. Department of Education.

National Head Injury Task Force. (1985). *An educator's manual.* Framingham, MA: National Head Injury Foundation.

Needleman, H.L. (1992). Childhood exposure to lead: A common cause of school failure. *Phi Delta Kappan, 74*(1), 35–37.

Needleman, H.L., et al. (1979). Deficits in psychological and classroom performance of children with elevated dentine lead levels. *New England Journal of Medicine, 300,* 689–695.

———. (1991). The long-term effects of exposure to low doses of lead in childhood: An 11-year follow-up report. *New England Journal of Medicine, 322,* 83–88.

Neel, R.S., Meadows, N., Levine, P., & Edgar, E.B. (1988).What happens after special education: A statewide follow-up study of secondary students who have behavioral disorders. *Behavioral Disorders, 1,* 209–216.

Nelson, K.B., & Ellenberg, J.H. (1986). Antecedents of cerebral palsy: Multivariate analysis of risk. *New England Journal of Medicine, 315,* 81–86.

Nelson, N.W. (1993). *Childhood language disorders in context: Infancy through adolescence.* New York: Merrill.

Neubert, D.A., Tilson, G.P., & Ianacone, R.N. (1989). Postsecondary transition needs and employment patterns of individuals with mild disabilities. *Exceptional Children, 55,* 494–500.

Newcomer, P.L., & Barenbaum, E.M. (1991). The written composing ability of children with learning disabilities. A review of the literature from 1980–1990. *Journal of Learning Disabilities, 24,* 578–593.

Newell, W. (1991). ASL is not a four-letter word: Deaf education can dance with the boogieman. In S. Polowe-Aldersley, P. Schragle, V. Armour, & J. Polowe (Eds.), *Profession on parade: Proceedings of the Fifty-fifth Biennial Meeting, Convention of American Instructors of the Deaf and the Sixty-third Annual Meeting of the Conference of Educational Administrators Serving the Deaf, New Orleans, Louisiana, June 1991* (pp. 74–75). Silver Spring, MD: Convention.

Newland, T.E. (1976). *The gifted in socioeducational perspective.* Englewood Cliffs, NJ: Prentice-Hall.

Nietupski, J.A., & Hamre-Nietupski, S.M. (1987). An ecological approach to curriculum development. In L. Goetz, D. Guess & K. Stremel-Campbell (Eds.), *Innovative program design for individuals with dual sensory impairments.* Baltimore: Brookes.

Neitupski, J., Hamre-Nietupski, S., Donder, D.J., Houselog, M., & Anderson, R.J. (1988). Proactive administrative strategies for implementing community-based programs for students with moderate/severe handicaps. *Education and Training in Mental Retardation, 23,* 138–146.

Nihara, K., Foster, R., Shellhaas, M., & Leland, H. (1981). *AAMR adaptive behavior scale: School edition.* Monterey, CA: Publishers Test Service.

Noonan, M.J., & Kilgo, J.L. (1987). Transition services for early age individuals with severe mental retardation. In R.N. Ianacone & R.A. Stodden (Eds.), *Transition issues and directions* (pp. 25–37). Reston, VA: Council for Exceptional Children.

Northcott, W. (Ed.). (1984). *Oral interpreting: Principles and practices.* Washington, DC: Alexander Graham Bell Association for the Deaf.

Northern, J.L., & Downs, M.P. (1991). *Hearing in children* (4th ed.). Baltimore: Williams & Wilkins.

Oakes, J. (1985). *Keeping track.* New Haven: Yale University Press.

Oller, D.K., & Eilers, R.E. (1982). Similarity of babbling in Spanish- and English-learning babies. *Journal of Child Language, 9,* 565–577.

Oller, D.K., Weiman, L.A., Doyle, W.J., & Ross, C. (1976). Infant babbling and speech. *Journal of Child Language, 3,* 1–11.

Oller, J.W., & Damico, J. (1991). Theoretical considerations in the assessment of LEP students. In E.V. Hamayan & J.S. Damico (Eds.), *Limiting bias in the assessment of bilingual students* (pp. 77–110). Austin, TX: Pro-Ed.

Orelove, F.P., & Sobsey, D. (1987). *Educating children with multiple disabilities: A transdisciplinary approach* (pp. 285–314). Baltimore: Brookes.

Orelove, F.P., & Sobsey, R. (1991). *Multiple disabilities: A transdisciplinary approach.* Baltimore: Brookes.

Ortiz, A., & Maldonado-Colon, E. (1986). Reducing inappropriate referrals of language minority students in special education. In A.C. Willig & H.F. Greenberg (Eds.), *Bilingualism and learning disabilities: Policy and practice for teachers' and administrators* (pp. 37–50). New York: American Library Publishing Company.

Ortiz, A.A., & Wilkinson, C.Y. (1991). Assessment and intervention model for the bilingual exceptional student (AIM for the BEST). *Teacher Education and Special Education, 14,* 35–42.

Osborn, A. (1963). *Applied imagination.* New York: Scribners.

Owens, R.E., Jr. (1995). *Language disorders: A functional approach to assessment and intervention* (2d ed.). Boston: Allyn & Bacon.

Padden, C. (1980). The deaf community and the culture of deaf people. In C. Baker & D. Cokely (Eds.), *Sign language and the deaf community: Essays in honor of William C. Stokoe* (pp. 89–103). Silver Spring, MD: National Association for the Deaf.

Padden, C., & Humphries, T. (1988). *Deaf in America: Voices from a culture.* Cambridge, MA: Harvard University Press.

Pahl, J., & Quine, L. (1987). Families with mentally handicapped children. In J. Oxford (Ed.), *Treating the disorder, treating the family.* Baltimore: Johns Hopkins University Press.

Paneth, N. (1995). The problem of low birth weight. *Future of Children, 5*(3), 19–34.

Parasnis, I. (1996). Interpreting the Deaf experience within the context of cultural and language diversity. In I. Parasnis (Ed.), *Cultural and language diversity and the Deaf experience* (pp. 3–19). New York: Cambridge University Press.

Parke, B.N. (1989). *Gifted students in regular classrooms.* Boston: Allyn & Bacon.

Patterson, D. (1987). The causes of Down syndrome. *Scientific American, 257*(2), 52–57.

Patton, J.R., Beirne-Smith, M., & Payne, J.S. (1990). *Mental retardation* (3d ed.) (pp. 77–116). Columbus: Merrill.

Paul, P.V. (1998). *Literacy and deafness.* Boston: Allyn & Bacon.

Paul, P.V., & Jackson, D.W. (1993). *Toward a psychology of deafness.* Boston: Allyn & Bacon.

Paul, P.V., & Quigley, S.P. (1990). *Education and deafness.* New York: Longman.

Pauls, D.L. (1990). A review of the evidence for genetic factors in stuttering. In J.A. Cooper (Ed.), *Research needs in stuttering: Roadblocks and future directions.* (ASHA reports, #18). Rockville, MD: American Speech-Language-Hearing Association.

Pembrey, M. (1992). Genetics and language disorder. In P. Fletcher & D. Hall (Eds.), *Specific speech and language disorders in children* (pp. 51–62). San Diego: Singular Publishing.

Pendarvis, E.D., Howley, A.A., & Howley, C.B. (1990). *The abilities of gifted children.* Englewood Cliffs, NJ: Prentice-Hall.

Peterson, H.A., & Marquardt, T.P. (1990). *Appraisal and diagnosis of speech and language disorders* (2d ed.). Englewood Cliffs, NJ: Prentice-Hall.

Phelps, D. (1994). Retinopathy of prematurity: A neonatologist's perspective. In S.J. Isenberg (Ed.), *The eye of infancy* (2d ed., pp. 437–447). St. Louis: Mosby-Year Book.

Pintner, R., & Patterson, D. (1917). A comparison of deaf and hearing children in visual memory span for digits. *Journal of Experimental Psychology, 2*(2), 76–88.

Polloway, E.A., Epstein, M.H., & Cullinan, D. (1985). Prevalence of behavior problems among educable mentally retarded students. *Education and Training in Mental Retardation, 20,* 3–13.

Polloway, E.A., Patton, J.R., Payne, J.S., & Payne, R.A. (1989). *Strategies for teaching learners with special needs* (4th ed.). Columbus, OH: Merrill.

Polloway, E.A., Patton, J.R., Smith, J.D., & Roderique, T. (1991). Issues in program design for elementary students with mild retardation: Emphasis on curriculum development. *Education and Training in Mental Retardation, 26,* 142–150.

Polloway, E.A., Smith, J.D., Patton, J.R., & Smith, T.E.C. (1996). Historic changes in mental retardation and developmental disabilities. *Education and Training in Mental Retardation and Developmental Disabilities, 31,* 3–12.

Powell, T.H., & Gallagher, P.A. (1993). *Brothers and sisters: A special part of exceptional families* (2d ed.). Baltimore: Brookes.

Pugach, M.C., & Warger, C.L. (1993). Curriculum considerations. In J.I. Goodlad & T.C. Lovitt (Eds.), *Integrating general and special education* (pp. 125–148). New York: Merrill/Macmillan.

Quay, H.C., & Peterson, D.R. (1983). *Behavior problem checklist: revised.* Coral Gables, FL: University of Miami.

Quigley, S.P., & Paul, P.V. (1984). *Language and deafness.* San Diego: College-Hill.

———. (1986). A perspective on academic achievement. In D.M. Luterman (Ed.), *Deafness in perspective* (pp. 55–86). San Diego: College-Hill.

Ramirez, M., & Casteñeda, A. (1974). *Cultural democracy, bicognitive development, and education.* New York: Academic Press.

Ramsey, E., & Walker, H.M. (1988). Family management correlates of antisocial behavior among middle school boys. *Behavioral Disorders, 13,* 187–201.

Raph, J.B., Goldberg, M.L., & Passow, A.H. (1966). *Bright underachievers.* New York: Teachers College Press.

Rapport, M.K. (1996). Legal guidelines for the delivery of special health care services in schools. *Exceptional Children, 62,* 537–549.

Raths, L.E., Wassermann, S., Jonas, A., & Rothstein, A. (1986). *Teaching for thinking.* New York: Teachers College Press.

Ratner, V., & Harris, L. (1994). *Understanding language disorders: The impact on learning.* Eau Claire, WI: Thinking Publications.

Reichard, A. (1995). The value of prenatal testing. *Exceptional Parent, 25*(8), 29–31.

Reichle, J., & Keogh, W.J. (1986). Communication instruction for learners with severe handicaps: Some unresolved issues. In R.H. Horner, L.H. Meyer & H.D.B. Fredricks (Eds.), *Education of learners with severe handicaps: Exemplary service strategies* (2d ed.) (pp. 189–219). Baltimore: Brookes.

Reis, S.M., Neu, T.W., & McGuire, J.M. (1997). Case studies of high-ability students with learning disabilities who have achieved. *Exceptional Children, 63*(4), 463–479.

Renzulli, J.S. (1977). *The Enrichment Triad Model.* Mansfield Center, CT: Creative Learning Press.

———. (1978). What makes giftedness? *Phi Delta Kappan, 60,* 180–184.

———. (Ed.). (1986). *Systems and models for developing programs for the gifted and talented.* Mansfield Center, CT: Creative Learning Press.

———. (1996). Schools for talent development: A practical plan for total school improvement. *School Administrator, 53* (1), 20–22.

Renzulli, J.S., & Reis, S.M. (1985). *The schoolwide enrichment model: A comprehensive plan for educational excellence.* Mansfield Center, CT: Creative Learning Press.

———. (1991). The schoolwide enrichment model: A comprehensive plan for the development of creative productivity. In N. Colangelo & G.A. Davis (Eds.), *Handbook of gifted education.* Boston: Allyn & Bacon.

Reynolds, M.C., Wang, M.C., & Walberg, H.J. (1987). The necessary restructuring of special and regular education. *Exceptional Children, 53,* 391–398.

Richardson, G.A., & Day, N.J. (1994). Detrimental effects of prenatal cocaine exposure: Illusion or reality? *Journal of the American Academy of Child and Adolescent Psychiatry, 33,* 28–34.

Rimm, S.B. (1986). *Underachievement syndrome: Causes and cures.* Watertown, WI: Apple Publishing Company.

Roberts, J.E., Wallace, I.F., & Henderson, F.W. (1997). *Otitis media in young children.* Baltimore: Brookes.

Robertson, C.M., & Finer, N.N. (1993). Long-term follow-up of term neonates with perinatal asphyxia. *Clinics in Perinatology, 20*(2), 483–500.

Robinson, A. (1990). Cooperation or exploitation? The argument against cooperative learning for talented students. *Journal for the Education of the Gifted, 14*(1), 9–27.

Roedell, W. (1989). Early development of gifted children. In J. van Tassel-Baska & P. Olszewski-Kubilius (Eds.), *Patterns of influence on gifted learners: The home, the self, and the school* (pp. 13–28). New York: Teachers College Press.

Roedell, W.C., Jackson, N.E., & Robinson, H.B. (1980). *Gifted young children.* New York: Teachers College Press.

Roessing, L.J. (1982). Functional vision: Criterion-referenced checklists. In S.S. Mangold (Ed.), *A teachers' guide to the special educational needs of blind and visually handicapped children* (pp. 35–44). New York: American Foundation for the Blind.

Rooney, K.J. (1988). *Independent strategies for efficient study.* Richmond, VA: J.R. Enterprises.

Rosen, L.A., Gabardi, L., Miller, C.D., & Miller, L. (1990). Home-based treatment of disruptive junior high school students: An analysis of the differential effects of positive and negative consequences. *Behavioral Disorders, 15,* 227–232.

Rosen, M., Rice, D.R., Walsh, K.K., Hartman, E.M., & McCallion, P. (1992). Developmentally disabled people grow up: Needs and resources in the post-school years. In W. Stainback & S. Stainback (Eds.), *Controversial issues confronting special education: Divergent perspectives* (pp. 285–298). Boston: Allyn & Bacon.

Rosenberg, M.S., Wilson, R., Maheady, L., & Sindelar, P.T. (1992). *Educating students with behavioral disorders* (pp. 87–112). Boston: Allyn & Bacon.

Rosenshine, B., & Stevens, R. (1986). Teaching functions. In M.C. Wittrock (Ed.), *Handbook of research on teaching* (3d ed.) (pp. 376–391). New York: Macmillan.

Rosenthal, I. (1992). Counseling the learning disabled late adolescent and adult: A self-psychology perspective. *Learning Disabilities Research and Practice, 7,* 217–225.

Rosenthal, S.L., Cohen, S.S., & Biro, F.M. (1994). Sexually transmitted diseases: A paradigm for risk-taking among teens. In R.J. Simeonsson (Ed.), *Risk, resilience, and prevention: Promoting the well-being of all children.* Baltimore: Brookes.

Ross, M. (1986). A perspective on amplification: Then and now. In D.M. Luterman (Ed.), *Deafness in perspective* (pp. 35–53). San Diego: College-Hill.

———. (Ed.). (1990). *Hearing-impaired children in the mainstream.* Washington, DC: Alexander Graham Bell Association for the Deaf.

Rostron, A., & Sewell, D. (1984). *Microtechnology in special education.* Baltimore: Johns Hopkins University Press.

Ryan, K., & Cooper, J.M. (1998). *Those who can, teach* (8th ed.). Boston: Houghton Mifflin.

Sabornie, E.J., Kauffman, J.M., & Cullinan, D.A. (1990). Extended sociometric status of adolescents with mild handicaps: A cross-categorical perspective. *Exceptionality, 1,* 197–209.

Sacks, O. (1989). *Seeing voices: A journey into the world of the deaf.* New York: Harper Collins.

Sacks, S.Z. (1996). Psychological and social implications of low vision. In A.L. Corn & A.J. Koenig (Eds.), *Foundations of low vision: Clinical and functional perspectives.* New York: American Foundation for the Blind.

Safer, N. (1997). IDEA opens the door to a better future for students with disabilities and special educators. *Teaching Exceptional Children, 29*(60), 1.

Safran, S.P., & Safran, J.S. (1996). Intervention assistance programs and prereferral teams: Directions for the twenty-first century. *Remedial and Special Education, 17*(6), 363–369.

Salisbury, C.L., Evans, I.M., & Palombaro, M.M. (1997). Collaborative problem-solving to promote the inclusion of young children with significant disabilities in primary grades. *Exceptional Children, 63,* 195–209.

Salvia, J., & Ysseldyke, J.E. (1998). *Assessment* (7th ed.) Boston: Houghton Mifflin.

Sameroff, A.J., & Chandler, M.J. (1975). Reproductive risk and the continuum of caretaking casualty. In F.D. Horowitz, M. Hetherington, S. Scarr-Salapatek & G. Siegel (Eds.), *Review of child development research* (Vol. 4) (pp. 187–244). Chicago: University of Chicago Press.

Sandall, S.R. (1997a). The family service team. In A.H. Widerstrom, B.A. Mowder & S.R. Sandall (Eds.), *Infant development and risk* (2d ed.). Baltimore: Brookes.

———. (1997b). The individualized family service plan. In A.H. Widerstrom, B.A. Mowder & S.R. Sandall (Eds.), *Infant development and risk* (2d ed.). Baltimore: Brookes.

Saunders, J., & Espeland, P. (1986). *Bringing up the best.* Minneapolis: Free Spirit.

Savelle, S., & Fox, J.J. (1988). Differential effects of training in two classes of social initiations on the positive responses and extended interactions of preschool-aged autistic children and their nonhandicapped peers. In R.B. Rutherford, Jr. & J.W. Maag (Eds.), *Monograph in Behavioral Disorders: Severe Behavior Disorders of Children and Youth, 11,* 75–86.

Scanlon, D., Deshler, D.D., & Schumaker, J.B. (1996). Can a strategy be taught and learned in secondary inclusive classrooms? *Learning Disabilities Research and Practice, 11,* 41–57.

Scarborough, H.S., & Dobrich, W. (1990). Development of children with early language delay. *Journal of Speech and Hearing Disorders, 33,* 70–83.

Scheuermann, B., & Webber, J. (1996). Level systems: Problems and solutions. *Beyond Behavior, 7*(2), 12–17.

Schiff-Myers, N.B., Djukic, J., McGovern-Lawleer, J., & Perez, D. (1993). Assessment considerations in the evaluation of second-language learners: A case study. *Exceptional Children, 60,* 237–248.

Schildroth, A.N. (1986). Residential schools for deaf children: A decade in review. In A.N. Schildroth & M.A. Karchmer (Eds.), *Deaf children in America.* San Diego: College-Hill.

———. (1994). Congenital cytomegalovirus and deafness. *American Journal of Audiology* (July).

Schirmer, B. (1994). *Language and literacy development in children who are deaf.* New York: Maxwell Macmillan International.

Scholl, G.T. (1986). *Foundations of education for blind and visually handicapped children and youth: Theory and practice.* New York: American Foundation for the Blind.

Scholl, T.O., Hediger, M.L., & Belsky, D.H. (1994). Prenatal care and maternal health during adolescent pregnancy: A review and meta-analysis. *Journal of Adolescent Health, 15*(6), 444–456.

Schon, D.A. (1990). *Educating the reflective practitioner.* San Francisco: Jossey-Bass.

Schuler, P.A. (1997). Cluster grouping coast to coast. *Newsletter of the National Research Center on the Gifted and Talented* (Winter).

Schumaker, J.B., & Hazel, J.S. (1984). Social skills assessment and training for the learning disabled: What's on second? Part I. *Journal of Learning Disabilities, 17,* 422–431.

Schumaker, J.B., & Lyerla, K.D. (1991). The paragraph writing strategy instructor's manual. Lawrence, KS: University of Kansas.

Scruggs, T.E., & Mastropieri, M.A. (1996). Teacher perceptions of mainstreaming/inclusion, 1958–1995: A research synthesis. *Exceptional Children, 63*(1), 59–74.

Seidenberg, P.L., & Koenigsberg, E. (1990). A survey of regular and special education high school teachers and college faculty: Implications for program development for secondary learning disabled students. *Learning Disabilities Research, 5,* 100–117.

Shea, T.M., & Bauer, A.M. (1991). *Parents and teachers of children with exceptionalities: A handbook for collaboration* (2d ed.). Boston: Allyn & Bacon.

Sherburne, S., Utley, B., McConnel, S., & Gannon, J. (1988). Decreasing violent or aggressive theme play among preschool children with behavior disorders. *Exceptional Children, 55,* 166–172.

Shiono, P.H., & Behrman, R.E. (1995). Low birth weight: Analysis and recommendations. *Future of Children, 5*(3), 4–18.

Shutz, R.P., Williams, W., Iverson, G.S., & Duncan, D. (1984). Social integration of severely handicapped students. In N. Certo, N. Haring & R. York (Eds.), *Public school integration of severely handicapped students: Rational issues and progressive alternatives* (pp. 15–42). Baltimore: Brookes.

Shuy, R. (1988). The oral language basis for dialogue journals. In J. Staton, R.W. Shuy, J.K. Peyton & L. Reed (Eds.), *Dialogue journal communication* (pp. 73–87). Norwood, NJ: Ablex.

SIECUS Report. (November-December 1988). *Sexuality and the developmentally disabled: An annotated SIECUS bibliography of resources.* New York: Sex Information and Education Council of the United States.

Sienkiewicz-Mercer, R., & Kaplan, S.B. (1989). *I raise my eyes to say yes.* Boston: Houghton Mifflin.

Sigelman, C.K., & Shaffer, D.R. (1991). Environmental and life-span development. *Life-span human development.* Pacific Grove, CA: Brooks/Cole.

Silliman, E.R., & Wilkinson, L.C. (1994). Discourse scaffolds for classroom intervention. In G.P. Wallach & K.P. Butler (Eds.), *Language learning disabilities in school-age children and adolescents* (pp. 27–52). New York: Merrill/Macmillan.

Silverman, L.K. (1990). A tribute to Leta Stetter Hollingworth. *Roeper Review, 12*(3), 133–134.

Simeonsson, R.J. (Ed.). (1994). *Risk, resilience, and prevention: Promoting the well-being of all children.* Baltimore: Brookes.

Simon, C.S. (1991). Functional flexibility: Developing communicative competence in speaker and listener roles. In C.S. Simon (Ed.), *Communication skills and classroom success: Assessment and therapy methodologies for language-learning disabled students.* Eau Claire, WI: Thinking Publications.

Simpson, R.L. (1988). Needs of parents and families whose children have learning and behavioral problems. *Behavioral Disorders, 14,* 40–47.

———. (1989). Agreement among teachers in using the revised behavior problem checklist to identify deviant behavior in children. *Behavioral Disorders, 14,* 151–156.

Simpson, R.L., & Souris, L.A. (1988). Reciprocity in the pupil-teacher interactions of autistic and mildly handicapped preschool children. *Behavioral Disorders, 13,* 159–168.

Siperstein, G.N., Leffert, J.S., & Widaman, K. (1996). Social behavior and the social acceptance and rejection of children with mental retardation. *Education and Training in Mental Retardation and Developmental Disabilities, 31,* 271–281.

Skiba, R.J. (1989). The importance of construct validity: Alternative models for the assessment of behavioral disorders. *Behavioral Disorders, 14,* 175–185.

Skinner, R. (1990). Genetic counseling. In A.E.H. Emery & D.L. Rimoin (Eds.), *Principles and practice of human genetics* (2d ed.) (Vol. 2). New York: Churchill Livingstone.

Skutnabb-Kangas, & Toukomaa, P. (1976). *Teaching migrant children's mother tongue and learning the language of the host country in the context of the socio-cultural situation of the migrant family.* Helsinki: The Finnish National Commission for UNESCO.

Slavin, R.E. (1988). Synthesis of research on grouping in elementary and secondary schools. *Educational Leadership* (Sept.), 67–77.

———. (1990). Ability grouping, cooperative learning and the gifted. *Journal for the Education of the Gifted, 14*(1), 3–8.

Slentz, L., Walker, B., & Bricker, D. (1989). Supporting parent involvement in early intervention: A role-taking model. In G.H.S. Singer & L.K. Irvin (Eds.), *Support for caregiving families* (pp. 221–238). Baltimore: Brookes.

Smith, C.R. (1985). Identification of handicapped children and youth: A state agency perspective on behavioral disorders. *Remedial and Special Education, 6*(4), 34–41.

Smith, J.D. (1989). On the right of children with mental retardation to life sustaining medical care and treatment: A position statement. *Education and Training in Mental Retardation, 24,* 3–6.

Smith, T., & Lovaas, O.L. (1997). The UCLA young autism project: A reply to Gresham and MacMillan. *Behavioral Disorders, 22,* 202–218.

Smith, T.E.C., & Dowdy, C.A. (1989). The role of study skills in the secondary curriculum. *Academic Therapy, 24,* 479–490.

Smith, T.E.C., Finn, D.M., & Dowdy, C.A. (1993). *Teaching students with mild disabilities.* Orlando, FL: Harcourt Brace Jovanovich.

Smith, T.E.C., Price, B.J., & Marsh, G.E. (1986). *Mildly handicapped children and adults.* St. Paul, MN: West.

Smith, T.M. (1994). Adolescent pregnancy. In R.J. Simeonsson (Ed.), *Risk, resilience, and prevention: Promoting the well-being of all children.* Baltimore: Brookes.

Snell, M.E. (1988). Curriculum and methodology for individuals with severe disabilities. *Education and Training in Mental Retardation, 23,* 302–314.

Snell, M.E., & Drake, Jr., G.P. (1994). Replacing cascades with supported education. *Journal of Special Education, 27,* 393–409.

Snider, V.E. (1997). Transfer of decoding skills to a literature basal. *Learning Disabilities Research and Practice, 12,* 54–62.

Snow, C.E., Burns, M.S., & Griffin, P. (Eds.). (1998). *Preventing reading difficulties in young children.* Washington, DC: National Academy Press.

Snyder, L.S., & Downey, D.M. (1991). The language-reading relationship in normal and reading disabled children. *Journal of Speech and Hearing Research, 34,* 129–140.

Sobsey, D. (1994). *Violence and abuse in the lives of people with disabilities: The end of silent acceptance?* Baltimore: Brookes.

Solomons, G. (1983). Child abuse and neglect. In J.A. Blackman (Ed.), *Medical aspects of developmental disabilities in children birth to three* (pp. 31–37). Iowa City: University of Iowa.

Sontag, J.C., & Schacht, R. (1994). An ethnic comparison of parent participation and information needs in early intervention. *Exceptional Children, 60,* 422–433.

Sparks, S.N. (1984). *Birth defects and speech-language disorders.* Boston: College-Hill Press.

———. (1993). *Children of prenatal substance abuse.* San Diego: Singular Publishing.

Sparks, S., & Caster, J.A. (1989). Human sexuality and sex education. In G.A. Robinson, E.A. Polloway, J.R. Patton & L.R. Sargent (Eds.), *Best practices in mild mental disabilities.* Reston, VA: Division on Mental Retardation of the Council for Exceptional Children.

Sparrow, S.S., Balla, D.A., & Cicchetti, D.V. (1984). *Vineland adaptive behavior scales: Interview edition, survey form manual.* Circle Pines, MN: American Guidance Service.

Spungin, S.J. (1990). *Braille literacy: Issues for blind persons, families, professionals, and producers of Braille.* New York: American Foundation for the Blind.

Stainback, G.H., Stainback, W.C., & Stainback, S.B. (1988). Superintendents' attitudes toward integration. *Education and Training in Mental Retardation, 23,* 92–96.

———. (1993). Schools as inclusive communities. In W. Stainback & S. Stainback (Eds.), *Controversial issues confronting special education* (pp. 29–43). Boston: Allyn & Bacon.

Stainback, S., Stainback, W., & Ayres, B. (1996). Schools as inclusive communities. In W. Stainback & S. Stainback (Eds.), *Controversial issues confronting special education: Divergent perspectives* (2d ed.) (pp. 31–43). Boston: Allyn and Bacon.

Stallman, A.C., & Pearson, P.D. (1990). Formal measures of early literacy. In L.M. Morrow & J.K. Smith (Eds.), *Assessment for instruction in early literacy* (pp. 7–44). Englewood Cliffs, NJ: Prentice-Hall.

Start, J.A., Kiernan, W.E., Goldsburg, T.L., & McGree, J.J. (1986). Not entering employment: A system dilemma. In W.E. Kiernan & J.A. Stark (Eds.), *Pathways to employment for adults with developmental disabilities* (pp. 199–204). Baltimore: Brookes.

Starko, A.J. (1986). Meeting the needs of the gifted throughout the school day: Techniques for curriculum compacting. *Roeper Review, 9*(1), 27–33.

Sternberg, R.J. (1985). *Beyond IQ: A triarchic theory of human intelligence.* New York: Cambridge University Press.

———. (1991). Giftedness according to the triarchic theory of human intelligence. In N. Colangelo & G.A. Davis (Eds.), *Handbook of gifted education* (pp. 45–54). Boston: Allyn & Bacon.

———. (1997). What does it mean to be smart? *Educational Leadership, 54*(6), 16–20.

Sternberg, R.J., & Clinkenbeard, P. (1995). A triarchic view of identifying, teaching, and assessing gifted children. *Roeper Review, 17,* 225–260.

Stetson, F. (1984). Critical factors that facilitate integration: A theory of administrative responsibility. In N. Certo, N. Haring & R. York (Eds.), *Public school integration of severely handicapped students: Rational issues and progressive alternatives* (pp. 65–82). Baltimore: Brookes.

Stinson, M., & Lang, H. (1995). Full inclusion: A path for integration or isolation? *American Annals of the Deaf, 139*(2), 156–159.

Stoel-Gammon, C. (1992). Prelinguistic vocal development: Measurement and predictions. In C.A. Ferguson, L. Menn & C. Stoel-Gammon (Eds.), *Phonological development: Models, research, implications* (pp. 439–456). Timonium, MD: York Press.

Stokoe, W. (1960). Sign language structure: An outline of the visual communication system of the American deaf.

Studies in Linguistics Occasional Papers No. 8. Washington, DC: Gallaudet College Press.

Stoneman, Z., Brody, G.H., Davis, C.H., & Crapps, J.M. (1987). Mentally retarded children and their older same-sex siblings: Naturalistic in-home observations. *American Journal of Mental Retardation, 92,* 290–298.

————. (1988). Childcare responsibilities, peer relations, and sibling conflict: Older siblings of mentally retarded children. *American Journal of Mental Retardation, 93,* 174–183.

Storey, K. (1997). Quality of life issues in social skills assessment of persons with disabilities. *Education and Training in Mental Retardation and Developmental Disabilities, 32,* 197–200.

Storey, K., & Provost, O. (1996). The effect of communication skills instruction on the integration of workers with severe disabilities in supported employment settings. *Education and Training in Mental Retardation and Developmental Disabilities, 31,* 123–141.

Stotland, J. (1984). Relationships of parents to professionals: A challenge to professionals. *Journal of visual impairment and blindness, 78*(2), pp. 69–74.

Strain, P.S., & Odom, S.L. (1986). Innovations in the education of preschool children with severe handicaps. In R.H. Horner, L.H. Meyer & H.D.B. Fredricks (Eds.), *Education of learners with severe handicaps: Exemplary service strategies* (2d ed.). Baltimore: Brookes.

Stuckless, E.R., Avery, J.C., & Hurwitz, T.A. (Eds.). (1989). *Educational interpreting for deaf students: Report of the National Task Force on Educational Interpreting.* Rochester, NY: National Technical Institute for the Deaf, Rochester Institute of Technology.

Sullivan, C.A.C., Vitello, S.J., & Foster, W. (1988). Adaptive behavior of adults with mental retardation in a group home: An intensive case study. *Education and Training in Mental Retardation, 23,* 76–81.

Summers, J.A., Behr, S.K., & Turnbull, A.P. (1989). Positive adaptation and coping strengths of families who have children with disabilities. In G.H.S. Singer & L.K. Irvin (Eds.), *Support for caregiving families* (pp. 27–40). Baltimore: Brookes.

Swanson, H.L. (1993). Principles and procedures in strategy use. In L.J. Meltzer (Ed.), *Strategy assessment and instruction for students with learning disabilities* (pp. 61–92). Austin, TX: Pro-Ed.

Swanson, H.L., Cochran, K.F., & Ewers, C.A. (1990). Can learning disabilities be determined from working memory performance? *Journal of Learning Disabilities, 23,* 59–67.

Swarthout, D.W. (1988). Enhancing the moral development of behaviorally/emotionally handicapped students. *Behavioral Disorders, 14,* 57–68.

Swenson-Pierce, A., Kohl, F., & Egel, A. (1987). Siblings as home trainers: A strategy for teaching domestic skills to children. *Journal of the Association for Persons with Severe Handicaps, 12*(1), 53–60.

Taylor, S.E. (1983). Adjustment to threatening events: A theory of cognitive adaptation. *American Psychologist, 38,* 1161–1173.

Taylor, S.J., Lakin, K.C., & Hill, B.K. (1989). Permanency planning for children and youth: Out-of-home placement decisions. *Exceptional Children, 55,* 541–549.

Taylor, S.J., Racino, J.A., & Walker, P.M. (1992). Inclusive community living. In W. Stainback & S. Stainback (Eds.), *Controversial issues confronting special education: Divergent perspectives* (pp. 299–312). Boston: Allyn & Bacon.

Teplin, S.W., Burchinal, M., Johnson-Martin, N., et al. (1991). Neurodevelopmental, health, and growth status at age six years of children with birth weight less than 1001 grams. *Journal of Pediatrics, 118,* 768–777.

Terman, L.M. (1906). Genius and stupidity. *Pedagogical Seminary, 13,* 307–373.

Terman, L.M., et al. *Genetic studies of genius.* I. *The mental and physical traits of a thousand gifted children,* 1925; II: *The early mental traits of three hundred geniuses,* 1926; III: *The promise of youth,* 1930; IV: *The gifted child grows up,* 1947; V: *The gifted group at mid-life,* 1959. Stanford, CA: Stanford University Press.

Terman, L.M., & Merrill, M.A. (1973). *Stanford-Binet Intelligence Scale—Third Revision Form L-M.* Boston: Houghton Mifflin.

The new IDEA: A brief review of selected new statutes. (1997). *The Special Edge* (July-August), 6.

Thompson, L., Lobb, C., Elling, R., Herman, S., Jurkiewicz, T., & Hulleza, C. (1997). Pathways to family empowerment: Effects of family-centered delivery of early intervention services. *Exceptional Children, 64,* 7–18.

Thurstone, L.L. (1924). *The nature of intelligence.* London: Kegan Paul, Trench, Trubner.

Todis, B., Severson, H.H., & Walker, H.M. (1990). The critical events scale: Behavioral profiles of students with externalizing and internalizing behavior disorders. *Behavioral Disorders, 15,* 75–86.

Torgesen, J.K. (1977). Memorization process in reading disabled children. *Journal of Educational Psychology, 69,* 571–578.

Torrance, E.P. (1969). Creative positives of disadvantaged children and youth. *Gifted Child Quarterly, 13,* 71–81.

————. (1984). *Mentor relationships: How they aid creative achievement, endure, change and die.* Buffalo: Bearly Limited.

Treiman, R. (1993). *Beginning to spell.* New York: Oxford University Press.

————. (1993). Participatory research on cognitive coping: From concepts to research planning. In A.P. Turnbull, J.M. Patterson, S.K. Behr, D.L. Murphy, J.G. Marquis & M.J. Blue-Banning (Eds.), *Cognitive coping, families, and disability.* Baltimore: Brookes.

Turnbull, A.P., & Ruef, M. (1997). Family perspectives on inclusive lifestyle issues for people with problem behavior. *Exceptional Children, 63,* 211–227.

Turnbull, A.P., & Turnbull, H.R. (1997). *Families, profes-sionals, and exceptionality: A special partnership* (3d ed.). Upper Saddle River, NJ: Merrill.

Turnbull, H.R. III, Buchele-Ash, A., & Mitchell, L. (1994). *Abuse and neglect of children with disabilities: A policy analysis.* Lawrence, KS: Beach Center on Families and Disability, University of Kansas.

Turnbull, H.R., Turnbull, A.P., Bronicki, G.J., Summers, J.A., & Roeder-Gordon, C. (1989). *Disability and the fam-ily: A guide to decisions for adulthood.* Baltimore: Brookes.

Tuttle, D.W. (1984). *Self-esteem and adjusting with blindness.* Spring, IL: Charles Thomas

Tymchuk, A.J., Hamada, D., Andron, L., & Anderson, A. (1990). Home safety training with mothers who are mentally retarded. *Education and Training in Mental Re-tardation, 25,* 142–149.

U.S. Advisory Board on Child Abuse and Neglect. (1995). *A nation's shame: Fatal child abuse and neglect in the United States.* Washington, DC: U.S. Department of Health and Human Services.

U.S. Bureau of the Census (1995). Statistical Abstract of the U.S., 1995. Washington, DC: Government Printing Office.

U.S. courts affirm the need for a full continuum of ser-vices. (1996). *CEC Today, 3*(6), 4–5.

U.S. Department of Education. (1995). www.ed.gov. IDEA/amend95.backgrnd.html.

U.S. Department of Education (1996). *Eighteenth Annual Report to Congress on the Implementation of the Individuals with Disabilities Education Act.* Washington, DC: U.S. Department of Education.

Vahidi, S. (1998). I learn, therefore I am: Descartes ideol-ogy in Cyberage. *The National Research Center on the Gifted and Talented Newsletter* (Winter), 5–8.

van Tassel-Baska, J. (Ed.). (1989). Introduction. *Patterns of influence on gifted learners: The home, the self, and the school* (pp. 1–10). New York: Teachers College Press.

Vander Zanden, J.W. (1989). *Human development* (4th ed.). New York: Knopf.

Vaughn, S. (1991). Social skills enhancement in students with learning disabilities. In B. Wong (Ed.), *Learning about learning disabilities* (pp. 409–440). San Diego: Aca-demic Press.

Vaughn, S., Schumm, J.S., & Arguelles, M.E. (1997). The ABCDEs of co-teaching. *Teaching Exceptional Children, 30*(2), 4–10.

Verharren, P., & Conner, F. (1981). Physical disabilities. In J.M. Kauffman & D.P. Hallahan (Eds.), *Handbook of spe-cial education.* Englewood Cliffs, NJ: Prentice-Hall.

Vernon, M., & Andrews, J.F. (1990). *Psychology of deafness.* White Plains, NY: Longman.

Vernon, P.E. (1989). *Intelligence: Heredity and environment.* San Francisco: Freeman.

Villa, R.A., Thousand, J.A., Meyers, H., & Nevin, A. (1996). Teacher and administrator perceptions of het-erogeneous education. *Exceptional Children, 63*(1), 29–45.

Voeltz, L.M. (1984). Program and curriculum innovations to prepare children for integration. In N. Certo, N. Har-ing & R. York (Eds.), *Public school integration of severely handicapped students: Rational issues and progressive alter-natives.* Baltimore: Brookes.

Walker, B. (1989). Strategies for improving parent-professional collaboration. In G.H.S. Singer & L.K. Irvin (Eds.), *Support for caregiving families.* Baltimore: Brookes.

Walker, H.M., Severson, H., Stiller, B., Williams, G., Haring, N., Shinn, M., & Todis, B. (1988). Systematic screening of pupils in the elementary age range at risk for behavior disorders: Development and trial testing of a multiple gating model. *Remedial and Special Educa-tion, 9*(3), 8–14.

Walker, H.M., Todis, B., Holmes, D., & Horton, G. (1988). *The Walker social skills curriculum: The ACCESS Program.* Austin, TX: Pro-Ed.

Walker, N. (1985). Impulsivity in learning disabled chil-dren: Past research findings and methodological in-consistencies. *Learning Disabilities Quarterly, 8,* 85–94.

Wallace, G., Larsen, S.C., & Elksnin, L.K. (1992). The na-ture of assessment. *Educational assessment of learning problems: Testing for teaching* (2d ed.) (pp. 1–29). Boston: Allyn & Bacon.

Wallace, G., & McLoughlin, J.A. (1988). *Learning disabili-ties: Concepts and characteristics* (3d ed.). Columbus, OH: Merrill.

Wallach, G.P., & Miller, L. (1988). *Language intervention ad academic success.* Boston: College-Hill.

Walsh, K.K., Rice, D.M., & Rosen, M. (1996). Options and choices in residential service delivery. In W. Stainback & S. Stainback (Eds.), *Controversial issues confronting spe-cial education: Divergent perspectives* (2d ed.) (pp. 267–278). Boston: Allyn & Bacon.

Ward, M.E. (1986). The visual system. In G.T. Scholl (Ed.), *Foundations of education for blind and visually handicapped children and youth: Theory and practice* (pp. 35–64). New York: American Foundation for the Blind.

Warren, D.H. (1984). *Blindness and early childhood develop-ment* (2d ed.). New York: American Foundation for the Blind.

Watlawick, J., Beavin, J., & Jackson, D. (1967). *The prag-matics of communication.* New York: Norton.

Weaver, C. (1991). Whole language and its potential for developing readers. *Topics in Language Disorders, 11*(3), 28–44.

Wehman, P., Wood, W., Everson, J., Marchant, J. & Walker, R. (1987). Transition services for adolescent age individuals with severe mental retardation. In R.N. Ianacone & R.A. Stodden (Eds.), *Transition issues and di-*

rections (pp. 49–76). Reston, VA: Council for Exceptional Children.

Wehmeyer, M., & Schwartz, M. (1997). Self-determination and positive adult outcomes: A follow-up study of youth with mental retardation or learning disabilities. *Exceptional Children, 63,* 245–255.

Wehmeyer, M.L., & Kelchner, K. (1994). Interpersonal cognitive problem-solving skills of individuals with mental retardation. *Education and Training in Mental Retardation and Developmental Disabilities, 29,* 265–278.

Welsh, M.J., & Smith, A.E. (December, 1995). Cystic fibrosis. *Scientific American,* December, 52–59.

Werner, E.E. (1986). The concept of risk from a developmental perspective. In *Advances in special education* (Vol. 5) (pp. 1–23). Greenwich, CT: JAI Press.

Werner, E.E., & Smith, R.S. (1982). *Vulnerable, but invincible: A longitudinal study of resilient children and youth.* New York: McGraw-Hill.

Westling, D.L., & Floyd, J. (1990). Generalization of community skills: How much training is necessary? *Journal of Special Education, 23,* 386–406.

Whitmore, J.R. (1980). *Giftedness, conflict and underachievement.* Boston: Allyn & Bacon.

Whitmore, J.R., & Maker, C.J. (1985). *Intellectual giftedness in disabled persons.* Austin, TX: Pro-Ed.

Whitney-Thomas, J., & Hanley-Maxwell, C. (1996). Packing the parachute: Parents' experiences as their children prepare to leave high school. *Exceptional Children, 63*(1), 75–87.

Widerstrom, A.H., & Nickel, R.E. (1997). Determinants of risk in infancy. In A.H. Widerstrom, B.A. Mowder & S.R. Sandall (Eds.), *Infant development and risk: An introduction* (pp. 61–87). Baltimore: Brookes.

Wieseler, N.A., Hanson, R.H., Chamberlain, T.P. & Thompson, T. (1985). Functional taxonomy of stereotypic and self-injurious behavior. *Mental Retardation, 23,* 230–234.

Will, M.C. (1984). *OSERS programming for the transition of youth with disabilities: Bridges from school to working life.* Washington, DC: Office of Special Education and Rehabilitative Services, U.S. Department of Education.

Williams, G.J., & Haring, N.G. (198). Identification and assessment of behavioral disorders: A state perspective. In R.B. Rutherford, Jr. & J.W. Maag (Eds.), *Monograph in Behavioral Disorders: Severe Behavior Disorders of Children and Youth, 11,* 11–21.

Williams, R.G., & McHenry, P.C. (1981). Marital adjustment among parents of mentally retarded children. *Family Perspective, 15*(4), 175–178.

Williams, W., Vogelsberg, R.T., & Schutz, R. (1985). Programs for secondary-age severely handicapped youth. In D. Bricker & J. Filler (Eds.), *Severe mental retardation: From theory to practice* (pp. 97–118). Lancaster, PA: Lancaster Press, Inc.

Withrow, F.B. (1976). Applications of technology to communication. *Volta Review, 78*(4), 107–112.

Witte, R. (1998). Meet Bob, a student with traumatic brain injury. *Teaching Exceptional Children, 30*(1), 56–60.

Witty, P.A. (1940). Some considerations in the education of gifted children. *Educational Administration and Supervision, 26,* 512–521.

Wolfsensberger, W. (1972). *The principle of normalization in human services.* Toronto: National Institute on Mental Retardation.

———. (1977). The principle of normalization. In B. Blatt, D. Biklen & R. Bogden (Eds.), *An alternative textbook in special education* (pp. 305–327). Denver: Love.

———. (1983). Social role valorization: A proposed new term for the principle of normalization. *Mental Retardation, 21,* 234–239.

Wolk, S., & Schildroth, A.N. (1986). Deaf children and speech intelligibility: A national study. In A.N. Schildroth & M.A. Karchmer (Eds.), *Deaf children in America* (pp. 139–159). San Diego: College-Hill.

Wolozin, L. (1998). Teachers' Learning Center: A CD-ROM. Boston: Houghton Mifflin. In press.

Wolraich, M.L. (1983a). Myelomeningocele. In J.A. Blackman (Ed.), *Medical aspects of developmental disabilities in children birth to three* (pp. 159–166). Iowa City: University of Iowa.

———. (1983b). Seizure disorders. In J.A. Blackman (Ed.), *Medical aspects of developmental disabilities in children birth to three* (pp. 215–222). Iowa City: University of Iowa.

———. (1983c). Seizure disorders. In J.A. Blackman (Ed.), *Medical aspects of developmental disabilities in children birth to three* (pp. 31–37). Iowa City: University of Iowa.

Wong, B.Y.L. (1982). Understanding learning disabled students' reading problems: Contributions from cognitive psychology. *Topics in Learning and Learning Disabilities, 3*(2), 15–23.

———. (1991). The relevance of metacognition to learning disabilities. In B.Y.L. Wong (Ed.), *Learning about learning disabilities* (pp. 232–261). San Diego: Academic Press.

Wood, J.W. (1993). *Mainstreaming: A practical approach for teachers.* New York: Merrill/Macmillan.

Woodward, J., & Gersten, R. (1992). Innovative technology for secondary students with learning disabilities. *Exceptional Children, 58,* 407–421.

Working Group on Mother-to-Child Transmission of HIV. (1995). Rates of mother-to-child transmission of HIV-1 in Africa, America, and Europe: Results from thirteen perinatal studies. *Journal of Acquired Immune Deficiency Syndromes and Human Retrovirology, 8*(5), 506–510.

Wright, D., Pillard, E.D., & Cleven, C.A. (1990). The influence of state definitions of behavior disorders on the number of children served under P.L. 94–142. *Remedial and Special Education, 11*(5), 17–22.

Yell, M.L., & Shriner, J.G. (1997). The IDEA amendments of 1997: Implications for special and general education teachers, administrators, and teacher trainers. *Focus on Exceptional Children, 30*(1), 1–19.

Yetman, N.R. (1985). *Majority and minority: The dynamics of race and ethnicity in American life* (4th ed.). Boston: Allyn & Bacon.

York, J., & Vandercook, T. (1991). Designing integrated programs for learners with severe disabilities. *Teaching Exceptional Children, 23*(2), 22–29.

Ysseldyke, J.E., Thurlow, M., Graden, J., Wesson, C., Algozzine, B., & Deno, S. (1983). Generalizations from five years of research on assessment and decision making: The University of Minnesota Institute. *Exceptional Education Quarterly, 4,* 75–93.

Zeaman, D., & House, B.J. (1979). A review of attention theory. In N.R. Ellis (Ed.), *Handbook of mental deficiency: Psychological theory and research.* Hillsdale, NJ: Erlbaum.

———. (1963). The role of attention in retardate discrimination of learning. In N.R. Ellis (Ed.), *Handbook of mental deficiency.* New York: McGraw-Hill.

Zimmerman, G.J. (1996). Optics and low vision devices. In A.L. Corn & A.J. Koenig (Eds.), *Foundations of low vision: Clinical and functional perspectives* (pp. 115–142). New York: AFB Press.

Zirpoli, T.J. (1986). Child abuse and children with handicaps. *Remedial and Special Education, 7*(2), 39–48.

Zuk, G.H. (1959). The religious factor in the role of guilt in parental acceptance of the retarded child. *American Journal of Mental Deficiency, 64,* 139–147.

Zuniga, M. (1998). Families with Latino roots. In E.W. Lynch & M.J. Hansen (Eds.), *Developing cross-cultural competence* (2d ed.) (pp. 209–245). Baltimore: Brookes.

Name Index

Subject Index

Unique "bookends"
frame categorical chapters

Helping all teachers understand cross-categorical themes and become reflective practitioners

Framework 1

*C*ommon Issues for All Exceptional Children and Youth in Special Education

Framework 2

*C*ommon Issues for All Developing Professionals in Special Education and Related Fields